T0287451

DER PAYATZ

DER PAYATZ

Around The World With Yiddish Theater

HERMAN YABLOKOFF

Translated from the Yiddish by
Bella Mysell Yablokoff

Bartleby Press
Silver Spring, Maryland

Published by:

Bartleby Press
11141 Georgia Avenue
Silver Spring, Maryland 20902

Library of Congress Catologing-in-Publication Data

Yablokoff, Herman, 1903-1981.
    [Arum der velt mit Idish teater. English]
    Der Payatz : around the world with Yiddish theater / Herman Yablokoff ; translated from the Yiddish by Bella Mysell Yablokoff.
        p. cm.
    Includes index.
    ISBN 0-910155-28-3 : $24.95
    1. Yablokoff, Herman, 1903-1981. 2. Theater, Yiddish. 3. Actors, Jewish—Biography. 4. Jews—Belarus—Hrodna—Biography. 5. Hrodna (Belarus)—Biography. I. Title.
    PN3035.Y313   1995
792'.092—dc20
[B]   94-30515
                                                                         CIP

Manufactured in the United States of America

To my son, Jack

CONTENTS

1

Warsaw 1960

The imposing gates of the "Kremlin" had barely loomed into sight, when my taxi-driver suddenly pulled up short and asked that I please pay my fare. From his jittery behavior and baleful glances at the massive building that rose so mighty and formidable up ahead, I gathered he was trying to say, "Prosje Pana... if it's your wish to enter the Kremlin, the pleasure is all yours. As for me, sir, dziekuje bardzo!...thanks a lot! The going in is easy enough, my friend...it's the coming out!"

When I'd engaged the taxi in front of Warsaw's Grand Hotel, I had asked him to take me to the Soviet Embassy.

"Do Kremla?" he balked, his eyes popping at me. According to regulations, he could not refuse to drive me anywhere I wished to go. But, after we had covered part of the way, he tried to draw me into conversation in the manner of cab-drivers the world over—making comments on the freezing weather, the icy roads, and general small talk. I had the impression he was choosing his words. He guessed, from my attire no doubt, that I was a Westerner and he was feeling his way to determine who this strange fare might be.

"Where, may I ask, does the Pan come from?"

"From New York. I'm an American," I told him in my half-forgotten Polish. "An American!" he beamed at me over his shoulder.

Evidently, America labeled me a safe ally, for he straightaway poured out his frustrations at me as if I, America could rescue all of Poland, including him automatically in the bargain!

He tarred the Soviet liberators, the new Polish rulers, the Polish traitors, and the Jew-Communists and—the Kremlin! He spat in contempt and spewed forth a string of salty Polish epithets neatly addressed to Matushka Russeia—Mother Russia—and her blasted Kremlin thrown in for good measure!

"If I may ask the Pan," he inquired, "what do you do in America—business?"

"I'm not a businessman. I'm an actor...an aktor." I gave it the Polish pronunciation. I paid him and got out of the cab. With a grinding of gears, my inquisitive driver made a wide U-turn and took off as if the devil were after him.

The frost nipped at my face. Turning up my fur collar over my ears, I trudged uphill towards the huge building, on which fluttered the red banner with the Soviet hammer and sickle.

After the war, the Russians had erected the structure with several smaller

1

buildings adjoining it on a hilly site near Lazienki Park. This project, achieved through the contributions made by the Russian populace, was presented as a gift to the citizens of Poland as a symbol of solidarity and friendship. The Poles promptly dubbed it "The Kremlin," and avoided the area like the plague.

With a pounding heart I took the stairs and found my way to the entrance hall of the Soviet Embassy. An elderly, pleasant-faced woman examined my American passport. When she looked up, her eyes were two blue question marks. With a self-assured air—and in English—I answered her curious gaze:

"I wish to speak to the ambassador, please."

"Can I, perhaps assist you?" the lady inquired in Russian, which she then repeated in Polish. Getting no response from me, she resorted to English. "What is it you wish to speak to the ambassador about?"

"I would like to ask His Excellency to grant me a visa to Grodno."

"A visa to Grodno?"

"To Grodno," I stood my ground, looking her square in the eye.

"Grodno?" she shrugged, "Byelorussia?" Her expression implied, 'that's what I call American brashness! A visa to Grodno, no less...! An audience with the ambassador, if you please. Crazy...!'

Nonetheless, she reached for the telephone, and after a whispered conversation, an amiable smile appeared on her face. I breathed a sigh of relief. Apparently, I had met her approval after all. Handing back my passport, she bade me to follow her to a nearby reception room. I was to sit down, she indicated, and wait.

Thanking her, I sat down and—I waited.

Throughout my many years of roaming the globe, I learned—out of sheer necessity—to live by the key words: determination, tenacity, perseverance. In a word—guts! And I often think that, had I not lived by these words, I would probably not be here to tell the tale.

Why then, I wondered, was I now sitting in the Russian consulate here in Warsaw like a scared rabbit? Was it because of all the cloak-and-dagger-peering-around-corners-atmosphere around me? Or, was it the stories I had heard about the Iron-Curtain countries—Russia, Poland and others—stories, true or alleged, which made me shake at my own shadow?

Engrossed in these conjectures, I didn't notice the man standing in the doorway looking at me—or rather through me—with his piercing glance, but at his beckoning I jumped to my feet and strode beside him down a long corridor. Stopping at one of the doors, my silent guide waved me past him into a windowless room.

Staring down at me from a large portrait on the opposite wall was the face of Lenin. No trace of Stalin...? I wondered. A second wall was entirely covered by a map of the European continent. A few straight-backed chairs and an antiquated desk completed the room's furnishings.

A solemn, bespectacled gentleman in a dark, outmoded suit, rose from his desk as I entered and nodded in answer to my greeting. While he took his time examining my passport I kept my eyes riveted on his face. I wanted to find the key to his personality, a cue, maybe, as to what to expect.

After an interminable silence, he asked, "What can I do for you, Mr. Yablonik?" (my legal name in the passport).

"Sir, if possible," I managed to find my voice, "I would like a visa to Grodno."

"Grodno?" he repeated, shaking his head. Before he could utter no, I dove right in with a plea.

"Sir, I was born in Grodno," I explained. "As a boy, still in my early teens, I left my hometown and since then—for forty years now—I've been traveling around the world as an actor, a Yiddish actor. The fact that I have not become a world capitalist during all these years, nor that the Yiddish theater has made me anything resembling an American millionaire, is self-evident. I cannot even include myself in the category of the prosperous American tourists, who roam Europe at leisure. If I were scooping up all that gold in America," I continued on a jocular note, "would I now be in Poland on a concert tour, working for Polish zlotys, which I can't even take with me when I leave the country?"

At this point it crossed my mind that I had, of course been screened by the authorities before being granted my Polish visa. And my dossier surely contained the details of the personal appearances I had made right after the war in the D.P. camps in the allied occupied zones. And so I felt that I would rather bring up the subject myself.

"During the war, I was the producer and star of my own theater in New York, and gave it all up to devote a year doing all I could to help lift the morale of the displaced persons, who scattered over ninety-six camps throughout Germany, Austria and Italy. The only compensation I received was the acknowledgment expressed by the military of the occupied zones, including the Russians," I emphasized, "and the gratitude of the quarter of a million homeless in the D.P. camps, whom I entertained. There was no political motive, whatsoever, connected with my mission. It was simply an act compelled by human compassion."

Noting the suggestion of a smile on his sensitive face, I felt that my openhearted avowal had broken the ice.

"My family were poor, hard-working people in Grodno. In the end, they were destined to breathe their last in the ghettos, the gas-chambers and the crematoriums at the hands of the Nazi murderers. I don't think I shall ever again have another opportunity to revisit the place where I was born, where I spent my childhood. I know it is a difficult request. But, please, sir, won't you help me?"

"If you no longer have anyone left in Grodno, why are you so anxious to go there?"

"You see, sir, in 1929, when I was already in the United States, my father died. I went home for a brief visit shortly after, to erect a headstone on my father's grave. In the subsequent Holocaust I lost my mother, my brothers and sisters, their children and all the rest of my kin. Since I have no way of knowing where their remains are interred, I've come to regard my father's grave as the resting place of my entire family. It is for this reason that I wish to revisit my home-town once again...go to the cemetery and recite the Kaddish—the prayer for the dead at my father's grave."

Silence filled the room. Looking over my passport again, the man stopped to scan the small photo there, then glanced up at me as if to make sure my fea-tures corresponded with the snapshot.

"I do sympathize with you, and I'd like to help you," he said, "although I don't see how I can. We have come through some very difficult war years. The destruction is tremendous everywhere. Of course, we have already rebuilt a great deal and are still in the process of rebuilding. But Grodno...? Grodno is still a long way from encouraging visitors and tourists. In time, perhaps...but at present, Grodno can certainly not boast of the deluxe accommodations as you find here at the Grand Hotel in Warsaw," he smiled.

"But, sir," I hastened to assure him, "I am not looking for, nor expecting these comforts. If you could possibly grant me a visa for only two, or three hours, there would be no problem of accommodation. I won't starve. I'll manage some-how without food—or sleep, for that matter."

"But you would have to spend the night there because the Warsaw-Grodno train makes only one run a day."

"In that case, I can spend the night in the depot. In an actor's life there is nothing new in going hungry, or sleeping on a bench in a railroad station." This obstinate appeal brought silence again. Then, with a sudden impulse, he rose to his feet. "I have an idea!" he said. My heart leaped.

Going up to the wall-map he ran his finger along one line, then another, his brow wrinkled in calculation.

"Look," he indicated a spot. "This is the train route: Warsaw, Bialystok, Sakolka, Kuznica. Here is the Polish-Byelorussian border. Now it continues to Grodno, Vilna, Minsk and Moscow. I will issue you a visa to Moscow. Grodno, as you can see, is en route. On the way to Moscow, or back, you just hop off in Grodno. Of course, this is entirely at your own risk."

"Sir, unfortunately I cannot accept your generous offer. My stay in War-saw is limited. My concert appearances begin in several days. I don't believe I have the stamina for such a speculative undertaking. I thank you from the bot-tom of my heart, but..." Seconds dragged by in silence. The disappointment was more than I could bear. I had tried and...I had failed.

"Mr. Yablonik," said the man in a decisive tone as he handed me my pass-port, "go to Plaka Street #16. You will find the Polish travel agency, Orbis. Speak to the general manager. Tell him everything exactly as you have told me. If he is willing to give you an official receipt for the sum, in dollars, required to cover your time in Grodno, I will issue you a visa..."

"To Grodno?" I broke in, excitedly.

"Direct to Grodno."

"You mean today?"

"Today!"

Overjoyed at this turn of events, I felt encouraged enough to ask, "Whom shall I ask for when I return?"

Smiling modestly, he replied, "Just ask for me, the ambassador."

I made my way out into the wintry air. I still could not believe that the man was none other than the ambassador! For the life of me I could not figure out why he had decided to go out of his way to help me. Yet, I told myself, if I have come this far, I will go all the way. Hailing a taxi, I directed the driver to Plaka Street.

Occupying an entire building, the Orbis Travel Bureau was arranged in modern American style. People stood in long lines, obviously waiting for hours to accomplish their travel requests. To go anywhere out of Poland, it is necessary to present a passport with the required visa, a clearance from the police, and a special exit permit.

Observing these endless lines my heart sank. I ventured a phone call to Simon Zarkzhevsky, who had promised to help should I run into any snag here in Warsaw. It was a great relief when he told me to stay put, that he would try to contact someone in the travel bureau.

Sure enough, before long, a young lady, scanning the crowd from a stairway, called my name. She showed me to an upper-floor office, where I was received by a tall, congenial man. "I am Pan Sadowsky," he introduced himself, shaking my hand warmly. "Please be seated."

Offering me a Russian cigarette, he began to extol the virtues of our mutual friend, Zarkzhevsky. Without preamble, I delved right in with my request to visit Grodno.

"Grodno...Grodno?" he mumbled, ferreting through some travel brochures. "No, we have no instructions from Intourist in Moscow, regarding Grodno in Byelorussia—White Russia." As if I didn't know! Down went my spirits again.

"Please, sir," I implored, "the Russian ambassador did explain that Grodno is not yet prepared for tourists, but he agreed to grant me a visa providing you give me a receipt for the required sum, which I am ready to pay in dollars. Please, Pan Sadowsky, help me."

"Good!" he agreed. "I will give you the receipt!" This was too good to be true. I could barely contain myself.

A secretary brought in the required forms, but Sadowsky told her he would attend to it himself. 'What she doesn't know won't hurt her,' he implied with a discreet wink as she left. After he had filled in the necessary information and thumped out at least a half dozen stampings, I affixed my signature, counted out my twenty-four dollars and considered the transaction happily consummated.

All at once, Sadowsky's face fell. My God! I shuddered. What now?

"See here," he said, holding up my passport. "Your Polish visa is valid for one entry and exit, only! Once you leave Poland, how will you come back? They are very strict at the White-Russian border."

With sudden inspiration, Pan Sadowsky attacked the typewriter and pecked out a letter to the commandant of the border guard at Kuznica: "Due to the Chopin Centennial now in progress, many artists and musicologists from around the world, have assembled in Warsaw for the celebration. The gentleman presenting this letter is one of our American guests and is on his way for a short mission to Grodno, Byelorussia. Would the commandant at the border be kind enough to overlook this guest's one entry and exit visa, and permit him to return to Poland on completion of his mission there."

I hugged the man and clutching my papers, hurried out and grabbed a cab back to the "Kremlin." This time I inquired after the White-Russian Ambassador as if he were a buddy of mine.

He soon appeared in the hallway. "I'm sorry," he said, "but it's too late today. Please come back tomorrow morning. Officially, the embassy will be closed, but I will personally take care of your matter. Be here not later than nine o'clock, as I shall be occupied after that."

I remained standing on the broad terrace considerably drained. But my heart sang...I'm getting a visa! ...a visa to Grodno!

Turning my steps in the direction of my hotel, I fairly walked on air. The Grand Hotel in Warsaw had been newly built and was comparable in comfort to any first-class hostelry in Europe. A guest could avail himself of any type of luxury here—for dollars, that is. Realizing that I hadn't eaten all day, yet lacking the patience to enter any of the dining salons, I ordered a sandwich and a beer brought to my room and began to count the hours until morning.

* * *

My getting to Poland had not been an easy task. It took two years of wandering, and rather hard, grueling work. In August of 1959, I had set out from my home in New York on another of my theatrical tours around the world—a pattern I had been following for years. I began this tour in Argentina and continued on to other Jewish communities in South and Latin America. From there I flew to Israel, where I starred in my own repertory plays with a cast of talented actors, newly arrived refugees from Europe.

At the end of my engagement in Israel, my wife, the noted Yiddish actress, Bella Mysell joined me, and together we visited Istanbul, cities in Italy, Switzerland and other European countries. On arriving in Paris, Bella flew back to New York. There were many important things for her to look after. I remained in Paris, where I organized a troupe of attractive young performers. Some, who could speak Yiddish, I recruited from the French stage, and we played in Paris for months, as well as in Brussels and Antwerp.

During my stay in Paris I corresponded with Meyer Melman, actor and administrator of the Jewish State Theater in Poland. Having read in the Paris press that the theater was contemplating a guest tour of Israel, I offered to come to Warsaw and star and direct several plays with the remaining cast members, who were unable for one reason, or another, to leave Poland...I suggested Arthur Miller's *Death of a Salesman*, in Yiddish; also my adaptation of the classic operetta, *The Witch*, by the founder of the Yiddish theater, Avram Goldfaden, renaming it *Goldfaden's Children*.

The reply from Warsaw was not very enthusiastic. And so I continued with my performances in Paris, convinced that my desired journey to Poland was—in theater parlance—cold turkey!

In January 1960, still in Paris, I received an invitation from the Scandinavian Jewish Youth Association to do a series of concerts in Finland, Norway, Sweden and Denmark, and for a very attractive fee at that! I jumped at this exciting proposition. For whoever imagined that Jews—in numbers, that is— were settled in these far-flung Nordic regions and boasted a Jewish youth interested in Yiddish language and artists?!

No sooner did I start packing my wardrobe for my Scandinavian concert tour, when, out of the blue, I received an official invitation from the Cultural Organization of Polish Jews in Warsaw, to do a concert tour in Poland. Well, well, I thought...when it rains, it pours!

Hershel Smoliar, the general secretary of the Cultural Organization, implied in his letter that I was the first Yiddish artist from a foreign country to be granted a visa by Poland's Foreign Ministry, including work permits for me and my pianist, Renee Solomon. We were assured first-class passage, comfortable hotel accommodations and a handsome honorarium...in Polish zlotys, naturally.

I promptly wired that I was most eager to appear in Poland, but would only be able to do so after my Scandinavian concert tour. They agreed and assured me that our visas and work permits would be ready and waiting for us in Helsinki. And indeed, they were!

After winding up the tour, we left Sweden by train. Then, train and all we were transferred onto a Soviet ship, which took us to East Berlin. There, we boarded the Berlin-Moscow Express to Warsaw.

It was a crisp, frosty morning when we arrived at the Warsaw Terminal. Representatives of the Jewish State Theater and the Cultural Organization were there to welcome us.

The most moving moment was the unexpected reunion with my childhood chum from Grodno...the actor Avrom Khash, the only survivor of the well-known theatrical family, Kadish-Khash. I hadn't seen him in forty years. His wife, Nina, their young son, Chaim'l and little daughter, Nesha—a talented child actress—had all perished in the Holocaust. Avremel, as I used to call him, and his present wife, Tania, whose husband and children had also been annihilated, had only recently made their way back to Warsaw from Riga in Latvia.

From the moment of my arrival, Avremel stuck close to me. Our endless talks invariably led us back to the city of our birth, Grodno. We reminisced about the old days, when, as choirboys, we sang in the Great "Cold" Synagogue with the town cantor, Boruch Kaminetzky; about the time when, as children, we first set foot on the stage of the Grodno City Theater. We recalled the names of pals in our children's theater group, of whom only three survived: Avremel, Shimon Finkel, now one of Israel's leading artists and the cultural director of the Habima—and I.

When I confided to Avremel how strongly I yearned to set foot again in our hometown, he eyed me as if I'd gone out of my mind. He peered over his shoulder in fear of being overheard—a reflex from his own miserable years of exile in Russia. "Chaim," he admonished, "if you value your life, knock this idea out of your head!"

But my longing to visit Grodno was infinite, and I resolved to try though I'd heard of a number of VIPs who had sought clearance to visit White Russia only to have their efforts met with a categorical nyet!

Before leaving Paris, the French impresario Leonidoff, a former associate of Sol Hurok, gave me a letter of introduction to Simon Zarkzhevsky, chief director of the Polish Theatrical Agency in Warsaw. He and Leonidoff were in charge of the French and Polish artist-exchange program.

When I arrived in Warsaw, Poland was celebrating the centennial of the Polish-born Frederic Chopin; an event attended by a congress of esteemed musicologists from around the world. The main feature of the celebration was to be contest-recitals of Chopin works played by promising young pianists. This highly intricate enterprise was planned by Director Zarkzhevsky.

As a man involved with theater, I understood that this was certainly not the time to barge in on him with my letter of introduction. Still, out of courtesy to Mr. Leonidoff, I phoned and to my surprise, Director Zarkzhevsky invited me at once to his office.

"Sit down, sit down, Mr. Yablokoff," said Zarkzhevsky, "Make yourself at home as you would in your America!" he quipped. I handed him my letter of introduction. "Leonidoff!" he chuckled, "that old Don Juan! I heard he's on his way to Moscow... still interested in the Bolshoi for Paris."

As he read the letter, he interspersed it with some witty jibes at the expense of our mutual friend. I soon caught on that it was merely good-natured ribbing.

"Leonidoff, I see, thinks very highly of you," he winked. "Tell me, what can I do for you!"

"Perhaps you can help me. I would like to get a visa to Grodno. I've made inquiries, but it appears I'm up against a stone wall."

"My friend," he replied, rocking back in his upholstered swivel-chair, "with a request such as yours, the thing to do, is to go straight to the head—the Soviet head. You may succeed, and you may not. But, at least you will have the satisfaction of having dealt with the head, not the rear end..."

Laughing uproariously at his own joke, he called for his secretary and instructed her to reach a certain party on the phone, adding that he would take the call in private.

"I can't promise anything for sure," he said. "If it were up to the Polish government, it would be like that!" he snapped his fingers, "In a second! But it's up to...you know...the Kremlin!"

His secretary interrupted to say that the party was on the line. Zarkzhevsky left the room. When he returned, he scribbled something on a piece of paper and with his arm around my shoulder, walked me out to the corridor.

"Go directly to this address," he whispered, "and ask to be shown to the ambassador—the ambassador of White Russia, understand? If anything goes fluky, don't hesitate to call me."

* * *

In the morning, long before the appointed hour, I stood waiting at the door of the Russian embassy. Promptly, at the stroke of nine tolling from a nearby tower, I began to tug at the door. It was soon opened from within by a gracious lady. She showed me into the reception room and left. In my fidgetiness I picked up one of the Russian magazines from a small table and began to turn the pages, when I suddenly remembered that I had given the impression that I did not understand Russian. I dropped the magazine, unable to shake off the eerie feeling that I was being watched.

Finally, the ambassador appeared with my papers and passport. And there, stamped in Byelorussian, was a visa to Grodno—valid for 48 hours!

"Sir, how much do I...I mean the cost..." I stammered, aware that in Europe there is a charge for a visa.

"No charge," he smiled. "Consider it a present from the Soviet Union."

I was at a complete loss for words. But the ambassador read my deep gratitude in the tears that sprang to my eyes.

Hastening to the travel bureau, I took my place in one of the inevitable queues and waited my turn.

"A first-class ticket, please, for tomorrow morning's Warsaw-Grodno train, and back," I requested, handing over my passport and documents.

The clerk thoroughly examined my papers. Eyeing me speculatively, she turned to her co-inspector, and engaged him in a whispered conference. Judging by their expressions, something told me: don't count your chickens yet, Chaim...you're not traveling yet!

Sure enough, two strapping fellows—unmistakably secret-service men— showed up. Gathering up my documents and passport, they disappeared.

After an agonizing wait, Pan Sadowsky appeared, like an angel of mercy.

"Everything is in order," he whispered reassuringly. "The 'boys' had me on the carpet, demanding to know why, but I made it quite clear to them that your visa comes from upper echelons—the ambassador. It's all right now. They will sell you a train ticket. But don't pay in dollars. They naturally prefer dollars, but you must pay them in zlotys."

One of the secret-service fellows, returning at this point, looked disgruntled; frustrated, no doubt, that he failed to land a fish. Handing back my documents and passport, he instructed the clerk to sell me my train ticket. Elated with the outcome, I left the travel bureau happily pocketing my precious ticket, which read: Warsaw-Grodno and return. Valid March 6, 1960.

My friends at the Cultural Organization were dumfounded when I showed them my visa to Grodno. I had accomplished a feat which had hitherto been impossible, and they met my candid explanation that I had obtained my visa through quite normal channels with polite incredulity.

Accepting the news that I was indeed bound for Grodno, Hersh Smoliar eagerly asked me to give regards to his dear friend, the partisan Lazar Scheikowky, and to bring him a book newly published in Yiddish, *Jewish War Heroes at the Front and in the Partisan Groups*. He also gave me a letter addressed to Sarah Dworetzky, a highly revered revolutionary personality in Grodno. She was bound to be of valuable help to me, he said.

The most astounded person of all was my friend, Avremel Khash. Visibly shaken, he regarded me with suspicion, as if I had suddenly turned out to be a Russian KGB agent in disguise. Nonetheless, he made sure to caution me on how to handle myself on the other side of the Iron Curtain, and briefed me on what to say...and even more important, what not to say if I cared to stay alive. But most of all, I treasured the names he mentioned of the few Jews still to be found in Grodno; among them, the actor, Michel Trilling.

Returning to the hotel, I was sure that, after all the emotional ups and downs of the last two days; the running back and forth from embassy to travel bureau, I'd fall into an exhausted sleep.

Yet, for all my weariness, I could not sleep. I tossed and turned...no use. I could not stem my thoughts. They carried me, as if on wings, into the distant reaches of the long ago. The bygone years flashed before me with cinematographic speed, as if it all happened yesterday. And yet, almost sixty years had flown by...sixty years since I came into the world in my birthplace—Grodno.

2

Grodno

Grodno lies nestled amidst rising hills and deep valleys. The surrounding forests are dense with birch trees. Sprawling fields of green blanket the landscape. Bubbling springs, cascading from their primary source high up in the hills, form sparkling little waterfalls. Clear-running brooks and snakelike rivulets wind their way through the city; all bent on the same outlet— the historic River Niemen.

In the history of Polish-Lithuanian Jewry, Grodno comes into focus as early as the eleventh century, though it is alleged Jews may be traced as far back as the ninth century.

The first written documents referring to the presence of Jews in the region, dated 1389, contained special decrees set forth by the ruling overlord, Count Alexander Witold. Listing various privileges allotted the Jews, it stated that since there were sixty to eighty Jewish families, who already had their own houses of worship and learning, their own burial ground and shelter for the infirm, they were to be considered a Jewish community.

In 1495, all Jews were driven from the city, their goods and possessions confiscated. It was not until 1503 that Jews were allowed to return to Grodno. Permission to engage the services of a rabbi was not granted until the year 1547.

The first rabbi in Grodno was Nossen Shapiro, of blessed memory. In 1572, the rabbinical seat was held by the world renowned Mordicai Jaffe, may his righteousness protect us. He was known to the entire Jewish world as "Ba'al Halvushim," the Holy "Lvush."

During the seventeenth and eighteenth centuries, Grodno already held a prominent place in the autonomous organization of Lithuanian Jewry and developed into a center for Talmudic studies. The task of the Council of Lithuanian Jews was to circumvent unjust government restrictions and banishment. It also endeavored to combat the barbaric fanaticism of the blood-thirsty Jesuits, and worked to refute the fabricated accusations that the Jews ritually slaughtered Christian children to use their blood for Passover matzohs.

One of the first victims of such vicious accusation in Grodno was Eleazor of Verbelov. In 1790, on the 2nd day of Shavuoth, hordes of drunken, carousing Christians stood by as a red-robed executioner hacked the martyred Eleazor. The Jesuits then hung the severed parts of his body on four tall posts in the four corners of the city. After much intercession and considerable bribery, the

11

Jewish community succeeded in bringing Eleazor's hacked body to proper inter-
ment on Jewish burial ground.

The day of his tragic death was memorialized forever after. His grave, in
the old cemetery in Grodno, was considered a holy shrine, where the Jewish
people came to pray for deliverance in times of stress.

According to a census taken in 1906, Grodno had evolved into a predom-
inantly Jewish town. And it was their incentive that promoted agriculture, established factories, developed industry and made trade flourish. The Shereshefsky
factory was one of the largest and most productive cigarette factories in Russia.

Due to its terrain and surrounding hills, Grodno was a natural stronghold
and always served as a coveted point on military maps of eastern Poland. Time
and again Grodno found herself under siege, either by Polish nobility, Lithuanian overlords, Russian grand-dukes, Prussian counts, or any old band of neighboring marauders, which invariably inscribed many bloody pages in the Pinkes,
the Jewish community's book of records.

From 1389 to the twelfth of March, 1943, when the occupying Nazis
declared "Grodno, Judenrein," this community had, throughout the ages, born
oppression, persecution, bloodshed and exile; tortures which were sanctioned
and executed by the anointed rulers, themselves.

At the time I was about to make my entrance into the world, Grodno
was a province of imperial Russia, under the last ruler of the Romanov family:
Czar Nicholas II. His tottering throne was maintained by a corrupt clique of
autocrats, the Choranaya Sotnya—Black Hundred.

Exploiting their authoritative immunity, they plundered, raped and killed.
To deflect the anger of the long-suffering Russian masses, they turned the wrath
of the rabble against the only conceivable scapegoat—the Jew!

Yet, ironically enough, it was decreed that a bronze tablet, bearing on it
a special prayer for the Czar and his family, had to be displayed on the wall
of every synagogue and house of learning. On the Sabbath and holidays, following the reading of the Torah, it was mandatory for the cantor and his choir
to chant the prayer and sing the praises of the Czar Batushka—Little Father
Nikolai Alexandrovitch; his Czarina, Maria Feodorovna; the Crown Prince,
Alexei, and the entire royal family.

* * *

My parents knew little about world politics at the time they brought me
into the world. If the matter of being born had needed my seal of approval,
I might have declined the pleasure. Nevertheless, one fine day, sans fanfare,
on the 11th of August 1903, around the time of solemn observance of the fast
of Tisha B'av, I made my entrance onto the chaotic world-scene.

It was my mother's dearest wish to have another male child, so that she
could name him Chaim after her father, who had recently passed away. Thus,
the honor was bestowed upon me.

The mazel tovs lasted until after the brith. The Mohel, Reb Tzudick, performed the rites of circumcision as he intoned: "May his name in Israel be Chaim, son of Avram." He pronounced the traditional blessing, and to drown my shrill protests let dribble a few drops of sweet raisin wine into my mouth from his fingertip.

Family and neighbors drank l'chaim, nibbled a few egg-kichlach, helped themselves to a bite of herring, and following the after-meal prayer, my very first "banquet" was over.

As an infant, mother used to tell me, I was a champion crier. I could scream myself into a spasm until I was blue in the face; apparently displaying dramatic talent from the cradle. My best performances were delivered during the night, tormenting poor Mama and disturbing father's sleep. I had no way of knowing what my brothers and sisters were wishing me during these midnight concerts.

Eventually, I began making peace with myself and the world. Since I was already part of the living, I reasoned, I may as well hang on and see what the future holds. Let me live and see. Was I not named for my grandfather, Chaim? And doesn't Chaim in Hebrew mean life?

* * *

My maternal grandparents, Doba and Chaim Shillingoff, owned a strip of land, which bordered on the very edge of the "new" cemetery. The little house, in which they lived and raised their offspring, stood half on the open field and half on the rim of the cemetery.

For years my grandfather, and his heirs after him, were involved in lawsuits pertaining to this parcel of cemetery real estate. The city authorities claimed that the tract belonged to the city proper and demanded rent. Grandfather, however, turned a deaf ear and paid nary a kopeck. His argument was simple: he had legally, rightfully purchased this "estate" from a Lithuanian squire for a sum of so-much-and-so-much, in gilden, making it unequivocally the Shillingoff property forever!

These court proceedings cost my grandfather more than the whole bargain was worth. But he was not a man to be pushed around!

While these hearings dragged on, my grandparents did not sit around with arms folded. With the help of their three sons and four daughters, they turned their disputed piece of land into a fertile garden. They acquired a couple of cows, a few chickens and managed to eke out a living.

True enough, as grandfather would say: "A Rothschild, I'll never become! But, a roof over our heads, we have? Vegetables, dairy products and potatoes, are aplenty? Fruit trees, galore? A hen for the Sabbath, is available? Fresh, cemetery air, is free? So what have we to worry about?"

So there, on the edge of the cemetery, under the very nose of the Angel of Death they dwelt, like Adam and Eve in the Garden of Eden.

A Singular Romance

My mother, Leah, was born and raised in the little house on the edge of the cemetery. Her radiant face, dark sparkling eyes, shining raven braids and charming, ever-ready smile, were proof enough that the fresh cemetery air was no deterrent to her well-being. Carefree as a bird, she skipped over the pastures bare-footed, bubbling with the joy of life. She romped with the youngsters of the neighboring peasant folk, singing their songs, dancing their dances, ripening into her teens in the very lap of nature.

In the course of my many years as an actor, whenever, or wherever the repertoire demanded that I appear in, or direct Peretz Hirshbein's idyllic play, *Green Fields*, I always envisioned the role of Tzina, the uninhibited country girl, as my mother. No wonder my father fell in love with her!

Years later, settled in the United States, it was my Aunt Sarah Mankofsky, who filled me in on the details of their singular romance. When my father, Alter took one look at her sister Leah, he was instantly "cooked!"

Alter Yablonik, the poor boy from a needy, toiling family, did not suit my Grandfather Shillingoff, the landowner, as a suitable match for his daughter.

"A love affair?!" he stormed, "And with whom? A nobody! Alter?...David and Marya's son from shoemaker alley? Never! He'll never be my son-in-law!"

"It's Alter, or no one!" revolted Leah.

In sympathy with her daughter, Grandma Doba tried to intercede.

"Chaim," she reproved her husband, "since when do you consider poverty a disgrace? Alter is a very mannerly boy and very well versed in the Torah."

Leah's three brothers, Zelik, Shayeh and Shloimke, and her three sisters, Basha, Sarah and Tzivia, were divided into two camps—pro and con the match, respectively.

The sisters were against it, because, having a younger sibling beat an older one to the altar was not in keeping with custom. It might doom them to life-long spinsterhood.

Zelik, the oldest son, a promising young man, took the liberty of opposing his father for his old-fashioned stand.

"We are living in a new world, father!" he declared. "Time has passed when parents relied on a matchmaker to pair up a bride and groom, hitching up total strangers like a cow and a mule, not even allowing them as much as a peek at one another until after the chupa!"

Since Cupid always contrives ways to bring two loving hearts together, Leah and Alter discovered that the safest place for their trysts was the cemetery. Huddling behind gravestones, they poured out their hearts and pledged their undying love.

The climax to this cemetery romance could easily have reached tragic consequences. Leah declared a hunger strike. Gone was the sunny smile from her face. Days on end she sat by the window staring into space. Nights, she lay sleepless on her pallet, hot, burning tears wetting her pillow.

Late one night, grandmother slipped out of bed to have another look at her ailing daughter. Putting her hand on Leah's forehead, she was so startled at the feverish heat that met her touch, she cried out in alarm, "Chaim! Chaim! Wake up!"

Trembling, grandfather lit the kerosene lamp and hurried to Leah's bedside. Even by the dimness of the sooty lamp he could see that his young daughter was near death. There she lay, her limbs rigid, her eyes glazed, face aflame, her lips faintly murmuring, "Mama...Mama..." Grandfather broke out in a cold sweat, while grandmother collapsed in a dead faint.

"Zelik!...Shayeh!...Shloimke!" he roared at his sons, in helplessness. "Don't stand there like mules! Get Doctor Zamkov!"

It was near daybreak when the brothers drove in with the doctor. Shaken up, wisps of straw clinging to his clothing, the sleepy-eyed doctor clambered down from the farm wagon. Fumbling for his pince-nez, which dangled from a black ribbon around his neck, he clamped them irritably on his nose and in half Russian, half Yiddish, made it known that he was far from glad about this midnight call.

"We finally got here!" he grunted. "What kind of creatures camp out here in the wilderness—on the doorstep of a cemetery?! Overeat and drag the doctor out in the middle of the night!"

But after his first glance at Leah, he realized that she was a very sick girl, indeed. He ordered everyone out except her mother—according to the custom of having another woman present when examining a girl.

Finally, the doctor emerged, and from the expression on his face it was clear that Leah was in grave danger. The diagnosis: erysipelas of the face. For several weeks Leah lay in a stupor. Day and night, her mother and sisters taking turns never left her bedside, while her father and brothers padded forlornly about the house.

In accordance with traditional customs in aiding the sick, grandfather arranged for a minyan—quorum of ten men in the synagogue, to recite the psalms. Grandmother resorted to the primitive practice of measuring areas of burial ground with lengths of wicking, to be used in the wax candles for the synagogue. On the Sabbath, when the special prayer for the sick was offered, Leah was given the additional name of Riva, after her departed paternal grandmother, Riva, the Benevolent. My mother was henceforth called Riva-Leah.

After hovering between life and death for weeks, Riva-Leah's eyes fluttered open. She was barely able to make out the anxious faces of her family gathered around her. And vaguely, she discerned the shadowy figure of a young man, standing apart from the others.

"Alter?" she breathed, hesitantly.

This proved too much for the lovelorn young man and in one swift movement he was at her side sobbing his heart out. Two sparkling tears rolled down Riva-Leah's wan little face and a tremulous smile played about her lips, as in a dream she heard her father say, "Praised be the Lord! It is surely written in heaven that Alter and Leah are a destined pair. Then, who am I to interfere. Children, you have my blessing. Mazel tov!"

"By the Sweat of Thy Brow"

The marriage of my parents Riva-Leah and Alter was consummated, and on their first anniversary, Leah presented her husband with their first-born son— my eldest brother Velvel. Each year thereafter, dutifully observing the religious law of propagation, they added to their fast-growing choir, a new and squawking chorister, whose leitmotif was: "Mama, I'm hungry!" It was a jolly household, to be sure, but the wherewithal? ... that was something else again!

"The question of making a living, my children, is in the hands of the Lord," was Grandma Doba's consolation. But, until the Almighty took notice of their circumstances, Leah knew she had better rely on her own devices, such as: adding another cup of water to the barley soup and slicing the bread a bit thinner.

My father adhered to the philosophy that a man—especially a Jew—must readily accept and be content with his lot. For, "no matter how bad things are, they can always be worse." Having no trade, the problem of providing for his family was extremely pressing. His parents, Marya and David Yablonik, had denied themselves the barest necessities so that their son, Alter, could attend the yeshiva. Learning a trade, of course, would have been more sensible, my father realized, but how could he shatter his parents' dream of having their son become a rabbi? And so, he continued his studies at the yeshiva right up to the time of his marriage.

While it was true that Grandfather Shillingoff had lived up to his promise of providing the young couple with room and board, as was then customary, how long could a man, with an ever-increasing brood, continue to accept another's provender? He already wracked his brain over his two young daughters, Mariashka and Slavka, who were shooting up like saplings. Before long, they'll be ripe for marriage, and what is a father to do about their dowries...?

His sons Velvel and Shayke, he reasoned, will soon enough be finished with their schooling and be ready to go to work. Motke will also be earning his keep in time. So the infant boy, Chaimke, may not prove to be such an extra burden after all. Trying to cover his anxiety from his wife, he playfully teased her. "Well, well, Leah'le, our household is really expanding, 'kein ein ahore'—no evil eye! And you, my dear, were so worried lest you be barren, like our biblical Mother Sarah, heaven forbid! Now, the Lord be praised, we have six children: four sons and two daughters."

At the sudden tears in mother's eyes, father realized his blunder. In enumerating the children, he had touched a sore spot in mother's heart. I was actually child number ten. There had been four others, who, alas, did not tarry too long. Niske, the undertaker, a bony, exceedingly elongated figure of a Jew, would appear on the occasion of these heartrending losses. Unceremoniously wrapping the tiny, short-lived infant in the skirts of his long, black caftan, he would make hasty, long-legged strides along his well-trodden path back to the new cemetery.

* * *

Grandfather Shillingoff's eldest son Zelik had begun taking on contracts for government jobs: paving streets, sidewalks and laying roads. In a short time, Uncle Zelik became a wealthy man. The Shillingoff Buildings, a complex on Zamkova Street, took up a square block and became a landmark in Grodno.

In addition to his brothers, Shayeh and Shloimke, Uncle Zelik also hired his brother-in-law, Alter, and they became a crew of road pavers.

Thus, my father, the would-be rabbi, toiled with his calloused hands to the end of his days, true to the Bible: "By the sweat of thy brow, shalt thou eat bread..." In time, the paving crew appointed my father as their foreman.

The business of street-paving was a spring-to-fall occupation. It still did not solve the problem of keeping the wolf from the door during the long winter months. Necessity, being the mother of invention, it occurred to my father that, during winter's inevitable sleet and slush, there would be a fair demand for the mending of rubber galoshes. Wasting no time, he invested in some sort of gum-adhesive, a bottle of benzine, liquid shoe-blacking, a small file and a cobbler's knife. He collected a heap of old, discarded galoshes for patchwork and hung out a homemade shingle.

The house was turned into a workshop, and galoshes began to pile up. My brothers and sisters learned the art of this intricate operation and pitched in with the repairs after school hours. Even Mama lent a hand in her infrequent spare moments.

My Father, The Road-Paver

I was growing up, and every day brought new wonders. There was the first time mother took me to market, where the haggling at the smelly fish stalls on Troitza, the bustling at the meat shops in the compound of the synagogue court bewildered me and made me claw at my mother's skirts.

As time passed, I was no longer content to stare and wonder. I soon reached the pestering stage. I heard grownups using the words roader and reader in referring to my father and I puzzled over it.

"Mama, what is a roader?" I wanted to know. Preoccupied with one of her endless chores, she paid no attention.

"What is a roader, Mama?" I persisted.

"A roader, my child, is a worker, who paves roads and streets, understand? Father is a roader. May the Lord help you find a better trade."

"And what is a reader, mama?" I pursued.

"Your father," she said, a smile now lighting up her face, "is a reader, my son. A reader of the Torah—in the synagogue."

For a time I toyed with the similar words, reader-roader... If father is both of these, I puzzled, why was mama so pleased with reader and so displeased with roader?

The enigma solved itself when mother entrusted me for the first time, to take the noonday meal to father. Balancing the earthen pot, wrapped in a red kerchief, I set out on my errand.

The broken rhythm of the steel hammers striking the stones created a curious blend of sounds. The paving crew sweated at their labors. In old, worn pants, their tattered sleeves rolled to the elbows, caps pushed to the back of their heads, some of the men squatted cross-legged on the ground, while others worked on their knees. Inching backwards as the work progressed, the men laid stone by stone, filling in the spaces with dampened sand.

Down on one knee, his back bent low, my father was hard at work. Great drops of sweat, trickling down his forehead, ran down his face and into his silver-threaded beard.

"Great day, father!" I pitched my voice even higher to outshout the clanking hammers. When father caught sight of me, his expressive eyes shone with genuine affection. "Chaimke! You?! ...You've brought father his noon-meal?" Rising, he wiped the perspiration from his face with his shirtsleeve, and brushed the sand from his knees.

"How times flies!" he remarked, looking at me, visibly moved. "Chaimke, a grown boy!"

My Father, The Reader

On a Sabbath morning, my father took me along for the first time, to the big Hayyei-Adam Synagogue. The myriad of colorful tints created by the sun's rays, filtering through the tall stained-glass windows and fusing with the long-burning memorial candles, fascinated me.

The sanctuary was packed with men and boys, while the womenfolk, in accordance with Orthodox law, were separated in the upper section of the synagogue. The trustees, mainly the rich and prominent townspeople, the custodians and disciples, in silk and wool prayer-shawls embroidered at the neck with gold and silver, sat up in front by the east wall, on either side of the Holy Ark. Members of the middle class, who could not afford the expense of reserving a seat annually, filled the mid-section of the sanctuary. In the rear, near the laver at the door, huddled in frayed, time-yellowed prayer shawls, stood the very poor.

The seats in the women's gallery were also assigned according to the status of the family. The only pauper woman privileged to a front seat was the prayer prompter. Since she was one of the few able to read the text of the prayers, she kept the other women abreast of the services.

On the Bima, the large pulpit in the center of the sanctuary, stood the revered Reb Chaim-Leyb Zupovitch. Originally from the village of Eishishok, he was known affectionately as the Eishishker Rabbi.

And there, between the trustee and the rabbi, stood my father. His prayer-shawl draped over his Sabbath garb, the black yarmulke on his head, and his well-tended beard, all lent him dignity and stature.

The little bells dangling from the gold-encrusted crowns that adorned the wooden rollers on which the holy scriptures were wound tinkled softly, melo-diously adding a mystic, ethereal atmosphere. On the high pulpit lay an open scroll of the Torah, its coverlet a gold-and-silver embroidered velvet vestment.

The beadle, with a specific lilt, called the names of those who were to come up for an aliyah, the blessing of the Torah; which every Jew is to observe beginning with the day of his bar mitzvah. Thus, called upon, the worshiper approached the pulpit, placed a kiss on the Torah and intoned the blessing.

With an Oriental-like cadence that caressed the ear, my father's voice rang out. He read portion after portion of the Pentateuch according to the weekly series of the Torah, giving each word the traditional intonation.

It is a familiar oddity among Jews in communities around the world that, during the reading of the Torah, many members of the congregation feel com-pelled to take a breather... sauntering outdoors, as one might do during an inter-mission at the theater. Even those who remain in their seats are guilty of using this period for a little private shmoozing.

But, whenever my father officiated as reader of the Torah, folks always remained in their seats listening to him as attentively as they would to a good cantor.

That Saturday morning, walking home after prayers, I clung tighter than ever to the work-roughened hand of my father. I strutted beside him, proud of the praise awarded him at every step. Emulating him I nodded to the friendly greeting of "Gut Shabos." My young heart was ready to burst with reverence and love for my father. I was overwhelmed by the aspiration to become both a roader, as well as a reader of the Torah, exactly like my father!

Not long afterward I realized half of my ambition. Barely seven, I stood on a little bench in the very same Hayyei-Adam, and I intoned the weekly portion of the Torah and the "Haftorahs," imitating my father's every nuance, every cadenza and embellishment.

My father was extremely fond of cantorial compositions. Yet, despite his very pleasant tenor and knowledge of the age-old prayer chants, he never con-sidered himself a cantor. During the High Holy Days, the worshipers in the small prayer houses, too poor to afford the services of a cantor, always relied on my father to officiate without compensation.

It was in the little synagogues of the tailors, the soldiers and droshky-drivers that I began as a choirboy with my father, in a choir that consisted of one singer—me!

"B'Rosh Hashono Yi Koseivun—On New Year's Day, the decree is inscribed."
I sang out loud and clear, in my boyish alto, as we ushered in the New Year.
I was not yet able to read, but under father's tutelage, I learned the text of
the prayer by heart. The congregation would pick up the traditional melodies
and together we sounded like a real choir.

My father's original folk-melodies and liturgical compositions, which he
taught me, remained in my memory. Years later, I wove them into my Yiddish
theater songs and eventually made them popular around the world.

* * *

My parents waged a fearful struggle for the daily existence of our growing
family—especially with the unmistakable symptoms of yet another hungry
mouth on the way. The fact that our new addition would not arrive solo, but
be accompanied by a soulmate, a twin—and two girls at that—was something
none of us bargained for!

As it happened, one of the tiny creatures did not remain with us very
long. Thus, Niske, the undertaker, appeared again and carried the little half-
soul off to her eternal rest.

The remaining half of the twin could not decide whether to stay, or follow her sister. For a while it was touch and go with this little one. She kept
the family in constant suspense. But, hang on, she did. And so our frail little
half-twin remained the youngest member of our family—my baby sister, Rochele.

With the birth of the twins, my mother's childbearing trials were over.
Out of the twelve children she had brought into the world, five had not sur-
vived. And so we remained seven in all: Velvel, Shayke, Mariashka, Slavka,
Motke, Chaim and Rochele.

3

School Days

I was six when I was admitted to the Hebrew school called Cheder Msukon. The school was attended by children of the Jewish intelligentsia, Zionists, and boys and girls from well-to-do families in Grodno, to whom the high cost of tuition at Cheder Msukon was no problem.

I did not fit into any of these categories, but I was allowed the privilege of attending the school as a special concession to my father, who was regarded by everyone as the "intelligent pauper."

The Russian government schools, such as the Marinska and Real Gymnasias, offered the conventional curricula of secular studies; while the Talmud Torahs and yeshivas held to their strictly religious programs. The gymnasias did not accept Jewish students readily, and so, between the two diverse forms of education, the Cheder Msukon was considered the most preferable school for Jewish children.

The language taught there was Hebrew—except for the class periods in which the students were also taught Russian. Yiddish, considered a jargon, was taboo.

The difficult choice Jews were faced with, in regard to religious versus secular education, was not felt as sharply in Grodno, as in other Jewish communities of Eastern Europe. Parents who were against schools of secular courses only sought to protect their young from becoming engulfed in revolutionary ideals. Such teachings, they maintained, invariably swept youth into perilous currents. This theory of "what you don't know won't hurt you" played right into the hands of the Czarist oppressors whose interest it was to keep the people in ignorance.

My parents knew only too well of these dangers. Didn't their eldest son, Velvel—and even Shayke—already cause them enough heartache with their revolutionary activities? Father blamed it all on the heretical books they read. Consequently, their third son, Motke, had to be content with attending the Talmud Torah and the girls, Mariashka and Slavka, with learning to read and write under a tutor, who came to the house once a week.

How my father brought himself to sanction my attending classes with boys, who sat bare-headed and shared the same school bench with girls, I'll never understand. As for Mama, she was in seventh heaven that her Chaimke was going to school with the children of "refined" families. Father was not completely sure that the school was germ-free of revolution, but the deciding factor was that Cheder Msukon was dedicated solely to Hebrew...and how the social revolution in Russia could possibly be brought about in the holy language of Hebrew was beyond his imagination.

Shayke volunteered to contribute toward my tuition out of his earnings as a mechanic at Shereshefsky's cigarette factory and Mariashka, as a salesgirl in Elkins' clothing store.

At last the day arrived. After father left for morning prayers, Mama began to fuss over me. She washed, scrubbed, slicked my hair in place and got me into a new suit—cut down from one that Motke had outgrown. Pulling on my first pair of new boots by the bootstraps, I delighted in them, so skillfully fashioned by my Uncle Berel in honor of the occasion.

Adjusting my shiny-visored cap on my head, I paraded before Mama for inspection. She beamed at me. Then, suddenly overcome, she clasped me in a tight embrace.

"Why the tears, mama?" Shayke teased, "one would think you were sending him, like Isaac, to the sacrificial altar!"

"Don't be so funny!" Mama retorted, drying her eyes on her apron and busying herself with comforting the baby, Rochele, whose birdlike chirps from the cradle meant it was time she was fed.

"Well, come on, big boy, let's go," Shayke said. He had volunteered to enroll me in school on his way to work. With rhythmic squeaks of my new boots, I tried to keep up with my brother's long strides.

The schoolyard was already buzzing like a beehive: boys and girls milled about, waiting for the bell. Catching sight of me in my odd-looking outfit, they hailed me with shrieks and guffaws.

Mercifully, the bell sounded loud and clear, hurrying my tormentors to the school entrance. Clutching my cap, I stumbled after my brother as he led me through a long hallway. Stopping at one of the many doors, Shayke knocked.

"B'vakeshah—please come in," answered a voice from within. Shayke opened the door and pushed me in ahead of him.

Seated at a desk was the principal of Cheder Msukon, Yeshua Levine—an elegant man, with a crop of thick, black hair, his dark features framed by a small rounded beard and mustache trimmed in the French fashion. His coal black eyes took us in.

Explaining the nature of our visit, Shayke listed my assets: I was an obedient child...I had a quick mind...I was not entirely a beginner, since I had already mastered the alef-bez. I could also read the prayers out of the sidder, thanks to father's tutoring. And I was already assisting my father as a choir-boy. In short, I had enough credits to enter the halls of learning at Cheder Msukon.

Plucking at the ends of his mustache, Herr Levine listened patiently and, with a smile, threw me a question in Hebrew. "Ma shimkha habibi?" Even if I

had understood, I was too awed to answer. I just twisted my cap and stood with my eyes glued to the floor.

"What is your name, my friend?" he repeated in Yiddish.

"Ch - Chaim..." I stammered. "Chaim Yablonik."

"Chaim! A fine Hebrew name," he nodded, coming from around his desk. And without further ado he looked behind my ears, parted my hair—to make sure I didn't have the "third plague of Egypt"—looked into my throat and inspected my teeth. "We're very strict about cleanliness," he explained.

Thanks to mother's scrubbing I passed my physical with flying colors.

"Your brother tells me that you're a choirboy. Is that so? Yofi, yofi—that's nice. What kind of voice do you have, Chaim? A bass, or a tenor?" he jested, turning back to his desk.

"I...I...don't know."

Finished with the preliminaries, the talk turned to the business at hand. Taking heart, Shayke pointed out that, undoubtedly, there were richer people in town than we, not that we expected anything for free, heaven forbid. But, would the esteemed principal be kind enough to show us some consideration?

Herr Levine stated that my tuition would be ten rubles a month. There was a slight hesitation in his voice when he said ten. He probably expected us to faint at the mention of it.

Yet, in astonishment, I heard my brother agreeing to these terms. He was actually thanking the principal for his generosity in charging us no more than ten rubles a month!

When Shayke shook the principal's hand in the manner of a merchant closing a deal and turned to go, I emitted a screech to shame a factory whistle. "I wanna go home!"

Shayke was mortified at my outburst, but not Herr Levine. Scenes like this had erupted in his office more than once. Putting his hands on my shoulders, he gave Shayke the eye to take off. He lifted my chin and looked directly into my tear-filled eyes.

"Come now, Chaim," he gently admonished, "what is this crying? This does not suit a big boy like you."

Herr Levine smoothed my hair in place, took me by the hand and led me toward one of the classrooms. The hall echoed with the voices of children singing with gusto and feeling. Accompanied by the vibrating tones of a concertina, the song went to the very core of me, stirring an irresistible urge to join in that lovely Hebrew song: "I long for my Homeland."

As in a dream, I walked beside Herr Levine and entered the room whence came the sweet music.

"I am the singing teacher," Reuben Vigderovitch introduced himself after a whispered exchange with the principal, and added, "what is your name, little boy?"

"Chaim," I answered courageously, "Chaim Yablonik."

"Children, this is our new pupil, Chaimke," Herr Levine told the class. "Let us bid him Shalom."

A chorus of Moishelech, Shloimelech, Rivkelech and Leyalech greeted me with a resounding, "Shalom, Chaimke, Shalom!"

* * *

Forty years later, during one of my performances at the Public Theater on Second Avenue in New York, I had the honor of introducing from the stage my first teacher, the principal of Cheder Msukon in Grodno, Dr. Yeshua Levine.

By a coincidence, I learned that he was living in the United States, engaged as a pedagogue in a Brooklyn yeshivah. I immediately called him and was elated to find that he remembered me. I invited him to my running production of *The Magic Melody*.

Our meeting, after forty years, was indescribable! Tears gushed to my eyes when I beheld my dearly remembered teacher, now a stooped little man, his hair and beard snowy white—except for the same fiery twinkle in his eyes.

At the end of the performance, I had the extraordinary pleasure of welcoming my venerable guest, whom the entire company and audience greeted with rousing applause.

How vividly there flashed before me the scene in the classroom that first morning in Cheder Msukon forty years ago, and how clearly the sound of the children's voices rang in my ears, as they welcomed me with their, "Shalom, Chaimke, Shalom!"

Quarantine

Nobody needed to prod me mornings to get ready for school. Who is to say whether it was the revelation of a new and exciting world that filled me with such a desire for learning, or...Esterke?...a little girl, who shared the school-bench with me. With the first glance, her sky-blue eyes captured my heart.

More than once her nudge, or warning kick under the desk, alerted me that the teacher was calling on me. Seeing me lost in a cloud, the class would burst into laughter.

I must admit that at first I did sit in class like a dummy; listening, but not understanding a word of the lessons conducted in Hebrew. All that father had crammed into my head from the prayer-book and the Bible proved to be inapplicable in Hebrew school. I had to start from the beginning.

The teachers were very patient and understanding. As for the children, they soon accepted me. When I finally began to speak, read and write Hebrew, I made rapid strides and became one of the best students in class. My forte, nevertheless, was in the singing periods with our teacher Vigderovitch. Here, I really shone. One chord from Vigderovitch's concertina was enough to send my boyish alto soaring, as I reveled in the children's Hebrew songs. With eyes closed, I poured out my heart and soul in my first "Shir Hashirim"—Song of Songs—for Esterke...

One day, after school dismissal, as I stood waiting to walk Esterke home, I was surprised to find my sister Slavka waiting for me at the gate. Slavka, brown as a gypsy, her flashing eyes almost as black as her braids, was already, at the age of twelve, beginning to show signs of burgeoning, her slight figure visibly straining against the tautness of her calico dress.

"We'll have to stay at Grandma's for a while," she said. "Those are Mama's orders. I've already taken Rochele there. Motke is very sick and we have to stay with Grandma."

"Motke is sick?" Vaguely, I remembered that before I left for school in the morning, mother and father seemed very upset. It then occurred to me that, for the last few nights, Motke had not shared the sleeping bunk with me. From snatches of conversation, I gathered that father had banished my brother Velvel from the house and I simply assumed that Motke chose to sleep by himself, on Velvel's bunk.

"Slavka, I won't go to Grandma's!" I rebelled in panic. "I want to go home to Mama!" And turning on my heel, I headed for home. Terrified and panting, I reached the house. The door was locked.

"Mama! Mama, let me in...let me in!"

Mama appeared at one of the closed windows and frantically gestured at me to go away. Slavka caught up and gasping for breath, pleaded with me and hugged me as she tried to pull me away from the window.

"Look, look up there—on the door," she pointed. "See that sign?" Lifting my blurred eyes to the door, I saw a square of paper. Printed on it in big, black Russian letters, were the words: QUARANTINE SMALLPOX.

During my brother's illness, we younger children stayed with father at Grandma Doba's house, while the older ones were put up with relatives and friends. Only Mother remained shut in—quarantined with her stricken son. Every morning at daybreak, father brought a basket of food and medication to leave outside their bolted door.

After some weeks, the crisis broke. Following a lengthy process of disinfecting and scouring every nook of the house with strong-smelling sprays, we were allowed to return home.

Mother was a shadow of herself. One would think it was she, rather than Motke, who had suffered the dread smallpox. And father, whose hair and beard had grown grayer during these harrowing weeks, hied himself to the synagogue to offer a prayer to the Almighty for sparing his son.

4

Auditions for a Cantor

Grodno had a reputation as a city of great enthusiasts for cantors, concert artists, and the theater. In fact, an impressive number of outstanding personalities in all phases of art and literature were born in Grodno, though for the most part, their development and artistic achievements were accomplished elsewhere.

Actors, musicians, cantors and other such colleagues around the world, in whose spheres I've spent more than half a century, have always prided themselves on any recognition they received in Grodno, especially cherishing a good review in the *Grodno Moment*.

Pertaining to cantors, Grodno had—up until the Nazi Holocaust—contributed an interesting chapter in the history of Jewish life in Eastern Europe. Veteran cantors, discussing cantorial history in Grodno, will to this day invariably recall with deep reverence, the name of Reb Yoshe Slonimer. They cannot forget his unique style, his masterful interpretation of prayers, let alone his vocal technique. Elder townspeople, who had the privilege of hearing him, still relate wonder-tales of his divine stature and legendary personality.

The demise of Reb Yoshe Slonimer caused a great tumult in Grodno; the question on everyone's lips was: "Who is to be Reb Yoshe Slonimer's successor?"

There ensued endless discussions, debates, arguments, even quarrels, but no decision could be reached. Stalemated again and again, what was there to do but call another meeting! Even during services in the synagogues and little prayer-houses, the discussions often became so heated that they led to fisticuffs. The tension mounted, but still no decision—and no cantor!

One must understand the pattern of Jewish life in that era to fully appreciate how important a role the cantor and his choir played in the community. On Friday nights, folks looked forward to listening to a sermon given by the rabbis in the prayer-houses. Even the mid-week visit of an itinerant preacher, heard in the interval between dusk and evening prayers, was a diversion; especially when our community was visited by such renowned preachers, as the Bialystoker Magid—the father of the well-known Jewish writer and poet, B.I. Bialystotzky. At such times, even the biggest synagogue hardly accommodated the numbers who came to relish every proverb, every moral of these spiritual experiences.

It was characteristic of Grodno Jews to idolize their chosen town-cantor, especially one as exalted as the late Reb Yoshe. No wonder they were at a loss in finding a worthy successor. The issue dragged on for months.

Finally, someone came up with a solution: Auditions! Every Sabbath, a different cantor would perform the services for the approval of the majority, until the congregation decided on the "one."

Grodno was soon inundated by impressive cantors of every type: tenors, basses, baritones with, or without falsettos, or mezzo-voces.

Friday nights, right after the prayer of "Hashkiveynu," the buzzing of exchanged opinions could be heard throughout the synagogue.

The result was that the congregation heard enough cantors to last them a lifetime. The consensus of opinion, however, remained the same: "No, he is not the one for Grodno."

One fine day, another applicant arrived: the Krementchuker Cantor. The moniker Krementchuker certainly added nothing to his prestige. Nevertheless, if the cantor from Krementchuk wished to audition—fine! Was there anything better to do? It was agreed to let him officiate on a Sabbath, which happened to fall on Shabat Hagodel, the Sabbath before Passover.

What an impressive tableau the choir made, in their black robes, their neatly folded prayer-shawls and high yarmulkes. They stood in two rows beside the raised Bima in the center of the sanctuary. Prayers to usher in the Sabbath were always held on the Bima, instead of at the pulpit up front by the Holy Ark.

Sergei, the choir leader, distributed the music folios and the congregation waited to hear this near contender, the Krementchuker Cantor.

A dark-haired young man, his face framed by a trim, black beard, slowly approached the Bima and carefully limped up on the platform. He turned his gaze on the choir leader, a pleasant smile playing about his lips. Sergei, taking this as a signal to begin, softly blew a note on his little pitch pipe. After sounding the tone la, he then sustained it by humming. The impression was that he was cueing in his choir. In reality, he was tactfully giving the cantor the right key; for all too often, the nervous candidate would start off in the wrong key, throwing the choir off base.

The Krementchuker, however, didn't just rely on Sergei's little pitch pipe. Reaching into his vest pocket with his left hand—another awkward movement that made it obvious there was something wrong with his right hand—he produced his own tuning fork. Giving it a little bite with his teeth, he then brought it up to his ear. Nodding at Sergei, he indicated his *la* did indeed correspond with that of Sergei's little pitch pipe.

With a decisive thump on the reading stand, the beadle called out, "Kabolath Shabat!...come, let us welcome the Sabbath!"

With a mighty and totally unexpected roar of, "O come, let us sing unto the Lord..." the cantor's resonant tones shook the rafters. His dramatic tenor reverberated throughout the Great Synagogue, electrifying his listeners. The entire sanctuary was instantly stunned into a breathless silence that prevailed to the very end of the prayers.

The people couldn't believe their ears! It was incredible that a voice of this magnitude could emanate from the throat of such a young man—with such skillful interpretation of the prayers! Incredible to think that the honeyed tones could flow from his slightly distorted mouth, which resulted from a partial paralysis that affected one side of his body.

That Friday night, as the congregation dispersed, people wended their way home in a spellbound hush, a magical premonition that Grodno was on the eve of an historic event.

Before daybreak, we could hardly get anywhere near the Great Synagogue. My father and brother Motke, with me in tow, managed to wedge through the crowd that kept growing. They came from far and near, pushing toward the entrance. But many were obliged to remain standing in the courtyard, for there no longer was any room in the synagogue.

After the reading of the Torah, the auditioning Krementchuker Cantor stood aloft before the open Ark and delivered the prayer, "Uvnukho Yomar" (When the Ark rested) which thoroughly enchanted the congregation, its utter sweetness melting every heart. And when he came to "Khadesh Yomeynu K'kedem" (Renew our days of old), he executed the most intricate modulations and fanciful coloratura passages. Upon reaching the last word, "K'kedem," he struck a ringing high C with such power and resonance that the candles spluttered and the chandeliers vibrated. Still holding the high C he closed the Ark, drew the curtains and descended the sixteen steps to the cantor's lectern. Only then, did he end this spectacular finale in a glissando, which, in the same breath carried him into the traditional incantation of "Yis-ga-dal, v'yis-ka-dash..."

Neither the quiet interlude of the "Shmone-Esrai" (silent prayer), nor the beadle's rapping on the reader's stand, quelled the excitement that took hold of the congregation. Unabashed, folks hugged one another in ecstasy.

"Mazel tov!" they congratulated each other. "At last Grodno has discovered the cantor she had hoped and waited for—the right one!"

The hallowed Reb Yoshe Slonimer had finally found a worthy successor in the person of the Krementchuker Cantor, Boruch Kaminetzky!

5

The Great Synagogue

The Great Synagogue's courtyard encompassed a substantial area at the very edge of the city. Built of brick, with huge doors and tall windows all around, the structure was so immense that to heat it properly was impossible. It was known, therefore, as the "Cold Shul."

The spacious Bima in the center of the sanctuary was flanked by four massive columns that reached to the vaulted ceiling. Twin stairways at either side of the pulpit led to the hand-carved Holy Ark, which dominated the center of the east wall. Catching the reflection from the multicolored windowpanes, the crystal prisms of the great chandeliers cast mystic lights on the golden lettering over the Ark: "Dah Lifnay mi Ato Omed" (Know ye before Whom ye stand).

After listening to the choir during the audition of the Krementchuker Cantor, I was no longer satisfied to sing with father during holidays in the little prayer-house of the soldiers. Come Rosh Hashanah and Yom Kippur, I would meander into the big sanctuary to listen to the choirboys. I was envious of their flowing black robes, their little white prayer-shawls, their four-cornered yarmulkes, the impressive music folios spread before them on the stands. How I yearned to be a real, bona fide choirboy! How I envied my brother Shayke!

"Shayke," I pleaded, "take me along when Sergei is rehearsing the choir. Yes? Will you take me? Will you?" I nagged. But he wouldn't hear of it.

I was struck by an idea. Where is it written that I had to sit inside the rehearsal room? Why can't I listen from the outside? As soon as Shayke left for choir practice, I hied myself to the big courtyard, chose a spot on the grass beneath the window of the rehearsal room, and "tuned in." This was how I eventually learned the entire repertoire by heart.

Sergei, the choir leader, took each section individually. Listening to the altos, I instinctively felt that their part was best suited to my voice and followed the altos note by note. After absorbing all I could from these choir sessions, I lay awake half the night going over the haunting melodies in my head.

One fine evening, as I squatted in my usual spot below the window, entranced with the new and beautiful composition Sergei was teaching the choir, I was only vaguely aware of a group of boys playing at a little distance. The group decided to make me the target of their stone throwing. A sudden crash of shattering glass startled me, but before I could pull myself together and "make tracks" as the other kids did, the assistant beadle, Khone-Leyb, had me by the ear.

"Sheygetz!" he raged. "Blasphemer! You'll break windows of a holy place, will you?!...I'll break every bone in your body!" he roared, hauling me into the rehearsal room.

"It isn't true! I didn't break the window! I didn't throw any stones! I was just sitting on the grass listening to the singing..."

"Well then, who threw the stone?" the beadle stormed. "Answer me, you sheygetz!"

"I don't know...I didn't see..." I stammered, struggled to keep from bursting into tears. "I didn't do it!"

"Yablonik," a mild voice uttered. It was Sergei addressing my brother. "Seat the boy next to you. Let him listen. And you, nightingales," he said turning to the choir, "let's take it from the beginning."

I never expected this outcome. I promptly forgot all about my burning ear. For the privilege of sitting in on a rehearsal with the choir, it was worth it!

They launched into their new composition, "Hayon Haras Olom" (This day the World was called into Being). I quietly started to hum along with the altos. Warming up, I soon forgot that I was there merely as a listener, and, with eyes closed, began to sing louder and louder. Completely carried away, I failed to realize that I was singing by myself because Sergei had signalled the others to keep mum and let me carry on alone. The jest paid off. A burst of laughter brought me up short, causing the last note to stick in my throat—which only brought a greater explosion of hilarity. I jumped up ready to flee, when Sergei's friendly voice stopped me.

"Hold on, little Yablonik! Come here, boy. I must say, that's a mighty fine voice you have. Tell me, how do you come to know the 'Hayom Haras Olom'?"

"I learned it by listening. I listened outside...by the window."

Finding this rib-tickling, the choir broke into fresh gales of laughter. Since their rehearsal had already been disrupted, they felt they might as well have a little fun and asked me to sing. Needing very little coaxing, I obliged with father's entire repertoire.

Walking home with Shayke that evening, there was only one thing that remained to be accomplished: to get father's assent to Sergei's proposal that I join the choir as a full-fledged member.

Father agreed and Mama was simply elated. "What a joy! Imagine my son, my Chaimke, like his big brother, a regular choirboy at the Great Synagogue!"

* * *

The news that I had become a choirboy brought me quite a measure of prestige in Cheder Msukon. My association with adults also had a great influence on my general development. I applied myself more diligently to my studies, and I learned to conduct myself more like a grown-up.

One of our teachers, Herr Bloch, had a favorite expression, which intrigued me. When a pupil failed to grasp one of his explanations, he would admonish,

"Open your head!" This always struck me as very funny: how do you open your head! It soon became clear to me. My head did begin to open as I absorbed the varied subjects we were taught.

My school chum, Zvi Belko was, unquestionably, the boy with the open head, the best student in school. The teachers predicted a great future for him in science. And their predictions came true. He received his doctorate at a very early age, but subsequently perished in the Holocaust.

Cheder Msukon augmented its faculty by engaging a teacher who taught Russian. She was a spinster; tall, slender, her hair in a chignon at the nape of her neck, her manner of dress, prim and immaculate. A gold-rimmed pince-nez hung from a chain fastened to the lapel of her jacket. This was my teacher, Berta Isaacovna.

The boys took a great shine to her. We began to vie with one another in running her errands. I, too, sought favor in her eyes and interpreted every smiling look in my direction as a sure sign that I was her chosen love. My romance with Esterke!—kid stuff! Berta Isaacovna! This was the real thing! This was love, like in the Bible...like Jacob and Rachel, Amnon and Tamar... Samson and Delilah...

I began fussing over my appearance: primping in front of the mirror, slicking down my mop of black hair with Shayke's hair pomade, rubbing shoe-wax on my boots, buffing them over and over.

"What am I supposed to wear—the same old rags again!" I harassed Mama every morning. "Why must I be different from the other boys?! They come to school all spruced up. But me, I have to go looking like a shlepper!"

"A boy like you, Chaimke, should consider our circumstances," was Mama's ready answer. "Your father's earnings, such as they are—God forgive me—are not enough for our bare necessities. It's a good thing people trust us 'on the book'...Better pray to God that we are able to pay for your schooling. We are a few months behind as it is. How long do you think they will keep you there for nothing?"

Mother's argument was justified, of course, but go argue with a fool in love. Especially when he is up against so much competition. In time, naturally, I had to face the unsuitability of this "match." To stifle my unrequited feelings, I threw myself into my studies with even greater zeal. I spouted Hebrew like a chatterbox. And when our teachers instructed us to practice the language at home, Mama bore the brunt of it; as if she didn't have enough to distract her, I kept jabbering at her in an unfamiliar tongue.

* * *

The first commendation I received in school was in a letter-writing contest. We corresponded with school children in Palestine. In my letter I expressed my innermost feelings toward Zion; my yearnings toward the land that flowed with milk and honey; where every Jew would sit peacefully in his own vineyard, in the shade of his date trees, relishing a glass of milk and a slice of challah spread with honey…

This letter won me the second prize. The first prize went, as usual, to Zvi Belko. Nevertheless, when it came to our singing sessions with Vigderovitch, no one could compete with me.

The happiest time for me was Chanukah. Our instructor rehearsed us thoroughly in the holiday songs, and chose me to sing the prayers for the blessing of the candles.

Thus, my first appearance as an actor and singer was made on Chanukah, on the school's little makeshift stage. In the children's traditional playlet, *Hannah and her Seven Sons*, I played the youngest son, who refuses to kneel before the idol god. The biggest success I scored was in the scene where I bid my mother farewell. Accompanied by Vigderovitch's concertina, I sang the liturgical composition, "Man's Origin is Dust."

After the holiday presentation, refreshments were served. Meted out to each child was a slice of salami in a roll; a glass of sweetened tea, and a little bag of candy—a treat I relished but once a year—on Chanukah.

Neither can I forget Arbor Day—the New Year of the Trees, celebrated on the fifteenth day of Shevat, when figs, dates and carob were distributed among the children in honor of the holiday.

And how can I forget the outings on Lag Ba-Omer. We gathered in the schoolyard bright and early on the spring morning, laden with provisions, a small keg of drinking water, bows and arrows, kites, slings and other such diversions. Marching in step to the beat of a small snare drum, we set out to spend the day in the fresh air.

Near Grodno was the green Sekretter forest. Along the way we usually halted on Sabatchi Gorki, close to the Tartar's cemetery. If we made our way to Lasosna, through Kalozha, it gave us a chance to view the ancient and quaint little Cossack church on the crest of the hill. Then we'd be rowed across the Niemen.

Joyfully returning to town at dusk, we marched, singing and laughing as we crossed the Niemen river over the pontoon bridge, or sometimes by way of the hawser-drawn punt.

The Niemen

The central attraction in Grodno was the age-old Niemen. The river lay only a stone's throw from the Great Synagogue compound. In the wintertime, we'd coast down to the river on sleds, ice skates, or simply on our rear ends. Summertime, we would hop like wild goats from one hillock to another, peeling our clothes off piece by piece as we went, racing the rest of the way stark naked, to throw ourselves into the cool ripples of the crystal-clear waters.

It fascinated me to see the Niemen change according to weather and season. At the approach of the High Holy Days, around September, when legend tells us: "...even the fish in water, tremble," the Niemen already waged its annual struggle against the oncoming winter's freeze. In vain did it churn and toss choppy waves in the air. Slowly, like a mighty Hercules caught in heavy chains, the river succumbed to winter's icy breath.

Frozen solid, the commanding Niemen was no longer so forbidding. People ventured out on its smooth, glistening surface in horse-drawn sleighs as freely as on the open road. Young folks and little children went skating and sledding, with utter abandon. At times, the river did crack here and there, claiming victims. Still, this did not deter traffic from moving back and forth on it as confidently as on solid ground.

Thanks to its freezing, there was always an ample supply of ice to store in the ice-shacks. This was not only a boon in the sickroom, it also took care of the citizen's daily needs year-round.

At last, at the first hint of spring sunshine, the Niemen began to rouse from its torpor. By Passover, bursting with renewed energy, the river sent great cracking chunks of ice tumbling in the air like rubber balls. Fiercely, old river Niemen came to life again, its currents rampaging anew on their way to mysterious places.

Once again, fishermen took to spreading their nets, and the river obligingly filled them with plenty of fresh pike for the Sabbath and holidays—gefilte fish for the rich, and little smelts for the not-so-privileged.

Steamboats began their regular cruises, carrying passengers to Cruzkenik to take mud baths for rheumatism. Long transports of logs also started floating downstream to far-off destinations. Little rowboats swayed in rhythm with dipping oars propelled by romancing twosomes. Rocking the boat by a sudden swell, the river playfully interrupted a lover's kiss, or listened dreamily to heart-warming folk songs accompanied by the sweet sound of balalaikas and mandolins, and quite often acted as the silent witness to vows of eternal love, whispered under the moon.

During the "nine days"—from the first day in the month of 'Av, until after Tisha B'av—it was forbidden to dip in the river since it was alleged that the Niemen delighted in drowning humans during this period. The saying "Mi bamayim"—who shall perish by water—reminded us throughout the nine days of the flood that inundated the world. And each year the Niemen seemed to say, "People of Grodno, beware! You are in the shadow of a new and bloody deluge, which does not have its equal in the entire history of man!"

The Jews of Grodno failed to sense this forewarning. And now, a river of blood and tears flows through the city of Grodno; the blood of our nearest and dearest have rendered crimson the waters of our beloved Niemen.

6

On My Way to the Border

After my sleepless night in Warsaw, I arose before daybreak and, without waiting to be awakened by the operator's ring, was at the Warsaw terminal a full hour before train-time, ready to be on my way to Grodno.

In my heavy trenchcoat, custom-made in Buenos Aires; fur collar, a gift from a furrier in Helsinki; Norwegian fur "papakha" on my head and my sturdy Swedish galoshes—I looked like a dyed-in-the-wool Muscovite.

My baggage consisted of an overnight valise, in which I'd packed some underwear, a few shirts (one of which wrapped around the Yiddish book I carried as a gift for the partisan Scheikowsky), an extra sweater and sundry articles I planned to leave in Grodno. At the last moment, for something to while away the hours on the train, I threw in a pocket edition of an Ellery Queen detective story.

The only two friends who came to see me off were my pianist, Renee, and my Grodno chum, Avremel Khash. The car reserved for first class seemed very sparsely occupied.

I boarded the train. Soon, the conductor's shrill whistle, followed by a toot from the engine, signaled our departure. From a window in the corridor, I waved to my friends and watched their forms recede until I could only make out their fluttering handkerchiefs waving me a happy journey.

Neither the ever-increasing clatter, nor the screeching of the wheels over frozen rails, seemed able to drown out the pounding of my heart. Was this a dream, I wondered. Was I really on my way to my home town?

Entering my compartment, I found myself alone in a section meant to accommodate eight. As the landscape sped by my frosted window, I strained to catch a glimpse of the outskirts of Warsaw. The devastation of the Hitler occupation was still very evident. Row upon row of recently built houses flashed by, all of them with the same look of military barracks.

The train glided over the icy bridge spanning the Vistula River, the same old Vistula, now frozen, immobile, as if numbed in silent mourning for the six-hundred-thousand martyrs of Warsaw, the largest Jewish community in all of Europe! What enormous torrents of bloody waters have flowed here during the past turbulent years! The Warsaw we once knew, is no more... and is never again to be...

* * *

Sitting alone in my compartment, wrapped in retrospective thought, it occurred to me that I hadn't even breakfasted. Right now, I thought, what wouldn't I give for a piece of black bread and some kosher cold cuts of the Warsaw I knew years ago! In fact, I'd settle for the bread alone. I had neglected to include some provision for the journey. I figured I could grab a bite in the dining car, but just my luck—no such thing on this train.

My theater colleagues were well acquainted with my lifelong habit of arming myself with bread before going on a trip. These slices of pumpernickel came in handy more than once. I can recall when a morsel of bread was not to be had for any amount of money—and times when bread was easily available, only the money was not. So, "better to have and not want, than want and not have!"

How vividly this reminded me of an amusing episode in 1951, on one of my flights to Israel. Among my fellow passengers on El Al, I met a delegation of the Workmen's Circle, headed by their president Yechiel Eberil. It was during the height of the summer tourist season and the plane was jampacked. We took off from New York, and about seven o'clock were served a kosher, but very meager dinner. Along about 2 a.m., I noticed Mr. Eberil ambling up the aisle.

"Hello there, my friend, are you asleep?" he whispered, stopping at my seat.

"No. But why are you up and about at this hour? Aren't you feeling well?"

On the contrary, I feel too well!" he replied with characteristic humor. "I feel so well my stomach is growling and won't let me sleep. I wish I could sink my teeth into a pastrami sandwich from a Second Avenue deli!"

"Sorry, I can't produce a pastrami sandwich," I chuckled, "but I do have something I can treat you to—a fresh slice of pumpernickel.

Accepting it gratefully, he thanked me and went back to his seat. In about fifteen minutes there he was, back again. This time, he pushed a miniature bottle of cognac into my hand and remained standing by my seat.

"Tell you what, Yablokoff, let's trade. For every slice of bread, I'll reciprocate with another cognac. Is that a deal?"

To this day, whenever we happen to run into each other, Mr. Eberil is sure to remark, "Ah, Yablokoff, my friend, that delicious black pumpernickel on the plane to Israel! I'll never forget it!"

Bialystok

"Bial-y-stok!...Ten minute stop!" the conductor rasped out.

People, laden with bundles, crowded the station's platform ready to make a dash for it the moment the train stopped. I failed to recognize the station. It did not in the least resemble the Bialystok depot I remembered from bygone years.

Shoving each other, the people were more shabbily dressed than those in Warsaw. Their style of clothing seemed to date from World War I. Poverty was stamped on everyone.

On the platform, accessible from either roadbed, stood a wooden snack-shack. Quite hungry by now, I followed other passengers off the train to grab a bite. We were waited on by an elderly woman whose fingers were frozen stiff. The best she had to offer was bread, rolls, cheese, smoked herring (Bialystok's smoked herring and fish had been the city's specialty before the Holocaust; a business run exclusively by Jews), sausage, little paper bags of hard candy, chocolate bars, cigarettes, pipe tobacco, matches and small bottles of cider.

I bought a roll, a wedge of cheese, a bottle of cider and a small bag of caramels. With this epicurean repast tucked under my arm, I hurried back to my coupe and dug right in.

Several passengers opened the door of my compartment. Finding me the only occupant there, they made ready to drag their bundles in and keep me company. But, along came the conductor. Giving them a meaningful look, he mumbled something in Polish, whereupon they nodded a hurried "psheprasham!" and backed off.

It disturbed me. Here I occupied an entire compartment, while others had to squeeze together like herrings in a barrel.

The conductor blew his whistle and we were on our way again.

"Next stop...Sakolka!" he announced.

Sakolka, a small town, but what memories these names awakened. Sakolka...Bialystok!...

Bialystok, in fact, was on my concert schedule. The directors of the Jewish Cultural Association in Warsaw felt that, inasmuch as Bialystok's Jewish community now consisted of a mere ninety or a hundred Jews, it would hardly be worth dragging myself there to give a concert.

Bialystok?!!...with so few Jews? Unbelievable! All the more reason to give my concert there! These souls, I contended, were more in need of a moral lift and a bit of entertainment than those in Warsaw. The Association finally agreed, but as for the town of Sakolka, they told me, there were no Jews there at all.

It had turned very cold in the train. The farther east we traveled, the frostier it became. I snuggled deeper into my upturned collar and pulled my papakha well over my ears to keep warm.

I peered through the grime-covered windows. In vain did I try to catch a glimpse of the tall spire of the clock tower, a well-remembered landmark in Bialystok. The train only sped faster and faster, while everything vanished in the drifts of fallen snow.

Bialystok!...with a mere ninety, or a hundred Jews! It was hard to imagine. Bialystok, which had had forty-five to fifty thousand Jews! And Sakolka, with no Jews at all?!...

The names of these two cities were carved in my memory. Now, they only stirred anew the many painful emotions linked to my eldest brother Velvel, in the year 1905.

The Raid

With the blanket pulled over my head—a habit, to this day—I lay on the bunk I shared with my brother, Motke. The others in the family were sound asleep, while I lay half awake, lost in my childish fantasies.

Suddenly, the baker's dog, Malchik, began to bark. His yelping soon ended in a howl as if someone had stepped on his tail. Then came a sharp bang on our door, which rattled the window panes and sent a shudder through the little house. The tumult in the courtyard, the pounding on the door and the shutters grew louder.

"Open up! Open!...you accursed, scurvy Jews!" voices shouted. "In the name of the law, open up. Police!...this is an obisk!...a search!"

Terrified, I sat bolt upright. I held my breath, only my eyes strained into the dark to seek reassurance from my father, my mother and brother Shayke. I clung to Motke, who was also sitting up now, frozen with fright.

"Open the door!" the pounding and the threats continued, "or we'll break it down and tear you apart, you damned revolutionaries!"

I heard the hushed sound of someone tiptoeing in the dark, the creak of a drawer being opened, a rustling of papers...and sensed it was Shayke puttering around. Agile as a cat, he tiptoed to Rochele's cradle, fussed there for a moment and sprang back into his bunk.

The door groaned under the heavy blows of rifle-butts. A match flickered in the dark. With trembling hands, father groped for the kerosene lamp on the table. Igniting the wick, he replaced the smoky glass and bare-foot, in his nightshirt, carried the lamp to the door.

"Who is there?" he asked, knowing only too well. At the very first thrust on the door, he knew, and his heart stood still. They had come for Velvel!...his blessed son! It was almost three weeks since Velvke left the house...and he, his own father had driven him out.

"Shema Yisroel...Hear O Israel," his lips murmured, "God Almighty, watch over us and protect us!"

"Open the door, Jew bastard!" boomed a voice. "Open!"

Like a man resigned to meet his Maker, father removed the wooden bolt of the door. Police, drunk as lords, burst into the house giving father a shove that made him hit his head against the wall, almost dropping the guttering lamp.

"Oh, Alter!" cried mother in anguish. And we, echoing her hysteria, cried out, "Father...father! Oh, please don't hurt father! Have mercy!"

"Shut up, or we'll finish the lot of you!" barked one of them, gruffly.

The invaders rummaged in every corner, pulled out the drawers of the commodes and dumped the contents on the floor. Like pigs at a trough they sniffed and poked their snouts into everything, grunting with rage because their pillaging hadn't brought any results.

"Get the hell down off your bunks!" roared the gendarme in charge of the search. "Get a move on, you anarchists!"

Trembling, we slid to the floor and stood there in our nightshirts, teeth chattering with cold and terror. Mama and my two sisters stood huddling in their bedsheets and blankets, desperately trying to hide their nakedness. Roaring with laughter, the raiders pulled their coverings loose and leered at them.

They ripped open our pallets, strawsacks, pillows and eiderdowns, releasing feathers and straw all over the place. When they came upon Rochele's cradle, they stopped a moment to observe the little creature, who lay there soaked—not in tears alone. Considering it hardly worth the trouble, they merely pulled her coverlet aside as a perfunctory investigation and that was that. Shayke's instinct had paid off. What he had so hurriedly hidden under the baby's mattress was a batch of forbidden proclamations and a revolver.

"Where is your son, jid?" the gendarme abruptly demanded.

"Which son?" father barely managed to utter.

"You know damned well which son I mean. Don't play dumb with me. Your son the anarchist!"

"My children are all good, honest children, sir."

Don't give me any back-talk, you lousy jid!" he roared. "I ask the questions and you answer, understand? Now then, how many sons do you have?"

"Four sons, sir," murmured father.

"Four, eh? Good! Where are they?"

With an unsteady hand, father pointed at me, at Motke, at Shayke... and now, he thought, this is the end. We are doomed.

The gendarme, looking Shayke over from head to toe, winked at one of his aides and then barked: "Come here, you revolutionist! What do they call you, scoundrel?"

"I am not called scoundrel," retorted Shayke in flawless Russian. "My name is Shayke Abrabovitch Yablonik."

Like the crack of a whip, he slapped Shayke across the face, leaving a red imprint of five fingers. Shayke's hand flew to his cheek. He gritted his teeth, but uttered not a peep. With the groan of a wounded lion, father lunged forward, while Mama moaned in helpless agony. And we, children, wailed at the top of our lungs.

"If you insist on being such an impudent dog, you'll get more of the same!" rasped the gendarme. "A proud jid, what? And what is your occupation, you..."

"Shaykele, answer the honorable man," pleaded Mama between sobs. "Take pity on your mother. Answer."

"I attend trade school," Shayke murmured, his eyes ablaze with defiance.

"Trade school, eh?" the gendarme kept at him, "and what do they teach you there? How to stir up revolution against our beloved father, the czar?"

"I am a student at the..."

"Trade school! I heard, I heard! We'll check that later. You have another son," he said, turning to father. "His name is...his name..." he pawed in his leather folder to make sure.

"His name is Wolf, sir. Wolf Yablonik," father answered in misery.

Like a tiger preparing to pounce on his prey, the gendarme took a deep breath and with exaggerated casualness, inquired "Where, may I ask, is your son?"

"He is...he...he hasn't come home yet."

The gendarme almost choked in a wild burst of laughter. "Well, well! So he hasn't come home yet. It's four o'clock in the morning. Your children are good, decent children are they? Well, where is he, your son? Answer, jid!" In despair, father buried his head in his hands. "I'll tell you where your son is," thundered the gendarme, "behind bars! We caught him, that terrorist, together with the other three assassins. Caught all of them in Bialystok, the Christ killers. That bastard son of yours threw a bomb—a bomb! He'll hang by his neck! And you, jid, you can all thank your Jewish God that we didn't find any proclamations, or weapons here. We were sure we'd find a whole arsenal. You ought to be packed off to Siberia, anyway, you Jew bastards!"

With a command to leave, they stormed out cursing and spitting. We remained standing as if welded to the floor. Velvke arrested?...a bomb?...chains?...hanging...?

My brother's arrest stirred up the entire city. The police had rampaged throughout the night with their searches and arrests. That very evening at a secret meeting in the woods, fellow revolutionaries gave fiery speeches:

"Comrades! Brothers and sisters! Four of our invaluable party members have been seized. We are well aware of the fate that awaits these imprisoned fighters, who have sacrificed themselves to fulfill their mission for the proletariat. They have delivered our protest against the sadistic treatment received in the jails of Russia by our brothers and sisters, the political prisoners. An eye for an eye!..."

Mounted Cossacks suddenly descended on this secret gathering in the woods, cracking their whips left and right. Yet even this brutality failed to quell the shouts of: "Down with the Czar! Long live Wolf Kropotkin!"

My Brother, The Anarchist

Velvke, a delicate youth barely eighteen, was of medium height, with jet-black hair, regular features and big dark eyes like mother's. And already he was playing an active role in the Grodno revolutionary movement. Though Velvke possessed an innate drive for education, he did not have the opportunity to accomplish more than a few grades in the Talmud Torah and trade school; whereupon he went to work in Charin's bookbindery. While he labored long hours for a pittance, other boys his age, whose families could afford it, were parading around in their smart Gymnasia uniforms.

The abortive revolution of 1905, which followed the Russo-Japanese War, only added more fuel to the people's resentment toward the czarist regime. All the golden promises made by the ruling autocracy to pacify the workers and the peasants soon fizzled out. The double-crossing tyrants promptly dissolved the Duma, the parliament—never very representative of the people to begin with—and a new wave of terror began to smother all liberal thinking in Russia. With renewed despotism, they proceeded to liquidate everyone suspected of participating in any revolutionary movement.

Velvel began his activities with the PPS (Polska Partja Sosjalistyczna) and then joined the anarchist-terrorists, throwing himself into their movement heart and soul. He listened to the fervent speeches of the intellectuals, who always began by elaborating on the enslavement and poverty of the local working class, which suffered unmercifully under the yoke of exploitation in Grodno, as in other corners of Russia.

Velvel came to realize how limited, how unfulfilled, is the individual who is uneducated. He avidly took to reading whatever material he could lay his hands on: books, journals, old newspapers and periodicals. His drive toward learning and probing into the core of things soon motivated several party members to tutor him, and before long he became one of the leading young fighters for freedom and justice under the pseudonym of Piotr Kropotkin, the anarchist.

My brother Shayke and our cousin Fraydke, Uncle Shillingoff's eldest daughter, were also active in the movement.

Fraydke was a charming girl, a gymnasia graduate, whose wealthy parents lovingly indulged in all that her heart desired. A young lady of many attributes, she was indeed the pride of the family. Fraydke dreamed of a career in medicine and intended to further her studies at the University of St. Petersburg. But there arose the problem of a residence permit. Areas outside the Tchertah—beyond the Pale—were restricted to Jews. The one recourse she had was to acquire a yellow identification card issued only to registered prostitutes. Other Jewish students with similar aspirations were obliged to avail themselves of these permits of residence, but Fraydke could not bring herself to accept this. Her father's influence and generous palm-greasing was of no help either.

Bitterly disappointed, Fraydke was forced to remain at home, in Grodno. Inevitably, she was caught up in the tide of revolution.

Fraydke admired Velvke's strides in self-education, and she beamed with pride as she listened to her cousin's fiery speeches, delivered in fluent Russian. Thus, a rare friendship and a close, spiritual bond sprang up between them.

* * *

Shayke, who had also become involved in the revolutionary movement, was Velvel's exact opposite. He was taller, round-faced, with brown eyes more like father's, and he had a shock of sandy brown hair. Shayke was a placid boy by nature. At the trade school where he learned mechanics, it was said that he had a "pair of golden hands." Shayke could take apart and put back together anything from a pocketwatch to a locomotive.

Shayke and Velvel, hardly two years apart, belonged to two different ideological groups. Velvel expounded the theory that the best and quickest way to emancipate the proletariat was through terrorism: an eye for an eye! Shayke, on the other hand, was for the milder form of socialism prescribed by the Jewish Labor Organization, the Bund.

The odd-looking characters my brothers befriended robbed father of his sleep. The smallest sound stirred him out of bed. Mother suffered in silence, but she too, could not shut an eye until her sons were home and accounted for. She was just as disturbed as father, but to keep peace she often tried to defend the boys by finding all sorts of excuses for them.

This only angered father all the more. "Mark my words, Leah, your sons will bring catastrophe on us. No good will come out of Velvke's poring over that dangerous, sacrilegious drivel. And Shayke, too! Make refined men out of them, you urged. Educate them, you said! Well, what did they learn—how to shout 'Down with the czar!'?"

Neither reason nor anger could persuade Velvke to give up his revolutionary activities. The situation finally reached the point where Velvel was forced to leave the house. This turn of events had its effect on Shayke. Officially, he dropped his activities with the Bund and channeled his youthful energies into other outlets such as, bicycling, mandolin-strumming and choir-singing. But, secretly, he helped his comrades repair, rehabilitate and clean old shotguns, rifles, pistols—antiquated weapons dug up from "Bogdan Khmelnitzky's Era."

In his free moments, Shayke puttered around with gunpowder, bullets, shells, cartridges and dynamite. He turned the outhouse into a secret ammunition dump. Shayke was suspected of having manufactured the bomb that had dragged Velvel into such disaster.

* * *

To father, the arrest of his son was a devastating blow. "Woe is me," he cried, "that I should live to bear such disgrace! My son, a convict! Alter's son, a criminal!" He was tortured by conflicting emotions. On the one hand, he thought: "My son wouldn't listen to me so let him stew in it!" Then again, he knew it was his duty to go to Bialystok and find an advocate to plead clemency for his son. He had to do all in his power to save him.

Mother pawned the silver Sabbath candlesticks for the necessary fare, and together they set out for Bialystok fervently hoping for a miracle. The miracle, however, did not come to pass. They were not permitted as much as a glance at their son.

Velvel's arrest had also dealt a mortal blow to our cousin Fraydke. She had known of the assassination plot and was tortured by a stricken conscience. She locked herself in her room; wouldn't eat, sleep, or talk to anyone. When she did speak, her words were incoherent. The doctors warned that she be watched, for she was suffering from a melancholia with suicidal tendencies.

Fellow-workers collected money and engaged an advocate to plead the case for each of the four accused assassins. Whatever leniency the advocate was able to wrest from the benevolent judge, was as follows: two of the four prisoners were to be hung. A girl in the group was given fifteen years penal servitude. And the mercy extended my teenage brother was the sentence of ten years solitary confinement in the Schlusselburg Fortress in St. Petersburg, to be followed by exile to Siberia for the remainder of his life.

At these horrendous tidings father rent his garment, removed his shoes and sat on the floor—the rituals observed in mourning the dead.

"Leah... mother!" he wailed in soul-stirring agony, "we have lost our son. He is dead...'Boruch dayan hoemess' (Blessed be the Judge of Truth)."

And cousin Fraydke lost her mind completely. She had made several attempts at taking her life, and although there were moments when she seemed quite lucid, murmuring: "Velvke, let us go to St. Petersburg. I have my identification card"—she always slipped back into her melancholia until her troubled heart and tortured spirit were stilled forever.

* * *

"Sakolka!...Five minute stop!" the conductor yelled, startling me out of my reverie. Sakolka! And right on cue, I couldn't help thinking in theater jargon. My thoughts were indeed revolving around Sakolka, dredging up the events involving the two towns, Bialystok and Sakolka, 1906.

To The Rescue

Information trickled out of Bialystok's underground that Kropotkin (Wolf Yablonik) was to be taken with other prisoners from Bialystok to the jail in Grodno, by way of Sakolka. His comrades promptly discussed plans on how to snatch him out of the etape. Since Sakolka lay midway between Bialystok and Grodno, it was the most likely rest point for the marching convoy, making it the most logical site for their rescue. As part of the plan, father had to get the job of surfacing the yard of the Sakolka jail. His crew was to be put to work on the project, leaving the rest to Wolf's comrades.

It was a far-fetched plan, but father grabbed at it like a drowning man at a straw. To everyone's surprise he cooperated with all their instructions, despite the danger he knew was involved in such a conspiracy.

Sure enough, before long, the ringing of steel hammers echoed around Sakolka's prison-yard. According to strategy, father and his crew made it their business to strike up a camaraderie with the guards; treating them to an occasional swig of vodka from the bottle, or presenting them with a full krutchok, Russian half-pint, to take home.

In a corner of the yard stood the toilet shack. When a prisoner needed to make use of it, he was escorted by a guard who held a loaded rifle to his back. The guard waited outside the door of the latrine. If the prisoner took longer than the guard deemed necessary, he knocked on the door with the butt of his rifle and barked, "Hurry up there, you bastard. Don't take all day! Let's get back to the cell!"

It was this privy that played the main role in the plot to rescue my brother.

At last the etape came trudging into the village of Sakolka. With a chain-clanking rhythm, dragging swollen feet, the prisoners shuffled past the curiosity seekers who lined the streets.

Among these shackled dregs of humanity, father caught the pitiful sight of his son. Like a dog on a leash being dragged along, Velvel was chained hand and foot to the other prisoners. Blinded by the tears that streamed down his face, father stood rooted to the spot. He didn't dare make a move lest he draw unnecessary attention, or cause suspicion that he, or his fellow-workers, had any interest in the prisoners.

When Velvel was finally allowed to drop his weary limbs on his allotted cell bunk, his ears caught the familiar sound of hammers striking stone; a sound he knew so well from early childhood. What a sweet, nostalgic reminder of home and loved ones. His heart quickened. But who, he wondered, can they be?

The riddle solved itself upon his first visit to the latrine. He recognized the dear, familiar face of his father, his uncles and cousins, who were gallantly swinging away at the cobblestones in the yard, going about their work in feigned ignorance of his presence.

Prisoners were forbidden to speak to anyone, but Velvel knew that something was afoot, and understood that he was expected to wait for instructions. Friends began sending him the permitted food packages, which were, of course, thoroughly examined before reaching the inmates. Still, Velvel probed each item in the package minutely until he found what he was looking for. Baked into a loaf of bread he found a note that read: "Kropotkin, on such and such a day, at such and such an hour, ask to be taken to the latrine. Loosened boards on left side of back wall need only slight push. A wagon, loaded with sand, will be waiting in back. Crawl in. Leave rest to us. Do everything as outlined. Long live freedom!"

The family crew of pavers waited for the designated hour with a silent prayer in their hearts. Their part of the rescue was to distract the guard by staging a sudden squabble. Everything was going according to plan. The sand wagon was to get Velvel out of the prison grounds. Nobody would suspect anything, because the wagon had been making trips in and out of the yard quite freely. In one of the side streets, a larger wagon piled with hay would be standing by. As soon as Velvel was transferred from wagon to wagon and hidden in the hay, he would be trundled off to the Prussian border and smuggled into Germany. The sand wagon would bide its time, driving around the side roads until the alarm was sounded. By that time, it would be all over but the shouting! The prison staff could damn well go ahead and search until doomsday!

Father had been advised to go back to Grodno, so as not to be on the scene during the escape. If anything went wrong, he would have a bona fide alibi: he knew nothing of the conspiracy.

The crucial moment was finally at hand. Velvke appeared in the yard as scheduled, with the armed guard at his heels. He entered the latrine and shut the door. The guard took up his watch, pacing back and forth. The wagon stood waiting on the dirt road in back of the shack, with a comrade dressed as a local peasant on the driver's seat, ready with reins in hand. The pavers were just about to go into their planned rumpus, when all at once, the door of the latrine opened. Out stepped Velvke—and in the routine manner, was led back to his cell.

A stunned, heartbroken, "Oh!" rose from the depths of every man in the yard.

Velvke's note, subsequently smuggled out of prison, explained his action: "At the last moment I could not bring myself to further jeopardize the lives of my father and my family. I have already caused them enough misery. I must make peace with my fate. My undying gratitude for undertaking the perilous risk on my behalf. Comrades, do not despair! The ultimate hour of freedom is at hand. Down with the czar! Long live the revolution!—Kropotkin."

7

The Grodno Jail

Russian prisons were filled with many innocent victims doomed to long-term sentences. The Grodno jail was no exception. Political offenders, those fortunate enough to be spared the gallows or the firing squad, were thrown together with murderers, thieves, perverts, prostitutes, and the venereally diseased.

These unfortunates were flogged across bared buttocks for the slightest act of disobedience. Their only weapons against their inhuman treatment were frequent hunger strikes.

With the pledge of the freedom-song on their lips, they bade brave farewells to comrades, who were exiled with etapes to the fortress of Schlusselburg, Petropavlovsk, or various other prisons in Russia. Long chains of shackled martyrs often wended to a living grave in far-off Siberia.

The walls of the narrow prison cells were covered with revolutionary slogans, like last wills and testaments left for inmates who were destined to follow. The straw-filled pallets on the iron cots were infested with fleas, lice and bedbugs. The constant battle against these flesh-devouring, blood-sucking demons made sleep impossible. The small window near the top of the wall afforded neither light, nor air—as proved by the ashen faces of the inmates.

In the code of the prison's wall-language, the tapped-out communication was relayed from cell to cell: "New 'lodger' brought in during the night... another house-guest of the czar... Kropotkin..."

Obtaining a pass to visit a political prisoner was no easy matter; especially one like my brother, who refused to take orders even behind bars. Promptly, upon his arrival in jail, he began to rebel against the cruelties meted out by the prison guards. To keep him in line he was whipped. When this failed to dampen his protests, he was thrown into solitary confinement.

* * *

Visiting hours were held on Saturday afternoon. Father had forbidden us to go and see Velvel at any time; particularly since it would have to be on the Sabbath.

"A fine way to spend a Sabbath, I must say!" he grumbled bitterly, "Visiting in jail with a son, a convict!" The Sabbath was merely a convenient excuse for the restriction. In truth it was because of his rankling chagrin at Velvke for having, at the last moment, defeated the well-laid plan for his escape from the Sakolka jail.

45

"Such a devoted son!" he seethed. "He wanted to spare his mother and father! First he cuts our throats and then he feels sorry for us! To me, he is dead...dead! Do you hear me? I never want to hear his name again!"

The frequent quarrels on this subject inevitably upset our Sabbaths, casting a heavy gloom over the entire household.

My sister Mariashka and my brother Shayke did sometimes manage to slip out and bring Velvke a little package of food prepared by Mama without father's knowledge. He would never tolerate the toting of packages on the Sabbath—and to jail at that.

"Sending gift packages to your precious meshumed (renegade)?" he once upbraided her. "If I find out that you've sent him as much as a crust of bread, I'll leave this house and you'll never see me again! It would be more of a mitzvah on your part if you threw the bread to the birds. Your dear son has made his bed—now let him lie in it!"

Mother kept silent. She knew it was the agony in father that spoke out. Summoning every ounce of strength, she tried to carry on for the sake of the rest of her family.

A custom we well observed, when Shabat Shirah rolled around, was to set food out on a window ledge for the birds: bread crumbs, groats, stale challah, bits of leftover "cholent," to the sparrows' delight, since Shabat Shirah falls in mid-winter, when everything is steeped in snow, and the little feathered creatures are unable to forage for themselves.

The custom of feeding the birds was one in which I participated with great childish satisfaction; especially after father had explained its origin. When the Romans set fire to the Holy Temple in Jerusalem, countless swallows flew overhead carrying water in their bills to put out the flames. For this brave deed, all birds are henceforth to be rewarded with food during the winter months.

It happened to fall on Shabat Shirah that I became acquainted with Grodno jail, where Velvke spent several months, waiting to be exiled to the Schusselburg Fortress in St. Petersburg.

"Chaimke," Shayke had whispered, "Velvel has been asking me to bring you along sometime. So, on Saturday, after we eat, I'll take you."

I had seen my brother Velvel so seldom at home, I hardly knew him. The curiosity of visiting this brother, the object of such constant bickering, and the thought that I would actually be inside of a prison, filled me with an awesome dread. Yet I lived in a state of excited anticipation.

That Sabbath, coming home with father from the synagogue, I sat at the table unable to swallow a bite. What a good time the birds are going to have with my portion of food, I thought. Halfheartedly, I joined in the singing of "Zmiroth," and kept alert for Shayke's signal to slip out of the house.

Mama, aware of our plan, had a parcel of food tucked away for us to take along. But, as luck would have it, father discovered it.

"So, a food package...all neatly wrapped for your convict son!" he shouted.

"Well, why don't you, yourself get all dressed up, Leah, and go have a little visit with your son in honor of the Sabbath?!"

Enraged, he flung open the door and hurled the parcel across the yard, scattering its contents all over the snow. In an instant, a swarm of birds swooped down and, with grateful chirps, devoured the feast.

Well...after all, it was Shabat Shirah, the Sabbath of Song.

The Visit

A crowd of visitors had already gathered at the outer gates of the prison, when Shayke and I got there. Almost all carried a parcel: food to supplement the scant and unappetizing fare of the prison, and also a bit of tobacco, or some cigarettes. The food parcels had a peculiar way of shrinking after prison inspection: the choicest morsels, undoubtedly, disappearing into the gullets of the gluttonous jail keepers. But go sue them!

At last the gates opened. Two black-uniformed guards collected the issued passes and glowered at the visitors, who pushed and jostled one another to get in as quickly as possible, so as not to lose a precious moment.

I tagged after Shayke across the big prison yard into a musty room with gray walls. It was divided down its length by three wire-mesh partitions, which separated the visitors from the prisoners. All communication had to be held in Russian, so the guards, moving up and down between the partitions, could understand. Topics of conversation had to be kept within prescribed boundaries.

The eager questions and answers flying back and forth between visitors and inmates were punctuated by sudden bursts of weeping. The din in the congested room grew steadily noisier, so that it became necessary to outshout one another in order to be heard. The guards only added to the tumult by hurling threats at the prisoners and abusive remarks at the visitors.

The air grew heavy with a stinking mixture of perspiration and damp boots. It made me nauseous. The shouting, the smell and the strangeness of it all made my head swim.

"Chaimke, Chaimke, look there!" Shayke nudged me. "Look, there's Velvke!"

A youth, in gray prison garb, was hustled in from a side door. The guard ordered him to take up a place at the wire mesh facing us.

"Velvke!" Shayke called to him, "Velvke!"

Oh no! It can't be! I thought. Is that Velvke? My brother? There must be some terrible mistake! The ashen color of Velvke's face was almost one with the drab clothing that hung on his thin frame. The round cap on his head hid the gruesome fact that his dark crop of wavy hair had been shorn to the scalp. His gentle eyes smiled at me. Hypnotically they drew me, kissed me and gave me consolation. I was too young to grasp the meaning of the strange flame that burned in my brother's eyes, but they were to haunt me the rest of my life.

What it was my brothers were shouting to each other I could not hear, nor make out. I was fascinated by Velvke's big black eyes, set deep in their shadowy sockets, glowing with an unearthly, feverish flame. There was love and compassion in them, infinite tenderness and forgiveness; the eyes of a martyr resigned to sacrifice himself for the welfare of mankind. An indescribable feeling gripped my young heart and, suddenly, tears stung my eyes and ran down my cheeks. Every detail of my brother's image became etched in my mind.

After this short, but unforgettable visit, Shayke took me home and promptly went off again. Father was lying down, taking his customary nap after the Sabbath meal. Mother was quietly puttering with the dishes, while Mariashka and Slavka, glumly gazing out the window, kept sniffling and intermittently blowing their noses. Motke's head was buried in a prayer book. Rochele was wide awake in her cradle.

Shayke and I had apparently missed the real thick of a quarrel between mother and father, which must have ensued after we left.

Still shaken, but careful not to awaken father, I curled up in a chair. Resting my hands on the arm, I put my head down and fell asleep, only to be disturbed by morbid dreams.

After a while, the ponderous bells of the Russian church began to toll, and were soon followed by the Polish church. The doleful clanging in the quiet of the dusk created an air of mysticism and they summoned the worshipers to vespers.

Mama fetched the earthen teapot of tepid water, which she'd been keeping warm in the folds of the eiderdown. Wordlessly, she poured a glass of tea for father and set it on the table. He arose, and ignored the tea. "Evening prayers!" he gruffly announced, and, slamming the door, was gone.

Motke and I exchanged glances and without a word agreed that we had better lose no time in following father to the synagogue.

As we neared the big Hayyei Adam, voices were already raised in the ancient prayers ushering out the Sabbath Queen—the Day of Repose. Louder and louder the chanting rose, as if intent on drowning out the persistent and deafening church bells.

* * *

That night, the frost crept into the very marrow of my bones. My teeth chattered as I lay snuggled close to Motke; each of us pulling at the covers in a vain attempt to warm up. The hours wore on and finally, very late in the night, fatigue triumphed over the cold and we feel into a deep sleep.

A sharp rapping on the shutters startled us awake. A breathless voice was calling behind the frosted windows, "Shayke...Shayke! Wake up! Hurry! They're taking your brother to the railroad station. Wake up, Reb Alter! Hurry to the depot. Your son is being led away with the etape!"

In the confusion, everyone threw on whatever clothing was at hand and ran into the street. People from every corner were hurrying to the railway station. Breathlessly, I followed them as far as the post office. Crowds had already gathered there—Jews and non-Jews alike—anxiously craning their necks in anticipation of the transport of prisoners.

The cold beams of a full moon fell upon the frost-pinched faces of the crowd. Some vigorously rubbed snow over their benumbed ears and noses, while others kept swinging their arms back and forth across their chests, as they stomped on one stiffened leg and then the other.

All at once, an ominous hush fell over the crowd.

"Here they come... here they come! Merciful God!" lips murmured in stifled anxiety. The unmistakable clanking of chains could be heard in the distance... the crunching of footsteps on crisp snow... the hollow clop-clop of horses' hooves. Louder and louder these sounds echoed as they drew closer and closer.

A mournful wailing broke out around me even before the procession moved into sight. It made my hair stand on end and pricked my scalp like needles. The rattling of chains grew steadily louder. The weeping and lamenting became even more unbearable. And then, an awesome sight unfolded before me.

A convoy of soldiers leading the etape, tramped into view; menacing figures bundled to the teeth, clad in heavy, long-skirted greatcoats, bulky felt coverings over their boots, tall fur hats down to their eyes, topped by huge hoods securely tied over their heads. The fixed bayonets of their loaded rifles were trained on the crowd.

Following this avant-garde, the prisoners dragged into view. Hulking apparitions, they were, their backs bent under tattered blankets, or shawls of every hue, heads wrapped in rags, torn scarves and kerchiefs, their legs bound up in burlap, twined with rope. The steel manacles welded to the connecting chains, fettered their frozen hands and feet.

Flanked on every side by gendarmes on foot and Cossacks astride horses, the grim procession was enclosed as in a steel trap. The flashing of swords and the terrifying whooshing of whips kept the onlookers in cowering abeyance. The nervously prancing horses, bringing up the rear, drove the prisoners on like sheep being herded to slaughter.

Petrified, I stood rooted to the spot. A warm wetness ran down my thighs, making my pants cling to my legs. In mortal terror, I had lost control...

Suddenly, a wisp of a girl, with the agility of a cat, tore herself from the crowd and slipped through the barricade of soldiers. Hurling herself at one of the living corpses, she screamed hysterically, "Velvke! Velvke! My dear brother!" Brutally, two gendarmes flung her back against the curb and crackling whips rained on the huddled form of my sister Slavka.

Swept along by the surging crowd, I followed the funereal procession, desperately trying to single out my brother. In vain did I stretch my neck over the marchers to catch a glimpse of his face, his eyes. But the exiles had to keep their heads lowered. Any attempt to look up was promptly met by the crack of a whip, or the thrust of a rifle-butt.

At the station, a fresh detail of guardsmen restrained the crowd, whose weeping and clamoring became intolerable. Somehow, I managed to slip through the cordon.

By the dim glow of the sooty lanterns along the platform, I huddled behind a post, and watched them load the human cargo.

A string of wooden freight cars, on outmoded springs and wheels, stood waiting on a siding. Their snow-covered roofs, doors and small iron-barred windows were strung with long icicles. The prisoners lumbered up the high steps into the boxcars and were swallowed by the cold, cavernous dark.

A shrill whistle from the locomotive, a hissing of white steam, a puffing of black smoke, a tentative screech of frost-bound wheels and then, as one car bumped against the other, the train slowly began to move.

To my amazement, from somewhere within the shadowy dungeon, a voice rose in song. Instantly, other voices picked up the strain, until the singing spread throughout the length of the crawling hell: "Arise, ye victims of enslavement."

The wheels turned faster and faster, the laboring engine in its unsteady rhythm chugged louder and louder, tooted shriller and shriller, but could not drown out the inspired singing of the "Internationale," which seemed to soar to the very heavens.

My frozen fingers curled into hard fists as my eyes stared after the taillight of the caboose, until it became a tiny red dot in the distance.

* * *

Durov's Circus

My first public appearance, save as choirboy in the Great Synagogue and the heyder concerts, took place in the arena of Durov's Circus.

Large, colorful posters proclaimed the exciting news that the famous Russian circus and animal show was coming to town.

One day, during choir practice, we learned that the circus director was looking for boys and girls to take part in a pantomime, a sequence to be portrayed specifically by children. Each participant would receive ten kopecks a performance.

Well, the ten kopecks... although nothing to sneeze at... were beside the point. The main attraction was seeing, free of charge, a circus with real wild animals, such as I had only read about in school books and seen on little picture cards.

Lucky for me, father had taken on a paving job in a small town outside Grodno. Unable to resist the temptation, I joined several other boys and went off to accept the "engagement" at Durov's Circus.

A gnome-like little man, his shaggy mane flowing down the nape of his neck à la impresario, was sorting a group of boys and girls according to type.

The sequence was to portray a royal wedding attended by all the crowned heads of Europe, including their respective queens and entourages. Thanks to my swarthy complexion, I was cast as the ruler of Italy. Arrayed in royal robes, a small beard glued to my chin, a pair of mustachios, a crown on my head— and behold, I became King of Italy! For my queen, I was paired off with a cute and equally dark complected "shiksele" about my own age. She too, was costumed and bejewelled in royal fashion, with a shimmering crinoline gown and adornments befitting a queen. The rest of the boys and girls were also out- fitted according to the countries and nationalities they represented.

We were seated in small replicas of regal couches, each drawn by a span of six plumed and beribboned ponies, and driven by youngsters dressed as coach- men and footmen. As the ringmaster announced the arrival of each monarch and his retinue, the bank struck up the anthem of that particular country and we, in turn, rode into the arena. Sitting up stiff and pompous in our royal car- riages, we nodded haughtily and waved in response to the clapping of the audi- ence. It required no great talent, but, who could deny the thrill of such a jaunt around an arena in a pony-drawn coach, winding up with ten kopecks to boot?! To top it off, we also had the privilege of watching—at close range—the antics of the clowns, the magicians, acrobats, wire-walkers, flame swallowers and see the ferocious lions, tigers and bears claw at their cages and bare their fangs!

The greatest attraction was Durov's "Pig Act." The pigs, cleverly done up in uniforms, easily recognizable as those of high-ranking Russian officers, acted out an entire satire at the expense of the czarist regime. The audience rocked with laughter, grasping the revolutionary propaganda behind this daring bit of comedy more readily than they would from a lecture given by the most persuasive agitator. In fact, this ingenious pig act cost the circus their permit. Durov and his menagerie were run out of town by the city authorities right smack in the middle of their smashing success.

When we showed up for our pantomime the next day, there was no longer a sign of a circus, nor any of its trappings. The little gnome had absconded with my first theatrical wages! Yet I had to keep my mouth shut. If ever my father found out that I had become a circus performer, I'd find myself in a far greater predicament than having lost my pay of seventy kopecks.

8

All in the Family

A new peril threatened our family. My brother Shayke was due for military service. Friends, relatives and neighbors came up with all sorts of advice guaranteed to save my brother from the ordeal of serving in the czar's army in addition to the standard recourse of self-inflicted handicaps. Still, after long deliberation, it was resolved that in Shayke's case, the wisest and "healthiest" way out was to smuggle him across the border into Prussia, and let him make his way from there to America.

But Shayke would have none of it. "The Russian ogre won't devour me! Aren't there hordes of Jewish soldiers in the Russian army? So I won't be the only one. Three years of military service? Nothing to it. I'll come back safe and sound and live out the rest of my life right here in Grodno!" There was no use arguing the point. He was determined to serve.

As if this were not enough, the family was faced with yet another problem—my sister, Mariashka. She had grown into an exceptionally attractive young girl, albeit a bit on the plump side; a round-faced, blue-eyed dumpling who liked to pass herself off as older than her eighteen years. Her salary as a salesgirl was a great help to the family.

Mariashka's acquaintance with a young fellow called Khoneh Abramowitz created an upheaval in the house. Khoneh, who was orphaned at a very early age, had been obliged to fend for himself and his little sister, Tzirele. When Khoneh grew up he went to work in a tannery; an arduous and most unpleasant kind of occupation, although it did pay well. As soon as Khoneh felt a few rubles in his pocket, he began playing the big shot. He took to dressing like a dude; frequenting a restaurant, where he could order a gourmet meal; thus, earning himself the reputation of a glutton, a spendthrift! "Disgraceful!" people shrugged, "no good can come of him!"

Khoneh hung around Mariashka every free moment, unburdening his heart to her, and her alone; berating his kin, who didn't give a hang about him and his little sister. No longer, he confided, would he be at the mercy of anyone who felt like kicking him around, oh, no! He was strong as a bull!

The compassion in Mariashka's heart soon turned to love. She knew, nonetheless, that she would have a hard time convincing her parents that Khoneh, the tanner of raw hides, was her destined mate.

The sweethearts held their meetings secretly—that is, until it reached Shayke's ears, whereupon Mariashka promptly received an ultimatum.

"To begin with, you're too young to be keeping steady company. Secondly, couldn't you find a better suitor than Khoneh the tanner? And third, if I ever catch you with that character, I'll slap your face! And, as for your 'beloved,' I'll break every bone in his body!"

Undaunted, Mariashka let all this bluster go in one ear and out the other.

Whether Shayke was truly keeping an eye on her, or whether it was purely by accident, he ran into the lovebirds head on, strolling along Sadova Street. He did not slap his sister's face, but the look he gave her was enough to send her marching home, alone. Neither did this encounter between the two future brothers-in-law lead to a scuffle. They merely glared at each other like the entrants at a cockfight and went their separate ways, bitter enemies.

Mariashka cried her heart out to Mama. And Mama could do nothing but talk the matter over with father. The match wasn't much to their liking either, but they couldn't help recalling their own nearly-wrecked romance. Father told Mariashka she could bring her young man to the house, for if they wished to spend time together, home was the proper place.

Shayke made it his business not to be present during these visits. In time, however, the ruffled feathers were smoothed and Mama acquired an extra guest at the table. Mariashka and Khoneh were, unofficially, engaged. As time went on, even Shayke relented in his disapproval of Khoneh, although deep down, their early animosity rankled in them for the rest of their lives.

* * *

Shayke subsequently answered the call to military duty. As soon as the doctors at the induction center took one look at him, they pronounced him godyn—fit to serve the czar—and he was inducted into the army.

Shayke was assigned to the artillery in Kolomna, near Moscow. We went to see him off at the station on a Saturday morning. Father preferred not to come along, for it would mar the Oneg Shabat (Joy of the Sabbath). Mother, too, chose to remain at home. Witnessing Velvke, her firstborn, being dragged off to the Schlusselburg Fortress, was still too fresh in her mind. At parting with her second son, she was strangely silent and dry-eyed.

Returning home from the station, we sat around the table utterly glum as Mama moved about, absent-mindedly serving the Sabbath meal. Opening the iron door of the oven, she lifted out the cholent and temporarily placed the pot on the floor. In a quick motion to rise, her head struck the open oven door with such force that it knocked her to the floor, the blood oozing down her face. We rushed to her aid, all of us in tears. Yet Mama herself did not cry. It was as if she had no more tears to shed.

The Betrothal

Khoneh was also about to be conscripted into the army. But, having no appetite to serve the czar, he planned to head for America. Mariashka was beside herself. America... my God! One heard such awful tales about fiances going off to America only to disappear, leaving prospective brides with nothing but the promise to be sent for. Time would pass, the young husband-to-be would never again be heard from, and the bride would either be put back into "open stock," or remain a spinster.

Our parents gave a great deal of thought to Mariashka's situation. Was she, or was she not engaged? Father took heed of his friend, the Eishishker Rabbi, who advised him not to rely on miracles, but to get the couple formally betrothed. The good rabbi drew up the traditional Tnoiem (betrothal agreement). The family gathered at the house to wish them mazel tov, drink a toast l'chaim, sample the honey cake and bid Khoneh Godspeed.

Arriving in New York, Khoneh went directly to the home of Mama's sister, Aunt Sarah and Uncle Israel Mankofsky. They had been settled in America for some time. Khoneh soon anglicized his name to Henry, and went to work as a fur cutter, saving every dollar to purchase a steamship ticket for Mariashka.

The long winter evenings found Slavka, Motke and me busily plucking the eiderdown to stuff the pillows and huge billowy comforters for Mariashka's trousseau. Mama had saved a little knipl—nest egg—toward her daughter's dowry out of her earnings. Mama had, of course, heard that in America, the custom of dowry was outmoded. Nevertheless, did it mean she had to let her daughter leave home like a pauper, heaven forbid?!

At last, Mariashka's waiting was over. Her passage arrived with the necessary affidavits, stating that Henry Abramowitz requested his betrothed, Mariashka Yablonik, to join him in America.

My Uncle Shloime Shillingoff, one of Mama's brothers, had already been to America and had, in fact, made out very well financially. But he had worked like a slave in what he called Columbus's Golden Land. So he saved up his dollars and came back to Grodno. Eventually, he married a girl named Reichel from the nearby village of Azior and settled there. (Uncle Shloime, his wife and their children Avremel, Shifra and David perished in the Holocaust. Their two surviving sons, Joseph and Wolf Shillingoff, are now in New York.)

Uncle Shloime's American-made suit, pointed toe shoes and snappy wide-brimmed hat did, indeed, make an impression around town. But his tales about the golden land did not create too favorable a picture in my mind. If things were really as rosy as painted, why did my uncle come running back to Grodno?

The marvels of the golden land failed to generate any great enthusiasm in me. My heart fairly quaked at the thought of my sister going off to a country where people slaved and sweated from dawn to dusk. The only marvels I grudgingly found in favor of the country were the decorative New-Year cards sent to friends around town at Rosh Hashanah. One type of card in particular caught my fancy: a little replica of the Holy Ark, with folded doors that opened to display a miniature Torah. How my heart yearned to own such a little Torah! Not as a toy, heaven forbid, but because father had been teaching me to be a reader of the Torah. With all the flurry going on at the house, I was hesitant to ask Mariashka to send me such a little Sefer-Torah from America.

Considering all the excitement and trepidation involved with my sister's leaving, Mama bore up like a veritable Joan of Arc! This, then, is how her children leave the nest and go out into the wide world! Velvke, to Siberia; Shayke, to serve the czar; and now Mariashka!

Mariashka was father's favorite, although he never displayed it openly. But now, when it came time to part with her, he couldn't very well hide his emotions. Under no circumstances could he be persuaded to come to the station to see her off. He wished to keep the illusion that his Mariashka had simply gone off to work and would return at day's end...

With Shayke no longer at home, Motke automatically took up the role of big brother. Having completed his studies at the Talmud Torah, he considered himself quite the adult. Taking me by the hand, his firm grip indicating that from now on I was to be his charge, we marched to the railroad station to see our sister off to America.

Slavka, in turn, assumed the responsibility of older sister. Taking Rochele up in her arms, she and Mama rode to the station in a droshky, while a group of relatives followed. At the last minute, father—apparently having a change of heart—came puffing up to the station to catch another parting glance at his eldest daughter, knowing that she was going away forever...

Mariashka stood at the open window of the railway car and waved her handkerchief at us. Summoning all the courage I had, I ran alongside the moving train and shouted, "Mariashka! Please, send me a Leshona-Tovah card from America...the card with a little Sefer-Torah in it!"

* * *

Time passed and we had no word from Mariashka. We feared the worst. When the postman, at long last, delivered a thick packet from America, enclosed was, not only her letter containing the goods news that she had landed safely, but a clipping from the *Jewish Daily Forward,* dated 1912, with a photo of Mariashka. The article revealed that some difficulty had indeed arisen, which held up her entry into the United States. The HIAS stepped in and took up her case. It was only after Henry, in the presence of the immigration officials on Ellis Island and the HIAS representative, pronounced Hareyat (I take thee...), that Mariashka was permitted to land as the legally wedded wife of Henry Abramowitz. In fact, the letter was signed: from your devoted daughter and son-in-law, Mary and Henry Abramowitz.

Enclosed in the same large envelope was a handsomely decorated card with the Holy Ark, opening to display a little Sefer Torah.

With her emigration to America, fate had decreed, there and then, that none of my dearly beloved brothers and sisters should remain alive in the subsequent Holocaust, but Mariashka and I, Chaim.

9

The Fortress

Our economic situation was dark after Shayke's induction into the army and Mariashka's emigration to America; notwithstanding the few cents earned by Slavka, who was helping out in a little grocery store.

Motke had no alternative but to help father in the menial job of street-paving. Our cousin, Michel, who was raised in our house after the death of his father, followed suit and also became a paver.

As for me, I completed my studies at the Cheder Msukon and the most I could look forward to in furthering my education was to enter the yeshiva. I was admitted without having to pay for tuition.

World politics was a subject I knew nothing about, nor understood. In fact, the word politic was non-kosher in our house. All the more wonder that Czar Nikolai's bloody regime should turn out to be such a boon to us.

Grodno, holding a key position so close to the Prussian border, needed to be re-enforced against a possible German attack in the event of war. Consequently, the czar decided to build a fortress on the Western terrain of Grodno, which proved to be a gift from heaven.

Father got the job of paving the fortress grounds. As a Jew, his chances of landing such a plum would normally have been slim, but, since Grodno had no non-Jewish street pavers at the time, who could lay the type of roads necessary to withstand the rolling of heavy artillery, father drew the lucky number. Before long, the fortress, on the Fehrstadt side of town, began to expand.

As foreman of the crew, father hired extra men, Jews and Gentiles who were ready to work. The boom was on! And not only in Grodno. The peasants in the outlying villages also enjoyed the fringe benefits. They were hired to drive their farm wagons, hauling the necessary stones, gravel and sand required for the paving job.

Our existence was a good example of the phrase: "it's either all, or nothing!" When at last, after a lengthy spell of joblessness for my father and his crew, along came a fortress to build, the city fathers also decided to resurface all the main streets in town. Father would gladly have passed up this extra job. The city officials were notoriously delinquent paymasters. But, since he could not afford to tussle with the city authorities, the paving crew broke their backs from sunup to sundown in order to squeeze in the additional city project.

When the work called for still more hands, father recruited a number of non-Jews from other crafts and began teaching them the skill of stone-paving. Our family crew was not exactly pleased that father was teaching these strangers a trade, which they'd come to consider primarily their own. Their uneasiness may have been prophetic, for, in the very near future—under Polish regime—these same grateful gentiles would organize their own paver groups and compete with our men, blocking them from available jobs.

10

A Guest in Town

In the year 1913, Russia celebrated the 300th anniversary of the Romanov dynasty. In honor of the jubilee, Grodno opened her new concrete bridge across the Niemen, connecting Fehrstadt with the city proper. Until then, people were obliged to make their way to and from the suburb of Fehrstadt by way of a narrow pontoon bridge, strung over a relay of small boats.

The Jews in Grodno awaited the opening of the new bridge with trepidation. For, it was rumored, that the populace could expect the presence of an exalted guest in town: the ceremony would be presided over by none other than the "Little Father" himself—the czar Nicholas II.

An official state-proclamation substantiated the rumor of the czar's impending visit, adding that the "Batushka" would be accompanied by his little son and heir, Czarevitch Alexei.

Panic gripped the Jewish community. Still fresh in everyone's mind was the assassination of the prominent Peter Stolypin. Nor had the Jews gotten over the false accusation of ritual murder made against the martyr, Mendel Beiliss; only recently set free after years of imprisonment. The least provocation, or discourtesy toward the anointed ruler, could evoke bloody vengeance upon Jews throughout the entire Russian empire.

The leaders of Grodno's Jewish community called a meeting to work out a welcome program. They also decided to contact the underground anarchist-terrorist organization and warn the hotheads that Jewish life lay in their hands. Paying homage to the czar in song was assigned to Kaminetzky, the city cantor. Our choirleader Sergei rehearsed us in the Russian anthem, "Bozhe Czarya Khrani" (God protect the Czar). We practiced the anthem over and over, to give each syllable the perfect Russian accent. With our very lives at stake, was there any choice?!

Our choir vestments had long become shabby. But now, thanks to the upcoming celebration, a whole new wardrobe was ordered: robes, yarmulkas and prayer-shawls. In fact, the preparations for this historic visit brought a wave of unprecedented prosperity to the town's tradespeople.

Father and his co-workers toiled day and night, repairing and paving the parade route. Heaven forbid that a member of the royal entourage should trip over a loose pebble! Jewish life wouldn't be worth a snuff of tobacco!

The city authorities continued to issue proclamations—a new one every other day. Sidewalks and housefronts were scrubbed. Portraits of the czar and the crown prince were prominently displayed in shop windows. The main streets were steeped in a sea of Russian flags.

At long last, Judgment Day arrived. At dawn, military marches echoed through the streets. The army bands were escorting the detachments to their designated positions in the parade. I slipped out of the house and hurried to Saborna Street, imagining myself marching in rhythm with the soldiers.

The marching infantry, with gleaming bayonets on their rifles, took up their places in long rows down either side of the street. Several Cossack details on Circassian horses, all of them one color, galloped by. The Cossacks, evidently, had been assigned as an honor guard to escort the czar's retinue. Their whips, which so frequently came down on the backs of Jewish revolutionaries— or Jews in general—were, on this occasion, to protect the anointed royal visitors. What struck me as most unique was the Cossack band. They played their instruments sitting astride their mounts.

The sidewalks became jammed with people pushing and elbowing their way for a vantage point. The crush was becoming unbearable.

The courtyard of the synagogue and the little side streets were packed with thousands of Jews. The official order had clearly stated that no one was to remain indoors, but to be out on the streets to hail His Royal Highness!

Arrayed in their Prince Alberts and high silk hats, the committee of the merchants' guild took the lead, and the procession of Jews moved forward. Carrying the ornamented Torahs beneath a chupah held overhead, walked the rabbis, trustees and beadles.

Soon, a detail of gendarmes blocked the way. There was no room on Zamkova Street, they claimed, and wouldn't let us continue. After much pleading, they only let pass the cantor, the choir and the official delegation. Hordes of people and children remained stuck behind us in the side streets.

The bells of the Russian Tzerkva began to toll and almost immediately, the bells of the Polish Cosciol, as well as the little German church picked up the cue. From the Place-Parade, near the Boulevard Square, the strains of the Russian anthem reached us. The bands on Zamkova and other streets, including the band of the Fire Volunteers, chimed in with their own rendition, so that when one orchestra began, another was in the middle of it, or just finishing the last bars. It created a real mishmash. The hurrahs bursting from thousands of throats, heralded that the royal procession was nearing.

A closed, black sedan came moving closer to us. The command "Present Arms!" and the wild shouts of salutation from both the military and the surging crowds were deafening.

Cantor Kaminetzky's voice rang out with: "Baruch Habah" (Bless the arriver), and we, our hearts fluttering, sang out, "Bozhe Czarya Khrani..."

The black sedan, flanked by mounted Cossacks, came abreast of us. The rabbis intoned the traditional: "Blest be He, Who bestows of His Grace upon mortals."

My eyes strained into the closed windows of the vehicle and there they sat, Czar Nicholas II and his heir, the Czarevitch Alexei. I had anticipated something superhuman and awe-inspiring in the features of the mighty ruler of Mother Russia. Instead, I saw a pallid, lackluster countenance. The small, darkish blond beard and thick mustache gave him the look of a run-of-the-mill peasant. The Czar and his heir apparent, both in military uniform, sat rigid, with an almost theatrical haughtiness, gazing into space, never deigning to acknowledge the representatives of the Grodno Jewish community with as much as a glance.

Suddenly, a thunderous explosion rent the air, making the ground beneath us tremble. Stunned, we remained open-mouthed, rooted to our places. Another boom echoed and still another. The firehouse horses set up a frantic whinnying, rearing up on their hind legs and straining at their harnesses. In panic, the sea of humanity surged into the roadway. The Cossacks drove their mounts into the midst of the throng, their bared swords and whips cutting a path for the czar's sedan, which promptly took off.

Later it was learned that this was no assassination attempt on the czar and his heir, although many a palm in Grodno was itching to square accounts with the "Little Father." At the moment the Jews of Grodno were about to present His Highness with the traditional golden tray bearing bread and salt, the age-old custom of welcoming royalty, the artillery detail on Kalozha hill began a 300-gun salute in honor of the 300-year anniversary of the Romanovs.

The parade continued for the rest of the day without further incident. The Czar cut the ribbon, officially opening the new bridge; attended the receptions and balls arranged for the royal guests, who spent the following nights guzzling and making merry.

Only two years later, in 1915, during the First World War, when Grodno was occupied by the Germans, the Jewish community tendered the very same welcome to the new ruler, Kaiser Wilhelm II.

Jewish children waved German flags, Jewish representatives greeted the conqueror with the traditional bread and salt on a golden tray, our Great Synagogue choir sang the German anthem, "Deutschland, Deutschland über Alles," and the rabbis intoned the blessing: "...Who bestows of His Grace upon mortals."

How strangely different were the two historic visits! Czar Nicholas, who came with his crown prince on a visit to one of his own Russian provinces, drove through the streets of Grodno cowering in the depths of a closed vehicle. The anthem we sang, "God Protect the Czar," seemed most appropriate.

Kaiser Wilhelm, on the other hand, visiting the occupied territory of Grodno, rode in an open motorcar sitting up arrogantly, the sharp spike on his war helmet glinting in the sun, while from every direction voices sang out: "Deutschland, Deutschland über Alles!"

11

Yiddish Theater—In Russian

L arge placards, with hand-printed letters in Russian, bore the announcement: Yakob Guzik and his Yiddish Troupe coming to Grodno! The performances would be given in the huge circus-arena.

It is possible that the elegant City Theater was being occupied at the time by a Russian company of players; but it is more likely that the powers that be were reluctant to allow Yiddish actors with their "Jew-plays" into the City Theater. Be that as it may, the airy circus-arena proved more than adequate for the Guzik company.

The chances of obtaining the governor's permit to perform in Yiddish being out of the question, the announcement stated that the cast would present their Yiddish repertoire in Russian.

People in town needed very little urging to patronize the performances. What a treat it was to see the well-known musicals, comedies, and dramas; listen to the familiar tunes; laugh and enjoy the genuine Yiddish folk humor, and forget personal and worldly problems. True enough, people were aware that the plays would not be performed in their mother tongue, but no matter. At least, there was no restriction against the music, so heartwarmingly Yiddish, and played by a big orchestra.

The theatergoers in Grodno also knew that no restriction was going to deter the actors from getting some of their lines across in Yiddish whenever possible. In fact, a sharp eye was usually kept out for the chance appearance of an inspector. At a warning signal from the lookout, the actors would instantly switch back into Russian, even breaking into song with typical Russian tchastushkes (jingles), or a living Kazatchok (dance), and the inspector would declare the performance "legit." But the minute he was out of sight, the actors would again resume their roles in Yiddish.

In Russia and in the Polish-Russian provinces, there was no lack of Jewish wandering troupes. On the European theatrical horizon, there had also arisen the names of such American guest-artistes, as Boris Thomashevsky, Jacob P. Adler, Sigmund Mogulesko, Jacob Silbert, David Kessler, Sigmund Fineman, Max Rosenthal, Malvina Lobel, Dinah Fineman, Kenny Lipson and Berta Kalisch.

In our part of the country, Yakob Guzik and his troupe scored great success. The arrival of his huge entourage was equal to the advent of a circus.

In addition to his large cast of comedians, tragedians, juveniles, character-actors, romantic leads, prima donnas, ingenues and heavies, Guzik also brought his own chorus group. The younger singers among them doubled in the dance numbers. Truckloads of costumes were carted along for the historical Goldfaden operettas, as well as countless props for their extensive repertoire. The orchestra too, with Winocur as conductor, was part and parcel of the traveling company.

Guzik opened with Boris Thomashefsky's *Dos Pintele Yid*, (loosely translated, The Core of Yiddishkeit), a play which requires a number of choirboys, plus the special role of a Bar-Mitzvah boy, called Yisrolik.

These youngsters were usually recruited from the local synagogue choirs. And so, Guzik's chorus captain soon came to consult with our choir leader about engaging several of our boys. He assured Sergei that we would of course be compensated for each performance and that, the one chosen for the part of the Bar-Mitzvah boy, would of course, receive a somewhat larger stipend.

At first, I shrank from even considering this proposition. After my experience with Durov's Circus, where they'd skipped off with my pay, I was very wary of such promises. But more than anything, the temptation to trod the boards of a legitimate stage, with professional actors, proved irresistible. I agreed to go along with the rest of the boys for the audition, although my heart was in my mouth lest my father get wind of it.

We reported to the arena theater, where the troupe's comedian, a fiery-haired character called Kazhdan, looked us over and heard us sing. It was his job to select one of us for the role of Yisrolik. Me—he ruled out immediately. "Too small for a Bar-Mitzvah boy!"

The role called for an alto, but the taller boys in my section were at the voice-changing stage. Blending with other voices, their cracks and squeaks weren't noticable, but to sing solo—oh, no! Kazhdan wouldn't have it! In the end, whether or not I could pass for thirteen, he had to settle for me.

Thus, it was fate that maneuvered me into my very first role on the Yiddish stage, with professional artists, playing a Bar-Mitzvah boy, before I myself, had as yet reached that status.

The impresario-entrepreneur-star-director was Yakob Guzik, himself. His wife, Rosa, a hefty soubrette and their three young daughters, Lolka, Hanna and Bubi, affected airs like those of a royal family at a coronation. Everyone hung around: musicians tootling, principals vocalizing, dressers handling costumes...all waiting for the scenery to be set up so we could begin the dress rehearsal.

My Debut

A narrow wooden ramp, built especially for the production, ran from the back of the house to the stage. The choirboys, clad in robes, skullcaps and prayer-shawls, were to file up the ramp to the stage, carrying little prop Torahs, and singing—in Russian:

Our Torah, our Torah,
Blest be our Torah.
Israel shall live, we pray,
To shine forever and a day...

As the Bar-Mitzvah boy, I stood center stage, surrounded by my parents and other characters in the play. All were assembled to welcome my friends, marching up the ramp to greet me on the occasion of my Bar Mitzvah. I had very few speaking lines, but did have several numbers to sing. I was able by now to sight-read music. Kazhdan had written out the notes for me and I managed to memorize the melodies overnight.

When the boys finished singing their part, the orchestra modulated into the key for my solo. With a quivering heart I braced myself to begin. I opened my mouth but no sound came forth. Up to this point I had been accustomed to the accompaniment of a concertina; but to sing with a full orchestra... this was a new and bewildering experience. I was completely overwhelmed by the violins, the cellos, the bass and some brass instruments I had never seen before. Only the sharp tap-tap of Winokur's baton and his impatient "Nu! Nu!" shook me out of my sudden freeze. Kazhdan, thoroughly exasperated, nudged me from behind and grunted, "Come on, you klutz, sing!" The conductor gave the sign for the orchestra to repeat the introduction. I took a deep breath and in a shaky voice, began my solo:

In every land, in every place,
The Jew alone, has had to face
A life of exile and despair,
A homeless stranger, everywhere...

I became so moved by the words that, little by little, I began to warm up. By the time I got to the refrain: "Yidele, dein kroin iz dos Pintele Yid," my nervousness was gone. I threw myself into the song heart and soul, ending up with pathos on the concluding words: "Ich blayb trei dos Pintele Yid!" (I remain true to that core of Yiddishkeit). As I sustained the last note, the entire cast applauded. Not just for my singing, but because this was the way Herr Guzik directed the scene.

"Good boy!" exclaimed Kazhdan, giving me a hearty slap on the back.

Guzik pinched my cheek. "Khorosho! (Good!)" he said, speaking half Russian, half Yiddish. "For a rehearsal, that's very good. But for the performance, see that you don't do it in your pants! Ponyemaiyesh—understand? Do you see the gallery up there? That's where people will be sitting. So you have to open your mouth and give! Ponyemaiyesh? You must deliver!"

This was a most valuable piece of advice to receive at the very outset of my "theatrical career." Throughout the ensuing years of my association with theater, I held this to be a lesson of major importance: to make sure that my audience can clearly see and hear everything that is happening on stage, no matter where they are seated, or whatever price they paid for admission.

My first professional debut was a success. I delivered, as Guzik demanded of me. And while I ached to tell my parents of my success so they could be proud of me, I managed to keep my theater involvement a tightly kept secret.

Every one of Guzik's performances in Grodno was a sellout. The repertoire included "A Mentsh Zol Men Zein" by Anschel and Moshe Shorr; "Die Amerikanerin," "Hantche in Amerike"; "Mein Veib's Man" by Hyman Mysell. This was also presented under the title "Sammy, the Buffoon" and was originally brought to Europe by Clara Young, who toured with it and became a famous star in the soubrette role of Bella. (Its author, Hyman Mysell, had, obviously, given the heroine of the play the name of his daughter, my wife, Bella Mysell Yablokoff.)

Guzik's spouse, Rosa, was excellent as "Hantche" and as "Die Amerikanerin." Both of these comedies required that the characters she portrayed put on a pair of trousers in order to disguise herself as a man; certainly a risque stunt in those days. The pants would definitely have been more preferable on a trimmer figure, but the viewers marveled at the daring of it and thoroughly enjoyed the shock!

Guzik's productions, even those of lighter genre, were produced on a lavish scale—never thrown together slapdash. In the large Jewish communities of Odessa, Minsk, Vilna, Grodno and Tialystok, not to mention Warsaw, or Lodz, a producer had to gird himself pretty well, in order to pass muster and achieve financial success.

Smaller communities also reaped the benefit of getting to see these professional performances. Almost all of them had their own little amateur theater groups, which often sprouted young talent, who eventually found their way into the professional companies.

When news got around town that Guzik and company had finally been granted a permit to give several performances in Yiddish, and that these would include Avrom Goldfaden's *Shulamith, Bar-Kochba* and *Akeides Yitzchok*, tickets were snapped up immediately. As for me, I stayed glued to the theater; I hung around to watch the rehearsals and lived in a bewitched world.

The Goldfaden operettas made a lasting impression on me. To this day I regard them as the most precious pearls in the Yiddish theater repertoire. Aniuta Femova, the conductor's wife, sang the role of Shulamith, and Guzik truly outdid himself in the role of the romantic hero, Absolom. His nasal tenor was particularly suited to the sweet lullaby, "Raisins and Almonds." And when he assumed the role of the heroic Bar-Kochba, he affected a throaty tone as he bravely declaimed: "Arise, my people, Sons of Judea!" Guzik also cut a most imposing figure as Abraham, in *Akeides Yitzchak* (The Sacrifice of Isaac).

Walking home from the theater, I couldn't help but imitate Guzik's manner of speech, and singing. Nor could I resist mimicking Kazhdan, the red-haired comedian; his clowning as the wild black African Tzingentang, his lame-footed Papus in Bar-Kochba and his Ishmael, the dim-witted Arab in the *Sacrifice of Isaac*. Walking along, I quoted all his jokes and puns, aped his hilarious mannerisms and repeated all his ditties and catchy rhymes. It became my ambition to become an actor-singer like Guzik, or a comedian like Kazhdan. I planned to sneak away from home, leave everyone and everything and join the Guzik troupe in their wanderings around the world. Bitten, at last, by the acting-bug, my destiny was sealed: to dedicate my life to the Yiddish theater.

August 1, 1914

WAR! MOBILIZATION! These words, in bold type, sprang up overnight. War posters were plastered right over Guzik's theater-placards announcing a new play, *Broken Hearts*. The proclamation read: All men ranging in age from 20 to 45 are to report for military duty in the courtyard of the magistrate!

I was not yet able to grasp the full impact of the bloody word war. For me, nothing existed outside the theater. That historic morning of August 1, 1914, with father, Motka and Slavka already gone off to work, I heard mother murmuring to herself, "Shayke will surely be first at the front." I couldn't imagine what upset her so.

It was only out on the street that I realized something really ominous was afoot. People stood in knots around the posted mobilization orders. They read the fearful words and silently turned away. Some, shoulders hunched, trudged on to work, while others returned home to prepare themselves for army duty.

The very air around the market was already filled with an avid undercurrent of hoarding; buying up all sorts of food items and household necessities, just in case!

The taverns and inns were abustle with out-of-town merchants and traders hastily packing their bags to return home. The streets echoed with the sound of marches as military bands escorted troops to the railroad station.

When I came up to the arena-theater, I found everything in a turmoil. Guzik and his family, as well as a good many of his performers and staff had lost no time in vacating. Most of them traveled with illegal passports, and some, to evade the military or for political motives, made straight for the larger cities, where it was easier to "get lost."

That night, the announced play, *Broken Hearts,* by Z. Libin went on with Kazhdan and several others who remained. Whether they felt compelled to keep faith with the theater's tradition: "the show must go on," or because they sought to realize a few more rubles toward traveling expenses, the Yiddish actors did indeed stick to their post, winding up their advertised performance in the face of an onrushing storm—the First World War!

* * *

The official order to report for military duty had to be heeded promptly.

Helter-skelter, a man had to grab a few belongings, bid his family goodbye
and go off to sacrifice life and limb for Mother Russia. My sister Slavka's
fiance, Itche Nemeisky, a strapping, good-looking, muscular fellow, was one
candidate the doctors didn't even bother to examine. One look at him was
enough! They welcomed him like a rare find. Between Slavka's hysterics and
Mama's commiserating sobs, the atmosphere at home was anything but joyous!

Father's state of mind was certainly unenviable. The Russian government
owed him and his crew a considerable sum of money for the project at the
fortress. Those in authority were suddenly out of reach, and father's repeated
attempts at knocking on doors were futile.

As the Jewish recruits were getting ready to leave for their assigned destinations, the rabbis declared a Day of Fast. All the Jewish soldiers assembled
in the Great Synagogue, where Rabbi Moshe-Jehuda Rabinovitch led them in
reciting the Tfilath Haderech (a prayer before a Journey), and the Vidui (a
prayer of atonement said on Yom Kippur, or on the threshold of death).

A solemn atmosphere hung over the holy place, the tall candles flickered
as if this were the night of Kol Nidre. Cantor Kaminetzky, in his deepest tones
began: "Out of the depths have I cried unto Thee, O Lord..." (Psalm 130).

A deathlike silence fell upon the sanctuary. During my solo: "Yea,
though I walk through the valley of the shadow of death," a weeping broke
out. I continued singing until I blended in harmony with Cantor Kaminetzky,
whose voice rose to the heights of his phenomenal range.

Rabbi Rabinovitch, in white robe, yarmulka and prayer-shawl, slowly
ascended the steps to the Holy Ark. His flowing white beard lent a mystic
holiness to his patriarchal countenance. All eyes were fastened on him as he
opened the doors of the Ark. Bowed before the Holy Scriptures, he stood
there for some time, swaying from side to side in deep prayer. Slowly, he
turned to the congregation. In a weak voice he bade all soldiers repeat the
Vidui with him. As if under a hypnotic spell everyone murmured the solemn
words: "Oshamnu Bogadnu..."

Suddenly, an agonized cry broke from his lips. "God Almighty!" he
implored. "If any one of these children of my flock be destined to come to
harm, let me, O Lord, be the sacrifice!" He then began to falter. In vain did
he try to support himself by reaching out for the open doors of the Holy Ark.
Thus, with arms outstretched, he sank to the floor.

Standing around the pulpit below, we were all too stunned to move. It
was too late. Rabbi Moshe-Jehuda Rabinovitch had drawn his last breath... the
first Jewish casualty of the First World War.

12

At the Polish Byelorussian Border

"**K**uznica! Last stop! All out!" the conductor bellowed. "This train returns to Warsaw in half an hour!" Kuznica is a little town that lies on the Polish-Byelorussian border. Beyond this point, the stretch of land up to Lasosna, the stop before Grodno, is considered no-man's land.

The small, low-roofed structure squatting between the railroad tracks was the custom-house and checkpoint for document control. On the other side stood a mammoth locomotive, its flags flying the hammer and sickle.

Taking my small valise in hand, I clambered from the high steps of the train and followed the other passengers to the checkpoint.

They had already formed two lines: one for document examination and the other, at the customs counter, for baggage inspection. Two uniformed inspectors—male and female—pawed over every rag in their bundles as if they were the costliest silks. The inspectors' appraisal of each item determined the value and the tax required from each passenger. The sum had to be paid on the spot—and in cash—or else their baggage would be confiscated. The babble grew loud with bickering. Unperturbed, the customs inspectors listened to the pleas and protests, but remained adamant.

"Passport, porzhe Pana!" a Polish officer addressed himself to me. Taking his time, the officer examined my passport from cover to cover, reading the names of the various countries I had already visited on this tour.

"Excuse me for not asking you to sit down," he apologized in halting English, "there are no extra chairs."

"Don't let it bother you," I replied, "I sat on the train all the way from Warsaw. But thanks just the same." Oh, good, I thought, a friendly officer! Everything is going smoothly. I'll soon be on my way to Grodno.

"Psheprashem Pana," said the officer, begging my pardon. "I've just noticed that your visa to Poland is valid for only one entry. Are you aware that if you now exit Poland, you will not be permitted to return?" As if I didn't know! But blessed be Pan Sadowsky of the Orbis Travel Agency! He certainly had foresight! I handed over his introductory letter.

The officer gave it his full attention, but shook his head. "This is all very well," he observed, "but I cannot assume the responsibility of checking out your exit from Poland without a re-entry visa. I am sure the Russians will not let you cross their border, and you will not be allowed to re-enter Poland at any point of the border. Do you wish to remain in no-man's land? No, you must go back to Warsaw and get a new re-entry visa."

Sick with disappointment, I asked when I could get a train back to Warsaw.

"In about fifteen minutes. The same train that brought you here will be returning to Warsaw. There won't be another 'til tomorrow at this time."

"How long would it take me to obtain a new visa!" I asked.

"Who can tell?" he shrugged. "Maybe six months…a year…"

"Let me cross the border, please," I explained that my stay in Poland was limited.

The officer took up my documents and went off to an adjoining room. Utterly dejected, I stood and waited while the haggling and quibbling around the room continued. The passengers whose baggage was being withheld were finally obliged to dig into their purses.

My Polish officer finally reappeared. "I will pass you through," he said, "but at your own risk. If the Russian officials on the other side of the frontier refuse your entry, you must bear in mind that you will be detained there because the border back to Poland will be closed to you. It's for you to decide. The Russian train has already been waiting an extra ten minutes at our request. Decide now."

"Yes, check me out!" I exclaimed in a burst of determination. "Come what may, now that I've come this far, I will not turn back!"

The officer began to jot down some writing on the page that bore my Polish visa. But just as he did, something within me took a quick turn. Are you crazy? You may be stuck there forever! Don't do it!

"I'm sorry to trouble you, officer," I quickly said, "but I have changed my mind. I'll take your advice. I won't run the risk. I will turn back to Warsaw."

Instead of being annoyed, he seemed pleased at my change of heart. Quickly erasing what he had written, he put down at the side of the page the one word— valid. "Now run, quick!" he smiled approvingly, pushing my passport at me. "You can still catch your train back to Warsaw!"

I grabbed my valise and made a dash for it. The conductor helped me up the steps of the car just as the train began to move. The Soviet train also chugged out of the station, albeit in the opposite direction.

Out of breath I sank down on the bench, miserable and completely spent. Maybe I had better drop the whole undertaking. It wasn't meant to be, that's all! On the other hand, would I be able to make peace with myself for having forfeited this opportunity?! All through life my premonitions had saved me more than once. Could it possibly be, I tried to console myself, that my last-minute premonition not to cross over on Russian soil would also prove to be in my favor?

I sunk in recollections of my childhood years, when at the outbreak of the First World War, I found myself a refugee, starting out as a "boy entertainer" and desperately longing for home.

13

In Exile

Grodno had barely recovered from the sudden death of Rabbi Rabino-vitch, when it was hit by a new and devastating decree: "All Jews must leave the city of Grodno within the week. Exempt from this ukase are only those engaged in wartime projects: professionals such as doctors, advocates and rabbis, as well as city officials and those working at trades essential to the war effort. All elderly Jews and women and children, without exception, will be evacuated by special trains to the interior cities of Russia."

The Jews attributed this shattering ukase to the fact that our city lay so close to the Prussian border. How could the Czar take the risk of allowing the Jews to remain in this strategically sensitive area, when even the Yiddish language was so similar to German? The Jews would surely communicate with the enemy and sell out the city of Grodno, lock, stock and barrel!

It was, therefore, safer to pack them off to Russian provinces far removed from the border. My father and his crew were among those privileged to remain. Street-paving became essential. The military vehicles and heavy artillery had to roll through the streets unhampered. They often left potholes, which needed immediate repair. Father had no idea when they'd be paid for the work, but it was work they were forced to do.

My sister Slavka's job also fell into the category of wartime occupation. She worked at the Shereshefsky tobacco factory, and the army, of course, had to be supplied with cigarettes.

So, with my brother Velvel locked up as a political prisoner, Shayke in the army, Motke working with father, and Mariashka in America, the only dangerous characters in our family to be banished from the city were my mother, my baby sister Rochele, and I. We were the menace that threatened to deliver the city of Grodno into the hands of the German Army!

Our impending journey intrigued me: to be going somewhere on a train was a brand-new experience to look forward to. To me, the passenger cars looked like moving palaces; the locomotive, like some prehistoric monster. I pictured Mama, Rochele and me, lounging like lords in one of those luxurious railway carriages.

Before taking off, mother gave Slavka instructions on how she was to look after father, Motke and cousin Mikhl. She must prepare a good, home-cooked meal; remember to change the bed linen regularly; have a clean white shirt ready for father on the Sabbath; do the family wash once a week, boiling the clothes thoroughly in the washtub. Until mother's safe return, God willing, Slavka was to be in charge of housekeeping. Finished with her instructions, Mama finally dissolved into tears. And father, throughout this tense and trying period, had grown strangely tight-lipped.

* * *

Early dawn on the day of our departure, I went to the synagogue with father, not only to recite the pre-journey prayer, but to take leave of my rabbi, the Eishishker, and bid my friends goodbye.

Walking back from prayers in silence, father suddenly stopped. "Chaimke," he began. The tenderness with which he uttered my name went straight to my heart. "You're a big boy now, my son. Almost Bar Mitzvah."

"I could be Bar Mitzvah even now!" I boasted. "I know the blessings and I can read the weekly portion of the Torah. I only need to go over it once or twice."

"Son, you will be Bar Mitzvah, God willing, according to Jewish law, when you reach thirteen." Clasping me close to him, he then placed his hands on my shoulders and looked straight into my eyes. "Chaimke," he said, "promise me that, no matter where you are, you will be a decent boy; say your prayers three times a day and observe the Sabbath wherever you and Mama find yourselves, do you hear? Take care of Mama and your little sister. You will be the only one to look after them. You know Mama is not too well, and Rochele is a frail child."

Shaken by this sudden responsibility, I clung to him even closer. "Where are they sending us, father?"

"God only knows!" he sighed. "What can I do, son! The good Lord will surely watch over you."

A remarkable feeling took hold of me. Father was actually entrusting me with the responsibility of a grownup. If so, I decided, then I must act like one. I'm not a boy anymore.

From that day forward, more than a year before my Bar Mitzvah, I began to feel and behave like an adult—a circumstance which stood me in good stead in my years of growing up.

* * *

On reaching the railroad station with our bundles and wicker baskets, we found hundred of men, women and children already gathered there, pushing, jostling and bickering.

The Zionist leader, Leyb Jaffe, and other community leaders were present to oversee the evacuation, not to mention the Russian military force.

After a half day of waiting, along came a railroad officer with a squad of gendarmes in tow and delivered the terse command: "March!"

Thrown into confusion, the crowd began to gather up their pieces of baggage at random and, for the umpteenth time, to bid loved ones farewell. The gendarmes hurried the evacuees along.

Picking up a large pack, I hoisted it to my shoulder and took Rochele firmly by the hand. Impatient lest the others snatch up the best seats in the choice compartments, I implored Mama to shorten her farewells, and out we hustled to the platform to board our train.

There was no such thing in sight! Instead, the throng of refugees went plodding after the railroad officer, who led them over the wooden ties between the tracks. We were herded on for about a quarter of a kilometer and there, on a siding, stood a long string of boxcars, the type used for transporting cattle.

People were obliged to lift their children in through the gaping doors and climb in after them. Women needed a boost so they could crawl into the cars on hands and knees. The din that reached our ears from the bawling children and the hysterical protests of the struggling women told us there and then what to expect out of this journey!

As soon as one car was filled to capacity the doors were rolled shut and another thrown open. Quick-thinking Motke swung himself aboard an opened car. Father and Mikhl promptly threw our baggage in and helped Mama, Rochele and me climb up. Unrolling a blanket on the floor in a corner of the car, Motke got us settled, and hurriedly kissing us goodbye, sprang down.

Except for a large pot-bellied stove, the car was bare. In a few moments, we too, reached our quota of human cargo. When the doors were rolled shut, we found ourselves in utter blackness. Bewildered we huddled even closer to each other. The children, frightened by the dark, let themselves be heard, and parents found it impossible to soothe them. Before long the air began to reek of sweat and urine. There were no facilities and the little ones, unable to restrain themselves long enough for someone to come up with a pot, or a container, relieved themselves on the floor. Folks were afraid to open the doors. The gendarmes had strictly forbidden it, and nobody dared open a door and risk catching a whiplash across the face. At last a shrill blast from the locomotive startled us. A sudden and violent convulsion sent the car swaying and shuddering.

"They're hooking us on to a locomotive," astutely observed a fellow evacuee for our benefit.

"You don't say! Mazel tov!" cracked another. "Happy sledding, everybody!"

Tooting and shrieking, the engine began to puff and pull, which only brought on a fresh outbreak of weeping and wailing: "We're moving. God only knows whether we shall live to return."

"Don't cry, Mama," I begged, putting my arms around her. "I'll take care of you and Rochele. I'm not a child anymore. God will watch over us," I repeated father's expression to comfort her. "I'll work, and you and Rochele won't want for anything. You're my responsibility. Father entrusted me to look after you." At this, Mama clasped me so tightly, her tears ran down my face.

After several hours there was a rush of cool air in the car. Some of the men had managed to wedge open the rolling door so we could, at least, draw a fresh breath. Hurtling along in the chill autumn night we watched the sparks from the engine fly past us. Soon, a squabble started as some hollered, "Close the door. You want the children to catch pneumonia?!" while others demanded, "Leave the door open, we're smothering!"

After a while, children asked for food and there began a rustling of parcels in the dark. Most of the food items were of the spicy, thirst-inducing variety. The congestion and the stuffiness in the car only created a greater thirst, turning it into a serious problem. Those who had a bit of fruit or a candy to suck on were able to pacify a child for the moment. But water? Not a drop.

Early dawn, the train stopped at a little way station to water the engine. Men threw the doors wide open and hurried to the water tower. The rail workers must have understood our plight, for no doubt we were not the first transport of refugees. Not only did they allow us to drink as much as we wanted and wash our hands and faces, but advised us to bring out as many utensils as we had and fill them with water to take along. We promptly produced all kinds of receptacles and gratefully filled them. We had no recourse but to drink from the same pots and bottles that had been used during the night for other purposes...

I persuaded Mama to venture down from the car and freshen up. Once out in the morning air, we all felt a great deal better. Stretching our legs was pure joy. The little stop in our journey was soon over. Thanking the rail workers for the water, we climbed back into our boxcars.

The rest of the day passed uneventfully. After the sleepless night, everybody dropped off. When we awoke it was nightfall again. We still had water. At any rate, it was no immediate problem. The government apparently had not deemed it necessary to provide for the refugees. Who were we, after all?!

The train stopped. The men climbed down, prepared this time with every available container. It was night, but at least we got water. All vessels rinsed and refilled, we climbed aboard again to rattle through another night.

Things took a bad turn. Children came down with fever. Whether it was the water, the fruit, or the food, which had become spoiled by now, the little ones—and some adults, too—kept throwing up. Nerves grew frayed, people became annoyed with each another and found reason to quarrel. Resignedly, we stayed put in our little corner, Mama reaching out now and then to touch our foreheads.

Our long echelon of cars rattled on with a grating, monotonous clatter.

I lay curled in a ball on the floor, my head resting in Mama's lap, while fantasies kept going around in my head. Softly, I began to hum the tune of "God, in His judgment is always right." Another melody that haunted me was, "There'll come a time of iron trains," and I saw myself in historic raiment, singing the heroic role of Absolom, in Goldfaden's musical legend, *Shulamith*. Ever so softly, I went on humming the lullaby, "Ay-liu-liu-liu," and at the refrain, I was so carried away, I sang out: "Under Yidele's cradle, there stands a pure white little goat." My voice rose in fervor as I continued with "Raisins and almonds, these will be your calling, so sleep, Yidele, sleep."

My singing stopped the children's whining and the sick from groaning. Maybe it wasn't a fitting thing to do—singing of all things, under the circumstances! I braced myself for a scolding from my mother and a possible tirade from the others.

"Hey folks, this youngster, bless his heart, sings like a bird!" exclaimed a fellow refugee, near us. "So sleep, Yidele, sleep," he imitated, warbling the song in a guttural voice. A ripple of laughter erupted in the darkness—the first sound of laughter since we left home!

"Hey, boychik!" someone called from the depths of our car, "where did you learn to sing so beautifully!"

"With Kaminetzky, our city cantor, in the Great Synagogue," replied Mama, supplying the information with a decided pride in our voice.

"With Cantor Kaminetzky! Well, no wonder!" voices commented. "A choirboy!"

"If that's the case, why let ourselves die of boredom in this trap!" our closest neighbor resumed. "Give us a song, boychik. Something with schmaltz—a song that'll go straight to the pupick (bellybutton). Do you know any more of those Yiddish songs?"

"Sure I do." I replied, encouraged by mother's pride. "I know a lot of songs from the Yiddish theater."

"Yes," said Mama, "my Chaimke has already sung in the Yiddish theater—with real actors!"

I could sense, even in the dark, that she had spoken with a meaningful look that implied: "You see, my son, you thought your singing in the theater was a secret eh? But, your mother knew right along where you were spending entire evenings—with the actors!

Sheepishly, I buried my head in her lap. I was so ashamed. Yet she had known all the time. Still, the gentle caress of her hand as she stroked my hair, told me that she didn't hold it against me.

From every corner of the car, voices clamored, "Yes, yes, sing something. Let's forget our misery for a while."

Mama, feeling my forehead and reassuring herself that I had no fever, murmured, "Sing, Chaimke, sing."

My First Concert

So there I sat in the dark, on the cold floor of a cattle car—a refugee boy from Grodno—giving my very first concert for an audience of exiles hurtling toward Russia.

I sang my entire repertoire: Hebrew songs learned in school, cantorial airs from the synagogue, Yiddish and Russian theatrical songs and the most familiar folk tunes were picked up by my listeners, creating an impromptu community sing. And so, the night sped by. When dawn came creeping up, I fell asleep utterly drained, my head cradled in Mama's lap.

Our status in the car instantly rose. We became "celebrities." Everyone began making a fuss over us. Even our little corner became roomier. Our neighbors congenially squeezed together so we might be more comfortable. Mama was so flattered, so proud of me.

At the next water stop, my "fame" spread to the refugees in the other cars and behold, they began pulling at me to ride a distance with them so I could sing for them too. At first, I balked at the idea, afraid to leave Mama and Rochele even for a moment. But Mama, herself, persuaded me. "Go, dear," she encouraged me. "Sing for the people. You'll be earning a mitzvah."

Thus, I started a "concert tour," entertaining our fellow refugees in the adjoining cars. I sang for them, gave imitations of the red-haired comedian, Kazhdan, and my antics, grimaces and jokes, made them roll with laughter. I felt like a full-fledged actor and at every little way station clambered from car to car, repeating my routine like a bona fide guest artist.

My success made me forget our own plight. It made up for my extreme unhappiness at being torn from all that was dear and familiar, at being whisked off to some strange, unknown world. I could only console myself with the realization of my dream. I was an actor! And the sound of applause and shouts of bravo rang sweet to my ears.

* * *

The longer our journey dragged, the longer our stops lasted. In one particular spot we were stuck for days, never moving an inch.

"It's because we're coming close to a big city," one of our know-it-alls explained. "In wartime, the trains are filled with passengers a lot more important than the likes of us. The tracks must be cleared for the military and their weaponry. So we have to yield the right of way to the express trains. After all, we're just refugees, not passengers!"

Provisions were now sadly depleted. Mother still had a bit of food left. Whether it was because she had begrudged herself an extra bit, saving it for my sister and me, or because others—while they still had something to spare—had pressed tidbits on me for my singing, it was Mama who became the purveyor. Not only did she feed Rochele and me, but managed to stuff a bite of food into the hungry mouths of the other children.

To make matters worse, our Rochele became alarmingly ill, burning with fever. And there we lay, huddled on the floor in misery, in hopelessness, utterly convinced that this was surely the bitter end.

Minsk

Jarred by the bumping of car against car, I knew we were coming to a stop. There was a babble of voices on the outside and, to my amazement, they were speaking Yiddish! They must be refugees like us, I thought, from an earlier transport. Sliding back the doors we stared in disbelief. Countless men and women stood along the side of our train, holding baskets and steaming teapots.

"Where are you from!" they called to us.

"From Grodno!" we eagerly yelled back, "Grodno!"

"Shalom Aleichem! Shalom Aleichem!" they welcomed us.

"Where are we?"

"In Minsk!"

"Minsk?! Oh, my God! What day is it?"

"Friday. Where are they taking you?"

"Who knows! To hell, for all we know!"

"You need food, yes!"

The men sprang from the cars and gratefully accepted bags of food, while the women of Minsk poured steaming hot water from their kettles and brewed the tea that wafted up an aroma of ambrosia.

"We've been shlepping along like this for more than a week," our refugees lamented, unburdening their woes for the Minsker angels of mercy. "Jews are being banished from every Russian-Polish community!"

"And we have been meeting these passing transports, trying to help any way we can," explained these good people of Minsk. "It is our duty as Jews."

We also learned that the chief rabbi of Minsk, heading a delegation of prominent Jews, was interceding with the city commandant to permit our transport to remain in Minsk, in care of the Jewish community.

Rochele lay in mother's arms, her dark eyes looking up at me, luminous with fever. She seemed so pitiful, I was ready to burst into tears.

A man peered into the car. He looked to be of medium height, in his late thirties, with a small, rounded beard. Waggling a finger at me to come closer, he asked, "What's your name, young fellow?"

"Chaim Yablonik."

"I'm Shlomo Nekhes," he said and shook my hand. I felt an instant warmth at the touch of his calloused grip—so much like my father's toil-roughened hand.

"Is that your mother?"

"Yes, my mother and my baby sister, Rochele. She's terribly sick," I stammered, fighting back tears.

"Would you like to come home with me?" he asked. "I have a son, too.

His name is Dovidl, a little older than you. Well, would you want to come home with me? Your mother too," he added, seeing the look on my face.

"And Rochele?"

"Of course. Leave it to my wife Basha, she'll take care of her. Are you coming?"

"Yes, yes!" Mama called to me. "I heard the good man. He's an angel from heaven!"

Shlomo Nekhes climbed up into the car, and between us we managed to get our belongings ready. We followed him to his wagon on the other side of the station. A fellow refugee, catching up with me, stuffed a wad of paper money into my palm. At my startled look, he smiled broadly and whispered, "For your singing, Chaimke. We collected this money."

"A collection? For me?" The word collection struck me as something for paupers, beggars. I thanked the man, but refused to accept the money.

"Take it, Chaimke, take it!" he persisted, pushing the money at me. "You earned it. It will come in handy. If the Almighty spares me and I do get back to Grodno, I will surely tell your father what a fine son he has."

I had to run to catch up with Shlomo. Reaching the wagon, I threw my bundle in the back and swung myself up next to Mama. Shlomo flicked the whip to the horse's flanks and off we went, driving through the streets of Minsk to the home of Shlomo Nekhes.

"Look, Mama," I nudged her, "our Grodno refugees made a collection for my singing. I didn't want to take it, Mama. A man just forced it into my hand."

"A collection! Charity! Woe is me," she murmured.

"No, no, Mama," I tried to soothe her. "It is not charity. I earned it honestly, as an actor and a singer."

At New Kamarovka

The horse plodded along at a pace no better than our cattle train. Shlomo's repeated grunts of giddap and impatient reminders to the old nag that it was Friday, and that housewives would soon be kindling the Sabbath candles, fell on deaf ears. Pulling four passengers plus baggage was difficult enough when going downhill, but to pull such a load uphill—especially the hills of Minsk— was beyond the old mare's strength.

Meanwhile Shlomo pointed out the lovely thoroughfares of the city: "This is Zacharievski, and that one is Gubernaterski. Soon, very soon, we'll be home." Approaching the last climb before Kamarovka, he got down from the wagon, took hold of the checkrein and led the horse up the incline. She snorted and stumbled and finally made it.

Kamarovka was an old section of Minsk. Now, a new area was being developed, referred to as New Kamarovka. The glow of Sabbath candles shone through many a window. A woman and a boy of about fourteen stood waiting at the gate.

"I am Basha," said the woman rushing up to us. "Here, give me the child and come into the house. Come. My Shlomo will bring your things in." Gently, she took Rochele from mother's benumbed arms and nestling her close to her breast carried her into the house.

"Dovidl has run for the doctor," said Shlomo to put our minds at ease. "With the help of the good Lord, the child will get well."

The warmth of the little house permeated my very being and I breathed with relief. Mama sat shaken and frightened. It was all too much of a strain on her. I knew that she was subject to fainting spells, and from her pallor and difficult breathing I recognized the symptoms and rushed over to Basha.

"Do you have any vinegar?" I asked, "My mother...she's fainting!"

When Basha came back from the kitchen with a bottle of vinegar, I snatched it from her hands. I held the bottle so Mama could breathe the vinegar. When she rallied a little, I soaked my handkerchief—a bit grubby by now—with vinegar and bathed her face and neck. Coming to, she began to cry.

"Mama, Mama, don't cry. The doctor will be here and Rochele will get well. Please don't cry."

"Let her cry, child," said Basha, "let her cry herself out. She'll feel all the better for it."

Dovidl rushed in with the doctor, an elderly, benign-looking Russian. He promptly gave his attention to Rochele. Glancing up at Mama and me every now and then, he shook his head.

"A frail little one," he remarked to Mama in Russian, "exhausted by the strenuous journey, poor child. A slight congestion of the lungs. But we'll catch it in time. Let her get a good night's sleep and rest. Tomorrow, you can give her a little soup. She'll recover."

Mama reached for her purse, but the doctor waved her proffered fee aside. Mama thanked him and the good doctor was gone.

"Leah," said Basha, calling mother by name like an old friend, "go wash up and comb your hair, you'll feel better. It is Shabos and soon, very soon, we'll eat. Don't despair, Leah, we'll manage."

"Yes, yes, of course!" Shlomo picked up Basha's words of consolation. "How can it be otherwise? Can anyone predict the whims of our beloved Ruler? At present he is hustling Jews out of Grodno. It could easily be the other way around, and Grodno Jews would be helping us. Who will help a Jew if we don't help each other?"

"The Almighty will reward you for your good deed, your kindness to my children and me," uttered Mama through tears. "We don't want charity, heaven forbid! My husband gave me money, and he will send more."

"We'll square our accounts some other time," interrupted Basha, as she led Mama to an alcove, where she could freshen up.

Shlomo was already murmuring his Sabbath prayers, as he stood facing the wall to the east. It was too late to go to the synagogue. Dovidl and I promptly joined him and recited our prayers with fervor. Turning around, as is customary for the prayer: "Crown of thy husband, come in peace; let joy and gladsome song increase," I noticed Basha toting a large tureen of steaming noodle soup, which left a heavenly aroma trailing behind. And my mother followed with a stack of dishes.

Finally, seated around the table, Mama and I ate our first home-cooked meal as orkhim (guests) with these poor but generous Jews, in Minsk. We also learned that Shlomo had come to the station with horse and wagon to help refugees from the train—pending permission from the city officials to have them stay in the city. After waiting there all day and the Sabbath drawing ever closer, he just didn't have the heart to leave with an empty wagon. And so, he decided to take anyone he could to his own home. As fate would have it, he chose us.

Finished with our delicious Sabbath meal, our benefactors began planning our sleeping arrangements. Lending a hand, I helped drag in several long boards from the stall. We placed them on wooden stools against the walls, propping chairs at one end. Basha then covered these wooden planks with down-filled comforters. After more than a week of wallowing on the cold, hard floor of a cattle-car, my bed of planks made me feel like a prince... and I fell asleep in the middle of Krishme (bedtime prayer).

* * *

Shlomo Nekhes, an orchard-renter, made a modest living supplying the fruit, wholesale, to the vendors in town. The income also made it possible to send Dovid to the Rialno School.

When Shlomo brought us the tidings that our entire Grodno transport was given permission to remain in Minsk, we cried for joy.

When Dovid took me to see the refugees, I was appalled to see rows upon rows of makeshift bunks and folding cots put up in the upper, women's sections of the synagogues, with sheets strung between them in a vain attempt at privacy. These were temporary quarters until the community could arrange shelter for them in private homes, but with new transports arriving daily, bringing carloads of fresh evacuees to be cared for, the result was that they remained in the synagogues until the end of the war.

After this visit, our poor little house in New Kamarovka seemed like paradise to me.

I wrote a letter to father telling him of our safe arrival and reassuring him that we were with good, kind people in Minsk, enclosing the address. Whether my letter would reach Grodno was something I doubted very much. Nevertheless I posted it.

Mother again broached the subject of contributing to the household, no matter how little. Finally, after some discussion, they agreed on a minimal sum that would include everything—just so we might feel at home.

I thought it was high time for me to start looking for work. But Mama was far more concerned about my schooling. She decided that since I was a graduate from Cheder Mesukon, where, in addition to Hebrew, we had been taught Russian, it would be worthwhile for me to try my luck at the Russian Rialno School.

Shlomo took me to the school director and explained our circumstances. After testing the extent of my knowledge of Russian, I was admitted to the second grade of the school, free of tuition.

To order a school uniform was a luxury we could not afford. So, Mama sewed some brass buttons on an old jacket of Dovid's, fixed a new strip of ribbon around my cap and there I was—a ready-made gymnazist!

Basha, having no other children but Dovid, became as attached to Rochele as if she were her very own. She fussed over her and plied her with all sorts of goodies, until our little "half-twin" began to blossom into a real cherub.

We had still not received any word from father, and mother spent many a sleepless night worrying over husband and children back home in Grodno. I, too, was terribly homesick. I missed my pals and I missed performing and singing. It was so bad, I actually lost my appetite—an ailment I never suffered before. Growing pains, Basha called it.

* * *

One frosty afternoon after school, Dovid and I decided to take a brisk stroll through the streets of Minsk. Coming upon Tartarski Street, we stopped to gawk at a huge mosque.

"A church without a cross?" I wondered aloud.

"It's a Mohammedan church," explained Dovid. "They don't believe in the cross."

We passed the Svislotch River, all frozen over, like our Niemen back home. Meandering on to the old marketplace, we came to a large courtyard sprawled halfway up the hill. It was studded with various little houses of prayer. Entering the court we remained standing before the impressive Great Synagogue of Minsk.

"What are you boys looking for?" inquired an old man suspiciously. Before either of us could answer, my ears, catching the sound of a choir practice, began to tingle.

Unwittingly, I blurted out, "I am a choirboy. I want to see the choir leader."

"Spektor is busy rehearsing," the old man replied. "Cantor Kopshtik is with him. But go in, you'll find them in the side room."

Seated at the head of the table was, as I surmised, Cantor Kopshtik. The choir, going over a composition with their leader, stopped to stare.

"I am a choirboy. From Grodno...A refugee..." I stammered. The mention of Grodno, and the word refugee, produced an extraordinary effect.

"You're a choirboy? Then sing something," commanded Spektor.

To this day I don't know how they estimated the real quality of my alto from this abrupt and unexpected audition. I myself did not recognize my voice. I shook with fright at my own daring and my tones came out wobbly.

"You read music?" Spektor asked. I nodded, yes.

After a short conference with the cantor, Spektor said, "Sit down next to Yasha over there, with the altos. But don't sing, just listen."

My heart jumped with joy! I'm a choirboy again!

The reason I was so readily snapped up became clear to me at the very next session. Yasha Gordon, a boy of about fifteen, was the leading alto, the soloist. Like other boys his age, Yasha's voice had begun to change. Since no other alto good enough to replace him had as yet popped up, the poor boy struggled with his solos the best he could. He neither wanted, nor needed, to stay on in the choir for the sake of the few rubles, for Yasha came from a well-to-do family.

The Gordons owned a winery directly across the synagogue court. Yasha lived there with his father and sister, who kept house for them after the death of their mother. Yasha felt relieved and happy at my coming. He hoped I could take over so he would not have to go through his agony anymore.

Yasha was, undeniably, a great favorite at the synagogue. To fill his shoes was no easy challenge. The congregation sympathized with him. They couldn't forget his beautiful singing during the years his voice was in fine form.

At one of the rehearsals, Spektor instructed me: "Yablonik, don't sing along with the choir. Just look at me. Watch my hand. If I give you the signal, you take the solo. Otherwise Yasha sings, understand?"

I was issued a black robe, a yarmulka, a prayer-shawl, and I girded myself for my "debut" at the Great Synagogue of Minsk. I was sure that Spektor would not permit me to open my mouth to sing solo before the congregation. He would not take the chance. But why did he instruct me to keep mum and just listen. Why couldn't I sing with the choir?

That Friday night Shlomo and Dovid planned to attend the service at the Great Synagogue so we could then walk home together. I tried to talk them out of it. Why should they see me standing there like a dummy? The whole choir will be singing, and I will be staring into space with my mouth shut. For this, they have to make the trek all the way from Kamarovka?!

* * *

We stood on the Bima and waited to begin the Friday evening service, with Spektor whispering last-minute instructions at us. Cantor Kopshtik began the Kabolat Shabat. The choir picked up its own portion, while I stood—silent.

At the alto solos, Spektor did not as much as glance in my direction and I remained silent in accordance with his instruction. Yasha, standing beside me, made every effort to produce a ringing tone. He managed, somehow, to get through his solos during the Kabolat Shabat. The A'avas oylom, a composition beginning with "Infinite is Thy love as Thou didst manifest it through Israel Thy people" is a lengthy solo for alto, a veritable aria. The soloist sings practically the entire composition, backed by the choir. It is a solo which demands a voice!

Spektor gave Yasha the tone with his pitch pipe and nodded at him to begin.

Yasha cleared his throat...yet nothing happened. He looked at Spektor with the eyes of a chicken about to have its gullet slit.

The sanctuary was so quiet one could hear a pin drop. The cantor turned to Spektor. "Nu! What's all this stalling for?" he whispered, "Let's get on with the service!"

Spektor, white as a sheet, his expression one of complete resignation, lifted his hands and gave me the sign to begin.

I took a deep breath, remembering father's training, and began the solo. Pianissimo at first, as Spektor had coached me and then, with an increase of volume, swelled to a forte giving it heart and feeling. I threw my very soul into it, as if my life hung in the balance and only the A'avas oylom could save me.

Spektor stared at me in amazement. Warming up, he began to conduct with fire—so different from the rehearsals. I obeyed his every variation, and faithfully executed every nuance and phrase of the composition. At the end, when the choir joined me on the words: "Thy love through Israel" and I finished on a rousing finale, a storm of applause broke out in the synagogue.

"Quiet! Quiet!" the beadles rapped on the pulpit for silence. "Don't you know it is forbidden to applaud in a synagogue?!" When they succeeded in bringing the men to order, the clapping still lingered in the women's balcony.

And after my Hashkiveinu solo, there was no longer any doubt but that I had—in cantor's jargon—taken Minsk by storm!

As I was about to leave, who should be coming toward me, their faces beaming, but Shlomo, Dovid, and to my overwhelming surprise—my mother! Filled with pride she hugged and kissed me. Shlomo and Dovid were extremely pleased and flattered, for here were these prominent men of wealth urging me to be their Sabbath guest...even asking that I also bring my mother, yet I had chosen to go home with them to Kamarovka! The women crowding around us congratulated mother and wished her much nakhas in her son.

It created such a holiday spirit in the little house, we all stayed up late to enjoy a genuine Oneg-Shabat.

In the morning Basha whipped up a gogl-mogl (eggnog), and made me drink it. "It's good for the voice," she insisted. That Saturday morning happened to be Rosh Chodesh, the beginning of the new month, and Cantor Kopshtik was to officiate with the aid of the choir. The synagogue was filled to overflowing.

Yasha greeted me with words of praise, never displaying an iota of jealousy. I was unable, at the time, to evaluate this rare trait. Jealousy is such an accepted condition among artists. Looking back years later I fully appreciated this quality in Yasha. It inculcated a desire in me to help other young talents, who aspired to careers in the theater—a profession in which it is most difficult to achieve recognition, or be given some sort of break. Throughout my years as producer and director in the United States and other countries, my theater was always open to young people of talent; many who later went on to attain prominence on the American stage and films. I feel more than compensated when I hear them publicly crediting me with having given them their first chance to develop their craft.

That Saturday morning in the Great Synagogue, we took our places for Shakhris, the first part of the Sabbath morning service. Yasha sang with the alto section, while I took over the solos. My success mounted with each composition, and everyone had a good word for me.

Our choir leader, Spektor, was in no way impressed with my individual triumph. It was the combined success of his choir as a whole, and that's the way he wanted it.

"I had good reason for not entrusting you with a solo," Spektor told me. "One must be very cautious with youngsters like yourself. At rehearsal they sing like angels. But, put them in front of an audience! I figured that by Passover I'd have you ready enough to take a chance on you. You were just plain lucky! Now don't get a swelled head, you hear me? I don't put up with that nonsense."

But why, I asked, wanting to satisfy my curiosity, did he order me not to sing with the rest of the choir?

"A soloist must always save his voice, in order to be fresh when his solo comes up, understand? Even though I wasn't taking any chances with you, I thought…just in case!"

After services the beadle had news for me. "The president of the shul," he smiled, "wants to take you to his house for the Sabbath meal. You lucky boy!"

I still preferred to go home, or to Yasha's inviting house, where I had, on several occasions, sampled his sister's cooking. Nevertheless, Spektor himself advised me to go.

"Yes, go, go with the president. He's the one to determine your salary, see? At the same time, why not have yourself a good, solid dinner? They won't serve you any cholent," he grinned, "but you certainly will not come away hungry. Have you heard of Wisotsky Tea? Well, our president, a gilt-edged merchant of the first rung, is the representative of the Wisotsky Tea Company in Minsk, and he's richer even than Wisotsky!"

Dinner with the Rich

I stood and waited for the richer-than-Wisotsky president, while he listened patiently to several Jews, who were unburdening their problems in the hope of a little "favor." The common folk didn't stand a chance of being admitted to the rich man's office. But here, in a house of worship, having communed with the Almighty, the rich man was sure to be in a more receptive mood.

I was pretty hungry by now, but I stood obediently by and waited for my benefactor. At last he moved toward the door and I, his guest, ambled after him. In his high silk hat, suede gloves, long black overcoat with karakul collar, worn over his Prince Albert and striped pants, he strode along Gubernaterski—with me traipsing after him. Not a word did he utter all the way, except to hum a little tune as he went.

At last, stopping before a most imposing residence, he nodded for me to follow him in. A pretty young girl in the entrance hall took his hat and coat.

"Gut Shabbes," I greeted her in keeping with Jewish custom. The girl did not answer. How was I to know that she was a "shiksa"? My host mumbled something to her in Russian and letting me stand in the hallway, disappeared up a stairway.

I was in a quandary. Should I remove my cap, or not? How will I eat without it? Do the rich provide yarmulkas at the table, maybe? In deference to her I decided to remove my cap and my bulky lumber jacket. Taking my things she waved me into a dining salon and also disappeared.

The room was magnificent. The elegant furnishings, the gleaming glass cabinets with their sparkling crystal, china, gold and silver tableware... splendor, such as I hadn't even seen in the home of my uncle Shillingoff, the rich man of Grodno. Afraid to come in close contact with anything, I stood and waited until my feet began to ache. Finally, drumming up enough courage I sat down—unasked—on the edge of a plush upholstered chair.

A boy about my own age, in a sailor suit, stuck his head in the doorway. Eyeing me as if I were some outlandish specimen, he burst into raucous laughter and promptly took off.

From another room came the sound of a gramophone. A metallic recording of voice with instrumental accompaniment blared forth the current Russian hit, "Machish Khoroshi Tanyetz, tra-la-la-la-la" (The Maxixe is a lovely Dance). There was nothing for me to do but sit and listen. The recording was repeated once, twice...I was starved, and in place of food, I was being treated to "Machish Khoroshi Tanyetz!" As if this weren't nerve-racking enough, the boy in the sailor suit decided to lend his own vocal support to the one on the record. At the top of his lungs he gave out with, "Machish Khoroshi Tanyetz, tra-la-la-la-la!"

At long last, thank heaven, the maid came in and busied herself setting the table. Then, one by one they appeared; first the mistress of the house glided in wearing an elegant peignoir. She was a very attractive lady, much younger than her husband. I bounced up and had good enough sense not to assail her with my "gut Shabbes." In answer to her nod, I bowed. Then the president came in followed by his son, who was still humming. I was indicated a seat at the table and we all sat down.

Gleaming pieces of silverware were laid out at my place: forks, knives, spoons, large, small and smaller ones. The servant and her helper, an older peasant woman, kept bringing in platters of food, the likes of which I had never laid eyes on. My heart yearned for Basha's potato-and-bean cholent back in our humble surroundings in Kamarovka. Nobody spoke a word to me, except as a concession to etiquette: would I care for another bit of this, another spoonful of that?

When the compote was served, the president finally spoke. "You sing very well," he smiled at me. "Sing something, boy! Let my wife hear you, too."

"Yes, sing!" his son chimed in, "sing, 'Machish Khoroshi Tanyetz!'"

I rose from the table and, fighting back tears of humiliation, excused myself. "It's late," I said, "my mother won't know where I am. She'll be worried. Thank you for everything. Goodbye."

Out in the hall, the maid handed me my cap and my jacket, and I ran from the place as fast as my feet could carry me.

* * *

Spring

The ice on the Svislotch had already begun to break up, and the low-lying areas along the river banks were inundated. Sure sign of spring! Spektor began rehearsing the choir for the Passover Holiday and promised that I would receive something extra added to my stipend of six rubles a month.

One early evening, Mama came rushing toward me, beaming with joy. "Chaimke!" she exclaimed, "guess who's here! Our Shayke!"

Sure enough, close on her heels, came my brother in his military uniform and soon grabbed me in a bear hug. Shayke, who served as a gunner in the Russian artillery, had gotten a blast of gunpowder in his eyes when a nearby shell exploded. It was not too serious, but reason enough to get him his discharge.

Through my brother we also learned that father did receive our letters, only his answers never reached us. Shayke had thus gotten word from father to stop off in Minsk on his way home and bring us back to Grodno. This was easier said than done. To be allowed back into a region so close to the warfront was no simple matter. It required a top priority permit from high up. Fortunately, this help came through Yasha Gordon's father. No doubt, his influence in addition to Shayke's two medals—one for excellence in marksmanship, the other for good deportment—and his honorable discharge papers, carried enough weight. He was issued a special military pass for our re-entry into Grodno.

Shlomo, Dovid and Basha, of course, were happy for us. But we were each conscious of the pain of parting, having grown so close during our eight months together.

I was filled with sadness. Not too long before, I would joyfully have flown back to Grodno. And now, when I had become so well adjusted... What of father, I berated myself. My relatives, my friends? Where was my love and longing for them? Already forgotten?

Another difficult mission I had to face was to tell my choir leader, Spektor, that I was going home. With characteristic equanimity he listened to me as he pretended to be absorbed in the pages of a music folio. Finally, he looked up.

"Well, then, that's that," he observed in his unruffled way. "The synagogue will not disintegrate and I'm sure we will all survive. There are plenty of boys in Minsk with voices."

"Yes, yes, boys with voices," Kopshtik interjected, "but try and get me one with a voice like this youngster's!" This remark by the cantor was the highest praise I had yet received.

I bade my fellow choir-singers goodbye. As I was about to leave, Spektor stopped me.

"Wait a minute, Yablonik," he said, "here's a little gift for you— something to remember us by." He handed me the pitch pipe with which he always gave us the keynote.

(I treasured this little memento as one of my most precious gifts. In 1930 during one of my guest performances in Romania, two things were stolen from my dressing room: my gold watch—a wedding present—and the little pitch pipe.)

At the depot, Yasha and Zina were waiting with a good bottle of Passover wine to take home for the holiday. With tears in our eyes we took leave of our dear friends and pushed our way into one of the third class passenger cars. Here too, it was jammed with passengers, but what a difference from the cattle cars that brought us to Minsk!

Farewell, my dear friends, I waved. Farewell, Minsk. I couldn't help recalling Basha's parting words: "God knows if we shall ever meet again."

As fate willed it, she was right. Except for Dovid—under incredible circumstances—we never met again.

14

Home Sweet Home

We returned to Grodno just in time. Had we remained in Minsk over the summer, we'd have shared the same fate as the other unfortunates of our town, who were stuck in Minsk, in Yelisovetgrad, Woroniezh and other far-off places. Cut off from families to the very end of the First World War, some of them never did come back.

Father and Motke welcomed us with our own carriage, repainted and drawn by my old horse, Kashtan.

We drove to a new flat, rented by father in the meantime, in the courtyard of Zalutzky the baker, on Troitza Street. It had conveniences such as our old place never had: a sink with running water and—electricity! These modern conveniences made life a lot easier. What a delight! A twist of the tap and water flowed right from the wall! We were still obliged to go to the outhouse in the yard, but all in all, we were quite fortunate with the improvements in our new flat.

My brother Shayke soon got a job at the city's electric power plant, and Slavka was still at the cigarette factory. Father bought another horse, a mare, whom I dubbed Masha, and both he and Motke became coach drivers; father, driving by day and my brother, by night.

I went back to the yeshiva to resume my studies, but nothing seemed the same anymore. I considered myself quite grown up, a man of the world. Who could sit huddled over a Gemara, when the air was astir with portent?

Among my fellow-students in the yeshiva, were Rabbi Moshe-Chaim Shapiro (former Israeli Minister of Interior), Rabbi Moshe Bulvin (the principal of a yeshiva in Jerusalem), and other prominent personalities, whom I encountered in later years during my travels around the world.

The Brass Band of the Fire Brigade

From earliest childhood I felt drawn to music. The urge to master an instrument had taken hold of me the first time I heard the concertina played by our singing teacher in Cheder Mesukon.

The volunteer fire brigade had a very good brass band of its own. Among this group of amateur musicians were a number of ex-soldiers from the Russian army bands. For many of the young, aspiring musicians, the fire-volunteer band was the only "conservatory" in Grodno. I spent many a long evening listening to their practice sessions. Whenever the band was scheduled to play at a parade, the city park, or at some other municipal function, I always managed to make myself useful.

Mostly, I assisted the drummer, Alter Stolarsky. He had to tote the large drum, the snare drum, the stands, plus cymbals, a tambourine and the rest of the paraphernalia a percussionist cannot do without. As these trappings were too heavy to lug by myself, I annexed another boy to help me—Borke Labendz. He, in turn, brought along his kid brother, Eyshke, and together we hauled the instruments and equipment to and from functions.

My brother Motke, a volunteer fireman, prevailed upon Stolarsky to teach me an instrument. I began with a French horn, but lacked the patience for this sensitive instrument. I switched to the snare drum, fascinated by the rhythm. Having learned to read music in the choir, my will was so strong that I caught the hang of it in record time and soon became Stolarsky's assistant snare-drummer. Motke and my cousin Mikhl, another volunteer fireman, were the only ones who knew of my musical venture, but they kept it secret from my father.

* * *

In the beginning of the war, Russia won several victories over the Austrians. Germany, in the meantime, concentrated on Belgium, France and other neighbors to the west. Polishing them off one by one, Germany executed an about face and began smashing the Russians unmercifully.

After occupying Warsaw and the surrounding Russian-Polish territory, Germany laid siege to Brest-Litovsk, a maneuver that cut off all train transportation to Russia. The whole western front fell apart. The most important cities in Grodno Province tumbled: Suwalk, Augustov and the German forces began pushing ever closer to the city of Grodno, itself.

Reverberations of artillery could be heard in town, and splotches of fiery red, reflected against the night sky, could be seen in the distance. The Russians, before evacuating, were setting fire to their own cities.

Father gave me strict orders: I was not to stick my nose out of the house! Well, well, I thought, he had a good case! I was just the one to stay put! Me, with my irrepressible nature, wanting to see everything for myself. In Minsk I had become accustomed to being a free bird, not having to account to him. But, having sense enough to steer clear of any discussions with him, I kept to myself, and more or less, did as I pleased.

No sooner did father drive off with his droshky, I was out on the street taking in the goings-on around town.

The Russian government officials, the military brass and city commissioners, who had already evacuated with their families, forsook government buildings and private homes. Civilians openly broke into the deserted buildings and helped themselves to whatever was movable; articles, such as furniture, paintings, vases and lamps, were gone in no time. Even the walls were torn down, for wood also had its value. People who normally wouldn't touch a thing belonging to anyone else, were caught up in the contagion of looting, dragging home whatever they could.

The Jews in Grodno grew fearful. What if the retreating Russian soldiers took out their defeat at the front on the Jews? Losing no time, the community formed self-defense units. These militia were made up of Jews from all classes and were headed by the chiefs of the volunteer fire department. The actual muscle of the civilian defense were the butchers, carters, tannery workers and other strong-arm fellows from Yurzika and Fehrstadt. These brawny sons of the people could be depended on to defend Jewish life and property!

During this mass retreat, the army requisitioned countless horses and wagons from the civilian populace. The endless march stretched from Fehrstadt to the city proper via the new concrete bridge, which had been dedicated to the 300-year-old regime of the Romanovs. Also strung across the Niemen by a military detail were some pontoon bridges.

Shops along the main streets were tightly shuttered. The explosions that kept coming closer shattered windows and forced shopkeepers to board up their fronts to prevent more looting.

Women were mortally afraid to stick their heads out the door. The besotted, demoralized and lust-crazed soldiers spared no one...

Word got around that an army storehouse of wheat flour and salt had been broken into. People came running from every direction with burlap sacks, buckets and wheelbarrows to grab up what they could of these life-sustaining items. I too, could not resist taking advantage of this free grab bag. Hastening home to find a sack, I made a beeline to this treasure trove. I found men, women and children down on their knees scooping salt into every type of container. The flour, unfortunately, had been drenched with kerosene by the Russians, rendering it useless to the infiltrating enemy. Even the parts that had escaped the dousing had absorbed the odor of kerosene and so I had to settle for the salt.

Bent almost double under my sack of salt, I staggered along on my way home, when a Cossack, astride a tall horse, stopped me.

"Put that sack down!" he commanded, "and get going!" Just then, his eye caught the glint of the little gold ring on my finger, which Mama had given me on my twelfth birthday.

"Take off that ring!" Trembling with terror, I set the sack down and began to pull at my ring. I rugged and tugged, but it refused to budge.

Baring his sword, he wielded it as if he were about to cut my ring off—little finger and all! In panic, I let out such a piercing scream that the Cossack's horse reared up and neighed so wildly I expected his hooves to come down and squash me. Desperately, I yanked at my ring, but to no avail.

In the end, the Cossack spat out an involved combination of Russian cuss words and galloped off.

Hands shaking and knees wobbling, I lifted my heavy burden onto my back and continued on my way. I should have listened to father, I scolded myself. I should have stayed indoors instead of gadding about the streets at a time like this. I thanked my lucky stars that I still had my finger—let alone Mama's little gold ring!

My sack of salt saved my neck. It helped take the edge off father's wrath at my obedience. And no wonder! Who would quarrel with a sackful of salt to keep body and soul together in the face of an uncertain future?!

My Bar Mitzvah

In the middle of all the turmoil, my Bar Mitzvah cropped up! I don't suppose I could very well postpone a Bar Mitzvah just because of a war between Russia and Germany. I had waited for this day as one waits for the Messiah! Not in anticipation of the presents. In view of the state of poverty in which we were living, I could only expect to receive a big zero.

I was eager to have my Bar Mitzvah over with for another reason. My parents met my protests that I was no longer a child with: "Look who's talking. Why, you're not even Bar Mitzvah!" Up until the time a boy reaches this stage, his blasphemies and sins are credited in heaven to his father's account; which gives a father the right to lay down the rules. But, after the Bar Mitzvah, that's over with! Father will no longer be punished for my trespasses. These will be credited to my own account. And speaking of trespasses, I had already committed a few.

On August 11, 1915, I finally became Bar Mitzvah...with mazel! The following Saturday morning my relatives came to participate in the prayers, while my mother and sisters sat upstairs in the women's section of the big Hayyei Adam, gazing down at me with pride.

My father, I sensed, was not exactly in the highest of spirits. There was a hint of sadness in his eyes throughout the ceremony. It was as if his heart were telling him that I was far from following the path preached by the Torah; that I was drawn, instead, to an entirely different way of life.

After prayers everyone gathered round to congratulate us and have a bit of refreshment. Since schnapps was hard to come by, folks sipped raisin wine and ate mother's home-backed honik-leykakh—minus the honey. Thus, another Jew was added to the Nation of Israel: Chaim Yablonik.

* * *

In the meantime, Germany captured the cities of Lutsk and Pinsk. The whistling of shells and grenades could now be heard coming closer and with greater frequency to our town. Every explosion made the walls shake, and the earth beneath the houses tremble.

Folks took to their cellars, seeking shelter not only from the fleeing Russians, but from the German bombs that hailed the city from their "tin eagles" in the sky—a brand new menace—aeroplanes!

During all this bombing, our horse was locked in a little stall on Troitza near the old cemetery. The thought of Kashtan alone in a stable, with shells and grenades bursting all around him, was more than I could bear. Sneaking out of our yard-gate and keeping close to the houses, I made a dash for it all the way to his stall. Kashtan whinnied pitifully when he sensed my approach. Straddling the horse, I galloped him back to our courtyard and put him up in a narrow shed. Father was ready to quarter me alive for this stunt, but since I was unscathed and the horse safe, I got off with a good scolding.

A deafening explosion, sounding as if the world were coming apart, shook the walls of our cellar. The Russian demolition squad had detonated the mined bridges over the Niemen. The explosion set fire to the city's military quarters, as well as houses on the Fehrstadt side. The flames quickly spread to the bordering streets and developed into an inferno.

Suddenly, the bombarding stopped. Silence fell over the city. A gunshot here and there could still be heard, or the rat-a-tat of a Russian machine gun swiftly answered by a German hand grenade. The advance column of the frontal attack under Field Marshal Von Hindenburg had reached Fehrstadt.

The Russian commandant of Grodno Fortress had bragged all along that, come what may, the Germans would never come anywhere near our city. Nevertheless, it is an historical fact that, on September 2, 1915, "Der Deutsch" did indeed occupy Grodno!

15

The German Occupation

There is an old Jewish adage that warns: "Never wish for a new ruler, for who can predict how good his successor will be." Yet the Jews in Grodno waited impatiently for Kaiser Wilhelm's army to bring them salvation from the czarist yoke. Germany's siege of Grodno shook up all of imperial Russia.

During the first hours of the German occupation, their initial objective was to clear the city of the remaining Russian soldiers. Several of these units had entrenched themselves in dugouts, shooting at anything that moved. Shots, coming from behind buildings, attics, belfries of both the Russian and Polish churches, echoed until nightfall. In the end, the Russian soldiers, who refused to surrender to the Germans, were soon made short shrift of by a few hand grenades.

At all vital points, such as Grodno Fortress, the Russians had abandoned their heavy artillery and great stores of shells; by turning these abandoned cannons around, the Germans bombarded the fleeing Russians with their own ammunition.

Cautiously, people crawled out of their cellars and peeked through the cracks in the heavy courtyard gates. German soldiers in gray uniforms and spiked helmets were patrolling the streets, armed with automatic guns.

Pushing open the gates, we too, ventured out on the street. The dense, black smoke that came billowing toward us soon enveloped the entire city. Grodno was in flames!

When the Russians vacated Grodno, they also evacuated the city fire department, along with their horses and best pieces of equipment. This left the city at the mercy of the flames. The bell on the watchtower could be heard desperately clanging, but the fire volunteers—made up mainly of Jewish chaps— were afraid to budge, what with shells still flying back and forth. Still, when the volunteers recognized the sound of young Rubinsky's own silver trumpet blaring the frantic pleas: "Boys! Our Grodno is on fire! Hurry!" they had to have a heart of stone to ignore this call to the rescue.

Quick as a wink, my brother Motke and cousin Mikhl pulled on their uniforms. Fastening their belts, on which there hung a length of coiled rope and a hatchet, they grabbed their brass helmets and fled to the firehouse. I made tracks to the firehouse, myself. True enough, I was only an assistant drummer boy, nevertheless, still a fireman! When I got there, things were already underway.

A German sergeant requisitioned a couple of horses from the coach-drivers and these were hastily hitched up by the volunteers to the only handpump-and-ladder apparatus left by the Russians. The hose-and-water-barrel wagons had to be drawn manually, so I pitched in and helped pull one of them. Many buildings around the city were engulfed in flames, the frame houses crackling noisily in the hellish blaze.

The dynamited bridges lay half sunk in the river, smoldering, with chunks of concrete still exploding in midair. The waters of the Niemen sizzled and foamed with the wreckage. The acrid smell of dynamite, gunpowder and smoke seeped into our lungs and stung our eyes. The volunteer firefighters were at a loss as to how to tackle the problem. It was clear that our old, inadequate apparatus was not going to get us anywhere.

The Kobrinski military building nearest the destroyed bridge was left with only three of its walls standing. The entire front was blasted out. Leaning against one of its smoldering walls sat a Russian soldier holding a crust of black bread in one hand, a hunk of salami in the other. Thunderstruck, I wondered what on earth he was doing, sitting there and eating in the midst of the smoking ruins! But then I saw that one side of his face had been ripped away. No mouth and no chin. Nearby lay other casualties, their feet bare, or in their burlap wrappings, their boots already in the possession of the living...

* * *

Considering the odds, the volunteer firefighters gave an excellent account of themselves, getting the fire under control and earning a good reputation with the occupying Germans. The leaders of the volunteer group later became important in the administration of the city.

The Russian and Polish churches, standing in the very center of the city, were hardly touched by the bombardment. Still, their former splendor, their iron-clad prestige with Christian citizens, did indeed suffer. Into prominence now, came the little German kirche in back of the city park. Its worshipers, a small number of Grodno residents of German descent, were suddenly at the head of things, getting important appointments in the civilian city council.

"Deutschland, Deutschland über Alles!" they spouted at every turn, these overnight city fathers. And it was woe unto the individual toward whom they bore a grudge from the days of the Russian regime!

* * *

The sound of music echoed through the streets. It came from the Boulevard Square, where a German military band was giving a free open-air concert. The band, arranged in a semicircle, played military marches, waltzes, overtures and potpourris from Kalman and Strauss operettas. For an encore they struck a happy note with the Jewish listeners by playing a medley of popular Yiddish tunes, such as: "Chave, oy, oy, oy Chave!" and "Yoshke Furt

Avek." Delighted, those who were familiar with the words sang along with the band.

This friendly gesture of providing recreation for the people was interpreted as a reassuring sign, and the crowd applauded the Kapellmeister and his orchestra.

Standing around on the Boulevard, enjoying the music, made it easy to forget that, for the last several days we'd been living on a diet of rotting potatoes; plus a few beets, radishes and carrots that Mama managed to trade with a neighbor for a shaker of salt out of my sack.

Early mornings, Motke, Mikhl and I tramped to the outskirts of town to scour the fields in the hope of finding some potatoes that had not yet been dug up. And we were not the only ones. Using spades we did sometimes succeed in digging up a few potatoes, radishes, beets, or some stray autumn herbs and turnips. To tread about in the open fields was no small hazard. Shells lay embedded in the ground and could go off at the slightest touch. Here and there, we could also trip over the decomposed body of a Russian, overlooked for burial, and giving off a terrible stench. The biggest threat of all were the field rats. Large as cats, they brazenly paraded over the stubbly fields, gorging themselves on the dead.

As if our lot were not woeful enough, a German major took a shine to our droshky and Kashtan, our horse. Our weeping and imploring that this would deprive us of our only means of earning a living fell on deaf ears. In return we were given a piece of paper—a receipt, for a horse and droshky. Losing Kashtan was a devastating blow to me. It was very difficult to part with my pet, who followed me around like a faithful puppy, and whose life I saved at the risk of my own. Yet what could we do...stand up to a major?

War is War

The first days of the honeymoon were soon over and the Germans began to show their true colors. Plastered on walls around town were dictates that read:

No one is to appear on the street between the hours of six in the evening and seven in the morning.

Firemen, doctors and militia must immediately provide themselves with identification passes.

Anyone found on the street without a pass during curfew will be shot on sight.

Anyone harboring Russian soldiers must surrender them at once. Failure to turn them in is punishable by death.

Weapons of all kinds are to be brought to the police courtyard without delay. All articles of copper and brass: pots, pans, washtubs, samovars, candlesticks, metal doorknobs must immediately be brought to the courtyard of the police.

Smuggling, or trading in German military articles is punishable by imprisonment.

The entire populace, from the age of twelve, without exception, must promptly register with the police and get their identification cards. Children under twelve will be registered on the cards issued their parents.

Civilians encountering a German officer must remove their hats and step down from the sidewalk. For failure to obey—heavy penalties.

At given hours, everyone is to report at the designated bathhouses for the purpose of being deloused. Upon receipt of the bath-certificate, the individual may then apply for his food-ration card.

The only attractive aspect of all these orders was the indication that, at last, ration cards were in the offing. At the designated hour, we went to the compulsory baths to be deloused. One such bathhouse was rigged up in the courtyard of the jail and the other on Lipova Street, over in Fehrstadt. Men and women reported at different hours.

These enforced baths were certainly not to be confused with Sidrowsky's Bathhouse where steaming leisurely on the topmost bench made any pauper feel like a Rothschild. Upon getting undressed, all clothing was taken away to be disinfected. The children, naked, were shorn to the scalp. The military doctors were mainly on the lookout for symptoms of syphilis and other venereal diseases. If anyone's hair, or beard, struck them as less than 100 percent clean, these were immediately sheared off with a clipper. If it happened to be a woman, she had to resort to a sheytl. By the same token, a pious Jew would then be seen with his chin tied up in a kerchief, so he wouldn't have to appear in public with a bare face like that of a priest's.

After the clipping came the scorching shower. It burned like hell, but not until the order came was anyone permitted to step out from under the blistering spray. With skin already scarlet after the shower came the dousing of an astringent that stung even more. Our clothing—shrunken in the process of disinfection—was returned. And now, each was given a certificate proving that he, or she, had been deloused. The odor of this disinfectant clung to the clothing for weeks.

But at last, we got our ration cards. Standing in line at one or another of the bakeries, we waited eagerly for our loaf of bread. Receiving our rationed portion, we hurried home overjoyed, only to find that the bread could not be eaten. To feed the civilian populace, the bakers had been allotted the flour that was drenched with kerosene by the fleeing Russians! In the end, hunger conquered. Having no alternative, we filled our empty bellies with the evil-tasting bread.

The Germans had already occupied Vilna and were well on their way to adding Minsk to their conquests. The fear that the Russians might possibly return to Grodno had dissipated, leaving us no doubt that we were to remain German! The routine of living began to stabilize itself. Artisans were engaged to restore the wreckage left by the bombing. The re-opening of Shereshefsky's tobacco factory also helped to ease unemployment. Slavka, for one, returned to her job of cigarette-rolling, and Shayke was made chief mechanic at the electric power plant adjacent to the railroad station. Peasants began to drive into town once again with their farm products, but insisted on being paid in gold or silver. Russian rubles no longer meant anything.

Winter was almost upon us and the chances of street-paving jobs were nil. The hack-drivers who had succeeded in keeping their horses under cover were able to earn a few marks. But since our horse and droshky had been confiscated, father, Motke and even Mikhl remained—as the saying goes—holding the whip! And go make a living with that!

The city commandant, Major Schmidt, appointed several prominent citizens to confer with him on all Jewish affairs; for without his approval, nothing could be done. That being the case, the Jewish community decided that it was time the interruption of schooling be taken into consideration. How long were Jewish children going to hang around the streets, idle? As a result, permission was granted to re-open the Talmud Torah, the yeshiva, the trade school, now called "Handwerker Schule," where youngsters were taught, free of charge, carpentry, mechanics and other trades, including dressmaking and knitting for girls.

A new order was issued: "All institutes of learning are required to teach the language of the occupant—German."

Thus, at the yeshiva, in addition to the study of Gemara, we were taught the rest of our subjects in German.

Cantor Kaminetzky had left the city at the start of the German occupation, and Sergei was gone too. Nothing was the same anymore. After my success in the Great Synagogue in Minsk, my singing in the Grodno choir no longer had the same gratification for me.

16

Life Goes On

The first winter under the German occupation was a hard one. It wasn't easy to wean ourselves from the long-ingrained Russian laws and ukases, but it was even more difficult to adjust to the dictates of the Germans. The winter's blizzards and bitter frosts added to the hardships of the community. Firewood was at a premium. The severe weather brought fatal ailments to children in particular. We combed every corner of town for anything we could lay our hands on to warm up the house. A stick, a twig, a slat, or a piece of old, discarded furniture were real treasures. We lugged them home and into the oven they went! A new heating material was introduced—peat—except that the carbon fumes it gave off could put one to sleep forever!

All army personnel were being supplied with truckloads of huge logs, which needed to be chopped and sawed into kindling wood. This was the beginning of forced labor. Gendarmes swarmed the streets, rounding up every male who came their way. Their curt, "Bitte schön, kommen sie mal!" was an unceremonious invitation to come along and chop the logs. And there were other chores too, like dumping and cleaning the big garbage bins at the corners and cleaning the public toilets. Some civilians were taken in forced labor units to the outskirts of town and put to work clearing snow from the railroad tracks and main roads, which were impeding access to the city.

German gendarmes, in recruiting civilians for forced labor, had rounded up the Eishishker Rabbi, as well as my father and other elderly Jews as they were walking home from morning prayers on the Sabbath. They were hauled off to the military barracks and ordered to saw a load of logs under threat of severe punishment.

Terrified, the men looked to their revered rabbi with the bewildered question in their eyes: "Work? On the Sabbath?" The rabbi comforted them, saying: "Pikuach Nefesh—the saving of life transcends even the laws of the Sabbath." With these words, the rabbi, himself, picked up the ax and the men followed suit.

The ruthlessness of this act stirred up great bitterness and indignation throughout the Jewish community. But the leaders felt that it was dangerous to kick up an open protest, lest it bring even sharper decrees upon us.

* * *

I developed an insatiable hunger for reading. The city library, in addition to works in Russian and German, also had a small selection of books in Yiddish and Hebrew. I could hardly wait to come home from the yeshiva so I could settle down with my reading. More often than I can say, if I happened to be in the middle of a suspense-filled chapter, I committed the sin of reading the book hidden between the covers of the Gemara, even during studies at the yeshiva.

This period marked my initial acquaintance with the Yiddish works of Mendele Mokher Sforim, Sholom Aleichem, Jacob Dyneson, I. L. Peretz, and the writings of Bialik, Tchernichovsky and others, in Hebrew. I was enchanted with the folk songs of Avrom Reisen, Warshavsky and Kipnis, which I had already sung before. But my inspiration to compose theater songs definitely sprang from my first fascination with the recitations of Morris Rosenfeld and the poetic compositions by Shlomo Schmulevitch.

The widest selection of books at the library were in the Russian language. I pounced on the works of Leo Tolstoy, Dostoievsky, Gorki, Chekhov and Russian translations of Emile Zola, Guy de Maupassant and others.

Tolstoy's *Anna Karenina, War and Peace* and *Resurrection* gave me my first real insight into the tragic circumstance of my brother Velvel's exile to Siberia. How vividly these works brought back Grodno jail, my visit with my ill-fated brother and the unforgettable etape to the railroad station, where he was dragged off to the Schlusselburg Fortress. I was even more convinced that Velvel, of whom we hadn't heard in years, would never again be seen alive.

I didn't find it easy to grasp the full range of these profound works. There were far too many phrases in the Russian language beyond my ken. At times, I was able to inveigle Shayke to come to my aid, but he never explained things in depth—only perfunctory answers, as if afraid I might be drawn into the revolutionary stream.

Some books in Yiddish, which I was unable to find at the library, were loaned to me by my friend Zvi Belko out of his father's bookshop. I also borrowed some novels from him that were Yiddish translations by the Hebrew Publishing Company in New York of Arthur Conan Doyle, Jules Verne, Jack London and a novel called *The Indian Chief*, whose author escapes me.

The tales kept me spellbound. They carried me off to faraway places; to worlds hitherto undreamed of; to lands of strange races and even stranger ways of life. How intrigued I was by the hair-raising episodes of strife between the American pioneers and the red-skinned Indians; their life on the prairies and the new frontiers.

It was difficult to imagine how my sister Mariashka and her husband could live in America, in such threatening surroundings. No wonder we hadn't heard from them all during the war! I had nightmares about them lying dead somewhere on the prairie, scalped by the Indians!

* * *

With the first days of spring, the community came alive. One by one, shops around town re-opened, whether or not they had merchandise to sell.

The new German authorities reorganized the city fire department and appointed Harry Rubinsky as chief. Cousin Mikhl also joined the city fire department, doing himself, as well as us, a big favor by moving. We gained a bit more space in the flat, while he gained the status of having a sleeping bunk all to himself at the firehouse.

The fire-brigade band began to function again. The familiar sounds of trumpeting, fifing and tootling from above the magistrate stalls could be heard in the evening, as the musicians tried to firm their lips after the long winter layoff.

I felt reborn. I had a place where I could spend a few hours of an evening, learning to be a musician. No doubt, it would have behooved a yeshiva boy to stay at the synagogue and pore over the holy books, but who could resist the magnet that was drawing me to the band?!

With summer approaching, father landed a paving job. The Germans had re-opened the big military hospital, a huge complex of pavilions and wings to serve the army. Father's job was to surface the grounds surrounding the various buildings as well as the main approach to the hospital. This project was such an unexpected windfall, father didn't even ask how much he would be paid for his labors, nor from whom he was supposed to collect his money. Rounding up the remaining crew, with Motke now an equal partner, he went off to work. With father occupied, I was free—which meant that I spent entire evenings, even some daytime hours, at the rehearsal hall of the fireman's band.

The inducement to register officially, as a volunteer fireman, or member of the band, was the assurance of being exempted from forced labor. The county office was therefore furnished with a list of names and addresses of the fire brigade, including the band. The chosen few, belonging to the upper strata, promptly received their certificates of immunity. The rank and filers of the volunteer firemen waited all winter and did not receive any such identification, although the exemption pass was a necessary and most urgent need.

At Forced Labor

One evening, during band practice, we received an order to report early next morning at the police court. Well! Would I miss the chance of getting my identification as a full-fledged volunteer firefighter?!

The next morning, bright and early, before attending service in the synagogue, I hurried off to the police courtyard. Pretty soon others gathered, and not only volunteer firemen. Before long, gendarmes appeared and holding long lists of names, proceeded to call them out one by one.

I presently heard my name. "Here!" I replied and stepped up to the gendarme like a man qualified for a certificate as a fireman.

"Beschäftigung?" he inquired, asking about my occupation. As if I'd tell him that I was still a boy attending the yeshiva!

"Ich habe noch nicht keine beschäftigung." I have no occupation as yet, I explained in my Yiddish-flavored Deutsch, just to show him that, when it came to speaking German, I was no slouch, either. He told me to wait on line, so I waited.

In a little while, a few military hauling-trucks pulled in and the gendarmes ordered all those waiting on line to kindly pile into the trucks. Only then, did it dawn on everyone that this was a sample of German trickery: leading the fire-volunteers and others to believe they had been summoned to pick up their passes of exemption from forced labor. Recognizing the ruse, there ensued a tumult, an uproar and a hurried scattering toward the gate. But, stationed there, were gendarmes and military police. Armed with guns, they threatened to shoot.

"Gnädiger Herr Gendarme, there must be some mistake!" I pleaded. "I'm still a boy at the yeshiva. I was only recently Bar Mitzvah."

"Your name is Jablonik? Mor...Mordekhek?" he read, mangling Motke's name.

Realizing the error, I hastened to explain, "Motke," I corrected him. "That's my older brother. He's working with my father at the regional hospital. He is the fireman, not me. I'm only a boy, a drummer boy in the band. My name is Chaim, not Motke."

Motke-Shmotke. Boy-shmoy! All he knew was that his list called for a Jablonik, so what difference did it make to him, the blockhead!

Grabbing me by the collar with one hand and by the seat of my pants with the other, he tossed me into one of the trucks—and we were off! We rattled over the improvised bridge across the Niemen, through Fehrstadt and out of the city on the road to the fortress. Along the way we passed other groups of forced laborers, who were clearing the area of debris, and digging trenches.

By the time we reached our destination, the day was half over. With our innards shaken up and legs fallen asleep, we climbed out of the trucks. A guard ordered us to form two lines, soldier-fashion, while he held forth with a lecture. His German was over my head, but, from the way he emphasized the word desertiren (deserting), and the eloquent flourish of his revolver, I had no difficulty catching on. He also imparted the news that we had already missed the noonday meal. But if we behaved and put in a few hours of good work up to about six in the evening, we would then be rewarded with supper.

After a couple of hours of digging, lifting and bending, up-down, down-up and hauling unaccustomed weights on my back—on an empty stomach at that—I soon was convinced that I wasn't cut out for this type of labor. To stop and catch one's breath in the middle of the job was strictly verboten.

Finally finished for the day, we gathered up the implements and lined up four abreast. Flanked by armed guards we were marched off to our barracks. On the way, we passed long rows of wooden shacks, already abustle with other groups of forced laborers. Seeing us, they hailed us with cynical epithets and vulgar catcalls. Not to be outdone, our group retaliated in kind. All this rough exchange nevertheless, incurred no hostility. On the contrary, it provoked laughter—laughter fraught with bitterness over our common lot.

Our promised supper consisted of large slabs of bread with marmalade and ersatz coffee. Hungry as a wolf I welcomed even this. Evenings were still rather cold and nights even colder. Double-decker bunks, filled with straw, ran the length of the barracks. My nostrils were assailed by the penetrating smell of disinfectant—a losing battle, I discovered—against the bedbugs, lice and fleas that infested the straw sleeping pallets. Choosing an upper bunk, I climbed in, clothes and all, and fell into a dead sleep.

Five o'clock in the morning found us waiting in line at the latrines. I splashed cold water on my face and used my shirttail to dry myself. Breakfast was again bread and marmalade. The coffee tasted like lukewarm dishwater! We were each supplied with a rake, a shovel and an iron pick—tools, we were told, for which we were responsible. Shouldering these implements we trudged a few kilometers on the way to work. There was nothing I could do but resign myself to my fate and do as I was told. If only my feet weren't killing me! The stiff leather of my boots rubbed my feet so sore that every step I took was agony. The wrappings around my feet in lieu of stockings, chafed and irritated the back of my heels as well as my toes, causing blisters. But the work had to go on. "Arbeit macht das Leben süss!" (Work makes life sweet!) My co-workers knew that I was suffering and felt sorry for me. One of them told the guard that I was not strong enough to do this kind of work and explained that my being there was due to an error, anyway. The guard, himself, was convinced that something was wrong, since it was obvious, even to him, that I was only a boy. He told me to squat on the ground and rest.

Around the noon hour, large kettles of soup were brought to us and each worker was given a tin bowl and a wooden spoon. The cook meted out portions of bread and ladled out a measure of chickpea soup, with some stringy pieces of meat floating in it. I munched on the bread, but couldn't bring myself to touch the soup. The taste of non-kosher food was foreign to my palate and so I gave my portion of soup to the man who had spoken up for me.

"M-m-m," he smacked his lips gratefully, slurping spoonful after spoonful. "What a tasty piece of meat," he remarked, "horse meat!" That was all I needed! I vomited everything I'd eaten days before!

At the end of day I could barely limp back to the barracks. Not waiting for my ration of bread and marmalade, I climbed into my bunk. I wept bitter tears. It's your own fault, I chastised myself. You wouldn't listen to father. No! You had to be a fireman! You made your bed—now lie in it!

When I could no longer endure the torment, I begged one of the men to help me get my boots off. He tried, but my feet were too swollen by now. With the use of his knife, he cut away the pieces of leather and slit the boots open. I drew my first breath of relief. I tried to sleep but it was no use. I itched all over. Scratching only made matters worse.

The rest of the work-crew lay on their bunks already snoring their heads off. All at once, a fearful screaming and thrashing about came from the bunk beneath me. The fellow below was battling with a midnight visitor in his bunk— a field rat! My hair stood on end, prickling my scalp like needles. I was gripped by an overpowering compulsion, a yearning for one person—Mama! I must go home to mama, I kept repeating to myself. Yes, I must go home! And let them shoot me!

Except for the heavy snoring of the toil-weary men, the barrack was quiet. Slipping from my bunk and taking my cut-open boots and footwraps with me, I sneaked out with a ready alibi on my tongue: I'm going to the latrine…

Outside, I stopped and took a cautious look around. Nothing stirred. Edging my way along the outside wall, I headed for the shelter of the woods, expecting at any moment to get a bullet in the back.

There was some light from the starry sky, but the deeper I went into the thicket, the darker it grew. The brambles and stones cut into my sore feet, so that I had to sit down and wrap them in the rags. Picking up a fallen branch for support, I stumbled deeper and deeper into the darkness of the woods.

Limping along I held close to the trees bordering the road, so that at the slightest sound I could throw myself to the ground. All at once, I heard the unmistakable clatter of motorcycles and quickly took cover in the underbrush. I was scared to death! Could it be that they were already hunting for me, the deserter? Two military men on motorcycles whizzed by and disappeared down the road. They did not spot me, I breathed with relief. But my feet felt worse than ever. I couldn't go on. Utterly spent, I remained sprawled by the side of the road.

Out of the early morning mist, there slowly emerged a farm wagon piled with wood. The horse clopped along as if he knew the road blindfolded, while an old peasant on the driver's seat sat nodding, the reins dangling loosely in his hands. As the wagon slowly came abreast of me, I hailed the old man and asked him where he was going. Roused from his dozing, he pulled up the reins and sleepily grunted, "Fehrstadt."

Fehrstadt! My heart leaped with joy! So I'd been following the right road after all—the road home!

I explained about my swollen, bleeding feet and promised him the moon if only he would give me a lift across the Niemen into the city, or at least as far as Fehrstadt. I assured him that my father would reimburse him handsomely for bringing me home. He would, in fact, buy up his entire cartload of wood at any price he asked.

The peasant bobbed his head for me to climb aboard. In a wink I was beside him on the driver's seat. A smooch of his lips and the horse resumed his plodding gait, while the old man went back to dozing.

Riding on the wagon that morning, I prayed with a fervor I never felt before, a fervor my father would surely have sanctioned. I praised and thanked the Almighty with every fiber of my being for delivering me from the forced slave camp. Something about this miracle of my escape brought to mind the fanciful Hassidic tale I'd read by I. L. Peretz, *Maybe Even Higher.*

Can it be—the fantastic notion crossed my mind, that this peasant beside me on the driver's seat, who came to my rescue, is also a holy man in disguise? Eyeing the drowsing old peasant in his sheepskin jerkin, I had my doubts. Out of sheer exhaustion and the lulling motion of the wagon, I fell asleep.

Nudging me awake, the old man grunted, "Where to?" Rubbing my eyes, I realized that we had crossed the bridge over the Niemen—the crucial point of danger—for the bridge was patrolled at both ends, and if news of my escape had reached them by now, I surely would have been nabbed right there and then. Relieved, I directed the old man to our house.

Mama, filled with anguish, hugged and kissed me, while Rochele, afraid I might be whisked off again at any moment, clung to me for dear life! Father and Motke had already gone off to work, so Mama reimbursed my savior and did indeed buy up his cartload of wood. He left beaming, and no doubt praising the Holy Spirit for placing me across his path.

At sight of my feet, Mama was beside herself. She bathed and wrapped them in clean white strips torn from an old bedsheet. Easing my two bulky-bandaged feet into a pair of father's roomy galoshes, Mama packed a parcel of food for me to take to the hospital where my father and brother worked; an errand designed to get me into the grounds, where one of the doctors might, perhaps, do something for my bruised feet.

Father, Motke and the rest of the men almost crushed me with their hearty embraces. Open-mouthed with amazement, they listened to my tales of the labor camp.

Father asked one of the nurses if she'd be kind enough to do something about my feet. Unwrapping the rags, she caught her breath, so appalled was she at my wounds. Taking me into one of the wings of the hospital, she summoned a doctor.

After the doctor's ministering with scissors, or whatever else he did to trim the blisters—at which I closed my eyes and gritted my teeth—the nurse followed up with a cooling salve and yards of wide bandages. The instructions were for me to stay off my feet as much as possible. After this little ordeal, the kind nurse felt I needed a lift, and treated me to a generous slice of white bread spread with blackberry jam. She also hunted up an old pair of hospital scuffs and helped me hobble out into the yard. Settling myself on a convenient mound of sand, I waited to go home with father and the rest.

Much to my disappointment, it was decided that I had better not come back to the house. Gendarmes were sure to come looking for me. When my uncle Reuvke volunteered to take me to his house in Yurzika, father consented. They all agreed, the Germans would never find me in Yurzika.

Father's premonition proved right. That very evening, the gendarmes did indeed come to look for me. But everyone at home played dumb. They knew nothing at all. The gendarmes could search all they pleased...I had simply vanished.

During my first few days in Reuvke's house I was bored to death. The family couldn't visit me for fear they'd be followed. When I just couldn't stay put another day, my uncle took me along to the hospital to watch them at work.

I spent entire days on the grounds of this labyrinth. It was the ideal hide-out. My nurse dressed my feet in fresh bandages and usually rustled up a buttered roll and a glass of milk—to build me up—while I took life easy. But, after a while it began to pall on me. It was spring, with so many things I was bubbling to do, and here I was! Stuck all day in the yard of a military hospital, my feet wrapped in bandages and my evening spent, of all places, in the slum area of Yurzika! I couldn't stand it any longer.

On a Saturday morning, I decided to surprise father and show up for services at the synagogue closest to our house. It probably took Moses less time to climb Mount Sinai than it took me to drag myself up the steep hill from Yurzika to Troitza, but I made it.

Father was more than a little uneasy at my appearance in shul, despite the fact that the search for me had, seemingly, stopped. Everyone in the synagogue gave me a warm welcome. I was even honored with an aliyah.

At the end of prayers, how could I possible keep from stopping in at home, to wish Mama "gut Shabbes," give Rochele a big kiss, and by the way, enjoy some of my mothers cholent—her specialty?!

As we entered our courtyard—uh, oh!—a gendarme! Tall as a lamppost! He'd been waiting in ambush and quickly collared me. To no avail was Mama's weeping, nor father's pleading. The gendarme had orders to arrest me, so that's exactly what he did!

At the jail, prisoners, milling about the yard, greeted my arrival with cat-calls and obscenities.

The gendarme handed me over to a turnkey, who took me by the collar and, like a rag doll, tossed me into a cell. Slamming shut the iron-grated door, he disappeared.

Except for an iron cot folded against the wall and a stinking urinal in a corner, the cell was bare. The walls were covered with scribbled slogans and pornographic drawings. Leaning up against the wall, I let myself slide to the stone floor. Hours went by. Still shaken by the prisoner's jeering and the frightening thoughts evoked by the things they shouted: shooting, hanging. I dropped off into a nightmarish sleep. I woke up at the jangling of keys outside my cell. This is it! I was prepared for the worst.

"'Raus!" barked the turnkey. I followed him into the corridor. In the yard

I was handed over to a gendarme, who led me out of the prison gates, and back through the streets. I hobbled after him until we entered the court of a private residence. Delivered into the hands of the German soldier answering the doorbell, I was taken into an elegantly appointed room and left to wait.

At long last, a door opened and in strode a military man of medium height. His head was shaven as clean as his face. And clamped in his left eye, he sported a monocle. His impeccable uniform bore the insignia of a high-ranking German officer, an impressive array of medals covering his chest.

Seating himself at a desk he leafed through some papers and then, eyeing me sharply, his glance fell on my bandaged feet. Rising, he waved me to a chair and at his unspoken command, I undid the wrappings. Taken aback at the unsightly lesions on my feet, he shook his head and indicated that I re-wrap the bandages.

From a drawer in his desk he fetched a bar of chocolate and put it into my hands. I didn't dare not accept it, nor did I double-dare to unwrap and eat it.

"How old are you!"

"Thirteen, mein Herr," I replied.

"Why did they take you for forced labor?"

I explained as best I could in German. "They took me instead of my older brother. He is employed," I hastened to add, "He's working with my father at the military hospital."

"Why did you desert?" the officer asked. Here it comes; my heart sank.

"I didn't desert," I murmured. "I wanted to see meine Mutter, so I went home. I was homesick for meine Mutter..."

A broad smile spread across the officer's face. Putting his hand on my shoulder, he said, "Boy, go on home. Yes, go on," he repeated, still grinning. "Go home, zu deiner Mutter."

I couldn't believe my ears! Was I really free? I barely managed to utter a confused, "Danke schön, mein Herr."

It turned out that Shayke's friends at the power plant, mostly Germans, had interceded in my behalf with the topmost rung of the ladder. For this was none other that Major-General Schmidt, the German chief commandant of Grodno!

17

Sea, Sky and Theater

Every now and then a lecturer would show up in town, but these spoke at special functions for members of the various political parties that sprang up like mushrooms after a rain. When an occasional concertist did stray into Grodno, he was certainly not likely to be of world fame. What the folks missed more than anything was Yiddish theater; a play with a moral to lift the spirit, instill new hope and courage for a better tomorrow. Since the outbreak of war, there had been no theater productions. Last seen were Guzik's guest performances, when it was still compulsory to speak the lines of a Yiddish play in Russian. And so, the people were starved for a show tune and a bit of folk humor, and most important of all, have it performed in their mother tongue—Yiddish!

Shmulke Garber, a medic in a German clinic who happened to be a rabid theater lover, assembled a group of boys and girls and rehearsed them in *The Stranger*, a drama by Jacob Gordin. This enterprise proved to be the springboard for a renaissance of Yiddish theater in Grodno.

The spacious and magnificent City Theater suddenly seemed too small to accommodate the crowds that jammed the premiere of *The Stranger*. The play, given in Yiddish, created a tremendous stir in the community. It ran for several performances, attended by audiences sprinkled even with high-ranking German military.

The only "seasoned" actor in Garber's amateur group was Yitzhak Azarkh. The advent of Garber and his amateur group, Yiddish Art, was the answer to his prayer. Azankh had a genuine flair for the stage, quite versatile and never one to be choosy: it could be drama, comedy, musicals—no matter, as long as he was on the stage! And that was his way to the very end, until he walked the last mile with the rest of the Jewish community in Grodno, to the Nazi gas chambers.

Another professional actor, Michael Trilling, had just returned from touring the provinces. He was a handsome young man, with a ringing tenor, musically educated and quite adept at the piano—assets that made him ideally suited for the stage. Azarkh promptly got after Trilling with a proposition. They could form an operetta company on their own and make a fortune. When Trilling agreed, Azarkh not only purloined a few young talents from Garber's group, he also recruited several new ones.

The family of Sholom, the tailor, was blessed with sons and daughters, all of whom possessed beautiful singing voices and strong leanings toward the stage. The oldest son, Joseph, whose stage name was Khash, had begun acting with various troupes in Russia. Leah, a daughter, also won recognition as an actress in later years. Kadisch, another son, had a rare bass-baritone, and as an acquisition to the newly formed company of Trilling Azarkh was a great asset. The youngest son and only survivor of the well-known theatrical family is Avremel, known professionally as Khash-Grodner, now on the Yiddish stage in Israel.

For their first presentation they chose an American-Yiddish success play, *A Mentch zol men Zein*. For the chorus of this operetta, Azarkh recruited boys and girls from the shops and factories. The reed and brass instruments were supplied out of the firemen and army bands by my drum teacher, Alter Stolarsky, which of course, gave me an in at the theater. I toted instruments, ran errands and acquired my very first behind-the-scenes acquaintance with the intricacies of preparing a musical production.

The performance went over tremendously. And the biggest hit was scored by Kadisch Khash. He was unanimously acclaimed as a rising attraction on the Yiddish stage. A few years later, his theatrical firm, Kadisch Khash-Nehama (his wife), did indeed become one of the foremost musical companies in Poland and Lithuania.

Grodno audiences were very demanding. Troupes whose presentations were not entirely free of vulgarities, double entendres, or lewd mannerisms adopted by their couplet-singers suffered where it hurt the most—in the box office!

Garber produced *God of Vengeance* by Solem Asch; a play that created a great deal of controversy in those days. There were many who vehemently opposed the portrayal of life in a Jewish underworld.

The trio—Trilling, Kadish and Azarkh—produced *The Jewish Heart* by Lateiner and *The Holy Sabbath* by Fineman.

Garber put on a whole series of plays: Jacob Gordin's *Chassia, the Orphan*, Andreyev's *The Days of our Lives*, and Weiter's *The Mute*. In short, all at once there was nothing but sea, sky—and theater!

*   *   *

And now, a German theater company arrived in Grodno to present three operettas: *The Rose of Stamboul* by Leo Fall, *Biadera* and *The Chardasz Countess* by Emerich Kalman. This series of performances was for the entertainment of the troops and military personnel in town.

The entire company was under strict military discipline. They had brought along sceneries, furniture, props, lighting equipment and costumes for the principals, chorus and dancers. They also traveled with their own orchestra.

This was something I didn't care to miss and offered my services. I ran errands for the actors, fetched whatever they needed at the apothecary, even carted baggage to and from the lodgings where they stayed. My reward was the opportunity to witness the modern operettas that were the rage in Europe and eventually around the world.

The lavish scale on which these musicals were produced, the coordination and interaction of the professional artists, the projection of their lines and schooled singing filled me with wonder and awe. These spectaculars presented by the German company and, later on, the dramatic offerings I saw done by the Vilna Troupe, opened my eyes to the vast difference between professional craftsmanship and amateurish attempts.

The revelation remained with me as a valuable yardstick throughout my career around the world with Yiddish theater. In time I became even more aware of the important elements that go into the molding of a legitimate musical production: a realistic story line, a tuneful score, illusion and, above all, uncompromising discipline. These were the theories and principles I practiced during my many years as theater producer in New York. I always angled for a large stage spacious enough to accommodate my presentations, I surrounded myself with the foremost artists of every genre, and I went into my enterprise with an open hand and on the largest possible scale.

A Children's Theater Group

This burst of theatrical activity in my hometown had its effect on me, as well as on a good number of kids in our community. We organized ourselves as a children's theater group under the name Zion, changing it later to Cherut, Hebrew for Freedom. Our club room on Gorodnitchanski was duly festooned with colored streamers, the walls hung with pictures of Dr. Harzl, Chaim Weitzman, Mendele, Peretz and Sholem Aleichem.

My closest friend and club member was Ascher Dimant whose family ran a rooming house on Skidler Street.

A boy, about eleven, a shy, quiet youngster, began hanging around us. "Sh-Shimon Finkel," he stuttered his name. His parents ran a dress-goods store on Saborna Street. Actually, it was his mother who was the business head.

Finkel's passion was—theater! It breathed out of every pore of his being. To mention the subject of theater was enough to kindle a flame in his expressive eyes. Even at that early age he was well versed in the art, having read most of the classics in the Russian theater repertoire.

Finkel's parents, his mother in particular, were not at all pleased with his association with me. For when they learned that we were seriously planning on becoming actors, of all things—I was forbidden to show my face around their store. I was told, in no uncertain terms, that I had better let their precious son alone. Little did they know that it was their son who wasn't letting me alone with his burning ambition for the stage... and that I had my own troubles keeping my involvement from my own mother and father. All I needed was for them to discover that their yeshiva student was hell-bent on becoming an actor!

In recalling the beginnings of our mutual aspiration toward theatrical careers, my mind jumps to 1951. During my first visit to Israel, I experienced the joy of meeting Finkel's parents again. They were among the fortunate ones to have settled in then-Palestine before the holocaust.

Finkel's father embraced me like a long-lost son. His mother cried, "Chaimke! As I live and breathe, it's Chaimke!" Reaching out for me, she embraced and kissed me like a mother.

To cover my emotion, I jokingly asked, "Giveret (Madame) Finkel, will you run me out of the house now, for dragging Shimon away to the theater, as you used to do in Grodno when we were kids?"

Her eyes glistened with tears and her wan, emaciated lit up with pride as she looked up at her son. For just then, Finkel had scored fantastic success at the Habima, with his portrayal of Henrik Ibsen's classic, *Peer Gynt.*

"And you, Chaimke," she eyed me with pride, "I hear you too, are not such a small fish in your America!" Her smile conveyed gratification that another of her boys had made his mark in the world.

* * *

As youngsters we were faced with a problem. How was our theater group to acquire members of the fairer sex? If the adult amateur groups found it difficult enough to persuade young damsels to portray the female roles, how were we to expect girls to defy their parents and display such daring as to play together with boys?!

Fortunately, our problem was solved by Dimant's young sister Emma. She persuaded several of her friends to join the club. Emma herself was quite an eyeful, with her golden curls and blue eyes. (Years later, during the Polish regime, a Polish officer fell madly in love with her and because of her shot himself to death.)

A one-act play called *Cooked up a Mess* was translated for us from the Russian by a gynmasia student, Liova Halpern. The teacher, Sonia Staradub, agreed to direct us in the comedy and even brought her own young sister, Galia, into the group. For the second part of our program we prepared a revue, consisting of folk songs staged in makeup and costume. An outstanding hit was "I am a Coachman," sung by Israel Stotchik and me. Finkel did recitations, Joseph Binsteing led the children's chorus and Lolke Berezowsky play classical compositions on the piano. The Brothers Eliashev displayed their acrobatic skills with other members of the newly formed sports club, Maccabee.

Our debut was a great success and we donated the entire proceeds to the orphanage. When the all-important questions arose: what to select for our second vehicle, several held the opinion that we ought to stick to a revue program, but Finkel and I held out for playing three- or four-act dramatic works, no less, on the order of those produced by Garber's group. And we won!

One of the adults interested in our group was Moshe Weller. When he received a copy of *Der Intelligent* (the Intellectual) by Peretz Hirshbein, sent to him from Warsaw, he let me read it. I was instantly taken by the plot. The action might well have taken place in my own home; so similar was the story to that of my brother Velvel the revolutionary...so much like the struggle between him and father. Finkel was equally as enthused as I over the play, and when Weller expressed his own recommendation, everyone in our group agreed to do it.

Our directress, Sonia Staradub, happened to be occupied with Garber's production of Gordin's *Kreutzer Sonata,* and so, Israel Khomul, the photographer, volunteered to direct the play.

Special posters were printed, in German and Yiddish, announcing the play and the names of the cast. One of the bill-posters was prominently displayed near the Shillingoff buildings, where we were living at the time. I didn't dare use my right name, Yablonik, so I was billed as Yablokoff. This then, was the first poster to announce the professional name I chose while still a boy in Grodno—Chaim Yablokoff! Many years later, in New York, through a unique set of circumstances, Chaim became Herman.

I could not believe that my father, who had to pass this corner daily, hadn't already guessed who this Yablokoff might be. Could it be that he considered me a lost cause anyway, convinced that a rabbi, I will surely never be? At any rate I was so embroiled in rehearsals, I didn't give it much thought, except to hope that everything would somehow turn out right.

When we were well advanced in rehearsal, we tried on our costumes and makeup, and Khomul, our director, photographed us in various poses à la professional actors. These pictures were displayed in the windows of his photo studio on Saborna Street, where people stopped to gape at the sort of youngsters, who were presumptuous enough to present theater in the manner of adults, complete with photographs, bill posters and printed programs like bona fide actors.

We, the players, couldn't tear ourselves away from the show-windows, unable to get our fill of ogling and admiring ourselves. These photos remained in Khomul's showcase for years and years. Copies of them are still in my possession, as they are in the possession of Shimon Finkel, in Israel.

Our venturesome enterprise in putting on a Hirshbein play was met with interest. The community marveled that we youngsters should understand the psychology of this realistic drama and portray our roles with the insight of mature performers.

I played the title role of the Intellectual, who preaches justice and equality in the world. The director placed a pair of spectacles on my nose, tucked a couple of books under my arm and there I was, the conventional concept of an intellectual! According to the applause and the bravos on my behalf, I must have given a good account of myself. But Finkel—a stripling, not yet Bar Mitzvah—wearing a beard, a gray wig on his boyish head, portraying so true to life the complicated role of the old father with a paralyzed arm in a sling and dragged a lamed foot with the help of a cane, was absolutely remarkable.

My appearance in this weighty drama at the City Theater could have turned the premiere into a tragicomedy. Actors have a phrase for a performer who raves and rants to excess, whether or not the scene warrants it, "chewing up the scenery." In the third act of the play, the intellectual goes berserk. It is an intensely dramatic scene demanding the skill of a competent artist. But I, a novice, genuinely carried away by the situation, gave it my all.

Suddenly, a woman rose from her seat. Rushing down the aisle to the stage, she cried out in an anguished voice: "Chaimke! Stop screaming like that! Stop tearing your throat. Stop it, my son!"

My mother! And I had no idea that she was even in the theater! For a moment, the audience was completely nonplussed, but catching on to the situation, understood the deep concern of a mother.

The incident was recalled again and again in Grodno...with great hilarity.

18

The Yeshiva "Shaar Hatorah"

Since my formative years were so disrupted by war, the normal process of my education was thrown out of kilter. I floundered, I jumped from one thing to another; singing at the choir, playing around with theater, drumming in the firemen's band, studying only in spurts... a pattern that seemed aimless, with no preparation for the future.

Father, of course did not relish my hanging around, idle. In discussing it with his friend, the Eishishker Rabbi, the good man recommended that I enter the newly formed yeshiva for young adults, the Shaar Hatorah.

Students who wished to further their religious education after completing the four grades of the yeshiva had been obliged to set out for cities with known Torah-study centers as those in Telz, Maltch, Breinsk, Mir and others. Now, a yeshiva of this status, equipped to accept students from other towns, came to realization in Grodno during the German occupation.

Despite the wartime hardships, the Jews of Grodno, under the leadership of the religious social worker, Reuven Soloveitchik, established the Center Shaar-Hatorah. Out-of-town students were put up in private homes and took their meals each day at a different household, a custom known as "eating-days."

The students, poring over their Gemaras day and night, eagerly congregated to listen to the greats among the rabbis lecturing on chastisement, ethics and morality.

For me, Shaar Hatorah was most inspiring. I was transported by the melodic chants and haunting minor strains emanating from the throats of the yeshiva students. I felt carried away from the outside world with its mundane materialism. I was uplifted. I threw myself into the holy books, convinced that I had finally come to my senses. I decided I would indeed work hard and get my rabbinical ordination as my father hoped.

Alas, my resolution to settle down to a life of piety did not last very long. My new-found moral sense, which was to lead me on the religious path, was soon overcome by the temptation that had already gotten its hooks in me before—namely, the theater! The theater, and music, and my general hunger for knowledge of a broader and more worldly scope.

The Vilna Troupe

News reached our community that a dramatic club to present Yiddish plays had also been formed in Vilna. The organizers were Leyb Kadison, Jacob

Sherman and Alexander Azra. The pattern adopted for their artistic endeavors was to be based on the Stanislavsky method. At first they called themselves FADA (Farein fun Yiddische Dramatische Artisten in Vilna). Later, they became widely known as The Vilna Troupe. After much effort and intercession with the German authorities, they succeeded in getting a permit to present Yiddish theater in Vilna.

In May of 1917, the Vilna Troupe set out to play the provinces and eventually came to Grodno, where they scored tremendous success. Their repertoire included the literary works of Yiddish, as well as those chosen from world classics. The interplay of the cast was well integrated and disciplined. The accent was placed on the ensemble as a whole, rather than on any one individual. The hand of the director could be felt in every gesture, every nuance. The action in each scene was timed to the second. The natural tone and character-portrayals made everything come alive with stark realism.

The Vilna Troupe was exceptional in every respect and, of course, went on to become one of the most renowned theater ensembles around the world.

As for our children's theater group in Grodno, the Vilna players created the deepest and most lasting influence. Finkel and I went about in a trance, completely bewitched. If indeed, Shimon Finkel and I had harbored the slightest doubt about seeking theatrical careers for the future, the Vilna Troupe settled the question. Our resolution became firmer than ever—we would indeed become actors!

* * *

"Stancia Bia-ly-stok…!" rasped the conductor, yanking me back into the present. The train shuddered as if in convulsion and with an abrupt jolt, screeched to a stop.

Cold rushed in through the open doors. The temperature outdoors, according to the crystal trees encrusted on the windows, was surely below zero.

Passengers boarding the train vigorously shook the snow from their clothing. Travel between Bialystok and Warsaw was quite active and in just a few minutes the train was filled. No longer was I extended the courtesy of privacy. In my coupé, designed for six, we were now eight. And the tracked-in snow made it wet underfoot all through the car.

A toot from the engine and we were off again. None of my fellow passengers exchanged as much as a word all the way to Warsaw.

It grew dark in the car and my thoughts—even darker. My heart felt as heavy as if I were returning from a funeral. Again, the hammering at my brain: What a fool you are, Chaim! You had such a rare opportunity. You should have taken the risk and crossed the border to Grodno!

To escape these self-torturing recriminations, I buried my chin again deep into my fur collar and took refuge conjuring up memories of our children's theater group, "guest starring," if you please, right here in Bialystok!

19

They Roll with Laughter

Our children's theater group had become so popular in Grodno that our success also spread to the surrounding communities, and our director, Khomul, received an invitation to bring the children's group to Bialystok for guest performances at the Palace Theater. What an opportunity to see a metropolis like Bialystok and, at the same time, be seen as regular actors on the stage of the Palace Theater!

But what does Satan do?! Several days before our scheduled trip, along comes Shimon Finkel, the picture of despair, and brings us the tidings that his mother won't let him go!

We were sunk! Khomul, grabbing at his head, wailed, "I'm ruined! I gave my word, my signature! Bialystok is already flooded with bill-posters. All your photos are displayed in the show-windows. We must go!"

Refusing to give up, Khomul went to talk to Finkel's parents. But, immune to anything he had to say, she told him off in typical Grodno fashion, adding, "You, Khomul'ke, will not make an actor of my Shimon—and good-day to you!"

So we couldn't go, and that was that!

"I will play Finkel's parts!" piped up Avremel Khash. "I know them by heart. I watched the rehearsals very closely. The roles that Finkel plays are just made for me. By right, my father said, they should have been assigned to me in the first place. My brother plays fathers and characters and so can I!"

After Avremel's proposal, there was nothing more to debate. Settled! We're going to Bialystok!

Well, it was easy enough to imagine how Finkel felt. But I was even worse off. His trials were over. Mine had only begun. On what grounds could I possibly get away? I was reminded of Azarkh's philosophy: "If you want to be an actor, boychik, you must be prepared to make sacrifices. Forget about parents, home, wife, kids, hunger, cold...the main thing is—you play theater! When the curtain falls, and I hear the applause and the shouts of 'Bravo Azarkh...Bis!' I feel compensated enough for all the heartache and hardship."

My problem was happily solved by my brother Shayke. The Germans had transferred him to a job at the railroad yard inspecting and repairing the train locomotives. One day, while inspecting the underside of an engine, Shayke inadvertently touched a loose valve and released a blast of scalding steam. Miraculously, he escaped with a few minor burns, which healed after a while.

We were all terribly shaken up, and Shayke was inconsolable. How could this happen to him...who was supposed to be such an expert? Notwithstanding, I summoned enough courage to intrude my own troubles in him and confided my dilemma.

To my utter surprise, he agreed to come to my aid and forthwith came up with a plan. Considering his recent nerve-shattering incident, he explained to father, he would take a couple of days to relax. He would go off to Bialystok for the change, and take me along for company. Train fare would not be involved, since he was privileged to ride the trains for free. As for my fare, well, he would manage this too. Shayke was not lying to father. He only omitted the fact that I was going to play theater there. And this is how my first tour came about, as a "wandering star," in Bialystok.

Tickets for our performances were quickly snapped up. The novelty of children undertaking dramas by acknowledged playwrights created a sensation. Our first performance, *Der Intelligent,* was very well received. The audience, although not overwhelmed, considered that, for a group of youngsters, it was quite an achievement. The greatest credit was due Avremel Khash. We made no comparisons between his and Finkel's interpretation, but we all had to admit that Avremel certainly had spunk.

At our second performance, something happened which taught me a stage-lesson for the rest of my life. In the one-act comedy, *The Critical Patient* by Z. Wendroff, I played the part of a slightly inebriated husband, who tiptoes home late at night. Certain that his wife is asleep, he quietly begins to undress. He is down to his shirt and pants, when he hears his wife coming. To avoid a possible tirade, he quickly throws himself on the sofa and pretends to be deathly ill. As his wife hurries off to fetch something to revive him, he springs up again, but upon her return flops back on the sofa and moans as if he were dying. It develops into a very hilarious situation.

Having played the comedy in Grodno, I was prepared for the laughs. But in Bialystok, there I stood in center stage, unable to go on while the audience kept roaring. How long was this hilarity going to last?

"Psst. Psst, Chaimke." Glancing toward the wings, I saw my colleagues gesturing, desperately trying to convey something to me, pointing—at what? I hadn't the slightest notion what they were trying to tell me. The audience was still rolling with laughter.

Emma Dimant, playing my wife, came back on stage with an ice bag and a blanket. Coloring beneath her makeup, she whispered from the corner of her mouth. "The pants, Chaimke!"

I glanced down and I froze! The audience was howling, while I was ready to bury myself! The fly of my trousers was unbuttoned and a corner of my white shirt was peeping out for all the world to see! I don't know where I got the presence of mind, but turning away from the audience, I buttoned up and went on with the scene as though nothing happened. The crowd certainly got more comedy than they'd bargained for. But for me, it was the greatest tragedy.

This lesson has remained etched in my mind. Such incidents happen all too often to careless performers. I know of a popular actress who lost her silk bloomers right on stage. This, I vowed, must never again happen to me. Over my fifty years on stage, it has become second nature to me to check and re-check my apparel before making my entrance, an automatic reflex to guard against a recurrence of that episode.

Before the Storm

It was quiet on the western front, and even more so in our part of the East. This was the lull before the storm that changed the whole political picture of the world.

In the meantime, preparations were under way for Shayke's wedding. Expenses, according to custom, were defrayed by the parents of the bride, Yetta. It wasn't too long after this happy event that we also attended the ceremony of my sister Slavka's marriage to her fiance, Itche Nemeisky, recently back from the Russian army. And Motke, who fell in love with a girl named Sheyne-Libbe over in Fehrstadt, didn't lag too far behind, either.

Thus, our flat became a lot roomier, but at the same time, a lot lonelier—leaving only father, mother, Rochele and me.

* * *

I continued practicing with the firemen's band and enjoyed playing for the festivals that the volunteer firemen were beginning to inaugurate again in the city park. The crowning attraction was always the scintillating display of fireworks. At these affairs our orchestra usually opened with a concert program and then played for dancing. But something was missing. The park itself seemed to have a withered look—not at all as it used to be.

Borke Labendz, the boy I had previously made my assistant in lugging the musical instruments for my music teacher, now hung around doing the very same chores for me. By now I considered myself an expert drummer and began teaching him the snare drum. He said he was thirteen, but I took him to be no more than twelve. His father, he told me, had gone to war with the Russians and hadn't returned. He must have been taken prisoner. I felt sorry for him and sometimes threw him a few marks from my earnings at the private jobs I occasionally played with the band. And Borke dogged my footsteps, always eager to do my bidding.

20

The World in Upheaval

March 8, 1917:   Revolution in Russia.

March 9, 1917:   Moscow becomes the capital of Russia, replacing Petrograd

March 15, 1917:   Czar Nicholas Romanov II abdicates.

The almost bloodless revolution in Russia that erupted in Petrograd quickly spread to other major cities. Russian morale disintegrated. The fiery clashes of opinion—for and against the continuation of war—added still greater confusion to the already chaotic state of the land. The reverberations of the revolution were already being felt in Grodno.

The Germans became very smug. Let the Russians annihilate one another they sneered, so we, the Germans will have our victory on the eastern front without having to fire a shot. We will then concentrate on the western front and make hash out of the French, the English and the Americans.

Jewish party members of the revolutionary movement greeted the news of the Russian upheaval with great exuberance. At last there was the realization of the longed-for hour of social justice, for which mankind—including Jews—had made so many sacrifices. They waited impatiently for the liberation to reach our own community. Political parties in Grodno planned open demonstrations, but this, of course, was strictly verboten by the Germans.

The Zionists were transported by the news of the Balfour Declaration. A Jewish home in Palestine, they fervently proclaimed, would finally resolve the Jewish problem and bring salvation to the Jewish Nation.

The political uproar also had its effect on the money exchange. The German ost-marks, which had begun to amount to something, took a drop. Again, unemployment in the city became frightening, and people went hungry. Only the barbershops were busy, for these were the center to pick up the latest news and indulge in a little discussion on world politic. And, not too badly hit either was Ibersky of the bookstore. Certainly not through the sale of books, it must be said, but rather through the sale of tickets for the Yiddish theater. Revolution, or no revolution, activity in the theaters went on. Rehearsals were attacked with more vigor than ever; especially, since it became known that actors and artists would now hold the highest position in the new order of things in Russia.

* * *

On January 18, 1918, Leon Trotsky came to Brest-Litovsk to arrange a separate truce with Germany. Germany set forth stringent conditions, which Russia was forced to accept. The Russian army was too demolished to stop a German attack. With the eastern front secure, Germany transported her entire military to the western front.

On July 16, 1918, Czar Nicholas II, the czarina, and the thirteen-year-old czarevitch, together with the rest of the family Romanov, were led into a cellar and shot. Thus, fell the curtain on the 300-year-old Romanov dynasty.

Two weeks later, the allied armies forced the Germans to retreat from the western front. Germany met her Waterloo at Verdun. During the battle, the allies took 30,000 German prisoners. The American army continued to advance on Germany through the Argonne Forest. Germany capitulated, signing an unconditional armistice on November 11, 1918.

* * *

New winds blew across Europe. New boundaries were drawn. Provinces were cut up and divided among the countries who claimed their respective territories based on historical rights.

The collective nerves in Grodno were drawn taut. There was great concern over the fate that awaited the Jewish community. What sort of regime was now in store for them!

Political groups from different nationalities sprang up. They surrounded themselves with the demobilized soldiers of the Russian army, who originally hailed from the occupied zones; areas from which the Germans were now making such a hasty retreat. These military battalions were to return to their respective homelands, and reclaim them.

Organized with this in mind, were: Ukrainians, Byelorussians, Lithuanians, Poles and others. The Byelorussians, Lithuanians and Poles set their sights on Grodno and surrounding environs based on their historical rights. Before the German reservists, thoroughly embittered by the unexpected capitulation, could evacuate, the first Byelorussian and Lithuanian infantry contingents trooped in. Their uniforms were a conglomeration of German and Russian, but the tin shields attached to their caps proclaimed the emblem of their own particular countries. Before long, the Polish infantry also showed up. These were readily identified by the eagle cockade perched on their caps. The Poles stayed apart, keeping to themselves.

Officially, it was designated that Grodno and immediate territory belonged to the Byelorussians, with Vilna as the capital. The Lithuanians, it was understood, were merely in transit, pending reorganization. They would then march to their Lithuanian territories, with Kovno as their capital.

The Poles focused all their attention on Warsaw, where some shrewd political maneuvering was underway. They, too, set their sights on including Grodno, Vilna and Minsk.

The first Byelorussian infantry regiment that marched into Grodno took quarters in the very same barracks just inhabited by the Germans. To celebrate their White Russian independence, they arranged to have a military parade on the self-same Place-Parade, which had seen many a Russian and German parade. There was only one problem. The White Russians hadn't as yet gotten around to organizing their own band. Instruments would have to be ordered—and where could they be ordered in time of war? Besides, instruments entailed real money—gold! The problem was solved by the professional musicians in our firemen's band. Eager for the chance to earn something, they proposed that we be hired to play for their historic parade. Delighted, the Byelorussians agreed to pay a reasonable sum for our services.

We wore our faded firemen's uniforms. The emblem attached to our caps was the sole indication now, that we belonged to the First Byelorussian Infantry Regiment. On the day of the parade, we picked up our instruments and marched to the barracks on Schweitzarski Dolina, where the Byelorussians were already lined up. We struck up a march and led the regiment to the Place-Parade. We played a reviewing march, and the soldiers, with precise salutes, paraded past their commander-in-chief and other high-ranking officers. At the end of the ceremonies, we marched the regiment back to the barracks. We collected our money—in German marks (which were still in use), and that was that!

Gradually, Grodno became accustomed to the Byelorussian administration. There was special elation in the Jewish community since all street signs and signboards on places of business were to be printed in Byelorussian, Lithuanian and Yiddish...an omen auguring better times ahead for Jews.

All political parties renewed their activities. The Zionists carried out a manifestation to celebrate the Balfour Declaration. It was one of the biggest, most momentous demonstrations Grodno ever witnessed. Blue-and-white flags fluttered in the air. The demonstrators fairly soared to the heavens when our firemen's band for the first time—publicly—struck up the "Hatikvah."

The other political parties openly celebrated May Day, the workers' holiday. Marching through the streets, they carried their red flags. And, to the accompaniment of our band, sang the "Marsellaise."

After more than three years, our Yiddish newspaper was published again. Thus, word spread that anti-Semites, taking advantage of the chaotic state in Russia, were instigating pogroms in Jewish villages; killing, raping and robbing Jews of their possessions. People in our town were horrified, but took comfort in the belief that it could not happen in Grodno as long as our militia of "muscle men" stood guard. "Let this 'pogromchiks' dare to tangle with our brawny young men! Our Home Defense stands ready!"

* * *

Once again Yiddish theater companies visited Grodno. Appearing in concert at that time: Cantor Zavel Kwartin; Gershon Sirota with his daughter, Helena; Cantor Mordecai Hershman; Menachem Kipnis and Zamara Zeligfeld, as well as the noted baritone of the St. Petersburg Opera, Joseph Winogradoff.

The Vilna Troupe came to do Hirshbein's *The Smith's Daughters*, Bimko's *Thieves*, and *The Mute* by Weiter.

Our children's group did not remain idle, either. We put on Heiermann's drama, *The Eternal Jew*. I played the father; Dimant, the son, and Finkel, the priest, a role in which he again was outstanding. Under Khomul's direction we also did *The Carrion* by Peretz Hirshbein, where I played the leading role of Mendel and Finkel portrayed Akhbrush, the father. It was, no doubt, quite pretentious on our part to compete in this very play. Nevertheless, we came through with flying colors. Everyone agreed that Finkel and I were becoming fine actors.

A professional artists' organization was duly formed in Grodno, where Finkel and I, privileged nonprofessionals, were presented with membership cards. Almost fifty years have gone by and the prized membership card from the Grodno Artists' Organization is still one of the treasured possessions in my memorabilia.

* * *

April 26, 1919. It was Saturday afternoon. Folks were taking their nap after the noonday meal. The younger set hadn't as yet sauntered forth on their customary Sabbath-stroll along the main street, Saborna.

Rigged out in my Byelorussian musician's uniform, consisting of pantaloons and a Russian-style cap with the emblem of the First White-Russian Infantry Regiment affixed over the shiny peak, I leisurely strolled along on my way to the barracks. Our band was scheduled to play an open-air concert for the soldiers that evening.

Suddenly, a young fellow rushed up to me, and out of breath, asked "Are you heading for the Byelorussian barracks?"

"Yes, " I said, "why?"

"Something is up over there! The Poles. Watch your step!"

I had no idea what on earth he was talking about. The Poles?! What would they be doing at the Byelorussian barracks?!

Coming closer to the barracks, I saw that something odd was indeed going on. Soldiers, surrounding the barracks, were aiming machine guns at the windows! Several heavy cannons in the yard were also trained on the barracks, ready to fire; while guns, protruding from the windows, were being aimed directly at the soldiers in the yard surrounding them. My first impression was that this was some sort of practice maneuver by the Byelorussians.

The soldiers in the courtyard were wearing the cockade of the Polish eagle. These were Polish soldiers! To enter the premises was possible, but no one was allowed out. Too late to turn back I found myself herded into the confines of the courtyard with other Byelorussian soldiers just returning from town. Among them were several unsuspecting musicians like myself. Fortunately, both sides were holding fire, or else we, who were herded together in the open yard, would surely have borne the brunt of either broadside.

Somewhere, negotiations were going on among the Polish, the Byelorussian and Lithuanian military leaders The Poles were standing firm on their ultimatum that all Byelorussian and Lithuanian soldiers in the barracks had to leave their weapons and come out with hands raised. Also, they now considered all soldiers born in Grodno, or neighboring territories—regardless of their nationality—as automatically recruited into the Polish army, while those soldiers born in the Kovno region were to be escorted with full military honors to the Lasosna Road, on the way to their Lithuanian capital, Kovno.

To avoid a bloodbath the Byelorussians were forced to capitulate. The city was flooded with the first Polish ordinances, to clear the city and all its outposts of Bolsheviks. They also proclaimed that Grodno and her surrounding terrain had always been part of the liberated Polish homeland, and that the first regulars of the National Polish Army were soon to arrive.

That same evening we escorted the Lithuanian soldiers as far as Lasosna. With our band marching in the lead, the Lithuanians followed, carrying their flags, weapons and belongings. At Lasosna, we struck up the popular Russian march, "Old Comrade." The Polish soldiers formed long lines at either side of the road, and as they raised their rifles in salute, the Lithuanians marched by on their long trek to Kovno.

Returning to town we learned that our entire band of the fire department was drafted into the Polish army! Our vehement protests were to no avail. If we could play for the Byelorussians, we were told, we could most certainly serve the Polish liberators!

In vain did we plead that we were civilian musicians simply trying to earn a living, and that the instruments we played weren't even our own but the property of the fire department. The Byelorussians, we explained, merely hired us to play for them. If the Poles wished to do the same, we would be only too happy to play for them, too. But, to be soldiers! I, for one, produced my German passport, bearing my photograph and stating black on white that I was all of sixteen years old—a long way from qualifying for military service. As for Borke Labendz, the Poles could easily see that he was a mere boy. But proof, or no proof, nothing was able to sway them. They needed a band and we were it! So there we were…no longer permitted to leave the barracks.

21

In the Polish Army

A fresh Polish regiment arrived in town during the night. Pinning on the Polish eagle badge to our Byelorussian uniforms, we struck up the self-same "Old Comrade" march and led the soldiers to Parade Square for the first Polish reviewing parade. Playing for a parade was no novelty to us by now, having already done so for the Russians, Germans, Byelorussians and Lithuanians. But this first Polish parade remained in my memory. It was the first time we officially played the Polish anthem: "Jeshtche Polska nye Zginiela." (Poland has not succumbed.)

Soon after this, followed Polish ordinances and decrees, far from pleasant for Jews. The Polish legislative council in Warsaw, designated General Pilsudski, as Chief of State. And for the office of prime minister, the piano virtuoso Ignatz Paderewski.

Our forced service as a military band just as suddenly came to an end. A new battalion of Polish regulars arrived from Warsaw with a band comprised of recruits and volunteer musicians from various Polish cities. The bandmaster was Colonel Edmund Sinkevitch, his right-hand man, Master Sergeant Adam Kochanowski. The only Jew among the newly arrived musicians was Marek, an outstanding trumpet player.

"I'm a volunteer," he told us. "They would have drafted me anyway. As an enlisted man I was able to choose where to serve, so I picked the band."

Marek also said that about 300 Jewish boys from his province in Galicia had already volunteered for General Haller's army. (General Haller and his "Hallertchiks" soon became known as the cruelest anti-Semites in Poland.)

Sikevitch must have found out that he could not draft the firemen's band by force, and he released us. Musicians who played key instruments which he lacked in his band—including me—were those he wanted to retain, and so, he propositioned us to volunteer for a two-year term, promising all kinds of benefits and privileges. We would be permitted to sleep at home, if we chose. In preference to eating in the general mess hall, we would be permitted to take our daily allotment of provisions home to our families. And considering the meager monthly pay of a private, we volunteer musicians would join at once with the rank of sergeant, thereby raising our army pay. The colonel also added that, time permitting, we could play private affairs to augment our income. Military functions however, must come first.

For the professional musicians in the firemen's band, this was a great setup. With a good swig of vodka, they forthwith put down their signatures. What difference did it make whose army they served?!

Those who signed up were Esmond, a wonderful baritone horn-player, Martzinkevitch, a first-class cornetist who had once been a former Russian band-leader, and his brother, Fedka, on the French horn. Fedka was an easygoing fellow, but rarely, if ever, spoke to anyone except to nod yes, or no. At first it was thought that he became shell-shocked in the war. Actually, Fedka had suffered a most bizarre experience during his service as a musician in the Russian army.

Late one night, Fedka—as the story goes—had to go to the latrine. Crocked with vodka, he fumbled his way outdoors. It was a stormy night, but Fedka had to go. As he crouched, a gale-force wind blew the roof off the shed and sent it crashing down on his head! Fedka was barely extricated from beneath the debris, luckily all in one piece.

This freak accident left him with a slight brain impairment. Yet, he was still able to play his French horn and guzzle even better. He was forever smiling. But to hold a conversation, or participate in social amenities? Not Fedka! The Jewish musicians who also signed up as volunteers dubbed him the "Schlemiel."

Without discussing the subject at home, I too, signed up as a volunteer. Borke Labendz, still aping everything I did, followed suit. Then, after I'd signed all the necessary papers, Col. Sinkevitch informed me that the rank of sergeant, which he had promised me, was out! I was too young, he said. After I had served a year, conducting myself as required, he would recommend me for the rank of corporal.

What a letdown! I had already envisioned myself parading before my pals sporting the three stripes on my sleeve! Besides, the extra pay to which a sergeant is entitled would have come in so handy, and that was what I had in mind! But I had signed, and that was that!

When my parents learned about the numskull thing I'd done, there was a fearful row at home. It was only after I began bringing home packs of food-stuffs, including cigarettes for father, that they forgave my foolhardiness. I even managed to trade the meat, the pork fat and other non-kosher items in my rations, with the Christian musicians for dry products, such as bread, sugar, salt, flour, barley, or groats…things no longer available in the city.

Our band was assigned spacious quarters at the barracks, lined throughout with straw-filled bunks. Adjoining was another large barrack that served as our rehearsal hall and repository for the instruments.

Top boss over us was Master-Sergeant Kochanowski, a man in his late forties. He was short of stature, but broad-shouldered, with the mug of an ogre. Half Polish and half Russian, he was more or less easy to get along with. He played a baritone instrument and was friendly toward Borke and me. He had great regard for the musicianship of the other professional volunteers. They all shared the rank of sergeant and they very often drank together. But the chummy relationship with his subordinates in no way interfered with military discipline. In the tavern, it was one thing... back in the barracks, it was strict army regulations.

Our bandmaster, Col. Sinkevitch, was Byelorussian. A run-of-the-mill musician in one of the Russian bands during the war, he immediately hopped on the Polish political bandwagon as soon as Poland was declared an independent country. What with the chaotic state of things in Warsaw, it was easy enough to set himself up as a great musicologist and finally land a commission of organizing a military band as bandmaster. He cultivated a pair of thick mustaches like a Polish nobleman, and used every device possible to assume the looks of a dyed-in-the-wool Pole.

His musical education and ability fit into a thimble, but, whatever he lacked in musical knowledge, he made up in cussedness and arrogance. His breath always reeked of vodka. To cover up his shortcomings as a musician, he imposed upon us ever more rigorous military discipline. Rather than play the role of bandleader, he preferred the role of army colonel. He regarded us not as musicians, but as soldiers.

The other officers in our regiment were quite friendly toward us. They were rather proud of their band and especially sympathetic toward Borke and me—teenagers, after all. The army uniforms only emphasized our boyishly gangling figures. I wasn't even shaving as yet, and Borke—certainly not.

Col. Sinkevitch began taking Sgt. Kochanowski to task for not being strict enough in enforcing all the army regulations. Besides rehearsing, we were taken out daily for field drills and trained in saluting and in marksmanship. The Russian musicians, veterans of the Russian army, were acquainted with this routine, but we Jewish musicians found target practice a grueling experience. Which of us ever had anything to do with firing a gun?!

The only one who took to the gun was Borke. He became an ace shot in no time. The officers marveled at him. A boy like that, hitting the target square in the bull's-eye! Borke also quickly picked up the Polish language and spoke it with the accent of a born Pole. Even our Polish patriot Col. Sinkevitch stumbled over the words. And no wonder. His language was Russian!

I didn't cotton to this business of shooting, and even less to Polish. I stuck to Russian. In the beginning, it was tolerated. But when a strict order was issued to speak Polish exclusively, I was really in trouble.

"Hey, Moshka! Kuk no!" Sinkevitch mimicked a broken Yiddish, "Look! Look in the music!" If it was I indeed, who made the mistake, there was surely the devil to pay! His pig-face aflame with rage, his eyes swimming in liquor, he'd come down to me, allegedly to demonstrate how he wanted me to beat a phrase on the drum. He beat out each accent with his stick on my knuckles, and he usually ended his tantrum with a sadistic smirk of satisfaction, giving my cheek a pinch that made me see stars.

Sinkevitch soon moved his wife, Wanda, and his young son, Janush, to Grodno. Wanda, a full-bosomed Polish lade, was mad at her husband for dragging her away from a scintillating metropolis like Warsaw to dull and provincial Grodno.

The Colonel rented a flat near the military hospital and commissioned Borke and me to show his wife around town where she could select some household furnishings. But Wanda turned her nose up at whatever was available. Nothing pleased her, with the result that she vented her frustrations on her husband and he, in turn—on us! "It's your fault!" he stormed at Borke and me. "You are Grodno natives. And you know damn well where you Jews have hidden your best merchandise!"

Borke and I also had the misfortune of being burdened with their bratty son. Janush made our lives miserable. Yet we didn't dare put him in his place.

My Friend Stashek

Col. Sinkevitch dug up a new recruit—Stashek. Claiming that he needed an extra bass drummer during our marches, he took the muscular Stashek into the band. Actually, he wanted Stashek as a personal servant for himself and his family. But I was stuck with the chore of teaching this fellow the bass drum. It required no genius for anyone to grasp the "art" ... anyone, that is, but Stashek. He had no ear for music and no sense of rhythm. Much as I labored to get him to beat the drum in time with the march tempo, it was useless.

Stashek, hailing from peasant folk, was fair-headed, illiterate and docilely obedient. He was also a stutterer whenever he became nervous.

I felt sorry for Stashek and exerted every ounce of patience to teach him. He sensed my friendliness and was grateful. Borke wasn't at all pleased about my new protege. In fact, he was becoming very cocky toward me. After all, he could speak Polish, he could shoot, and as far as other army regulations and drills were concerned, he could now teach others. So Borke began to intrigue against me. He took up with Marek, the Jewish trumpet player and they both became exceedingly chummy.

Marek had shown very little interest, or loyalty toward his Jewish comrades, stopping at nothing to gain favor in the eyes of Col. Sinkevitch. The term servile Jew became very clear to me. The few Grodno Jews among the musicians began to watch out for this "brother-in-faith" as if for the devil.

Stashek had to rise earlier than anyone else in the barracks. He had to hike to the colonel's flat, where he cleaned and pressed his uniform, shined his boots, as well as those belonging to Wanda and Janush. His work really began when the honorable Madame Wanda arose. Heaven help Stashek if he inadvertently woke her. He then washed dishes collected from the day before, tidied up the flat, did a load of laundry, swabbed the floor, chopped a cord of wood, laid a fire in the stove, attended to Janush and then—only then—was he free to return to the barracks and get on with his lessons and duties as a drummer.

* * *

"General Pilsudski to visit Grodno." We read this notice on the Order of the Day for June 2, 1919.

A tumult ensued in the barracks, a shining and polishing of instruments, and rehearsals without end. We had to play at the parade and the banquet that was being arranged by city hall in his honor.

Col. Sinkevitch was wild with nerves. He anticipated that the parade and banquet would surely bring him a promotion.

New instruments arrived from Warsaw, gleaming and dazzling. The borrowed ones were returned to the fire department. We were all spruced up in newly issued uniforms.

He drilled us until we were out of breath. Marching and playing is not exactly the easiest kind of exercise. As for Stashek, I had troubles galore. He kept slam-banging the drum off beat, throwing everyone out of step. My heart was in my mouth lest he deliver the same kind of concert performance before General Pilsudski and his staff. My life would not be worth a damn!

The entire city was decorated with Polish flags, garlands of green and portraits of the eminent visitor. The sidewalks were choked with thousands of citizens elbowing each other for a glimpse of General Pilsudski.

Fortunately, Stashek did not ruin the parade. He came through safely enough. There was, however, one incident, which led to a tragic consequence.

The commander rasped, "Attention!" signifying the appearance of the general. The soldiers presented arms, the officers bared their swords and we struck up the anthem, "Jestche Polska nie Zginiela."

General Pilsudski and his entourage lined up according to rank. At the head of the procession marched the flag-bearers, with an honor guard on either side. Behind them, swords raised, marched the high-ranking officers, followed by their regiments. Executing a precise step in tempo with the band, they passed by the dignitaries and the guest of honor, who acknowledged their salute.

One of the officers in the parade was First Lieutenant Zemlanski, whom I happened to know. He was a fine and handsome fellow, over whom the fairer sex swooned. Gleaming sword in hand, he stood ready to march in review.

Bandmaster Sinkevitch gave the cue and we drummers launched into a series of rolls and drum variations setting the march tempo and beat for the paraders to pick up and fall into step, left foot forward!

The command rang out—March! Bandmaster Sinkevitch, his white-gloved hands raised, gave the downbeat and the band struck up the march.

Lt. Zemlanski stepped forward, marching proudly. Passing the reviewing stand with its top brass, he flourished his sword in a perfect salute and marched on, totally unaware of his inexcusable blunder. For, while his detail—to a man—marched in correct step: left-right, left-right—the only one in the lead, marching right-left, right-left, was Lt. Zemlanski, himself.

That very evening, news reached us that First Lieutenant Zemlanski committed suicide by shooting himself. Three days later, we marched in slow, measured step, escorting his body to the military cemetery, playing the mournful Chopin Funeral March. He had taken his life for such a foolish little mishap! Empty pride. What a pity!

The sad news, however, did not dampen the festivities tendered in honor of the commander-in-chief.

Our band was arranged outdoors on the broad terrace of the Old Castle. And while the guests feasted, we played overtures, potpourris, fantasies and contemporary selections. One of our trumpet players scored a hit with his solo of a polka-mazurka, displaying great technical skill in intricate passages.

The Pilsudski banquet did afford one memorable moment. In the middle of a dance number, our master of ceremonies gave the command: "Attention!" Spontaneously we rose to our feet. Attired in a plain black uniform, unadorned by medals, or decorations, stood the commander-in-chief of Poland, Josef Pilsudski—the closest I had every gotten to a general of such historic fame!

Shaking Sgt. Kochanowski's hand, he thanked us for our playing.

"And how do things go with you musicians in the Polish army?" the general addressed us directly.

"Very good, Sir General," we replied. "Wonderful!"

The irony of it! Oh, yes, I had it good. Me, and the rest of the Jews! The Poles had already begun to push Jewish workers out of their jobs, replacing them with unskilled Poles. Considering this new crisis, I was lucky to be in the army, where I was entitled to a daily ration pack that I could bring home to the family.

* * *

Things became more and more uncomfortable for us musicians; particularly for the few Jews among us. Marek eyed us with displeasure, as if it were our fault that he was a Jew. If not for us, he thought, he could more easily lose himself among the Poles.

Col. Sinkevitch drank continuously and was mad as a bull. The promotion he dreamt of failed to materialize and this only antagonized him, making him more sadistic toward us. Some days would pass without him even putting in an appearance—which was pure joy. Then, he would suddenly turn up dead drunk and in the middle of the night!

Falling out of our bunks helter-skelter, we'd pull ourselves together. And standing in our underdrawers, we'd wait in stiff military attention for the midnight spectacle to begin.

The colonel would launch into a lecture on patriotism, on the glory of Poland's history, the conspiracy between the Jews and the Bolsheviks to destroy "our" liberated Polish Fatherland. With the foulest oaths he jeered, "You are not worthy of the Polish uniforms you wear! Musicians, are you? My ass! Soldiers are what you should be! Instead, what are you? Guvno! Shit!

Our daily orders were tacked up on one of the walls in our barrack. He picked none other than poor, stuttering Stashek to read them. Breaking out in a cold sweat, Stashek struggled to read, with the colonel egging him on. "Faster, faster! I'll teach you how to be a soldier, you bastard!"

The older men in our outfit, army veterans, gritted their teeth in rage, but didn't dare stand up to him. Everyone knew he had pull in the uppermost echelons.

These midnight inquisitions only wound up when the drunken Sinkevitch collapsed on one of our bunks, snoring loud enough to wake up the dead. Sgt. Kochanowski and several others would take him by the shoulders and the feet and lug him into the nearby office, where a cot waited for him—just in case. Now we could go back to our bunks, but following such a performance, who could sleep?

In the morning, when the alcoholic colonel awoke, he didn't remember what happened during the night, or perhaps pretended not to remember. He certainly endeared himself to us more and more each day!

22

The First Seder

Spring! Only a few days before Passover. The warmth of the sun lifted our spirits.

After playing at the officers' casino until the wee hours, I had gone to bed rather late. When I awoke and lifted my head, everything spun round and round like a carousel. During the last couple of days I had experienced several weak spells, but paid no attention. With a great effort I climbed out of my bunk, pulled my clothes on and, weaving like a drunk, went to wash up. I had to steady myself against the washstand. I thought it best to report sick to the officer of the day. His advice was to go to the field hospital, which was the last thing I cared to do. It was rumored that before one could get to see a doctor at the lazaretto, one could sooner see himself in the next world. The preliminary exam was usually done by a medic—a former pharmacy clerk. The medic determined whether or not the patient's condition warranted the attention of a doctor.

There was also talk among the Jewish soldiers in our regiment that, should a Jewish soldier need to report sick, he'd better pray to fall into the hands of a Polish doctor, rather than one who is Jewish. For these doctors shook in their boots lest they be suspected of favoring a Jewish soldier and abetting him in shirking his military duties by feigning illness. In fact, they would not pronounce a Jewish soldier really sick unless they practically saw the angel of death hovering over him.

Notwithstanding, feeling sick as a dog, I dragged myself to the field hospital. I found an endless queue of soldiers waiting ahead of me. But, finally, it was my turn. It was obvious from the start that the medic who examined me didn't know his ass from his elbow. He took my temperature and said it was normal. But he did seem to recognize that I wasn't bluffing.

I was weak as a fly. And food was out of the question. The very thought of food made me retch. I couldn't consider going home. Why upset mother? Besides, private doctors and medicine did cost money. At the field hospital, at least, I was entitled to be treated for free. So I had to settle for Dr. Melnick, who happened to be on duty. I undressed, put on a white hospital robe and waited to be examined.

Dr. Melnick's unmistakably Jewish physiognomy was hardly an asset to his ambitions. His looks could have been the model for the anti-Semitic caricatures drawn on the placards displayed around the Polish cities. Even the flaw-less Polish he spoke did nothing to diffuse his Semitic features.

"Tzo yest?" he grunted, asking me what was the matter, without as much as a glance at me.

"I don't know," I murmured timidly.

"You don't know? Then what are you doing here? Did I send for you?"

My Polish vocabulary being so limited, I just stood there, tongue-tied.

"Speak, soldier! The language of our country, Polish!" he bellowed at me for the benefit of chance listeners, who might suspect that he was in cahoots with a fellow Jew.

"I don't know yet how to speak Polish." I foundered. "In school, we learned Russian, German, but Polish, a little I understand, but not speak."

"Well then, speak German!" he commanded by way of compromise. In my halting Yiddish-flavored Deutsch, I told him how sick I was feeling. The doctor then examined my heart, lungs, throat, eyes and ears; everything down to my genitals.

"Nothing is wrong with you! Look here, I'm on to these tricks. You don't have a fever, your heartbeat is regular, your lungs, in order. You don't have a clap, yet you have the gall to tell me you're sick?!" he shouted, to make sure his associates could hear his tirade at this Jewish faker. "Don't let me see you around her again! Get the hell out! And you better speak Polish, you hear? Polish! Understand?!"

Did I understand! I quickly pulled my clothes on and like an arrow darted out of the hospital. Back at the barracks, when I related my harrowing encounter to Sgt. Kochanowski, he shook his head in outrage and spewed forth a seven-layered combination of Russian cuss words at the son-of-a-bitch Jew-doctor. Personally, I was tempted to hurl even nastier names at him.

It is Jews of his ilk—the self-hating ones—who have always brought disaster and shame upon Jews in various lands. Fortunately, his type is but a tiny speck on the overall world-loom, on which there is woven in threads of gold, our Jewish folk history.

"Go lie down on the cot in my office," the sergeant advised. "Just stay there; nobody will bother you."

I thanked him and as I turned toward the office, whom should I run into but the colonel. Just what I needed! Sgt. Kochanowski explained that I was sick, and from their whispered conversation I could tell that they were both incensed—not at me, thank heaven—but at the doctor. Col. Sinkevitch peered at me. My woebegone face evidently touched some hidden spark of compassion in his heart—he was a father, after all.

"Would you like to go home for a few days?" he asked. "Tonight is Paska. All the Jewish boys are taking leave. You can take forty-eight hours. Stay at home and rest up. Take along your ration-pack and go on home for the holiday."

Pesakh?! My God? A shudder went through me. Tonight is the first Seder, and I had completely lost track! Of course I must go home. Mama will surely know what to do for me. The very thought put new strength in me. I got my holiday pass, picked up my ration-pack and heaving it over my shoulder thought what a boon these foodstuffs would be to the family. With revived spirits and anticipation, I hied myself home for the Seder.

Mama, already keeping an anxious eye out for me at the window, saw me coming and her face lit up. Everyone was happy to see me and made a big fuss over me.

"Chaimke," said Mama, "maybe you'd like to grab a little nosh before the Seder? Just to take the edge off your appetite a little. So what? Let it be the worst sin you ever commit."

"I don't want to spoil my appetite. I wait a whole year, you know, for your kneydlach, Mama," I begged off, feeling nauseous at the mere mention of food.

We took our places around the table. Father at the head, wearing his white robe and white yarmulka rested on the hesebeth—traditional seat of pillows—looking majestic, a real Melach (king). Mama, in her holiday best, seated opposite him, looked as radiant as the traditional Malke (queen). On one side of the table sat Slavka and her fiance, Itche Nemeisky, on the other, my cousin Mikhl, Rochele and I.

Father, raising his cup of wine, chanted the Kiddush, and I, as the youngest male, asked the traditional four questions. The "Ho lachmo anyo," (Behold the matzoh, symbol of the Bread of poverty) was never more apropos. It had indeed been a task for father to provide us with matzoh for Passover.

I thought the Seder would never end. Father wasn't omitting a line, or single paragraph in the Hagadah. It went on and on, until he was finally up to the "Chad Gadya." Everyone at the table joined in the singing. "Good Yom-tov," we wished one another. "May we all live to enjoy the Pesach Holiday next year in Jerusalem," to which mother fervently added her "amen!"

Something was definitely wrong. When Mama opened and prepared the sleeping bench for me, I gratefully fell on it like a log. Even with my eyes closed I could feel the house swaying, carrying me round and round. I was spinning, spinning and sinking…sinking into a deep sleep.

My mother later told me that in the middle of the night something woke her. It was my voice, hurling abuse at someone, cursing in Polish, in Russian, in German! My screaming and yelling woke up father. He jumped up as if the bed were on fire. Mama was fainting; Slavka and Rochele, huddled over my bench, were wailing, and I was ranting—using language that would make a Cossack turn red, my father said. He sent Slavka to fetch Doctor Weisbrom. After one look at me, he didn't mince words.

"It's a calamity," he said. "He must be moved at once to the Infirmary."

When the doctor noticed my uniform, it changed the whole situation. He was not permitted to move a soldier before making a report to the military gendarmerie. It was for them to determine what to do with me. He was not even allowed to write out a prescription without their knowledge. So, until all of this could be arranged, the doctor was only able to advise applying ice to my head. The doctor promised to notify the military authorities about my case, and was gone.

A hospital wagon pulled up in our yard and two orderlies, carrying a stretcher, came into the house. They sprayed carbolic acid around the walls, the furniture and into every crevice they could reach. They wrapped me in a blanket, and carried me down the stairs to the hospital wagon. The ambulance attendants carried me into the bathhouse, deposited me on a wooden bench and left. The routine of cropping my hair, bathing and preparing me as a patient was left to the orderlies in charge. So there I lay the entire day, waiting. Just my luck, Passover happened to fall on the same day as the Christian Easter and most of the hospital staff had gone off to town.

An orderly finally heard my moaning and groaning that scared him half to death, because the bathhouse is right next to the morgue. I certainly looked like a candidate for the morgue.

He got me on a stretcher and began to tote me from ward to ward. But no one wanted to admit me, since I hadn't been examined by a doctor. When they got tired of carting me around, they put me down, stretcher and all, in one of the corridors and went off.

A nurse found me. I kept moaning, "Mama, Mama." She didn't have the heart to leave me out in the hall, so she pushed and pulled until she managed to drag my stretcher into the ward. As the night proved quiet, she watched over me until the head nurse arrived in the morning. She ordered me taken out into the hall at once, and gave her the devil for taking me into the ward without a doctor's diagnosis and assignment.

It wasn't long before the doctor showed up for his morning rounds. Seeing me on the stretcher, he uncovered me and, discovering the red spots on my body, quickly snapped: "Transfer this patient at once to the isolation wing! And disinfect everything in this ward immediately! Typhus!

The Military Hospital

The monotone clanging of a bell nudged me awake. My eyes opened on a sea of white. Beds stood lined against the walls and, row upon row, down the middle of the ward. The persistent clanging of the bell kept coming closer. A soldier, in a white, short-sleeved surplice worn over his uniform appeared, carrying a long-stemmed cross bearing the crucified figure of Christ. Soon, there followed a priest, robed for mass. The thurible he swung to and fro wafted incense. Chanting, the priest made intermittent signs of the cross over the beds. Many patients—sitting up or flat on their backs—crossed themselves in response. With a scoop into the golden laver, the priest sprinkled holy water in the general direction of the beds.

Am I dead? I pondered. Was this a mass for me? Am I not to have a Jewish burial? Everything grew so hazy, I dropped off again into a state of oblivion.

Someone was wiping my brow. It was such an effort to open my eyes. But who was it, standing at my bedside?

"Chaimke, how do you feel, my son?" he was murmuring. "Chaimke, don't you recognize me, your father?"

"Father," I whispered, "is it really you?" He had come to see me! I was not dreaming. He was standing beside me and calling me Chaimke as he always did when he was pleased with me.

"And Mama, where is Mama?"

"Mother is here too. We are all here—as if we have ever left the gates of the hospital this past week. But they don't allow anyone in. Today, I don't know for what reason they told me to come in. Maybe tomorrow, God willing, Mama will come. Now keep this on," he said, tying a kerchief around my forehead. "Mother sent it along as a nostrum. In shul, at the reading of the Torah, I have given you an additional name, the name of David, after my father, rest his soul. You are now Chaim-David. I pray the name will bring you a full recovery and long life."

Was father sobbing? I felt that my senses were leaving me again...falling back into the dark abyss...

That very night the crisis broke. I was out of danger.

Life in the Ward

For the first few days following the crisis, I was so weak I could barely move. The doctors and nurses marveled at me. Considering my case, they had practically written me off. But then, was it any wonder that I remained alive? In addition to my name, Chaim (life), I now bore the name of my paternal grandfather, David. And this name too, has great meaning in Jewish history: "King David of Israel lives and will exist eternally."

The isolation wing of the hospital was overcrowded with typhus patients. In the course of the day—or night—one or more would be removed from bed and with a sheet drawn over their heads carted out of the ward. Some of the recuperating comrades would cross themselves, then in a matter of moments, the emptied beds were occupied again by new typhus patients.

The groaning and moaning throughout the ward now disturbed me frightfully. It was hard to believe that, only recently I, too, had come through these fever-tormented stages, carrying on like crazy.

The nurses got extra help from the post-typhus patients who as yet had not been discharged. They made themselves useful by passing out the thermometers, so that a nurse only had to check a patient's temperature and record it on the chart at the foot of the bed.

Most of these convalescing volunteers, fully recuperated and strong as horses again, should long have rejoined their regiments. Instead, they still puttered around in robe and slippers, acting so important one would think they were indispensable. Having struck up a cozy camaraderie with the nurses, they made merry half the night, singing and laughing for all they were worth! And alcohol being an easy-to-come-by commodity in a hospital, the revelers mixed it with cider, or soda-pop and caroused well into the night.

But to complain? Heaven forbid! This would be informing—an unpardonable transgression in the army. Besides, which of us was in a condition to break a few heads, when we all lay stretched out half dead!

When one of our fellow sufferers did get up the courage to ask the revelers ever so politely to be kind enough to keep the noise down, the answer was a barrage of cuss words. On top of this the poor fellow could burst his bladder before one of these bullies would deign to bring him a urinal. After this kind of treatment, we knew better than to squawk.

One of these bullies was a galoot called Yuzhek—meaning porcupine— and Yuzhek really looked like one. The sparse hairs on his head stood upright like the spines on a porcupine. Yuzhek had a ravenous appetite. If there was any food left on a patient's tray, Yuzhek was sure to gobble it up. The patients were mortally afraid of him—I, in particular!

As the chart on my bed stated that I was a Jew, Yuzhek enjoyed baiting me, "Hey, fellas, take a look at this 'soldier!' This Jew-boy! Look who's going to defend Poland!" he guffawed. "These 'zhids' squirm out of everything! This little bastard even wriggled out of the clutches of death!"

* * *

I was beginning to improve. The typhus spots that had covered my body and my face were slowly fading, and I was able to get out of bed. The doctor transferred me to another ward. It turned out to be the very one in which I spent my first night in the hospital, where the elderly nurse took me in and cared for me. She recognized me at once and went into length about her grandson who was also in the army and how my crying, Mama, Mama, had moved her.

When my mother was permitted to visit me and bring some of the tidbits I loved, she made sure that my friend, the kindly old nurse, also got to taste these delicious kosher morsels.

In the new ward, with about twenty other convalescents, I began at last to regain my strength. Food was ample. We were fed products which had long become scarce around town—all provided by the American Red Cross specifically for the hospitals. Of course, a good deal of it fell into the hands of speculators, but that was another matter. The meat was something I did without. Was I going to eat non-kosher products when the good Lord had just spared my life? I had never up to then touched non-kosher food and intended never to break this rule.

23

Sister Bronya

The head nurse was Lieutenant Bronya Vronetzka. The appellation nurse being referred to as "sister" in Polish, she was addressed as Sister Vronetzka, but in speaking of her informally, the doctors and nurses referred to her as Sister Bronya.

A green-eyed, flaxen-haired young woman, Sister Bronya was of medium height, with a shapely and athletic body; a pleasant woman, who could also be exceedingly stern when necessary. She was in her early thirties and stemmed from Polish people who lived near the Prussian border. Formerly a nurse in a German field hospital during the war, Sister Bronya was widowed when her husband fell on the Russian front, months before Germany's capitulation. After the upheaval in Germany she volunteered in the Polish army, and with her thorough experience as a nurse, soon became supervisor in our Military General Hospital.

The doctors buzzed around Sister Bronya like bees around a honey pot. She had no lack of admirers. Even the patients yearned for her attention—and I was no exception. This was the first time I was overwhelmed by such a tantalizing feeling. I considered myself pretty well versed on the subject of sex, but hadn't as yet been bitten by temptation. I had thrown all my adolescent energies into other activities, so who had time to chase after girls—and get involved?! But now, lying around in the hospital with nothing whatever to do to occupy my time, all my thoughts were on Sister Bronya.

The hours were long and monotonous. How long could I putter around in robe and slippers without a stitch of work to do?! Out of sheer boredom I began to help the nurses and orderlies in any chore I was permitted to do. This eager-to-please attitude of mine found great favor in her eyes. She called me Yablotchka, a diminutive of my name, meaning little apple, which was enough to transport me to the seventh heaven!

My assistance around the ward led me into a profitable little business. Mother had a pet phrase: "One only needs to have a bit of common sense," to which I added my own amendment: "If you have it—use it!" And I did just that.

Regardless of a patient's condition, he got a daily ration of ten cigarettes. Naturally, they merely collected in the bedside tables, just begging for someone to take them—and someone usually did. Well then, my common sense told me, why can't I be the someone? On my regular rounds I began cleaning out all the drawers and hoarding the booty. I shared my loot fifty-fifty with the smokers, as an extra bonus for keeping mum. The hospital attendants, I knew, would eventually lay claim to the cigarettes anyway, so whether or not I smoked, I felt that as a patient I had first claim to them.

In addition to my traffic in cigarettes, I acquired another profitable commodity—food! When the trays of food arrived in the ward, I helped the orderlies distribute them. After a while this chore was left entirely to me. Here again, there were those who couldn't touch their food and everything remained sitting on the tray: hard-boiled eggs, butter, cheese, fruit, white bread, marmalade. It seemed a crime to leave it there and have the attendants haul it away. So, I used my common sense. Before any of them could get moving and come to collect the trays, I had all the dry leftovers stashed away in a pillow case.

My best paying customers were in the ward of venereal cases: strapping galoots, their appetites in no way impaired by their predicament. Everyone in the hospital regarded them with utter disdain. What with the threat of war again in the air, these big oafs were spending their time lolling in the hospital, when they should be back at the base preparing to protect Poland!

I would not have dared to engage in such hanky-panky were it not for feeling secure with Sister Bronya. She was very pleased with my help, not only to the patients, but to her personally. I hung on her every word, ready to carry out her slightest wish. I became one of the privileged few who were allowed to enter her office. And pertaining to my various errands, I was there quite frequently. The two things in her room which invariably made me uncomfortable were the photo of her dead husband, the German officer, and the Virgin Mary I could see hanging above her bed behind the screen.

I was certain that Sister Bronya was on to my black marketeering. Still, as long as she acted as if she saw nothing and knew nothing, what was there for me to worry about? No wonder my feeling of gratitude toward her grew into a much warmer feeling…a feeling of outright physical desire. I was overcome with a passion for her that tormented me.

Did Sister Bronya sense my yearning for her? Did she, as a woman, much older than I—a woman who had already been married—detect, intuitively, the burning desire drawing me to her like a magnet? As if she would deign to bestow her favors on a young, skinny squirt with a shaved heat, I thought! A Jewish "suitor" if you please!

War Again!

The air was suddenly filled with rumblings of war. Relations between Poland and Soviet Russia were becoming more strained from day to day. Polish military divisions had taken up positions at various points near the Russian border, with frequent exchanges of fire.

At the hospital, the doctors became very strict. No one was allowed to remain a moment longer than necessary. No more malingering! A soldier was discharged, got his furlough according to his case—typhus patients got four weeks—and that was that: back to the regiment!

My friends, the boys and girls in our theater group, were deeply concerned over my bout with typhus. According to the discouraging reports they got, they had as good as written me off. When they learned that I had safely returned to the living, they came around in the early evening to keep me company. Not that visitors were permitted into the confines of the yard, but we could gab to our hearts' content through the iron grillwork at the gates. They brought me up on what was new in the world of theater. My friend Finkel was glad that I was still safe from being sent to the front. I cherished these visits from my pals and waited all day in anticipation of their coming around to cheer me. My family came to see me daily too. Everyone looked upon me as one resurrected.

My friend Stashek passed by the hospital every day on his way to serve the Sinkevitch family. Through him I caught up on the goings-on in the band. Everyone sent regards and were waiting for my return. The message from Col. Sinkevitch, himself, was that I hurry up a bit. Borke, according to Stashek, was trying to commandeer things in my absence. At any rate, Stashek said, it didn't appear probable that our regiment would be sent to the front. Our mission as a Grodno garrison, he explained, was to protect the city from attack and be the last to retreat.

*　*　*

"Sister Vronetzka?" I inquired tentatively, as I knocked on the door of her office.

"Yablotchka?" she called, "come in, the door is open."

Timidly, I stepped in. Sister Bronya was busying herself behind her folding screen, while I stood and waited, fully convinced that I was to be taken to task for my black-market activities; else why would she have sent for me this late in the evening.

In a little while, she appeared from behind the screen wearing an open peignoir that revealed part of her bare breast. I lowered my eyes in embarrassment, while she, brushing her long flaxen hair, broke into amused laughter.

"How do you feel, Yablotchka?" she asked.

"Good. I feel very good, Sister Vronetzka," I replied, not daring to raise my eyes.

"You feel good? Well, that's not good at all! Do you know that tomorrow the doctor must decide whether you are well enough to be discharged, so you can be sent to the front?"

Discharged from the hospital? My heart sank! I began to catch on. She was trying to tip me off to the fact that my answer was not very bright. For as soon as the rumors of war began, all patients scheduled to be released back to duty suddenly developed "relapses," so they could put off going to the front for as long as possible.

"I don't mind being discharged," I mumbled. "I'll go back to the band. I'm a musician. What I do mind is not being able to see you anymore."

"So, you want to be near me? How near?" she cajoled, moving closer to me, still brushing her shining hair. "Is this near enough?"

I caught glimpses of her partially bared breasts, her white underthings through the sheer robe; the eyelet-embroidered ruching of her camisole beribboned with little red bows. The perfume of her lithe body made my head swim. The blood pounded in my ears and every nerve in my body throbbed with a burning desire to touch her, take her in my arms and cover her with kisses. Do I dare? No! How could I take such liberties with Lieutenant Vronetzka?!

"What are you thinking about, Yablotchka?" her caressing voice broke in on my thoughts. "Would you like to remain here with me for as long as possible?"

"Yes, yes," I murmured, "I certainly would."

"I can work it out. But it's up to you to use your head. And this I'm sure you can do, judging by the shrewd little business you've been running on the side. You must also know how to keep a secret, understand?"

"I understand."

"How old are you, Yablotchka?"

"I...I am," I began, but how could I admit that I was not even seventeen as yet?! Was I to lie and say that I was older? What difference did it make? I felt like a grown man, a man in every sense of the word.

"You are a man, Yablotchka, a real man!" she said, still reading my thoughts in her uncanny way. I stood there like a clod, too naive to grasp what she was leading up to. With another little ripple of laughter she disappeared behind the screen. What was I supposed to do, remain or leave? She hadn't dismissed me.

"Lock the door and fasten the chain, and come here," she called to me. I began to tremble like a leaf. I locked the door, fastened the chain and turning round again, my eyes involuntarily fell on the photo of the German officer, her husband. As if under a spell, I stepped behind the screen. Bronya, in bed, lay stark naked, her underthings flung over the headboard directly under the icon of the Virgin Mary.

"Come here, Yablotchka, don't be afraid," she cooed, pulling me down beside her. "Look at me with those big, black, devouring eyes of yours," she coaxed, her own flashing green fire. "Kiss me!" Her lips burned mine as she tore aside my hospital clothing and pressed my nakedness against her breasts.

"Tell me," she breathed into my ear, "have you slept with a woman yet?"

"N-no, never," I whispered, hoarsely.

"Really? Then you're still a virgin!" she giggled.

Clutching at me passionately, and with wild abandon, she quickly reached up and put out the lamp...

"Jews to Palestine!"

Taking a stroll around the hospital yard, I came upon a young fellow squatting on the walk. Huddled in a hospital robe, his feet bare, the fellow was holding forth in loud and abusive tones, talking to himself in Yiddish: "I will not go to the front! You go! Go and get killed, you bastards!" He limped right past me as if I were some inanimate object.

"Why don't you want to go to the front?" I called after him in Yiddish. He stopped, and fixed me with a questioning look.

"You're a Jew!" he threw at me.

"Can't you hear that I speak Yiddish?"

"That's a lot of rot!" he replied belligerently. "The Jewish goyim also speak Yiddish!"

"I'm a Jew," I assured him. "My name is Chaim. What's yours?"

"My name is Zhamke, Zhamke Khayet. But they call me 'Zhamke-go-to-Palestina.' Murderers! They cut off the beards of old Jews together with half their faces. I saw this myself. They beat me, see? Broke my back...crippled my leg. They say I'm pretending to be out of my mind. Me, crazy? It's they who are crazy! The Polish murderers are crazy! I won't go to the front. Let them go and be slaughtered!"

This kind of talk made me jittery. I peered all around to make sure no one was listening.

"Want a cigarette?" I tried to distract him.

"Got one? Gimme!" Delighted, he inhaled deep into his lungs, savoring the smoke as he exhaled through his nostrils.

"Sit down, Zhamke," I made room for him beside me on the bench. "Where are you from?" I asked, in an attempt to draw him out.

"I come from Tchenstokhov. I'm twenty years old. My father is a shochet (ritual slaughterer). I studied at the yeshiva, but that wasn't for me. I cut off my ear-locks, and considered myself a genuine Polish patriot. At the first call for volunteers, I was one of the first to join the forces. It was hell! They made my life miserable. Over the slightest thing, it was: 'Jews, to Palestine!' Any dirty job that needed doing, it was 'Hey, Jew'—meaning me! Then, with war with the Bolsheviks ready to break out any minute, who was immediately sent to the front lines? The Jews! So, before you knew it, Zhamke was on his way to be slaughtered.

"The train I was on was packed with soldiers. The tracks on either side of the train were lined with Jewish people—they begged, pleaded to be taken aboard so they could somehow get back to their homes. The soldiers jeered at them. They grabbed hold of the outstretched hands of an imploring Jew, to help him climb up the steps of the car; and when he managed to reach the top, they flung him back to crack his skull.

"I kept silent. What could I do? Jewish girls, on the other hand, were readily hauled into the cars. Pushing them into the toilets, soldiers lined up and waited their turn with them as in a brothel. When they had done with them, the girls were tossed right out of the speeding train. But I kept my mouth shut. What could I do? I saw them get hold of a Jew with a handsome beard and long side-curls. Two of General Haller's beasts grabbed him. Using a bayonet, they sheared off one side of his beard, taking a slice of his face with it. The blood was gushing, the Jew was screaming with pain and then, something snapped in my head. I too, began to scream. I screamed my guts out. I threw myself at these butchers, but I got pummeled, beaten... they crippled me, see? ...my shoulder, my leg. When the train stopped here, in Grodno, I was taken off and brought to the hospital. They keep testing me. They say I'm putting it on, pretending to be crazy. I tell you, I will not go to the front."

Suddenly, he leaned close and whispered, "What do you think, am I putting it on, or am I really crazy? I don't know anymore. But I will not go to the front!"

Zhamke's account, horrendous as it was, sounded convincing; as told by a sane and lucid person. Was he indeed crazy? Was he acting? I couldn't make him out.

"Zhamke," I said, "why must you antagonize them? It only stirs them up so they beat you and tease you. It would be a lot better for you to insist that you do, in fact, want to be sent to the front. They would stop tormenting you, and with your condition being what it is, they would send you home, anyway."

Zhamke gazed at me, took another puff on his cigarette and watched the smoke trail away. By now, the courtyard had begun to fill with the ambulatory patients from the various buildings and their attendants. Spotting Zhamke, they jeered, "Hey, Jew-boy, will you go to the front, or to Palestine?"

Zhamke sprang up from the bench and at the top of his lungs began to scream: "Send me to the front!" And with this he began to crow like a rooster, "Cockadoodle-do! Send me to the front. Cockadoodle-do! I'll kill them all!"

I was thunderstruck. Chills ran down my spine. He ripped up stones from the walk, hurling them at his tormentors. Whatever he could lay his hands on he smashed against the windows. His screams were heard all over the yard. They finally dragged him away, still raving.

Later on I learned that he was subsequently convinced that he was being sent to the front. They got him into his uniform and with his pack on his maimed shoulders, an empty gun in his hand, he let himself be taken meek as a lamb, to his parents in Tchenstokhov.

* * *

Thanks to Sister Bronya's influence, I was still being kept in the hospital. The doctor undoubtedly would have discharged me, because it was quite evident that I was fully recovered, but it was a patient's temperature that was the deciding factor. My temperature, according to Bronya's reports, fluctuated. Normal in the morning and up several points in the evening.

Truthfully speaking, the monotony of hospital routine had begun to pall on me. If it were not for Bronya, I would have begged the doctor to release me. I let Bronya talk me into staying on at the hospital for as long as it could be arranged. Lately, however, my relationship with her had become strained. I resented her dictatorial attitude toward me in front of others. She treated me like a trained pup. I never knew when she was in earnest and when she was jesting.

I was especially chagrined during one of my mother's visits. Bronya herself had written out a special pass and greeted Mama very amiably. In fact, she made a point of praising me to her.

"If your Yablotchka were a little older, Mama," she said, "I might even want to marry him!"

Mama, of course, took it as a well-meaning joke: She'd want, would she?! So let her want—the shiksa! That's as far as she'd get! Chaimke, married? That's a good joke!

I was burned up. Bronya should have been more discreet. The thing that was really eating Bronya was the time I spent every evening with the girls in my theater group.

"Your girls are such silly young geese. You're drawn to them, aren't you. After all, they are zhidovkas."

The word zhid, in Russian, is a derogatory appellation for Jew. The proper term is Yevrey. In Polish there is the one term, zhidzhe. It depends entirely on the individual who is saying it, and in what manner, or context, it is used. Whenever I hear the word zhid, it never fails to strike a harsh note in my ear and almost always in my guts; be it said ever so lightly, without malice, or insult.

It reached a point where, instead of feeling free and easy with Bronya, I began to fear her. She sensed this constraint in me and this antagonized her all the more. To placate her, I would have had to stay away from the gate, knowing that my friends were gathered there to share the news of the day. This, however, was something I wouldn't give up.

One evening, quite early, as my pals and I stood at the gate, laughing and exchanging our usual banter, an attendant came up to me and announced: "Lieutenant Vronetzka orders you to return to the ward at once!"

Well, well! I thought, Lieutenant Vronetzka orders me, does she?! This made me so furious, I went right on gabbing with my friends, paying no attention to him. In less than five minutes, her face burning with wrath, Bronya herself appeared.

"Why haven't you obeyed my order?" she demanded in tight-lipped rage.

In the face of such an outburst I might, under different circumstances, have obeyed her command. But embarrassed before my friends, who stood there aghast and obviously puzzled, I stubbornly stood my ground. What will they think of me, being bared at and intimidated!

"I'll go back in a little while," I answered doggedly, "it's still too early."

"I command you to return at once, do you hear? You've had enough fresh air for one day and enough jabbering with your zhiddes! March!!" With this, she turned on her heel and stalked off.

The guard at the gate came up and dispersed my friends. Slinking back to my ward like a wounded animal, shamed and disgraced, I flung myself on my bed. All through the night I tossed and turned and finally came up with the decision: I must leave the hospital as soon as possible.

Of no avail were Bronya's remorseful attempts to make up. I remained adamant in my decision. I was well and I wished to be discharged. The doctor himself advised me to reconsider, warning me of a possible relapse. I told him that I was willing to take the risk and would bear the responsibility. Thus, notwithstanding Bronya's protests, the doctor had to discharge me.

On my way through the corridor I came face to face with Bronya, who had obviously been waiting for this encounter. I stopped, pulled myself up to my full height and, with military precision, executed a snappy salute. Smiling tremulously, tears welled up in her eyes. Only too well did she understand the sarcasm of my gesture. Throwing her arms around me she kissed me and murmured, "Dovidzenia, Yablotchka, you will come to see me, won't you?"

Without answering, I disengaged myself from her embrace. With a final salute and a sharp click of the heel, I turned and walked out. I drew a deep breath, filling my lungs with fresh air. I was free—free! I had entered the hospital, a boy. I was leaving it now, a man! Nothing could frighten me anymore. I feared no one. From now on I could fight my own battles. I was a man, by God—a man!

24

The Bolsheviks Are Coming!

During my furlough, I still went to the barracks every day to collect my rations and spend time with the musicians. Borke was not elated about my return. It took some of the wind out of his sails. However, I did get a fine welcome from Col. Sinkevitch and Sgt. Kochanowski. They were pleased with my daily visits; especially with my willingness to help out at the concerts.

Evenings, I always got together with Finkel and Dimant, and the rest of our young theater hopefuls. We'd hang out again at the mall, dreaming about our future plans. On occasion, knowing some of the musicians at the City Theater, we'd get in to see the Yiddish performances still going strong with visiting artists.

"Grodno News"

The headlines told us that a state of war now existed between Poland and Russia. The victorious Polish armies lay siege to Vilna, Bobruisk and Minsk. Drunk with triumph, the Poles swaggered as if they had conquered the entire globe. Our regiment was to remain in Grodno for the present. It was our task to defend the city, should a retreat become necessary. Not that the Poles even entertained such a possibility. But the wheels of war took a complete turn. Now, it was the Poles who suffered one defeat after another, retreating in panic, with the Bolsheviks on their heels.

Our regiment was no longer smug about being spared going to the front. If this turn of events continued, we feared we'd soon have the front coming to us!

Trains, jammed with the wounded, made stops at the Grodno railroad station. For the purpose of morale, our band greeted them with martial music, although it was quite obvious that many of these men would never march again, having left their limbs on the battlefield.

The ladies of the Red Cross greeted them with flowers. In typical Polish ardor, they expounded the glory of giving their blood in defense of their sacred Polish soil. Our band struck up the anthem, "Jeszcze Polska nie zginela poki mi zyiemy" (Poland has not yet succumbed, not as long as we still live). I couldn't help thinking of the popular parody: "Jeszcze Polska nie zginela, alba zginiet mushi" (Poland has not yet succumbed, but eventually she must!).

The streets were congested with army vehicles groaning under the heavy equipment and weaponry of the retreating army. Unrest flared up all over the city. Replacement squads, on their way to embattled areas, robbed Jewish shops; broke into wineries; got filthy drunk and molested civilians on the street. Bloody fights erupted between soldiers and military gendarmes; the latter nicknamed canaries because of the bright yellow trimming on their uniforms. The soldiers despised the canaries because they didn't have to go to the front, and demonstrated their animosity at every opportunity.

The streets were also alive with the women's army auxiliary. Most of these female soldiers were recruits of questionable reputation. In fact, their behavior was even cruder than that of their male counterparts. They would barge into a shop and grab whatever they could get their hands on. The canaries, faced with this situation, merely laughed and shrugged their shoulders. They knew better than to tangle with these rabid Polish patriots in skirts. Oddly enough, these soldier-gals found very little favor in the eyes of the men. The soldiers referred to them as the "hole-y" army.

The Jews in Grodno lived once again in fear. Retreating Polish soldiers had rounded up Jews in Pinsk, and without reason, stood them up against a wall and shot them.

The railroad tracks along the Grodno-Bialystok-Warsaw route were lined with Jews who were stranded, hoping for some way that would get them home. Whenever a train happened by, they clamored to be taken aboard. But the soldiers on these military transports only grabbed a few women and hid them in the toilets. After dozens of soldiers had ravished them, the women were unceremoniously tossed out of the speeding train. Word got around that any Jew with a beard had better not as much as catch their eye, or he was in danger of losing it with part of his face. Up to then, I had only heard tell of these atrocities. I often thought of poor, demented Zhamke. But, since our band now traveled the transport trains to other cities to furnish music in the departure ceremonies for troops being sent to the front lines, I too, became an eye witness to the beastly practices of the Polish heroes.

For the Jewish soldier, life became increasingly intolerable. The attitude toward the Jewish musicians in our band had also undergone a marked change. The slogans that popped up everywhere read that Jews were the cause of Poland's losing streak! Others said that Jews were Bolsheviks, and that they were selling Poland down the river to the pagan communists!

I was confined to the barracks and no longer allowed to sleep at home. Col. Sinkevitch didn't stop drinking. His midnight lectures on patriotism acquired a new theme—Jews! Again we stood in our underdrawers for hours, while he preached at us. Stashek, the stutterer, was again tortured to read out the tacked-up orders of the day. Even his right-hand man Kochanowski lost patience with him. To all appearances he was on our side, but since military discipline was to be upheld at all costs, we had to endure it and suffer in silence. Like it or not, Sinkevitch was still the Colonel!

Dovidl, My Friend

A trainload of Russian prisoners-of-war pulled into the Grodno railroad station. People came running from every corner of the city to gawk at the Bolsheviks. To keep the main tracks free, the string of cattle cars carrying the prisoners was shunted onto a siding.

Coming home from the barracks on a special pass, Mama greeted me. "Chaimke, a man stopped by to tell me that while he was at the station, one of the Russian prisoners there—a Jewish boy—asked him about a family by the name of Yablonik here in Grodno."

"Mama, did the man give a name? I mean the name of the prisoner?"

"Yes, he did mention a name. It was something like Narkes or Nemkes."

"Mama!" It suddenly dawned on me, "Nekhes! Shlomo Nekhes from Minsk! The family we stayed with, remember? His wife, Basha and their son, Dovidl! This must surely be Dovid! His father, Shlomo would be too old for the army. Dovidl, a Russian prisoner! I must go to the station right now, Mama."

I took a short cut to the railroad siding. A pitiful sight met my eyes. Some of the Russian prisoners were sprawling on the ground beside the tracks; others, slumping inside the boxcars, were unshaven; all of them, ragged and dirty. I saw no one standing guard over them. What luck! If, indeed, there were any guards in attendance, they must have been on the other side of the depot. There was no fear of prisoners escaping. Where could they go? My Polish uniform did not seem to faze them one way or another. They lay about in complete apathy.

I flipped out my army identification paper and perused it as if it represented an official military order. In an authoritative, commanding tone, I called out, "Nekhes? Dovid Nekhes!" I repeated this as I walked along the cars. At one of them, a bearded face appeared at the door. Staring at me with bewildered eyes, he slowly moved into the center of the doorway, the picture of despair. His pants were tattered, his blouse torn and dirty, his feet bare. He seemed uncertain whether it was his name I called.

"Nekhes!" I repeated, keeping my voice stern.

"Da!" he replied, yes, but my Polish uniform was enough to make him distrust me. But I recognized him, beard or no beard. This was Dovidl all right, with the well remembered crinkly hair.

"Dovid Nekhes?" I barked, "from Minsk?" At this, a light came into his eyes. He was beginning to catch on.

"Da, da! It's me!"

"Come with me at once to the Commandeer's office!"

It had grown quite dark and there was no one around. "Dovidl," I whispered, "don't turn, walk straight ahead. I'll follow you to make it look as if I'm taking you in for interrogation."

"Is it really you, Chaim?" he murmured, still bewildered. "Where are you taking me?"

"You'll see. The first thing we must do is get you into some decent clothing. Dark as it is, we still can't take a chance of anyone spotting you in those rags before I can get you safely into our house. My brother Shayke lives nearby. You'll wait until I can find you an old suit of clothes to change into."

Shayke hadn't come home from work yet and his wife Yetta panicked when I told her what I came for. My God, she wailed, that's all she needed, getting caught helping a Russian prisoner to escape! Hurriedly, she pushed me out with one of Shayke's old suits, a shirt and a pair of shoes.

Beckoning my escapee out of the shadows, I led him into the little shed in the yard where he could make a quick change. Shayke's things were too large for him, though not enough to make him conspicuous. We tore up his rags and hid them between the piled logs of wood. More at ease now, the two of us walked side by side like any two friends out for a stroll. I was saddened to hear that Basha, his mother, had since passed away.

"And where is your father?" I asked.

"Probably still in Minsk." Soon after the revolution in Russia, Dovid related, he was mobilized into the army. He was taken prisoner when the Poles advanced on Bobruisk. For weeks now, he and the others had been dragged around and shunted onto railroad sidings in various towns. Nobody seemed to know just what to do with them. The Poles were too busy retreating, so who, in all this pandemonium, gave a damn about captured Bolsheviks?

Along the entire journey to Grodno they suffered mostly at the hands of Polish civilians, who vented their wrath at the Russian prisoners for the defeat suffered by the Polish troops at the front.

When their transport pulled into Grodno, he immediately thought of us. Picking out a Jewish face in the curious crowd, he took a chance and asked the man to get word to our family so we'd know he was among the prisoners.

Mama threw her arms around Dovidl as if he were her very own long-lost son. Father, Rochele—all of us were excited and delighted with our surprise guest.

"Don't worry, Dovidl," Mama comforted him, "you're in good hands. It's 'bread for bread.' Consider yourself home amongst your own family."

Dovid began to relax. He described the bitter years of war; the peak of misery and suffering that came with the upheaval following the revolution in Russia. To have survived through all of it was a miracle. His father, he sighed, didn't even know that he was alive.

No repercussions arose from his disappearance. The days continued quietly. Dovidl was also careful not to attract attention. Why stretch his luck? In any case, he carried an old identification card of Motke's, so that if need be, he could show that he was a member of our family.

Eventually, through a rare opportunity, my uncles, the enterprising Shillingoff brothers, who had begun running a bus line, were able to send Dovid off to Vilna. He tarried there for a while, until the Russians occupied the city. Only then, we later learned, did he manage to make his way home to Minsk.

25

July 25, 1920

The Russians were inching their way closer and closer to Grodno. Vilna had already fallen. Cannon boom could clearly be heard at night. The fleeing Poles were making life so unendurable, that the communal prayer to the good Lord—ironically enough—was to speed up the arrival of the Russians, and the sooner the better!

It was a Saturday morning. Col. Sinkevitch sent for me. I found him still stretched out on the cot in the office, not fully sobered up.

"Listen, Yablonik," he said in a friendly tone, "we are evacuating the city. My wife and son must leave Grodno today. All our military vehicles are loaded to capacity with army equipment. Take Borke and Stashek and requisition a horse and wagon somewhere. You know where, you're a local boy. Load my household things on it and take my wife, baggage and all, over to the Fehrstadt side. Railway cars are waiting there to evacuate the families of officers. Tell Wanda I'll join them there shortly before departure."

Borke, Stashek and I set out to carry out the colonel's order.

"Our best bet is out on the Grandzhitz road," suggested Borke. "First of all, it's closer to Sinkevitch's house, and among the peasants in that vicinity, we are sure to get hold of a horse and wagon." Borke proved to be right. In the yard of a peasant's hut, we spotted exactly what we needed—a horse, and a wagon big enough for our purpose.

The peasant was simply beside himself at our request. "Panovie," his wife implored, "I beg you, don't take the bread out of the mouths of our children. Without the horse and wagon we will starve to death!"

I felt for them, but it couldn't be helped. I tried to assure them that, as soon as we had moved the colonel's family, we would return the horse and wagon.

"That's exactly what the Germans promised when they took all the horses I had at the time," he pleaded. To settle the situation, I offered to take him along. He could help us fetch and carry, and when we were through he was welcome to take back his old mare and wagon. The peasant accepted my offer with deep gratitude.

Pulling up at Sinkevitch's house, we proceeded to load the wagon with all the household effects, piling everything up as high as we could. Now, there was no room for all of us on the wagon. Naturally, Her Majesty Wanda and her Crown Prince had first priority. I wedged myself between them on the driver's seat and took up the reins, while Borke, Stashek and the peasant trudged behind the slow, creaking wagon like a funeral escort. The horse could barely pull such a load. Going uphill, the escorting trio were obliged to push with all their strength.

We were not the only ones trying to make our way across the Niemen to Fehrstadt. We were on a steep incline, when coming toward us was an automobile filled with high-ranking army personnel. The chauffeur honked his horn, demanding right of way. Our nag suddenly came alive. Startled by this mechanized, horseless contraption emitting loud, outlandish squawks, she threw a tantrum! She reared up on her hind legs like a show-horse at the circus. In desperation I pulled on the reins, but there was no calming her. The harder I pulled, the wilder she became.

Chairs came toppling out of the wagon, featherbeds, pots, valises and heaven only knows what! Wanda was screaming, Janush was howling and I, I felt that this was sure to cost me my life. Just before we reached the bridge, a group of soldiers on foot grabbed hold of the harness and mercifully checked our runaway steed. But strewn all the way from the top of the hill were Col. Sinkevitch's worldly possessions.

Wanda, her hair disheveled, glared at me like a tigress. In her rage, she hauled off and delivered two resounding smacks left and right across my face.

"You did this on purpose!" she screamed at me, seeking justification from the amused soldiers gathered around us. "You just wait!" she shook her finger in my face, "you'll get what's coming to you for this!" I stood there, wiping the blood from my nose, while she continued to hail abuse.

Borke, Stashek and the peasant were busy retrieving the things scattered on the road and with the help of the soldiers, piled everything back on the wagon. This time, the peasant climbed aboard and took up the reins himself.

"If you had let me do the driving, this wouldn't have happened," he berated me, adding fuel to the fire. "The horse knows me. She's used to me."

"Yes," I agreed. "You drive. I'll run down to the river and wash the blood off my face. I'll catch up with you." Wanda balked at boarding the wagon again and so they all followed on foot, bracing the load with their hands to keep things from tumbling out again. As soon as they were out of sight I ran as fast as my feet could carry me, the blood still streaming from my nose. Reaching as far as the New Market, I slipped into my sister Slavka's shoe store. In answer to her startled questions, I made light of it. "It's just a little nosebleed. It will stop in a moment."

I washed away the blood as my thoughts kept racing. Where shall I run to? Back to the barracks? Col. Sinkevitch will skin me alive! No, no, I must desert. If only I could hide somewhere until the Russians invade and take over the city! They are so near! But where can I go? The safest place after all, I decided, would be in the housing complex of Uncle Shillingoff's courtyard, where I was familiar with every cellar and attic.

At the corner of Dr. Zamkov's house, I heard my name called. "Hey, Yablonik! Stoi!" (Stop!) My blood ran cold. I recognized the voice. Sgt. Kochanowsky! I turned—and froze. Facing me from across the Boulevard Square, I saw four rifles aimed straight at me: the sergeant, Fedka, Stashek and Borke Labendz.

"Why didn't you report back to the barracks?" Kochanowski thundered. "We are evacuating the city. What the hell are you gallivanting around town for—thinking of deserting?!"

"I couldn't stop my nosebleed. I was just on my way back to the barracks, and I..."

"He is not on his way to the barracks!" contradicted Borke. "He is on his way home. He lives here!"

"Yes, I was going home to pick up a few things on the way to..." I glanced at Stashek. He was white as a sheet, the rifle in his hands, shaking. Kochanowski looked at me with murder in his eyes. Fedka, the moron, had a vacuous leer on his face, and Borke left no doubt that it was he who had me trapped.

"Come along!" the sergeant barked at me and turned to go.

"I'll just grab a few things. It will take a minute. My military coat," I begged him.

"Dobzhe," he conceded. "But we'll go along. Make it snappy. If you make the slightest move to take off, we'll shoot!" I started to walk and they followed me. Coming into the courtyard I went up the stairs that led to our flat, with Fedka on my tail. Mama was alone. She stared at me wide-eyed, obviously jolted by the sight of my escort, armed and ready to shoot.

"Mama," I explained with elaborate casualness, "we're leaving for a couple of days to lay a sendoff for a regiment being sent to the front." From the glib tone of my story and the strange circumstance of the soldier with the gun at my elbow, Mama gathered that it was safer not to ask questions. Instead, she busied herself helping me "find" things.

On the pretext that I was hunting for a mislaid article, I desperately cast about for a possible means of escape. Fedka remained outside the balcony door, convinced that he might as well station himself there, since I had no way of escaping from inside the house.

The entry room of our flat was, actually, the kitchen. The old-fashioned oven was so huge it completely blocked from view a low door, which led into a tiny alcove. This was used as a storeroom. I ducked behind the oven and into the alcove. It was completely dark in there except for thin strips of daylight filtering through the cracks in the overhead boards that covered the small opening to the roof. My hands explored the walls for a hole, a crevice, an opening of any kind...there were none. I climbed on top of an up-ended barrel and tried to push up the boards of the roof. I knew this must overlook part of the yard. With a good shove I loosened one of the slats and then another. Shoving them aside, I chinned myself up and got my head through the narrow opening.

Resting my elbows on the remaining boards I was able to support myself. And there I hung—neither up nor down, half of me dangling in the alcove. Suddenly, I felt someone taking hold of my legs and pushing me up. It was Mama! She had grasped the situation and was giving me a leg up! With her support, I pulled myself up over the little rooftop. From there, I jumped onto a larger, adjacent roof and still another. They spotted me from below and shots began flying at me from the yard and from the balcony. Like a cat I leapt through an open dormer window and disappeared.

Breathless, shaken, unable to get hold of myself after this hair-raising narrow escape, I lay sprawled in the middle of the floor in a dark, cavernous attic. Way over in the far corner of the attic, several heavy wooden beams stood propped together against the wall, and I wedged myself behind them. I heard the shuffling of footsteps. Through the narrow spaces between the beams I saw two military gendarmes. They stopped at the very spot I left only moments before. One of them moved in my direction. I'm done for, finished! Holding my breath, I pressed myself even flatter against the wall. Now the gendarme was so close to me, except for the planks, he could have touched me. This is it, I told myself. Chaim, your luck has run out. You'll never get out of this alive! The gendarme stood still, his ears cocked for sound. I didn't dare breathe. Finally, he turned away and called to his partner. "He's not here either. Let's have a look at the other end. We'll nab him all right. He can't have gotten far."

As their footsteps grew fainter, my knees buckled and I slumped in a heap behind the beams. Crawling out of my hiding place I tiptoed down the stairwell. On the second landing, a pair of hands firmly grabbed me from behind and pulled me into one of the flats.

"Stop running, you foolish boy! The entire courtyard is full of military police."

"My parents," I sobbed for this friendly neighbor, "they will be arrested because of me."

"Don't you worry. Nothing will happen to them. And you run back upstairs to the attic. The gendarmes won't be looking up there again. We'll let you know when it's safe to come down." He opened the door a crack, and cautiously peering up and down the stairs, gave me the nod to run. I quickly tiptoed back up the stairs and once again took refuge behind my lucky haven of wooden beams.

* * *

I later heard that a group of gendarmes forced their way into our house and they arrested mother and father and led them toward the gendarmerie. But, before they could get there, the Almighty came to their rescue. The street suddenly sprang alive with tumult and wild shouting: "The Bolsheviks are already on the outskirts of town! They will besiege the city at any moment!"

The gendarmes took to their heels and fled. So my parents went home.

"If only Chaimke had listened to his father! If only he had remained to study at the yeshiva," shrugged father, "we would have been spared all this heartache. But no, he had to play soldier! What a world we're living in!"

* * *

Huddled in my corner of the attic I could feel the walls of the house trembling at the blasts of machine guns that came steadily closer. Grenades, hurled from the fortress's artillery, whistled over the rooftops, exploding in the air with deafening reverberations in the empty attic.

The bombarding continued. Then, all at once I heard the roar of dynamite explosions blowing up the two bridges spanning the River Niemen. The Polish demolition battalion, before their retreat, destroyed the bridges. Dozens of horses and military vehicles, as well as hundreds of soldiers making their way on foot across the river, were blown to bits.

Abruptly, the firing stopped. Venturing out from behind the beams I peered through the chinks in the wall and could see Zamkova Street and the courtyard of the Russian church. A rider, with flashing sword in hand, galloped by on an unsaddled horse. Bootless and naked from the waist up, he wore nothing but a pair of pants and what looked like a derby on his head. A second rider soon followed. He too, was barefooted, but wore riding breeches, a worn German military coat and a cossack papakha on his head. Holding a hand grenade, he made several swinging motions and hurled it toward the square, where it promptly exploded. At the corner of the Russian church, the first rider slipped from his horse. Wounded, he crawled on hands and knees to the sidewalk and remained propped against the iron gate of the church. The rider who threw the grenade, also reappeared. Guiding his horse right up on the sidewalk, he pulled his wounded comrade up behind him and galloped off in the direction from which they came. These were the first reconnaissance scouts to advance on Grodno.

From the same direction, moving into my line of vision, came a droshky drawn by a single horse—the type of carriage driven by the upper class. The driver, in a cossack jerkin, a fur papakha on his head, held the reins in one hand, an automatic firearm in the other. The back seat of the droshky was rigged with a machine-gun. A women, wearing an army jacket, her head bound in a flower-print babushka, knelt in the tonneau of the carriage, her hands on the machine-gun. Peering in every direction, she seemed ready to fire at the least provocation.

The droshky continued at a slow pace toward the Place-Parade. The military-looking man on the driver's seat, I later learned, was Marshall Simone Budiony. The woman at the machine-gun—his wife. These two were among the very first to lay siege to the city of Grodno.

* * *

Budiony's cavalry, although first-rate fighters, did not have clothing to cover their bodies. And their weapons were a conglomeration of every outmoded type; not in the least to be compared to the retreating Polish Ulaner Brigade with their sleek horses and shining modern weapons.

Dusk had begun to fall. More red cavalrymen kept advancing. In passing the houses, they shouted warnings: Stay away from the windows, or we'll shoot! Polish soldiers, wherever you are, we order you to come out with hands raised!

Another barrage of gunfire rocked the earth. This was a bombardment from the Poles holding their last stand on the Fehrstadt side. One of the shells hit the lofty cupola atop the Russian church, directly opposite the spot in which I stood cowering in the attic. It turned into a ball of fire, igniting the roof of the church itself. The burning cupola threatened to topple over onto the house facing it—an immediate menace! I dashed down the stairs and found people frenziedly packing their belongings in a panic to flee. I made straight for our house. At sight of me, the family fell all over me, carrying on as if I had just returned from the next world.

I changed into an old, civilian suit and tossed my Polish uniform into the alcove behind the stove—my lucky escape hatch. I helped the family throw together a few necessities before fleeing the spreading fire of the burning church.

Mama wept as she packed. Her thoughts were with Shayke and Yetta, and their little son David, who were in Slabodka; Slavka and Itche in New-Market and Motke, his wife Sheine-Libbe and their infant daughter also named Rochele, were over in Fehrstaedt in the very midst of the bombardment. God only knew if they were still alive.

A thunderous crash rattled the window panes. What now, we shuddered. But we were soon reassured by a familiar voice: "Don't be alarmed," cousin Mikhl called to us, "it's all over!"

Mikhl had come with the city firemen to put out the blaze at the church. The cupola did crash, he said, but luckily into the churchyard. Nobody was hurt and nothing in the neighborhood was damaged. There were other blazes in town, and the firemen were finding it impossible to spread themselves so thin. So if fires were going to break out, Mikhl said, let them! There was nothing they could do.

*　*　*

At nightfall, the sidewalks and gutters were strewn with the prone figures of Russian cavalrymen, snoring heavily, yet holding on to the reins of their horses, ready to mount them at a moment's notice and gallop into battle.

During the night, the Poles retreated from Fehrstadt. Marshall Budiony's cavalry kept right on their tails, giving them chase the entire way to Bialystok, up to Warsaw.

The Russian construction battalion got to work and threw a pontoon bridge over the Niemen, permitting civilians to get into town.

Motke and Sheine-Libbe, with baby Rochele in her arms, anxiously burst into our flat. Our joy at seeing one another alive was boundless.

The streets suddenly came alive with tumultuous glee! Hordes of Polish prisoners were being paraded in nothing but their underwear. The Russian guards hustling them along were now decked out in their prisoners' boots and uniforms. Stumbling barefooted and practically naked over the cobblestones, these recent Polish heroes hung their heads under the curious stares of the Jews lining the sidewalks. One onlooker stepped from the curb and catching up with one of the marching prisoners shouted, "Here is my beard! Here! Would you like to cut it off?" he sneered and thrust his whiskers into the prisoner's face. "Why don't you cut it, you big Polish hero!"

A host of the women soldiers were also being paraded through the streets. The Jewish women jeered at them as they passed by. But undaunted, with characteristic defiance, they retaliated with barb for barb, insult for insult. "Wait, you zhidi!" they flung back, "we shall return and settle the score with you!"

"You won't live long enough to return!" the crowd retorted. It was a foregone conclusion that these soldier-women would not be returning so soon—if ever. They would be rotting in some hellhole in Russia for a long time.

Father, worried about my safety, considered it too risky for me to remain in the flat and decided that I had better spend the night in the home of my cousin, Kaike Rosjanski, who lived at the other end of the building, sharing the same long-running balcony. She and her husband would be taking a great chance, what with the possibility of the Poles trooping back to regain the city. Yet they agreed to have me stay with them. Haike bedded me down on the floor for the night, and in a little while, she and her husband and little son Yoshke were fast asleep.

I lay down fully clothed. Exhausted as I was, I still found it impossible to sleep. One thought kept hammering at me: I must leave. Even the Russians would have no use for me, a deserter—regardless of which army. Where will I go? As if this made any difference. Anywhere! If I'm caught, let it be somewhere away from here—removed from those who are so dear to me. Why should innocent people be made to suffer on my account?

At the first glimmer of daybreak, I slipped out on the balcony, determined to leave. Still, it was painful to go without a last, parting glance at my dearest ones. Tiptoeing along the balcony, I stopped at the window of our little flat and peered through the dim panes of glass. I must not awaken them, nor say goodbye, I told myself. I will merely press my lips close to the window. It was quiet in the house, with everyone asleep after the tumultuous night—everyone except father. Already swathed in talis and tefillen, he was murmuring his morning prayers, for it was no longer safe to go to the prayer house.

Thus, pressed against the window, my lips whispered goodbye, dear father …goodbye, dear Mama…farewell, my brothers, sisters…my loved ones…God watch over you…

Blinded by my tears, I tore myself away and turned to grope my way down the steps into an unknown world...

* * *

Warsaw!... I awoke as from a coma. Back in Warsaw? Already? The shrill whistle of the locomotive and the bustling of my fellow passengers told me that we were indeed approaching the Warsaw Terminal. Stepping over one another's feet to reach their baggage in the overhead racks, they elbowed their way to the corridor. With a screech over the frozen rails and a jolt that rocked everyone off balance, the train slid to a final stop. Still heavy-hearted, I took down my bag and followed the others out of the station.

Warsaw! The irony of it—when I should instead have been stepping off at the opposite end of the line—Grodno! As I walked out into the swirling snowstorm, I got a wet slap of snow in the face. An appropriate welcome, I thought, for my miserable mood.

The desk clerks in the hotel looked askance at me. Back already? Before I'd left early that morning, I had relinquished my room with the understanding that, upon my return from Grodno, which was to be three days hence, they would have a room ready for me. But here I was—back the same day. How on earth were they going to accommodate me when they were full up? I had no alternative but to spend the night in the lobby. However, when the "wheels are greased, they roll," an axiom that holds true even in the Poland of today. They finally discovered a room for me—not as choice as the one I had, but I was grateful for any place where I could lay my head down.

I freshened up and phoned down for a shot of 100-gram vodka, a Swiss cheese sandwich and a bottle of ersatz beer. Somewhat revived, I began to think: what am I to do now? The evening is still young. It is Saturday night and surely there is a performance scheduled at the Jewish State Theater. The actors will, no doubt, be nonplussed to see me there. In fact, I could hear them jeering: "Sure, sure, they'll permit him into Grodno just like that, the big shot!" And they'd be justified. For I, myself, felt embarrassed and bitterly disappointed. After all my running around, imposing on people and being cocky, my entire project had fizzled out like a soap bubble!

Yet, the prospect of remaining along all evening with my depressing thoughts didn't appeal to me, either. I went down to the lobby and got one of the hotel chauffeurs to drive me to the Jewish State Theater.

26

The Jewish State Theater in Poland

That night's performance of *Meylach Freylach,* a repertory folk-comedy, was not particularly impressive; although it was presented lavishly, as were all their productions. The star and art directress, Ida Kaminska, and her husband, business manager Meyer Melman, did not take part in this musical play. The leading roles were portrayed by Ruth Kaminska (Ida's daughter) and her husband, Karl Latowitch.

I had already attended other performances at the State Theater, admiring Ida Kaminska in her famous roles of *Mirele Efros* by Jacob Gordin and *Trees Die Standing* by Alejandro Casona. It wasn't long before some of the actors in the troupe buttonholed me with their grievances, grumbling—in strictest confidence—that the repertoire of the State Theater was geared solely to suit the anointed members of the Kaminsky family. In other words, things were still being run according to the old, prewar star system; except that now, all expenses were coming out of the pocket of the Polish government.

The only actor in the company who was occasionally allotted a substantial role was Chavel Buzgan. He had to be reckoned with, for he was a reputed party member. And because the theater was conducted on the basis of personal aggrandizement and state politics, with rigid army-barracks discipline, many actors did not stick with the troupe long. They defected when the company played in countries outside Poland and some managed to emigrate officially to Israel.

The Jewish State Theater, a comparatively intimate house, had a seating capacity of 384. As the Jewish population in Warsaw at the time was not large enough to fill the theater at every performance, the company was obliged to travel to other cities still harboring the remnants of Jewry.

The stage of the theater was spacious enough to accommodate large productions, and was well equipped with the proper flies for hanging stuff. It had a good supply of modern reflectors, spot lamps and a suitable dimmer board. The cast consisted of thirty-five performers, and their dressing rooms were ample and quite comfortable.

What impressed me most was the innovation of earphones, which had just been installed. For an extra fee, Gentile patrons, as well as Jews who did not understand Yiddish, could avail themselves of one of these transistor-units at the box office. Plugged into an outlet in the seat, they could listen to the play as it was simultaneously translated into Polish.

154

Backstage after the performance, the actors were flabbergasted at the sight of me. I was the last person they expected to see in Warsaw that evening. "What? Back already from Grodno? So soon?" Besieged by their questions, I had to recount all that transpired at the border in Kuznica, which, at the last moment, made me decide to turn back to Warsaw. My hometown pal, Avremel Khash, himself only recently arrived as a refugee from Riga, fully agreed with my decision. He was glad to see me back. But one of the actors, amazed to hear that I was afraid to enter Soviet Russia, remarked, "You? An American, afraid?! You have nothing to fear. What's all this fear of Russia, anyway? All the allegations against the Soviet Union are nothing by American reactionary propaganda. People who have a clear conscience and clean hands have nothing to fear. Such people are admitted everywhere in Russia."

"Well, my friend, let's summarize," I challenged this colleague of mine. "Your Jewish State Theater, magnanimously maintained by the socialist Polish government; your troupe, headed by the renowned Ida Kaminska, who is so warmly received in France, England and other European countries—with plans underway for a tour of the Americas, where the Jewish populace will undoubtedly also give your company a grand welcome, for the name of Ida Kaminska is well known in Jewish communities the world over. This adulation, of course, is due to her own individual talents, not to mention the aura inherited from her well-remembered mother, Ester-Rochel Kaminska, in whose name your theater was founded. Well, then tell me, my good friend, how is it that your Jewish State Theater of Poland is not invited to appear in the Soviet Union?

"I hear that a Yiddish folk singer from Kovno, Naham Lifschitz, and the outstanding singer Misha Alexandrovitch, as well as Anna Guzik, have a terrific success with their Yiddish concerts in Russia. The Jewish people idolize them. And Yiddish theater is also quite active in Vilna. Romania, in fact, has two functioning Yiddish theater companies. Why not negotiate exchanges with these troupes? Just imagine what a tour like this would mean for thousands of Jews, who still find themselves scattered throughout Russia and her satellite countries; how the people would welcome seeing Ida Kaminska, remembered as a great artist before the Holocaust. Where then is the barrier, my friend, that keeps you this side of the Iron Curtain? Can it be that you, too, are not kosher?"

My esteemed colleague gave me a withering look, but offered no retort.

Avremel Khash accompanied me back to the Grand Hotel. The snow had stopped falling and it was quite pleasant, so we trudged along.

"Chaim," said Avremel, "better talk as little as possible with these red artists. It won't do you any good."

"Who cares," I shrugged. "Since I couldn't realize my wish to visit my hometown once more in my life, I don't care if they run me out of Warsaw tomorrow!"

On reaching the hotel, I asked Avremel to join me in having a bit to eat. The large, ornately-decorated club off the lobby was crowded with dancing

couples, with men and women seated around tables indulging in sparkling con-
coctions from the bar and late supper specialties.

"Let's refrain from talking politics," said Khash. "Better tell me how you
liked tonight's performance of *Meylach Freylach* at our State Theater?"

"A performance, that's all. Nothing to crow about. It is possible that the
exalted title of State Theater misled me. I anticipated something entirely different in the performances I've seen here. In Russia, Germany, or France, during
the years before the Holocaust, when a theater was awarded that kind of status,
it was because it had earned it on the merits of outstanding artistic achievement. Here, in Poland, I feel that the emphasis on State Theater should rather
be attributed to the financial grants it receives from the state. The heads of
state are fulfilling this project with great generosity in recompense for the horror suffered by Jews. They deserve credit and do, indeed, receive this credit
wherever the troupe appears under the Polish banner. Such magnanimous regard
toward Yiddish art has been unprecedented even in the rich, powerful countries, the United States included, with its millions of Jewish citizens. I hope
and pray this high regard in Poland lasts though I find it difficult to believe.

"Much as any theater group would love to be subsidized, the assurance
of being provided with regular wages, I'm afraid, robs an actor of giving his
utmost at every performance.

"Avremel, my friend," I continued, "tonight's performance, if you'll pardon
me, reminded me of the semiprofessional performances you and I took part
in at the Grodno City Theater during the First World War. These were average
provincial productions without titles or pretenses of any kind. Yet they stood
on a high level and were produced without any outside help. Everything was
accomplished at the expense of the poor actors themselves, struggling on a
cooperative basis. To be sure, it was a hand to mouth existence, but we lived
in hope of finding a future in Yiddish theater around the world. I feel that Poland's
Jewish State Theater falls short of such expectations. The best insurance for
the life of a theater and its actors has always been—and still is—the support
of the public itself. Looking back over the years, I learned this very important
lesson soon after leaving home to wander around the world with Yiddish
Theater."

27

From Lithuania to the U.S.A.

A fter I left Grodno, I spent four years in Lithuania where I traveled with a group of actors. We considered ourselves lucky if we could scrape together the cost of a horse and wagon to take us to the next little town, let alone train fare to Kovno, the capital. But I dreamed of sailing to America—if only on a barge. And oh, how I dreamed! How I envied the actors, Pesach Burstein and Reuben Wendorff, who were fortunate enough to be emigrating to America.

Wendorff, taking along with him not only my everlasting gratitude for his friendly attitude toward me, a young, aspiring actor, but also carried a letter to my sister Mary and her husband Henry in Brooklyn. In it I wrote:

My dear Sister and brother-in-law,

Please help me come to America. I have been knocking about in Lithuania for almost four years. I am utterly alone and do not even have a proper passport. I cannot go back to mother and father in Grodno. I would be shot by the Poles for leaving military service without permission. Where shall I go? I beg of you, please take me to America. I am now a full-fledged actor, playing important roles with well-known actors in the United Yiddish Art Troupe in Kovno. My friend, Wendorff, is also bringing you photographs of the roles already allotted to me. Up to now I have played the title role in *Doctor Cohen* by Max Nordau; Levi-Yitzhak in *Green Fields,* and Itzik in the *Haunted Inn,* both by Hershbein; Lemach in *The Wild Man* by Jacob Gordin. I have also sung and played the role of Absolom in Goldfaden's *Shulamith.* My voice has developed into a tenor and our music director, Herr Stupel from Vilna, assures me that my voice will mature even more as I grow older.

I am enclosing reviews which have appeared in the Kovno *Yiddishe Stimme* by the editor, Reuben Rubinstein, and by Dr. Mukdoni. Dear sister and brother-in-law, I will not be a burden to you. I'm sure I can manage to support myself in America. Please send the necessary papers and steamship ticket as soon as you possibly can. My love and kisses to you,

Your Chaim

* * *

My sister and her husband, a furrier by trade and a good-standing member of his union, both belonged to the Grodno Branch #74 of the Workmen's Circle. They lived in Williamsburg, Brooklyn, not far from the Lyric Theater, which was under the management of Isidore Lillian. Upon receiving my letter, my sister hied herself to the Lyric Theater to persuade the manager to bring me to America without delay. She showed him my photos and assured him that the theater was sure to strike a gold mine in me, since everyone who sees my pictures agrees that I am a dead ringer for Rudolph Valentino—only much younger.

My sister, alas, was totally naive in the ways of the theater world. In those days, when a manager did go to the trouble and expense of importing an actor from overseas, the article had to be the finished product: someone like a Lebedeff, a Goldenburg, a Mikhalesko, or a whole troupe, such as the Habima, or the Vilna—who had made such a stir in Europe that echoes of their fame had already reached theater circles in New York. Young, unknown talents were not invested in. And those who managed to reach the shores of the Golden Land were obliged to go through hell and high water before the Hebrew Actors' Union would permit them to accept an engagement somewhere out in the hinterlands.

To become a member in the actors' union, one had to give an audition before the membership and be voted on by a secret ballot. This examination was held at a meeting specifically called for this purpose. It was not so much for the opportunity it gave actors or actresses to prove themselves qualified to join the family of Yiddish theater, but more as a formality. This practice found very little favor in public opinion and was sharply criticized in the Yiddish press. Young performers grew old before they were considered worthy enough to possess the coveted little membership card. There were veteran members known to be categorical no voters; always afraid their roles would be usurped by newcomers.

If anyone had told me back in those early days that I would someday be elected president of the Hebrew Actors' Union—for several terms at that—I'd say they were plumb crazy, or simply poking fun at a greenhorn.

Isidore Lillien, the manager of the Lyric Theater, did not grab me up as my sister hoped he would. He explained to her that the Yiddish theater in America was already knee-deep in actors.

Mulling this over in her mind, my sister thought: where is it written that my brother must be an actor? Aren't there fine young men in America making a living at trades other than acting? So, Chaimke will have no problem.

One fine morning, the bureau of the HIAS in Kovno informed me that they had received affidavits, plus $200 for my second class passage to New York. The money was to be used to purchase my steamship ticket and other incidentals through HIAS, not given me as cash on hand.

I then went to the Holland-American Line for my steamship ticket, second class, on the S.S. Rotterdam. After the additional purchase of my train fare— third class—Kovno-Berlin to Rotterdam, my sister's $200 were finished. The only person I bade goodbye was the kind director of the HIAS, who helped me get a visa from the American consulate. As for my remaining colleagues, friends and admirers, my departure had to be kept secret.

My worldly possessions consisted of one large straw-woven hamper and a battered old valise. In these I packed a few worn shirts, underwear, a student's cap and jacket for the role of Schneierson in *Hard to be a Jew* by Shalom Alei-chem; a Russian rubashka (blouse), a pair of boots, a shiny-visored cap, an old cut-away, a Prince-Albert with striped pants and an old-fashioned full-dress. This completed my wardrobe. How was I to know that these treasures could also be found in America? Hadn't I struggled and gone hungry enough in order to acquire this stage wardrobe at the Kovno flea market?

I also packed a collection of printed Yiddish plays and music by various composers and writers; several published volumes by Sholom Aleichem and by Peretz, whose monologues I had presented at my personal appearances in Lithuania. A young actor armed with such a repertoire is bound to be snapped up in America, I was sure. Again, how was I to know that all this printed material I was lugging could be gotten at the Hebrew Publishing Com-pany, or Biderman's bookstore on Second Avenue in New York, for a quarter a piece?

With no money to hire a porter, I hoisted one load on my shoulder and gripped the other in my hand. Several hours later I was on the train to Berlin. I sat on tenterhooks, fearful lest it had leaked out that I was skipping the coun-try and they'd be waiting to nab me at the Lithuanian-German border, where I could be yanked off the train. But, on we sped and were soon across the border into Germany. I drew my first breath of relief.

I wasn't worried about my finances. In Rotterdam, I knew I'd be entitled to food and lodging in the company hotel, which was covered by my steamship ticket, until sailing time. So, money or no money, I consoled myself, I'll man-age to get along until I reach Rotterdam. As if going hungry was anything new to me. The important thing was that I was on my way to America!

My supply of food lasted only until I reached Berlin. At the station, I was met by a German representative of the American HIAS. He was very kind and took me to their shelter for immigrants in transit, where I was given an ample meal and a place to sleep overnight. Early next morning, baggage and all, I was taken to the train bound for Rotterdam. The HIAS representative pointed out that my straw hamper and valise were much too big to take into the com-partment. On German trains they were very strict about excess baggage. It was only a matter of luck, he said, that I'd gotten away with it up to Berlin. Yet how could I tell the man that I didn't have as much as a broken penny to pay the charge for baggage!

At any rate, he helped me lift my hamper onto the rack and stowed my valise underneath a bench. I sat down among the other passengers and a few moments later was on my way.

A conductor came around to collect our tickets. Spotting my hamper on the rack, he had a fit. An outrage! he spluttered. Whose monstrosity is this? It must go into the baggage car immediately! He threatened to take me to task about it as soon as we reached the border. By a miracle he failed to notice my oversized valise under the bench. When the conductor left, scared out of my wits, I made my way through the cars to look for a possible hole in the wall, where I could stash my hamper.

In one of the cars I came across two Polish Jews traveling to Paris. Confiding my problem, I asked if they wouldn't mind keeping an eye on it until after we had crossed the border. They agreed. So I lugged it into their section, wedged it between the benches and went back to my seat.

One of the passengers in the compartment, a woman traveling with two children, was on her way to join her husband in America. Watching them eat sharpened my hunger, but I looked away, affecting indifference. Would I stoop to beg? Not if I starved! When the mother again fed her hungry youngsters, she came up with an odd-shaped yellow kind of edible, which the children seemed to relish. I had never before seen this strange-looking item. Whether out of courtesy, or whether the woman sensed that my furtive glances at the children indicated more than ordinary curiosity, she asked, "Would you, perhaps, like to have one of these bananas?"

Would I! I thanked her and took the fruit. Luckily, I saw the children peel theirs first, or I would have devoured the banana, skin and all.

Before the train reached the border of Holland, the conductor was back with an inspector in tow. He looked at the rack…looked at me…my hamper was gone…vanished!

"Wo ist die Bagage? Es war doch oben, nicht wahr?" he asked, puzzled.

"Ja, es war oben," I replied. "Now it is gone, see? You wanted money. Well, I have no money. So I threw my baggage out the window!"

The inspector's eyes bulged. Somehow his "yekke" brain (slow-witted) could not absorb such a thing. My fellow passengers, choking with restrained mirth, bore witness to the fact that I did indeed throw my hamper out the window.

"Schade, schade." (too bad…what a waste) the inspector kept mumbling. "Why did you throw it out? You must be mad!"

Sheepishly, he and the conductor backed out of the compartment, whereupon the passengers burst into hilarious laughter.

Rotterdam, Holland

The next morning I arrived in Rotterdam. Retrieving my valise from its hiding place and collecting my hamper, which stood securely in the next car, I dragged myself to the depot to inquire how to get to the hotel of the Holland-

American Line—on foot. On foot?! Was I crazy or something? It would take hours walking. Go tell them that I didn't even have the fare for a trolley. Jotting down the necessary directions I set out with my cumbersome baggage toward the canal, as instructed.

It was May, the weather was fine, the warmth of spring was in the air. I plodded along the main streets of Rotterdam on my way to the wharf, sweating like a beaver and stopping from time to time to catch my breath. After an interminable trek, I found myself at the canal—and here, I realized, was the end of the road for me—unless I swam across. Lights blinking on the other side of the water spelled out the name of the hotel where I was supposed to stay. Ferries and rowboats coursed back and forth, to and from the hotels on the opposite bank. But where was I to get the precious coin for the ferry to carry me across? I slumped on my hamper, the valise by my side, as people went by staring at me. Dusk was falling, soon to slip into night and there I sat, dejected and humiliated enough to die.

Suddenly, from a distance, I heard youthful laughter; boys chattering, girls giggling and—wonder upon wonder—they were babbling in Russian! Russian … in Holland? These young people, I thought, must surely be angels from heaven! Stopping one of the group as they came along, I asked, "Would you please be kind enough to direct me to the hotel of the Holland-American Line?"

"Sure, it's right over there," the young man replied, pointing across the canal. "We're all going that way, so come along with us." Taking hold of my hamper, he helped me onto the ferry. I don't know whether the boatman lost count of the number of passengers as we all piled in together, or whether one of the chaps paid for the whole group, but there I was, crossing the canal and thanking God for coming to my aid.

I later learned that these were Jewish students who had, for one reason or another, been barred from emigrating to America. Some because of eye trouble and some because of quota restrictions. There were hundreds of such immigrants in Rotterdam at the time, who found themselves stuck, neither here nor there. The younger ones managed to go on with their studies, biding their time until an opportunity presented itself whereby they could make their way to the United States, or some other country. In addition to aid from the HIAS, they were being sustained by Rotterdam's Jewish community.

The students brought me to the hotel and helped me into the lobby. What happened to me after that, I don't know. When I came to, people were fussing over me, rubbing my temples, my wrists, holding spirits to my nose, until a doctor appeared. Brushing the people aside, he quickly made his diagnosis.

"In heaven's name," he exclaimed, "don't crowd him. Don't you people realize the young man has fainted from exhaustion and hunger?!"

Next morning, fully recovered, I became acquainted at breakfast with the other residents of the hotel—the "family of the homeless." They had already heard about me—an actor on his way to America. The young people told me that, due to a storm at sea, my ship, the Rotterdam, would be late putting in to port and this would delay my departure by six or seven days. This did not strike me as an inconvenience. After all, I was getting regular meals, had a room to myself and the young people, more or less my age, were making it so pleasant. In fact, three of them, Rebecca, Boris and Max, immediately attached themselves to me. What I did miss, however, was having a few cents in my pocket. It was too embarrassing to confess to anyone that I was penniless. How long could I go on shnoring cigarettes, especially when I knew my newfound friends were, themselves, poor? Besides that, how could one sit around the hotel day in, day out, with the beautiful city of Rotterdam beckoning so invitingly from across the canal?

An idea struck me. I took a stroll to the bureau of the Holland-American Line located in the harbor near the hotel. Taking heart, I explained my circumstances to the office director and begged him to take back my porthole window, sell me a cabin without one, and give me the difference in cash. The director's first reaction was to talk at such an odd request. A transaction like this, he would have me know, was highly irregular. Nonetheless, he agreed to make an exception in my case. Exchanging my cabin for one without a porthole, he counted out the equivalent of five dollars in Dutch currency. I had the feeling that he had heard about me, the fellow who fainted from hunger upon his arrival at the hotel, or he would never have gone along with such a trivial business as refunding a porthole, of all things.

I left the office feeling like a Rothschild. The first thing I did was to buy a pack of Murad cigarettes. Then, getting on the ferry, I headed straight for the city proper, across the canal.

Rotterdam was steeped in masses of breathtaking, full-blown tulips, looking like myriads of red and yellow goblets. I spent a whole day meandering around town, unable to get my fill of all the lovely sights around me. Toward evening, back at the hotel I found my friends greatly concerned about my absence. They feared I'd gotten lost. When I related the saga of my porthole transaction, they had a good laugh and thought it an ingenious idea.

After supper we got together to gab and dance to the music of several scratchy records. This was the only recreation for these refugees who stagnated here, wondering and waiting to reach some permanent haven. The last few years had indeed been a sad way of life for them.

For an actor enjoying the relaxation of a social get-together with friends outside his profession, it is a familiar experience to have someone come up with, "Hey, we have an actor in our midst. So how about a song, or a recitation, eh? A little entertainment. Come on, give us a song!"

Such requests always rubbed me the wrong way. And I never complied— never throughout the years of my long career. This particular evening was no exception. But my friend Rebecca, sensing my negative reaction, got me out of the situation very adroitly.

"Listen, folks," she quieted their clamoring, "If we are so eager to hear Herr Yablokoff, why don't we arrange a regular concert with tickets and everything, as befits a professional artist?"

Her suggestion, I understood, had a two-fold motive. She was aware of my financial status. A concert, aside from affording me artistic gratification, she figured, could also net me a few dollars earned with dignity.

Rebecca's proposal was received with tremendous enthusiasm, and I too, was highly pleased with the idea. The first thing decided on—in order to save expenses—was to hold the concert in the large hall of the hotel. Then a problem arose: where could we get a piano? The hotel possessed no such thing. To hire a piano from the city and have it carted across the canal would be too costly. My friends suggested that I devise a program of monologues, and choose songs which the audience could sing along. In this way the problem would be solved and nobody, they assured me, would demand their money back.

Still, in scouting around for a piano, I learned that, staying in a hotel of the Cunard Line along the same bank was a Russian couple, a husband-and-wife team, both singers. They too, it seemed, had sought to arrange a concert in our hotel, but for the lack of a piano—without which they could not perform—they had to forego the plan.

I was instantly intrigued. Russians, or whatever, what difference did it make, they were fellow performers. Hiring a small boat to skim along the bank, I found their hotel. I inquired after the Russian singers and in a few minutes, a very personable, well-built man with a crop of reddish blond hair—a typical Russian, came up and introduced himself.

"I am Misha Koltunoff, and this is my wife, Rita." In a Slavic-accented Yiddish, he related that following the revolution in Russia, he and his wife had left for Romania and had been roaming ever since. They, too, were waiting to emigrate to the United States.

I found them to be a most pleasant couple and promptly offered them a proposition: in the event I managed to locate a piano, they could appear with me at my concert and we could divide the profit in three equal shares. Delighted, they immediately accepted my offer. What's more, they said they knew of a pianist who could accompany us—a Russian refugee, himself.

When I informed the concert committee about the two artists, they were inspired anew in their efforts to dig up a piano.

The S.S. Rotterdam finally arrived just as all the hotels lining the canal were abustle over our concert. It was an exciting event in the drab and monotonous existence of these rootless people. When the tickets were so eagerly snapped up, our committee regretted not having hired a larger hall. The committee ventured to ask the captain of the Rotterdam if he could possibly lend us a piano from his ship. The captain, a good-natured, lusty old mariner, said he could—and would! A few hours later, sure enough, a detail of brawny seamen, supporting an upright piano on their shoulders, came along and deposited it in our "concert hall." I sent word at once to my colleagues, the Koltunoffs: we're in luck! We have a piano!

The concert went off beautifully, a huge success morally and financially. The hall was packed beyond capacity, not only with the "homeless," but with Jewish residents from the city of Rotterdam, who came at the last minute in little boats, determined to be admitted if only as standees.

The seats of honor down front were reserved for the captain and his officers. They understood not a word, of course, but their applause was loud and enthusiastic. The Koltunoffs scored a great success with operatic arias sung in Russian and duets from Yiddish operettas. I read *The Magician* by I.L. Peretz; recited a humoresque, by Tunkeler; did a scene in makeup and costume from *Menachem Mendel,* by Sholem Aleichem and concluded with a collection of folk songs and popular theater numbers.

We three concertists came away with the equivalent of forty-three American dollars apiece. Considering the nominal price of admission, this sum represented a fortune. Everyone begged us to give another concert—in the city this time. But my ship was scheduled to sail in two days.

With my bankroll, I hurried off first thing next morning to the shipping bureau to repurchase my porthole, and travel to America like a real "star."

"Never mind about your porthole, Herr Yablokoff," the secretary smiled at me, and to my surprise went on to say, "You've been assigned a private cabin on A-deck, not only with a porthole, but a few extra conveniences. It's a present from the skipper for the pleasure you afforded us at your concert last evening." I was so moved by this gesture from the hearty old Dutch captain, it left me speechless. Overjoyed with my success I couldn't help thinking, maybe this is the beginning of my "seven good years..."

In the morning, bright and early, I dressed, patted my flowing black Windsor tie in place, surveyed myself in the mirror and concluded that—yes, indeed, I looked the picture of a genuine professional actor.

I boarded the S.S. Rotterdam with the warmest wishes from the entire immigrant community. All my friends came to see me off. My second-class cabin really made me feel like a celebrity.

On our third day out we ran into a squall that tossed the ship about like a toy. All the passengers were laid low in their berths, grappling with seasickness. At the beginning of the voyage, I wasn't feeling any too well, myself. I had never eaten so much food in my life. But the captain gave me good advice: "Get up on deck and walk!" And that's what I did. I took turns around the deck, back and forth from stem to stern. The huge swells rocked the ship, but I stuck to my guns and finally got my sea legs. I was one of the very few who showed up for my meals. What will be, will be, I decided. In the meantime, I told myself, as long as there is food on the table, dig in and eat while you can.

At long last, on the thirteenth day, our ship nosed her way into quarantine, a distance from the New York harbor. And there, detained because of the strict new quota laws, lay at anchor an armada of vessels from every port of the globe. Squeezing her way in among this backlog of ships, the Rotterdam also put down anchor. After three days in quarantine, along came some tug-boats to pilot us into a berth at the New York pier. As these little boats nudged us past the Statue of Liberty with her torch held high, I raised my eyes to this mighty symbol of freedom and refuge for the forlorn and persecuted of the world, and murmured a fervent prayer that she take under her wing still another homeless wanderer—me!

Legally qualified passengers were given immediate clearance to land. Those with undetermined status were transferred to Ellis Island, where their fate would be resolved.

Who Am I?

I was filled with fearful apprehension at the prospect of the American examination of papers. European inspections were something I'd become accustomed to. I had learned to concoct excuses and ruses and to "grease a paw" when necessary, so that most of the time I managed to squirm out of a tight spot. Having no experience with American inspectors, the thought of their examination made me shake. This was not Europe—this was America! To a European, the urgency of being armed with identification papers, documents, or passports is as vital as life itself.

Now, as I stood on the deck of the ship waiting to be called, I was reminded of a tragicomic episode that took place on a train traveling with Streitman's troupe from Schavel to Ponievezh. Before the trip I tried desperately to obtain a temporary identification paper with a residence permit in Lithuania, but without success. Yet it was imperative that I go along with the company. We finally came up with a plan. They had me lie down on one of the benches in our train compartment; my colleagues dotted my face with red spots of rouge, applied a wet cloth to my forehead, covered me up to my chin with several coats—and waited for inspection.

When the Lithuanian gendarmes came into our section, I lay motionless, staring into space and feverishly muttering, while our actresses went into weeping scenes. The actors wrung their hands and the children, who were dragged along wherever their actor parents went, added their own tearful whimpering.

Asked, "What's the matter with this fellow!" our company manager, Moishele Romanovsky, dramatically explained, "Typhus! Spotted fever! We're taking him to Ponievezh, to the Jewish Hospital. He'll probably not even make it. He's a goner. Typhus, you know!" With the speed of jack rabbits, the gendarmes took off. We held our sides laughing all the way to Ponievezh!

Thus, throughout my four years of knocking about in Lithuania, I struggled without a proper document. Every few weeks I managed to obtain a limited extension of a paper stating my name, age, occupation and place of birth.

This type of temporary paper was generally signed and stamped by some small town vodka-drenched police chief—for a substantial fee, of course.

Standing at the ship's railing, awaiting judgment day, I watched the cranes swinging steamer trunks and crates onto the dock. Deck hands were hauling the baggage of first class passengers, a few diplomats and American citizens, who of course were given prompt clearance to land. The pier below was teeming with people waiting to welcome the arrivals. The tumult was deafening.

A woman, holding a bouquet of flowers, was straining her voice to be heard above the din. "Chaim! Chaimke!" she shouted. My heart skipped a beat. Could this possibly be my sister, Mariashka? I didn't recognize her. I was still a small boy when she left for America.

"Mariashka?!" I called back.

"Chaim?!" the woman repeated, to make sure.

"Yes, yes, it's me, Chaim!" I yelled above the hubbub, certain now that it was my sister. And the man beside her, I guessed, was my brother-in-law, Henry. The elderly couple with them was surely my Aunt Sarah—my mother's sister—and her husband, Uncle Israel Mankofsky. And now we were all excitedly waving and shouting to each other—our first greeting in America!

A heavy weight was lifted from my heart. Here they were, to welcome me. At last there will be an end to my loneliness, to my wandering. They have come to welcome me with flowers.

A sailor came up and told me to report to the immigration inspector. I followed him and after waiting my turn on line, I handed over my papers.

"What is your occupation?" one of them asked, in English. From the blank look on my face he realized that I did not understand the language.

"Parla Italiano?" ventured another inspector. Getting no answer to this either, another fellow in the group smilingly asked, "Ir farshteyt Yiddish?" This promptly put me at ease.

"Yes, yes" I nodded, "ich bin a Yid." (I am a Jew.)

"Looking at you I'd have sworn you were an Italian," the Jewish interpreter chuckled. "The inspectors want to know your occupation."

"I am an actor...a Yiddish actor."

"How old are you?"

"Twenty, going on twenty-one."

"How much money do you have?"

"Eighteen dollars."

"Eighteen dollars? A real fortune!" When he translated this for the board of inspectors, they roared with laughter.

"In which theater will you perform?"

"I don't know yet."

"Do you have a contract with some theater in New York?"

"Not yet. But I'm sure to get one."

"What makes you so sure?" the interpreter asked, with more sobriety.

"My colleagues in America wrote me that the Yiddish theater in America needs young actors."

In a cold, impersonal tone, one of the inspectors held a speech in English for my benefit. Although I had no knowledge of the language, I got the message. It told me that a darkening cloud was gathering over my head. The interpreter translated his words for me: "Even if your ship had arrived a day earlier, before the new immigration laws became effective, I doubt very much that it would have helped your chances. You have no theater contract, you only have eighteen dollars, and as for your sister, or your aunt? Well, they are not considered relatives close enough by blood to alter your status. The new quota laws have only made your situation worse. You will have to be sent back to Europe.

"Sent back?! But where? I have no place to go!"

"I am very sorry. It is not up to us. It is the law. You're not the only one. Thousands of people from other ships will have to go back." The interpreter returned my posters, my pictures and reviews I'd spread before them as proof that I was an actor. The paper with my visa they set aside and this indicated the end of my interview.

My first impulse was to hurry back on deck to let my sister know that I was to be sent back. I got only as far as the door, when a sailor barred the way.

"Can't I see my sister?" I pleaded with the Yiddish translator. "She's waiting down on the pier."

"No. Just sit down over there and wait," he said, waving me to a corner of the room where others in the same predicament were seated. Completely benumbed, I sat down among them.

Hours later, we were instructed to take only our hand baggage and come along. The heavier pieces of luggage would be brought to us in due time. Led out on deck, my eyes desperately swept the pier to find my sister, but in vain. She had probably been notified of the crushing result of my interview and, brokenhearted, had gone home with her flowers, but without her brother.

We were led down a rope-ladder into a motor launch. The rest of our baggage was already there. Chugging past the Statue of Liberty, her burning torch now aglow in the harbor, we were taken to Ellis Island—the "Isle of Tears."

28

Ellis Island

E llis Island served as the main landing place for the sixteen million immigrants to the United States from 1891 to 1954. It was the clearinghouse where inspectors decided who could enter the country. The deportation of undesirables was also expedited via Ellis Island.

Jews nicknamed it the "Isle of Tears" for the rivers of bitter tears shed there by countless immigrants. The island, also called Castle Garden, was referred to by Jews as Kessel Gortn. This too, seemed aptly named. Kessel, meaning kettle in Yiddish, denoted the "kettle in the garden" that constantly seethed with human emotions, trials and tribulations.

When our launch deposited us on Ellis Island, the congestion was already so great there was hardly any room. Thousands of immigrants from numerous other ships were being detained there; men, women and children, in a conglomeration of types, races, and color, with bizarre variations of dress, had to orient themselves in any space they could find—even along the corridors. The lucky ones, the women with suckling infants, were assigned the narrow, double-decker bunks that lined the long, barracks-like lofts. Men had to bed down as best they could—on their bundles, a chair, or simply on the floor.

What struck me as ironic were the tall prison-like windows. Why the iron bars? Could anyone escape from this island except to jump into the river? I later learned that the bars were indeed a precaution. Some immigrants, on learning that they were to be deported, had in fact thrown themselves into the river. Others, detained for interminable periods, had become so despondent, they sought all sorts of measures to do away with themselves.

The noise, the tumult, the loud and incessant babbling of so many different tongues and dialects were bewildering, and the monotony made life intolerable. Men, sitting on the floor, played endless games of cards or dice; women, squatting on their bundles, exchanged experiences of life back in the old country, intermittently yelling at the children, who kept chasing through the halls like wild colts, screaming loud enough to wake up the dead.

* * *

By the time our transport reached the island it was past the supper hour. Some among us, more courageous, asked the guards, "When do we eat?" and were told, "Tomorrow morning. Breakfast at seven!"

Finding a spot in one of the corridors, I put down my baggage. Sitting on my hamper with a book propped on my knees, I began to pour out my heart in a letter to my sister and brother-in-law, imploring them to rescue me from this hell.

Several men squatted nearby. As long-time detainees, they were up on all the rules. They tried to convince me that it was useless for me to write, because my letter would never be mailed. However, I had already spotted a mailbox on the premises and thought, what would it be doing there if letters were never sent out? Nevertheless, since I was so determined, they were kind enough to let me have a few stamps.

About nine o'clock in the evening, it was lights out. Except for a single bulb left burning at the end of the hall, we remained in darkness. After twisting and turning from one position to another against my hamper, I decided to spread my coat on the floor and stretch out. And this was how I spent my first night in America.

* * *

Every new arrival was given a printed sheet of instructions. These were printed in several languages. Through a sort of German jargon with Yiddish letters, I read that, for Jews who preferred kosher food, there were specially prepared menus. One had only to register in advance as being strictly kosher. I was cheered somewhat by this information. It would, at least, throw me together with Jewish people, with whom I could communicate. I immediately applied for the table that served kosher food—strictly kosher.

We were treated to Branfman's salami three times a day. Later, it was learned that this same "kosher" delicatessen could just as well have been had at the nonkosher table. Still, it was more pleasant to sit among my fellow Jews.

New transports of immigrants from the steadily arriving ships were brought to Ellis Island almost daily. It was a good thing we were regularly given baths of disinfection, or we'd all be louse-infested. These baths were strictly enforced. The guards explained almost apologetically that this chaos was due to the new immigration laws and that they were simply not prepared to handle such an unprecedented number of people. We would therefore have to bear with it and suffer awhile until our fate would be resolved.

I still hoped for a letter from my sister—an answer to those I'd been sending her. Yet, there were none. I asked some of the Jews whether it was possible to have someone from the outside deliver a written message. I would even pay that someone five dollars. They only laughed at me.

"This is America!" I was made to understand. "You can't get away with such monkey business. No one from the outside is allowed near this place. Not even to pay a visit. The only ones who do come here once a week on Sunday are a priest, a reverend and a rabbi.

I had written a letter to my actor friend, Reuben Wendorff, but didn't have his New York address. If only I could get someone to take my letter to the Cafe Royale—famous even in Europe as the gathering place for Yiddish actors, writers and others connected in the field—I was sure Wendorff would get it. But how? And with whom?

Sunday morning, when the Jewish immigrants gathered for religious services, I joined them. After leading us through several prayers, the young, beardless rabbi held a sermon on Yiddishkeit, on tolerance, brotherly love, American democracy, freedom and justice. Several long-suffering individuals on Ellis Island, finding it difficult to contain themselves, interrupted the rabbi in the middle of his discourse and put questions to him.

"Rabbi, are you telling us about freedom and tolerance? Better tell us, if you will, how long are we going to be tortured in this prison?"

"You talk about brotherly love? About Yiddishkeit?" another interjected. "Tell us, please, what are the Jews in New York doing in our behalf—supplying us with kosher wurst?"

"Is this American justice?"

"Does American freedom mean that innocent people should be locked up like jungle beasts in a cage?"

Moved by these complaints, the rabbi immediately changed the text of his sermon. In simple, down-to-earth language, he spoke heart to heart with us. The immigration laws, he explained, were not directed solely at Jews as were decrees in the countries from which we had come. It was a law made for everyone alike. And American Jewry were indeed interested in helping us. "Representatives from the HIAS and other Jewish Aid Societies will even place bonds for you, should it become necessary."

After these heartening words, even the cheeky ones, whose inner woes had spoken out, apologized to the rabbi and warmly applauded him.

Managing to corner the rabbi, I told him of my plight and implored him to take my letter to the Cafe Royale on Second Avenue.

"No, no! It is against the law. I dare not undertake such a thing!"

"But, Rabbi," I beseeched him, "this is a matter of pikuach nefesh (saving a life). I can only tell you that my last recourse is the river." Looking cautiously about him, the good rabbi relented and took the letter I'd written to Wendorff.

There is much truth in the proverb: "A Jewish heart is beyond appraisal." By his deed, the rabbi earned his olam Haba (share in the world to come).

My First Audition

The days and nights dragged by. I neither saw, nor heard from anyone. I kept writing to my sister, to my aunt, and dropped my letters in the mailbox, thinking maybe, maybe the good Lord will yet perform a miracle.

One morning, a guard showed up with an order for me to follow him. He advised me to take along my baggage as I would not be coming back to this place again.

This is it! flashed through my mind. I'm being sent back. I dragged after the guard like one being led to the electric chair. I knew about the electric chair from a play called *Capital Punishment* by Moshe Shorr, which I'd played in Kovno with a guest star from America.

I was led into a huge auditorium. Seated on a large platform, as in a court, were three elderly men in long black robes. On either side sat secretaries and interpreters—men and women. The auditorium was packed with other immigrants who had been summoned for a hearing. Also present were city administration guests and newspaper people.

The Jewish interpreter administered the oath and I swore to tell the truth. He then explained that my case would now be heard by the board of inquiry.

"Don't be nervous, you're an actor, you say, so just answer the questions calmly and to the point. Only think before you answer. You understand me?" he emphasized. I realized that he was trying to warn me to be on the alert with my answers. As long as he was speaking Yiddish and I understood the questions, I would certainly tell the truth. I had nothing to hide.

The following is part of a stenographic report of the board of inquiry hearing on Ellis Island, June 12, 1924, in the case of Chaim Yablonik, and can be found in the files of the Immigration and Naturalization Department:

"Name and surname?"

"Chaim Yablonik."

"Place of birth?"

"Grodno, Russia…now Poland."

"Your occupation?"

"I am an actor. A Yiddish actor."

"Who is Yablokoff?"

"I am Yablokoff. It is my stage name."

"Are you sure?"

"I am sure."

"Maybe you are Yablonik and 'Yablokoff the actor' is really someone else?"

"I am the actor, Yablokoff. Yablonik is my family name."

"How long have you been on the stage?"

"Professionally, four years."

"How old are you?"

"Twenty-one. That is, I will be twenty-one on the eleventh of August."

"In what type of plays do you perform?"

(I listed a number of plays I had taken part in.)

"How much did you earn a week?"

"We played on a cooperative basis. I earned…well, it all depended…"

One of the judges leaned toward his two other colleagues and remarked something. From their reactions, his remark must have been something like: "If this young squirt is a professional actor, then I'm a shoemaker!"

From here on, all my replies were treated with derision. Their shrugs and head-shakings made it clear that they didn't believe a word I said.

"At the age of almost twenty-one you claim to be an established actor? Acting professionally for four years? When did you start—in the cradle?"

Thanks to the calm, tactful manner of the translator, I kept up my courage. "In 1916, I began performing in a children's group in Grodno. And since 1920 I have been a professional actor." With this, I presented my membership card of the United Yiddish Art Theater in Kovno.

"If you really are such a talent, how is it that you have not been imported to the United States on a contract?"

"I did have a chance to come on a contract, but the impresario's proposed salary was insufficient. I thought if I could possibly be seen in New York in my repertoire, I could earn much more."

I caught the hint of a smile on the interpreter's lips as he translated my answer, a sign that he approved. But the judges still shook their heads, as if my explanations were just so much drivel.

"How much do you expect to earn a week in the United States?"

"For a start, at least $150," I quoted at random. I had learned from the other immigrants that it was wise to quote a higher figure when questioned about earnings, since the country was not interested in encouraging the influx of cheap labor to compete with American workers.

"Why did you change your name to Yablokoff?"

"As a pseudonym—an accepted practice in the theater."

"You don't like the name, Yablonik?"

"I do...but..."

"Then why did you change it?"

"My father is a very pious man. He wasn't supposed to know that I'm an actor."

"You deceived your father? Then you're a liar!"

"No, no! It is the truth!"

"If you were capable of deceiving your father, why should we believe you?"

"I'm telling the truth."

"What languages do you speak?"

"Yiddish, Russian, some Polish and Hebrew."

"Hebrew? You mean Yiddish?"

Here, the interpreter stepped in to explain that except for the same characters in the alphabet, Yiddish and Hebrew were two completely different languages.

"How do you come to know Russian?"

"We were taught Russian as a second language at my Hebrew School."

"Are you a Bolshevik?"

"No!"

"It says here you have a sister in America. Will she be able to support you?"

"She will not need to support me. I've been supporting myself all of four years."

"How much money do you have?"

"About eighteen dollars."

This brought a burst of laughter in the auditorium. One of the judges threw his head back and roared.

"You expect to get along on eighteen dollars in New York? For how long?"

"I will seek employment in a theater. My colleagues who have come here will recommend me for a position in a Yiddish theater."

"Who are they?"

"Reuben Wendorff, Paul Burstein, Sholem Tanin and actors from the Vilna Troupe."

The interpreter explained that the Vilna Troupe was brought to America by the well-known Boris Thomashevsky and was at present performing in New York.

"Did you play with the Vilna Troupe?"

"No. I was in Lithuania. They were in Poland. But they know me."

The same questions were repeated over and over, and I stuck to my answers: I am both Yablonik and Yablokoff, the actor.

"If we permit you to enter the United States on a three-month visit, would you be satisfied?" According to the interpreter's tone as he translated this question, I felt sure there was a catch in it, and he was warning me not to fall into the trap. My answer was a decisive one.

"Honored gentlemen, please forgive me, but I cannot accept your generous offer. I can never go back—not now, nor in three months. I have no place to go. What good will it do me to stay here in this free land for three months, only to be flung back to...where?...to hell? To knock about alone, without as much as a proper passport? Gentlemen, this piece of paper I have is all there is to certify my identity. I paid for it with my earnings after months of toil. And it was valid only up to my departure from Lithuania. I want to build my future in free America, near my sister and her family. I will not be a burden to anyone. I am an actor, believe me. I beg of you, do not send me back. I will do my utmost to earn the privilege of becoming an American citizen. I will go to school to learn the English language. Please do not send me back!"

After a whispered conference, one of the judges addressed me directly. The interpreter translated: "We'd like you to prove that you really are an actor. Are you prepared to audition for us? To sing or recite something?"

"Yes!" I jumped at the proposal. "If you please, sirs, I will perform for you. I will sing, recite, whatever you wish me to do. I have my theater wardrobe in my hamper, and it won't take me long. If the honorable judges will permit me, I will get ready with makeup and costume."

Again the judges conferred with one another and came to a decision: "As it is practically noon, we will take an hour for lunch. This will also give you an opportunity to have lunch and prepare for your audition."

Eating, of course, was out of the question as far as I was concerned. I remained in the corridor to rummage for my music and makeup box.

I was alone in the hallway, except for some fellow in uniform, whom I took to be a guard instructed to keep an eye on me. Peering mysteriously up and down the hall, he soon came up to me and, in Yiddish, whispered, "Do you know Yankele Kirshenbaum?" This proved to be the last straw! Such out and out ridicule was more than I could take! With searing sarcasm, I answered, "Do I know a Yankele Kirshenbaum! I know many *more* important people than he!"

The guard gave me a peculiar look and took off down the hall. The chutzpa! Just because he is some officer with brass buttons, he thinks he can make fun of me? Why this stupid, meaningless question—do I know some Yan-ke-le Kirchenbaum! Does he take me for some idiot greenhorn to play jokes on? "You're going to America? Give my regards to my uncle, Yankele. Where does he live? Number one, New York." Ha, ha! This tired old joke I knew well enough from the American-Yiddish plays we did. What nerve!

Moments later, the guard was back. Sidling up to me, he again whispered in a mixture of Yiddish and English: "Excuse me, young man, don't be angry. I know you're nervous. To be in your boots...well, I wouldn't wish it on a dog. But you must control yourself, or you won't be doing yourself any good. No, sir! Yankele Kirshenbaum is a writer in the *Jewish Morning Journal*. He is doing all in his power to help you, understand? If it weren't for Yankele, do you think you would be called up today for a hearing with the Board of Inquiry? No, sir! Here, on Ellis Island, immigrants sit around and wait for months. Yankele is a friend of mine, a Galitzianer landsman, like me. He supplies me with free passes to the Yiddish theater. So why did you have to bark at me? Yankele is trying to help you, understand?"

Did I understand! I could have buried myself for embarrassment. With this blunder, thanks to my quick temper, I surely did bury myself.

"I didn't mean any disrespect," I apologized. "Yankele Kirshenbaum is certainly a great man. I meant to say that I know other important people. Forgive me. My nerves are on edge. I really don't know what I'm saying."

"Don't worry about it," he smiled. "You're still young, so you're hotheaded. You'll get older, you'll cool down all right. As I was saying, that Yankele—he's one terrific Galitzianer! He has shaken up all of New York on your behalf. So don't be arrogant, young fellow. Just go and belt out a couple of songs for the board, and good luck to you!" At the sound of footsteps, the guard took himself off.

Darn it, Chaim! I berated myself. Your tongue will be your ruination! Mama always said: "No one can do a person as much harm as he can do himself!"

Another guard came along and showed me into a small side-room off the auditorium. I began to put on makeup for the role of Lemach in *The Wild Man* by Jacob Gordin. If they want to be convinced that I am an actor, I decided, then I must present myself in an impressive, dramatic scene. I put on the idiot's wig, slipped into a torn, white shirt, removed my shoes...and I was ready.

My Jewish interpreter didn't recognize me when he came to tell me that the gentlemen of the board were waiting. In my bare feet, I padded after him into the auditorium. The number of people assembled exceeded even that of the morning's session. It had gotten around during the noon hour that some immigrant actor was giving a concert, so people came running from every corridor to witness this rare spectacle.

At the sight of my weird getup, one of the men on the board asked the interpreter what it was I was going to portray.

"An excerpt from *The Wild Man*, a play by Jacob Gordin," I supplied the answer.

"The role played by Jacob P. Adler?" the interpreter asked me, as he put stress on the famous name of Adler, for the benefit of the board.

"I have heard of Jacob P. Adler," I replied, "and I have read about this artist, but I have never seen him play."

Taking my place in the center of the auditorium between the raised platform of the board and the curious spectators, I threw my heart and soul into the highly tense and dramatic scene. At the end, a spontaneous applause burst from the voluntary audience—my fellow immigrants.

"What else do you do as an actor?" was the next question.

"I sing." At this, another burst of applause erupted, provoking a reprimand from one of the board, who reminded the crowd that they were on Ellis Island, not in a theater.

"Then sing something," he addressed me directly. The word sing, I understood.

"But in this makeup?" I appealed to the translator.

"It doesn't matter," he encouraged me, "go ahead and sing."

"Without a piano?"

"Without a piano. We're 'heymishe mentchen.'"

All I could do was to turn aside for a moment, snatch off my idiot wig, wipe away some of the character greasepaint with my shirttail, slip into my shoes, my jacket and step back into center. In a faltering voice I began the lullaby "Raisins and Almonds," sung by Absolom in Goldfaden's *Shulamith*...."In dem Bes Hamigdosh, in a vinkl cheyder" At this finish, the clapping echoed like thunder. I didn't wait to be coaxed and forthwith obliged with the popular, humorous folk song, "How does a King drink Tea?" The Jews among the crowd laughed delightedly at the funny lines. I read a monologue, "At the Photographer's" by Tunkeler. Here again, the Jewish immigrants roared with laughter.

"Do you know any Hebrew recitations?" the interpreter ventured on his own.

"Yes, I know 'Die Shkhitte Shtodt' (The City of Slaughter) by Chaim Nakhman Bialik."

The interpreter explained that what I was about to recite was a classic work by the greatest Yiddish poet. I caught the word poet, another similar word in Yiddish. I turned to face the board and began:

"Heavens above! Plead mercy for me...
Dead, is my heart,
No further hope..."

Into Bialik's immortal passages, I poured my own pain and loneliness, my own struggle to survive from earliest childhood through twenty-one years of my life.

"How much longer...?" I continued. "How much...?" My voice suddenly broke. Tears began to stream from my eyes. I couldn't go on.

A tense silence fell over the auditorium. After a pause, when the interpreter beckoned, I approached the Board of Inquiry. As the older of them reached over and pressed my hand, his words were translated for me: "Son, we are sorry that we had to put you through such an ordeal. It is the first time a procedure like this has been carried out on Ellis Island as far as I can remember. You have proved to us that you are an actor—a good actor. And so, young man, in lieu of flowers for your performance today, we are happy to present you with something which, we hope, will bring you a bright future. Here is your landing card for your permanent residence in the United States of America!"

The tumult that ensued in the auditorium was indescribable. A guard soon appeared and opened the door of an adjoining room and in came my sister, my brother-in-law and my aunt and uncle! We embraced, we kissed, we wept. They had all been waiting, locked in this room during my entire audition; held there, in case it became necessary to be called in as witnesses in my behalf.

As I hurriedly began tidying up and throwing my props back into my hamper, one of the guards handed me a bunch of papers—the letters I had deposited in the mailbox to my sister.

I picked up my valise, while my brother-in-law got a grip on my hamper and off we went to the tender that plied between Ellis Island and the harbor in downtown Manhattan. The shouts of good wishes and blessings from the remaining immigrants followed us from every direction. At the tender, I presented my litle red card to the guard in charge, and he allowed me to step into the boat like a real American.

Already seated there and apparently waiting for us was a rather stubby, rotund man, wearing a black, broad-brimmed fedora, a sturdy cane in his hand.

"Chaimke," said my sister, "this is the good-hearted gentleman who interceded for you, Mr. Kirshenbaum."

I gazed at this hearty man as he, in turn, took me in from head to toe over the rim of his spectacles. I was speechless with emotion.

"That's me," he smiled, "Yankele Kirchenbaum, the Galitzianer!"

Later, in the taxi, as we drove to Williamsburg, Brooklyn, my sister handed me a telegram. It had been sent to me at the address of the Holland-American Line in Rotterdam. As I had already sailed for New York, Rotterdam forwarded it to my sister's address in Brooklyn. The telegram read:

> We are sorry to notify you that, due to changes in the quota laws, your visa to America is null and void. We advise you not to board ship, for you will not, under any circumstances, be admitted to the United States.
>
> American Consul, Lithuania

We laughed through tears, overjoyed and relieved that I did not receive this telegram before embarking for New York. Arriving at my sister's apartment on Humboldt Street, her three youngsters, Sarah, Georgie and Harold gave their "green" uncle a royal welcome. Neighbors and Grodno landsleit kept dropping in, so that we talked half the night away.

I was greatly puzzled how my sister knew what was happening to me when she hadn't received the letters I'd sent. She explained that someone had personally delivered a letter of mine to the Cafe Royale, and that it had stirred up a whole rumpus because a Yiddish actor was being detained on Ellis Island! And he was in danger of being sent back! It took Yankele Kirshenbaum, who was not only the theater editor of the *Morning Journal*, but a reporter for the HIAS, to get things under way. "We must come to the aid of a young actor!" he stormed and thumped the floor of the Cafe Royale with his walking stick. "We need new faces on the Yiddish stage!"

At last, when my head touched the pillow on the snowy white bedding my sister prepared—the eiderdown pillows that mother had given her when she left for America as a bride—I sank into a peaceful sleep.

* * *

Early next morning, Henry went off to his job at the fur shop and Sarah was sent off to school. Georgie and Harold romped with their newly acquainted uncle, until my sister suggested that I take a little turn around the neighborhood and get the feel of being in America. The weather is so nice, she said, a lovely summer's day, so why don't I get some fresh air. It would do my good after my little "sojourn" on Ellis Island.

"Mary," I said, "I'd like nothing better than to go out and have a look around. I would sure love to see what America looks like. But how can I venture out

on the street without a document?" After my landing card was collected at
the little boat from the island, I was left with nothing but my expired paper
from Lithuania.

In vain were Mary's assurances. "Look, my dear brother," she said, "in America you don't need any documents. Here, it is strictly 'mind your own business.'
If you don't bother anybody, nobody will bother you. Take me, for instance.
It is twelve years that I am in America. I got married here, I brought three children into the world. So? Did anyone ask me for a document? Here, nobody
needs to register with the police. It's a free country!"

"Without a document," I insisted, "I am not going to budge from the house."
Realizing that she wasn't getting anywhere, my sister went to seek advice at
the neighborhood grocer's. She was told to take me to the Brooklyn district
court, where, for one dollar, they would issue me my first naturalization papers
and so, I would have a document.

The grocer, a sympathetic little man, understood the situation and was
kind enough to let his delivery boy take me down to the court house. My
sister offered me a few dollars, which I refused to take.

"I have my own money," I told her, "eighteen dollars. For my American
document I will pay with my own money."

The grocery boy took me via the elevated train to Borough Hall. In one
of the offices of this large building, he explained that I had arrived from Europe
only a day before, and because I was afraid to go out on the street without
a document, he had brought me here to get my first citizen papers. This produced such hilarity, such a commotion among the office staff, one would think
they'd been visited by a man from Mars. I had arrived only yesterday? And
I was already applying for my first paper? From the giggling and chattering
of the secretaries and typists, I could only make out the words, "Valentino...
Rudolph Valentino..."

One of them typed out an application blank, which I signed. I gave her
a one-dollar bill. She then led me to the judge's chamber. Reading from my
application that I was admitted to the United States only the day before, the
judge himself was impressed that here I was, the very next day, for my first
naturalization papers. Highly pleased, he swore me in and I left the Brooklyn
district court with a document as a future American citizen.

The same day, June 14, 1924, the following new item appeared in the
Jewish and American press:

Chaim Yablokoff, young Yiddish actor, auditions for the Board
of Inquiry on Ellis Island. In lieu of flowers for his performance,
he is granted residence in the United States.

29

A Sunday in Warsaw, 1960

The jangling of the telephone startled me awake. A voice cheerfully inquired, "Yablokoff? Did I wake you?"

"No, no," I replied. What else could I say? "Who is it?" I asked.

"Goldfinger. I heard you were back in Warsaw. How come? I was sure you'd be in Grodno by now. What happened?" I gave him a rundown on my experience at the border.

"It's Sunday. You won't be able to accomplish anything anyway, so let's meet and take a stroll around town."

"Good idea," I said, and we agreed to meet at the Cultural Organization of Polish Jews, which was located near the hotel. I had met Goldfinger in Paris when he came there on a visit from Poland—a very pleasant fellow.

The telephone rang again.

"Pan Yablokoff?"

"Avrom Morevsky!" I exclaimed, recognizing his voice at once.

"Shalom! What happened? Did the Russians shut the door in your face?" he chortled huskily. "Maybe it's for the good. Anyway listen, my friend, my wife and I would very much like to have you join us for dinner this afternoon. You can probably have a fancier meal at your Grand Hotel, but here at home, we'll have a better chance to gab about theater. I am very eager to hear all that's going on in the world—in our theater world, that is. What do you say, all right?"

He used the phrase all right to prove he still remembers a bit of English, having spent some time in England and in the United States. I gladly accepted Morevsky's invitation for dinner. I was preparing to get dressed, when again the telephone. It seemed that all of Warsaw knew by now that I was turned back from the border on my way to Grodno.

"Mister Yablokoff? Bardini speaking. Alexander Bardini. Remember me?"

"Bardini! Of course I remember you," I said, surprised. "How are you? And your wife and children? Well, well, I've already read that you are standing Warsaw on its ear with your production of the opera *Boris Godunov*! You can't get tickets, I hear—sold out months in advance!"

"It all depends," Bardini chuckled. "For you, Mister Yablokoff, I can still organize a ticket." (The word organize had become popular in the DP camps where I met Bardini after the war.)

"In fact," he continued, "how about this very evening? I would like to get your opinion of my production."

I had become acquainted with the well-known regisseur Bardini back in 1947, during my tour of the camps. He was one of the displaced persons in Germany. Working with a Yiddish theatrical group, Bardini produced *Shlomo Molkhu*, a play by A. Glantz-Leyeles, which was quite a success in Munich and other DP camps in Germany. After returning to Warsaw, Bardinin soon became acknowledged as one of the most outstanding stage and film directors in Poland.

* * *

I finally got dressed. What with invitations for sightseeing, dinner and the opera, the day promised to be a pleasant one after all. I looked forward to it as an antidote to my bitter disappointment at having failed to get into my hometown, Grodno.

The nerve center of Jewish life in Poland was the Cultural Organization of Polish Jews in Warsaw. In the headquarters' entrance hall one could find, stacked on a long table, Yiddish books, periodicals, journals, the daily *Folks-Shtimme*, and heaps of other Yiddish newspapers from various parts of the world, including some from the United States. The bookseller, an elderly Jew, affected the air of commanding an extraordinary cultural mission.

I found Goldfinger already there, waiting for me. We boarded a trolley and set out to observe the "new" Warsaw. Scanning the streets as we moved along, my heart wept. No longer was there a trace that these very streets once pulsated with a world of Polish Jewry. Farther on we alighted at the vast wasteland, the former site of the historic Warsaw Ghetto—now nothing but desolation. Nothing remains here but the Paviak Prison, with its own tragic chapter in the log of Jewish blood and tears.

With the feeling that I was treading on graves, I approached the imposing monument erected in hallowed memory of the brave martyrs of the Warsaw Ghetto Uprising. Its life-sized figures, carved of stone and bronze, created by the artist Nathan Rapoport, seemed completely forlorn against the bleak and awesome background of Warsaw's "Valley of Tears." I stood a long time gazing at it, motionless.

"What is your impression of this monument?" my companion's words broke in on my benumbed senses. "Truly a work of art, isn't it?" he proudly remarked.

"Yes, a work of art," I conceded. "Throughout my decades of roaming the globe, I have seen countless monuments—masterpieces of granite and marble, erected in memory of outstanding personalities for their achievements. These monuments, of course, are a source of great pride to their countries. But, this monument, erected in holy memory of the Warsaw Ghetto Uprising, is not only a memorial for the martyrs who perished here, nor should it be a memorial for Warsaw alone. It is a testimonial which ought to have the power to cry out to the entire world: 'Remember!' Remember well the epoch of horror when Germany's Ehrenvolk turned into bloodthirsty savages! Remember and never forget, nor forgive the marauders who annihilated European Jewry!

"Tell me, my friend," I said, "how long do you suppose it will be before this waste-area of the Warsaw Ghetto will be built up? How long will this monument be tolerated? For the present, the remaining Jews gather here once a year in a parade. The band strikes up 'Jeszcze Polska,' followed by fiery speeches; the crowd sings, 'Zog nisht keinmul.' (Never say the road you travel is the last), and that's it!

"This monument, I fear, will eventually acquire the same facade as hundreds of other famous statues around the world, what with homeless pigeons coming to roost and desecrate them. The only befitting monument on this bloodied soil of the Warsaw Ghetto should have been the area's devastation itself.

"Perhaps, if the Polish government had been approached in the immediate aftermath of the Holocaust—particularly in light of their benign attitude toward the surviving Jews—they might have been persuaded to issue a decree that the entire area be fenced off with a recreated replica of the original ghetto wall, and have this wall inscribed at the entrance gate, in every language known to man: **This Waste Area is the Everlasting Monument to the Heroes of the Warsaw Ghetto Uprising! A Memorial to the Six Million Jewish Martyrs Massacred by the Nazis.**"

My friend and I turned to the Gensher Cemetery, the only one left undisturbed in Warsaw. Among the tilted headstones and neglected graves, one monument stood out—that of the inventor of Esperanto, Dr. Ludwig Zamenhoff, born in Bialystok.

A little further on, with heads bowed, we stood at the Ohel-Peretz, the tomb in which lie buried the greats of Yiddish literature: I.L. Peretz, Sh. Anski, Jacob Dyneson, and the wife of Peretz. The enemy did not succeed in destroying this tomb. Directly opposite, we came upon the comparatively fresh grave of the writer and well-remembered theater personality, Moshe Broderson (1890-1956).

Heavyhearted, we retraced our steps and took the trolley back.

* * *

Avrom Morevski, renowned actor-director and his wife, the gifted pianist, Marie Lenzer, made me welcome at their home. Along with my compatriot Avremel Khash, we were soon joined by two other colleagues, Chaim Nisentzweig and Julia Flaum, an actress recently from Russia.

Morevski's small two-room apartment was neat, cozy and warm. The point of interest, naturally, was the piano on which our hostess, with genuine artistry, played several classic compositions after dinner. We also listened with great interest as Morevski related:

"I managed to remain alive in the Soviet Union, where I happened to find myself during the war years. I stood at the helm of the Yiddish City Theater in Bialystok and produced plays like *The Family Ovadis* by Peretz Markish. From Bialystok we traveled to Mohilev. One of our shining achievements there was the production of Lermantov's *The Spaniards*, translated by Kushnirov and directed by Norwid. We also did a revival of *The Tempest* by Shakespeare. The role of Prospero was assigned to the noted actor Shmuel Landau. But, imagine, at the first performance, Landau dropped dead, at the end of the first act!

"After Hitler—may he rot in hell—attacked Russia, our theater group was then forced to travel in freight cars. We could no longer return to our home base, Bialystok, for the city was already occupied by the Germans.

"By August 1941, I was performing in the Russian language theater. For three years I was the leading artist in a Cossack theater in provincial Balashov (now called Barenburg). And in 1956, I came back to Warsaw. I was most warmly welcomed here. The Yiddish State Theater accepted me into the company, provided me with a lodging and a stipend. But an opportunity to act, or direct? Nothing doing!

"In 1957, after a lapse of twenty years, I was finally given the chance to direct Anski's *The Dybbuk*. I had directed this play with three different Leahs! One of them was the young actress, Ketti Efron. When the company of the State Theater played in London, Ketti did not return to Warsaw. She defected and is now living in Paris.

"The acclaim I received for my direction of *The Dybbuk* was tremendous. That's great, wouldn't you say? Well, I've been idle almost three years now, puttering around the house in robe and slippers, waiting."

(Later, when I broached the subject of Morevski's grievance to the director of the State Theater, Ida Kaminska, she confided: "Morevski is a sick man. It's his heart. We are simply afraid to entrust him with a role. What if something happens, right on stage, heaven forbid?!")

"Tell me, Morevski," I said, "How would you sum up the Yiddish Theater in Poland?"

"From the standpoint of artistic achievement," he said, "the answer is rather subjective. What one individual may like may not please another. To our great sorrow we no longer have many Yiddish-speaking theatergoers. What we do have is the commitment of the Polish government to the minorities; particularly the Jewish minority. The maintenance of the theater institution and our other cultural needs is a vital factor in Yiddish cultural life. What other country today would come forth with a substantial subsidy to help publish my three volumes of memoirs, *There and Back*, in Yiddish? And I am already preparing my fourth volume. Jews, no matter where they are, ought to applaud this fact.

"As for the theater's future—who can prophecy? Let us hope. Yes, all we can do is hope!"

* * *

On a modest poster at the entrance to the temporary playhouse (the new opera house, close by, was still being completed), I read: Tonight! The Warsaw Folk-Opera Presents Mussorgsky's *Boris Godunov!*

Inquiring at the box office for the ticket my friend Alexander Bardini had promised to leave for me, I gave my name and was promptly given a seat in a loge near the stage.

The symphonic orchestra, close to a hundred musicians, was entirely made up of young people, not a single bald head among them. Jerzy Semkov, quite a young man himself, I noticed, conducted the overture with the fire of youth and the know-how of a veteran. The curtain rose and I was enthralled with the splendid decor. The sets and costumes, I learned from the program, were designed by a woman, Theresa Rozhowski.

Aside from the leading artists—each one a gifted actor and trained singer, the ensemble consisted of about 250 singers and dancers. All in all, they created the kind of spectacular presentation rarely seen in any country. I was particularly impressed with Bernard Ladin in the challenging role of Boris Godunov. Above all, I felt the greatest credit was due the director, Alexander Bardini. No wonder he was stirring up all of Poland. And thanks to the free hand given him financially, he was able to bring this fantasy of his to realization.

During the entr'acte, Bardini came along, and apologized for not meeting me earlier. He was very much involved, he explained, with television interviews and a dramatic youth group, which he was directing in a classic drama. As a matter of fact, the entire opera cast and other theatrical troupes in Poland were mostly comprised of young artists, studying in the conservatories and drama schools.

"Soon after the war," he went on to say, "notwithstanding the appalling devastation, the government immediately centered its attention on the young ones who showed ability and ambition toward art in any form. The Yiddish State Theater," he added, "is also deriving the benefit of the government's generous attitude to the cultivation of the arts. Now, if only we could get our own Jewish youth interested in a career on the Yiddish stage! The obstacle is that, the few talented ones among them prefer the Polish theater, in the language they know, rather than Yiddish, the language they don't know at all."

"My dear Bardini," I replied, "this is the lot of the Yiddish theater and the Yiddish actors all over the world. We always were the stepchild of Yiddish culture and creativity. Even in the United States, with its millions of Jews, they now present Yiddish plays on Broadway but performed in English! The U.S. government doesn't concern itself with theater enterprises. This is a private undertaking, a business like any other business.

"It's the same in all other countries, wherever Jews reside. Take France, or England. In South America, especially in Argentina, the sun did smile on Yiddish theater for a while. There too, things have changed. The language of the country being Spanish, our people are obliged to seek their entertainment in the Spanish theaters. Up to now, the only country in the world where Yiddish theater has had a chance to survive is Israel. So far, the masses of newly settled Jews haven't as yet learned Hebrew, and so they still patronize the plays given in Yiddish. But for how long?

"Yiddish youth? The language they speak is that of the country in which they happen to be born. To expect them to turn to Yiddish and Yiddish theater is absurd. If and when they do seek a theatrical career, they naturally turn to the language of their particular country. But aside from all that, the kind of theater idealists that we were are no more.

"I shudder even now, when I recall the trials I had to endure before I managed to get a job as an actor during the Golden Era of Yiddish Theater in America."

30

New York, 1924

"Shalom aleichem, colleagues! I am Chaim Yablokoff, a Yiddish actor, just arrived from Europe!" I introduced myself cheerfully, on my first visit to the meeting hall of the Hebrew Actors' Union, on the second floor of 31 East Seventh Street in Manhattan.

The smoke-filled hall was abuzz with the chatter of actors and actresses, many of whom were absorbed in playing cards. My genial greeting was met by a chilling silence. A few kibitzers deigned to throw a glance my way.

At a long table near the windows, a couple of actors were engrossed in newspapers lying spread on the table. An elderly actor, seated nearby, seemed to be gazing at nothing in particular, his hands resting idly on the head of his thick walking stick. Taking courage I approached him.

"I am Chaim Yablokoff, a Yiddish actor only yesterday admitted from Ellis Island. Shalom Aleichem," I greeted him, extending my hand. I remained standing, my hand outstretched, as the old man gave me an annoyed look and turned his head away. I felt as if I'd been doused with a bucket of cold water.

A young man, hurriedly leaving the table, warmly clasped my hand. "Shalom," he said, "my name is Israel Mandel. The actors think it is Mendl, a first name, so that's what they call me. But who cares, let it be Mendl," he grinned. "Anyway, Mandel rings better, and more theatrical, than my real name, Madzhevitzky. You must be the fellow from Ellis Island, Yablokoff, right? Kirshenbaum was telling everyone about you. I just read the item in the *Morning Journal*. Believe me, a lot of the characters you see here ought to be sent to Ellis Island for re-examination as actors. I assure you most of them would flunk the test! But you passed all right, according to the article. Naturally, otherwise you wouldn't be here, eh? Well, lots of luck to you!

"Now then, you passed examination number one. You'll still be required to go through the acid test on the little stage over there," he pointed to an improvised platform at the back of the hall. "That's where applicants seeking to join the Hebrew Actors' Union are ground up. Here, we call it an audition. Take my word for it, brother, doing an audition before the membership of the actors' union is a hell of a lot more traumatic than performing on Ellis Island. With the Board, perhaps, you can find a spark of sympathy. Here, in the union, the slaughter of candidates for membership is a free-for-all. But don't let it worry you. By the time the union will grant you an audition, you may very well be old and gray," he burst into good-natured laughter.

I didn't grasp Mandel's humor. What he said struck me as strange, bewildering talk.

"Let's get out of here," he said. "It's hot as blazes up here. If we're gonna be fried, let's better be fried on Second Avenue."

At the corner of Seventh Street, Mandel offered to treat me to a glass of seltzer with syrup.

"What will it cost?" I asked.

"Cheap as dirt," Mandel joked. "A whole nickel. It's worth it."

In my head I began calculating. A nickel? That's the twentieth part of a dollar. "I'm not thirsty," I tried to get out of it. But Mandel insisted.

"You're a guest," he said, "and it's my treat."

"I'll have a glass of plain seltzer," I agreed by way of compromise.

"Two cents, please!" he called across the counter.

"I did appreciate the refreshing drink and even more than that, Mandel's warmheartedness. Here was a sincere, down-to-earth person, with no actorish mannerisms. We strolled along Second Avenue, the Broadway of the Yiddish Theaters in New York, and I gratefully drank in the enlightening words of my newfound companion.

"Listen, Yablokoff," his tone more earnest now, "I have a sharp eye. You think I didn't notice what happened when you came into the meeting room of the union? It really got me. There are many intelligent union members, fine men and women, and some truly great artists. With these, you can get along. They are established! It's only the two-bit players, running scared of their own shadow, who behave uncivilly and eat each other up for a piece of bread. Now, you certainly don't look to be anybody's fool, so I'll try to give you a clear picture of the theater situation in America today. Don't build any castles in the air. Getting a chance to play theater is not easy. Maybe you'll be more lucky than others. Take me, for instance. I love the theater with all my heart. I came here from Toronto, thinking I'll be able to make a career in the Yiddish theater. But not a chance, unless you can break through the "Chinese Wall" and become a member of the union. So I work in a shop. But I hate it. I want to act. Still, a fella has to eat. And a landlord wants rent—so I'm forced to work, see? But my heart is in the theater. Every now and then, I take a day off, like today, to hang around the actors.

"You're pretty young, my friend," he further observed. "You appear to have all the assets needed on stage. They ought to grab you up with both hands. But, even if you land a little job somewhere in the sticks, you will still have to pray that there doesn't pop up some character who looks like your grandfather and claims that he is more entitled to your job than you are, because, you guessed it, he's a union man! In my opinion, you should try and contact someone who has an in with the representative of the union, Reuben

Guskin. I mean someone from the Labor Movement, the Bund, the Socialist Order, or the Workmen's Circle. Or, wait a minute! What city do you come from?"

"Grodno."

"Grodno? I'm from Radom. Let me see, I think the Grodno landsleit have a Workmen's Circle branch. Guskin is a real bigshot in the Workmen's Circle. If someone from the Grodno branch would put in a good word for you, this could carry some weight, see?"

"My brother-in-law and my sister," I said, "are members of the Grodno branch, #74."

"That's great!" Mandel brightened up, "Let your brother-in-law get to these people. They can do a lot."

Having arranged to meet my brother-in-law, Henry, at the fur shop where he worked, Mandel walked me to the subway station at Fourteenth Street. He instructed me to get off at Thirty-fourth Street. Someone would be sure to show me to the shop.

"And don't hesitate to ask anyone in Yiddish. All who work in that neighborhood are Jews. You'll hardly find a non-Jew in New York, anyway."

"Mandel," I said, deeply moved by his sincere interest, "I don't know how to thank you. You have opened my eyes to a lot of things. You are the first person in the theater circle to befriend me here in America and I'll never forget it. Let us remain friends."

We shook hands on it and I went down into the subway.

Grodno Branch

Henry, a cutter in the fur trade, was aware that I stood waiting for him in the hall of the shop, but not until six o'clock was he permitted to spare me as much as a glance. Every moment of the workday belonged to the boss. Finally, at the stroke of six, finished with his long day's labor, he greeted me and introduced me to his co-workers.

"This is my brother-in-law, Chaim Yablokoff, an actor," he said with such pride one would think he was introducing Jacob P. Adler.

"I'll wash up and change my clothes," Henry said, "then we'll have a bite to eat down on East Broadway." Riding in the subway, he continued, "A landsman of ours, Julius Satz, runs a restaurant on East Broadway near the *Daily Forward*. We'll meet a lot of people there from Grodno. In the long run, Chaim, you'll have to become a member in the Workmen's Circle. Even the bigwig of the actors' union, a politician, Reuben Guskin, sometimes eats there. It will be to your advantage to get acquainted."

My brother-in-law's words fit in with the advice given me by my friend Mandel. Maybe things will all fall into place—I hoped!

The restaurant was a real homey place. Satz, the proprietor, waited on his landsleit in person. They knew he could be depended on to come up with a little prohibition booze for a l'chaim, as well as a full course meal, pungent with Grodno specialties. These dishes were so reminiscent of home, I devoured them with relish.

My compatriots were disappointed that I could not relay any current news from Grodno, since I had been away in Lithuania the past four years.

Finally, the talk got around to the subject of the Workmen's Circle and how branch 74 was organized in 1906. Satz recalled a curious episode of that period: "When our Grodno branch was organized, the national board of the Workmen's Circle gave us a charter with the branch number 69. When we learned 69 was a number used by a branch suspended for building a syna-gogue and holding religious services, we vigorously protested to the main office. How could we, Grodno radicals, known Bundists and Socialists, be stuck with this ill-chosen number used by a fanatic religious group?! Our just demand was duly approved by the national board and they changed our branch number to 74."

Leaning confidentially toward Satz, I put the question to him very dis-creetly: "Do you think one of the landsleit could possibly intercede for me with Mr. Guskin, the representative of the actors' union?"

"What a question!" Satz replied. "Of course we can—and we will. I, myself, as an executive member of the national board of the Workmen's Cir-cle, will take care of the matter personally. Mr. Guskin will give you all the help he can as a future member of W.C. branch 74."

The Place That Never Sleeps

Leaving Satz's restaurant, Henry and I strolled all the way to Second Avenue at Twelfth Street, to the place that never sleeps—the Cafe Royale. The Royale was known to come fully awake only at midnight, when the actors and all those connected with the Yiddish theater gathered after showtime to keep the place buzzing into the wee hours.

Outdoors, in front of the cafe, lattice-work partitions screened off the little tables that were set out like European sidewalk cafes. These trellised enclo-sures and potted shrubs served as a summertime arrangement only, and reminded me of exterior settings in a Yiddish musical.

Of all the people there, who should spot me but Mandel. Taking me by the arm he ushered me into the cafe like a bridegroom being led down the aisle. At last I got my first look at the world-famed theater-cafe, about which I'd heard so much.

"As you can see," said Mandel, "this place is bursting with actors, actresses, musicians, entrepreneurs, writers and other professionals. The Roy-ale is also an attraction to the 'civilians,'" he laughed. "Where else can they get such a close-up of their stage idols, whom they can otherwise only wor-ship from a remote seat in the balcony? Everyone wants to rub elbows with theater people.

"Over there, on the right side of the cafe, the tables are reserved for the profession's uppercrust, the stars. The left side is occupied by actors of second, or third rung, as well as writers and the general public. Actually, there is no written law that says so. It just worked out that way and has become a tradition. When an actor, habitually on the left, happens to get an exceptionally good review in the theater pages of the Yiddish press, he wanders over to the right.

"The waiters, mostly Hungarian-American, know every patron inside out. The trombeniks, who take up free space at the tables, are never actually told to move. But, come dinner hour, the trombeniks make themselves scarce. They clear out and leave the tables to the regular customers, who can afford a good Hungarian dinner.

"In the rear of the cafe, hidden from view, is the card-players' haven. They can engage in pinochle to their hearts' content for as long as twenty-four hours at a stretch—the cafe never closes—and the stakes are fabulously high. It is said that the proprietor, Oscar Zathmary, won the Cafe Royale in a pinochle game."

Reuben Wendorff, who was appearing in the Bronx with the Vilna Troupe, came hurrying downtown after the performance, on a hunch that he'd find me at the Royale. "Chaimke!" he exclaimed, throwing his arms around me. "You're here! I told you yet in Kovno that you will be in America, didn't I? Welcome, my boy!"

The later the hour, the bigger the crowd and the Royale buzzed like a beehive. My benefactor, Yankele Kirshenbaum, strolled in and gave me an elaborate greeting. "Well, Yablokoff," he smiled broadly, "did you read what I wrote about you?" He then proceeded to give an account of my Ellis Island experience for all who would listen. Everyone laughed at the way he described it—and I laughed too. Thank God I was able to laugh over it now. Relating the details of my audition, he declared that it was the first time such a procedure ever took place in the history of America.

An elderly waiter, hovering over our table, and lending an ear to this tale, fetched an extra glass of ice water and placed it before me. "Ein schöner Junge, you are," he remarked, in a German-English jargon. "You want to be an actor? Aber, Jewish theater ist now kaput! Nicht gut, nicht gut," he shrugged and padded off to another table.

"That's Herrmann, the busboy," Kirshenbaum enlightened me. "Would you believe that this old-enough-to-be-your-father busboy is a wealthy man? Filthy rich, from the nickels he's been collecting in tips all these years. Just a nickel. That's all he asks for. He brings you a glass of water, pages you when you get a phone call, anticipates your leaving, brings your hat and coat, and helping you on with your things, puts his hand out for his nickel. Several buildings on the avenue and a few in the side streets are the properties of Herrmann, the busboy!"

"He can't even sign his name, this millionaire," laughed Wendorff.

"And he's a Shylock too!" another added.

"But he knows whom he can trust, all right!" said still another. This whole appraisal of Herrmann was summed up by Mandel in one phrase: "Nu, I ask you, do you have to go to college?"

Suddenly, a stir was felt. Guskin had come in. From every direction greetings followed him as he made his way to his reserved table close by the telephone booths.

This, I learned, was his night-time office. During the day, he was at his desk in the union. At night, he conducted union affairs at his little table in the Royale. With Guskin's arrival, the telephones began to ring without stop.

Kirshenbaum wanted to introduce me to Guskin, but I decided I would wait until my landsman, Satz, put in a good word for me.

Before leaving, Mandel and I agreed to meet the next day so he could show me around New York. By the time Henry and I shlepped home on the El to Williamsburg, the night was half over. Poor Henry would soon have to be up and off to work. He did, of course, enjoy mingling with theater people, but what the evening cost him in dollars must have been half of his week's wages.

Lying on my nice white bedding, mulling over all the discoveries I had made this first day in America, I was sharply reminded of my father's common-sense psychology: "Chaimke," he often repeated to me, "Important as it is to know what to do in a given situation, it is even more important to know what *not* to do." This advice now seemed to be the answer to a number of things that disturbed me this first day in New York. For one thing, I felt a strong aversion to certain tactics here. These very first impressions, and my later experiences, prepared me to combat the evils which reigned just then in the Yiddish theater, such as keeping out young talent, and the chauvinism of the self-anointed elite of the profession.

Henceforth, I made it a rule to steer clear of the right—the bourgeois side of the Royale. I swore never to borrow money from Herrmann, the busboy. I also vowed to extend a warm welcome to newcomers in the country and help them in every way possible.

31

The Hebrew Actors' Union

The Hebrew Actors' Union, local 1, was organized in 1887, and is one of the oldest unions in America. With the Yiddish typesetters union and the Yiddish chorus union, they helped organize the United Hebrew Trades in 1888.

In 1902 emerged a local 2 of the actors' union, with sole jurisdiction over the provinces. In 1903, there sprang up a local 5, with jurisdiction over the Yiddish vaudeville houses. When local 1, made up of the representatives of the legitimate theaters producing musicals and drama, introduced its stringent rules against accepting new members, it incurred not only the appellation, Chinese Wall, but gave way to still another local—#18.

The friction brought about by all this splintering certainly did the actors no good and did even less for the Yiddish theater. Finally, in 1922, a merger was accomplished, unifying the Hebrew Actors' Union with a membership of 350 performing artists.

A theater season ran thirty-eight consecutive weeks, with twenty-four Yiddish theaters operating throughout the United States and Canada—twelve of them in New York City.

The man who shaped the union into a sound organization was formerly the representative of the barbers' union. This man—born in Brobruisk and who was active in the Bund, the Socialist Organization, the United Hebrew Trades and the Workmen's Circle—was Reuben Guskin.

Guskin's office was a walkup on the third floor of the building. I climbed the stairs to the small reception room, sectioned off by a balustrade, and there a young lady sat busily pecking at a typewriter. According to my friend Mandel's description, I surmised she was the union's secretary, Rosel Pivar.

Several actors and actresses had come to discuss engagements for the coming season. It was easy enough to read from their demeanor which of them had already pocketed a season's job and which were still hoping to land one.

Remembering the welcome I'd received the day before on my first visit to the union's meeting hall, I quietly took a seat in the corner of the room. No one spoke to me, nor did I speak to anyone. A few did throw me a curious glance, but went right on with their conversation. Somehow, I didn't have the gumption to tell the secretary that I was there to see Mr. Guskin, so I sat in my corner and waited.

A door opened at the side of the room. I recognized the large head with the thick, silver-flecked hair, the long sideburns and the pince-nez clamped on his nose—Guskin! In the Royale he had seemed much taller. When his gaze fell on me—an unfamiliar face—he came over with a friendly greeting and tried to guess: "You are?"

"Yablokoff, Chaim Yablokoff."

"Ah yes, Yablokoff. Well then, come in, come in. This is Mr. Greenfield," he introduced a gentlemen of slight build, who sat at the side of the huge desk, twirling his mustache. "Mr. Greenfield is the president of our union," Guskin added.

"Yablokoff," I nodded, repeating my name. "I have just arrived..."

"Oh, that's you, the fellow from Ellis Island," Greenfield rose to his feet sizing me up with curiosity. "Yes, yes, I read about you. What a story! An audition on Ellis Island! Very piquant. We ought to suggest it to Jacobs and Goldberg," he chuckled, "a catchy name for an operetta, 'An Audition on Ellis Island!'"

Guskin asked me to sit down and took his place at the desk. All I could see above this mammoth desk was Guskin's leonine head. Such an important man, I couldn't help thinking—the leader of the actors' union and the Yiddish theater—and yet so short! Both men stared at me in silence, until I realized they were waiting for me to begin.

"I'm an actor," I ventured timidly, "a professional actor. I have been playing theater since 1917, while still in Grodno, my hometown."

Evidently recognizing my nervousness, Guskin broke in with a friendly note. "I read the item about you in the *Forward*. I didn't know about you being detained on Ellis Island. Had anyone called it to my attention," he remarked in his Litvak accent, "I would have done something for you. I only heard about you later, through Kirshenbaum in the Royale. Well, now that you are here, we'll see. I cannot promise you anything, understand. But we'll see. Do you sing?" When I nodded yes, Guskin and Greenfield, still fingering his mustache, exchanged glances.

"You sing. Well, we'll see. Circumstances in the theater right now, you understand, are not at their best, so what can we do? Do you dance?" After a slight pause, I again nodded yes. I did not regard myself as a dancer, but at the moment I felt it was important to say yes. If a bear can be taught to dance, I figured, so could I.

"You will have to make an application in the union, of course," said Guskin. "Promises I cannot make. Well, anyway, as far as a job in a New York theater is concerned—that's out. Maybe somewhere on the road. What do you think, Mr. Greenfield?"

Greenfield, who hadn't stopped preening the ends of his mustache, shook his head in a way that made it difficult to make out whether he agreed with Guskin's assertions or not.

* * *

"Well, how did it go?" asked Mandel, waiting for me out on the street.

"'We'll see!'" I quoted Guskin. "But, no promises," I ended on a hopeless sigh.

"We'll see? Well, that's better than nothing, isn't it? So what's there to worry about?" Mandel tried to laugh it off. "Come on, let's go to Ratner's on the avenue. It's a terrific place. For fifteen cents you get a bowl of mushroom-and-barley soup that'll fill you up to here—with as much bread and butter as you can stow away."

As we ate, I tried to unburden my mind of some things that were troubling me. "Why is it," I asked, "that everything here is so mechanical, so impersonal, concerning the theater? Actors talk about a job in the same way my brother-in-law refers to his job at the fur shop. Is the theater in America a shop? My brother-in-law talks about his furrier's union. If it were not for the union, he says, people would still be slaving under bloodsucking bosses for twelve and fourteen hours a day! Well, this I can understand. But, is theater in the same category? Is it a sweatshop? Are the actors laborers? The producers, exploiters? What about theater as an art?

"Guskin tells me that, whether or not I am needed in a theater, New York is out. I may have a chance on the road, he says, providing a manager will want to engage me. Now, why should a manager want me? Has he ever seen me perform? And how can he see me on stage if the union won't give me a chance to appear? In Europe, it was different; managers practically fought over young performers."

Mandel, eating his bread and soup, listened attentively, making no comment. It seemed he could not deny the truth of my observations. Instead, he went off on another tack.

"Tell me," he said, "have you ever heard of the poet, Shlomo Shmulevitch?"

"The one who wrote, 'A Brivele der Mamen?' (A Letter to Mother)? Of course. I sing his song. Why do you ask?"

"Shmulevitch arranges a concert every year. He makes a few dollars by selling tickets to his friends and landsleit. He and his children perform. Would you like to appear on his program? It's a benefit, you know. That means no pay."

"Well," I hesitated, "what is your opinion? I have implicit faith in you. You think I should do it?"

"I think you should! Let people see and hear you. It may even lead to a job."

Thus, on Mandel's advice, I accepted my first "thank-you" concert in America.

* * *

Several days later Mandel took me by subway to Shmulevitch's concert in Canarsie. We came early so I could run through my numbers with the pianist, who happened to be one of Shmulevitch's daughters. Mandel had also invited some of his pals to pass judgment on me. He himself was most eager to hear me, he said, for how could he possibly recommend a "cat in a bag"?

Shmulevitch introduced me as a sensation in America. Relating the Ellis Island episode, he explained that I was so good the United States government even gave me its seal of approval.

Whether I really made such a hit, or whether the applause was motivated by sympathy, I'll never know. I do know that I shook in my boots, as I do to this day every time I appear before an audience. I heard echoes of "bravo, bravo," but what truly shocked me was the whistling! My God, I thought, I'm done for! I'm finished! In Europe, whistling from the audience means you are a flop.

"Atta boy, Chaim!" exclaimed Mandel, slapping me on the back. "You're gonna be A-OK in America!"

"Didn't you hear them whistling?" I asked, feeling crushed.

"Are you nuts?!" he burst into laughter. "This is America, pal. When they whistle, it means you're terrific, a sensation!"

Shmulevitch, with the promise of recommending me to the managers of the Yiddish theaters, assured me that there would be a notice about the concert in the press. Mandel's friends all agreed that there was indeed a great need for young performers like me in America. And what could be younger than twenty-one?

"Going on twenty-two," I made sure to let them know.

Another Audition

Mandel called and asked me to meet him right away at the Royale. Grabbing my briefcase containing my theatrical credentials and a few sheets of music, I hurried to the Royale and met Mandel running toward me fairly bursting with promising news.

"Listen, would you go to play in Canada?"

"Are there any Jews there?"

"Jews?! And what Jews! Wonderful Jews! Heartwarming Jews! Tremendous Jewish communities!" replied Mandel, making an enthusiastic pitch for Canada. "I ought to know," he continued. "Didn't my sister bring me over from Europe to Toronto?"

"Fine. But who is going? When? Where? For how long?" I asked.

"Three actors have formed a partnership," he explained, "Sam Auerbach, Irving Honigman and Jacob Goldstein. They will be the bosses and pay wages. I've already spoken to Auerbach about you. He's interested. He's looking for a juvenile comedian to play opposite his wife, Sadie Scheingold. He wants to look you over."

"This is Mr. Sam Auerbach," said Mandel, introducing me to a tall, broad-shouldered man wearing black-framed glasses. "And these are his partners, Irving Honigman and Jacob Goldstein."

As we strolled back and forth in front of the Royale, these impresarios asked me all sorts of questions. A good-looking, neatly dressed young man presently came along and Auerbach introduced him as Sam Gertler.

"Gertler," added Auerback, "is already engaged in our company—as the romantic lead."

Following Auerbach into the Royale, I was led to a table on the left, to meet his wife, Sadie Scheingold, a slender woman, her blonde hair cut short, her features rather fair and delicate. She looked much younger than her husband. She, in turn, introduced me to Clara Honigman, a tall woman with reddish hair, her face heavily made up—the prima donna of the company. Another Sadie at the table, Sadie Goldstein, although not an actress, was to accompany her husband, Jacob, to Canada with their little daughter, Charlotte (now a noted actress in her own right, Charlotte Goldstein).

The Royale was full of the usual hubbub and Auerbach took me outside again, where we resumed our strolling up and down the avenue.

"You understand, we need a young bouffe-comedian as a partner opposite my wife. Sadie's a star, you know. As far as your outward appearance is concerned, we are unanimously pleased. You're young, you're good-looking. That's what the stage needs. But we'd like to hear you..."

"You mean, audition me? With pleasure!" I jumped at the suggestion. "I'm ready to sing, recite and perform for you. I have some music with me. Taking examination in America is not new to me anymore. I did it on Ellis Island and, thank heaven, I was lucky." Auerbach seemed relieved that I helped him out of his dilemma. It is not easy for an actor to put another actor through the trial of an audition. "We can do it now. Why put it off? This way, you'll know at once whether or not I am suitable."

I was most anxious to audition immediately, because I was afraid to let the job slip through my fingers. Let it be Canada, or the end of the earth, I figured, as long as I could join a professional company and play in an honest-to-goodness theater.

The three couples came out of the cafe. Honigman, dark-complexioned and lanky, informed us officiously, "I hired a room in Webster Hall." They led the way, while Gertler, Mandel and I trailed after them.

At Webster Hall, a short walk from the Royale, we were shown into a large room strewn with litter from a previous meeting. A player-piano stood at the far end, but I didn't venture to ask who was going to play. Heavens, no! It might antagonize my future employers. Then I saw Sadie Goldstein approaching the piano. At her first discordant ripples, chills ran down my spine. And she, I shuddered, is going to accompany me?! I'm finished before I even begin, I told myself.

As if reading my thoughts, she explained apologetically, "A concertist, I am not! I never was, though in my younger days I played much better. I'm really a bookkeeper, a secretary, but Mr. Honigman asked me to..."

"Sure!" Honigman interjected, "Where was I supposed to look for pianists all of a sudden? Did we come here to listen to a piano recital? We came to hear if this young man can sing. What's the big deal, Sadie?"

Auerbach, his wife Sadie Scheingold, Clara Honigman, with Gertler, Goldstein and Mandel, all backed themselves into the far corners of the room.

I started by reading Tunkeler's humorous monologue, "The Photographer." Nobody laughed. I asked Sadie to play the introduction to one of my lighter numbers, "Don't Overshoot your Mark." She began, but I failed to recognize the melody, or the key in which she was playing. To get it over with, I sang without the help of accompaniment. On the finale, Sadie did manage to strike a chord to help me out on the last note. A thin ripple of applause reached me from the corners of the hall.

"Enough now!" came Goldstein's chronically husky voice. "Let's go."

"Why?" retorted Honigman, quite adamant. "What about a little dance?"

Calling on every nerve in my body, I began hopping around for all I was worth. To the tune of a lively Russian "Kazatzki" I hummed my own accompaniment. Bending at the knees, I thrust one foot forward, then the other in true Cossack style. I twisted and turned like a whirling dervish. Sadie, becoming inspired, began to bang out her own interpretation of a Russian "Kamahrinski."

"All right, all right!" Auerbach called out angrily. "That's enough! Don't you have a limit, you bulbenick?" I broke off my twirling and to my amazement found that Auerbach's irritation was directed at Honigman, not at me.

"Aren't you ashamed of torturing a young actor like this, you bulbenick?!" he glared at him. "Good, Yablokoff! Very good," he then said, turning to me. "I compliment you, that was swell!"

Sadie Goldstein and Honigman walked ahead to the Royale, while Auerbach and I stopped at a candy store.

"Have something, Yablokoff," he insisted. "But drink slowly. We can't have you catching cold. What will you drink?"

"Seltzer with cherry syrup, please," I ordered, feeling that I truly earned it this time.

"Mister Yablokoff (again, the Mister, it sounded so strange to me), I want to engage you." he finally came to the point, "providing the union will give you a privilege. We will have to fight for you in order to get you permission to play with us, see? We, ourselves, are not managers; we're actors too. Yiddish theater is not what it used to be. The situation on the road is no better, either. But we have to make a living, so we formed a partnership—not cooperative, you understand. We will pay our company wages. It's a tremendous risk today to guarantee weekly wages—thirty-six weeks at that! You are not a union member, and we cannot pay you very much. The most we can offer you is forty-five dollars a week. The union scale is fifty-five dollars."

Forty-five dollars a week? In Lithuanian money, in Kovno—I began figuring—this sum would be tantamount to a million. Every week? That's what the man said, I was sure. In Europe, salaries were paid by the month; shares were divided every two weeks, if there was something to share. But, forty-five dollars a week! Who ever dreamed of such good fortune? How was I to know that it was mighty difficult to stretch it, to cover rent, food, clothing, laundry and other necessities for the stage; especially when an actor must always present a decent front.

"Now, Chaim (after this, Auerbach called me by no other name), you will have to forgive us for the nonsense of the examination. As if I didn't know right off that you are okay. But that Honigman, my partner—stubborn as a mule. He insisted, you understand, and when he gets stubborn. Well, can I quarrel with him before the season even begins? You won't demand more salary, will you, now that we closed the deal?" he laughed.

Before catching the El back to Brooklyn, I took Mandel aside. "Tell me," I asked. "Why did Auerback call Honigman bulbenick?"

"Don't you know what a bulbenick is?" he stared, highly amused.

"Of course I know. A bulbe is a potato. So, an actor with a 'hot potato' in his mouth, fluffing his lines, mispronouncing words, turning sentences upside down, is called a bulbenick."

"Bravo! So you want to know why Auerbach called him that?" Mandel laughed fit to burst. "Because Honigman is known throughout the world of Yiddish theater as the King of the Bulbenicks!"

32

Toronto

Our company traveled to Toronto by Pullman—a luxury I certainly could never have afforded in Europe. Before leaving New York, Auerbach asked whether I needed a few dollars in advance. Did I? And how! Reaching for his wallet, Auerbach said, "Will twenty-five dollars be enough for now? I will let you have more in Toronto. You will need it until you get your first paycheck. According to the union rules, we pay only from the date we begin to play. For the weeks of rehearsal, there is no remuneration. The exchange on the Canadian dollar is ten percent less than the American dollar right now." Handing me two crackling ten-dollar bills and a five, he declared, "We'll deduct it from your salary at five dollars a week, O.K.?"

What else could I say, but nod, O.K.?

The first one to befriend me was Sam Gertler, a most congenial young man. He was married, but was traveling alone. His wife, Anna, had gone to stay with her parents in Missouri for the time being. His weekly salary of fifty dollars would not suffice for both of them. Besides, he had already collected a few hundred dollars in advance from the management during the summer layoff.

Gertler had experienced many of the ups and downs of the Yiddish theater—mostly downs. He was not yet a union man and was obliged to struggle on the road with nonunion companies. Considered a good actor, a real asset in a troupe, he was also considered a "good boy," which was a better recommendation than talent, when it came to joining the union. Still, he was unable to crack the "Chinese Wall." At present, Gertler was more than happy that he'd gotten to play with a union company. This, in itself, was an achievement.

"What you want to do first thing is start learning English. The parts you will be playing in this repertory company are usually sprinkled with a good many American idioms and wisecracks. Here is lesson number one: this car is called a 'sleeper.' The bosses sleep in the 'lowers.' You and I—the plain buck privates, will climb into the 'uppers,' get it?" he grinned.

Upper or lower, it didn't make a particle of difference to me. How was I going to grapple with the English words I might have to deliver on stage? And that was only headache number one. I had still another and greater headache... my Litvish accent! In Kovno, of course, we performed in the Lithuanian dialect, as did the Vilna Troupe. In America, the Yiddish stage had adopted the Wolhyner dialect. How on earth was I going to fit in with my Lithuanian accent? I was sure to create a dissonance with the other players that would jar everyone's ears. The audience would laugh, I feared, not only at my English, but at my Yiddish as well. On top of that I had another problem. Before leaving for Canada, Auerbach made sure to remind me: "Chaim, don't forget to take along your papers to present at the border." Again documents!

"Our company," Gertler explained, "is traveling on a special manifest from the immigration department. Sometimes the inspectors ask that you identify yourself and sometimes they just take your word for it. These fellas can smell whether or not you are kosher." And with this reassurance, I climbed into my upper and dropped off to sleep.

A commotion in the car woke me. Uh-oh! I thought, the border!

"Toronto!" the conductor bellowed.

Toronto?! I gaped in astonishment. What about the border? Well, how do you like that, I congratulated myself. Who could have guessed that we crossed the border a few hours earlier, while I was peacefully snoozing in my upper?! And here we were—in Toronto, Canada!

The Jewish Community

Arriving at the station we found a crowd of people waiting to greet us. Most of the members of our company, having played in Toronto at various times in the past, were well known to these welcomers. The only unknown one, of course, was me. As I stood waiting at the edge of the group, a young fellow came up to me. He was so small of build, and boyish, I took him to be much younger than his actual age. With an impish twinkle in his eye and a broad, unmistakable Yiddish-Polish dialect, he introduced himself.

"I am Chanineh," he stated. "Everybody in Toronto knows Chanineh. I'm a tailor—when I'm working," he grinned. Mostly, I assist the dresser at the Standard Theater, where you'll be playing. You must be Panie Yablokoff. I read about you in *The Morning Journal*. Are you single, or already a cooked goose?" Sensing that I didn't quite appreciate his humor, he went on to explain. "You see, I have to know how to arrange a place for you to stay. What I mean is, are you married, single, what?"

"I'm single," I said.

"Then I can recommend a very nice place for you, a room without "landsleit" (bedbugs). Not expensive, either. This woman, a widow, a fine Jewish lady with two daughters. She'll make it reasonable. Come."

"What do you call reasonable?" I had to make this clear at the outset.

"From a hundred dollars a month, she'll give you change," he winked. "Leave it to Chanineh."

The Standard Theater on Dundas and Spadina avenues had been built expressly for Yiddish theater and was owned by a Toronto businessman, Isidore Axler. Chanineh took me to a very pleasant house not far from the theater. The landlady showed us the room. It was furnished with a bed, a dress, a small table and a chair. In addition to the lamp on the table, the landlady promised to let me have a bedlamp to attach to the headboard so I could read and study my lines at night. I was also permitted to use the general bathroom and take a bath whenever I pleased. I rather liked the little room. It was immaculately clean. And with the house being so close to the theater, as Chanineh pointed out, I would save trolley-fare.

And now to the point: how much? Chanineh gave me a sly wink. By now I knew it mean leave it to Chanineh! Taking the landlady aside for a private negotiation, he soon announced, "Panie Yablokoff, it will cost you twelve dollars a month. The landlady wants fifteen, but I told her I don't hear so good on this ear. If Chanineh says twelve, she'll take twelve! Cheap enough?"

After a quick mental calculation, I realized that, even in Lithuanian money, it was a bargain. I agreed to move right in. Lugging my things into the room, Chanineh let me in on a secret.

"Panie Yablokoff," he whispered, "you know why the landlady agreed to the twelve-dollar rent? When she suddenly laid eyes on such a handsome guy like you, she figured, she's got two grown daughters. Let a young fella roam around the house. Who can tell? So take my advice, watch out! You know that song: 'You need to be wed, like a hole in the head?' Take me, I'm older than you and still a bachelor, thank heaven!"

This was my first encounter with my friend and admirer of many years to follow, Chanineh Englander.

* * *

The weather in Toronto was delightful, the climate dry and summer still hanging on. Our opening was scheduled for the close of Rosh Hashanah. I found the pace of the city to be serene, easygoing, utterly unlike the clamor of New York. Its shops, however, laden with all that one's heart could desire, were eye-catching and attractive very much like New York. Ambling along the clean wide streets, I couldn't get enough of all I saw and heard around me. They call this a provincial town? Why, it's a metropolis!

The theater was located in the very heart of the Jewish section. Yiddish was spoken at every turn. Directly across the street from the theater were two kosher restaurants. One was owned by a man named Wechsler, the other was run by the parents of Goldie Eisman, the young actress, who was to join our company whenever a suitable role came up. I was a frequent patron in both these restaurants, since I could order whatever I liked in Yiddish. In fact, I began to make up for the many time I went hungry in Europe. Gertler, on the other hand, went easy on his food. He had to watch his figure. After all, he played the lover roles and was wary lest he develop a pouch. He couldn't afford a potbelly. In Honigman's opinion, I would do well to put on a few pounds. Playing opposite Sadie, he thought I looked too youthful.

"Is that bad?" said Chanineh, always with a quip. "That's like complaining the bride is too beautiful!"

Out in front of the theater I saw placards that read: Famous Cantor and double choir will officiate in this theater during the High Holy Days. At a little table, a Jew sat outside selling tickets. To me, this was a new phenomenon! In a theater?! Rosh Hashanah?! Yom Kippur?! I asked Chanineh about it.

"Why not?" he replied. "You can just as well pray for a good year here too. Very simple. The stage is set with the Holy Ark from the play *Dos Pintele Yid*, and they place a genuine Torah in it. Center stage they put down the Bima from *The Dybbuk*. For the pulpit they set up the stand used in the *Yeshiva Bokher*, and there you have a ready-made synagogue!"

This manner of worship did not sit well with me at all! A theater is a theater, and prayers, I felt, should be conducted in a real synagogue.

* * *

Rehearsals were finally begun. The theater was comfortable to work in, the stage spacious enough for any type of production. The stars (our bosses) occupied the on-stage dressing rooms, while Gertler and the rest of us settled ourselves in the basement, Chanineh's domain. He was in charge of our wardrobe, while the official dresser, Gurevitch, took care of the actors in the dressing rooms on stage. The women had their own wardrobe mistress.

We rehearsed a musical comedy called *Sadie is a Lady*, starring Sadie Scheingold and directed by Irving Honigman. I was cast in the role of an effervescent young chauffeur, given to boasting. Luckily, I was always a quick study and learned my lines overnight. But I was jittery lest I slip up on my dialect. Worst of all, I knew I was murdering the English expressions in my part. Yet to change them into Yiddish was something our director, Honigman, would not allow.

"We must keep some of the English in," he insisted, "or you will sound like a greenhorn chauffeur just off Ellis Island!"

How on earth was I to portray the image of a typical American, when I didn't have the vaguest conception of such an animal? At rehearsals, I suffered the tortures of hell. The tires of an automobile, I pronounced as tiress. It was Sadie, herself, who helped me the most. She displayed a world of patience. I listened and watched her lips as she taught me to enunciate each syllable correctly.

Sadie, a born American, of actor parents, Annetta and Abe Scheingold, sister of the prominent actor-singer Joseph Scheingold, grew up on stage. The tremendous responsibility of the success or failure of our opening play rested on her shoulders. As my partner, she had to act with me, sing with me, dance with me and—in theater parlance—I could easily "louse her up"!

She tutored me with patience, for she truly felt my sincere desire to make good, despite the fact that the genre of bouffe-comedian and dancer was not my forte at all. This type of role in a musical comedy depends mostly on the fast spiel, the catchy song and the snappy American dance steps which were foreign to me. I thought Honigman was right when he put me through my paces, auditioning me in New York.

We rehearsed our duet and Honigman even allowed me to sing a number on my own; a couplet I had that was suited to my part. I finally had the prose and the English words under control. If only we were to do a waltz, a polka, a kazatzki, I would have been able to get along. But a soft-shoe, a tap dance, a buck'n wing, a Charleston? Not for Chaim's feet! Still, if you must, you must! The closer we came to the premiere, I danced! Not as gracefully as Fred Astaire to be sure—but I danced.

I breathed easier, and began taking note of the technical preparations for the performance. This was something that keenly interested me from the very beginning of my career. Other actors, I noticed, didn't care to delve into this end of the business at all, but I was fascinated with the American methods of building sceneries and producing lighting effects.

Before the opening we went through several dress rehearsals with scenery, lighting and the orchestra of six musicians, led by Shaye Fleishman on the fiddle.

The audience in Toronto, the same as in Jewish communities in Europe and America at the time, patronized the Yiddish theater not only to see a new or popular play, or a favorite performer who had created a name for himself. These only added spice to the evening. In those days the majority came to the theater for the sake of theater, itself. It was a vital, spiritual experience.

Soon after the First World War, masses of Jewish immigrants began to flock to America. They knew no English. Radio was in its infancy. So where could a poor immigrant go to find solace and forget his daily cares other than to the Yiddish theater? Here, he could have a good cry, a good laugh, learn moral behavior, enjoy a Yiddish song, a bit of ethnic humor, meet landsleit, all in the Yiddish theater.

When the new and very strict U.S. Immigration laws came into effect, our Jewish masses set their sights on Canada, making their way to cities like Toronto, Montreal, and as far as Winnipeg. The Jewish "wandering stars" followed them. That was how our theater bloomed in the newly developed communities in Canada. For anyone in that era to say that a Jew was ashamed of his language was equal to saying that he was ashamed of his own parents. The erosion of assimilation hadn't as yet set in. It was the golden epoch out of which the Yiddish theater derived artistic as well as financial benefits.

The crowds came, primarily, to see a good play, and if they didn't enjoy it, it still didn't mean that they vowed never again to set foot in the Yiddish theater. Indeed not. Nobody found fault, or blamed the actors for ruining the Yiddish theater. They always knew that there would be another play next week, a better, one, of a finer caliber, to meet their approval. At least, it gave way to controversy and theater was alive and booming!

My First Appearance in Canada

Our opening performance went over quite smoothly. The cast was very well received and so was the play. From the report Chanineh gave me as we gathered in Wechsler's restaurant after the show, it seemed that I too, made a good impression.

"You think the people in the audience don't know that you are a greener? So what if a few English words don't sound like the King's English? You think this ruined the masterpiece? They've seen worse than you. All right, so you don't dance—but you sure can sing! All the people were saying that with your voice, you should be cast in the romantic roles to sing the love songs, because you're a handsome guy. With a head of hair such as Chanineh should only have! See, I've already got a moon showing on top of my head. You should have seen the girls in the theater. I've got a sharp eye. They were dropping dead over your big black eyes! So don't worry, you conquered Canada!"

From Chanineh's observations, I concluded that I didn't do so badly after all. And when the critic, Hersh-Meyer Kirschenbaum (Mandel's brother-in-law) gave me favorable mention in the *Jewish Journal*, I was in seventh heaven. Most of all I was happy that I did not, in any way, spoil the success of my partner, Sadie. She scored a tremendous hit. The audience loved her from seasons past. Nobody could mar her success. For the courage she gave me, for her comradeship in preparing me for my first appearance in a new country and in a role not suited for me, I always tendered her my respect and appreciation.

My friend Gertler was praised as a good-looking romantic lead, a fine actor, but what about singing?

"I suppose according to the law of theater—and the union—" Chanineh kibbitzed, "only the stars get born with everything. If our theatergoers had anything to say about casting, it would be you, brother Yablokoff, who would be playing the romantic, singing lovers in the operettas, instead of being stuck with the silly bouffe-comedians."

And sure enough, it wasn't too long before this actually came to pass.

* * *

My first-earned salary in Canadian dollars trembled in my hands. The question confronting me, was what shall I do first with the money? I knew I would have to live on a very tight budget. If one didn't earn enough, I realized, one could find himself in deep trouble even in America—or, Canada, for that matter.

The management was deducting what Auerbach had advanced me in New York from my pay. I also had to begin putting away a dollar toward the $150.00 I needed to send to the Hebrew Actors' Union with my application. Besides, I figured, shouldn't I be sending a few dollars home to my parents in Grodno? In answer to my letters telling them about my job, my father immediately wrote that I must watch every dollar and be sure not to squander this "fortune."

I was faced with another problem: how was I to acquire a few suits of clothing! I didn't have a decent stitch of clothing to my name—not onstage, nor offstage. It was a lucky break that my first role required a chauffeur's uniform, which was supplied by the management because it was a union rule that, costumes other than conventional street wear, had to be furnished by the theater management.

I wore my chauffeur's uniform through most of the show. For my one change, I managed to piece together an outfit from my own rags.

Chanineh recommended a man's tailor to Gertler and me; a theater patron who was willing to make up a few suits to order on credit. Fashionable at the time were narrow pants, long, narrow jackets fitted at the waist, with narrow lapels, single-breasted with three buttons. Gertler ordered three suits, so I also ordered three suits in different colors, as well as a winter overcoat.

Decked out in our new wardrobe, Gertler and I looked real sporty during the season in Toronto; although it did take us all season to pay out the tailor. But, after the season, when we got back to New York, we looked like a pair of yokels! During this time, men's apparel had undergone a complete change of fashion. And that was how we blew a season's profits, remaining where we started—with nothing to wear!

Yiddish Theater in Detroit and Buffalo

On account of Sunday's blue law in Toronto, theater performances were forbidden. And so, our management made arrangements with the impresarios in Detroit and Buffalo to have our company play their respective cities on alternate Sundays.

In Detroit we played at Orchestra Hall, home of the Detroit Symphony, a big and beautiful concert hall. Our Sunday performances always brought large audiences, despite the fact that Detroit had its own steady union company playing all week in a small theater, under the management of the actor-director Misha Fishzon and playwright Moshe Schorr.

During our first Sunday performance in Detroit, an incident occurred that cost me great aggravation. And what I did in turn was hardly commendable, I must confess. We knew that our train back to Toronto would be leaving right after showtime, scheduled to the minute. Occasionally, trains did give a theater company a few minutes grace if the show happened to run over, or the stagehands needed extra time to load the sceneries. This particular evening our Detroit audience began arriving late. Naturally, we could not start the show with half the crowd still in the lobby. There was no recourse but to hold the curtain.

Everybody backstage was delighted at the prospect of playing to such a huge house; especially our bosses, who were elated over the big box office. The stage was so enormous and the dressing rooms so remote, my colleagues joked: "We need roller skates to get us to and from our changes!" This in itself helped slow up the performance. In the first act, the actors took their time stretching each line to make the most of their parts, thereby dragging down the tempo of the show. After the intermission, more valuable time was lost waiting for the crowd to settle back in their seats. By the middle of the second act, it became evident that, if we didn't put a move on, we'd be spending the night in the railroad station. So, suddenly the mad rush was on!

The number I sang in this show was in the second act, and was really the highlight of my part. Now, since the spot in which I sang it was so close to closing, it was cut out. If they had cut my throat, it would not have hurt as much. And by cutting out my song, it practically left me with no part at all in the second act, except to hang around backstage for curtain calls.

What the hell was I going to take bows for? For doing nothing?! I raged inside of me. What am I here, an extra in a mob scene? I gritted my teeth, working myself up to a pitch. Now they are trying to beat the clock—at whose expense—at mine? Why? Because I'm the greenhorn?!

As my part in the show was over, I went to the dressing room, picked up my valise and marched off in the direction of the railroad station. Let the rest of the cast take the bows and revel in the applause—not me!

When the curtain fell, and my absence was discovered, it set off an alarm. It never occurred to anyone that I could possibly find my way to the station by myself. All they knew was that I had vanished, and that I had surely gone astray. Worried as they were, they still had to grab their things helter-skelter and make a dash for the depot in whatever transportation was available.

They found me in the waiting room, where I sat, torn between eating my heart out for pulling such a stunt on the company and licking my wounds over my actor's pride. My friend Gertler, surmising that I must be hungry, hurriedly bought some delicatessen sandwiches at the buffet and shoved one into my hands.

Aside from Gertler, no one spoke to me. In the train everyone ignored me and went to sleep in their berths. I sat up all night in the lounge of the men's room, dozing, and chastising myself for having displayed such unprofessional behavior. In the morning, Jacob Goldstein tried to make me see how wrong I was. Cutting my number, he assured me, was not done to hurt me. Sometimes, these things happen in the theater, and something, or someone, has to be sacrificed.

The only one, of all people, who applauded my action was "good boy" Gertler.

"Boy, do I envy you," he said, "for having the guts not to let yourself be stepped on. If I had your spunk, Chaim, I would be getting the romantic leads as I'd been promised when they engaged me. Now, I hear, Honigman is going after these roles and I will be stuck playing villains!"

33

The Family Fleischman

Shaye Fleischman, our orchestra leader, born in Ostrovca, and his wife, Chaya, from Kielce, with their four sons and two daughters, were known in Toronto as the most musical family in the city. Except for mother Fleischman, each member of her brood played an instrument.

The oldest son, Max, a violinist, and daughter, Jennie, pianist, had already been acknowledged in Canada as wunderkinder. After the two were graduated from the Toronto Conservatory of Music, Max was sent to Paris to further his studies with a famous violinist. Jennie remained with her father on the job as pianist in the Yiddish theater—a job she held from a very tender age.

Manny, another son, also played the violin. But, since the Yiddish theater could not afford more than one fiddler, and that was papa Fleischman, Manny took up the trumpet. Dave, still a youngster, already showed promise as another pianist. Fay and Sol, the youngest ones, had also begun practicing musical instruments, but failing to show any particular talent, the family put them down as musical "duds."

Fiddling and tooting could be heard at the Fleischman residence from morning till night. When the kids in the family finished practicing, the pupils filed in for their lessons, so that the house constantly echoed with music.

Mama Fleischman, a vivacious little woman, while not a musician herself, was quite a connoisseur of classical music and musicians. She could be off in the kitchen preparing enormous pots of food for her family, but let a wrong note or false chord reach her ears from the other side of the house, she'd yell: "Stop bluffing! Read the music!"

* * *

Our first few musical plays of the season had been brought along from New York by the management with the original texts and scores intact: *Tzipke Fire,* by Samuel H. Cohen, *Palestinian Love,* and *The Step-Child of the World* by Isidore Lillian. The latter was a great success wherever it played, because of its timely theme: It takes place before the League of Nations, where the Jewish people claim their rights to Palestine in accordance with the Balfour Declaration.

On weekends we also produced the melodramas by Harry Kalmanowitz, Louis Freiman and William Siegel. In the middle of the week we gave special performances of Yiddish classics.

As the season progressed I found myself involved in various chores aside from my job as an actor—extras not included in my contract. But having obliged with one little favor, such as composing a musical ensemble, I was thereafter drawn into other tasks. I was even bestowed the honor of conducting the first act of an operetta called *The Jewish Star,* music by David Hirsch.

As Jennie, our pianist, was finding it dificult to make out the Yiddish lyrics scribbled beneath the notes in her piano part, I helped her rehearse our singing group. They became so accustomed to my way of leading them, they sang very well, but without me they fell apart. To save the situation, Auerbach came up with a plan. Since my part didn't begin until the second act, I could conduct the orchestra during the first act and hold the group together. In the second act where their singing was less complicated, I would go on with my part in the play. This arrangement did not exactly suit our orchestra leader, Mr. Fleischman. But it did, very much, please his daughter, Jennie.

Cooking up play after play in the custom of stock companies in the provinces, I had no alternative but to write lyrics and compose music for the rest of the cast. This meant spending additional hours in the theater with Jennie at the piano. When finished—and if her father wasn't there—I would walk her home.

Jennie was about nineteen. Not a beauty and a bit on the plump side, she nevertheless had an interesting face dominated by extraordinary gray eyes, with a dreamy look that I found most compelling. Wholly absorbed in her music, she too, had ambitions for the concert stage. But her parents could not sustain the cost of cultivating more than one concertist—her brother, Max. He had gotten a scholarship, so he went off to Paris. She had also won a scholarship, but it was her lot to remain in the theater with her father; especially since it was doubtful that he would be engaged without her at the piano. Actors didn't want to learn their music via the fiddle anymore. They preferred the piano. The piano was the backbone of the orchestra, small combination that it was. Every performer knew that, with Jennie at the piano, their worries were over. She was an orchestra by herself, they maintained.

Though Canadian born, Jennie spoke a fluent Yiddish. To me, this was an important factor. Here was a young lady with whom I could communicate. To seek out the company of some young girls in town was something I neither had time for, nor was I prepared to spend the money such socializing would cost.

I could see Jennie only in the theater, at rehearsals during the day and evenings at performance. To spend time with her after the show at a restaurant was something her father would never allow. First of all, he still lived by the moral code of Ostrovca: a decent girl doesn't go out on a date with a fellow who is not her fiance—and without a chaperone at that! Secondly, Fleischman did not care to encourage his daughter's friendship with an actor. His talented daughter was surely destined for something better than that!

I was so completely wrapped up in playing theater, studying roles and juggling my salary that I didn't realize how Jennie felt toward me. She never indicated by as much as a word, or a hint that she was far from indifferent toward me. She was not talkative to begin with. And although I had become exceedingly fond of her, it never occurred to me that, out of our innocent walks together, there would develop a deep affection. How could I possibly contemplate any such thing as a future together? I had only just arrived in the country and wasn't able even to support myself. Get married? Crazy!

Literary Plays

It was in our midweek repertoire that I truly came into my own as an actor, playing the literary works of Peretz Hirshbein, Sholom Aleichem, Jacob Gordin, Z. Libin, Fishel Bimko, Leon Kobrin, Itzhak-David Berkowitz and Sholem Asch. From the years I played in Lithuania, I knew these popular classics as well as I knew my own name. In Toronto I was now again receiving high praise, both from the audience and from the critic Kirshenbaum, for the interpretation of my roles. It was a pleasant surprise for my fellow-actors that I, the young bouffe-comedian, could grasp at the very heart of the characterizations my parts called for.

My pal, Gertler, on the other hand, was greatly in need of sympathy. Honigman and Auerbach were allotting themselves the leading male roles and assigning Gertler the villain parts. He took the hissing and booing personally.

Very successful in our literary offerings was our dramatic leading lady, Henrietta Schnitzer. A beautiful woman, tall and lissome, she cut a most alluring figure on stage. Credit was also due her husband, Louis Schnitzer, an impresario and financier of the first Yiddish Art Theater in America, under the artistic leadership of Jacob Ben-Ami, Emanuel Reicher and Rudolph Schildkraut. This enterprise eventually led to the establishment of the Yiddish Art Theater, directed by Maurice Schwartz. Henrietta Schnitzer was undoubtedly a great asset to our company in Toronto.

Another member of our troupe who gave an excellent account of himself was Jacob Goldstein. He stood out like the genuine talent he was. One of the very few in our midst who knew the art of makeup, he used this skill like a master. His daughter, Charlotte Goldstein, who later became an actress of note in the Yiddish Art Theater, surely inherited a good share of talent from him.

* * *

A dramatic group of young Zionist students from the University of Toronto invited me to direct them in a play to be given in Hebrew. The idea appealed to me tremendously and I agreed to help them. Directing an amateur group was not new to me. I had already done this with success when I coached the dramatic group of the Trade Union in Kovno. It was the first Yiddish performance permitted by the Lithuanian government in the newly built State Opera House in Kovno's municipal park.

My Toronto students and I decided to present Herman Heierman's play, *The Eternal Jew,* translated into Hebrew by one of the group. I had played it in Yiddish with Leonid Sokoloff at the Narodny Dom (People's Theater) in Kovno. I did not follow Sokoloff's direction. Technically, it would not have worked because the group was to perform on an improvised stage. Here, I felt, was an opportunity to try out my own wings as a director and block out my own structure for the play. I sketched all my formations and guidelines of action in a notebook and came prepared for rehearsal.

Directors, under whom I had worked up to this time, including those I encountered later on, carried no such blueprints. I had no difficulty with my dramatic group and the performance created a genuine stir in town. My stock in the community soared overnight.

My fellow actors too, began to see me from a new angle. My friend, Chanineh, of course, was ready to burst with pride. What's more, my new endeavor found favor in the eyes of the Fleischman family—and admiration in the eyes of Jennie, toward whom I felt more and more attracted each day.

Adding my honorarium received as director to my scraped-together savings, I made up the $150 required for membership, and sent it off with my application to the Hebrew Actors' Union. It bore the co-signatures of four union members.

I received a receipt for the sum accompanied by a letter from Reuben Guskin telling me that my application would be acted upon by the executive board of the union and that they would grant me an audition in accordance with the union by-laws. In the event I did not pass the audition, my money would be refunded.

Around March, it was customary in those days for the New York star attractions to set out on the road, making personal appearances. It was with the greatest anticipation that I awaited the American luminaries of whom I had heard so much about.

The first of these to come to Toronto was Max Gable. His wife, Jennie Goldstein, whom he'd helped to make famous, remained in New York to continue her season at Gable's People's Theater on the Bowery. He had brought, instead, Jennie's sister, Esther Goldstein. His arrangement with our management was to play for a percentage from the gross receipts. To keep an eye on the box office, he brought along his son, manager Harry Gable.

The first play produced with our New York star was *The Great Moment,* a highly successful melodrama he had written with Steinberg. According to custom, before starting rehearsals, Gable read the play. Several actors in our troupe had played with this noted guest, but I was totally unknown to him, and I really shook at the prospect of playing with the legendary Max Gable—director of his own theater; playwright of a score of successes, regisseur of productions which invariably scored fantastic hits in New York and wherever else they played.

When Gable finished reading his play, the cast applauded. Naturally, I joined in the applause. Gable observed us with a cynical smile.

I couldn't help wondering how we were going to install the rain effect that played such an important role in the melodrama. According to the New York press, crowds were storming the theater, curious to witness the publicized spectacle of spectacles—the cascading of hundreds of thousands of gallons of water on stage.

"Who is going to play David Papper's role?" Gable asked. This was so odd, I thought. Instead of naming the character in the play, he was referring to the actor who was playing the role in the New York company.

"Papper's role should go to Sam Gertler," Auerbach replied, aware that Honigman was sharpening his claws to pounce on this particular part himself.

"Gertler?" Gable wavered. Sizing him up over the rim of his spectacles, he tossed Gertler the handwritten script, saying, "All right, let's see what you can do with this plum! And now," he went on, "who will play Charlie Cohan's part?"

"Yablokoff!" a trio of voices responded, as my three bosses pointed at me.

"Who?" Gable again adjusted the pince-nez he wore on a black string around his neck. "Oh, yes. Well then, let it be Yablokoff," he sighed, resigned no doubt that this surely spelled disaster for his production.

Honigman ventured, "Who will play Frances Sinkoff's part, if Sadie isn't playing?"

"Esther, of course," said Gable flatly. "That's why I brought her with me. She had seen the play many times in New York and knows the musical numbers too. She'll be all right."

"Esther Goldstein?" So went the whispers behind Gable's back. "Is she going to play the ingenue? Since when is she an actress? Can she sing? Dance? And what about a privilege from the union?! Oh well, having Max Gable as a brother-in-law makes everything kosher!"

Next morning, at the first rehearsal, while the rest of the cast desperately struggled with their smudged and scribbled-over scripts, Gertler and I spouted our first-act lines by heart. We had a burning ambition to show Mr. Gable that he could depend on us.

"Well, how do you like that?!" he marveled at us. "These boys have learned their parts overnight! I wish my New York actors were that good! They are still depending on the prompter for every word. Senile! That's what they are! Listen to these fellas—that's youth for you! This is what we need. New faces! But, pardon me, we have a union, if you please! Will some of those cronies stand for new members?!"

The Great Moment proved to be just as huge a success in Toronto as in New York. Credit for the rain effect was unquestionably due to Honigman and a stagehand. Together, they masterminded the machinations of it so craftily, the audience could have sworn these torrents of water poured from the very heavens.

Business was great. Sam Gertler turned in an excellent performance. Gable was highly pleased with him and Gertler, of course, walked on air. Also complimenting me for my handling of the role, he said, "Oh, if only you were a union man. I could certainly use you in my theater." At my explanation that I had already sent in my application, Gable laughed.

"An application? First of all," he explained, "you will have a mighty long wait. Secondly, if they do take you in, you will have to wait your turn in line. And as a 'liner' you won't be permitted to play in New York for three years. After that, you'll be too old," he joked, "and God knows, we already have enough character actors in the union as it is!"

Gable produced several of his success plays with us: *Her Great Secret*,, collaborated with Louis Freiman; *Mother's Wedding Gown*, with S. Steinberg; *The Street Girl*, built on Yushkevitch's drama, *In Town*, in which Gable played his crowning role of the shoemaker.

Gertler confided to me that Gable wanted to engage him for next season at his New York theater—providing he had been admitted into the union by that time. Gable also promised to speak to Guskin, the manager, and to President Greenfield, about putting Gertler on the list of candidates scheduled for auditions.

Gertler had already flunked one audition eight years before. How much longer must he wait? About the three-year waiting line—well, Gable said, this hurdle could also be overcome, somehow. Let him first of all become a member. I knew what this long-awaited break meant to Gertler, and I wished him good luck from the bottom of my heart.

* * *

The next attraction after Gable was the musical-comedy couple, Minnie and Louis Birnbaum. They put on an operetta called *Avremele, der Rebbe,* by Harry Kalmanowitz, music by Philip Lawkowsky. Soon after this, Gertler received the news instructing him to report for his audition in the union. Evidently, Gable's intervention had brought results. The special auditions-committee in New York had assigned Gertler two excerpts from two separate plays. One, from the role of Gregoir, in Jacob Gordin's *Kreutzer Sonata* and the other from *Longing Hearts* by Gable and S. Steinberg.

This was certainly a time of turmoil for Gertler. He couldn't eat, he couldn't sleep. And although he knew his assigned roles, having played them many times, and gave every line tremendous feeling, he was in a state of panic.

There was no doubt in the mind of anyone in our troupe but that he would be admitted into the union by a landslide. Everybody liked Gertler, and the union members in our company took no chances. They each sent off letters to their colleagues in New York, importuning them to attend Gertler's audition and give him their yes votes. And what was more important, they were to canvass more yes votes among the other members.

At night, after our performance, Chanineh and I accompanied Gertler to the train for New York. His audition was scheduled for the next morning. In this way he would be spared from one night's show, only. We sent him off wishing him Godspeed and the best of luck to return as a full-fledged union man.

The next day everyone moped about with fluttering hearts. We were in the midst of preparing a new show, but nobody was in the mood for rehearsal.

About 5 p.m. we were informed by telegram: Gertler did not make it! Backstage, a pall hung over us, all through that evening's performance. We knew only too well what a devastating blow this was for our colleague and our hearts went out to him.

Next morning, when the train from New York slid into the depot, there I was, waiting for the crestfallen Gertler. The moment he laid eyes on me he broke into tears. He looked as if he had shriveled overnight. It pained me just to look at him. We wended our way home and I could not find the words to comfort him.

"Why? Why?" he kept repeating.

Why, indeed! There was a good reason for Gertler's failure. As soon as it got around that Gable wanted him for the coming season in New York, certain so-called "friends" got together and voted him out.

If this could happen to Gertler, I thought, what could I possibly expect in the Yiddish theater, in America?

* * *

When the once-glamorous Malvina Lobel came to Toronto as guest artist, she was already an ailing and resigned woman. Several actors remarked: "If she were not the sister of Rose Greenfield and Betty Jacobs, prominent as the actress wives of union president Greenfield and theater director, Jacob Jacobs, would the management bring her as an attraction? Never! The woman is passe!"

My fellow actors were dead wrong. The audience received Madame Lobel with warmth and reverence, remembering her earlier appearances there. In her heyday, she had appeared in New York with David Kessler, Jacob P. Adler, Morris Morrison and Boris Thomashevsky. She had also toured England, Poland, Russia and Romania, and was the first actress on the European stage to play Bisson's *Madame X* and Walter Brown's *Every Woman* in Yiddish. It was her success play, *Madame X*, in fact, that Malvina Lobel produced with our company in Toronto.

True enough, in the first part of the play she was no longer the young alluring woman whom men were supposed to fight over. But in the latter, highly dramatic scenes, she gave a magnificently moving performance, creating stark realism.

I was assigned the role of the young lawyer who is unaware that the woman he is defending against a murder charge—a woman who only identifies herself as Madame X, is his own mother. Many variations of this melodrama have been produced on the Yiddish stage, but none can compare to the original.

The high spot of my role was the lengthy, heart-stirring defense plea, which the young advocate holds before the court. I asked Madame's permission to rewrite my part's German-style prose into modern Yiddish. I had had enough of twisting my tongue over the mixture of Yiddish-English hodgepodge in my roles; did I now have to cope with the stilted, outmoded Deutschish Yiddish?

At first, Madame Lobel balked at the idea. My role had been played by countless actors in Europe, in America and in South America. All of them spoke the prose as written and it was good. Why should I suddenly want to change it? If I speak a pure Yiddish, she contended, I will sound like a Jewish lawyer and the play is definitely not of Jewish life.

"Besides," she said, "I am on stage throughout your monologue and there are moments when I must react on your lines. I am accustomed to the original script and if you change it, I am afraid it will take me out of the proper mood and hinder my reactions."

Well, I thought, she's got a point there. But, I suppose, lacking the strength to debate with me any further, she agreed to let me have my way— with an ultimatum: if, during rehearsal, she found that it distracted or threw her off in any way, then I had to go back to the original text.

At rehearsal, Madame Lobel sat and listened as I delivered my defense speech in an unadulterated, literal Yiddish, and the tears streamed from her eyes.

"I would never have believed," she admitted, "that the same prose could ring so beautiful, so warm and soul-stirring, in plain 'mameloshn!' The Yiddish has given me new inspiration to act."

When Malvina Lobel asked me to write my version of the role into her script, I took it as the greatest compliment.

Eight years later, when I was finally granted an audition in the actors' union, one of the two roles I was to portray was the lawyer from *Madame X*— in Yiddish!

Jacob Ben-Ami

Upon learning that our guest star was to be Jacob Ben-Ami, I was enthralled. Who could have dreamed that in my very first year in America I would have the privilege of playing with the world-famed Jacob Ben-Ami?!

I had heard about him in Kovno. As one of the famous Peretz Hirshbein Players, Ben-Ami was, even at that time, featured as a leading artist and regisseur. I had also read of his activities on the Yiddish and English-speaking stage in America and knew about his association as star and director with Arthur Hopkins and the Theater Guild.

During that period Ben-Ami had very little time to devote to the Yiddish theater. His production of Sven Lange's play, *Samson and Delilah*, created a stir on the American stage. In Yiddish, his guest performances were made only on special occasions. Thus, his engagement with us in Toronto imbued the entire community with a festive mood.

We opened with Ben-Ami's Yiddish version of *Samson and Delilah*. Up to this part of the season we had already plowed through a good many productions of every sort: operettas, comedies and dramas. Our approach had been earnest toward each of them. But working with Ben-Ami proved to me anew, how lucky the performer, who must all too often spout a lot of gibberish, or portray robots instead of flesh-and-blood people, can feel in a play of cultural value with a director who doesn't merely expound literary stage art, but actually practices what he preaches. Such a personality was—and has remained—Jacob Ben-Ami.

Although I was not enchanted with the play—the inflated raves in the American press may have led me to expect much more from the story—I was impressed with the artistic direction that went into it. What a difference, I thought, between a Gable-type melodrama with its theatrical gimmicks, and a Ben-Ami production, well thought out and consistent down to the last nuance. It is the difference between a burlap sack, crudely basted together, and a fine piece of linen, delicately stitched in silk.

I reveled in the natural tone, the realistic interplay, the coordination of the stage settings, props and lighting. I paid close attention, eager to learn how a performance of this caliber can be brought to life in the hands of an accredited director.

Samson and Delilah drew a huge attendance at every performance, including intellectuals we had rarely seen in the theater. No doubt, the name of Ben-Ami pulled them in. Yet, despite the biggest box-office receipts, we still could not risk running the same play for more than a week. We went ahead rehearsing *Green Fields* by Hirshbein and *The Idiot* by Dostoevski, both starred and directed by Ben-Ami. Business was exceptionally good and the management wanted to hold our guest over for another week or two.

During the season we had already produced several plays of Ben-Ami's repertoire. In Europe, it was not at all unusual to repeat the same repertory plays featuring different guest artists. In fact, it was a curiosity to compare the interpretation of one performer with another in the same role.

But, on the road, as well as in New York itself, no producer would take a chance on repeating a show that had already had its run; unless it was a special benefit for an organization, or a testimonial performance for one of the cast. It only gave customers an excuse to say they'd already seen the show, and keep away. Sometimes the box office even felt the pinch with a new play, if its title sounded familiar. Notices would have to go out assuring the public that this was a new show, never before presented!

We faced a real problem in Toronto. What was Ben-Ami to play for his extended engagement? Goldstein surprised me by requesting, "Yablokoff, maybe you have a play for Ben-Ami?"

I gaped at him, flabbergasted. "Yes," said Goldstein. "Maybe you have some script or other from the European repertoire. You, yourself showed me a wicker hamper full of manuscripts you brought along from the old country."

"I do have something!" I suddenly recalled, *"The Cantor of Vilna* by Marc Arnstein. Yes, I believe this drama would be most suitable for Mr. Ben-Ami!"

I had taken part in this play with Leonid Sokoloff in Kovno. The Vilna Troupe had also presented this fine drama. The leading role of Yoel-Dovid, the cantor, was just right for Ben-Ami. I had, in fact, long entertained the idea of playing this role myself someday, when I had reached a more mature age. The plan I had formulated was to produce it as a play with music, rather than a straight drama.

That same evening after the show, Ben-Ami asked me to join him for coffee. This was such an honor I could feel my head swelling like a balloon. I had already told him about my plan to rework and redirect it someday.

"Look," he said, "the management wants me to stay on for another week. I have read the play and I like it. The role is entirely new to me and I can see that directing this play is complicated. Time is short. To work on a new role and involve myself at the same time with directing...well, this is quite impossible. I would appreciate it very much if you would do me a personal favor and direct the play for me."

I couldn't believe my ears. Me? He was asking me to direct Jacob Ben-Ami?!

From the first day I'd set foot on stage, back in Grodno, it was my wont to hover in the wings during rehearsal absorbing whatever the director was doing—artistically and technically. The play could have been given for the umpteenth time, yet I still hung around soaking up every detail as if it were a premiere performance. And if I had to dress in the basement, or on the top floor, I changed in a hurry and flew back to my post in the wings to watch the audience reaction. I confess I do the same to this day.

During that season in Toronto we played several works with which I happened to be familiar. I made no pretense of original direction. I simply made use of the details gleaned from Sokoloff and Mikhailov in Kovno. I also helped out a good deal with the literary plays. Yet the credit in the programs always went to either Honigman, Auerback, or whoever was playing the leading role.

I trembled at the idea, but how could I turn down the request of such a gentleman? And how could I let slip such an opportunity, which can come up in the theater only once in a lifetime, to direct a play with Ben-Ami?!

The news that I was going to direct *The Cantor of Vilna* hit the troupe like a bombshell. But I assigned the roles accordingly and allotted myself a small, incidental part of a blind, elderly character, who lies huddled on the upper ledge of a huge, old-fashioned European oven.

It was Ben-Ami who, at the very first rehearsal, established the proper attitude of the cast toward me as their regisseur. He asked questions every step of the way and heeded every move I indicated in the mise en scenes.

Honigman took over the responsibility for scenery, furniture and props, built down to the last detail of my instructions. I invited my group of drama students to come—minus pay—to fill out the general background of people. The result was most rewarding.

The play was enthusiastically received. If one is destined for success it seems to come full circle. Not only did I receive praise as a director, I was also given acknowledgment for the characterization of my minor role, the ninety-year-old man.

Bessie Thomashevsky

The last attraction of our Toronto theater season was Bessie Thomashevsky. She was a most congenial person, a delight to work with. Although past her middle years, her animated features radiated an impish charm.

Bessie did several of her repertory plays with us, appearing in roles in which she had endeared herself everywhere. We played *The Imported Wife* by Moshe Richter and *Today's Women* by Harry Kalmonowitz. The crowds flocked to see her and thoroughly enjoyed her lively antics on stage. Most people actually wanted to see her do her former hit parts: *Hantche, in America,* or *Der Greener Bokher.* But Bessie was wise enough to realize that though these shows might bring in more money to the box office, these were roles in which she had to sport pants. And this no longer suited her figure.

The Doctor's Wives by Leon Kobrin was an outstanding success. In her tragicomic role of Minke, the servant girl, Bessie emerged as a first-rate artist. Her down-to-earth portrayal of this hoydenish domestic aroused laughter amid tears of compassion. There were actresses who tried to imitate her style, but could not compare to her in the least.

I played the part of Itzik, the butcher boy, opposite Bessie, a role originated by the exceedingly popular Sam Kasten in New York. Here, my experience of playing bouffe-comedians was a great help in acquiring the buoyancy that characterized Itzik, the plain-spoken, homespun butcher boy, with whom Minke, the servant girl, although married to a doctor, is in love.

When Bessie Thomashevsky expressed her approval of my acting, I was thrilled beyond words. She promised to put in a good word for me in New York. And she kept her promise. When she was asked to appear in *The Doctor's Wives* in a New York theater, she insisted that I be given a privilege to play the part of Itzik. The actors' union complied with her request and I appeared with her at the plush Second Avenue Theater in New York—the mecca of show business.

A Testimonial

A testimonial performance—a benefit—was a momentous event in the life of an actor. The sweet bit of acknowledgment he received from colleagues, friends, and from the public meant equally as much to him as the few extra hundred dollars he stood to profit. It was also his privilege to choose any play in which he felt he could star for that special evening. A benefit performance always brought with it an air of holiday excitement, not only backstage but in the audience as well.

The first such evening in Toronto was held in honor of our leading lady, Sadie Sheingold. My personal tribute to her was a little gold wristwatch, bought on time from a jeweler friend, a theater-devotee, out of my scrimped-together savings for the friendship and compassion she had shown me, an aspiring newcomer. Sadie was deeply moved. In fact, everyone in the troupe thought it was a very praiseworthy gesture on my part.

I could not afford presents for the others in the company as each testimonial came up. But what I was able to do, instead, was even more appreciated. Rarely did anyone have the original score that went with the play selected for their particular evening, and I would often be approached with the plea: "Please, Yabby, do me a favor like a good fella and write a little song, or a little duet for me." It was always a little this or that. Actually, it often meant a big number, a good-sized duet, if not an entire ensemble to fit the continuity of the play. I couldn't let them down; especially, when it offered a good excuse to get together with Jennie at the piano. She would meet me at the theater, and her father had to accept that we were working on some special material for someone's upcoming benefit.

One day, Auerbach took Gertler and me aside and offered us a most attractive deal. Since Gertler and I could scarcely have amassed a fortune out of our season's earnings, he would try, he said, to work out a joint benefit performance for us. And this, despite the fact that neither of us had any benefit proviso in our agreements. The house would grant us an evening on a fifty-fifty basis; fifty percent from the gross receipts for the management and fifty percent for Gertler and me to share.

We grabbed at Auerbach's proposition! We were broke, anyway, so what did we have to lose?

34

Jennie and I

There is hardly anything in life more tragic than being alone in the world, and lonely. This feeling was beginning to creep up on me as I contemplated the approaching summer hiatus. I had become thoroughly integrated into Toronto's way of life, its atmosphere so reminiscent of Europe, so close with my fellow troupers, that it was like being part of a family. It was difficult to think that, soon, very soon, each of us would be going his own way. Even more difficult to accept was that I would be parting with my dear Jennie, with whom I found it so easy to talk, and who occupied my thoughts so much in the after-theater hours, as I lay alone in my lonely little room.

During my frequent walks with Jennie, seeing her home after rehearsals, I often poured out my innermost thoughts for her. She absorbed my words but rarely commented on them. Yet, despite her reticence, I sensed that she felt a deep compassion for me and fully sympathized with my being so alone in the world.

Passover soon rolled around. The Yiddish theaters never performed on the first Seder night. In fact, it is a union regulation in America that this night belongs to the actors, as does the night of Yom Kippur. And, although the theater is dark, actors were still paid for this holiday night.

Who prevailed upon Jennie's father to invite me to the first Seder, I could not be sure. But it certainly came as a great surprise. I had never been asked to their home before. I learned that my invitation was motivated by Jennie's younger sister, Fay. She was a great fan of mine and could not imagine a more desirable suitor for her sister than me.

That Seder night among the Fleischman family, I was vividly reminded of my own home in Grodno; the home from which I was gone close to five years. The warm, family atmosphere gave me the feeling of being back at the Seder table with my own dear mother and father, for whom I was so homesick— my own brothers and sisters, whom I missed so terribly.

After the Seder, Max, the oldest son, home from Paris for the holiday, took up his fiddle, Jennie took her place at the piano, and together they played duets until late into the night.

After the guests were gone, Jennie saw me out to the porch. I don't know where I got the courage, but suddenly I took her in my arms and kissed her.

On my way back to my lonely room that night I walked on air. There were no further doubts in my mind but that Jennie was my destined bride.

* * *

The next evening after the show, Goldstein stopped me. "There's something important I would like to discuss with you," he said. "Get dressed so we can go for a little walk."

Removing my makeup and quickly changing, I was eager to hear what Goldstein had in mind. As we walked along I sensed that he was uncertain as to how to begin.

"Look, Yablokoff, it's not pleasant to butt into someone else's affairs. It's always healthier to mind your own business."

"As for instance?" I asked. "Please tell me—what on earth did I do?"

"You see, Jennie's father spoke to me today," he finally came to the point. "I have known the Fleischmans for years. Fleischman hasn't the nerve to talk directly to you. He's not even sure there is anything to talk about! Well, it's about Jennie. I've known her since she was so high. I know you don't belong to the category of actors who would simply turn a girl's head. We are all convinced that you are a straightforward, decent young man. Jennie is a well-brought up girl. The fact that she's in love with you is obvious. And from all appearances I gather that you are not exactly indifferent to her, either. The season will soon be over. You'll be leaving and the girl will remain brokenhearted. I know I sound like the last act of a melodrama. But, you see, I'm a friend of the Fleischmans, so pardon me for taking the liberty of asking you point blank; are you serious about the girl, or is it one of those romances that actors joke about: 'I loved you, but the season is over'? Don't hold it against me, Yablokoff. I promised I would speak to you."

I was bewildered. We continued our walk in silence, as I tried to gather my thoughts, "I don't hold it against you," I said. "On the contrary, I'm grateful for your being so outspoken. I find myself in a terrible dilemma. I'm all alone... there is no one with whom I can talk things over, or ask advice. I have infinite confidence in your friendship. It's true that Jennie is very dear to me. But to commit myself now to anything. It would be tantamount to a crime. I've been in the country only nine months, with no outlook for the future. I don't know English. Out of my earnings this season I won't have saved a nickel to see me through the summer. I wish I could at least pay back part of what I owe my brother-in-law for the cost of bringing me to America. Besides, I must help my parents in Grodno. Their circumstances are pretty sad. The Poles are blocking Jews from getting any work. I can't even support myself. And with debts hanging over my head, is it right for me to fall into the same pattern of family life that Gertler leads? Like struggling in Toronto, while his wife is with her folks in some other state? The way I see it, it would be the height of irresponsibility! It would mean taking an innocent girl and bringing her nothing but unhappiness. Don't you think so?"

"Yes, I see your point," Goldstein conceded. "But it is not as tragic as you imagine. If you are really in love, then all this figuring and calculating doesn't mean a thing. Love always finds a way."

"Well, meanwhile, I'm thinking of going to New York. Let me see what the near future will bring," I offered as a tentative concession. "I'll look for a possible theater engagement, or perhaps find some other type of work. And if it is to be, then..."

"Then may be too late," Goldstein interrupted. "Don't forget, Jennie was born in this provincial town, where everybody knows what's cooking in his neighbor's pot. Your leaving Toronto will put her in an awkward position. People like to gossip, you know. Is it any wonder that her parents are so concerned? It could very well hurt her reputation in the community."

Sensing that I had no defenses against his arguments, Goldstein forged ahead like an expert matchmaker.

"Jennie is a girl who can pull her own weight anywhere! She has a pair of golden hands. A girl like that, a graduate from the Toronto conservatory, is an excellent match for you. She can be a great asset to you in your stage career. I'm quite confident that you will land a good job for the coming season. You and Jennie, a couple like you. My God, you are bound to be grabbed up! Think it over."

The following day, Jennie did not show up for rehearsal. She, evidently, knew about my talk with Goldstein and was too shy to face me. That same evening, I asked her to wait for me after the show, instead of going directly home with her father, because I had to see her and talk to her about something very important.

Neither of us uttered a word all the way to her house. Jennie suggested we sit on the porch for a while, since the night was so spring-like.

The stars were out. The street was quiet. Hesitantly, I began by pouring out my innermost feelings. I explained my situation down to the last detail. Jennie agreed that it would be folly to make any concrete plans for our future at this particular time. "I am willing to wait," she assured me, "but my parents won't like the idea."

We came to the conclusion that the best thing for us to do was to become formally engaged. We could wait to be married until I had settled on something tangible. Meanwhile, I would go back to New York at the close of the season and look around for an opening in a theater; perhaps even find one for both of us. Then, we could marry in Toronto, or elsewhere. This, we felt, was a sensible arrangement, one that would also meet with the approval of her parents.

"Hymie!" a voice suddenly broke in from an upstairs window. It was Jennie's mother. It was the first time I heard my name anglicized to Hymie. "It's late.

Why should you walk home at this late hour? You'll soon have to get up for rehearsal. You may as well sleep here the remaining few hours till morning. I prepared Max's bed for you. Come in, the two of you, it's late! Haven't you had enough talk? Tomorrow is another day—come in!"

I needed no further coaxing. This unexpected invitation to sleep over, and calling me by my first name...let it be Hymie...was proof enough that the Fleischmans were ready to accept me into the family.

* * *

While preparations for our engagement were going on at the house, I was involved with the benefit I was to share with Gertler. I had decided on the play, *Hard to be a Jew* by Sholom Aleichem, and staged it according to Reuben Wendorff's interpretation. Gertler played Ivanov the Gentile student and I, the role of Schneierson, the Jewish student. We happened to be exceptionally well cast for these two opposite characters.

Our performance went beautifully. The theater was packed both by Gertler's fans and mine, as well as the general public, all of them filled with curiosity to ogle the actor, who was soon to take a Canadian bride.

Our benefit performance brought us honors and presents. The important thing was that between us we shared a nice few hundred dollars. Gertler needed it badly and I, equally as much.

Jennie assured me that she could do without an engagement ring—an iron-clad tradition in respectable families. Still, I had a surprise for her. My reliable theater buff, the jeweler, had prepared a diamond ring no groom need be ashamed to present to his betrothed. The good man surely made no profit on me.

I put in a call to my sister Mary in New York. Judging by her frigid mazel-tov, it was clear that she wasn't overjoyed. "You only just got here, and already you need a rope around your neck?" she berated me. "What's your hurry?!"

I held off writing the news of my engagement to my parents. They would surely think I had gone out of my mind.

Our engagement was held on Sunday. The company was no longer play-ing in Detroit and Buffalo, so our Sundays were free. It was open house and all through the day guests arrived to eat, drink and wish us well. Besides our theater staff, there were many friends of the bride, with relatives and landsleit from Papa Fleischman's side, as well as the Silversteins from Mama Fleischman's side. And from the groom's side—only me.

35

Gossip at the Cafe

Arriving in New York I handed my brother-in-law a crackling $100 bill toward paying off my passage to the United States. And to my sister's peevish comment, "What was your hurry in becoming engaged? Afraid you'd remain a bachelor?" I made no reply.

My friend Gertler and I took daily strolls, stopping in at the union to inquire if there were any prospects for out-of-town theaters for the coming season. Here, nothing had changed. Tables on the right were occupied by the elite, and tables on the left by those lower in rank. The pinochle was still going strong in the rear.

I did, nevertheless, learn something. Certain actors, hanging around and taking inventory of the crowd, would step out to the nearest phone booth and call the Royale to have themselves paged. This was to make some manager, sitting there, aware of their popularity. Good old Herrmann, the busboy, who always answered the phone, was wise to this byplay. As soon as the actor came back in, he would announce in his loudest tones: "You just had a call from a Broadway producer!" This, too, could earn Herrmann an extra tip.

Mandel, resuming his role as guide, pointed out: "See that table over there, that's the great Aaron Lebedeff. He became a star in America overnight. And sitting with him is Leon Blank."

"Now that's what I call an actor!" interjected Gertler, who, after a time, actually began imitating Blank, his idol.

"Who is the attractive lady at the next table?" I asked.

"That's Bella Mysell, with her husband, the composer, Alexander Olshanetsky. Bella is the daughter of the actor, Hyman Mysell. She's starring as prima donna with Aaron Lebedeff at the National Theater."

This was how I got to know the outstanding luminaries of the Yiddish stage. There was Joseph Rumshinsky, known as the dean of composers, the handsome star Michal Michalesko, and another young composer, Sholem Secunda. In a little while, the queen of Second Avenue, Molly Picon, strode in with her husband Jacob Kalich. They were accompanied by a tall man in a black hat. This was their representative and road-booking agent, Edwin A. Relkin.

Over in a corner, deep in conversation with the literati, was the director of the Yiddish Art Theater, Maurice Schwartz.

Outdoors, at one of the little sidewalk tables, I noticed Samuel Golden-burg. I had a tentative agreement with him—and this was to be kept hush-hush. He had contracted for the Amphion Theater in Williamsburg.

Other Yiddish stars were away for the summer, guest starring in Europe, South America and elsewhere. Before the opening of the New York season they were sure to show up at the Royale. Where else could they discuss theater politics, and maybe pick up a hint via the grapevine of some composer's well-guarded leitmotiv (theme song), already brewing for the next musical in a competitor's theater?

And so, like the rest of the clientele, we sat around sipping iced coffee topped by a blob of scalded milk, with ears and eyes open for gossip.

Yiddish Vaudeville

All during the summer, the Prospect Theater in the Bronx presented Yiddish vaudeville. People streamed there from every neighborhood. True enough, in those days before air conditioners, it was a sweaty proposition. But people didn't mind. A man could remove his jacket, treat himself and his lady to a cooling container of ice cream, or lemonade bought right in the theater, and enjoy a Yiddish variety show. These vaudeville programs were run by the Yiddish theater stagehands: Louis Lapidus, Abe Kantrowitz (Pete), and Morris Shapiro. They too, found it difficult to push through the summer layoff, so they became "impresarios" and paid wages to the artists and the rest of the staff.

They offered a new attraction every week: Pesach'ke Burstein, in tails and high hat, a cane tucked under his arm, sang, danced, whistled his catchy tunes and the customers didn't let him off the stage.

I greatly enjoyed the sketches played by such popular vaudeville couples, as Ziegenlaub and Rubin, Louis and Florence Weiss, Anna Zeeman and Joseph Tantzman, Louis Kramer and Rose Wallerstein.

Nellie Casman and Annie Lubin were tremendous favorites. Their material, punctuated by suggestive gyrations, were chock-full of double entendres, but the audience lapped it up.

An outstanding attraction at the vaudeville theater was a young boy in his teens. His voice was appealingly sweet and lyrical. This youngster, Seymour Rechtzeit, was a natural heart-and-soul singer. The brother of actor Jack Rechtzeit, he later became an actor, too. At that particular time, Joseph Rumshinsky's operetta, *The Rabbi's Melody*, had created a stir. A very poignant number in it, called "Ich Benk Aheim" (I Long for Home), was sung by the incomparable Ludwig Satz, who made the song a favorite to this day. Yet when this boy undertook to do a number so closely associated with the star, Ludwig Satz, the theater shook with applause for his self-styled interpretation.

Gertler and I, on a pass, hardly ever missed these weekly bills. And having initiated my pal as another patron of the Second Avenue cafeteria, we would then head downtown to sustain ourselves with a bowl of soup and plenty of bread and butter, for all of fifteen cents.

My New Impresario—Hollander

It was on the boardwalk at Coney Island that I met the actor-director, Isidore Hollander. Since he had an appointment with friends in nearby Seagate, we arranged to meet on the boardwalk. Some of the first among our theater people to settle inside the "gate," a private enclave, were Moshe Richter, Samuel Goldenburg, Sholem Perlmutter, Maurice Schwartz and Ludwig Satz.

"Guskin recommended you to me," Hollander said. "He knows that you have a signed agreement with Sioma Goldenburg at the Amphion Theater. The union won't allow it, Guskin told me, so you may as well as forget it. With the Hollander Troupe in Montreal, you will stand a chance of getting a union privilege."

The contract I had signed with Goldenburg was a step forward for me: to play with such a renowned artist like Goldenburg—and in a theater in Brooklyn. It was not Second Avenue, of course, but it was still New York. Let alone the seventy-five dollars a week I was supposed to get—a whole thirty-dollar raise from my Toronto pay! Of course, Goldenburg's stipulation in the agreement read that I had to get the permission of the union. Without this approval our agreement would be null and void.

"I was told that you can also compose a musical number, if necessary," Hollander went on to say. "How much salary do you want, Yablokoff?"

"Mr. Goldenburg promised me seventy-five dollars a week," I said.

"Sioma Goldenburg promised?" he burst into laughter. "It's easy enough to promise but try and get it. I don't want to merely promise, I want to pay! You're still a little green, so maybe you don't know. Tell him, Mandel," he said, "can I pay such a price? With such tremendous expenses? Impossible! I know how much you were paid in Toronto. Well then, I'll raise you a five-spot. I assure you that in my Hollander troupe you will play 'better theater' exactly as with Goldenburg. How long do you think he will last in the Amphion Theater in Williamsburg? You tell him, Mandel," he urged my friend to back him up, although Mandel refrained from taking part in the haggling. "I can give it to you in writing that, after New Year's I will have Goldenburg as a guest in my Monument National Theater, so you'll still have a chance to play with him if it means so much to you. An easy fellow, he's not! Ask Mandel."

Hollander engaged me for fifty dollars a week. The minimum union scale was fifty-five, but it was shrewd business to chew off at least a fiver from a non-union actor. He also promised me a fifty-dollar advance on my salary. This money, I decided, would go toward a trip to Toronto to visit my bride-to-be.

After escorting my future director as far as the gate, I dropped in at the nearest candy store to put in a long distance call to Toronto, to tell Jennie the good news. Jennie was elated at the prospect of having me in Canada for the season. I was planning to spend a few weeks with her, I told her, until the start of rehearsals in Montreal.

I spent three weeks with Jennie and her family. My future in-laws treated me like a son. Jennie's older brother, Max, had not returned to his studies in Paris. He was getting all kinds of offers from American symphony orchestras, and since Toronto had no future for him as a concert violinist, he was earnestly considering settling in New York.

This idea appealed to me as it did to the Fleischmans. Max would go to New York first, where he could join a symphony orchestra, and in time we would bring the whole family over. They did not see much of a future in Toronto. And to depend on the Yiddish theater for the upkeep of such a household was not a solid proposition, anyway. After our marriage, Jennie would of course be coming with me to New York, as I had no intention of settling in Toronto. This way we would all be together in one city. The second son, Manny, could get a job in any orchestra, and their father might even find an opening in a local Yiddish theater. All the actors knew him well, having worked with him one season or another in Toronto.

As for Jennie and me, it was difficult just then to make any definite plans. Our marriage would have to wait until I was settled in Montreal.

Thus, sending off some photos of Jennie to my parents and telling them of my betrothal, I spent part of the summer in Toronto until time came for me to join the Hollander Company in Montreal for the 1925-26 season.

36

Montreal, Canada

To this day, whenever I visit Montreal, it strikes me as a small facsimile of Paris. With its large French population, French is as much the official language as is English. Most commercial ads, billboards, street signs and such are in both languages. Although the city's politics have largely been dominated by the Catholic Church, Montreal is a vibrant, convivial town.

Its Jewish community, which took root in the middle of the eighteenth century, has grown to impressive numbers through the years. In fact, Montreal is still one of the very few North American cities where a company may find it quite profitable to play Yiddish theater.

The Monument National Theater on St. Laurent and St. Catherine streets was a building owned by Catholic priests. Seminars were held there and one could meet nuns and priests going in and out of the building. Some of them often dropped in to watch our performances. Ensconced in the balcony, they seemed to enjoy witnessing a Yiddish play and listening to Yiddish songs.

The employees at the Monument National were mostly Frenchmen, who spoke little English. These French stagehands, amenable fellows, did not belong to the stagehands' union in Canada. The musicians, on the other hand, did belong to the musicians' union. Since the theater was part of a Catholic institution, they evidently overlooked this irregularity and worked together, union or no union, a situation which would never be tolerated in the States.

The brass instruments in the orchestra were played by musicians from a military band, who often showed up for a matinee in their army uniforms, coming straight from marching in a parade.

Our cast was comprised of Isidore Hollander, an actor suitable enough in certain roles. But as a "star," he allotted himself parts which, unfortunately, did not suit him at all. His wife, Hanna Hollander, was a talented, sensitive actress, but she too was not always right for the roles she played. Others in the cast were Moseh-Ber Samuylov, a product of the German and Romanian theaters. He was an imposing figure on stage, tall and trim, with thick, white hair; a qualified actor, who always strove to project his lines in a resonant tone to counteract a chronic huskiness. Leon Seidenberg, a younger, well-disciplined actor from Maurice Schwartz's Art Theater, and his wife Leah, a talented dancer, who performed as soloist in our musical plays. Clara Margolin, a prima donna, was the wife of journalist Dr. Abraham Margolin of Chicago. Ida Gropper, excellent in matronly roles, had just finished playing Mrs. Cohen in the American hit, *Abie's Irish Rose.* Chaim Towber, a young actor recently from Russia, and a couple called Adela and Mordecai Schwartz.

The main character actor and comedian in our company was Jacob Zanger, an outstanding performer who made a hit with the Montreal audience from the very first performance. Zanger was another newcomer in America.

A great asset to the Hollander company was Diana Goldberg, a vivacious actress of about sixteen, with all the attributes for becoming a first-rate soubrette. And since I was engaged for the roles of bouffe-comedian, I was teamed with the teenaged Diana. Later in the season I was cast in the singing romantic leads opposite our leading lady, Hanna Hollander.

The difficulty in organizing a suitable company for an out-of-town theater was involved with fitting the repertoire to the cast, rather than casting according to the repertory. These were the main ills that led to the breakdown of Yiddish theater in the provinces; the same ills which, later on, also had a hand in undermining the Yiddish theater in New York. On the road, the union had to extend privileges to nonunion actors for work out of town. The young and the unknowns among the newly arrived had no choice. But by the same token, it was thanks to these young ambitious ones that the hinterland breathed anew. These fresh talents complemented the troupes in a way that made it possible to present a diversified repertory of plays.

* * *

The Hollanders had come to Montreal stocked with an assortment of plays. The theater entrepreneurs, Jacobs and Goldberg, to whom they were related, had supplied them with melodramas and musical comedies of all sorts. They had also armed themselves with many of Joseph Rumshinsky and Jacob Kalich's hits, in which Molly Picon had starred on Second Avenue for the last several years. Among them were such spectaculars as *Gypsy Girl, The Rabbi's Melody, Katinka,* and the operettas: *The American Rebbetzin, Tzipke, The Stepchild of the World, The Rabbi's Court,* and *Love, in Palestine.* I carried off the William Schwartz singing roles much better than Hanna Hollander was able to handle the sprightly roles created by the inimitable Molly Picon; roles which would better have suited little Diana Goldberg. But the Montreal audiences loved to see Hanna Hollander on stage, regardless of what type of role she chose to play.

Outstandingly successful was Avrom Goldfaden's classic operetta, *Shulamith,* with Clara Margolin in the title role. I was assigned the male lead of Absolom, and in addition I directed this spectacular, earning a special mention in the press and in the program. I modernized and formulated my own interpretation of this classic. It went over so well, we presented *Shulamith* on four consecutive weekends. In a provincial theater this was considered a sensation. Most effective, for the shepherd scenes, was the innovation of using live sheep. We even ribbed one another backstage, saying that the sheep were the real stars of the show. They were the talk of the town!

We followed this spectacular with *Bobbe Yachne,* also by Goldfaden. Jacob Zanger was terrific in the role of the old sorceress, while I played the quick-silver character of Hotzmach, the peddler. We also did *Bar-Kokhba,* and *Akeides Yitzhock.*

It seemed to be my lot—as in Toronto—to fill every gap. No matter what the genre: singing romantic? odd character? bouffe comedian? It was I who got elected! For the dramatic repertoire of our Literary Thursdays, I was needed more than ever, since I was familiar with these particular plays, having done them during my four years in Lithuania and, only the season before, in Toronto.

Literary Thursdays

Midweek performances, especially Thursday nights, have always been con-sidered poor for theater business. Jewish housewives are busy preparing for the Sabbath, which tends to keep the family at home. To boost up these weak Thursdays, we arranged a series of dramatic plays from the store of Yiddish, as well as world-acknowledged literary works.

In these straight dramatic plays, Hanna and Isidore Hollander were out-standing. Another actor who did himself proud was Leon Seidenberg, a product, after all, of the Yiddish Art Theater.

The writer and musicologist, Israel Rabinovitch (father of actor David Ellin), was the editor and drama critic of the local Jewish daily, *The Canadian Eagle.* His praise and sometimes healthy measure of criticism were highly respected by the actors and public alike.

In the beginning of the season, Rabinovitch had seen me cavorting in the light, song-and-dance roles, in which he preferred to see the American-born Hymie, or Irving Jacobson. How could I measure up to their nimble dancing feet and aptly delivered wisecracks? But I can't forget Rabinovitch's appraisal of my efforts in the drama, *Thieves* by Fischel Bimko. I quote:

> When I saw the young actor, Chaim Yablokoff, in the char-acterization of Velvel Svitnick, the shoplifter, I truly regretted the lot of this young artist, who is so often forced to take part in non-sense, because nonsense, it seems, pays off better than true art on the Yiddish stage.

The Canadian winter blew in early and with full force. Temperatures dropped below zero; trolleys struggled to crawl up the hilly streets; snow chains jangled on the frosty air. Yet this did not keep young people and tourists from venturing out in the horse-drawn sleighs that glided up and down the slopes of Mount Royal.

The weather in no way hampered the normal activities of the city, nor did it frighten away the public from attending the theater. Our regular devotees—

and there were many—didn't miss a single production we gave. The prominent Bronfman family even made sure to reserve the same seats for each new show. Whenever I paid a visit to Sadie and Samuel Bronfman at their office across the street from His Majesty's Theater (later changed to Her Majesty's Theater), I was sure to come away with a gift bottle of Seagram's Royal, encased in its blue drawstring sack—which I referred to as the "tefillen zekl."

The first guest artist to appear with us in Montreal was Samuel Goldenburg... just as Hollander said he would. I waited for this event with great anticipation. A suave personality, he was tall, masculine and lithe, with thick, crinkly, dark brown hair. This artist was indeed blessed with many attributes. Besides his melodious singing voice, he possessed yet another attraction. He accompanied himself at the piano.

Goldenburg opened with *The Romanian Kretchma,* a melodrama by Harry Kalmanowitz, embellished with appropriate musical numbers. His repertoire consisted of *Shir Hashirim* (Song of Songs) by Anschel Shorr and Joseph Rumshinsky; *The Tree of Life* by Kalmanowitz; *Sanin* by Artzibashev, and August Strindberg's *The Father.* As regisseur, Goldenburg made no compromises at rehearsal. He was very demanding, and often downright brutal with actors. Whether he cajoled or harassed, he tried to draw the maximum out of a performer. And he succeeded in molding his players into characters so convincing that, although some of his vehicles may have been far from a literary caliber, they were accepted with great interest and appreciation. I learned a lot from this gifted man, both as an actor and director.

Good Advice

Our theater manager, Ike Mitnick, called me into his office.

"Listen, Yablokoff," he said, "there are still a good many weeks to the end of the season, and our pianist is giving up his job. Do you think your fiancee, Jennie, would come to Montreal and replace him?"

Overjoyed, I replied, "Jennie is in New York now, playing at a theater. I will call her this very evening."

Jennie was elated at the prospect of joining me. She would have to give the management a week's notice, according to union rule, but directly after that, she would catch the first train to Montreal. We also agreed that I'd begin making the arrangements for our wedding. There was no sense, we felt, in being separated any longer.

When I relayed her answer to Mitnick, he made me sit down and listen.

"I know you're not exactly a man of wealth," he began, "and I also know that a wedding costs an arm and a leg. I have a plan so that instead of spending money, you will make some money. The best idea for you is to get married on stage. And this is nothing new," he hurried to explain. "Actors have done it before. We'll arrange a testimonial evening for you and we will share the income fifty-fifty. You will do a play of your choice, as you normally would on such an occasion. After the show the audience will remain as wedding guests, and your colleagues in the company will escort you and your bride to the canopy on stage. You've made a good name for yourself in the city, Yablokoff, and the people like you. With an attraction such as a real wedding on stage, I assure you that we will sell out the house in one day! It can net you about seven or eight hundred dollars. You can't thumb your nose at a sum like that. So what do you say?"

I was dumfounded! To be married on stage? My God, this was sure to come off as a farce! And he was expecting me to make this decision on the spot?! "Oh, no," I said, "I must give this a lot of thought..."

The more I mulled this proposition over in my mind, the more I had to admit that Mitnick's advice was the only solution to my situation. The Fleischmans were not in a position to undertake wedding expenses. If we should indeed arrange to have the wedding ceremony on stage, I would be able to send, not only for my sister and brother-in-law, but for the whole Fleischman family. And Jennie and I would still salvage a few hundred dollars.

I saw no other solution. The only thing to watch out for was that the ceremony be conducted with decorum and proper solemnity, so that, in no way would it resemble the finale of a Yiddish musical comedy, which invariably winds up with a song-and-dance wedding.

* * *

Jennie's arrival in Montreal inspired me anew. I vowed to work even harder at attaining a meaningful and creative career. And I was so proud when everyone at the theater remarked that, with Jennie at the piano, the orchestra suddenly sounded as if it had been augmented by additional musicians.

The Basbaums, with whom I boarded, also arranged a private little room for my bride, and even worked out plans in their roomy house to give us proper accommodations after we were married. They treated us like their own and we felt completely at home with them. The date chosen for our combined testimonial-and-wedding was March 18, 1926.

* * *

In the meantime, more guest artists arrived. We welcomed the well-known team of Liza and Jacob Silbert. Jacob, a tall, broad-shouldered, prepossessing man; Liza, tall, svelte and chic, with the face of a beauty queen, had traversed the world and were greatly admired wherever they appeared.

The following attraction was the great Sarah Adler, wife of Jacob P. Adler. She appeared in the drama, *Without a Home* by Jacob Gordin, and in *Resurrection* by Tolstoy. None of us doubted that Sarah Adler was a most gifted actress, but at this stage of her life, one could only glimpse a spark of her former glamour. It was sad to see that she no longer had the strength to carry such demanding roles, as Katusha Maslova, which had made her so famous.

Montreal then welcomed the popular comedian Jacob Jacobs and his wife, Betty, with their partners, the dramatic actors Nathan and Rose Goldberg, who balanced their varied repertoire. People came in droves to see their sensational New York hit, *Yente Telebende,* a riotous comedy based on B. Kovner's installments running in the *Jewish Daily Forward.*

Our next star was Leon Blank. It was a surprise to everyone that Blank was coming to Montreal to appear with our company, since he usually went on the road with his own cast, and only after the close of the New York season.

His first production was *The Three Brides,* a melodrama by Isidore Zolotorevsky. In New York, the young actor, Jack Rechtzeit, had scored outstanding success in this play. People, who had been accustomed to seeing him in light singing-and-dancing roles, were surprised by his versatility in portraying the straight, dramatic part of a son who strays from the righteous path. It brought him high praise from the critics and public alike. How flattered I was, when Blank assigned Rechtzeit's part to me.

Leon Blank was a character actor in the full sense of the word. A big, well-built man, he had a way of punctuating his characterizations with humorous little quips and songs. All this created a quality so peculiarly his own that anyone trying to imitate him would be said to be using a "Blank-istic" style.

Some of his other hits we played were: *The Watchman* and *The Drunkard* by William Siegel, and *The Broken Home* by Simon Wolf.

When we said goodbye at the end of his engagement, I truly felt that I had made another good friend in the family of the theater, who would drop a kind word about me in New York. And oh, how important this was!

A Wedding on Stage

My directors and fellow actors thought I was some kind of crackpot to choose Gordin's grim drama, *The Wild Man,* for my benefit performance. But I felt that the contrast from playing this unkempt, shaggy-haired half-wit was necessary before appearing as the bridegroom, decked out in full-dress and high hat, with every hair in place. Besides, it was one of my best roles. And I was right! At the end of the performance, I received rousing bravos and applause from the packed house.

Both our families, Jennie's and mine, had come to Montreal and were now waiting in the wings as the stage was being set up for our wedding. Standing under the chupa (canopy) with my bride, beautiful and resplendent in white, I uttered the Hareiyat. And, at the traditional breaking of the glass, the entire house responded with a thunderous Mazel Tov!!

* * *

To sum up the season of 1926-27, we presented some seventy plays, over thirty-eight weeks. I had come to Montreal single, and returned to New York a married man, with my wife, Jennie.

37

Our Honeymoon

We moved into a furnished room on East Eighteenth Street in Manhattan, where we spent our honeymoon. It was conveniently close to the "theatrical mart," the Cafe Royale, and the Actors' Union. Anyway, my hope for membership in the union did not materialize. Considering the countless applications gathering dust in the filing cabinets made by applicants who had—in the interim—flunked one, or two auditions, I knew my chances for membership were nil.

Some of the union people I worked with told me that, in view of my scant two years in the United States, I ought to thank my lucky stars that the union had extended me privileges to work. My only consolation was that the two seasons I had played in Toronto and then Montreal had run longer than those in New York; which meant a lot to me, moneywise, and that there were good reports about me circulating in the Royale. By now it was known in the profession that I was a "useful" actor, with assets made-to-order for a road company.

Jennie, as it turned out, also had to forget about playing in a Yiddish theater in New York. The special Jewish Club of the Musicians' union, local 802, barred newcomers from the Yiddish theaters in New York, no matter how essential they happened to be. The priority for these jobs was held exclusively by the chosen club members, whether or not they knew which end of an instrument was up! Considering that the club had even blocked the composer-conductor Alexander Olshanetsky, what was Jennie to expect?

I was not permitted to work in New York by the actors' union—despite some promising chances for an engagement; and my wife was not permitted to play in New York by the musicians' club! The only way we could hope to work together would be somewhere on the road. But, even there, the question was: where could we find an opening to include both of us? The theaters out of town had their own local musicians and there was surely no lack of pianists. Meanwhile, the summer dragged on, and our meager savings were beginning to dwindle.

About this time, Jennie complained that she wasn't feeling too well, and we went to see a doctor. It didn't take him long to come up with the diagnosis.

"Your wife is pregnant, Mr. Yablokoff," he informed me cheerfully. "She's in the third month." This was all we needed! But we took it as calmly as we could.

Unexpectedly, Mr. Guskin asked us to appear at a thank-you concert. It was for an annual picnic arranged by the Socialist Organization in a park near Coney Island. Naturally, we complied and happily had a big success, which was even more important than the few dollars we did not receive—and could well have used. It offered us the opportunity to be seen and heard in the circles of Yiddish social and cultural life in New York.

Approaching us for a return engagement-without-pay, Guskin invited us to spend a whole weekend at the Workmen's Circle Camp on Sylvan Lake in New York. We were, of course, expected to entertain for our room and board. But I was pleased that Guskin and his wife would also be spending the weekend in camp. I was most eager to have him see us on stage. Our programs were enthusiastically received and we were highly complimented by the camp committee and by Guskin, himself, which was indeed a great source of encouragement for us.

* * *

Several weeks later I ran into Guskin at a chance encounter on the avenue. He stopped me to ask, "Look, Yablokoff, would you want to take a job at a theater in Los Angeles?"

"Los Angeles?!"

"Yes. Los Angeles has a rapidly growing Jewish community. Our people are settling there from all over the States, even from Canada. And they are theatergoers," he added. "Last season we had a union company playing there for months. They made out very well, too. This coming season the theater in Los Angeles will be managed by Sam Auerbach, Sadie Sheingold and Harry Feld. What do you say?"

At the mention of Auerbach and Sadie Sheingold, my spirits soared. They were my first directors during my initial season in Toronto! And they certainly knew my wife, and her talent. I got Jennie and we both went to find Auerbach at the Royale.

He greeted us like long-lost relatives. "This is Mr. Feld, our new partner," he introduced us. "Has Guskin spoken to you yet about Los Angeles? Are you coming with us?"

"I certainly do want to come along with you," I said, "but there is something I must tell you. You see, Mr. Auerbach, my wife...well, we're expecting..."

"What?! Already?" he stared at us in amazement, "What was the hurry?"

"Sam!" Sadie reproved him. "Enough with your silly comments!" Visibly moved, Sadie, who had no children, threw her arms around Jennie. "Good luck, my dear! I wish both of you all the best in the world!"

"O.K., O.K., lots of luck, and mazel tov!" said Auerbach. "After all," he grinned, "whose name is signed on your betrothal document? Auerbach, eh? Well, then, I guess fate wants me to be 'Sandek' at the brith, as well! When are you due, my dear Jennie?"

"Around the end of January," replied Jennie, blushing guiltily, as if her being pregnant had upset our apple cart.

"So why worry? There's more than six months to January. You can play until it's time for your confinement. After the baby arrives, with God's help, we'll find a good woman to take care of it so you can come back to your place at the piano. Come, let's take a stroll and talk it over."

Once out on the avenue, Auerbach came straight to the point. "Now then, how much do you want a week?"

"Look, Mr. Auerbach," I began, "before we discuss anything I would appreciate your advice. Do you think it is right for me to drag my wife off to such a faraway place in her condition? Here, in New York at least, we would be near Jennie's parents. They are contemplating leaving Toronto and settling in New York. We also have my sister here, and my aunt, but, in California with Jennie expecting and all alone."

"Why alone?" Auerbach refused to listen, "and where will you be, her husband? Won't the whole company be there? What do you think Los Angeles is—a wilderness? We have already played there several times. As a matter of fact, Sadie and I are contemplating making our home there. Don't you suppose babies get born in California, too?" Seeing that I was at a loss, he made me an offer. "Yabby," he said, "we will pay you a hundred dollars a week."

"For both of us?" I asked, feeling terribly let down.

"What else—for you alone? What are you, a star? Do you belong to the union? Do you realize what the traveling expenses to Los Angeles are going to cost us? A fortune! And by the way," he informed me, "the train fare back to New York is paid by the actors themselves. This is the working agreement with the union, and you're no exception. To L.A., we pay. Back—you pay. Didn't you pay your fare back from Toronto and from Montreal? Well, Yablok-off, let's make the deal and good luck! Isn't it worth everything to have Jennie, in her condition, escape the New York winter?" he threw in as an extra inducement. "California is a Garden of Eden! Sunshine! Palm trees! Pineapples, a nickel a dozen! Oranges that grow beneath your window! Jennie will be delighted. The baby, too. Now then, what do you say?"

What could I say? In our circumstances $100 a week was certainly better than nothing. I agreed, but with a condition: a testimonial performance! Let me at least realize a few extra dollars, I figured, so that after the season we'd have train fare back to New York.

On Our Way West

In 1926, California was still thought of as a primitive, sparsely inhabited frontier. If it were not for Hollywood, the mecca of filmdom, the world would hardly have been aware of the burgeoning metropolis called Los Angeles, a city more than 3,000 miles from the tumultuous pulse of America—New York!

Today, when one can fly to L.A. in less than five hours, it is difficult to imagine that in those years an express train took six days. And the trains of that era certainly had none of the comforts of today's modern express trains that tear across the country in a scant seventy-two hours—air-conditioned, showing the latest films, so the passengers may not be bored, heaven forbid.

Despite all the physical discomfort, our Jewish "wandering stars" made it to Los Angeles somehow and brought Yiddish culture to the newly sprouting Jewish communities.

Before leaving New York, Auerbach advanced me $100. This sum had to see us through the interim before we could collect our wages. That same day I got a letter from my father in Grodno, telling me that my youngest sister, Rochele, had become engaged to fine young man, called Hershel Kanatzky. He had just returned from the Polish military service and they were soon to be married.

Up to this time, my father had in no way hinted at the state of their circumstances; although, knowing the situation in Poland, I surmised well enough how bitter the conditions were. This time, however, father wrote: "Chaim, if you can help out toward Rochele's wedding, you will have earned a great mitzvah."

My father's words were enough for me to take my entire advance, and with Jennie's consent, sent it off by telegraph as a wedding gift for my sister Rochele—the half-twin—and her husband-to-be, Hershel.

For our journey to Los Angeles, Jennie packed a parcel of food, and we boarded the train—flat broke! Yet, I wouldn't think of asking Auerbach or Feld for another advance. During the day we traveled tourist—in the coach section. At night we retired to our berths in one of the sleeper-cars. In the morning, it was back to the coach again. The first day out, several of our fellow actors went to eat in the dining car. Jennie and I made do with the provisions we brought along.

We stopped in Chicago to change trains for Los Angeles. This was practically a half-day's stopover, and who should show up at the station to hail our troupe, but the impresario of Chicago's Palace Theater, Elias Glickman, with several of his Yiddish actors in tow. It was a very pleasant break in our journey.

The next morning, when our colleagues trailed off to the dining car for breakfast, Jennie and I remained in our seats. At the call for lunch, the company again took off for the dining car—and we sat. Came dinner time—we sat! Harry Feld finally said, "Why don't you people come along and eat with the rest of us?"

I had to confess that we would be only too happy to join the company. But, for this pleasure, one was expected to pay, no? I then told him what I did with the $100. Obviously moved, Feld handed me a crackling fifty-dollar bill.

"You see, my dear," I reassured my wife, "you can never go lost among theater-colleagues! Come, let's go eat in the dining car."

To pass the tedious hours, most of the company played either pinochle, or poker, while I stayed glued to the window, marveling at the vastness and beauty of America's landscape.

The most difficult part of the journey was crossing the desert, through New Mexico and Arizona. The heat was unbearable. In lieu of air conditioning—a long way off yet—there was a revolving ventilator, which only succeeded in blowing the hot desert air in, rather than out!

We were coming closer to California, and sure enough, there they were—the palm trees! The train made a stop and we climbed down to stretch our legs and get a breath of fresh air; except that, by comparison to the heat outdoors, the inside of the stuffy car was almost a delight!

Indians milled about the depot offering carved figurines, beaded necklaces and handwoven rugs for sale. I couldn't believe that I was seeing them in reality. As a boy in Grodno, I had read about their bloody battles with the white infiltrators and was fascinated by their bravery. Now, seeing them in the flesh: placid, resigned, begging us with silent glances to buy their wares, I felt sympathy for them. Poor Indians...what they'd come to...

38
Los Angeles

At the Los Angeles Terminal we were met by a horde of people. The company's arrival had been announced in the Yiddish *Los Angeles Forward* and *California Voice*. In addition we were hailed by a band of Mexican musicians. The proprietor of the Capitol Theater, where we were to play, was a Mexican Jew, so in keeping with their custom he arranged to welcome us with music.

Among the welcomers were the theater devotees, Joe Wasserman, an exporter of walnuts, Cantor Carr, and the semiretired actor, David Sheinholtz, with his wife. There was no lack of reporters and photographers, either. In short, we were greeted like film stars arriving in Hollywood. For me, this was a new encounter, but I liked it. (Receptions of this sort, as I experienced in later years, were extended to Yiddish actors only in Buenos Aires.)

We decided to rent a furnished room near the theater. For one thing, it was easier for Jennie, and it saved us trolley fare to and from the theater.

The city of Los Angeles was in constant expansion, and so was the Jewish community. A considerable drawback, however, lay in the city's inadequate transportation. Happy indeed was the fellow who owned a car.

* * *

The Capitol Theater was on Spring Street near Broadway, right in the heart of town. It was not far from the office of the *Jewish Daily Forward*, managed by Julius Levitt, or the office of the Los Angeles branch of the Workmen's Circle, whose most active members happened to be my own townspeople from Grodno: Counsellor Harry Sherr, Dr. Kavanocki, Victor Menacker, Sol Levine, Abraham Lewis and Jack Kay. The editor of the other Yiddish newspaper, the *California Voice*, was Dr. Zekiel Wortzman.

There were several kosher Hungarian restaurants near the theater, but as they were too expensive for us, we ate at the Penny Cafeteria. Each food item in this place was priced to the penny. For instance, a complete meal could amount to fifty-nine, or sixty-three cents, or more—but figure to the penny. There were salads and fruits, the likes of which I had never seen before—certainly not in Grodno. The decor of the cafeteria was designed to simulate a tropical garden. The setting and the piped-in organ music created a delightful and even exotic atmosphere in which to dine. And last but not least, the price was right... to the penny.

Our season of 1926-27 was to open directly after Rosh Hashanah. The players in the company, besides me, were Sadie Sheingold, Fannie Reinhardt, Julia Varadi, Pauline Fogelnest, Sam Auerbach, Harry Feld, Sam Fogelnest, Yitzhock Wernick, Adolph and Annie Freiman. The prompter, Chaim Podlias, and orchestra conductor, Jeanette (Jennie) Fleischman.

Our first production was *The Romanian Wedding,* an operetta by Moshe Schorr, the musical score by Peretz Sandler—a hit that had captured audiences not only in New York, but wherever else it played. This vehicle gave us an excellent start in Los Angeles. Peretz Sandler's tuneful score, the costumes, the dances, the sets, the acting and singing of the cast created a furor.

The young prima donna, Julia Varadi, a new arrival from Hungary, made a fine partner to Harry Feld. Although she struggled with the Yiddish language, her singing made a great hit, particularly with her many fans among the Hungarian Jews.

Sadie and I had no difficulty handling our leading roles. I fell right into stride with the lively bon vivant, and found the musical numbers made to order for the range of my voice. The dances were choreographed by Sadie, and the play was staged and directed by me.

Acquiring singers and dancers for the show was no problem. The town was already overrun by young hopefuls hanging around Hollywood, seeking to make careers in the movies and starving in the process. Scores of them came to beg for a job in our chorus. One young girl, about seventeen, performed some solo dances in our production. And this girl, who was brought to our theater by her mother, later emerged as the glamorous Mexican star, Dolores Del Rio.

The Yiddish and American press sang our praises, and many world-famed film stars of that period came to see our Yiddish performance.

Jennie, having arranged the music, led the orchestra as she played the piano. She was greatly admired and received a good share of the applause. She could not very well conceal that she was pregnant and our steady theatergoers, the women in particular, would come down the aisle to the pit, to ask solicitously how she was feeling.

I talked Auerbach into introducing the "Literary Thursdays," as we did in Montreal. These special literary works also proved to be a great drawing card in Los Angeles.

At every new premiere, a limousine driven by a liveried chauffeur would pull up in front of the theater and deposit an elderly couple. We were very much impressed when we learned that the venerable gentleman was the founder of the famous Warner Brothers Studio. Mr. Warner and his wife had their regular reserved seats in the front row. Seated so close to the orchestra, they soon became quite friendly with Jennie.

One evening, attending one of our plays, Mr. Warner asked her whether she and her orchestra could play a weekly program of Jewish music on the radio station that was conducted by his son, Jack Warner. Jennie invited them backstage after the show to meet me and the rest of the company. Listening to their plan of introducing a Yiddish radio program in Los Angeles, I was filled with enthusiasm.

"Why only orchestral music?" I ventured to ask. "If indeed there is an opportunity to broadcast a Yiddish program, why not include singing?"

"Singing?! Yes, by all means!" they agreed. "We want to present the Jewish communities in and around the city of Los Angeles with a gift: a weekly radio program in Yiddish!"

They proposed that I take over the supervision of the programs and leave the rest to them. Getting paid for the broadcasts was the furthest thing from my mind. It was the prospect of singing on the radio that interested me—a new medium, after all. Harry Feld, too, was eager to take part in the program.

Only Auerbach balked at the idea. "Sing on the radio! It's sure to take away from our business! If the people can hear you sing at home, for free, they'll keep staying at home!"

"On the contrary!" I countered. "It will be announced that we are the Yiddish artists of the Capitol Theater! It's great publicity, don't you see?" After much persuasion, I finally got him to allow us to sing on the radio.

Introductions to our program were done in English by Jack Warner, himself. The senior Warners came every week to listen to the broadcasts right in the studio, and took keen delight in it. I doubt whether there was a single Jewish home with a radio in it that didn't tune in to our weekly programs. We continued with these broadcasts for a good many months, and the envelopes handed to us after each program, containing fifty-dollar checks, came in very, very handy. For Jennie and me, the extra hundred dollars a week was plainly a boon from heaven!

Who could have imagined, at the time, that my singing on the radio would also be the beginning of my career as a Yiddish radio and stage artist?!

A big asset in our company was the singer-actress Fannie Reinhardt. The quality and range of her voice was exactly like that of a man's—a lyric baritone. Her delivery of liturgical compositions was truly something to listen to and admire. As a resident of Los Angeles, she was very much involved in local welfare activities. She was married to Dr. Morris Reinhardt, a dear man and a dedicated physician. He recommended the prominent Doctor Lambord of Santa Monica Hospital. Out of courtesy to Dr. Reinhardt, he assured me that he would charge only a quarter of the fee he normally received from his patients among the Hollywood celebrities.

Our radio programs for the Warners also gave us entree to the movie lots and studios in Hollywood, where we could watch the filming process.

* * *

Our company was rehearsing Joseph Lateiner's Biblical operetta, *Joseph and His Brethen,* with a new score by Peretz Sandler. I did not take part in it so I could be free to conduct the orchestra during Jennie's confinement. As the play called for a large cast of characters, we recruited several actors among whom was a fellow called Max Romberg. He was sort of lanky, with reddish hair slightly tinged with silver, and was rarely seen without his broad-brimmed hat and a book under his arm. Our actors poked fun at him. But I couldn't take their badgering this frustrated, but gentle soul and tried to befriend him. He, in turn, became strongly attached to Jennie and me. Nothing seemed too difficult for him to do for us.

I was getting more and more jittery about the birth of our baby. Yet things, I learned, have a way of falling into place. Auerbach had cousins in Los Angeles, a Mr. Kruger and his wife, Frieda. And Frieda had become exceedingly fond of Jennie, doing little errands for her and often visiting with us backstage. This fine woman insisted that we were not to worry. Since she was childless, and had more time on her hands than she knew what to do with, she said she would be more than happy to help take care of our newborn infant.

One evening I was already in makeup, ready to go on, when Jennie said she was feeling kind of peculiar. This threw me—and everyone else—into a dither. A rush call went out from the box office to our standby pianist and to Dr. Reinhardt. They both came flying to the theater.

Dr. Reinhardt assured me that I needn't be alarmed. He would drive her to the hospital and call Dr. Lambord, her obstetrician.

"But, Doctor!" I said, beside myself, "I can't come along. I have to go on!"

"There is time enough," he calmed me. "Most likely, we will have to wait all night, anyway. Even after the performance, you can still come to the hospital to do your waiting."

We finished the show. No one in the cast quite knew what he was saying or doing, and I—even less. The atmosphere in the audience was also apprehensive. For, as soon as they saw another pianist in Jennie's place, they knew her time had arrived. They took turns running to the box office, even barging in backstage, to ask: "Well, what did she have—a boy or a girl?"

For me, it was all a nightmare. I felt like a brute! I was downright ashamed to be standing on stage, playacting before an audience. What sort of husband would fail to be at the side of his wife in the most exalted moment in her life, when she is bringing forth their firstborn?

I thought the last curtain would never come down. Hurriedly dressing, I discovered that, just my luck, not one of my friends who owned a car happened to be around that night. And the Santa Monica Hospital was a whale of a distance from the theater!

Running for the streetcar, I heard someone yelling behind me, "Yabby, wait! I'm coming with you!" It was Max Romberg. I was deeply moved and grateful. And although I was in no mood for talk, he sensed this and rode all the way to the hospital with me, in silence.

I had much to think about as we rattled along. My heart ached for my wife, who must in these sacred moments of her life be all alone, torn from parents, from family. I blamed myself! Will the theater with its wanderings, enable us to lead a normal family life? Support my wife and child? I must find some other means of a livelihood. I need a home. I now have a family to care for. Theater? Nonsense! This is a project for the footloose and fancy-free, with obligations to no one—not for me!

In the maternity ward of the hospital, everything was hushed and dimly lit. A nurse informed me that my wife was in the delivery room. Max sat with me in the half-lit waiting room. I urged him to go home, pointing out that he would not get a trolley until morning, if he waited any longer. Why should he sit up a whole night? But he begged to let him stay. So there we sat and waited while I smoked one cigarette after another.

About 4:30 in the morning, the nurse finally put in an appearance.

"Come," she beckoned, very quietly. I followed her She helped me into a white robe, covered my mouth with a gauze mask and ushered me into a brightly lit room. The sudden glare bouncing off the various surgical instruments blinded me. Dr. Lambord murmured, "It won't be long now."

On a long, operating table, her knees propped up, lay Jennie, swathed in white sheets. At her groaning I made an attempt to go to her, but the doctor motioned me to remain at a distance. Jennie's groans coming louder and louder sent the doctor and the nurse quickly to her side. I was rooted to the spot. I didn't know whether the doctor wanted me to stay in the delivery room, or leave. Holding my breath, not daring to move, my eyes followed the miracle of birth. I grew dizzy, ready to faint. I shut my eyes and turning my head away, prayed for it soon to be over.

Around five o'clock in the morning—January 31st, 1927—a piercing scream forced my eyes open. I saw the nurse holding my newborn baby by its feet, head down, spanking its little bottom, until the little mite began to wail. Dr. Lambord, looking drained, came over to me.

"Congratulations, Mr. Yablokoff," he patted my shoulder, "It's a boy!"

"An 8-and ¾ pounder!" added the nurse, beaming, as if she herself had produced this miracle.

"Well, how did you like this phenomenon of creation?" Dr. Lambord smiled. "You see, I strongly believe that every husband should witness the birth of his child."

"May I go to my wife, now?" I asked, completely humbled.

"Yes, but only for a moment. She's worn out. Believe me, she did not have it as easy as playing the piano! She'll soon be moved to her room and after a good long sleep, she'll come around, all right."

"Jennie?" I whispered through the gauze over my mouth. "Mazel tov, my dear!" A glazed look passed over her eyes, but she soon rallied to the fact that it was I, standing beside her. "Mazel tov!" I repeated. "We have a little son!"

"A son?" Tears welled up in her eyes. "Is he all right?"

"Is he all right? And how!" I assured her, holding back my own tears. "Do you hear his screams? That's our son, delivering his first concert," I quipped.

A feeble smile quivered on her lips. Then her eyelids drooped and she was asleep. The orderlies came to move her to her room. Still dazed, I found my way back to the waiting room, removing my robe and mask.

"Mazel tov, Yabby, mazel tov!" Max threw his arms around me, "A boy, wonderful! There'll be a brith! And we'll drink l'chaim!" He was so elated, he practically danced with joy.

Dawn was coming up as we left the hospital. The cool of the early hour felt good. There was no early-morning transportation back to downtown Los Angeles, and so we decided to walk. It was some hike from Santa Monica to the theater! When at last we neared the center of town, the hustle-bustle of the day had already begun. The first thing I did was to send a telegram to the Fleischmans in New York, where the whole family was settled now. I also sent a telegram to my sister and brother-in-law and one to my aunt and uncle. As for my parents, I decided to write them a letter. A wire to Grodno was too expensive, and besides, it might frighten them.

At rehearsal, the actors greeted me with hearty congratulations. All our friends were delighted, and Frieda Kruger was altogether transported with the news that Jennie had given birth to a boy. "Why the ecstasy over a boy?" I joked. "What if it had been a girl? Would we have refused to accept her, heaven forbid?"

The telephone in the box office kept ringing incessantly—and not only to reserve tickets for *Joseph and his Brethren*. People were curious to know whether the pianist had given birth yet and whether it was a boy or a girl.

At the performance that evening, everyone in the theater was already aware that I had become a father. As soon as I stepped into the pit to conduct the orchestra, I was greeted by a spontaneous mazel tov and a hearty round of applause.

After the show I called the hospital again. Frieda, who hadn't left Jennie's side, told me that mother and child were doing fine, and that the baby—in her own words—was a real handsome "buster!"

* * *

The department stores in Los Angeles had established the custom of sending gifts to every native-born child in California. The greater part of the population at the time was comprised of families who had only recently migrated from other parts of the United States and Canada. Therefore, a native-born son, or daughter, was considered a VIP. Hospitals made every such birth known to the various business people and they promptly sent in gifts—layettes of every kind, including toys. The shops didn't lose anything by this generosity, for together with their presents they enclosed folders and catalogs, advertising the merchandise they had for sale: every item under the sun that a little newcomer could possibly need. When next I arrived at the hospital, Jennie's room was already stacked with a variety of presents; such as I would immediately have to go out and shop for.

Jennie wanted to name our son after her maternal grandfather, Jacob. As my own grandfathers already had names given after them, I agreed whole-heartedly. I liked the name Jacob. Jacob—son of Chaim.

The Bris

Our friend David Scheinholtz helped me bring my wife and baby home in his car. He also suggested that we have the brith take place at his bungalow, where guests could be accommodated outdoors on his spacious patio. We could set up the tables and chairs right under the blue of the sky, surrounded by trees and flowers. The idea greatly appealed to us.

Frieda was still hovering close to mother and baby, clucking over them like a mother hen.

"Frieda," I joked, "your husband will divorce you. You have practically left him flat and moved in with us."

"My husband won't divorce me," she replied, "and if he does, well, my life doesn't mean that much, anyway," she suddenly dissolved into tears.

"Frieda!" I exclaimed, taken aback. "What kind of talk is that? What's wrong?"

"I don't know how to tell you what's pressing on my heart. I'm not demand-ing, or saying that you must do this for me," she wept anew. "Hardly anyone I know would do it. But I keep thinking that you, perhaps, would be big-hearted enough to grant me this wish. You see, God has not seen fit to bless me with a child. And my dearest wish is to have a name after my father, rest his soul. I've been thinking that maybe you can find it in your heart to add my father's name to the one you will give your little son. God will bless you and your child for your good deed. You will have given me the greatest gift in life!"

The bris attracted more guests than we expected. The Scheinholtzes, with Frieda's help, prepared, cooked and baked a whole variety of dishes. There was no lack of drinks, either. Among the guests were Dr. Lambord, Fannie and Dr. Reinhardt, as well as the Warners who came in their chauffeur-driven lim-ousine. People kept coming and going throughout the day. Honors were be-stowed upon Sam Auerbach as Sandek, Sadie Sheingold and Harry Feld as Kwatters. The Mohel intoned: "As a son of Israel, his name shall be Jacob-Ari, son of Chaim." Jacob for Jennie's grandfather and Ari (lion, in Hebrew) for Frieda's father.

We, and our theater-family, called the baby Yankele. Later, Yankele became Jackie and eventually gave way to Jack—my son, Jack Yablokoff.

* * *

Our season at the Capitol Theater continued successfully. My wife, however, was still not completely recuperated. The doctors advised that she get
more bed rest. She couldn't go on with her job at the theater. For one thing,
we didn't wish to entrust the care of the baby with others; secondly, Jennie's
weakened condition simply forbade it. During the day, Frieda and Mrs. Scheinholtz helped her all they could, until I would get home from the theater. The
doctor also advised to wean the baby from breast-feeding and put him on the
bottle. Tired as I was and groggy with sleep, I was obliged to get up several
times during the night to warm the baby's bottle.

The wages I now collected were cut in half. My wife received nothing.
When I asked Auerbach how come, he became indignant. "We're paying a sub-
stitute, aren't we?" he retorted. "You don't expect us to pay double, do you?
Friendship is friendship and business is business."

I was glad enough that the season was coming to a close. I looked forward
to being back in New York now that Jennie's folks were settled there. it would
be nice to spend Passover with them. But how were we going to get there?
After paying the Hollywood obstetrician, the hospital bill, the cost of the bris
and the month's rent—out of my half salary at that—I was sure we wouldn't
have enough to cover train fare with a compartment to accommodate us and
the baby. We could not very well travel with an infant in a railway coach, especially since Jennie had to be lying down most of the time.

"Yabby," suggested Scheinholtz, "maybe you, the wife and the baby would
come along with us to spend a weekend at Marietta Springs? The weather is
fine now, so let's go. It's a resort with hot springs and mud baths. It may even
help Jennie get rid of her aching back. It's the favorite spa with our Jewish residents. The Auerbachs and Felds are also planning to take a few days' vacation
there. So, let's spend a few days together before you leave us."

My wife and I were willing, but how would we take the baby? Up to this
point, the little fellow had been sleeping on a pillow placed in a drawer pulled
out of a dresser. It hardly paid to invest in a crib or a carriage. These were
things we planned to buy in New York. So, rummaging in her attic, Mrs. Scheinholtz came across a straw-woven basket. She padded it and lined it with blue
sateen, and Yankele traveled with us to Marietta Springs, ensconced in his laundry basket as cozy and comfortable as in a royal crib.

The hotel at the springs was filled with guests; most of whom were our
theater-patrons, who knew us very well. The mud baths did nothing to help
my dear Jennie. But the concert I arranged there helped us very much indeed.

During my entire program, with Jennie at the piano, our little son, conveniently stationed in the wings, lay in his basket never uttering a peep, as
his mother and father were putting forth all their efforts to earn the traveling
expenses back to New York.

Bidding farewell to many of our dear friends who came to see us off, we
were finally on our way East.

Our compartment was rather a narrow affair: double-decker bunks, a wash-basin, toilet, and beyond that, no room to move around. I made Jennie lie right down. And resting the baby's basket on two stools, I made arrangements with our porter to fill and warm up a baby bottle at given hours. I promised him a quarter each time he would bring a bottle to our compartment. Needless to say, the baby got fed to the minute. It was not so much for the quarter tip, I'm sure, as for the sympathy felt for us. Our friends had provided us with food aplenty for the journey, and any extras we needed were brought to us from the diner.

I bathed my little son in the small basin twice a day. It wasn't very com-fortable, but he loved it. When crossing the desert, the heat was so intense I had to bathe him more frequently. Lying in my upper berth I was unable to shut an eye. I was afraid to fall asleep. Jennie might want something, or the baby might cry and I wouldn't hear him. I got a bright idea. I took the belt from my pants and buckled one end around my wrist, letting the rest dangle within Jennie's reach. I told her to give it a good tug to wake me if she needed anything. But, falling into a deep sleep from sheer exhaustion, I rolled over and—up flew the belt—way beyond her reach. Well, so much for my bright idea.

Arriving at last at Grand Central Station, we were met by the entire Fleisch-man family and, of course, my sister and her family. What joy it was to be together again, and above all, to share their thrill in seeing the baby for the first time.

The theater season in Los Angeles ran twenty-eight weeks—a record for the Yiddish theater. We did thirty-three plays, including concerts and a weekly radio program—a first! The only riches we amassed from this season, 1926-27, was our son, Yankele!

39

New York, 1927

Back from California, we found the New York theaters already preparing new productions for the Passover holiday. The theatrical agents, Relkin and Weintraub, were bustling between the cafe and the actors' union in the throes of booking road tours for the various companies soon winding up their New York run.

My first mission was to drop in at the union to see Guskin.

"What about my audition for membership?" I asked him. "My application and $150 initiation fee have been filed in your office for almost three years."

"Well, for this year, it's too late. Auditions are held during the winter. You wouldn't have come all the way from California for the audition, would you? So, we'll see, maybe next season. Anyway, you're on the list."

My new address was in the Bronx. Jennie, the baby and I had moved in with the Fleischmans. The seven-room railroad flat was hardly adequate to accommodate all of us. My mother-in-law could not be blamed for bemoaning the rambling house they'd given up in Toronto. Still, we managed to celebrate a mighty fine Passover Seder together, hoping for better times to come.

Mama Fleischman and sister Fay adored our little Yankele. Leaving him in their care enabled us to go see what was cooking on the Yiddish Rialto.

At the Second Avenue Theater, I was tremendously impressed by Joseph Rumshinsky's operetta *Czarevitch Feodor*. The book by M. Asherowitz, one of the noted writers in the *Forward*, was based on the boyhood years of the czarevitch. The incomparable Molly Picon, portraying the young Prince Feodor, with William Schwartz as Boris Godunov and Max Wilner playing the court jester, enthralled me. An operetta, I thought, should by all means be done with the artistry displayed in this production by the director Jacob Kalich.

Rumshinsky had written a terrific score, but our enjoyment of it was marred by the large orchestra, which—under his baton—overpowered the singers and dominated the entire action on stage, with the result that the singers, in their effort to be heard, were forced to strain their vocal chords.

Having read, while still in Los Angeles, about the auspicious opening of the newly built Yiddish Art Theater on Second Avenue at Twelfth Street, we were most anxious to take in one of their performances. They happened to be playing *Human Dust* by Ossip Dymoff. It was not one of Dymoff's best works and was not very successful. But the fine acting by Maurice Schwartz, who also directed the play, and his well-chosen cast greatly impressed me.

Also, the recently built Public Theater further down the avenue was starring Aaron Lebedeff in a light, but rather banal musical comedy, *The Little Millionaire*. Nevertheless, Lebedeff's personality, aplomb and grace, his ringing tenor and special style of delivery, made it plain why he had become an overnight sensation in America.

A Summer Job

My coming to America apparently brought my sister and her husband good luck. Henry, an expert cutter of furs, had grown tired of slaving for others, and after negotiating a deal with a former boss became a partner in a small fur shop on Seventh Avenue. In the art of processing furs, Henry was a master. He and his partner were soon swamped with orders for fox scarves, muffs, collars and cuffs, and before long they realized a small fortune.

My sister forthwith rented a large apartment in a new building near the ocean at Brighton Beach. They bought the finest furniture and a shining new car. It was not everybody who could afford to own an automobile at that time. They even acquired a black, sleep-in maid and began hobnobbing with others of the nouveau riche; throwing parties and spending summer weekends in the mountains.

I asked Henry how I could find some kind of job that would tide us over the summer—be it any kind of work. After a long consultation with his partner, they agreed to take me on. Of course, I knew nothing about furs, and since it was a union shop, I was only allowed to do chores like sweeping up, unpacking the raw skins, or removing them from the stretcher boards on which they were nailed. I also had to deliver bundles of the finished fur collars to the coat manufacturers up and down the length of Seventh Avenue.

I dreaded the thought of coming face to face with some actor who might know me. I would surely want to bury myself under the bundle of furs I was shlepping. But shlep, I did! I had a wife and son to support.

At the end of the week, I waited eagerly to see what my first pay would be. I imagined myself coming home and handing over my salary, so that all at home could see that I was not lazy, not shirking my duties, but determined to earn a living. When Saturday came along, I was handed an envelope. With trembling fingers I tore it open and took out my first pay—fifteen dollars.

I was crushed! In the washroom of the shop I scrubbed myself of the day's grime and the fur that clung to me. Putting on my white shirt and tie, I changed into the clothes in which I'd come to work that morning and off I went—to the Royale. It was then and there I made my decision: I would rather go hungry as an actor than seek fortune in any other field. No matter what fate had in store for me, I vowed, I would remain an actor—an actor on the Yiddish stage.

* * *

In bold type, headlines flashed around the world: Charles Lindbergh Flies the Atlantic Solo in his Plane, The Spirit of St. Louis!!

Oh, I thought, if only I could fly. Back to Europe, where an actor could play Yiddish theater without the worries of audition in the union, without begging for a privilege, or landing a job! But, go fly! Easier said than done. I was no longer the footloose traveler of before.

Announcements in the press were already listing a good number of theater openings for the coming season of 1927-28, including *Greenberg's Daughters* by M. Underschlager, directed by Maurice Schwartz at the Yiddish Art Theater; *Reyzele*, starring Molly Picon at the Second Avenue Theater; and *Der Litvisher Yankee*, an operetta by Alexander Olshanetsky performed by Aaron Lebedef and Bella Mysell at the National Theater.

Under *Theater News* I also read that the actors of the Vilna Troupe had formed a partnership for the coming season with Oscar Green, the proprietor and manager of the Hopkinson Theater in Brooklyn. This company was to be dedicated to a literary repertoire in the tradition of the Vilna Troupe.

One day, Oscar Green, a very prepossessing gentleman, stopped me in front of the Royale.

"Would you be interested in taking an engagement for the coming season at my Hopkinson Theater?"

"Would I be interested?!

"You see," he went on, "Samuel Goldenburg and my former mother-in-law, Liza Silbert have praised you very highly. If you are interested, my associates will talk business with you. Engaging the cast is their job."

"And what about a privilege from the union?"

"I think it will be all right," Green winked at me, reassuringly. "You just come to terms about salary and we'll do the rest. I have spoken to Guskin about you. I'm sure he will be amenable, otherwise, he would immediately have said no."

After this encounter, I didn't budge from the cafe. And pretty soon along came two of Green's fellow entrepreneurs, Schneier and Schorr. We sat down to talk business and I asked for eighty five dollars a week. I finally took the engagement for seventy. The union scale was fifty five dollars. I also agreed to write the musical numbers for the forthcoming production without any extra pay.

They would gladly have engaged my wife too, they explained, fully aware of her capabilities. But, the Jewish Musician's Club would not permit her to play. Besides, they had already engaged Joseph Brody, as leader and pianist of a small orchestra.

Jennie was not too pleased that I had accepted the engagement without her.

"Do we have a choice?" I tried to placate her. "Would it be better to travel with a baby in the sticks? Besides, this is a big chance for me to be seen on a New York stage for the first time. And what about the fifty dollars I already have as an advance on my salary? Isn't that something to consider? Don't you know we are broke?" Nevertheless, it led to harsh words—our first quarrel.

* * *

The Hebrew Actors' Union always held a general meeting prior to the opening of the theater season. The representative of the union, Reuben Guskin, gave his annual report regarding the past and the future of the theatrical profession. Invited were also various members of the press. Union members were expected to pass approval and to give praise to Guskin for all he had accomplished during the year on behalf of the union and its membership. Then came the issue of ratifying engagements at the theater for the coming season.

I sat in the Royale awaiting the outcome of this meeting with great trepidation. According to the talk in the cafe, there would be fireworks. I had been officially engaged and Guskin had indeed promised to work out a privilege for me. The membership, I feared, would never allow it. Especially, since I was not the only nonunion actor in the cast. Others engaged were; Lazar Zelazo, Moshe Feder, Moshe Tarlovsky and Rose Birnbaum (Zelazo), noted actors of the Vilna Troupe. I was sure the ax would fall on me—an unknown in New York.

Guskin always sought to imbue these tense meetings with a festive spirit. It was definitely His Day! He would arrive in his holiday best, a boutonniere in his buttonhole, like a bridegroom at his wedding. Excerpts of his report— practically the same year in, year out—could later be read in all the Yiddish newspapers. To wit:

> The Yiddish theater is experiencing a crisis. The reason for this can be blamed on the actors, themselves. Our union people refuse to take engagements out of town. And it is the provinces themselves, in fact, that are the backbone of the Yiddish theater in America. New York alone cannot furnish jobs for all...Yet, despite this great crisis affecting the theaters, there will still be a greater number of actors employed this season than last year at this time. And many more are sure to be absorbed into the stream.

I waited for news of my verdict at the union meeting. The telephone rang again. It was Oscar Green "It's O.K.," he said. "The union has granted you a privilege. I'll tell you the rest later."

Most of the actors, dressed fit to kill, collected in the Royale after the meeting. And Guskin, all aglow, like a star following a premiere, entered, escorted by his entourage: Jean Greenfield, Louie Goldstein, Charlie Cohan and Abe Sinkoff. He took his place at a large table reserved for the occasion, with people congratulating him left and right for his excellent report on the state of the union. Noticing me at a discreet distance, he beckoned me to come over. In a low voice he filled me in on the official decision.

"It's all right, Yablokoff," he said, "You can report tomorrow for rehearsal at the Hopkinson."

* * *

The theater was located on Hopkinson and Pitkin avenues in Brownsville. As it turned out, we really had a name cast, with such artists as Bella Bellarina, Liza Silbert, Tillie Rabinowitz, Boris Auerbach (no relation to Sam), Helen Blay, and others. Our opening play, *Children do not Forget* was a drama by Z. Libin. Joseph Brody and I collaborated on the musical numbers. Brody had for many years been the composer for the famed David Kessler, for whom he had written some very outstanding compositions that are remembered and sung to this day, like *Mizmur L'Duvid* and *Altashlicheinu* (Do not forsake us). He was a quiet, easy-going elderly musician and very pleasant to work with.

Moshe Schorr and Chaim Schneier impressed upon us that the musical numbers had to emerge out of the action and be smoothly integrated into the continuity of the script. The song's insertion in the middle of this true-to-life play should not jar the critics or the sensibilities of the most finicky connoisseurs.

The singing and dancing in this play was to be provided by Tillie Rabinowitz and me. Tillie was cast as a housemaid and I, as her boyfriend, a housepainter's helper. If we were suddenly to break into song and dance, it would surely turn the literary style of the drama into another cheap melodrama, or trite musical comedy.

Mr. Libin, the author, a sentimental little man, white-haired, hatless, with a pleasant smile that almost never left his face, listened attentively to my observations. Gazing at me with his pale blue, benign eyes, he bobbed his head in agreement with everything I pointed out. As a matter of fact in his opinion his drama needed music like a hole in the head.

"What are you saying, Mr. Libin?" protested Oscar Green, aghast. "No singing? Here in my Hopkinson Theater? And you expect the audience to accept that? Why, they're already singing and dancing even in Maurice Schwartz's Art Theater! But, Yablokoff has a point. The songs must be inserted cleverly, so that—as the saying goes—'the wolf is sated and the lamb remains intact' so I'm sure he'll find a way."

"Mr. Libin," I said. "If you could possibly alter the script a little for instance: the simple housemaid and her boyfriend want to become vaudeville entertainers and are constantly dragging around to amateur night contests. This will give us stage license to sing, dance and amuse the audience in a plausible way. It will appear that we are rehearsing our act for the amateur night routines."

Mr. Libin, inspired, brought us new material chockful of entertaining situation. I then wrote several comic numbers, to which Brody set music and they evolved as musical scenes rather than the same old theater duets. They became part of the action, so that it seemed the scenes could not have been played any other way.

* * *

Riding the subway to and from the Bronx to Brownsville during the rehearsal period was pure punishment. And would only be worse after the show opened, I contemplated. By chance, I discovered an unfurnished three room flat to let on Amboy Street, a few blocks from the theater. It could have been a good deal brighter and more airy, but the rent was reasonable. One can't have everything. Oscar Green took me to a second-hand furniture dealer, where I bought a bed, a dresser, a kitchen table and few chairs for $200—which Green advanced me. Equipment for the baby, we already had, and so that same week, we became residents of Brownsville.

Rehearsals lumbered along with difficulty. Chaim Schneier as director blundered a little until we finally found our way out of the woods. Tillie Rabinowitz and I scored a big hit, thank heaven. The audience enjoyed our antics tremendously and called us back for encore after encore.

None of the theater critics derided our play as a piece of song-and-dance trivia—the way they usually downgraded a melodrama laced with "vocalizations." Nobody took us to task for disrupting the plot with a song and dance out of the blue. And I was given all the credit.

My friend Kirschenbaum gave me a very fine mention in his weekly *Theater Portraits* under the caption "New Faces on the Yiddish Stage." He wrote: "I am wholly gratified that I helped get this young actor released from Ellis Island three years ago. The Yiddish stage in New York is greatly in need of young talents such as, Chaim Yablokoff."

Critics from the American press were lured all the way out to Brownsville by our publicity man, Max Karper. They also received our play with high regard. Our success was also the topic of the day in the Royale. The self-styled crystal-gazers had predicted that our format would be too literary for the clientele of the Hopkinson Theater. But their predictions fell flat. We ran *Children do not Forget* for months. In a local house where it was customary to come with a new show almost every week, this was a record!

We also produced Leon Kobrin's play *Door Number Three*, a dramatization of his novel *The Professional Bridegroom* which dealt with prostitution. Our management resorted to the old tried and true advertisement: Children under 16, not admitted. That did it! The public beleaguered the box office for tickets!

There is really no crystal ball in show business. If one strikes it, it goes all the way. If not nothing will help. We happened to strike it pretty good that season, while the other theaters did not. Our second weekend play, *Her Last Dance* by Abraham Bloom, was such a huge success in our theater that Max Gable and Jennie Goldstein made a special trip to Brownsville to see it. They liked this melodrama so much that they bought the rights and soon produced it at their People's Theater in Manhattan. But it failed to click. So, who can possibly foresee these things, or supply the answer?

We also did a play called *Why Husbands Leave Home* by Harry Kalman-owitz. Playing a small character part, I introduced, for the first time, Moishe Nadir's humorous song "Der Rebbe Elye-Meylech." It was such a terrific suc-cess, the audience clamored for encores. When Moishe Nadir, himself, came to hear my interpretation he was so inspired, he wrote an additional verse for my encore—a verse that had not yet been printed in the original copy. I was very flattered to say the least. This song, which I have since introduced all over the world, is popular to this day. The original piano arrangement was made by the composer, Abe Ellstein. It is now considered a folk song.

* * *

Jennie's parents finally moved into a house of their own in Boro Park. Since I was occupied at the theater seven days a week, with daily rehearsals, evening performances and matinees on Saturday and Sunday, she and Yankele spent more time in Boro Park than in our flat. I couldn't blame her. She was lonely. She didn't know any of our neighbors and it was difficult being so alone with the child. At the Fleischmans who managed to acquire an old baby grand, she could practice her concertos or play duets and trios with her brothers. She and the boy often stayed over at her parents' home.

Needless to say, when I came home from the theater tired and hungry, I would find myself alone. I hardly had an opportunity to spend time with my son. While I did understand my wife's need for company, it was far from conducive to a harmonious marriage.

Bertha Kalish

At Passover, our company at the Hopkinson Theater was joined by a guest star, the celebrated Yiddish-American actress, Bertha Kalish. I was all aquiver. As if I ever dreamed of playing with this great lady, who was so renowned, not only on the Yiddish, but on the American stage as well.

Madame Kalish was quite tall. She was stately, beautiful and possessed of a speaking voice that was likened to the deep, mellow tones of a cello. The play in which she was to appear was a melodrama by Moshe Schorr *The Only Way* directed by the author himself.

At the very first rehearsal, Madame Kalish made us feel that she was indeed, the great artist she was famed to be. Her boundless energy was truly something to marvel at. Suffering as she did from an eye ailment, which subsequently blinded her, it frustrated her and made her irritable. This probably accounted for her stern and demanding attitude toward the actors.

One of our actors, Meyer Sherr, an incorrigible jester, was a tall, ruggedly built individual. Jokingly, he would say, "Go 'way, or I'll belt you one!" Yet he was gentle as a lamb.

In this play Meyer Sherr played the incidental role of a Russian officer. As Meyer happened to be Galician, it was impossible for him to get his teeth into this typically Russian character. We sat around for hours while Madame Kalish tried, unrelentingly, to mold Meyer into a Russian.

"No, no, no! That's not it!" she thundered at him. "Mr. Sherr, you must try to assume the image of a stern Russian officer—a Gentile!!! Not a Jewish peddler on Orchard Street!"

Meyer looked at her, smiled, and tried again and again. But it only went from bad to worse.

"No, no," Madame Kalish wouldn't let up. "Now you sound like a rabbi! I want you to bring out the typical Gentile."

Meyer, sweating, but still smiling, answered in an unruffled tone, "Madame Kalish, why upset yourself? It will be all right. You want me to be a typical Gentile...a goy? Fine. But you'll have to wait till Sunday."

Taken aback, as we all were, Madame Kalish fixed him with a puzzled stare and demanded, "What do you mean?"

"Very plain, Madame Kalish," replied Meyer with a straight face, "Sunday, early in the morning as soon as the churches open, I shall go and have myself converted. Then, I'll be a genuine Gentile!"

We survived the rehearsals with Madame Kalish, and the performance brought very substantial receipts into the box office. The play was not a smash—just another melodrama. But, the magic of Bertha Kalish was truly astounding. Her diction in delivering her monologues, her laughter, her weeping were all modulated so masterfully that it could well have been a virtuoso playing on his instrument—the cello. We forgave this fabulous artist for her harsh treatment of us at the rehearsals. It was worth appearing with her.

* * *

Another guest artist soon followed. This was the effervescent character-soubrette, Nellie Casman, in a musical comedy written by her husband, Shlomo Steinberg. She played the role of a boy cantor, which suited her perfectly, right down to the pants she wore. The audience loved her.

When I heard that we were soon to welcome the star, Bessie Thomashevsky, I was delighted. I had already been initiated in her repertoire during my first season in Toronto. This time she came with a melodrama by Harry Kalmanowitz, *Women, Guard your Home.* One of the key male parts, called for an elderly character-comedian, who could sing and dance. The likely choices in our company, Lazar Zelazo and Moshe Silberstein, immediately set their hearts on this role. Zelazo, however, was not a singer, while Silberstein, a good actor and comedian did sing and dance. Yet, instead of either of them, Bessie cast me in the part.

I knew right off that this was not going to win me too many well wishers in the union. Silberstein took this as a terrible blow to his ego. He had had to relinquish many a role during the season in favor of Zelazo, who was after all an actor of repute, an artist with the status of the Vilna Troupe. But, the affront of taking a role just tailor-made for him, and giving it to me, a new-comer, a nonunion man—this was the last straw!

He ran to the union with his complaint. And that was no help because, according to the ruling of the executive board, guest artists had the right to cast their plays as they saw fit. So, if Bessie Thomashevsky wanted me for the part, then that was that!

Silberstein became my bitterest enemy. I would gladly have turned my part over to him, just so I could remain a "good boy" in the eyes of union members.

Bessie's performance was so successful in Brownsville that the manage-ment of the Second Avenue Theater made a deal with Oscar Green to exchange companies. Molly Picon and her cast would move to the Hopkinson Theater, and Bessie would take her company to the Second Avenue in Manhattan.

This turn of events created a revolution in the union: how dare they per-mit four nonunion people to play at the Second Avenue Theater?! The four actors in question were forthwith replaced by union members. Feder and Tar-lovsky of our troupe, were out. Zelazo wasn't in the show anyway, so that left me, the only nonunion man in the cast. Silberstein remained to play a lesser role.

My success enraged Silberstein all the more. One of the numbers I did in the show, was a couplet of mine, called "Don't Overshoot the Mark"—a surefire hit. Finished with the song, I had to make a dash up the stairs for quick change before the finale. At one performance, just as I rushed in to make my change, Silberstein picked up a large tin of face powder and threw it square in my face. All I could do was wipe my bloody nose, change and get back on stage for the finale.

When my brother-in-law learned of the incident, he came backstage ready to maul my assailant. I had all I could do to restrain him. "Leave him alone, Henry," I pleaded, "he's a union man! He can ruin me! Leave him alone!"

* * *

At the plush Second Avenue Theater, I was constantly amazed that the management should countenance the undisciplined behavior of the men in the orchestra. The Yiddish theaters were, of course, still dominated by the Jewish Musicians' Club—run specifically by their leader, Morris Vatman, a drummer who couldn't read music. But he was a very good politician in the musician's union and everyone in the theater trembled before him.

I observed that the musicians were in the habit of slinking out of the pit in the middle of a performance, disappearing into the cellar to play cards. As soon as they began weaving their way out one by one from among the stands, the audience reacted as one, "Uh-oh, the orchestra is leaving, there won't be any more singing!" And when the men crawled back into the pit, you could hear the rustle in the theater: "Aha! The orchestra is back. Somebody is going to sing." During this exodus—and not exactly on tiptoe either—there may have transpired the most crucially dramatic moment, or perhaps the most rib-tickling scene on stage, but nobody paid attention. All eyes were on the fumbling musicians. More than once a performer remained standing on stage open-mouthed, ready to sing, only to discover that the orchestra was not in the pit. They were too absorbed in their card game to mind the cue. Only when the frantic stage manager flew down the steps to rasp, "Hey, musicians! Come on!" did they begin to scramble one at a time through the narrow doorway from under the stage. Whichever musician reached his stand first, would start the introduction, while the others staggered in to catch up several bars later. The last one, always, to reach his drums was the beefy Mr. Vatman, who made his presence known by a loud thud on his bass-drum: Vatman is back...so there...sing!

One incident in particular had upset me terribly. At the rehearsal, Vatman banged away at his drums, deafening everyone. Bessie Thomashevsky, who tried to go through her number, could hardly hear herself.

"Mr. Vatman," she begged, "please, not so loud."

"Hey, you!" he retorted, "don't you teach me how to beat a drum. Better learn how to sing in your old age!"

My blood boiled. This boor! The gall to talk this way to a lady, an actress, a world personality! yet I was in no position to take a stand. But I never forgave him for it, and some years later I did indeed pay this Mr. Vatman back several times over for his cussed arrogance.

* * *

Zalmen Zilbertzweig, a congenial young writer from Europe, came to see one of our performances. He was in the United States to promote his project of publishing a lexicon of the Yiddish Theater.

"The Yiddish theater in America hasn't as yet shown much confidence in me and even less optimism in my project. Everyone assures me that if I do succeed in getting such a lexicon published, I will have earned great credit for my accomplishment. I know that credit is an important commodity in America, and that's exactly what I've been feeding my wife and son in Europe for the past two years—credit! It's time that, in addition to the credit, the Hebrew Actor's Union and the actors themselves should create some funds for the lexicon."

Anyone trying to enhance, or dignify the status of the Yiddish theater was all right with me. Without hesitation I sent the lexicon committee all of ten dollars—a sum which represented a fortune to me then.

Over a span of years, under the auspices of the Hebrew Actor's Union, Zalmen Zilbertzweig did manage to publish six volumes of the *Yiddish Theater Lexicon*. It is truly a monumental life's work dedicated to the Yiddish Theater.

* * *

The managers of the other theaters were beginning to make plans for the coming season while our play with Bessie Thomashevsky was still doing business on Second Avenue. Summer was approaching and already it was hot, but people kept coming so we continued to play. I was very tired, and had to ride the subway from downtown Manhattan to Brownsville every night. Jennie and Yankele were still staying over with her parents. During the day, having no rehearsal, I traveled to Boro Park to spend time with them. Then, in the evening, it was back to the theater, I wished the season was over. This, for me, was no family life at all.

"There's one more attraction following Bessie into the Second Avenue Theater," said Oscar Green. "Julius Nathanson is scheduled to play. And Nathanson will be needing an actor like you, Yabby. I'm sure the union will allow you to work with him. You really ought to consider the job, summer is only just beginning, why not make yourself some extra money?"

I agreed to play with Nathanson and reported the following day for rehearsal. Out of our entire Hopkinson company, I was the only one there. Nathanson's cast of actors were all new faces to me. I just stood to one side of the stage and waited for rehearsal to begin.

The production was to be a revival of a Boris Thomashefsky and Rumshinsky operetta, *Di Chazente* (The Lady Cantor). Most of the cast had already played this production. The director was the veteran actor, Kalmen Juvelier, and Rumshinsky was to conduct. Julius Nathanson, the star, handed out the scripts. As he gave me mine, everyone looked askance at me. Suddenly, an elderly actor—who shall remain nameless—pointed at me and in a voice loud enough for all to hear, kibitzingly said, "Hey, boys, and who is this 'dreck'?"

Without a word, I handed back my part, and walked out of the theater.

That season of 1927-28, I had appeared in twenty-six plays over a period of forty-two weeks. The important thing to me that season was having the opportunity to prove my talents as an actor, not only in Brownsville, but also on Second Avenue. True enough, in the process, I had also won myself a few "good friends" in the union! As for privilege to play next season in New York, I knew this was something I had better forget despite getting several such bids. I had made too much success for a nonunion actor. And to boot, I had broken the rule of being a "good boy," by refusing to take humiliation and walking out on a job. I decided, no matter what, I would not be a good boy anymore!

40

Detroit

For the 1928-29 season, I was engaged in Littman's Peoples' Theater, in Detroit. The producers were my old friend, Sam Auerbach, and Abraham Littman. Having no other alternative I accepted this engagement, especially to be with Auerbach and his wife, Sadie Sheingold, with whom I had already played in Toronto and Los Angeles.

My wife could not be engaged. The pianist there was Abe Grushkov, a native Detroiter. Besides, she had no desire to just tag along with me, having gotten a taste of what it was like to be alone with the child while I was constantly at the theater. In New York, at least, she was near her family, but Michigan? I promised that as soon as we were settled in Detroit, I would send for her sister Fay to pay us a visit, so she could have company.

We gave up our little flat on Amboy Street and I sold our furniture to a peddlar for a piddling sum. In Detroit we rented a furnished room with kitchen privileges in the home of the Winokur family—the parents of actress Sally Josephson. Our prompter, Oscar Ostroff, also lived there.

The large community of Jews in Detroit had its very own newly built theater with a capacity of over 1,000 seats. The stage of Littman's Peoples' Theater was not overly large, but adequate enough for any type of production. The theatergoers were very proud of this achievement because the building had been erected solely for Yiddish theater at the cost of $250,000, a small fortune at the time.

The architect, Morris Finkel, had provided every possible comfort and decor for the audience, not to mention the gilt cherubim around the proscenium. There was only one little thing he forgot: dressing rooms for the actors! And when was this omission discovered? After the theater was completed. Well, one could hardly demand that the theater be rebuilt just for the comfort of the actors! So, we had to make the best of it.

On the third floor, way up under the roof, where the flies were hung, several cubicles were partitioned off, and the actors each got their corner where they could change and makeup. In the summer one could stifle up there and in the winter one could freeze. But this was only the half of it. The real hardship was running up and down the three flights to make our changes. It was hard enough on the men. But, the women, for whom it was a never-ending process of on-with-a-costume, off-with-a-costume, it was pretty rough. In a pinch we changed in the wings. Climbing up and down that spiral stairway during the nine shows a week, we referred to ourselves as the angels in Jacob's dream, ascending and descending the ladder to heaven!

Aside from forgetting the actors when blueprinting the plans for the house, the credit for the incentive of building this Yiddish theater in Detroit was definitely due to one man—Abraham Littman. The title impresario described him to a tee! He even spoke with haughty authority!

Upon my recommendation, we opened with Z. Libin's *Children do not Forget*. I had the book and music intact from the season before at the Hopkinson Theater. The play, as well as the cast, were received with tremendous enthusiasm.

Among the actors, with whom I had not played before, was my Grodno compatriot, Wolf Shumsky. He and his actress wife, Fela Landman, had wandered over half the globe after the revolution in Russia. They found refuge in Harbin, China as did many Russian Jews, before emigrating to the United States. Shumsky was a fine actor, a cultured, learned and intelligent man. He had also created a name for himself in Russia, as a composer, violinist and playwright. In fact, he wrote the very popular operetta, *Liovka Maladietz* in which Aaron Lebedeff made his debut in New York.

The character-comedian role in our production was played by Jack Shargel, a recruit from American vaudeville and burlesque. Although he struggled with Yiddish, he managed to wade through the tough spots. A spry sort of fellow, Shargel kept his audience in stitches. With him in Detroit was his wife, Birdie, who in time, also became a Yiddish actress.

Outstanding of course was the singer-actress, Esther Field. She was known to New York radio listeners as "Di Yiddishe Mamme," and was often referred to as the Jewish Kate Smith. With the rendition of one of her liturgical compositions, she was always sure to stop the show.

I had officially been engaged to play bouffe-comedians, and as such I often worked opposite our character-comedienne, Clara Rosenthal, a gal with a powerful voice—a "belter." We sang duets, danced and were a great hit with the audience.

Another very fine actor was David Reitz. He had come to the United States with his wife and two young sons from Australia and was subsequently engaged with us in Detroit.

My two closest pals in the company were Isaac Arco, the stage manager and spare actor, and Oscar Ostroff. Ostroff, who had been brought over from Romania by Misha Fishzon, remained in Detroit as a prompter. He later made his career in the Yiddish theater as an impresario, playwright and radio commentator in Chicago and eventually in Los Angeles.

Some of our staunchest theater fans were the Jewish "boys" from the notorious Purple Gang on Twelfth Street, where our theater was located. Their "activities," such as they were, never kept them from attending all of our shows. Every now and then we would lose one of these admirers through circumstances graphically described as a rub out in the tabloids. Yet in the theater, one would never suspect that these fellas were any such thing as mobsters.

Interestingly enough, when one of our actors was burglarized, our devoted fans got wind of it, and assured us that the missing stuff would turn up—as indeed it did! Before long the stolen goods were returned and the burglar got a few bones broken for his daring to lay hands on the worldly possessions of a Yiddish actor!

* * *

Playing in a provincial city for an entire season was hard labor. We had to come up with a new show every weekend—and I mean new, not something warmed over. During the week we filled in with popular stock plays out of the Yiddish repertoire. We also inaugurated the "Literary Thursdays." So, day in, day out, we were up to our necks in rehearsal. There was just time enough to eat and hurry back for the evening's performance.

In addition to my regular duties as an actor, I had to compose music and lyrics, write out texts and sometimes direct a play. In addition, I was obliged to participate in Altman's Yiddish radio hour. There was no extra remuneration for this. It was only for the publicity of announcing our program of the week.

Under these circumstances, the peace and harmony between my wife and me didn't last very long. And how could I blame her? Her situation was far from enviable. She was fully prepared to go back to New York to stay with her parents; whereupon I kept my promise and sent for her sister. Fay came to Detroit and stayed with us to the end of the season.

The Flu Epidemic

As if we didn't have enough tribulations, the Almighty sent us a plague right smack in the middle of winter—the flu! Theater business fell off. Radio and newspapers cautioned people to stay away from crowded places. Schools were closed. And the weather spread a cold damp blanket over the entire city; a dampness that penetrated one's bones, affected one's lungs, throat, nose and ears. Even those who had not as yet succumbed, dragged about in a lethargic daze. Yet, we didn't miss a performance. Epidemic or no epidemic the show must go on!

Our guest star at the time was made Madame Bertha Kalish. We were rehearsing for her opening vehicle, *In the Middle of the Road*, a drama by Moshe Schorr. I knew that she wasn't easy to work with; only this time it was worse.

The one who bore the brunt of her caprices in Detroit was Wolf Shumsky. Since he had the leading male part, all his important scenes were involved with Madame Kalish. He endured her demands with patience. Shumsky was a quiet, gentle person by nature, trained in the discipline of European theater. Swallowing Madame's harassment, he tried, with every ounce of strength to interpret his role according to her wishes. But it was no use. Shumsky only floundered all the more. His confusion was due to the flu, which must already have gripped him, weakening his resistance.

The premiere was set for Friday evening. That morning, general rehearsal was called for nine o'clock. We were still rehearsing at six. And through all those hours Bertha Kalish had relentlessly bedeviled this poor man. The rest of us hung around the theater, nobody daring to go home, let alone have something to eat. We sent out for sandwiches and coffee and began climbing the three flights to make up and dress for the performance.

Shumsky remained on stage, slumped in a chair. Stopping to comfort him, I said, "You'll be great in the part. After tonight's performance, Madame Kalish will praise you to the skies. I know her from Hopkinson. That's the way she is at rehearsal, very demanding."

"Chaimke," he said affectionately, "if only I can live to see this over with! I'm cold...cold..." he repeated, his face a waxy yellow. Finding a cape backstage, used in *Bar-Kochba*, a historical play we did the night before, I threw it around him and climbed to my dressing room.

Before long, people began straggling into the theater for the premiere of *Middle of the Road*. For Wolf Shumsky, it was "the last road" for half an hour later, an ambulance was called and the doctor, declaring him critical, took him to the hospital.

The performance was not cancelled, only delayed. Madame Kalish had, of course, bargained for perfection on stage, but when it was a question of jeopardizing her share of the gross, she was prevailed upon to go on with the show, having David Reitz step into Shumsky's role. Reitz's part was taken over by Harry Jordan.

The theater was packed. Bertha Kalish lured the people out despite the flu warnings. The curtain went up and she was enthusiastically received and presented with flowers. In her traditional after-curtain speech, she thanked and praised each performer for helping make her premiere such a colossal success. And through it all, Wolf Shumsky lay dying of a cerebral hemorrhage.

David Reitz did an excellent job considering the circumstances. We all admired and marveled at him. The next day, Reitz himself, began feeling under the weather. But he made nothing of it. Weren't we all complaining of one thing, or another? He merely indulged in a groan, or two, and played the matinee performance. Come Saturday evening, he was very dull and lifeless in his part. Madame Kalish was visibly upset, but held herself in check. She, as well as the rest of us, was still quite shaken over Shumsky's condition.

The next day, I noticed David Reitz coming up the street to the theater supported by his two frightened young sons, one at each elbow.

"David!" I exclaimed, as I ran toward them, "What's wrong? How do you feel?"

"Not too good, I'm afraid," he murmured. "Maybe something I ate. But you know, the show must go on," he smiled, feebly.

The only thing I could do for him was to keep him from climbing those three flights to his dressing room. Arco and I screened off a corner backstage with a panel of scenery and helped him get ready. His boys, together with his wife, who soon came running, helped him with his changes throughout the matinee. Between shows, Arco and I lugged a sofa from the set and made him lie down. Nobody needed a thermometer to read his temperature. He was burning with fever. I called emergency. And when the ambulance came, they took David Reitz to the hospital along with his family who refused to leave his side. That evening, Harry Jordan stepped into Reitz's part, while Ostroff took over for Jordan and the show went on. People applauded...Madame Kalish held her curtain speech...and none of us knew—least of all the audience— that Reitz was no longer among the living.

All of us at the theater, joined by many a Detroit citizen, escorted his body to the station, where it was placed on a train for New York. He was laid to rest on the plot of the Yiddish Theatrical Alliance at the Mount Hebron Cemetery. Our company subsequently arranged a benefit performance to help his widow and children return to Australia.

Not long after, Shumsky too, passed away. Thus, again joined by a large crowd of mourners, we escorted our deceased colleague to the train for New York. And Wolf Shumsky also came to rest on the burial ground of the Alliance.

Laugh, Clown, Laugh!

I for one did, not succumb to the flu, although I lived in constant fear for my wife and child. I did nevertheless develop a cough—and such a hacking cough I had to brace myself against anything at hand. Our good theater friend, Dr. Kleinman kept me immune to the flu, prescribing a wonder drug—booze! It evidently proved to be my savior. Not that this prescription was easy to fill. It was during the Prohibition and there wasn't a legal drop to be gotten. I was obliged to settle for bootleg stuff. The boys of the Purple Gang came to the rescue. They supplied me with the best cognac smuggled direct from Windsor, Canada. They even provided me with a convenient hip flask. So, I gulped my "medicine" for all I was worth—doctor's orders!

My wife, her sister and Yankele, having been kept away from crowds were also safe, thank heaven.

A rumor spread in New York that the actors in Detroit were dropping dead one after another. So the top stars, naturally, gave us a wide berth. Even the lesser luminaries were afraid to venture near our theater. When Auerbach and Sadie left the company, the entire burden of continuing our season fell on my shoulders. I took over the responsibility of directing, staging and taking part in every type of play. Any suitable old script I was able to dig up in Littman's archive, which he hoarded like a treasure—on it went! We struggled to keep the theater going until some new attraction would have mercy and come to rescue the season.

Our "Messiah" finally arrived: Samuel Goldenburg. Worn out as we were, we gathered new strength to prepare for his opening show, *The Romanian Kretchma* by Harry Kalmanowitz. While our days were spent in rehearsal with Goldenburg—another hard taskmaster—I still held the fort evenings, "starring" with our new leading lady, Rosetta Biales, who had come to replace Sadie Sheingold. Titian-haired, slender and elegant, with a keen understanding of the classical repertoire, she proved to be a great asset to our theater.

During that particular era, plays were three and four acts long. Performances often ran as late as midnight. Rehearsals, of course, began bright and early in the morning. All this would not have been so bad if only I could have caught up on sleep, but the minute I dropped off, little Yankele would start fussing and crying. I had become an actor, I joked, so that I could sleep late—what a joke!

One morning, even the alarm clock worked against me. It didn't ring, although I was sure I wound it. I hadn't slept a wink most of the night because my little son cried and cried. Neither Jennie nor I was able to soothe him. It was heartbreaking, but we couldn't understand what disturbed him so. He was not talking yet and we had no way of knowing that he was being tortured by an ear inflammation. Toward morning, when he calmed down, I fell into a deep sleep and relied on the clock to wake me for rehearsal. When I awoke with a sudden start, I realized I'd overslept!

Pulling my clothes on, I dashed water on my face. Shaving was out of the question, and there was no time for coffee, either. Under the door of the vestibule I picked up a letter and saw that it was stamped—Grodno! My heart quickened. It was several weeks since I last heard from home.

With the letter in one hand, the apple in the other, I hurried out. From the handwriting on the envelope I knew at once that it was from my brother Shayke. I couldn't wait to read it. Continuing on the run, I tore open the envelope, eager to glance at the opening lines, at least. It read: Dear Brother, Chaimke, by now you must surely have heard the sad news. Our dear, beloved father is no longer with us... he passed away...

I started to cross the street, too stunned to grasp the full impact of these dreadful words: my father, dead? It can't be! My father?!

The honking of horns raucously warning me to get out of the way drove me back to the curb. Suddenly, I turned and ran back to the house. Breathlessly, I reached the door, but halfway up the stairs I broke down. Hearing the hurried footsteps, Jennie opened the door and discovering me in such a state that she called the theater to tell them of my tragic news.

Mr. Littman and several of my colleagues came rushing to the house, not only to console me, but to persuade me to play the evening's performance.

I was not to worry about today's rehearsal for Goldenburg would, of course, excuse me.

"You have our deepest sympathy," said Littman. "but you know, we have absolutely no one to take over for you. Under the circumstances, even a rabbi would sanction your performing tonight. If you don't come to play, Yabby, I will be forced to close the theater."

Distraught beyond words, I was persuaded to go and discuss my situation with the rabbi at the little shul on Twelfth Street. I would then abide by his ruling. The rabbi took into consideration the extenuating circumstances peculiar to my profession. He also took into consideration the plight of the other theater families, who would be deprived of a living if the theater closed.

The good rabbi then gave consent to my working that same evening, with the promise that I will recite the Kaddish in memory of my father three times daily, for the entire year of mourning—a promise I religiously fulfilled.

I performed that evening. And painfully enough, the number I had to do expressed the very grief I was suffering. The words: "Lakh, lakh, Payatz!"(Ven dein hartz oif shtiker vert tzurisn, lakh, lakh, Payatz...)

When your heart is torn with pain and sorrow,
    Laugh, laugh, you Clown!
Though your grief will still be there, tomorrow,
    Laugh, laugh, you Clown!

You are only a plaything, a tool
To make people laugh is the rule—you fool!

When you feel your tears are burning,
    Laugh, laugh, you Clown!
Never show the world your pain, your yearning,
    Laugh, laugh, you Clown!
Just be amusing, appealing,
You are a clown without feeling...So,
    Laugh, laugh, you Clown!

Ironically, this was the very song that brought me tremendous popularity later on via the radio and on the stage. It was the start of my career around the world.

41

Lyric Theater in Williamsburg

For the 1929-30 season I was engaged at the Lyric Theater, a Yiddish playhouse in Williamsburg, Brooklyn. The entrepreneurs were Sam Auerbach and Misha Fishzon—my fourth season with Auerbach and Sadie Sheingold. But, again Brooklyn! Brooklyn, not Second Avenue, the Yiddish Broadway! Well, I consoled myself, at least it was still in New York, not "Siberia," as I had named the hinterland theaters with their eighty odd plays a season, leaving an actor ready to fall flat on his face!

The Jewish Musician's Club finally agreed to let Jennie play, on the premise that she was engaged as a composer. I rented an apartment on Hooper Street, not far from the Lyric, and during the hours that Jennie and I were occupied, her sister Fay volunteered to take care of our little son.

Our first production was *The Cabaret Singer* by Abraham Bloom, with original music composed by me and arranged by my wife, Jeanette Fleischman. We played this musical for eighteen weeks, the longest run a play had ever enjoyed at the Lyric Theater.

I had finally made the transition, from the light, bouffe-comedians to the singing, romantic roles. And it was very gratifying to receive the warm praise in the press, predicting a bright future for me on the Yiddish stage.

The season was very successful. Every play seemed to go over big, running weeks at a time. I wrote several hit songs that season and *The Clown*, which I sang in *The Cabaret Singer*, became an instant hit in New York. What more could an actor wish for? Yet the uppermost thing in my mind was to go to Europe and arrange to have a tombstone erected on my father's grave.

The last time I saw my father was in 1920 when I had left home. I arrived in the United States in 1924. I knew that in order to apply for citizenship I had to reside in the United States for a full five or more years, and I was counting the days until I would be eligible for my naturalization papers. I had been yearning to make a trip back to Grodno to see my family. And more than anything I wanted to sail with an American passport in my pocket.

At last the day came and I applied for citizenship. It was exactly five years from the day I was released from Ellis Island. I did, however, have misgivings about having spent two seasons out of the country when I played in Canada. The judge in the Brooklyn district court, where my hearing took place, did at first advise me that I wait two more years before I even contemplated leaving the country. But in looking over my citizenship application, he noticed that it was dated exactly one day after my arrival in the country. This pleased him tremendously.

"Look," he remarked to the others in the chamber, "this young man really has his heart set on becoming an American citizen. Only one day after his arrival in the States, he lost no time in securing his first naturalization papers. There are people in our country who have been here for forty, fifty years, they have raised families, made fortunes, and never given a thought to becoming citizens."

Turning back to me, the judge said, "In your case, Mr. Yablonik, I will make an exception and endorse your application. I am taking into consideration the fact that, as an actor, you are obliged to travel outside the border sometimes in order to make your living. But, your heart, I am sure is in the United States."

He then proceeded to ask me the required questions, which, thank heaven, I answered correctly. My two witnesses were Sam Auerbach and Irving Honigman. With one of his inevitable blunders, Honigman almost did me in, right there!

"How long have you known Mr. Yablonik?" the judge asked him.

"About five years," he replied.

"About is not satisfactory enough!" the judge pointed out. "A witness must know the applicant all of five years, or more."

Fortunately, Auerbach came to the rescue. "Your Honor," he interposed, "Mr. Honigman happens to be famous for his bloopers. When he says about he actually means more than five years."

At this, the judge threw his head back and had a good laugh. At last, I was sworn in and I left the court, a full-fledged American citizen.

* * *

When Misha Fishzon proposed that I come along with him to Europe to star in Yiddish theaters there, I was in seventh heaven. The name Misha Fishzon was a theatrical trademark. Aside from his prestige as a member of the Fishzon dynasty in Europe, he had made his own name in the world of theater.

I considered Fishzon's offer an opportunity to make up my traveling expenses and perhaps earn a little besides. It suited my plans perfectly, for it was certainly not within my means to take such a junket purely for the sake of visiting my family. My wife and I did manage to save a few hundred dollars that season at the Lyric. But this money was to take care of her and Yankele during my travels in Europe until I could earn something.

I began casting about for a few extra hundred dollars to cover the cost of a monument for my father's grave. My only solution, I realized, would be the old reliable source: a benefit performance. And I made an agreement for such an evening with the management of the Lyric Theater on a 50-50 basis.

The date for my testimonial performance was set. And I chose once again to play Gordin's drama, *Der Wilder Mentsh* (The Wild Man). The theater proved too small to accommodate the crowds that came, not merely to do me honor, but because the play had not been seen in years. No actor dared to appear as Lemach, the crowning-glory-role of the chief eagle himself, the late Jacob P. Adler. His "patriottn" would have hooted such a chutzpenik off the stage!

My announcement of the play did indeed stir up a kettle of fish among his old devotees in the Cafe Royale. Nevertheless, my new adaptation of the drama, the staging and interpretation of the unfortunate, mentally handicapped Lemach found favor even with the Adler patriots, who came prepared, I learned, to give me the "bird." They saw a different characterization, they said, not a mimicry of their revered Jacob P. Adler, and gave me their stamp of approval.

I was overjoyed at this triumph, not to mention the several hundred dollars I derived out of that unforgettable testimonial performance.

Again, my wife and I gave up our little flat on Hooper Street. Our acquired pieces of furniture were again sold for some trifling sum, and Jennie, taking our little Yankele, went once again to stay with the Fleischmans in Boro Park.

Packing up my wardrobe, such as it was, plus several plays and music, I boarded the French liner, Ile de France, and off I went—to Paris.

Paris, 1930

The crossing was tedious and uneventful. Fishzon, of course, traveled first class, and I didn't begrudge him this pleasure. The purser was kind enough to oblige me with a pass and I spent most of the time with Fishzon in first class, anyway.

After depositing our baggage at the Hotel Moderne in Paris, we went straight to the Lencry Theater and found the company already waiting for us. As our premiere was scheduled for the following week (Yiddish actors are notoriously quick studies), there was no time to lose for rehearsal. I read our opening play, *The Poor Millionaire*, a comedy by Michaelson, which I was to direct. I had also written the songs and lyrics. But more important than anything to me—an unknown in Paris—was that I had a splendid part in the play, showing me off to the best advantage.

Paris throbbed with Jewish life. And Yiddish theater was a going concern. It surprised me, therefore, that such a large Jewish community in this great cosmopolitan city had never managed to acquire a more suitable playhouse. Performances were held in the little Lencry, near the Place de Republique, known to Jews as The Pletzl.

The theater had a tiny stage with stationary scenery that was made of tin. Painted on one side of these metal panels was the replica of a room, serving as the interior setting of anything from a poor dwelling to a palatial salon. On the other side of these tin wings, was an exterior background, giving the illusion of a forest, a flower garden, or a tree-lined street. The Jewish theatergoers in Paris had apparently become accustomed to this static scenery.

Business was tremendous. The drawing card, of course, was Misha Fishzon. For me to be co-starring with such an acknowledged stage personality was a great step up the ladder. Considering that young, unknown talents are not readily given such opportunities, Misha Fishzon did make it possible for me to be seen and heard in Europe, not only by large audiences, but in well-suited roles and in a variety of plays.

While Fishzon took the straight dramatic characters, I did the romantic leads, singing my own compositions; songs totally new in this part of the world, where they became instant favorites.

We stayed on in Paris for about two months, producing a variety of plays, and thoroughly enjoying the adulation. It must also be said that performers around town—even those just visiting, or passing through Paris—immediately copied, word for word, note for note, all my songs. Many young aspiring actors (whom I shall not name), later made their careers in Europe using my repertoire without my permission.

We would have continued playing in Paris, or gone ahead with our plans for guest appearances in Poland and Romania. But I wanted to no longer put off my trip home to Grodno. And so we decided that Fishzon would go on to Romania and wire me from there at my mother's address, telling me where to meet him. At a special testimonial evening in my honor, where I surprised my audience by switching from lover to the character role of Lemach, I bade my newfound admirers in Paris a fond farewell. Escorted by friends and colleagues, I embarked on my journey via Berlin and Warsaw to Grodno.

Warsaw, 1930

On the train from Berlin to Warsaw, I became acquainted with a fellow passenger, an emissary from Palestine, with a mission for Jews in Poland. From him I learned that that the Habima Troupe was appearing in Berlin, and that my boyhood chum from Grodno, Shimon Finkel, whom I hadn't seen for ten years, was now a member of the Habima. I was beside myself with frustration. Oh, if I had only known! What a joyous reunion it would have been. To think that here we were in the same city and missed each other.

Finkel, he said, had studied with Max Reinhardt at his Berlin Dramatic Workshop and had recently been accepted into the Habima, a highly coveted achievement for a young actor. It was truly gratifying to know that Finkel too had attained his goal of becoming a professional actor.

Arriving in Warsaw early in the morning, I spent the day there until train time for Grodno, late that night. I naturally visited the Yiddish Actor's Guild and was warmly hailed by actors, who had already heard of my success in Paris. I received many propositions to play in Warsaw. Since I had a contract with Misha Fishzon, I referred them to him in Paris. We would undoubtedly play in Poland, too, I explained, but meanwhile I was on my way to Grodno to visit my family.

I also stopped in at a center that buzzed with intellectuals, Yiddish writers, artists and many other people of culture. They sat around, sipping tea, nibbling on egg biscuits, and discussing Yiddish and world events. With great interest they listened as I relayed greetings from writers in New York and Paris.

Guest starring in Warsaw was Ludwig Zatz, as well as a number of other performers from America. And they all did well. It was the very peak of a glittering era for Yiddish theater in Europe.

And yet, the anti-Semitism in Poland has not let up. At the universities, Jewish students had to sit in back of the classroom, on benches separated from the rest. The economic situation for the common Jew was very grave. A general boycott prevailed over Jewish places of business, Jewish tradespeople and workers. Polish officials and tax collectors laid siege to Jewish possessions, confiscating them for government taxes. Yet, the love of theater was so strong that Jewish people even pawned household articles to buy tickets for a Yiddish performance.

I got together with Ludwig Satz, his wife Lillie, his three little daughters and his group at the Bristol Hotel. The American actors Moshe Silberkasten and Gitel Stein were there too, and we all went for a stroll.

As we meandered along the Saxon Garden, where the revered I.L. Peretz, Avrom Reisen, Sholom Asch and other greats of Yiddish literature had often walked, my friend Silberkasten filled me in on all the latest theater news, recently brought in from New York. We jabbered away in Yiddish until Gitel Stein, nervously peering around, tugged at my sleeve. "Lower your voices, " she admonished in a whisper, "See those students over there? Let us speak English, please." Yes, indeed, there were very unpleasant incidents in Warsaw.

In the evening I went to the Kaminsky Theater to catch Ludwig Satz in the first act of the comedy *The Bandit*, a great performance. During intermission, I took leave of my colleagues and hurried to the station. On the way I stopped to buy some of Warsaw's famous kosher delicatessen. Armed with a kilo of cold cuts, a loaf of black bread fresh from the oven, I boarded the night train to Grodno.

Although the compartment I happened to be sharing with a Polish major was in first class, it was shabby with worn upholstery and only dimly lit. I felt very uncomfortable in such close quarters with a Polish military man, since I was, legally, still considered a deserter of the Polish army. I made no attempt to enter into conversation with the major, nor did he encourage it.

Tired as I was I couldn't doze off. My mind was too full of the many events in my life during the ten years in which I had wandered over a good portion of the globe, yet it had brought me very little recognition as an actor and still less, materially. After traveling in Europe for almost three months and after my great success in Paris, I was barely able to save enough for travel expenses to Poland. This was besides the money which I had wrapped in an undershirt and tucked between the music sheets in my folder. I would not have touched this money if I were to starve, for this was to pay for the headstone on my father's grave.

The glimmer of dawn was beginning to break through. Standing at the window, I watched the sky as it turned a lighter blue. And the stars growing paler finally vanished, giving way to the burst of brilliant sunrise. My eyes followed the fields as they flitted by, dotted here and there with wooded areas and little running streams. The peasant huts and farm sheds hadn't changed one iota in the ten years I'd been away. Cows were already in pasture, relishing the grass freshened by the morning dew. Peasant folk were doing their morning chores exactly as their forefathers had done generations before them. Not a thing had changed.

I wondered if anyone would meet me at the station. At first I was going to come as a surprise. But this, I feared would be too much for my mother's health. So, I sent a telegram to my brother Shayke, telling him when I would arrive, so he could relay my message to others in the family. Did he get my wire? Did he tell mother?

We passed Lasona...Ferstadt...and chugged over the trestle spanning the old River Niemen. Approaching the station with a clatter as cars bumped one against the other, the train finally came to a stop. Before I could turn from the window, the Polish major had already made it to the exit and was gone. Losing no time, I too, quickly gathered up my baggage and hopped off.

42

Grodno, 1930

I saw no welcomers on the platform. Evidently, the old regulation was still in effect—keeping this area clear of all but railroad employees and the police. People collected in the waiting room.

I scanned every face and suddenly my heart stood still. There she was! My mother! Yes, it was she, and standing beside her was a man I didn't know. But his eyes, I'd seen those eyes before. Could it be? Of course! My brother Velvel. The brother I had seen only twice in my life—twenty-five years ago. Once during a visit in jail and again when he was dragged off in the middle of the night with the etape to the Schlusselburg Fortress.

In a split second I was in my mother's arms. Holding me in a tight embrace, covering my face with kisses, she murmured over and over, "Chaimke, Chaimke. My son."

Velvel and I soon threw our arms around each other like the long-lost brothers we really were!

"Why mama, why?" I repeated, "why wasn't I told that Velvel is alive and in Grodno?"

"We'll explain, later," she whispered.

"Shayke got your telegram about an hour ago," said Velvel. "We didn't have a chance to tell all the others because mother and I immediately hurried to the station to meet you. The rest have all gone off to work. But my wife Chaya will relay the news of your arrival to the rest of the family."

Mother had aged although her face still retained traces of her former charm. The white hair now peeping from under her kerchief was rather becoming, I thought. She looked neat and trim, which only accentuated her frailness.

Velvel showed the ravages of his exile. It was stamped on his face. The clothes he wore hung pitifully on his slight form. Helping me with my baggage, Velvel hailed a droshky. With a Polish driver? Where were the Jewish drivers of old? Another occupation denied them?

Turning into Zamkova Street, we passed my Uncle Shillingoff's building complex and stopped at a court where mother was living with Velvel and his little family. His wife, Chaya, and their two little boys, who were also named Shayke and Chaim'l, ran to meet us. We embraced and kissed and everyone tried to help with my baggage.

The flat had three small rooms; a tiny alcove for mother, a bedroom for

Velvel and his wife and the general family-room for cooking, eating and where
the two boys slept. In mother's room, opposite her bed, stood an extra sleeping
bench with a straw-filled mattress. This had been arranged for me. Mother
simply wouldn't hear of me staying at the hotel, or the inn.

On second thought, I felt I was indeed better off staying at the flat. I had
no wish to hand over my American passport to register with the police, as
I would have to do at a public lodging-house. The only discomfort I'd be obliged
to bear, was making use of the communal toilet in the yard, a convenience
I had long gotten away from in America.

Velvel was in a hurry to go to work. It was late, but better to put in a
few hours, he said, than nothing at all. His job at the bookbinders did not bring
in much to begin with. Chaya urged him to take along some food for his lunch,
which reminded me that I had a whole loaf of untouched black bread and the
Warsaw cold cuts tucked away with my things. I unwrapped the package and
the mouth-watering aroma filled the room. but Velvel wouldn't think of indulging himself in a morsel of this gourmet treat merely for a noontime snack. He
settled for a slice of bread and declared that the meats will serve well as a treat
in the evening.

"We'll manage a bottle of vodka too," he said, "so when the others come
in, we can drink l'chaim in honor of you, Chaim!" The play on words pleased
him, for there was just a hint of a smile at the corners of his mouth.

Giving each child a gentle pat on the head, he left. Chaya busied herself
with household chores, while Mama suggested that I lie down and rest after
sitting up all night on the train. Gratefully, I stretched out on the sleeping bench
and made Mama come and sit on her bed, so we could talk our hearts out.

As Mother Related

"Father was on his way to the shul early morning to pray with the first
minyan, as he always did," she began. "At the corner of Skidler Street, he suddenly felt weak. It was his heart. He had to stop and lean against a wall for
support. He asked a passerby for help, but the man, it seems, was in a hurry
to get to work and didn't stop. Father barely made it to the synagogue. He
put on his tallis and tefillin and collapsed. They brought him home and he
died in Velvel's arms.

"The whole city escorted your father to his eternal resting place. They
carried him on a litter past all the synagogues and little prayer houses where
he had spent the days of his life. The rabbis spoke very highly of him in their
eulogies, God rest his soul.

"Life without father has been very difficult for me. But as my mother,
may she rest in peace, used to say: 'Life must go on. May a mortal never be
put to the test, such as he can become accustomed to.' The adjustment is very
hard. I did make one decision; never to go and live with any of the children.
'Alone, your soul is your own.' I rented this little flat and settled down to a

widow's way of life. Saturday afternoons and holidays I take a walk to visit the children and I'm always a welcome guest. For myself, I don't need much. From the money you send me, Chaimke, I even manage to save a few zlotys to slip to one, or another of the family—whoever needs it the most. And they all need it, my poor children. To help all of them would take the wealth of a Rothschild.

"Your brother Velvel is the worst off and the most to be pitied. Chaya is a sweet, lovable wife, an able housekeeper and, as you see, they have two lovely children. We get along beautifully. But for Velvel everything goes butterside-down. To spare them rent money, I had no recourse but to take them in here with me. What else could I do?"

"Velvel's political past is certainly no help toward holding a position. He has to be careful of every word he utters. The Polish police keep an eye on him. This is the reason we didn't write about his homecoming from Soviet Russia. Mail is censored. The less the police know about his past, the better.

"Yes, my son, you really have been keeping me alive, sending me to Druzkenik to take the baths for my rheumatism. May God give you good health, Chaimke, and enable you to earn enough for your little family, your wife, Jennie, and your son, Yankele. The fact that you have never forgotten me is no secret to the family. But that you are not a wealthy man is known only to your mother. Everybody here thinks that in America everyone is a millionaire. Especially an actor who travels around the world the way you do must surely be gathering up fortunes in gold. I wish to God it were true, my son!" she ended with a sigh.

"Who needs money, Mama!" I jested. "I'm richer than Croesus! The public paid for this trip and they also paid for father's monument. My riches are deposited with the audience. As long as I am on the Yiddish stage and people accept me, I'm a wealthy man. I have a dear wife, herself a musical artist, I have a wonderful little son, so I'm richer than rich. As a matter of fact, just say the word, Mama, and I'll take you right back with me to America!"

Mother had remained her old courageous self, never shedding a tear even during her account of father's passing. But, at this moment, what I noticed glistening in her eyes told me that these were tears of happiness, the kind she had rarely shed in her lifetime.

* * *

Mother prepared lunch, an old favorite of mine—fried herring. She remembered how I used to relish it as a boy. Now, sharing this delicacy with Velvel's two youngsters, I was amused to see that they too licked their fingers over it.

My brother Motke came running to welcome me during his noon-hour break from his temporary paving job. How toil-worn he looked! He would be back in the evening, he assured me, with his wife, Sheyne-Libbe and the children.

In a little while, my sister Slavka burst in, breathless, leaving her husband to mind the shoe store. Throwing her arms around me and kissing me, she lamented, "Our dear father didn't live to see you, Chaimke, I suppose it wasn't destined."

Shayke was the only with a steady position, working as a mechanic at a printing shop. He and his family were also expected in the evening.

When I asked mother about my baby sister Rochele, she hesitated. Rochele's husband, Hershel, she said, was mad at the whole family. She did not believe he would let Rochele and the children come to see me. When Chaya brought them the news of my arrival, he had said, "If the American millionaire needs us, let him come to see us here."

I decided that I would put aside my pride and indeed go to visit them. Not see my sister Rochele? The idea! When Velvel returned from work we sat down to our meager evening meal and soon after, the family began to gather.

Despite the tumult and hubbub of voices around me, I could not shake off the feeling that, any moment, the door would open and in would walk my father. I could not make peace with the thought that I would never see him again. Although everyone avoided mentioning him in my presence, I could see him standing before me, large as life.

Motke was going to come with me to order the gravestone. The epitaph would be composed and prepared by the Eishishker Rabbi, father's lifelong friend. My brothers also insisted that they too, contribute toward the cost of the stone—according to each one's means. I protested, but they were adamant. They felt that they too must share in this solemn obligation.

Velvel did not participate in the evening's general conversation. He seemed ill at ease. I still hadn't had a chance to talk with him, and I was anxious to learn how he'd lived through those ten years of hard labor in the Schlusselburg Fortress, how he'd survived in Siberia, and how was it that after sacrificing his life for the Russian Revolution, he returned to Poland.

It was late when everyone finally left. Little Shayke and Chaim'l had long fallen asleep. And while mother and Chaya were putting things in order, I asked my brother to come out for a breath of air. Leaving the courtyard gates, we strolled toward the square.

As Velvel Related

"I served my full ten-year sentence at hard labor. Most of the time I was kept in solitary, completely separated from the world."

I noticed that he had difficulty with Yiddish, substituting Russian expressions and idioms.

"It is punishment enough," Velvel went on,"to be isolated from the outside, but to be pent up in solitary can destroy a human being altogether! My physical suffering was easier to bear than my spiritual agony." He then showed me the permanent ravages left by the iron chains that had bitten deep into the flesh of his wrists and ankles. It was horrible to see.

"After serving my sentence at the fortress," he continued, "I was sent off with the etape to Siberia. This was truly the most gruesome chapter of my life. I have described my experiences in writing, both in the Fortress and in Siberia. Some of these articles were published in Russia soon after the revolution, under my pseudonym, Kropotkin. I still have a few manuscripts lying around. But who can think of these things now? I have to watch my step. To the Polish secret police I'm still a Communist. It is very difficult to talk about the past. The bitter disillusionment in the very things in which you believed, and in those in whom you placed your trust, gnaws at your guts. I endured all the horrors with the hope of freedom and justice for all mankind, not only in Russia, but all over the world. And the time did come. The revolution reached me in Siberia. I was set free from that hell and brought to Moscow.

"My political past immediately placed me in the highest rank of the revolution government, and I was appointed to the office of commissar of the executive body in Moscow. I threw myself into my work heart and soul. The war still raged and Russia had no contact with the region of Grodno, I was convinced that during the upheaval of those war-torn years, there could no longer be a trace of anyone in our family."

"When the war ended I was in charge of approving travel permits for the tens of thousands of refugees, who found themselves in the area of Moscow and who wished to return to their hometowns—former Russian territories—from which they'd been evacuated at the outbreak of war.

"Reviewing one of these applications for exit permit, I happened to notice the word Grodno. I sent for this applicant, a woman. I learned that she was indeed a native of Grodno and that she herself was uncertain whether she would find any of her family alive. I saw to it that she got her necessary papers and begged her to inquire about my family. Correspondence was out of the question. But in this way, mother and father learned that I was alive and in Moscow. It was some time after that news of the family also reached me."

"New political winds began to blow across Russia. Ideological splintering set in. Yesterday's party comrades suddenly became today's power-seekers and bloody enemies. This shift in Russia's political scene didn't spare me, either. To save my life I was forced to leave in a hurry. I supplied myself with the exit papers of a refugee from Poland returning home. Thus, I succeeded in smuggling myself into Grodno.

"I got married. My wife, Chaya, a dear, unassuming woman, is wholly devoted to me and to the children. I am surrounded by my own flesh and blood, yet I still live in a prison—a spiritual prison. Now, there remains nothing but incomprehensibility and uncertainty. Belief? In what? In whom? Hope?! For what?

"Grodno's youth is again brimful of idealism. They often reproach me for standing aside. We must combat the Polish oppressors, they argue. And of course they are right. The Polish revolutionaries had also preached equality and justice before they came into power. Now, they have become oppressors far worse than the czarist torturers. Jews, in particular, are not allowed to lift their heads. Pogroms, boycotts, night raids and arrests. Political offenders in custody are tortured by methods even more meticulous and scientific than ever. After all, they had good teachers in the practice of oppression, torture and rule. I'm still wondering why they have let me be.

"Father's death was a terrible blow to me. I didn't really know him. He was a fine man, father. He forgave me for everything. And he died in my arms. I couldn't help him."

By the time we turned in, half the night was gone.

* * *

I was up early next morning. Mama was already offering me a glass of chicory before I was fully dressed.

"Mama," I quipped, "as an actor, I'm not accustomed to eating this early in the morning. I'll take a little walk, maybe I can work up an appetite."

Slipping out of the courtyard, I turned toward the synagogue compound—the big, cold synagogue where I spent my childhood as a choirboy and as a student in the upstairs yeshiva. There it stood, its facade somewhat weather-beaten, but intact.

I strode down Cemetery Lane, alongside the old burial ground that stretched all the way to Troitza Street. The old tombstone rising above the fence had also remained undisturbed. I came across the big Hayyei Adam Synagogue, where my father, rest his soul, was Reader of the Torah, and where my Bar Mitvah was held.

I had started out on this little tour of the city with a quivering heart, suspecting every passerby to be a representative of the secret police. At any moment, I feared, I would be grabbed by the collar and arrested; for the fact remained: I was a deserter. Walking back, I tried to keep off the main streets.

My Sister, Rochele

A dim stairway led me to a garret on Gorodnitchanski Street. Holding on to a shaky banister, I climbed the creaky stairs. At my knock, a woman's voice asked, "Who is there?"

"Rochele!" I called out, "It's me, Chaim!"

The door flew open. A woman, small and disheveled stood in the doorway staring at me, wide-eyed. "Chaim?" she wavered a moment in disbelief. "Chaimke! You've come! My heart told me you would!" she cried, falling into my arms. I held her close, unable to speak. Was this my little sister, Rochele the surviving half of a twin? I would never have known her! Skin and bones, she was. So frail, it broke my heart.

"Come in, Chaimke, come in!" she urged.

Her husband, Hershel, seated morosely at his cobbler's bench, made no move.

"Shalom aleichem, Hershel," I said, extending my hand, "how are you?" He shook my hand but didn't deign to rise.

"Forgive us, Chaim," Rochele tried to cover up for his rudeness. "We didn't expect you so early. I'm not even dressed properly or combed. These are our children. This one is Mayer'l and this Avremele, named after our father, blessed be his name. And this is our little daughter, Zeldele. Children, this is your uncle Chaim from America. Give your uncle a kiss."

The children, too shy to do her bidding, clung even closer to their mother, who looked no more than a child herself. I offered them some chocolates. Such lovely, pretty children!

Hershel had a very sympathetic face in spite of its embittered expression. He was at odds with the whole world; especially with our family, including me. And more with me, perhaps, than with the others. He expressed his complaints: "When I came back from the Polish army after the war, did I even dream of getting married?! Did I have a zloty to my name? My earnings as a shoemaker, working for the blood-sucking exploiters, were so little that I, myself, starved ten times a day! But, your father, may he rest in peace, and the others in your family, promised to help me open my own cobbler's stall somewhere on the street. We were also promised that, until I could get on my feet, you would send us some help from America. After the $100 you sent as a wedding gift, we never received another zloty from you. My outlook of running my own little stall went right out the window. I have to struggle up here in this garret, doing patchwork to take care of my wife and children, may they be well and strong. Is this justice? Ever since your father passed away, there is no one for whom I can unburden my heart. Everyone has his own troubles, I know, but I was plainly deceived."

Tears sprang into Rochele's eyes. She looked at her husband and bit her lips. Hershel, realizing that he'd gone too far, suddenly took up a mouthful of cobbler's tacks and proceeded to hammer them, into the sole of a shoe.

I didn't resent his tirade. On the contrary, he had my full sympathy. From his standpoint he was right, of course. His grievance against me, the "American millionaire" was certainly justified. How could he know my true financial status? Was there any such thing as a poor man in America?

"Hershel," I said, "believe me, I have not forgotten you. I was simply unable to help you. My circumstances are such that, aside from the few dollars I can spare for mother, it is very difficult for me to help the rest of the family. You may very well include me in your category of katzunim—paupers," I commented wryly. "I too, have a wife and a three-year old son to support. I have traipsed to Canada, to California, there and back, in these few years. It's not as easy as you may think to get somewhere in America, especially in the

Yiddish theater. There's a saying: 'America is a free country. Everyone is free—
to go barefoot and hungry!'"

My frankness impressed both my sister and her husband. Pushing his work
aside, Hershel listened to my explanation with interest, showing no small amazement at my tales-of-fortune in the golden land. After a lengthy silence, picking
up his work again, he turned to his wife.

"You see, Rochele," he remarked with irony, "it's the same thing everywhere. That's America for you! The bourgeosie exploit and rob the poor worker
all over the world. The only land that is free is Soviet Russia! That's where
justice and brotherhood reign. The time is near when we, the oppressed masses,
will bring social revolution into Poland. When the workers and peasants of
every land will unite, the proleteriat will reign throughout the world!"

Hershel's political ideology didn't surprise me. I had already learned from
the family that he was a confirmed communist, and that he held an important
position in the party. Obviously, the tragic history of my brother Velvel's life
had no effect on him. I couldn't help but think back on Velvel's words last night:
"Grodno's youth is again brimful of idealism, the same as I was at their age.
Yes, history repeats itself."

I didn't have the heart to go without leaving them some money. Figuring
that I would have about sixty dollars left from the cost of the tombstone, I
decided to divide part of this between Rochele and Velvel. As long as I had
my train ticket and return passage to New York, I believed that ten dollars would
hold me until I reached a city where I could play and earn my expenses. So,
upon taking leave, I pushed twenty five dollars into Rochele's hand. She hugged
me and burst into tears on my shoulder. Hershel finally got up from his work-
bench and together, they and their children, saw me downstairs, with the promise to come and spend the evening with me at mother's house. I felt that
my visit had renewed a measure of peace and contentment in their lives.

* * *

Back at mother's flat, I found a telegram from Fishzon. He was already
in Romania, and had made arrangements with the impresario Maurice Ziegler
for our guest appearances. He advised that I hurry things up and start out for
Galatz, where we were to begin our tour.

The telegraph office was located in the post office building just opposite
the brikhalka, the mall. So off I went to wire back that I would, of course,
be on my way as soon as I possibly could. I received a telegram from Louis
Goldstein in New York. He had become the manager of the Laundale Theater
in Chicago and wanted to engage me for the coming season as the romantic
lead. I wired back that I was on my way to Romania and would write him
from there.

43

Untitled

T he gravestone we had ordered for my father was ready and the unveiling was to take place immediately following the Sabbath. That Saturday, accompanying mother on her weekly rounds to the children, I realized how wise she was in choosing to be a periodic visitor. The family welcomed her with love and respect.

Walking back, I wondered in what way I could bring a little cheer into Mama's drab existence. I had noticed some theater posters around town and knew that the prominent Boris Thomashevsky was appearing that evening at the City Theater.

"Mama," I ventured, "why not come to the theater with me tonight? The renowned artist, Boris Thomashevsky from America, is playing, and I'd like to see him."

"So, why should you want me underfoot, Chaimke? Go and enjoy yourself."

"No, Mama, come, it will do you good. If you don't feel up to it, then I'll stay home with you." At this, she relented a little. Once we were home, she took time to change and spruce up and was ready to come along to the theater with me.

In those years, it was quite the vogue for a man to sport a cane. Actors, in particular, wouldn't think of sallying forth without this "status symbol." And an actor's cane was something to behold! With handsomely embossed heads, gold and silver monograms, these walking sticks were gifts from admirers and friends, usually presented on the occasion of an actor's testimonial performance. I too, carried a cane. But, to carry it in Grodno? On the Sabbath? I wouldn't dare! Dusk had already fallen, but it was still the Sabbath! I did, however, want to come to the theater that evening like a genuine stage personality jauntily sporting my cane. Mama read my thoughts.

"You want to take your walking stick? Go ahead, take it. In the next world— after 120 years—it won't be me they'll be punishing for your sin of carrying a cane on the Sabbath!" She looked at me and smiled. But I didn't take it.

As there was still time before the performance, I went backstage to greet Mr. Thomashevsky. Remembering every little nook of the theater from child-hood, I could have found my way to the stage door blindfolded. Nothing seemed to have changed.

Through the open door of a dressing room, I recognized Thomashevsky's imposing figure. Robed and in makeup, he sat staring moodily into the mirror. Wearing a flowered robe, Mme. Ruth Reneé, who was appearing with him, stood pressing something.

"Hello," I greeted them from the doorway. "I am Chaim Yablokoff, an actor from the States." Thomashevsky turned from the mirror to fix his gaze on me. "I don't know if you remember but I played with you, Mr. Thomashevsky, when you came to Toronto, at the Standard Theater about five years ago. My name is Yablokoff."

"Yes, yes, I remember now. What are you doing here, in Grodno?"

Briefly, I explained about my mission in my hometown. The reason for Madam Reneé's coolness dawned on me later. They had not been doing well on this tour, and even Grodno didn't promise much of a turnout. It made her very uncomfortable to have an actor from back in the States witnessing their poor business. Before you know it, this would reach the Royale Cafe in New York and furnish the actors with something to gossip about...

From an adjoining dressing room, in makeup and costume, came Ola Lillith and Willy Godick, a pair of young performers to fill out the bill. This duo had become exceedingly popular in Europe, and Thomashevsky engaged them as a good drawing card.

"Yablokoff?" said Ola when we were introduced. "We've heard about you, from Paris." And Godick added, "We also know that you are bound for Romania. You see, there are no secrets in the theatrical profession. Herr Thomashevsky has promised to help us come to America."

"America! Ah, yes," Thomashevksy sighed. "I have brought over entire companies from Europe, the Vilna Troupe and others. I always gave young talent a chance. Yablokoff!" he pointed at me, "a good actor! Yes, I remember now. Toronto, right? He's still young, needs more experience, but he's got what it takes. We need such versatile performers. Years ago, I would have snapped him up for my theater. Now, the Yiddish theater in America has taken the wrong turn—downhill. What do they feed the audience? Straw! I'm sure you have heard about the elaborate productions I gave in my day!

"Right now, the largest and most dedicated audience for Yiddish theater is in Europe. Unfortunately, the economic crisis is so great, the public hasn't the means to patronize the theater. Boris Thomashevsky has come to play, but where are the people who used to storm the theater for tickets in advance?"

"They'll show up!" I reassured him. "If I know my Grodno audience, they'll come!" Trying to bolster his mood, I struck a jocular note. "In the meantime, Mr. Thomashevsky, would you be kind enough to write out a pass for my mother and me, so at least there will be two more customers to applaud?"

A bell sounded for the opening. The house as I looked around seemed neglected. The well-remembered glitter was lacking, yet it was still a magnificent theater.

The performance, in its framework of "kleinkunst," was presented on a very fine level. Ruth Reneé, a prepossessing woman with a rich and lovely voice, stirred the audience with her singing. The duo, Lillith and Godick, in Hasidic garb, won the hearts of the people with their charmingly staged folk duets. Ola Lillith was especially outstanding in her solo numbers, a truly gifted interpreter of Jewish folklore.

The biggest hit, of course, was scored by the veteran star himself, Boris Thomashevsky. In a one-act playlet with Ruth Reneé, *You and I*, Thomashevsky portrayed various characters from his popular plays. He sang several of his compositions and received well-deserved adulation from the audience. My faith in Grodno's theater lovers was justified. Despite the difficult period reigning in the community, the theater was packed.

Eight years later, after a performance of my production, *Sammy's Bar Mitzvah*, in New York's National Theater—known by then as Herman Yablokoff's National Theater—I had the honor of saluting Boris Thomashevsky, as he sat in a loge, watching the show. In response to the thunderous ovation that greeted him, he rose to his feet and addressed himself to me, on stage:

"Herman Yablokoff, with your dynamic aspirations, your scope, your reverence for the theater and for the highly esteemed public, you remind me of the golden era of Yiddish theater in America when I, Boris Thomashevsky, was in my prime. In you, Mr. Yablokoff, I see a reflection of myself, the young actor-producer!"

His words have remained in my memory as the greatest compliment I ever received in the fifty years of my life on the Yiddish stage.

The Unveiling

The next morning, our family and friends gathered for the unveiling of my father's monument. I had not yet been to the cemetery, and a sea of gravestones met my eyes as I entered the wide gates. To either side of the long path stood the tombs and mausoleums of the departed holy rabbis, blest be their names. In times of despair, people came here to pray and to leave slips of paper bearing written petitions to the Almighty.

Next to the rabbis were laid to rest the men of wealth and prestige in the community. Their graves were marked by mausoleums of black granite and other costly tombstones of various shapes and design. My gaze fell on the striking sculptured figure of an angel with crumpled wings on the grave of the short-lived poet of *Sunny Verses*, Leyb Neidus.

We walked along the path that led to the row where my father was laid to rest. Gathered around the grave, we waited for Rabbi Zupovitch to perform the unveiling ceremony. Mother and Rochele wept aloud. Slavka became hysterical and had to be led away. I stood as if made of stone. The rabbi's touching eulogy only reached my ears as from a remote echo. Brother Velvel uncovered the gravestone. Beneath the Star of David the inscription, in Hebrew, read:

In Eternal Memory

Our eyes shed tears at the passing of our dear father.
A man, humble, righteous and God-fearing
In deep faith he gave of himself
With dedication to charity and good deeds
All the days of his life.

Reb Abram (Alter) Son of David Yablonik
Passed away on the 2nd day of Av. 1929
May his soul be bound up in the bond of eternal life.

Together with my brothers I recited the Kaddish. Our old friend, Homul, the photographer, gathered the family around the gravestone and snapped a picture for me to take back to my sister Mary in America. She had not as yet been told of father's death. (This photograph remains all that is left of my mother and family after the Holocaust.)

Friends and family slowly began to leave. I could not tear myself away from the grave. Is it all over? I asked myself. Is this all there is to it? For more than a year I lived with the hope of fulfilling my duty in erecting this memorial to my father. What did I not do to accomplish it! And now, what? Again leave Mama? Leave my sisters, my brothers and their families?

I wanted a moment to myself at the grave. Sensing my feelings, the others moved away and left me alone. With my arms around the stone, I broke down.

"Father," I cried, "why wasn't I destined to see you alive once again? I had yearned so much to see you. Forgive me for all the anxieties I caused you. Forgive me..."

* * *

After seeing mother home, I went out to walk a while and collect my thoughts. As I neared the Boulevard Square, I noticed two men in uniform several feet ahead of me. My heart gave a little quiver. I had carefully been avoiding any encounter with army personnel, lest I be recognized by any of my former army buddies. To avoid making it obvious that I was trying to lose them, I continued walking behind them a little, looking for a side street to slip into. Just my luck, they turned their heads and my blood ran cold. There was no mistake. Even after ten years, I recognized both of them! My Sergeant Kochanowsky and the Jewish bass-player, Suchalnitzky, with whom I had played in the Polish military band before I deserted.

Whether or not they recognized me was something I didn't care to contemplate! I made a beeline for mother's house.

Realizing the danger that threatened me, mother and I at once began to plan how I could leave the city unnoticed. To go to the depot and board a train was too risky. I could easily be detained and arrested. We decided that Motke would take my baggage, and I would follow him to Fehrstadt. There, my cousin Meyer Shillingoff, who ran a busline, arranged my transportation to Warsaw. Even after I saw myself on a train bound for Romania, I still trembled for fear of being yanked off at some point along the way. When we stopped at the frontier between Poland and Romania, I held my breath until the Polish conductors got off the train and the Romanians took over.

Mulling over everything that transpired during the eight days I spent in Grodno, I couldn't shake off the eerie feeling that something ominous hung in the air, threatening everyone and everything. The most painful moment for me was bidding my mother goodbye. I have never forgotten her last words: "God knows," she sighed, "whether I shall ever see you again, my son."

"You'll see me, Mama," I comforted her. "I'll send for you soon, and we'll be together in America!"

44

Romania, 1930

Galatz, a very important city in Modavia, is divided into the "old town" and the "new." The latter part commands a clear view of the Balkans and dominates the River Danube and its tributaries: the Pruth and the Sereth, whose waters empty into the Black Sea and flow on to Istanbul.

At the time of my arrival, the political state of Romania was fraught with tension. The royal throne was occupied by the eight-year-old King Michael, the grandson of the late King Ferdinand. Michael's father, Crown Prince Carol, was forced to forfeit his right to the throne because of his illicit love affair with the fabulously beautiful Magda Lupescu, a Jew. The rumor in the country was that he was coming back to Bucharest to retake the throne from his son. In June of 1930, Carol did indeed return and was recrowned King of Romania.

These political upheavals, nevertheless, did not affect the keen interest of the Jewish people for Yiddish theater. The expression actors often use in describing a city where one can expect a sizable turnout is "The people regard the theater to be the most essential next to bread!" This could definitely have been said of the Jewish communities in Romania—the very birthplace of Yiddish theater.

It was in 1876, in the city of Jassy, that Avrom Goldfaden founded the Yiddish Theater. Since then, this medium of entertainment has been active not only in Jassy, but in Romania's capital city of Bucharest, in Czernowitz, Braila, Botoshan, Raman-Pokashan, and of course, Galatz, which became one of the key theater towns. In 1880 this city saw the world premiere of the Biblical operetta, *The Sacrifice of Isaac*, authored by Avrom Goldfaden, known as the Father of Yiddish Theater.

It was here in Galatz, that Misha Fishzon and I began our guest performances. Some of our most outstanding artists had guest starred at one time or another in Romania: The Vilna Troupe, Esther-Rochel Kaminska with her company, Boris Thomashevsky, Molly Picon with Jacob Kalich, Joseph Buloff, Luba Kadison, Celia Adler and countless other celebrities.

The Jewish youth of Romania were so enamored of these visiting stars that after a performance they would unhitch the coach-horses and personally pull the carriages to escort the prevailing favorite to his or her particular hotel.

Playhouses were rather few in Romania. There was the popular Zhignitze Theater run by Isaac Goldenberg, but for the most part performances were held during the summer in open-air theaters. Among the trees and greenery of the city's park areas, stages were built, complete with dressing rooms and scenery. The open-air theater in Jassy, known as Pomul-Verde (Green Tree), and Axelrod's Garden in Czernowitz were the most preferable.

In Galatz, we also played in a garden theater. Tables and chairs were set up along the hedges, and during intermission the people were served drinks and light delicacies, while a gypsy girl-orchestra played for their entertainment. One could spend an evening in this atmosphere till dawn, enjoying the show, eating Romanian specialties, drinking the sparkling wine, listening to the exotic gypsy airs, and even letting oneself go, in a Romanian dance!

* * *

Maurice Ziegler, the distinguished impresario of the company with whom we played, was the prototype of a Viennese theater director. His wife, Rosa, an attractive, buxom actress, their three daughters Ella, Sevilla and Erna, their son-in-law Muni Pastor were the mainstays of Ziegler's troupe. In fact, Pastor (Sevilla's husband) became Ziegler's right-hand man, helping him run his theatrical enterprise. The orchestra leader was the young violinist Marcel Kreizler, who now lives in Israel. Child parts were played by Ella's little daughter, Charlotte (actress Charlotte Cooper, now in New York).

The Ziegler players were warmly welcomed wherever they appeared, especially Sevilla. Her beauty, her slender grace and magnetic charm, captured the hearts of the public. She played all the soubrette parts in Molly Picon's repertoire. And whenever her father was stuck for an American or European attraction, she filled that bill herself, and very successful too. Sevilla Pastor is now a reputed artist of the Romanian State Theater.

I had never before played in an open-air theater. What if it should rain in the middle of a performance, I wondered.

"That," explained Ziegler, "all depends. For instance, if it rains during the first act, it is the actors' loss. The money must be refunded, or the tickets exchanged for another performance. But if the first act is over, then it may rain, storm, or hail—this is the customers' tough luck! The money belongs to the company!"

The actors did resort to a bit of chicanery: if they suspected a possible shower during the first act, they immediately stepped up the tempo of things, so that in no time flat the act was over—curtain! And the evening's receipts remained with them!

Our engagement in Romania was highly successful. My songs caught on, right off. The cast, mainly comprised of young people, were a pleasure to work with.

I played the leading roles in *The Blind Clown* and *The Poor Millionaire*, while Fishzon did the character parts. In *God of Vengeance* by Sholem Asch and *Tree of Knowledge* by Jacob Gordin, Fishzon played the heavy dramatic parts and I carried the character comedians. It may have been our luck, or the luck of the patrons, but it never rained all the time we played in Romania. The time I spent with Misha Fishzon and the Ziegler Troupe was a joyous and most memorable interlude in my wander-route around the world.

I decided that I would remain with the company as long as I could. America, I told myself, can wait. The out-of-town cities with their eighty-odd plays a season, I surely won't miss. And the actors' union is not yet ready to grant me membership...so I'll remain in Europe where I'm a welcome guest.

At the same time, common sense told me that these were only empty conjectures. Remain in Europe? And what about my wife, my son? Have I no responsibilities? A telegram from my wife stated that I had been engaged for the coming season with Chicago's Laundale Theater, and that she expected me back in New York as soon as possible.

And so, putting aside the pleasure of being dined and wined by friends and admirers, I began making plans for my departure.

Before leaving Romania, I wrote my friend Shimon Finkel to let him know that instead of taking the direct train route Bucharest-Paris, I would go via Berlin, so we could meet there.

With a reluctant but hearty goodbye, I took leave of my dear colleagues, who all came to see me off on the first leg of my trip home to the United States.

* * *

After what seemed like an endless journey, the train stopped at the Berliner Bahnhauf. And there he was, my boyhood chum, Shimon Finkel! He had come to meet me with yet another friend from Grodno, Bennie Nesvizhesky. Bennie was in Berlin studying for the rabbinate.

Our meeting was a most moving experience. When I left Grodno, we were all in our teens. Now, as grown men, after a span of ten years, we had each embarked on different pursuits in life: Finkel, a member of the Habima; Bennie, soon to become a reform rabbi, and I, a Yiddish actor in America. We felt rather strange with each other, but in a little while, the stiffness was gone and we felt as close as in the "good old days."

Finkel was happy at the personal regards I gave him from his parents I had so recently seen in Grodno. And although I did not see Bennie's folks, I did notice that his father's shingle, "Parisian Tailor," still hung securely at its corner, a good omen, I assured him, that all was well.

The furnished room I occupied in the home of a German family in Berlin was very comfortable, clean and reasonable. I was treated with the utmost courtesy. Who, in his wildest dream, could then have imagined that these highly civilized, cultured and well-mannered Germans were already on the brink of turning into savages trying to conquer the world, slaughtering millions of human beings...six million Jews among them?!

Stopping in at Finkel's lodging, I noticed stacks of plays lying around— mostly dramatic works in German and Russian. On his night table lay an open copy of *Hamlet*, in German, which he was diligently studying. His wife, Batami, he told me, was a dancer with the Habima and happened to be in London just then. The plan was to meet in Palestine.

The Habima Troupe had been formed in Moscow after the revolution. Later, they appeared with outstanding acclaim in the chief cities of Europe— and eventually, of course, in America. Their only obstacle was the language in which they performed—Hebrew. Since there were mighty few communities around the world where Hebrew was spoken, the only likely place, they decided, where the Habima could exist, was Palestine. Meanwhile, they tarried in Berlin to rehearse and shape up several plays before establishing their home base in what was then Palestine, now Israel.

I was getting anxious to get back to my family and make preparations for my engagement in Chicago. Finkel and Bennie saw me to the Bahnhauf, where we said goodbye and promised to keep in touch.

Before leaving the city, my train made several stops along Berlin's "Unter den Linden" route, where we picked up other passengers bound for Paris and other points out of the country.

As I sat gazing through the window, whom should I see standing on the platform and grinning, but Finkel and Bennie! What a surprise. And what an unexpected delight to see those two again! They had caught the subway and arrived at the station even before my train. We had a hearty laugh, and waving goodbye again, they were gone.

At the next such local stop—lo and behold—my pals popped up again. They kept pulling this zany stunt as we moved along, beating the International Express at each stop. Even my fellow passengers became intrigued with this hilarious contest and we all laughed our heads off.

* * *

At the last local stop in Berlin, in 1930, I said goodbye to Bennie for the last time. He was among the first victims of Germany's gruesome infamy. Finkel and I met years later at the airport in New York.

It was in 1948, when David Ben-Gurion proclaimed the Jewish State of Israel. President Harry S Truman, in the name of the United States, was the first to acknowledge this historical event. Almost immediately, the Arabs attacked Israel. Firing on Jewish settlements, they also strafed the airport in Lod. The plane that was to fly the entire Habima Company to New York for their scheduled guest performances barely managed to take off between the barrages.

As a representative of the Hebrew Actors' Union, I went to the airport to welcome the troupe. Their plane was late. And since they were to give their premiere of *The Dybbuk* that very evening, I arranged for a motorcycle police-escort to get them directly to the theater. With the Habima, of course, there came my very dear chum, Shimon Finkel. Yes, eighteen years had passed since our last meeting in Berlin.

45

Chicago—What A Town!

Chicago's vast Jewish population always regarded Yiddish theater as an integral part of life. The impresario Elias P. Glickman, who for thirty years managed the Palace Theater, always presented the popular New York stars: Adler, Kessler, Thomashevsky, Morrison, Kalish, Lipsin and others of that generation.

Chicagoans also patronized the Independent Vaudeville Theater, managed for many years by the actors Adolph and Jennie Gertner. Here, the people enjoyed seeing the veteran performers Philip and Sally Weisenfreund, with their son Muni, who later rose to fame on the American stage and screen as Paul Muni.

The Yiddish theater season in Chicago lasted longer than in New York. As soon as New York's thirty-six-week run was over, the headliners struck out for the road, with Chicago as one of the main goals on their itinerary.

There were two daily Yiddish newspapers in Chicago: *The New York Forward* edited by Jacob Siegel, and *The Jewish Courier*, whose editor was Dr. Melamud.

The Laundale Theater, known as the million-dollar house, stood on Twelfth Street and Crawford Avenue, in the heart of the Jewish neighborhood. I had never seen such a splendid theater. It had been built as a motion picture and vaudeville house. But with changes taking place in the neighborhood, it was no longer profitable to run it as such, and was subsidized by Chicago's Democratic party as a Yiddish enterprise. The Jewish vote meant a great deal at election time. For a political party to subsidize a Yiddish theater was something of a first in America.

I had come back to the States only a few days before the company was ready to set out for Chicago. This left me little time to spend with my wife and son. Jennie had been re-engaged for another season at the Lyric Theater in Brooklyn, so we decided she and Yankele, whom we now called Jackie, would remain at her parents' home, while I would be away in Chicago. At least the union had granted me permission to play there.

* * *

The Cafe Royal in Chicago—the gathering spot for show people—was a duplicate of the Cafe Royale in New York. Located on Twelfth Street, later

287

named Roosevelt Road, the cafe was originally run by the veteran actor Mendel Teplitzky. When I came to Chicago, the place had been taken over by Morris Mason, a member of the town's Dramatic Circle.

Aside from being a restaurant, the Royal was a place where people could celebrate special occasions: bar mitzvahs, graduation parties, and where stranded nonunion actors in need of funds to continue their shlepping around could arrange a little recital in the back room.

Our opening night was a gala event. The dignitaries of the city's political and social strata, Jews and non-Jews, were the invited guests. The chief "members of the wedding," of course, were the representatives and politicians of the Democratic party, who held reign in the city.

The performance of *The Candy King* went over big. The million-dollar theater simply delighted the hearts of the Jewish public. To see Yiddish theater presented in such a palace was certainly a great pride. The audience even tolerated the after-curtain speeches delivered with political overtones: "Devoted Democrats, we have provided you with a Yiddish theater and we hope you will remember us come election time..."

The editor and drama critic of *The Forward*, Jacob Siegel, praised the production and the cast—even me, for my lyrics and special compositions. The public, he added, was now eagerly waiting to see me on stage in the following plays.

The *Courier's* critic, Dr. A. Margolin, also wrote a very favorable review of *The Candy King*, although privately he confided that he did not hold with mixing politics with theater.

In the midst of all the excitement of the opening, I felt like an outsider. I was utterly miserable. After only a three-day visit with my little family on returning from Europe where I enjoyed such tremendous success, I had to come to Chicago and do every chore under the sun, except show myself on stage!

Since I was not appearing in our first show, the theater's managers, Nelson and Goldstein, asked me to arrange a special Laundale Theater radio program. And so, in a short time, the public came to know me through my regular broadcasts on Miller's radio station before they even saw or heard me on stage. Nelson stuck me with still another project: to appear in concert at the Democratic party's political rallies. So, though the season had just begun, Nelson was already receiving credit form his political bosses for my contributions at their gatherings.

Backstage Politics

Charlie Nelson made me all sorts of promises for the future. Whenever he ran into any dispute with Julius Nathanson, the star, his parting retort would be: "Look, you can quit if you like. We have Yablokoff in the company. He'll do equally as well as you!" Small wonder then that I found little favor in his eyes. Nathanson felt—and rightly so—that I was being held as a whip over his head. It was very uncomfortable for me. And I could hardly wait for the season to close so I could hie myself back to Europe. I had received many bids offering me the best possible terms to come as guest star.

Nelson assured me that, as soon as Nathanson's ten-week contract terminated, I would star in a play of my own repertoire. My friend, Louis Goldstein, didn't even deem it necessary to wait, and forthwith proposed that I make my first appearance in Chicago on the first available Thursday night. He recommended that I play Zolotarevsky's *Yeshiva Bokher*. This play, he contended, would draw a big box office on a plain Thursday where there were no benefit tickets to bank on.

Nelson jumped at the suggestion and I myself was intrigued with the idea. Certain plays of a bygone era are usually accepted as Yiddish classics. The story of the *Yeshiva Bokher* is more or less based on Shakespeare's *Hamlet*. When it is properly cast and directed, people will always go out of their way to attend.

No sooner did I begin preparing for the title role, when Nathanson's patronizing cronies went to work on him: "Julius, are you crazy? Why give this nonunion man such a chance?! You are the star here! You should play the *Yeshiva Bokher!*"

Well, it wasn't difficult to convince Nathanson that he could tackle this intensely dramatic, singing role although it was not his genre at all. Considering that the prevailing star had the right to cast a play as he saw fit, the result was that I did make my Chicago debut in the *Yeshiva Bokher*, only I was assigned the role of Todros—the villain in the piece.

My makeup for this character consisted of a long, thick black beard, an appropriate nose molded out of putty, with eyebrows thickened—à la Rasputin. Donning a pair of knee-length pants, long white stockings, slippers, a black caftan tied with a sash and the traditional hasidic fur hat, I was disguised as Todros all right!

My fellow actors could not believe that it was really me. Where did I learn this art of makeup? To fashion such a beard? Shape such a nose? How could a young actor like me be adept enough to transform himself so completely?! And my stock also soared with the audience, who puzzled about this new character-actor Yablokoff.

The rancor between Nathanson the star and Nelson the manager put me in a very awkward position. I told Nelson that I would not be held as a threat over anybody. I would just as soon hand in my notice and go back to New York. Yet, despite our star's lack of goodwill toward me, I still went on working on the musical numbers needed for his upcoming productions. With Ruby Osofsky, a talented young pianist, pounding the piano in the pit every night and on matinees, we found it more convenient to work on the necessary material after the show. In the wee hours with a cup of coffee to revive us, we'd be ready to come to rehearsal.

Abraham Teitelbaum, in charge of directing the straight dramatic plays of our repertoire, began preparations for the production of *Motke, Ganef* (Thief) by Sholem Asch. It needed a larger cast, so several players were annexed from the Dramatic Circle in town.

Teitelbaum cast himself in the title role of Motke, a part I had played successfully in Lithuania. But, here again, as director, it was Teitelbaum's prerogative. To me, it was adding insult to injury. He cast me in two different portrayals: in the prologue as the underworld character Kanarik and in the later scenes as Motke's one-eyed father, Leyb. With this double assignment, I made my second appearance on stage at the Laundale Theater, and was once again praised for my makeup and versatility in switching from one type to another. The press lauded me highly, but the audience knew only from their program that this, or that, part was being played by an actor whose name was Chaim Yablokoff. They still had no way of knowing what I actually looked like.

"Natasha"

In the operetta, *Gypsy Prince* by William Siegel, I finally appeared as a young man, unbearded and undisguised. I played the part of a Russian officer, a young anti-Semite who perpetrates the cruelest deeds according to the plot. To compensate for casting me again in the role of villain, Nathansan magnanimously gave me permission to insert a song—if I so wished. How the devil could such a despicable character face an audience and give out with a song?! No actor, playing a cad, would dare. No matter how beautifully he sang, it could only draw boos and catcalls from the audience. The exceptions, of course, are to be found in opera, in Moliere's farces, in Gilbert and Sullivan, and in the satirical characters in the Yiddish repertoire, such as Papus in *Bar-Kochba*, or *The Witch*, and other diabolical and fanciful operettas, for whom there is written appropriate comic material. Did I expect to be applauded for singing after committing the murderous acts my role demanded? Nonsense.

Wracking my brain, I thought of a popular song, "Natasha." A recent arrival from Europe, Pincus Lawenda, making his debut at the National Theater in New York, had created quite a stir with it. "Natasha" is a romantic ballad, translated from the German, with a lilting melody, easy for an audience to sing along.

The opening scene in *Gypsy Prince* takes place in a garden-cafe, where I and several fellow-officers are making merry. This gave me an idea. If I could do my number at the beginning of the play, before the audience had seen me in my true colors, I could take a chance and sing "Natasha."

"All right, sing whenever and whatever you like," Nathanson brushed me off. "I have my own things to take care of."

Since the theme of the song deals with the lament of a betrayed lover, I believed this ballad would be the most appropriate choice for my part. The frustration of an unrequited love might even explain the motives of his villainy.

At the premiere of *Gypsy Prince*, with the audience barely settled in their seats, there I was, singing "Natasha"... and the miracle happened! I had to repeat it several times, "Natasha, Shvartze Natasha." And for the rest of the show the audience even forgave the low-down things I was obliged to do.

The backstage intrigue was set into motion immediately after the first performance: "Julius, what gives? Is Yablokoff the star here?" The sly ones needled him. "Natasha is a show-stopper, didn't you hear it? Anybody can sing it. So why not you, the star?"

Without any hesitation, Nathanson informed me that at tomorrow's matinee he himself would sing "Natasha." When Nelson heard about this, he gave Nathanson an ultimatum: "Yablokoff sings 'Natasha' or another musical goes into rehearsal immediately! The people who phone in for reservations are already asking who the new actor is that sings 'Natasha' and the answer from the box office is—Chaim Yablokoff!"

Chicago really flipped over the song and me, as they did over Lawenda in New York. On the street, or in the cafe, the glances that followed me and the whispers I heard were: "There goes Natasha. That's Natasha!"

Some years later Julius and Anna Nathanson gave up acting to settle in Los Angeles, where they ran an antique shop. We eventually became very good friends. I visited them in California and the entire Chicago chapter was entirely forgotten.

46

Star Attractions

I t soon became apparent to me why Chicago was called the "windy city." Its gales blow from the four corners of the earth and sweep you off your feet. When the heavy snows and sub-zero temperatures also descended upon the city, the bite was immediately felt in the box office. Our deficits, however, were covered by the Democratic party, and we hoped that the party would continue to do this.

Our next star attraction was Betty Frank. She was the daughter of the veteran actor Jacob Frank and the daughter-in-law of the renowned Leon Blank. A talented, vivacious soubrette, she was a great favorite in Chicago.

Betty opened with the New York hit *A Wedding in Town* by William Siegel. Here, I had the good fortune to be cast in the role played by Aaron Lebedeff. I also had the male leads in the other of Betty's productions and nothing could have afforded me more gratification.

Scheduled next was the producer-playwright and star Max Gable. But, at the last minute, Gable was unable to make it, and so, Nelson and Goldstein prevailed upon me to put on one of the plays I had done in Europe.

Considering the cold, things were hardly conducive for people to venture out to the theater even with the lure of a bona fide, imported star! Why then, should I stick my neck out? Still, with the necessity of keeping the theater going I had to take on the responsibility of directing and playing in my adaptation of Bloom's play, *The Blind Clown.* My song, "The Clown," had already won popularity in Chicago through my continued radio programs.

Our management didn't scrimp on the production. Special sets were built and new costumes ordered. Most of the cast applied themselves to their parts with the same integrity they had shown other directors and leading artists. Some, however, did as they chose, which was a great source of aggravation to me. But, on the whole the play emerged as a very fine musical production. Surprisingly enough, business was in no way worse than it had been with our visiting stars. Naturally, this was a boost to my prestige in the eyes of the public and even more so with the managers of the Laundale Theater, who immediately wanted me to sign up for the following season.

Celia Adler

Returning from a highly successful European tour, Celia Adler was engaged as guest artist with our troupe. She was accompanied by her husband, the actor and theater veteran Jacob Cohen, who acted as her business manager.

Miss Adler's opening play was a melodrama, *Outpour* by L. Malach. The action deals with white slavery in Brazil. I had not yet seen Celia Adler on stage since my arrival in America. And now, working so closely with her, I was able to appreciate her innate artistry.

In *Outpour*, I played a lonely young man, referred to only as "der blonder." This blond intellectual helps the unfortunate girls, forced into slavery in Brazil, by writing letters for them in Yiddish to their parents back home in Europe. One of these captive prostitutes, with whom the young man is deeply in love, was masterfully portrayed by Celia Adler.

The play stirred up differences of opinion among the critics and theatergoers. It was daring indeed to handle such a sticky subject. It also recalled a similar controversy years back over the play *God of Vengeance* by Sholem Asch.

The rest of the plays we did with Celia Adler were more in keeping with Yiddish melodramas. Celia scored not only as an artist; she and Jacob Cohen won everyone's affection by their outgoing friendliness.

Michal Michalesko

Having won tremendous acclaim in New York after his arrival in the States some years earlier, Michal Michalesko also became a great favorite in Chicago. He was soon engaged by Elias Glickman to appear at his Palace Theater, where he starred for two consecutive seasons. Michalesko was one of the most handsome actors on the Yiddish stage. Not since Boris Thomashevsky were theatergoers—especially women—so taken by the physique of a stage personality. A magnetic and debonair figure, with crinkly, light brown hair, adding extra charm to his features, Michalesko presented the classic image of a matinee idol.

His devoted wife, Anna (Anjou), watched over him like a doting stagemother. Anjou took care of her husband's business interests in the theater and was not so much concerned with his financial gains as with his success on stage. Without Anjou, Michal hardly ever made a move.

An actor in the full sense of the word, Michal, whose baritone was of a middling quality, sang with heart and feeling. Blessed with a natural gift for cantorial interpretation, he was readily supplied in every production with at least one liturgical composition—a sure-fire hit!

Michalesko opened at the Laundale Theater that season in Bloom's operetta, *The Jewish General*, the score by Alexander Olshanetsky. Easygoing and placid by nature, Michalesko rarely displayed much temperament, not even on stage. Rehearsals with him did not exactly ignite any sparks of inspiration.

Michalesko's premiere was a sensation. When he made his entrance, decked out in the dazzling white uniform of a general, with all the brass trimmings, the roof almost caved in with thunderous applause.

Other productions we did with Michalesko were *The Last Dance*, libretto by Louis Freiman, score by Alexander Olshanetsky, and *The Damaged Man*, a theme on the order of Tuler's *Hinkerman*. I was most impressed with Michalesko in the role of the Biblical Abraham in Goldfaden's *Sacrifice of Isaac*. In this, he presented a most awe-inspiring, patriarchal figure.

In theater circles, Michal was held to be a great sport. Money just slipped through his fingers. He was a card-player, a pastime he never gave up to the end of his days. Anjou tried her best to hold on to her husband's earnings, but when her precious Michal had a yen for something, she indulged him like a spoiled child.

With Leon Blank in Milwaukee

Another popular attraction in Chicago was Leon Blank. Having played with him in Montreal and Detroit, I was familiar with his repertoire: *The Drunkard, The Watchman, Three Brides, The Broken Home,* and others.

Our management also arranged for him to perform at a large theater in neighboring Milwaukee, a city with quite a fine Jewish community. The play was *The Drunkard*. There wasn't much of an advance sale on tickets, so we were resigned to playing for empty seats. Then, at the last moment, the community woke up. It was getting close to curtain time, yet we could not very well start the show with most of the customers still milling in the lobby, clamoring for tickets.

Becoming a little nervous, Blank rasped, "Time to start! We can't wait all night. At this rate we'll never make the last bus back to Chicago! Yasha," he commanded the stage manager, "start the show!!"

To Yasha, an order was an order. He killed the house lights, brought up the foots—the stage lights—and gave the orchestra the signal to begin.

The actors in the opening scene were already well into the action of the play, when there ensued a hullabaloo. "Put the curtain down!" the people shouted. "Start the show from the beginning!"

It was no use. We had to lower the curtain and begin at the beginning. As the performance had gotten off on the wrong foot, other things seemed to go butter-side down.

The most upsetting incident was caused by a violinist in the pit. Leon Blank loved to have his dramatic scenes enhanced by the soft, soulful strains of a muted violin. This mood music, in theater language, is referred to as melodrama. In order to give the violinist the direct cue for the melodrama, Blank had a little signal of his own. He would touch the right lapel of his jacket. This, he instructed the violinist at rehearsal, meant: start to play... but ever so softly, with the mute on your strings. Blank would then touch his left lapel as a signal to stop playing.

Toward the end of the first act, as Blank was ready to go into his dramatic monologue, he put his hand up to his lapel. The violin player, alert for his cue, got to his feet, and instead of playing pianissimo as instructed, turned to face the audience, lifted his violin and, as if on a concert stage, attacked the strings with gusto and "schmaltz." The forte he gave out could have been heard in Chicago!

Dumfounded, Blank broke off in the middle of his monologue, his eyes glaring. Some of us, shushing from the wings, tried desperately to make this virtuoso pipe down. But he paid no attention and sawed away at the strings! Facing the audience, how could the fiddler see that Blank had almost ripped the lapel from his jacket in a wild attempt to stop the recital?

I dashed down to the cellar and through the opening to the orchestra. I managed to persuade the fiddler to cut it and sit down. He looked daggers at me, but sat down.

Blank concluded his first act without benefit of "melodrama." As soon as the curtain fell he flew down the cellar steps ready to strangle the concertist.

"Didn't I tell you to play pianissimo? Pian-i-s-s-i-mo!!! And to play sitting down?!"

"What do you mean pianissimo?" the fiddler bristled. "There are parents here tonight, of kids I give violin lessons to. Do you want them to think that I, their teacher, am some kind of klezmer? I am a graduate of the St. Petersburg Conservatory! When I play I have to be seen and heard. I'm an artist! You will be leaving after the show, but I—I live in Milwaukee!"

For the rest of the performance, Blank did not touch any part of his lapel, for fear that, in place of a soft, muted melodrama, he might bring on another rousing concerto from the Misha Elman of Milwaukee.

* * *

I was still getting proposals from Europe to appear as guest artist. I often discussed the situation with Jennie over the telephone. But she was categorically against my leaving the country again. Our son was growing up and needed his father around as much as possible. At least we could spend the summer together, she contended, and if nothing else materialized closer to home, I could then take another season in Chicago.

In the end, with the offer of a substantial raise, I agreed to another winter in Chicago for the season of 1931-32.

I returned to New York and joined my family. While it did my heart good to see how tall and handsome my little son had grown, it also saddened me to think that, in all too short a time, I would have to leave again.

The summer layoff didn't last long; theater seasons then lasted longer and started earlier. Before I knew it, it was Labor Day and I was back to my furnished room, all set for my second fling at the Laundale Theater.

47

Back in Windy City, 1931-32

Our guest artist for the first ten weeks was Samuel Goldenburg. I was delighted. I hadn't seen this great Yiddish artist since we worked together in Montreal.

Goldenburg had not lost any of his aplomb, but he seemed to have little luck with the repertory he had acquired from the hack writers during the summer. Our manager, Nelson, had insisted that Goldenburg produce new plays—vehicles never before seen in Chicago. This was rather a tall order.

Goldenburg's first production took me by surprise... a gangster melodrama, of all things! What interest, I wondered, could such a theme hold for our Jewish clientele? When Goldenburg told me there was no part for me in this opus, I was relieved. I busied myself, instead, collaborating with the music director, Morty Glickman, on the musical numbers for the show and resumed my radio programs and the concerts for the Workmen's Circle forums.

It was a presidential election year and Herbert Hoover, the incumbent president, as well as the Republican party, were being blamed for the disastrous Wall Street crash of 1929 and for the depression in the country. Our sponsors, the Democratic party, sought to capitalize on the Laundale Theater by stimulating Jewish audiences to vote for their favored candidate—New York's governor, Franklin Delano Roosevelt.

The premiere at the Laundale with Samuel Goldenburg was an auspicious affair. Among the invited dignitaries was the mayor of Chicago, Anton Cermak. (He was subsequently shot to death in Miami on February 13, 1933, during an assassination attempt on the life of president-elect, Franklin D. Roosevelt.)

Goldenburg's initial offering was not a success. He portrayed the role of a gangster who led a double life. Even his outstanding attraction of singing and accompanying himself at the piano—a feature his audience always admired and anticipated—did not click. How could an audience muster any enthusiasm to applaud a mobster?

Consequently, business fell off and we went into rehearsal of an operetta by Siegel and Olshanetsky, *The Garden of Love*, in which the middle-aged Goldenburg appeared as a romancing young soldier, while I was assigned the role of an eighty-year-old grandfather. The box office did not improve.

Goldenburg finally hit his stride again when he came up with his old reliable repertoire: *The Romanian Kretchma,* Tolstoy's *The Living Corpse, Song of Songs, Sanin* by Artsebashev, and business improved considerably.

The last play Goldenburg did at the Laundale Theater was a drama by Meyer Schwartz called *Under One Roof,* set in a town in Eastern Europe. The opening scene takes place in a stable. At dress rehearsal when our manager, Nelson, saw the stage transformed into a humble stable by Goldenburg who demanded realism, he came running backstage on the verge of an apoplexy.

"What the hell are you making out of my million-dollar theater—a dung heap?!"

Nelson was certainly not initiated into anything like "literary theater" and we had all we could do to persuade him to let us at least play off the week. In the meantime, we had no recourse but to somehow "beautify" the stable, much to Goldenburg's mortification.

Goldenburg regarded me as a understanding younger colleague. During our free hours we spent time together, chatting at the Royal, or strolling and discussing theater. I learned a lot from him.

Shortly before Goldenburg's return to New York, I happened to stop by his dressing room and found him seated before the mirror, his head in his hands, crying like a baby.

"Sioma," I exclaimed, "what happened? Why are you crying?"

He raised his head, the tears trickling down his face, and groaned, "My hair! Oh, God, my hair! A bald spot! Sioma Goldenburg with a bald spot!!"

"Don't take it so to heart," I tried to console him. "It's not noticeable, certainly not from the stage. Many a young romantic lead would want to have your head of hair, instead of having to resort to a toupee!"

"This is surely the beginning of the end! Finita la commedia!" he cried.

I found it hard to realize at the time what a terrible blow it is for an actor when he first discovers that he is losing his hair. Many years later I too got a taste of this bitter pill.

I am always reminded of Goldenburg's tragic reaction: "Baldheaded! This is surely the beginning of the end! Finita la commedia!"

* * *

The second attraction of the season was the very popular couple, Misha and Lucy Gehrman. Their type of family-oriented plays held tremendous appeal for the older generation, who easily identified with the conflicts depicted in their parents-versus-children melodramas.

The leading role of mother, who sacrifices herself for her children, was of course portrayed by Lucy. Misha was content to play a secondary role: a devoted friend, or old admirer, who has for years adored the struggling widow. But this didn't seem to have any adverse affect on their private lives, which is not always the case with professional couples.

Chicago audiences welcomed the Gehrmans. Their performances achieved a higher level than plays of this caliber often fared in other hands. Working with Lucy Gehrman was not what one would call comfortable, however. Her natural and utterly realistic style of speaking lapped over into the other performer's lines. An actor would expect a definite cue from her—which he seldom got. And if he did wait for her to run out of prose, he would get an impatient "nu" under the breath, meaning, what are you waiting for?

In all fairness it must be said that Lucy's stepping on another's lines, or failing to give the exact cue, was annoying only to her fellow actors, not to the audience. On the contrary, it added to the realism, speaking on until interrupted, as one would in real life. The thing was to know when to interrupt. The actors did not appreciate this foible of hers and were often quite riled by it.

He Who Laughs Last

All the business transactions of the Laundale Theater were made at the little branch of the United States Bank around the corner. It was also quite convenient for the actors. The only one who did not have his savings in the bank was me. I kept my "capital" in a savings account at the U.S. Post Office. Why the post office? I had to go there anyway. Every Monday morning before rehearsal, I would go to send a money order to my wife in New York, and occasionally I would also send some money to my mother in Grodno. For this, I certainly had no big transactions that required a bank. So, when a clerk in the post office suggested I open a savings account right there, I became a depositor with Uncle Sam.

My fellow actors poked fun at me. "Yablokoff doesn't trust the bank. What a greenhorn!"

One fine morning, in the midst of rehearsing a new play with the Gehrmans, our benefit manager, Max Kreshover, came running up the aisle to the stage.

"A catastrophe! The United States Bank has failed!!" he spluttered breathlessly.

I'll never forget the scene that followed. For a second everyone froze as in the tableau before curtain in Gogol's *Inspector General*. Then, panic broke loose. Flinging down their scripts, they bounded over the footlights, scrambled over the seats and ran to the doors crying, "Oh, my God, my savings!!"

And so, the only one who escaped the collapse of the U.S. Bank unscathed was—me. I was no longer the butt of their ribbing. "The luck of a greenhorn!" they bridled with envy. "He put his money in the United States Post Office! Nu, do you have to go to college?"

48

Audition in the Hebrew Actors' Union

"The Hebrew Actors' Union is calling a number of applicants to report for audition." When I read this notice in the *Daily Forward,* my heart leaped. Maybe this time, I prayed, I too will be among the lucky candidates. Then, when Marty Baratz, another nonunion actor in our company, received a letter from the union notifying him to report for audition, I asked my friend Goldstein about my own chances.

Marty's father, Goldstein explained, was a long-time politician in the union and so he interceded for him.

"Louis," I pleaded, "you're a politician in the union. You're my friend. Why don't you intercede for me?"

"I'll be frank with you," he said. "You were also on the list, but we couldn't spare you from the theater. Who could possibly take over for you during your absence? Your train trip to and from New York alone would take two days."

I was fit to be tied. "Just because I can't be replaced for a couple of performances I have to lose my chance of an audition in the union? I've been waiting for this opportunity almost eight years! If you won't let me go I'll be forced to quit my job right now and go back to Europe!"

Both Goldstein and Nelson contacted Guskin and Greenfield in the union and got them to put me in the very next group of candidates.

At long last, the awaited letter from the union arrived. I was to report for audition on the 24th of February, 1932.

I called Jennie right away to relay the good news, and asked her to meet me at the union. I would go there directly from the station. "And please, Jennie," I added, "bring Jackie with you so I can at least have a look at my son before I take the train back to Chicago."

The Inquisition

On a tiny makeshift stage at the back of the hall, each applicant was required to perform before the assembled members, who would then vote yes or no by secret ballot.

Two very small closed-off areas—one on each side of the stage—acted as dressing rooms: women on one side, men on the other. Each contender, according to the genre indicated on his, or her, application, was to perform excerpts from roles selected out of two plays. These were assigned in advance by a special audition committee. It was up to the applicant to find these sometimes obsolete scripts and study them. Singers were required to do a scene from a musical. They were permitted their own accompanist, or were provided with one. A prompter would give cues from the side of the stage, if the scene called for dialogue.

According to the prevailing rule, the applicant had to draw two-thirds of the affirmative votes in order to be accepted as a member. The votes were also counted by a designated committee. Of course, there were always the chronic no-voters, who voted no on principle.

Reuben Guskin never meddled. He had to show his impartiality. The handling of these auditions was not only a mockery, it was a downright disgrace! The union was constantly castigated by the press for this barbaric treatment of new, young talent, as well as of some acknowledged, professional performers. Many famous celebrities had, at one time or another, been obliged to step out on this two-by-four platform, only to be voted out, because they were too good and might threaten some other member's job.

I was not quite so naive, even then, to think it advisable to accept each and every aspirant without benefit of experience, or apprenticeship in a theater; especially when there weren't any Yiddish dramatic schools where they could acquire the training for the craft.

To my way of thinking, I would have a committee chosen of directors, playwrights, composers, choreographers, producers and other representatives of the performing arts (except actors and official theater critics), to be in charge of judging new aspirants seeking to become professional artists and union members. According to genre, the applicant would be allowed to appear in a suitable role on the stage of a theater—and before a paying audience, with the proceeds earmarked for a special theater fund. At such a performance the critics could then be invited to express their opinion.

When an applicant has made a favorable impression, the committee could recommend him or her for acceptance into any theatrical union.

My Audition—At Last!

In the morning, after an eighteen-hour journey, the "20th Century" finally glided into Grand Central Station. Jennie was there to meet me and we taxied straight to the union. Jackie, she assured me, would be brought there by Grandpa Fleischman.

Louis Goldstein did accomplish one concession for me with the committee. I was permitted to do a scene from *The Blind Clown* and sing my own composition, "The Clown." Jennie would accompany me. For the second part of my program, I was given the monologue of the lawyer in the drama, *Madame X.* This lifted my spirits somewhat because I knew both roles like my own name.

Arriving at the union I immediately went into one of the crowded little side rooms to make up and dress. I was scheduled first on the list so I could make my train back early in the evening.

The members began filling the hall. In a little while along came Sam Gertler, Jacob Zanger and other colleagues with whom I'd worked the past eight years. They squeezed into my "cell" to wish me luck and bolster my courage.

The proceedings were opened by President Jean Greenfield. When I heard him pronounce my name, I understood he was introducing me. Jennie attacked the keyboard with the theme of "The Clown," and I, in my Pagliacci costume, took the few steps to the platform.

There was a tentative ripple of applause. I launched into the monologue that led into my composition and waited for Jennie to play the introduction. Casting a quick glance in her direction, I thought she seemed disturbed. What could it be? Still, she began to play and I sang. Finishing on the finale of the number, I went off to change, and was followed by the sound of applause.

As the lawyer in *Madame X*, I delivered the highly dramatic address for the defense and received a rousing applause from the membership.

The result: the only candidate voted in at that audition as a member of the Hebrew Actors' Union, with a big majority was me! And yet having proved my professional ability, I had come mighty close to failure, winding up as I did, with twenty-seven no votes to prove it!

Who could have thought that a campaign had been launched to bar me from being admitted into the union?! The instigators were Marty Baratz, Irving Grossman and their friends. Well, Baratz's grievance may have been understandable—the crust of me to demand a note for the money I had loaned him! The only solvent member in the troupe, I lent him $200 toward the balance of his initiation fee in the union and train fare for the audition. I learned that he was boiling mad at my chutzpah in asking him for a note. I was therefore a lowdown, no-good character. But Grossman's hostility was something to puzzle over. As it turned out, I had my friend Louie Goldstein, indirectly, to thank for this.

Irving Grossman, a very fine actor and singer, had been engaged that season with Ludwig Satz at the Public Theater in New York. Business was very poor. The actors hadn't seen a paycheck in weeks. The manager of the Public Theater airing his woes in a letter to his buddy Goldstein in Chicago, wrote that, on top of other ills, they were having trouble with Irving Grossman. They were preparing a new operetta, which might pull them out of the red, but Grossman refused his part saying that he would under no circumstances play a villain. And they were stuck.

Big-hearted Louie replied: "Grossman giving you trouble? Throw him out! I will spare you Yablokoff for a few weeks." In the end of course, Grossman gave in and played the part. But, since there are no secrets in our profession, he got wind of the suggestion to "throw him out of the theater" and was convinced that it was written with my consent. And this was utterly ridiculous. How could I, a nonunion man, do him out of a job? Instead of using a little common sense, he used this opportunity to get even with me by helping to instigate the membership to vote against me.

During my change for the second part of my audition, the gang went to work among the voters. "Don't dare give this candidate a yes vote," they bullied, "he must be defeated!"

Jennie, catching on to this plot against me, sat at the piano in tears.

The one who really saved my neck was the actress Emilia Adler. "Nobody dare give this candidate a no vote!" she countered loudly, "this young actor is giving an excellent performance!"

"What kind of outrage is this?" others joined in the protest. "Agitating against a candidate in the middle of his audition? Unheard of! It's against the rules of the union!"

The gang of twenty-seven voted no, while the rest of the 255 members voted yes.

Coming out into the hall after my audition, I came face to face with Irving Grossman. "Yablokoff," he said, offering his hand, "I congratulate you. I want you to know that I'm a straight-from-the-shoulder guy. Those twenty-seven nos you got...I hung them on you. You can tell it to my friend Louie Goldstein in Chicago. Now that you're a union man, you can both throw me out of the theater!"

"Listen!" I said, mad enough to strangle him, "you've made a terrible mistake! I've waited eight years for this day, and you could have ruined me because of malicious theater gossip!"

Guskin stepped in. "It's all over, and you're in, Yablokoff! Come on, shake hands with Grossman and forget it. Don't stand there, you have to make your train back to Chicago."

Throughout all this commotion in the union, my little Jackie waited for me with his grandfather. I barely had time to bid him and his mother hello and goodbye. How I yearned to remain in New York. But, grabbing a cab back to the station I was soon on my way to Chicago to wind up the season as a union man, only to wait three more years as a "liner" for the right to be engaged in New York.

* * *

In 1949 I was elected as president of the Hebrew's Actors' Union. Discussing the issue of auditions with our representative, Reuben Guskin, I observed quoting from Mark Twain, "Everybody talks about the weather, but nobody does anything about it." Everybody condemns us for the auditions, yet nobody, in all these years has done anything to abolish them."

"My, my Yablokoff, but you're naive, if you'll pardon my saying so," Guskin laughed. "Believe me if you had campaigned for president on the platform of abolishing the auditions, you would have not have gotten as many as five votes! The actors feel that since they were made to go through the ordeal, why should others get off so easy?"

It took time, but we eventually liquidated this inquisition. To the union's credit, applicants, returning from service in the armed forces, as well as survivors of the Holocaust, who managed to reach our shores, were accepted as members exempt from initiation fees and auditions. Now, young actors, who have a chance for an engagement, can easily become members of the union. The motto, one might say, has become the Haggadah quote: "Let all those who are hungry, enter and eat." The only sad part is that there aren't enough engagements now to go around...

49

From Bad To Worse

I returned to Chicago just in time to make the evening's performance. My colleagues congratulated me warmly on becoming a union member. Marty Baratz, of course, was mighty uncomfortable. Everybody knew what happened in New York.

Business at the Laundale Theater went from bad to worse. The economic situation in Chicago was no different from that of the entire nation. Unemployment, hunger and want reigned throughout the country. Still, we did our best to struggle along.

Our next attraction was Max Gable. I had played with him in Toronto, my first engagement after arriving in America. This time he came to Chicago not as a single star, but with his now famous wife, Jennie Goldstein.

Jennie had begun her career on the Yiddish stage as a child, developing over the years into a first-rate actress. Although she was short and plump as a butterball, it did not detract from her appeal and her pretty face. She could always hold her audience. In addition to her attributes as a performer and singer, Jennie later displayed a talent that very few actresses can boast of—theater management. She proved to be as expert and shrewd as many a male business manager.

In Gable's successful melodramas, Jennie usually depicted a woman betrayed. Audiences shed buckets of tears over her pitiful lot. The name Jennie Goldstein became synonymous with having a good cry. In the Depression this was hardly an asset. People were beset with enough troubles. If, and when they ventured out to the theater, they wanted to forget their problems. The committees who bought benefit tickets for their organizations also insisted on light comedies and musicals.

Jennie, born in America, was not hampered by the English language like a good many of us Yiddish actors. She compiled a humor-filled routine of monologues and songs in English, transforming Jennie, the tragedienne, into a fun-and-laughter comedienne.

I was very pleased with the advent of Max Gable and Jennie Goldstein in Chicago. I was familiar with the repertoire and played the most suitable roles. I was also cheered by the thought that the season was drawing to a close and that I would soon be on my way home to New York. My only regret was that I would have to give up my weekly radio program, which had become so popular during my two seasons in Chicago.

It so happened that the actor, Chaim Towber, with whom I had played in Montreal, was stranded in Cleveland. When the theater there closed, he came on to Chicago bringing his family with him. His circumstances were unenviable. I decided I would make him the offer of taking over my radio spot. Towber was elated. Inheriting a program which had already cultivated a tremendous listening audience was no small windfall.

Fire!

During a Sunday matinee performance with Max Gable and Jennie Goldstein, we experienced a fire that brought my two seasons in Chicago to an unexpected and climactic end.

The theater that afternoon was filled. I was standing in the wings—as per habit—watching an intensely dramatic scene played by Jennie and Gable. Next to me, the actress, Ethel Dorf, who stood waiting for her cue, suddenly whispered, "Yabby, something is smoldering. Don't you smell it?"

"Yes," I sniffed.

"Look!" Ethel suddenly pointed, staring upward, "up there! Something's burning up there!"

A 1000-watt bulb in one of the spot lamps in the concert border had burst. It had ignited the border hanging close behind it! No one on stage or in the audience was aware of it. A puff of black smoke and a lick of flame shot out from above. A quiver went through me. With as much calm as I could muster, I stepped out on the stage and walked down to the footlights. Utterly flabbergasted, Jennie and Gable broke off their dialogue and stared at me as if I'd gone crazy. The audience was also taken aback. What on earth was I doing?

"Mister Glickman," I cheerfully addressed our orchestra leader, "please play the theme of our last show!" and without waiting, sang out loud and lively, "Don't worry, brother…live and laugh!"

Glancing up at me from the pit, Glickman noticed the flame licking its way around the proscenium. He quickly caught up with me at the piano and the orchestra followed him. I knew the fire department would be alerted from backstage, so it was a question of diverting the audience for as long as I could. I had experienced many fires in the little makeshift stages back in Lithuania where we used kerosene lamps for footlights. Panic could kill more people than the fire itself.

The moment the first tongues of fire leapt into full view, the audience pulled back with a horrified "oh!" and froze in their seats. I waited for the asbestos curtain to come down behind me, as I instinctively felt it would. There was no use trying to console the audience that there was no immediate threat to them since the fire was confined to the stage and would soon be under control. I'll never forget the panic that followed. Women broke into hysterics, children shrieked, while their menfolk desperately tried to pull them along to the exits. The ushers, who managed to throw open all the side doors, pleaded with the surging crowd to stop shoving. They only got clawed and clobbered for their effort.

When the last of the frantic mob squeezed it way out, I leapt over into the pit, scaled the railing, and together with Glickman and the rest of the musicians made it to the nearest exit. The streets were already clogged with fire trucks.

Except for the dense smoke, the theater itself escaped damage, but the stage was badly gutted by the flames, and the dressing rooms got a thorough soaking, leaving all the costumes waterlogged. No one in the company, or stage crew, was harmed. It was a miracle that no one in the audience was trampled. The only ones who suffered were the ushers, poor fellows.

I was even given credit in the news reports for trying to calm the audience, or there might indeed have been casualties.

The management tried to restore some of the scenery and continue to play, but it just didn't go and the palatial Laundale Theater closed.

Menasha Skulnik

For the season of 1932-33, I was engaged at Oscar Green's Hopkinson Theater in Brooklyn. The enterprise's star and partner was Menasha Skulnik.

As a matter of fact, I was not too keen on taking an engagement anywhere. My heart was set on guest-starring on my own, in Europe. But, as my son was suffering persistent earaches, I just couldn't leave the country. Ever since the infection he'd developed during our stay in Detroit, when a doctor had lanced an abscess in his ear, Jackie was having trouble.

My wife had taken him to a known ear specialist, who said the child would outgrow it in time and to just continue with the ear drops. Still, worried as I was, I decided to forego all my European plans and tend to the care of my son. We kept taking him from one doctor to another, much to Jackie's tearful protests, but still no improvement.

My savings from both seasons in Chicago were rapidly dwindling, and so I had no recourse but to take the job at the Hopkinson.

Menasha Skulnik was an actor who always appeared as just another member of the cast, a comic character. Small and sprightly, done up in outfits that were deliberately outsized or undersized and put together from different vintages, he topped them off by a squashed, boat-shaped little hat. The audience always convulsed with laughter at his funny walk; the mincing step, the high-pitched voice that unfailingly delivered his punch lines with the most precise timing. All this became a trademark on the Yiddish stage. Despite his pale, deadpan makeup and dull-witted mannerisms, his large, expressive eyes twinkled with the impish charm of a lovable schlemiel.

Between seasons, Menasha and his actress wife, Sarah, had made several trips to Buenos Aires, where they appeared with great success.

Summing up his career for me, he said, "You know, Yablokoff, I often asked myself, how come I'm such a big hit in Buenos Aires? Down there, I'm a star while here I always play second fiddle to get a job. Are the Jews in New York any different from the Jews in South America? That's why I decided to try my luck and go out on my own. I didn't have the capital to invest in a big theater on Second Avenue, so when summer came along and my season with the Gehrmans at the Twelfth Street Theater was over, I made a deal with Lowenfeld and Garfinkel of the Lyric Theater in Williamsburg. I was to play a weekend on my own. If it proved profitable, we'd do another weekend. Putting together a company, I produced a comedy, *The Great Wage Earner*, and despite the hot weather people flocked to the Lyric. I then made the same arrangement with Oscar Green at the Hopkinson. Here too people came from all corners of the city to see the 'new' comedian, Menasha Skulnik."

"Business was so good it baffled the profession. 'What is this?' they said. 'During the height of the season, we, the Second Avenue big shots, played to empty houses. Now, along comes this bit player, Menasha Skulnik, and stirs up such prosperity! And where? In the little local houses in Brooklyn!'

"Oscar Green recognized a potential drawing card in me," Skulnik concluded, "and has taken me on as a partner and star at his theater."

And it was Green who persuaded me to join the company, pointing out that as Skulnik would, of course, play his comic characters, I would do the straight, dramatic and singing roles...the lover.

My wife could not be engaged at the Hopkinson, although she had already created a name for herself at the Lyric Theater in Brooklyn as Jeannette Fleishman, pianist-composer-conductor. But the "Jewish Musician's Club" was still wielding its power and Green was forced to hire Samuel Grechtman—an old club member.

Once again Jennie and I set out to hunt for an apartment close to the theater. Luckily, we were able to rent a three-room apartment at the corner of Bristol Street. We were delighted. Everything was fresh and bright, with an elevator yet, to spare us climbing the stairs...the fifth floor this time. Acquiring some new furnishings, we even bought a piano on installment and once again set up housekeeping in Brownsville, Brooklyn.

* * *

Bella Mysell

At the first rehearsal, I became acquainted with the rest of the cast. I knew that the leading lady, who would be my partner, was the well-known actress Bella Mysell. She was a great favorite on Second Avenue, appearing as prima donna opposite such stars as Aaron Lebedeff, Samuel Goldenburg and Michal Michalesko. It surprised me, in fact, that she would engage herself in an "off-Broadway" theater like Hopkinson, but I asked no questions. Instead, I began wondering how I was going to measure up to her as a partner.

Our opening play, a comedy by Israel Rosenberg, was titled, *Mister Schle-*

miel. It was not a success. A second play was quickly put on—and it was worse. A third—disaster. We were stumped. But why? Only a few weeks earlier, in the heat of summer, as Skulnik had told me, no one could get near the theater for the throngs who crowded to the box office to see Menasha Skulnik. What happened?

In my opinion, the answer was plain: Skulnik had allowed himself to be misled by close friends, who contended that the star must always win the girl in the end. So, despite the theatergoers, to whom Bella and I were obviously suited as lovers, and who applauded our romantic duets so enthusiastically, Skulnik's so-called advisors insisted that they knew better!

Consequently, the plays—each in turn—were doctored in a way to have the girl turn me down...the fella she really loves...and decide to marry the schlemiel! And to justify the switch, they made a villain out of my role. Such manipulations were quite bizarre and pretty corny to say the least.

Quite often after the show, people—mostly women—would wait for Miss Mysell at the stage door. "Bella! How can you marry Skulnik?" they'd rib her. "Yablokoff, such a handsome young fella you don't like? You only want that schlemiel? Where's your common sense?"

I, on the other hand, got another kind of reception, "Yablokoff, how can you let a girl like Bella slip through your fingers? Are you a man or a mouse?"

Skulnik's fans didn't spare him, either. "Where do you come off playing the loverboy?" they kidded him. "We want to see Skulnik, the poor schlemiel!"

Business was going from bad to worse. We played nine performances a week, and rehearsed day in, day out, cooking up new plays one after another. From the salaries agreed upon, we received half, or a quarter, and at the end of a strenuous week, we often went home empty-handed.

In the six years I played on the road and the two seasons in New York, I had experienced a variety of situations, but this was my first encounter in America of working without being paid.

I was surprised that the union didn't do anything about it. As a new member I refrained from protesting. There were others in the company with far more experience than I in such matters. If they were keeping silent, it probably meant we had to grin and bear it. William Epstein, the company's union deputy, told us that he had discussed the matter with Reuben Guskin and that his reply was: "You want to close the theater? Close it! Do you think the situation in the other theaters is any better? I'll talk to Skulnik and Green. We'll see what we can do."

Der Payatz

In 1932, a young radio artist, known only as, "The Street Singer" became the sensation of the air. His style, with accordion accompaniment, created the illusion of listening to an Italian street singer strolling along the banks of Venice. His theme song, "Marta," the romantic air from the opera of the same name, became the rage, selling the sheet music and recordings by the hundreds of thousands of copies.

Who was this troubadour who sang so melodiously? The mystery kept his popularity soaring around the country.

In time the enigma was duly solved at the Cafe Royale, the Yiddish theater grapevine where secrets didn't remain secret very long. It was learned that the Street Singer was Jewish; he was born in Kaminietz-Padolsk, Russia; he had even tried his luck in Yiddish theater out in Los Angeles, and in Philadelphia with Boris Thomashevsky.

Blessed with a sweet tenor voice, Arthur Tracy then began hanging around the American theater circles until he gained an in with Columbia Broadcasting Company and subsequently began his career on radio as the Street Singer. The idea of remaining nameless was ingenious, it made him a sensation overnight.

Singing on radio was no novelty to me by now. Our Hopkinson theater company was also engaged in presenting weekly programs on WFOX to boost business. I usually sang a duet with Bella Mysell, as well as a single number from my own repertoire. I might add that we received no extra pay for this.

My next-door neighbors on Bristol Street were the Yiddish actors, Bertha and Sidney Hart. They were no longer active in the theater, although Bertha did occasionally get a small part. To eke out a living for his wife and their young adopted son, Hart devoted his time to selling radio commercials to the various Jewish firms in Brownsville.

One night, coming home after the show, I met Hart in the elevator. "How about stopping in at my apartment for a glass of tea?" He invited me in and we sat in his kitchen having a quiet little chat.

"Tell me," he finally said, "would you be interested in a weekly fifteen minute radio program?"

"What do you have in mind?"

"A program in Yiddish. You'll sing a few of your songs."

"OK," I said, "what have I got to lose?"

"Until I get a sponsor to pay for the program, I won't be able to compensate you. Jeanette will of course accompany you. I can't pay her either. Meanwhile, until I get a sponsor, I'll try to get some free time from the bosses of the station—nice Italian fellas. And then, if a few dollars do come in, I'm sure you and I will not need to go to court to square things between us."

Hart and I drank l'chaim to our new venture.

The prospect of my very own program did appeal to me. It wouldn't be like making a pitch for the theater, as I'd done. The program, I felt, must have an individual style that would intrigue listeners. The Street Singer flashed across my mind. Why couldn't I do the same? Why not come up with some sort of novel title, like..."der Payatz," for instance? Under such a pseudonym I could present a varied program: dramatic compositions of recitation and song, romantic ballads, light comedy. Above all, I'd guard against being connected with the actor, Yablokoff, now playing with Menasha Skulnik. I must be presented on radio exclusively as the "Phantom of the Air—Der Payatz."

My plan of presenting myself as Der Payatz struck Hart as a great idea. Enthused, we agreed to keep the whole idea a secret.

The weekly spot for my program began the following Wednesday, from 7:15 to 7:30 P.M.

Hart opened with the intro: "I am proud to present the Phantom of the Air, Der Payatz!" Jennie began the theme that was to be my signature, and with pathos, I sang out, "When your heart is torn to shreds with sorrow—laugh, laugh, Payatz!"

After doing three of my compositions, interspersed with recitative, I closed again with my theme, "Laugh, Laugh, Payatz!"

I had only time enough to grab the subway for the evening's performance. No one in the theater company, or in the box office happened to catch any part of this Payatz program, which was just as well. Why should they recognize the voice and know that it was me, making an ass of myself? Phantom of the air, indeed!!

Next morning, Hart breezed in with news. "They just called me from the studio and told me that, right after the broadcast, the phones didn't stop ringing. This morning too, everyone is asking, who is the Payatz, the Clown?! They've already received a stack of mail addressed to the Clown."

Two days later, on Friday, when I had to sing again on our Hopkinson Theater radio hour, I thought this is it! My voice will be recognized; this will surely give me away. Yet strangely enough, the calls and letters to the station continued. The postcards praised my choice of material and style of delivery. So different, they wrote, not the run-of-the-mill radio fare, but rather like a theater presentation, which kept them glued to the set. So, who, they wanted to know, is the Clown?

Hart brought around a pleasant young man, short and bespectacled, whom he introduced as Norman Furman. He was an English-speaking agent, who dealt with radio sponsors and radio artists.

"So you are the Payatz?!" he said, warmly shaking my hand. "I like your program. Great idea! 'When your heart is torn with sorrow, laugh, laugh, Payatz," he warbled to prove that he had heard me. "Darn good material. Good reflection of Jewish life in present day America. It gets you right here!" he touched his heart. "Who writes your stuff?"

"What do you mean, who?" interposed Hart, boastfully, "he does, the Clown, himself!"

"Well, Mr. Clown, I will try to get you a sponsor." And he kept his promise. Several days later, Hart had good news.

"Mazel-tov!" he beamed. "Furman has got us a thirteen week contract with Klein and Zwerling's Department Store right here on Pitkin Avenue!"

Norman Furman became my personal representative, handling my programs. Thus, my broadcasting career really began. Eventually, it brought me recognition, not only as a radio artist but as a stage personality, around the world.

* * *

At the Hopkinson, we prepared a new musical comedy with Skulnik as the schlemiel, of course. *Getzel Becomes a Bridegroom* was an overnight hit. The former alibis for poor business—weather, economic crisis, war veterans selling apples—no longer held water. The Hopkinson Theater was jam-packed at every performance. Even "Broadway" traveled to Brownsville to catch the new sensation. Yes, Menasha Skulnik had finally made it!

I gave some serious thought to this about-face. What was it that had brought the theater to life when up to now, with the same Menasha Skulnik, it had been ignored?

Mulling it over I came to the following analysis. To the credit of most character actors and comedians on the Yiddish stage, they possessed the skill of transforming themselves into a variety of types. They would never dream of playing a new part with the same makeup and interpretation of a character they had previously created. In appraising a Yiddish actor's talent the emphasis was on his versatility. Should a critic write that his performance was always the same, it would break his heart.

A character actor relied on beards, mustaches, wigs, noses and chins reshaped with putty, spectacles, outfits of various style, color and origin, headgear of all forms—indicated by the author, director, or by an actor's own conception.

Depending on the character, the actor adopted a gruff basso, or a falsetto, a stutter, a limp, a pronounced nasal tone—anything to create something different.

Actors on the American stage, or in Hollywood, have often expressed envy of this specific talent endowed Yiddish performers. They admitted that once they had won acclaim in a certain type-portrayal, they were stuck with it. There were of course such successful one-character stars as Charlie Chaplin, Buster Keaton and W.C. Fields, to name a few. They were so great, who would want them to change their image?

During the years that Skulnik played characters under the direction of others, he too had resorted to devices that made him appear different in each role. But now, on his own, he decided to stick to one type of lovable patsy who is still smart enough to know what's best for him.

In the beginning of our season, he was led astray by well-meaning friends, who wanted to make him into something completely out of character. Instead of being funny, these plays turned out to be ridiculous. The public wanted the funny little caricature whose hilarious capers had them in stitches. And that's what they got in *Getzel Becomes a Bridegroom*. Despite the hard times that prevailed everywhere, people came to the theater. We had success at last.

Our English publicity man, Max Karper, released a press item including a picture of Bella Mysell and me in a romantic pose from the show. The provocative caption read: "Romance in the Air." This sort of ballyhoo has always been show-business practice, of course. But, it still didn't sit too well with my wife, nor with Bella's husband. Businesswise, it probably added spice, and speculation. There was no sense getting upset over it.

The theater was jammed at every performance, yet our salaries were still half or less of our weekly wages. The management claimed that, prior to our hit play, they had gone into debt over their heads and that these debts had to be paid off first.

My radio program, I must say, was going great, but after splitting up the money with my two agents, Furman and Hart, there was nothing much left.

With household expenses to meet and doctors treating my boy, I finally got up enough courage to appeal to the union. "Mr. Guskin," I said, over the phone, "when business at the Hopkinson was so bad, pay or no pay, we worked. But now, when business is so good, why shouldn't we get our full salaries?"

"We'll see," came Guskin's stock answer, "I'll take it up with the executive board."

That same evening, after the first act, we had a visitor backstage, the actor Max Kletter. Taking me aside, he whispered, "Tell me, Yablokoff, are you leaving the show? What happened?"

"What?!!" I stared at him, dumbfounded. "Who the devil spread such a rumor?"

"I had a call from the theater," Kletter explained, "telling me to come and observe your part because you were leaving, and they wanted me to take over."

Catching on, I said, "Wait a minute. Now I get it! For daring to call the union they now want to throw me out. I'm a trouble maker, see?" What irony! I thought. Here they were, all set to replace me with Kletter, a non-union man, after my waiting eight years to be granted this privilege! "So, if they want to kick me out for that," I said, "so be it!"

"Oh, no!" Kletter exclaimed, "nothing doing! If they offered me a stack of gold, I wouldn't take away your job. That's why I came directly to you. I had to make sure. Believe me, I need a job. I too, have a wife and child to take care of. But, let them get themselves another boy—not me!"

After the performance, I took the bull by the horns and had it out with the bosses. "If you and the entire company consider it fair," I said, "that all other employees in the theater should be paid in full, while we actors—in the face of such thriving business—should work for pennies, it's OK with me!"

I could not afford to lose my job.

Herman Yablokoff

The Yablonik family at the grave of
Alter Yablonik, 1930

Top left: *Goldele, the Baker's Daughter (Goldele, Dem Becker's)*

Top right: *Papirossen*

Bottom left: *Der Payatz*

Bottom right: *The Wild Man (Der Milder Mentsh)*

Top: Publicity Photo

Bottom left: Captain Pinkerton in the Madame Butterfly segment of *Papirossen*

Bottom right: *Hard to be a Jew (Shver tsu Zein a Yid)*

Bella Mysell and Herman Yablokoff in *Give Me Back My Heart*

Bella Mysell

Publicity insert from the *Forward* Art Section

Below: Max Kletter
Right: Chorus from
The Magic Melody

Above: Sidney Lumet in the
film version of *Papirossen*

Right: Gloria Goldstein and
Yetta Swerling

Top left: Yidl Dubinsky, Anna Toback, Esther Saltzman, Leo Fuchs, Dave Lubritzky and Anna Thomashefsky

Top right: Composer and conductor Ilia Trilling

Bottom left: Helen Magna and Buddy Douglas

Bottom right: Feivish Finkel (in sailor suit)

Yablokoff in the D.P.
Camps

50

Papirossen

I was now broadcasting from station WEVD in Manhattan. The popularity of Der Payatz gained momentum from week to week. Norman Furman, my representative, fully convinced that I was headed for a great radio career, began building castles in the air.

Having exhausted my radio repertoire, I began casting about for fresh songs. And this was not easy, for I had developed an individual style, so that I had to write my own material. My songs were mostly built on real-life stories. Then, I remembered that in 1922, wandering with troupes in Lithuania, I was inspired to compose a song I never really got to sing. Fresh in my mind at the time was the plight of thousands of little orphan boys and girls dragging about the streets in Russia, during the years following the Revolution. Starving, and demoralized in body and soul, these homeless waifs roamed the city streets like packs of stray dogs, seeking means to stay alive.

As I myself was torn from home and family, these gruesome tales haunted me. It took me back to the time of the German occupation in Grodno during the First World War, when, as a boy, I trudged the streets selling papirossen, cigarettes, to earn a few pfennigs. Influenced by this moody recollection, I wrote "Papirossen."

During my first years in America, cast in light comedy roles, my song "Papirossen," a tale of lament, was certainly not suited to my song-and-dance genre. But, searching for something new in my radio repertory, I thought this would just be the thing!

Summoning my neighbors, Bertha and Sidney Hart, I tried the song out on them. Tears sprang to their eyes. "What a song!" Bertha sniffled. "It really tears at your heartstrings!"

They thought "Papirossen" was not a suitable name. People might joke about it: why cigarettes? why not cigars? But I remained adamant. I stuck to my original title and decided to introduce it on my very next broadcast.

My partner, Bella Mysell and my sister Mary, were among the few who knew I was the Payatz. My sister didn't miss a single program, and kept my identity to herself. This was no easy task for her in the close community of Seagate, where she lived. The temptation to show off was too great. Bella, however, had no opportunity to tune in because at that hour, she was already on her way to the Hopkinson Theater for the evening's performance.

Eagerly, I waited for my next broadcast. I did two other songs, and then introduced "Papirossen." I sang the first two verses and it went very well. Even the engineer in the control room smiled approval at me through the plate glass partition. Meanwhile, the hands of the clock moved steadily forward. My program was running late and before I knew it my time was up. Unaware that I was taken off the air smack in the middle of the third verse, I kept singing.

Later, I thought, oh, God, that does it! The song is ruined! A flop! How could it be otherwise, when I was cut off at the crucial point in the story, just before the climatic end? Heartbroken, I left for the theater to do the evening show.

"Yabby, your sister called," Green stopped me as I walked in, "she wanted to talk to you."

I had to go on in a matter of minutes, but I called her right back.

"Chaimke!" she exclaimed, breathless with excitement, "what is that new song you did on the radio this evening? Why didn't you finish it? It's something out of the ordinary!..."

Oh, great! Go tell her why I didn't finish it!

"Out of the ordinary?!" I retorted with bitter irony, "you mean, out of the ordinary lousy!"

"Chaimke! What are you saying! I tell you the song is beautiful! Your sister is a maven..."

"OK, OK, Mary, if you say so. I've got to run now. It's curtain time."

Backstage, during the performance, I related this aggravating incident to Bella.

"Well then, sing it again on next week's program," she comforted me, "only do it first instead of leaving it for last. That way you'll be sure to get the whole song in."

In the morning, my phone rang. "Yabby, it's me, Furman. They called me from Klein and Zwerling. Their phones haven't stopped ringing. Everyone is clamoring to have the Clown sing 'Papirossen' again on his program!"

The following week, naturally, I complied with this overwhelming public demand and sang, "Papirossen" in its entirety. After the broadcast it seemed as if there was nothing but sea, sky and Papirossen! Thousands of listeners inquired whether the song was published and where they could buy it. My sponsors, the Klien and Zwerling department store, lost no time and had the lyrics printed with my picture as the masked clown. These were mailed to their customers on request, or distributed right in the store with every sale. They also had soft pillows manufactured of satin, with the head and shoulders of the masked clown in costume embroidered on one side and on the other, the printed words of the chorus of "Papirossen."

The furor of my radio program finally became known to my colleagues at the theater and in the Cafe Royale. The kibitzers, of course, took it with a grain of salt. "A flash in the pan," they said.

Meanwhile other sponsors, the Al Entin and Samuel Mogelevsky Clothing Stores began impugning Norman Furman to get the Payatz on their radio
time. The top hit on my program was without question "Papirossen." If the
fans had their way, they'd have singing it, week in week out.

"See? I told you so, Chaimke," my sister repeated over and over, bubbling
with pride. "I told you your sister is the real maven!"

The song is still sung in many different languages and is, to this day, one
of the most popular in Yiddish repertoire all over the world.

I Sell "Papirossen"

In the November election of 1932, Franklin Delano Roosevelt was voted
into office. He was sworn into office in March 1933; a ceremony now held
in January. The entire country was in a state of despair, the likes of which had
no equal in American history. Most banks across the land had failed. Million-
aires lost their fortunes overnight, and the plight of the worker and businessman was indescribable. Everyone felt trapped in a sinking ship.

All eyes were on President Roosevelt. His famous phrase, so emphatically
expressed at his inauguration, "There is nothing to fear but fear itself," did help
to bolster American morale.

Roosevelt's first act was to declare a moratorium on all banks: they were
closed from the sixth to the ninth day of March, after which, until the New
Deal went into effect, only small sums could be drawn.

Under these trying circumstances, the business of our hit play, *Getzel* with
Menasha Skulnik, fell off considerably. For the company to expect full salary
was now out of the question.

One day, my Jackie was sent home from school with a note from the nurse,
asking us to do something about his ear. A neighbor recommended another
specialist, who advised having the boy's tonsils removed. This, in his opinion,
would automatically relieve his ear trouble.

"Usually, a tonsillectomy is done in the spring, but in this case, I deem
it advisable not to put it off. I recommend that he have this operation done
at once." All very well and good, only where was I to get the money for the
operation?

One evening as I sat in my dressing room making up, there was a knock
at the door and two skinny little men shyly stepped in. They looked like the
two comic characters, Bobbchinsky and Dobbchinsky of Gogol's *Inspector
General*. I could barely refrain from laughing.

"We are the Kammen Brothers," one of the two said. "I am Jack and this
is my brother, Joe. We're partners—music publishers on Roebling Street in Brooklyn. I manage the business and my brother Joe is a pianist and music arranger."

For the life of me I couldn't tell which was which. They looked like two
peas in a pod, wearing the same suits, ties and hats.

"I also play in the Romanian Rathskellers on the lower East Side," interceded Joe. "The people who patronize these places are always requesting your songs. And the singers down there get some pretty fat tips for singing them, too. Now, everybody wants to hear 'Papirossen.'"

Looking daggers at his brother, Jack the businessman, seemed to imply: "Idiot! Who's asking you to butt in with your palaver about Papirossen?! Now, he'll want a million dollars for the song!"

"So you are the Clown?" Jack tittered. I was startled enough when his brother mentioned Papirossen, but this last remark floored me.

"Where did you learn that I am the Clown?"

"You see, we managed to get to you... hee, hee, hee," brother Jack tittered again. "It wasn't that easy, but you see, we did. Anyway, we have a business proposition for you. We'd like to buy the rights to your song, "Papirossen." His brother nodded in agreement. "We want to print it, words and music, with your picture as the masked Clown."

I couldn't believe my ears! Here was I, worrying about money for the tonsil operation, and these two angels come along and...!

"Is 'Papirossen' copyrighted?" Jack asked eagerly. "We are interested in buying the copyright of the song."

"I did copyright Papirossen in my name," I replied, "and I will not sell the copyright to anyone for any amount of money. I am willing to sell you the Yiddish publishing rights to the song. And in consideration of the money you will advance me now, you will not have to pay me royalties for the publishing rights for the period of twenty-eight years, during which the copyright is valid. All other rights to Papirossen shall remain mine."

"Well, if that's the way you want it, Mr. Clown, then all right," Jack readily agreed, with Joe bobbing his head. "How much, for instance, would you want for the right to publish the song?"

Quickly, I calculated that $200 would pay for the tonsillectomy as well as the premium on my insurance policy that was about to lapse.

"Two hundred dollars," I replied and peered into the mirror, expecting to see the two publishers fall in a faint.

"Two hundred dollars? Oy!!" the Kammen Brothers exclaimed. "Have a heart, Mr. Clown. For the copyright of the best songs we don't pay more than twelve to fifteen dollars! Ask the composers Rumshinky, Secunda. They'll tell you. But $200 only for publishing? How can we do it?!"

"I can't make it any less," I stuck to my price. I turned back to the mirror to put the finishing touches on my makeup, while the brothers backed into a corner and put their heads together.

Coming out of their huddle, Jack said, "Two hundred dollars is a fortune of money. The songs sell for a quarter a copy. The printing alone costs an arm and a leg. But if you insist... hee, hee, hee," again the giggle, "we're willing to pay it. Give us a copy of the song and we'll prepare it for the printer. Just as soon as President Roosevelt orders the banks to open we'll give you a check.

You can trust us. We can't do anything anyway, until you sign a contract. In the meantime let my brother Joe look over the music. He will have to make a simple piano arrangement so the kids can play it. The mothers are good customers for these popular Yiddish songs. Meanwhile, we'll prepare a check and a contract."

"Look my friends," I said, "I need the $200 very urgently and in cash. If you can get me the money not later than tomorrow at this time, then it's a deal—if you can't, forget it."

"OK, we'll try to get it for you. You understand, it's not that we don't have the money," Jack explained apologetically, "but the banks are closed. We'll try."

When they left my dressing room looking crestfallen, my conscience bothered me. I felt that I had embarrassed them with my demand, as if I didn't trust them. And my father, rest his soul, taught me to always give a man the benefit of the doubt. Where indeed, were they to get the cash, with all the banks closed? I decided that I would give them the publishing rights to the song even if they didn't get the money right away.

The next evening, the brothers came to me with a paper bag containing $200 in silver and bills of small denomination collected from whomever they possibly could. I signed a contract and they took leave, thanking me and feeling highly gratified.

Thanks to this transaction I was able to pay my insurance premium, as well as the cost of my son's tonsil operation...which, I'm sorry to say did not effect the desired cure for his troublesome ear.

The Kammens sold hundreds upon thousands of copies of "Papirossen" throughout the ensuing years, as well as other hits of mine, which I'd given them the right to print. Their publishing business grew, and they moved from Roebling Street at the foot of the Williamsburg bridge to a new and modern building on Broadway.

The firm—Kammen Brothers—became a noted publishing house for all types of popular and classical music. My greatest gratification has always been that Jack and Joe Kammen themselves have admitted on numerous occasions that the publication which put them on their feet was my song, "Papirossen."

51

The Play's the Thing

According to my agreement with the management—Skulnik and Green—
I had a testimonial performance coming to me. I debated with myself
whether or not to risk running one in the face of such unfavorable
economic times. In addition to the general misery, the weather had become
sleety and sloppy. Who would care to venture out to the theater, on an ordinary weeknight to boot? Oscar Green advised me to go through with a performance in spite of these odds.

"No matter how much it brings in," he contended, "it will be found money.
We will supply whatever you need for the show. You won't have any expenses
and you will get 50 percent of the gross."

It sounded reasonable enough. I was faced, however, with a big question:
what sort of play could I come up with that would attract people to the box
office on a plain old weeknight?

As Shakespeare was supposed to have said: "The play's the thing." I began
searching for a vehicle suitable for me and for the occasion. Approaching some
of the playwrights hanging out in the Royale, I asked them to sell me the rights
to a new play for my benefit performance. Some ignored me completely.
Another scribe wisecracked, "If I had a new play, would I need you? I'd sell
it to one of the regular stars."

William Epstein, one of the actors in our company, taking me confidentially aside, said, "Yabby, I understand you're looking for a play for your
benefit. I have a script for you. That is, it's my wife's. She wrote it. She's not
a professional writer, you know, but read it. Maybe you can do something
with it."

I found its drama rather interesting and plausible. Technically, however,
the play left much to be desired. What attracted me was the climax. The leading character, an opera singer, is forced to appear and sing before an audience,
after learning of a great personal tragedy. It brought to mind the libretto of
Leoncavallo's opera, *I Pagliacci*. If I could revise the plot and adapt it for a drama
with music, I figured the play could be called *Der Payatz*.

I set to work rewriting the script. When the company heard that I was
planning to do this play, some of the encouraging remarks were: "Epstein has
been peddling his wife's masterpiece for years. Nobody would touch it with
a ten-foot pole. What does a housewife know about playwrighting?!"

Notwithstanding, I sat up nights, working on the script, the lyrics, music and blocking of the action. I would have to direct it myself, I knew. Instead of an opera singer, I turned my role into a radio singer, who is known under the assumed name of Der Payatz. I was also inspired to try out an effect, which was an innovation at the time, especially on the Yiddish stage.

Sound equipment had not yet been implemented in theaters. A singer had to be blessed with a strong pair of pipes to project into every corner of these vast theaters with their balconies and galleries. It was no place for crooners who had to rely on megaphones à la Rudy Vallee. I take the credit for being one of the first to introduce amplification on the Yiddish stage, even before it was installed in the American theaters. Of course, houses like the Roxy, Paramount, and Radio City Music Hall were already experimenting with public-address systems for their spectaculars, but even there, they were not yet successful in getting the bugs out of the equipment. The unperfected mechanism was subject to rasping noises of static and feedback; or else the entire system of amplification conked out altogether.

Norman Furman brought around a young man who was experimenting with sound. His name was Moe Asch, and Moe was forever tinkering with electronics. Not only was the young man happy to practice at my expense, he also proved a godsend to me.

After rehearsal one afternoon, Moe told me he would not be able to come to the theater next day. "What's happening tomorrow that you can't be here?" I asked. "Without you on the job, our whole radio effect will turn into a de-fect!"

"I'm sorry, but I have to meet my father at the pier. He's due back tomorrow from Europe."

"Your father? From Europe? Who is your father?"

"Yabby!" interjected Furman with surprise, "You mean to say you don't know who Moe's father is? His father is Sholem Asch!"

"Sholem Asch?! You mean 'The' Sholem Asch?"

"Yes, 'The!'" said Moe. "Can I help it if Sholem Asch is my father? He's arriving tomorrow and I want to meet him at the boat."

"How come you never mentioned it?"

"I don't want to ride on my father's coattails. I'm just a simple mechanic. I might detract from his laurels," he grinned.

After my first association with Moe Asch, he continued working with me for many years, experimenting in my various enterprises. Eventually, he became top-notch in his field of electronics and acquired his very own recording and transcription business.

* * *

In the announcements of my testimonial performance, as well as for the programs, I omitted my name. The ads read: "The Phantom of the Air" will be seen for the first time on stage, at the Hopkinson Theater in *The Clown*, a musical drama by Esther Epstein; music arranged and conducted by Jeanette Fleishman; staged and directed by—The Clown.

My cast of players were in a rather irritable mood: "Again we have to fall out of bed for rehearsal? For one performance, yet, as if we didn't already have a bellyful of rehearsals this season—and for half wages at that!"

In their opinion it was a waste of effort. It was sure to be a fiasco—a flop, morally and financially. Nevertheless, after I'd read my revised version of the play, their moods changed and the play went into rehearsal.

Advance tickets were selling nicely, Green told us, and judging from the way things were going, he expected a sellout. To me, this sounded like wishful thinking. But, as it turned out, Green was right. Despite the snowy, frosty Thursday night, my performance brought a sellout. Every member of the cast gave his very all toward the success of the play. Actors are like that, once they're in harness.

Behind a gauze drop, the audience saw what looked like a broadcasting studio. Spotlighted in my Pagliacci costume and half-mask, I stood before a microphone. As I sang out, "When your heart is torn to shreds with pain and sorrow," the audience, which instantly recognized my signature on the air, broke into thunderous applause. The tag line, "Laugh, Laugh, Payatz," was already drowned out in the din.

The number that truly electrified the audience was the one I sang for the first time, live on stage, "Papirossen!" At the end of the performance, the crowd shook the theater apart with their shouts of "Bravo!"

When the show was over I thought, there goes my "mystique." The secret is out! By now, everyone in town will know that the Clown is none other than Chaim Yablokoff. But not so. For some reason, I was still able to keep my two identities apart. As far as my listeners were concerned, I was still the "phantom of the air,'" and they still addressed their mail to Mr. Clown.

My benefit netted me quite a few dollars. And now I was impatient for the season to end. All sorts of plans were beginning to revolve in my head as to how I could combine radio and stage to my advantage. With the addition of the new and successful play I now owned, I hoped that, with a little luck, I too, like Skulnik, could venture out on my own and become somebody in the theater.

Green wanted me to repeat several performances of *Der Payatz*—on nights that were slow.

"A success like that should be exploited," he urged, "don't let it cool off. Strike the iron while it's hot."

I thanked him for the advice, but packed the script away and decided not to touch it until the good Lord granted me the opportunity to produce it on my very own.

* * *

I have often tried to define the factors that brought about my successful radio and stage career. There was certainly no lack of fine Yiddish radio singers at the time...with far better voices. So what was it that the Clown created, which had such special appeal for audiences? Granted that my aura of mystery, the wondering who this phantom of the air was, did much to stimulate curiosity and excitement. But the impelling feature was the clown's laughter-through-tears style of repertoire; an elusive figure, who vividly interprets in song and recitation, the romance, drama, even tragedy in the true-to-life compositions he brings to the people; themes of consolation, hope, encouragement, the feeling that all is not lost; everyone has his share of problems; the world is a stage and each of us is a clown. Is your heart full of sadness? Laugh, laugh, you clown! have faith and hope for a better tomorrow...

In 1946-47, after the Holocaust, during my concert tour of the European DP camps, I became convinced that people can sooner be eased from the depths of despair by tales of woe reflecting their own suffering and turmoil, rather than by prescribed lighthearted entertainment, whose diversion could backfire: "You have it good, so you can joke and laugh! For us, there is only heartache and tears..."

* * *

With the coming of spring 1933, the country became more optimistic. Roosevelt's New Deal began to take root. Banks reopened, a good many of the unemployed millions went back to work. Business, in general, stabilized. The depression eased up.

For the Passover holiday, it was arranged to have Menasha Skulnik's company change places with that of the Prospect Theater in the Bronx. These exchanges were known as the subway circuit. Up to Passover, in accordance with the settlement the union had worked out with the management, we would receive only 50 percent of our salaries. But, starting at the Prospect, we would be paid our weekly wages in full.

Our show *Getzel Becomes a Bridegroom*, went over as big in the Bronx as it did in Brownsville. Business couldn't be better.

In this particular show I had a number to do, "Rosalie," dedicated to my sweetheart in the play. It was just a lighthearted couplet, not what you'd call a showstopper. If Skulnik hadn't needed to make his change for the finale, during this time, the show would have survived just as well without my "Rosalie." The hour was late and, at this point, the audience was only waiting to see the outcome of the plot—which didn't take much to figure out—and go home.

One night, singing "Rosalie" as usual, I embellished it with a little dance step. For an encore I repeated the chorus, giving Skulnik a little more time, and thought I was through. But the crowd continued to clap, whistle, shout and stamp their feet. What is this? I puzzled. How come such success all of a sudden? Skulnik, waiting in the wings, was impatient.

"No, come on! It's late," he hissed.

His no didn't do any good. The clamoring did not subside. Amid the tumult I caught shouts of "Papirossen! Sing Papirossen. Sing, Payatz!"

My blood ran cold. So that's it! There's been a leak somewhere! I felt like a thief caught red-handed. I acted as if I had no idea what the people were demanding of me, and shuffled off the stage.

Skulnik made his entrance. Instead of the spontaneous burst of laughter that always exploded at the sight of Getzel, this schlemiel of a bridegroom, in high hat and tails reaching to the floor, the audience kept yammering for the Clown! With difficulty we managed to get through the finale and bring down the curtain.

I was prepared for some angry remark from Skulnik, but he said nothing. Since I fully suspected some public release from the theater had pinned me down as the Payatz, I was so burnt up I followed him to his dressing room.

"Listen, Menasha," I said, "after this lowdown trick of divulging my identity, which is sure to ruin everything I've accomplished on radio up to now, I'm finishing my engagement here as of this Sunday. Please tell Mr. Green to pay me my full salary for the week, as promised. I am through!" I left him standing there completely nonplussed and ran upstairs to my dressing room.

Oscar Green, who came puffing up the stairs, pleaded with me not to leave. He swore that neither he, nor Skulnik had any hand in releasing any publicity about me.

It wasn't too long before I discovered the item in the paper and knew it was our regular publicity man who had spilled the beans about my dual role. It was very thoughtless of him, to say the least. Skulnik certainly needed no extra boost for his show. He was great enough on his own to bring the crowds, and already popular at this point as Uncle David on the Molly Goldberg radio program in English. But, to a publicity man, a scoop is a scoop and it must not be passed up, even if someone gets hurt. And someone usually does! In this case, the old blurb "Write what you want about me, only spell my name right," didn't work!

52

The Slippery Uphill Climb

On leaving the Hopkinson company, I found myself forlorn and rather jittery about the future. Giving up the chance to earn another few weeks' salary did not please my wife, much less my in-laws. It was a rash and hot headed thing to do. To leave a paying job and go chasing rainbows to become a big shot, a star, was plain crazy in their opinion. At any rate, my in-laws made it clear that I was not to depend on their support.

Still, with the few hundred dollars from my benefit, I began to plan for my first theatrical venture. When my wife once again took our son to go and live with her parents in Boro Park, I sold our furnishings for the third time since we were married and took a room at the Broadway Central Hotel in Manhattan. This was the beginning of the end of our marriage.

The Lyric Theater in Williamsburg was available. In the profession, this house was considered to be a jinx. Except for Skulnik who had played successfully during the spring, no one was able to do any business there. Notwithstanding, I negotiated with the proprietors to rent the theater for a weekend of five performances. They agreed on condition that their expenses be deducted first from the gross. This deal was hardly in my favor, yet having no alternative I signed the contract.

Shakespeare may have said, "What's in a name?"... but to me, this now presented a problem. Should I use my stage name, Chaim Yablokoff or go by my radio moniker as I did for my benefit performance? Perhaps I could combine the two. But the title of my play was also *Der Payatz*, which could be very confusing. It needed mighty careful consideration before I launched my first project.

I came to the conclusion that my real name was out of the question. It is pretty rare for a supporting actor, no matter how gifted, to suddenly be billed as a star. In my case, after three seasons in Brooklyn, I was known only as a featured player in a neighborhood theater. Although I may have managed to stand out in the parts I played, promoting myself overnight as an attraction meant taking an awful chance.

Granted, there is no law in America that says one can't become a self-made man. If not in America, where else? What did bother me was the doubt whether I really had what it took to attract an audience for more than a one-night stand. Was I living in a fool's paradise? After a weekend at the Lyric I could easily wind up as a "fallen star"—a dud! And in addition to burying my few invested dollars, I would have to bury myself in disgrace.

I was also well aware that the name, Payatz conjured up the image of one who clowns, cavorts…a buffoon! I had misgivings that the name would not present me with the desired dignity, in the eyes of the intellectuals and the press. My radio listeners, who knew me only as the Clown, were familiar with my dramatic and folk-style programs on the air. They, I felt, would surely not confuse me with the bulbous-nosed circus clown, or some slapstick comedian, but see me rather like Pierrot, the sad but jesting character of French and Italian folklore. I could only hope that those who came would recognize for themselves that my play reflected my serious-minded approach to the theater.

Taking all this into consideration, and on the advice of Norman Furman, I decided to disregard my name and bill myself as the Phantom of the Air, starring in the musical play Der Payatz.

I notified Reuben Guskin at the union about having rented the Lyric Theater and said I was ready to engage a company.

"Now?!" he asked, taken aback. "But it's summer. All the theaters in New York are closed, and you first want to open? And where, of all places, at the Lyric? People have stopped coming there even in the height of the season. Do you have so much money to burn?!"

Deep down I felt that Guskin was right, yet everything within me kept prompting: it's now or never! Take the chance! "Mr. Guskin," I said, "I am determined to go through with it."

"All right then," he shrugged. "Leave a list of the cast you intend to engage with Miss Pivar. I will talk business to them."

Inexperienced as I was in the intricacies of union politics. I made my first blunder. I did not leave a list with Miss Pivar. Why must Guskin engage the actors for me? Why can't I negotiate with them, personally? I would still have to come to him, anyway, to approve and verify each engagement.

Bella Mysell and the original cast that played in *Der Payatz* with me at the Hopkinson were on the road with Skulnik, so I couldn't have any of them. I shrank from approaching the anointed Second Avenue artists, knowing that they would only be doing me a favor by taking the job. Yet I wanted to surround myself with the best performers possible, so I went ahead on my own and engaged a cast most suited to the characters in my play. For Bella's part I engaged Gertrude Bulman, and the others were Abraham Teitelbaum, Peter Graff, my old pal, Sam Gertler, Abe Lax, Louis Hyman, Rose Wallerstein, Rebecca Weintraub, Tillie Rabinowitz and a child actress, Gloria Goldstein. I engaged a prompter, a stage manager and my brothers-in-law: Manny Fleischman as orchestra leader, with Dave Fleischman at the piano.

By engaging the company without first consulting Guskin, I committed an unpardonable sin, which caused me great difficulties in my future dealings with him. This touchy snag in our relationship lasted a long time and was anything but helpful to me when I needed his favor during my slippery climb uphill. I was just not his man.

My radio sponsors permitted me to use their air time during my broadcasts to announce my performance at the Lyric Theater. I also placed ads in the Jewish dailies, of which there were a goodly number at the time. I had posters plastered on every available wall in Williamsburg and show-cards placed in neighborhood store windows.

Louis Markowitz, a young man with a remarkable gift for drawing ran a small printing shop, where he specialized in lithographs and advertising material in multicolored prints for the theater. Admiring my ambition and courage in doing things on a larger scale, he turned out a poster for me that was a real beauty!

The sceneries and sets were done by the Saltzman Brothers; the sound system by Moe Asch; and the lobby was decorated with pictures of the cast. For the box office I engaged Joe Costa, the young Italian from the Hopkinson theater and waited for news of an advance sale. Days passed and not a nibble, not even a call to inquire as to who's playing?...what's playing?...where, when?...dead!

"At the Lyric, they don't buy tickets in advance," said Joe, trying to console me. "Here, the people come the last minute, same as at the Hopkinson. That is, when Molly Picon is playing or Skulnik. But, the Clown?" he grinned, "I'm sorry, Yabby, for the Clown, I can't guarantee you."

With a heavy heart I started rehearsals and my troubles only began. I had meticulously blocked out every move, every mise en scene of the play. But not every member of the cast was ready to take my directing. One of my actors, eyeing me with sarcasm bristled, "After forty years on stage are you going to teach me how to act?!"

Another came up with: "What's the big to-do? Are we going to make a run of this play? It's only a lousy five performances!"

I asked them to please memorize their lines as I did not intend to have a promptor's box—although I had engaged a promptor according to union rules. This threw the older actors into a panic.

"We must do away with the promptor's box on account of the microphones I'm having planted in the foot lights," I explained, "or else the audience will hear the promptor sooner and louder than they will hear the actors." In the end I had to compromise by having the promptor cue them from the wings.

I couldn't sleep nights. Like a lion in a cage, I paced my hotel room. If the play should turn out looking the way it did at rehearsal—and if business should prove bad at the box office, where would I get the money to cover all the expenses, for which I alone was responsible? I knew I would have my creditors as guests in the theater, waiting to collect their balances in cash. Guskin was right. Did I have so much money to burn? And maybe my in-laws were also right. What kind of lunacy indeed, to venture out on my own?!!

At my long awaited opening, a few hundred local residents showed up at the box office. Most of them brought the special poster-passes, entitling them to a reduction in price for allowing my show-cards in their shop windows.

There is a Jewish saying: "The smaller the crowd, the greater the simkhe— the greater the festivity. Well, the crowd was small, but there could not have been more enthusiasm if the house had been packed to capacity. The audience applauded and cheered. Financially, I knew I was in the soup, but morally, we all felt that the performance had taken the people by storm.

The next morning, Saturday, I tried to call the box office and couldn't get through. The lines were busy. A good omen. I took the subway to Williamsburg and found a crowd of people lined up to buy tickets. An hour before curtain time the street was mobbed with people trying to elbow their way into the lobby for the matinee. But, by now the sign was up: sold out. The same thing took place before the evening's performance. The constant ringing of the phones was deafening. People also kept reserving tickets for Sunday's two shows.

The proprietors Lowenfeld and Garfinkel proposed that I extend my arrangement with them for another weekend. I agreed with the condition that I get 60 percent of the gross receipts, with no guarantee whatever for their expenses. They accepted most willingly.

After Sunday's matinee I had enough to pay my company and other employees their full wages in cash. My share of the evening's performance, I calculated, would cover my bills and maybe leave something for me, too.

After Sunday's matinee, Sigmund Weintraub, a former actor came backstage. His theatrical agency, Relkin and Weintraub, guest stars and entire Yiddish theater companies which were customarily booked on the road following the New York Season.

"You have a fine performance, Mr. Clown," Weintraub complimented me. "You're turning Williamsburg upside down, I see. And after the Lyric, what? Do you have any further plans?"

"To tell you the truth, Mr. Weintraub, up to the last minute, business here looked pretty hopeless. I really don't know how or why the public did show up at the last moment."

"Leave it to the public!" he smiled. "In my book, the word-of-mouth publicity is still the best kind of advertisement. During the week they'll talk about you and your show in the shops, the market and on the telephone! You'll see."

"Mr. Weintraub," I ventured further, "what are the chances of the Relkin and Weintraub office representing me and getting us a theater to play in?"

"I'll talk it over with Relkin. Come up to the office tomorrow morning. We'll see. It's turning hot and humid. But theater business is unpredictable, so who can tell? Give the people a good show and they'll come any time of the year." I always remembered this veteran's advice.

Monday bright and early, I put in an appearance at the Relkin and Weintraub office, located in the building of the Maurice Schwartz Art Theater. Weintraub introduced me to his partner, Edwin A. Relkin, who was more interested in his telephone conversation. It involved Schwartz and his current sensation in New York, *Yoshe Kalb*, a play by I.J. Singer.

Relkin was a swarthy man, with a shock of inky black hair that fell over his forehead almost touching his bushy black eyebrows.

He answered another call, gruffly. "How much did you take in last week?" he asked, speaking to one of the company managers calling in from the road. "How much? Ten thousand? Terrific! Colossal! You'll do twenty next week. Send me my commission special delivery!"

Later, I learned that he was a great exaggerator. Whether he took the call in his office, or across the street in the Royale, he would repeat the figure quoted to him, doubling the amount for the benefit of listeners. He spoke no Yiddish at all.

"What's your name again?" he finally turned to me, "the Payatz? What's that? Oh, the Clown? Yeah, yeah, Weintraub told me. You're playing at the Lyric? How much did you take in last week?" I mentioned the sum. "You're kidding! In that dump? That's more than Molly Picon did in Pittsburgh! Do you want to play the Prospect next week?"

"Mr. Yablokoff is being held over at the Lyric for next weekend," interjected Weintraub.

"Oh, you're held over? All right then, I'll get in touch with Willie Pasternack at the Prospect and see what I can work out for you."

Thanking him I left the office and crossed the street to the Cafe Royale. It was still pretty early. The place was sparsely occupied.

In a little while Alex Cohen came in. "Alex! What are you doing in New York? You're supposed to be on the road with Menasha Skulnik. What gives?"

"It's all over," he shrugged. "Business was rotten. The whole company came back by Greyhound. The news of your success reached us even in Philadelphia. I was real happy for you," Alex said, slapping me on the back.

I offered him the management of my enterprise. I knew that Alex Cohen was the most honest and trustworthy of theater managers, and I was happy when he accepted my offer.

I took off for the union. Judging by Guskin's acknowledgement of my greeting, I sensed that he did not have very pleasant news.

"Mr. Yablokoff, I hear that you intend to play another weekend at the Lyric. Why didn't you notify the union?"

"That's why I'm here, Mr. Guskin. Business was very good and the bosses are holding me over for another weekend."

"Who is going to play?"

I stared at him, "My company of course. I spoke to them and they are willing."

"Some are willing and some are not. Actors are actors. To you, they said one thing and to me, another."

"What is the issue?" I asked, startled. "I must play off the weekend. I signed a contract. It was announced from the stage. I ordered printing, and I am also negotiating with the Prospect Theater."

"The Prospect? For when?"

"Right after the Lyric for a full week of nine performances."

"The company wants a raise," Guskin finally came out with it. "Business, I heard, was very good, so..."

"A raise? Already? How much? I just started."

"Give them an extra 15 percent on their wages. And oh yes, there's something else. Gertie Bulman is leaving town for the summer. So is Abe Lax. Teitelbaum is going to Europe. You'll have to replace them. The rest of the cast will play."

"What am I going to do about replacements? I have only till Friday to rehearse."

"You can engage anyone you like. Here, take this roster of members and let me know."

I took the list of names and walked back to the Royale. I sat brooding over the roster of actors. There wasn't much time to ponder over it.

"If Bella would agree to play," I thought, "she would save the situation. She knows the show, and I'm sure she remembers the part and the music. Besides, Bella Mysell is a name, and I would have a co-star who would add prestige to the enterprise."

I called Bella and was tremendously relieved when she agreed to it. We arranged to meet at the Lyric that very evening for rehearsal. From the list of names, I decided on Boris Auerbach. He was one of the bosses for whom I worked at the Hopkinson in 1927-28.

Hurrying back to the union I showed Guskin my contract for the Prospect Theater, and reported the engagement of Bella Mysell. I also said that I intended to engage Boris Auerbach.

"Bella Mysell," he said, "is OK. Auerbach too. I'll speak to him. Now you still need a comedian. Engage Jacob Wexler."

This really threw me. Wexler? I was sort of afraid of Wexler. He was a politician in the union and hard to handle, I'd heard.

"Yes, engage Wexler," he repeated. "You can do that right now. He's waiting in the other office. Miss Pivar!" he called, "please send in Mr. Wexler!" Turning to me he threw in a hint. "If he should want a few dollars more, come to terms with him. He's the vice-president of the union, you know."

"Naturally, I'll come to terms with him. Do I have a choice? I'm forced to come to terms with everyone. After all, I've already signed a contract."

Guskin's only answer was a half-smile. And of course, I engaged Wexler.

* * *

The advance sale for the second weekend at the Lyric Theater was terrific.

I concentrated all my attention on the rehearsals, the administrative work and advance publicity for the Prospect Theater. From the cartons of mail sent to WEVD addressed to the Clown and postmarked Bronx, it was clear that I had many listeners there, too. Would there be enough of them to fill such a tremendous house as the Prospect?

Contrary to the consensus expressed by the know-it-alls in the Royale, the performances at the Prospect Theater surpassed all expectations. The stage crew met all my requirements for scenery, sets, lighting and props. Moe Asch installed extra microphones in this huge theater. And a truly great asset to the entire production was the augmented orchestra I insisted on. This was conducted by the very talented Harry Lubin, who later became a composer-conductor with his own symphonic orchestra in Hollywood and television.

My co-star, Bella Mysell, scored tremendous success, delighting the audience with a colorful Spanish song, "Clavelitos," often sung by the opera star Lily Pons. Her name—as I knew it would—added much prestige to the play.

Yet no one from the Yiddish press deemed it worthwhile to travel to the Bronx to review The Clown. Just the same, business couldn't have been better. And this, in spite of summer, without air-conditioning! Men sat in shirtsleeves, women fanned themselves with their programs, but nobody stirred from their seats to the last curtain.

For the second week I no longer had to guarantee the first $1500 of the box office, as agreed upon the first week. We played on the same 50-50 basis as all the established star attractions.

How often I thought of Sigmund Weintraub's words: "The best kind of publicity is by word of mouth! Just give the people a show and they'll be there with bells on!" And indeed they were throughout the solid month we played at the Prospect Theater with our nine shows a week.

* * *

The popularity of my radio program and the success of my show came to the attention of Loew's Theater Circuit. They were scouting for radio names to book into their movie houses that still presented vaudeville programs and personal appearances. Norman Furman got me a contract to headline a vaudeville program at Loew's Boulevard Theater in the East Bronx.

"It's a trial engagement," said Furman, "they want to convince themselves of your box office appeal and decide whether your type of material warrants featuring you as a headliner."

I wasn't overly enthused about the idea, although the money was certainly attractive. Why, on earth, would they want me, a Yiddish radio singer in an English-speaking vaudeville house? Even though the Boulevard Theater was located in a predominately Jewish neighborhood, they rarely presented performers from the Yiddish stage—except Molly Picon, who had already played the

Palace on Broadway. So where, I thought, do I fit in with my entire Yiddish repertoire?!

"If you make good at the Boulevard," Furman urged, "they'll book you into other Loew's houses in New York and around the country. Try one week. If you don't care to continue, you'll be paid well for the week and you can call it quits."

Vaudeville theaters usually began their new programs on Friday and changed the bill every week, or twice if it was a split week. Music rehearsals were held Friday at 10 A.M., and at noon the current movie went on. This was then followed by the stage show.

That Friday, as I neared the Boulevard Theater for rehearsal, I stared in amazement! A huge banner was strung across the street with large block letters spelling out: Personal Appearance of The Phantom of the Air—The Clown. And the same words in electric lights glared from the marquee. The sidewalk had already been cordoned off and people stood in long lines waiting for the box office to open.

I opened with a song currently popular, "Play, Fiddle, Play" by Emery Deutch. Singing it in English I followed it with my Yiddish translation. 'Shpiel, Fidl, Shpiel." For the rest of my turn I did a cycle of songs from my Yiddish repertoire and the audience wouldn't let me off the stage. The highlight of my program, of course, was "Papirossen."

"The street is jammed with people!" Furman rushed into my dressing room with excitement. "Management is sure it will continue like this for the rest of the week!" And so it did.

The Loew's managers conceded that nobody had ever brought such business to the Boulevard. The staff from the main office came to gawk at me. I was immediately booked for the following week—again in the Bronx, only this time, at the Paradise Theater on the Grand Concourse.

"This is another challenge," said Furman. "At the Boulevard, you know, they cater to mixed clientele, mostly Jewish. But the Paradise draws a majority of non-Jewish people. So, Yabby, if you bring big business at the Paradise, the entire Loew's Circuit will open to you. You can name your own price."

The Paradise Theater was appropriately named—a paradise indeed. This palatial house seated over 3,000 people. The symphonic orchestra, under the famed conductor, Don Albert, consisted of more than sixty musicians, and the other acts on the bill with me were big names in vaudeville. I had been warned that the theater's patronage was largely Gentile and not receptive to Jewish performers, no matter how good they happened to be. The Grand Concourse at the time, was not the overwhelmingly Jewish neighborhood it later became. I was told that even such greats as Sophie Tucker and Eddie Cantor were jittery when appearing at the Paradise.

"I'm in for it, all right!" I worried. "How can I get up there and concertize in Yiddish, for an English-speaking, non-Jewish audience?"

"I feel very confident," said Furman soothing me, "that you will be a hit here, too. And you will bring tremendous business!"

Furman's predictions came true. My opening show did come across beautifully, although I was never so nervous, or relieved, in my life. On Saturday I had to do four shows instead of the usual three. And Sunday after my early broadcast on WEVD, it was almost impossible to get near the theater.

Working the continuous shows in vaudeville was tantamount to hard labor. Hanging around the theater from morning to night was more wearing than the performance. How the typical vaudevillian was able to take this routine year in, year out, was beyond me. Many of them traveled with their families. Between shows there was only time enough to send out for a sandwich and a cup of coffee and stay put in the theater, to charge up energy for the next show. If the weather was pleasant an actor could catch a breath of air out in the back alley, keeping his makeup on, maybe teaching the younger actors the tricks of the trade or writing a letter back home. Some used these intervals to brag to the others on the bill how they "stopped the show" in Peoria, how they "killed them" in Sheboygan, or about the big break awaiting them on the Coast. Their lives were not involved with anything outside of their ten or twelve-minute act.

Me and My Shadow

During the last few days at the Paradise, I noticed a man shadowing my every move backstage. If I tried to step out for a cup of coffee—lo and behold—the man was right behind me.

"Mr. Clown," he'd say, "just tell me what you want and I'll send out for it. It will be brought to your dressing room. Why exert yourself, doing all those shows a day?!"

"Who is that fella that keeps dogging my footsteps?" I asked Furman. "He annoys me!"

"That guy? Oh, he's the stage doorman," he brushed it off. "He's around to see that no autograph hounds pester you, or pilfer your dressing room while you're on stage."

One late afternoon as I tried to venture outdoors for a breath of air—there he was at my heels again—my shadow! After the last show, the guy actually followed us into the car when Furman and I went back to my hotel.

"Excuse me," he apologized, "I'm also going to Manhattan, so I hope you don't mind if I tag along."

This was the last straw! On reaching my hotel, I exploded. "Why the hell is this nudnick trailing me?"

"He's not a nudnick and he is not trailing you—he's 'tailing' you! He's a detective! The theater is doing such fabulous business, the cops were tipped off about a plot to kidnap the Clown for ransom, understand? We didn't want to alarm you, so we kept it secret. But now you know!"

When this kidnapping story broke, it was interpreted as a publicity stunt.

Nevertheless, the records show there was a plot to kidnap the Clown. Fortunately for me, the plot did not succeed.

* * *

To quote an old Yiddish saying: "Tie me up among strangers, but cast me amongst my own." I earned more in vaudeville than I could ever dream of earning in the Yiddish theater, yet I wasn't happy. The tiresome grind of four or five shows a day, the routine of singing the same stuff over and over was not for my temperament. I'd wake up in the middle of the night, terrified. What if I should become hoarse? I was only human. How long could my vocal chords hold out after so much abuse? I decided that vaudeville, for all its fabulous monetary gains, was not for me.

The Loews Theater managers deplored my decision. As for Norman Furman, he never changed his belief that I threw away the rare opportunity to achieve an outstanding career on the American stage!

53

By Public Demand

I went back to my first love—the Yiddish theater. The manager of the Prospect Theater proposed that I do a return engagement of *The Clown*, and offered me a very good deal, out of which I paid my leading lady, Bella Mysell. She now joined me wherever I played, so that we became a team. Business again was tops. We stayed on at the Prospect for weeks in which I produced two other shows, assembling different casts all the time: a musical I called *Natasha*, and another by Isidore Friedman entitled *Oh, Promise Me*. The public, however, still demanded *The Clown*.

Following the Prospect, we played at the Parkway Theater in Brooklyn. When Bernard Elving, actor-manager of the Metropolitan Theater in Newark came to Brooklyn to catch *The Clown*, he immediately invited me to star at his theater and put the play on with his ensemble. *The Clown* also scored a smash hit in Newark. Instead of the one week agreed upon, we ran the show for six consecutive weeks, breaking a record for this city. The Newark engagement stands out in my mind, for this was where we celebrated New Year's Eve of 1934. It was the first time in more than a decade that we all merrily toasted one another with legally purchased liquor. Prohibition had finally been repealed.

* * *

Louis Goldstein, the manager with whom I'd worked in Chicago, was partners now with Josh Gruber in Philadelphia's Arch Street Theater. When he asked me to appear at his benefit performance, I was in a spot. I knew that Chaim Towber, whom I had befriended in Chicago, leaving him to take over the radio program I ran for the Laundale Theater, was now presenting himself on Philadelphia radio as Der Payatz and I was plenty aggravated over it. I had never appeared in Philadelphia—not as Chaim Yablokoff, the actor, nor had they ever heard me on radio.

"Louis," I argued, "I can't play the Clown in Philadelphia. Don't you know that Towber has already played a benefit for himself at the Arch Street Theater using that name?"

"So what?" persisted Goldstein. "So he used the name. It wasn't your show he played, was it? Meanwhile, please, Yabby, come to my benefit. I can use the money. I'll announce you as Der Payatz, Chaim Yablokoff! Wait, I have a better solution. Since Towber's name is also Chaim, let's change your to…let me see...Herman! Herman Yablokoff, the famous Clown from New York! Listen to me. You'll sing a few of your numbers and the audience will eat you up—especially the song, 'Papirossen.' It's a sensation in Philly too."

Reluctantly, I promised to appear at his benefit performance. And this was how my name Chaim hereafter became Herman.

For this first concert in Philadelphia, I took along my musical directors, Manny and David Fleischman. Driving out through the Holland Tunnel, it began to snow. It became thicker and heavier by the minute, turning into a full-scale blizzard. We could not afford a heater, so there we sat, freezing to death. The trip took us from nine in the morning to eight o'clock that evening. The snowstorm had also hit Philadelphia, and I was sure this whole miserable journey was a complete waste.

Reaching the theater, I had the surprise of my life! I saw a sea of umbrellas, with people huddling under them, waiting for the gallery entrance to open so they could scramble for the unreserved seats.

There was no time to eat or rest. The concert was due to begin. Hurriedly, we made our preparations—me, in the dressing room and my brothers-in-law in the pit with the other musicians, for a quick run-through.

My misgivings about appearing in Philadelphia proved groundless. My frozen bones were soon thawed out by the heartwarming reception. That night, after a good supper, and with roads cleared, I returned to New York pocketing a signed contract for the Passover holiday at the Arch Street Theater.

* * *

Philadelphia has long been a great town for theater. Broadway companies have always considered it a good place for breaking in a show, while the Philadelphians themselves enjoy seeing these productions before they open on Broadway.

Yiddish theater also played a vital role in the life of the city's Jewish community, often with two or three theaters functioning simultaneously throughout a season.

Diligently, I began preparing for my Passover engagement in the City of Brotherly Love. The expenses on my share were enormous. Even with average business, it could easily cost me quite a sum—a gamble I could ill afford.

Getting a call from Nathan Fleischer to appear on his radio hour in Philadelphia, I gladly accepted. I drove in to do a few broadcasts in advance, and the box office slowly picked up. The requests for "Papirossen" began pouring in same as in New York.

The premiere was a slow beginning, opening as we did on the day of the second Seder. This was a notoriously slow night. Goldstein said, "But the show went over so big, you'll be playing to sellouts by the weekend." And he proved to be right again. "You can chalk up this triumph," he swaggered, "to the appearance you made at my benefit that snowy night, remember?"

Others insisted that the biggest boost came through my preliminary broadcasts.

I thought, if radio is to be my calling card, then, from now on that's what I must do in every city before I open there!

Due to the blue laws affecting certain cities at the time, Philadelphia theaters were forbidden to function on Sundays. Yiddish companies usually played those days either in Baltimore, or Washington, D.C. For our first Sunday in Baltimore, we did the matinee and evening performances at the huge Maryland Theater. Early Sunday morning, there I was at Youngelson's radio studio to deliver my magic calling card. And sure enough we packed them in at the Maryland. The tenure of appearing in Philly for Passover, with Sundays in Baltimore, remained mine for many years.

My success in these two cities was certainly a boost to my prestige on Second Avenue's Rialto and in the Cafe Royale—where it was most important. The booking agents Relkin and Weintraub, arranged a tour for me, covering Montreal, Toronto, Detroit, Cleveland, Pittsburgh, and Boston and its surrounding towns, like Roxbury and Chelsea.

* * *

My company and I began our tour in Montreal. This city no longer maintained a steady Yiddish theater; although the former managers, Ike Mitnick and Louis Shochat, did occasionally present an attraction. These, mostly, were celebrated stars with current shows fresh from New York runs.

I was far from confident about attracting business in Montreal, where I was known only as the supporting actor Chaim Yablokoff, who had played a whole season at the same Monument National Theater. Could I now descend upon them as Herman Yablokoff, the star, heading his own company?

My friend Shochat had arranged an advance broadcast for me. I left for Montreal before the company. On arrival Shochat explained that the big Municipal radio station of Montreal, where he'd bought air time for me, permitted singing and reciting in Yiddish, but announcements had to be made in English, or French.

For my introductory program I, of course, snag my Yiddish compositions, while announcements for my upcoming guest performances were done by Shochat in English. At my following broadcast I tried to get around this Canadian restriction. Since recitation in Yiddish was permitted, I made my own announcement, employing a declamatory tone with music for background and got away with it. No one could tell whether I was reciting poetry, or inviting my listeners to come see me in person.

Before my company arrived, the tickets for my scheduled performances were completely sold out. The Clown and Company created a sensation in town. And no one held it against me for changing my Hebrew name Chaim to Herman, or that, behind the mask of a clown, I presented myself as a star. On the contrary, I was accepted with the attitude, "Hometown Boy Makes Good!"

Before leaving Montreal, the managers proposed a return engagement with the same show. As a rule the profession frowns on such return engagements. If you've got a success you can keep the show going. But once you break off, it cools, and bringing it back can be a disaster. Nevertheless, as long as these local impresarios deemed it worthwhile to bring me back, with the same show at that, I felt encouraged enough to take the chance.

* * *

Toronto was another city that no longer ran a steady Yiddish theater. The Standard, which had been built for the purpose, had been converted to a movie house. I rented it though, and here too, I noticed the same pattern: a slow start, then the broadcast—and finally, success. The city's blue law sent us out on Sunday to play Detroit. And that was another community added to our list of devoted fans.

* * *

Boston treated us royally. Of course, Bella had played all these cities before, and always got a grand welcome. Whenever possible I would make her come with me to sing a number, and do a duet with me on radio, but all this knocking about, the packing and unpacking, was hardship enough and I didn't want to tax my co-star any more than necessary.

After Boston, we headed back to Montreal for our return engagement. All performances were sold out in advance before I even did my radio stint. I went again to the Municipal radio station, accompanied by Shochat.

Finished with my program I was asked to step into the director's office. "Here it comes," I whispered, "they've caught on to the fact that I made my announcement in Yiddish and the director is going to let me have it!"

It turned out that they had neither heard me speak, nor sing.

"I'm sorry to tell you, sir," the director informed me, "but your program was not heard. Something went wrong with the transmitter. We don't know how it happened."

As we stood there we heard a French program going on loud and clear and didn't know what to think. "Something is fishy here," I murmured to Shochat as we left. In the outer office, at every desk, the staff busily answered the incessant calls, repeating: "Sorry... transmitter trouble..."

The next day, Shochat was called to the studio to learn that it was sabotage all right! Perpetrated by some young Hitlerites, who had indeed tampered with the transmitter lines. The station director offered us free time the following day to do a special Yiddish program for the Jewish community of Montreal. This program, he promised, would be announced every hour up to broadcast time, with an apology to the listeners and to the Clown for this unfortunate incident.

Despite the anti-Semites, I sang and announced my program all in Yiddish to the great satisfaction of my people. As a matter of fact, this episode brought about the lifting of the ban on Yiddish being spoken. It also afforded me so much publicity that Mitnick and Shochat proposed still another return engagement with The Clown—a third one. And I accepted. The theater was jam-packed every time. Nothing like this ever happened to me, nor to anyone else in the profession as far as I knew.

Summer was upon us and I said that's enough. No more traveling. We were all exhausted. Back in New York, Norman Furman, who refused to give up, booked me into Loews Delancey Street Theater on the Lower East Side. Well, I certainly couldn't turn this down. At the same time, totally unbeknownst to me, Max Friedlander, who was the union deputy of my company, had taken it upon himself to promise Mitnick and Shochat that he would get me to lay still another five performances in Montreal! And of all times, the very same weekend I was scheduled for Loews Delancey!

"What's the idea?!" I demanded of Shochat on the phone.

"Friedlander assured us that you would play off the last five performances. And why shouldn't you?"

"I have another commitment that weekend here in New York, that's why! I will not come to Montreal," I stood firm. "It's getting to be ridiculous...four return engagements—it's crazy!"

In a call to Guskin at the union, Shochat complained that I was refusing to play and that the tickets had already sold out.

I was called to the union, and when I protested that Friedlander, who was not my agent, had closed the deal without my knowledge, this character just sat there grinning like the cat that swallowed the canary.

"Since you've already been advertised," Guskin declared, "it is only right that, according to professional ethics, the performances should be played off. Especially, when Shochat assures me that the tickets have already been sold out."

"Sold out? I don't believe them! Playing in Montreal cost me a fortune, not to mention the physical hardship involved, shlepping a whole company! I won't do it!"

The result was that angry, frustrated and bitter, I canceled the Loew's booking and dragged the company to Montreal to play the Payatz once more. The only concession granted me by the union was that the company would work with me on a co-operative basis. All expenses would be paid out from my share of the income and the balance divided by the company, share and share alike. I would not have to pay them their salaries as before.

Shochat's claim that all tickets were sold out in advance happened to be true. So here I had a chance of realizing a neat profit for myself and I, like an obstinate mule, insisted playing on a co-op basis, with each actor's share adding up to two weeks' wages for the one week. And while I lost a sizable sum by being forced to cancel my booking at Loews', my company magnanimously allotted me the same share they each received according to union scale.

It taught me a lesson for the future: never to rely on goodwill and fairness in the profession. Business is business!

* * *

The King of Song

The theater season was once again in full swing, while I found myself at loose ends. I could not go back to taking any engagements. I had to be my own boss. Only now, my biggest concern was getting a new play. A few writers did bring me their rejected scripts, but none of them appealed to me. They were the same old hackneyed plots. By this point in my career I had doctored dozens of plays, written lyrics and music for countless musicals, and had some ideas of my own.

Encouraged by Bella, I decided to try my hand at writing an original musical that would be tailor-made for both of us. Bella, herself, had turned down several offers, preferring to wait until I could come up with a new production.

I sat down to work out a story I had in mind. A musical romance, I called it *The King of Song*. In order not to use my name as playwright, I substituted my mother's maiden name, Leah Shillingoff. I wrote the lyrics, composed the music and gave this credit to Manny Fleischman, who arranged the score.

To my own and everyone else's utter amazement, *The King of Song* drew large audiences and was received with the most gratifying enthusiasm. The bleak and already written-off Amphion Theater in Williamsburg, where I presented the musical, took a new lease on life. The show ran for weeks and I did exceptionally well. For the first time the Jewish and American press deigned to come, and actually wrote some very favorable reviews. Everyone, naturally, was puzzled over this new playwright, Leah Shillingoff, who wrote *The King of Song*.

Relkin and Weintraub lined up a road tour for me with my new hit, but I had to put it off. The managers of the McKinley Square Theater in the Bronx, a 1,200-seat house, made me and my leading lady an offer to join their company and star in my new play. They extended me very favorable conditions. On Thanksgiving Day, we opened at the McKinley Square Theater with *The King of Song*, which ran for twelve straight weeks, playing nine shows a week, and did fabulous business.

* * *

My delayed tour throughout the States and Canada also proved most gratifying. People came to the theater to see *The King of Song*. For the Passover holiday, we again played the Arch Street Theater in Philadelphia, with Sundays in Baltimore. In a review in the *Philadelphia Jewish World*, the editor wrote: "Herman Yablokoff, known as the Clown, is by no means a clown. He is an outstanding stage artist, a gifted regisseur and an intellectual personality..." To me, this was the most beautiful tribute I had ever received.

54

Papirossen—A Musical Production

Despite my success in local houses and on the road, I was convinced that this would in no way further my career. Only on our Yiddish Broadway—Second Avenue—would I establish myself once and for all as an actor-director and producer on a par with the others.

The company managers heard of the tremendous business my productions brought wherever I played. Relkin made sure this information reached the Royale Cafe. Yet none of these impresarios took the trouble to come see for themselves. For them it had to be a direct import from Europe like Menachim Rubin, Itzhak Feld, Dina Halpern, Ola Lillith, Edmund Zayenda, or Leo Fuchs. And even these newcomers were not readily entrusted to carry a show by themselves. They were usually co-starred with older, more established luminaries.

The organization-committees that bought benefit tickets hardly ever cared what play was to be presented. What they wanted to know was: who will be the star? And they insisted on one or more well-publicized names, so they could more easily sell tickets over the summer. Since benefits were the backbone of Yiddish theater, these committees had to be catered to.

Benefits, usually bought in bulk, were sold to the organizations at reduced prices. Of course, the deposits, which were made in advance during the summer, were soon enough "eaten up" by management long before the opening. Along about mid-season, some theaters were often forced to close. The union was thus obliged to appeal to those that were still open to play off the remaining benefits and block tickets for free, or for the remaining balances, if any.

Under such circumstances, no producer or manager could risk jeopardizing his benefit and box-office business by engaging just any Johnny-come-lately to star on Second Avenue.

Season 1935-36

Joe Lasky, the general manager of the McKinley Square Theater, and brother to the actor Max Lasky, offered me a proposition: to join the combination of Schachter, Lasky and Goldstein, as star-director and equal partner to the business.

I would not be required to invest any money, Joe explained, nor be responsible for losses. In consideration, the three partners and I would draw an equal weekly sum, and the profits would be shared equally among the four of us at the end of the season. Having nothing in view for the immediate future, and the theater season almost upon us, I signed the deal.

I was at once confronted with the same old problem—a new play. Considering that "Papirossen" was such a sensation, I was struck by an idea. Why not write a play built around the story of the song? Bella was enthused over it and my partners liked the idea, too. The title, again, caused some differences of opinion, as it had over the song. Some suggested calling it "The Singing Cigarette-Vender" or "The Singing Papirossen-Maker," but I stuck to my idea. "The song," I said, "is called 'Papirossen,' and it's doing just fine, right? So my play will also be called 'Papirossen!'"

To be close to the theater, I moved into a furnished room in the Bronx. Engaging the actor-playwright Isidore Friedman as my collaborator, we promptly got to work on the script.

As a flashback depicting the childhood years of the lead character, I dramatized the story of the song into a short, silent film to be inserted as part of the action on stage.

For the ragged little boy in the story peddling cigarettes, I cast the actor Baruch Lumet's little son, who is now the prominent director of films and television, Sidney Lumet. For the girl portraying the part of Bella as a child, I chose her own little daughter, Anita. The other characters in this silent short were played by Alex Cohen, Leon Hoffenberg and Rose Schachter.

The location we chose was Mrs. Landman's Parkside Hotel in the Catskills. Driving up in three cars to this mountain resort with actors and equipment, we were prepared to shoot a thirty-six millimeter film. Thus, I became a movie director without knowing the first thing about it. With the guidance of our hired camera man, I did the best I could.

To simulate the background of a Russian park, we used a clump of trees and buses near the hotel. We also persuaded a few of the inevitable rubberneckers—who needed no persuasion—to don our rented Russian costumes and take part as passersby. To the relief of my partners, who cried that I was spending too much of their money on the production, these extras did not ask to be paid. They were only too thrilled to be "acting" in a movie. And Mrs. Landman, the proprietress, charged us no more than the regular weekend rates.

The only thing that worked against us was the sunny weather. The song "Papirossen" starts with: "A chilly night, a rainy night, and darkness all around... a shivering boy, huddled against a wall, a little basket in his hands..." And, as if to spite us, the sun shone bright as could be. It left us only one recourse—to become rainmakers. With a little ingenuity and an accommodating plumber on the premises, we accomplished it—we made rain!

The theater patrons who saw this film in the show shed many a tear over the poor orphan boy being drenched by the torrent of rain...

To have a sound track for the film would have been beyond our shoestring budget. So instead, on a long-play transcription, I synchronized the narration and music pertinent to the story. This was played on our P.A. system while the film rolled.

At the end of this fifteen-minute movie, the action resumed live on stage. This was where I did my ballad, "Schweig, Mein Hartz"—Hush, My Heart. This song ultimately became a worldwide sensation in 1948, known as "Nature Boy."

In creating vehicles for myself, I disregarded the old concept that a musical must perforce be mounted on a light-as-feather theme. Aside from the innovation of an inserted movie and other effects, I wove them around a realistic and absorbing tale.

I wound up the play's finale with a colorful fragment of the opera, *Madame Butterfly*. Since royalties for performing Puccini's music was another item not for our budget, my music director "altered" this particular sequence …and since the lyrics were sung in Yiddish, anyway, we hoped to get away with it. But, some competitor must have blabbed, for two gentlemen soon came around toward the end of the show, to convince themselves whether or not we were plagiarizing Puccini. Admittedly, it was close enough, and they came backstage to tell us so. Then, surprise of surprises! One of the gentlemen turned out to be a certain Signore Interrante, Bella's former singing teacher! He did not at first recognize her, in her Japanese raiment, bejeweled wig and Oriental makeup. But he was most proud of his pupil singing "Un bel di…" albeit in Yiddish of all languages! Signore Interrante, representing his opera association, was very kind and settled for a token royalty. It was worth every penny!

Among our group of young and attractive singers and dancers were the talented teenaged sisters, Claire and Merna Bagelman, featured singers on Abe Lyman's WBNX radio station. They later achieved wide acclaim as the Barry Sisters, and recorded many of my songs. Among the young people who volunteered to participate in the show were Marty Lerner and his sister Gladys, whose devoted friendship I value to this day. The business this play brought in had as yet been unprecedented in any local theater. And the highlight for me was the unrestrained applause for my stormy soliloquy, "The Dance of the Devils." It never failed to bring the house down. What more could an actor ask for?!

From every corner of the city, including parts of New Jersey, people came to see *Papirossen*. It's said that, when the Vilna Troupe played Anski's *Dybbuk* in Warsaw, the Polish street-car conductors soon observed where most of the people were getting off. Rather than call out the name of the stop, they alerted the passengers with a loud, "Na Dybbuka!" The same thing now happened in the Bronx. When the trolleys came to a stop at the corner of Boston Road and 169th Street, the motormen bellowed, "Passengers for Papirossen!" And sure enough, most of the crowd got off and made a beeline for the theater!

Incredible!

Once, during an intermission, Joe Lasky popped his head into my dressing room, saying, "Yabby, there's a woman in the theater asking to see you."

"Now, in the middle of the show? I'm sorry," I answered impatiently. "After the performance, please!"

"She says she has regards from Grodno."

"Grodno?" I jumped to my feet, ready to see her right away.

"I'll bring her back later," said Joe and left.

Who could it be? I was in constant touch with my mother, writing to her and sending her money. I had even sent her copies of my published songs. They had my picture on the cover and I knew this would afford her joy and make her proud. My songs had become popular in Grodno too. Some of my old actor-cronies would come to borrow these copies from mother and sing them to her. So who could it be, now in America?

After the show, sure enough, Joe escorted a woman into my dressing room.

"Mister Yablokoff," she began, timidly, "I am Mrs. Stern, and I have regards for you..."

"From Grodno?" I intercepted, eagerly. "Please sit down, Mrs. Stern, and tell me..."

"Well, not exactly from Grodno, but from Druskenik. You surely remember Druskenik."

"Yes, yes, of course. Are you originally from Grodno?"

"I was born there. But I've been a New Yorker now for years, living in the Bronx with my family. My sisters and brothers and the rest are still in Grodno, so I recently visited them. As it was during the summer, I thought I would take a boat-ride to Druskenik for a few days. You know how beautiful it is there in the summer with the sulphur baths and everything. So, one evening, as I sat on a bench under the trees, enjoyed the fragrant air, I thought of my husband and children back in the Bronx and I guess I got a little homesick. Sitting there in the quiet of the evening I began humming to myself—songs that I'd heard you sing on WEVD. I want you to know, Mr. Yablokoff, my family and I traveled from the Bronx to Brownsville to see your shows. So I kept humming your songs, like 'A Briev,' 'Give Me back my Heart,' 'My White Flower'...and softly, I began to sing 'Papirossen.' A woman, sitting near me, turned to stare at me with such a strange look, it sent chills through me. With trembling hands on my shoulders, she gasped, 'Where did you hear that song?'

'In New York...on the radio,' I stammered. 'There's a singer, an actor on the Yiddish stage. He is known as der Payatz. This is his song, Papirossen.'

'And you have seen him?' she asked.

'More than once,' I tried to calm her, she seemed so intense.

'How does he look, please tell me,' the woman pleaded.

'My dear, why are you so upset?' I asked her, 'Do you know him?'

'Do I know him?!' she burst into tears, 'He is my son, my Chaimke!'"

* * *

People were always coming backstage to greet me, and that's how I met

Dr. Max Ehrenberg, his wife Gussie, and their close friend Counselor Emanuel Storm. I immediately touched on the subject constantly on my mind—the worry Jennie and I were going through over Jackie's ear. The doctor, a most congenial man, a dermatologist himself, offered to take us to his friend, a nose, throat and ear specialist, Dr. Martin Ross.

My wife and I were separated by then and in order to take my boy to Dr. Ross, I needed her consent. The following day, of course, she herself brought Jackie to the doctor's office and after a thorough examination, he assured Jennie and me that he was confident about a cure. We had been through this routine time and again, but still we held out hope.

One evening, when Dr. Ehrenberg came into my dressing room, I could tell by the grim look on his face that something was very wrong.

"It's urgent that you and Jennie see Dr. Ross tomorrow. You don't have to bring Jackie."

My heart sank. I had a premonition that something terrible was about to happen. I phoned Jennie, and next morning, Dr. Ehrenberg and I met her in the doctor's office.

"When I first examined the boy," said Dr. Ross, "there was no doubt in my mind that I could clear up his ear condition in a few treatments. I had more X-rays taken this last visit, and I find that he must be operated on as soon as possible."

We were thunderstruck! An operation?! None of the doctors who treated him ever mentioned such a possibility, not even those at Johns Hopkins!

"I'm ready to consult with any other specialist of your choosing, if that's your wish. But, in my opinion, an operation is urgent."

"My God, Jennie," I murmured, "what shall we do?" Stunned, she looked at me, and replied, "I will not let my son be operated on!"

Dr. Ehrenberg arranged a consultation of several prominent physicians, and the necessity for surgery was the unanimous decision. I was in a terrible state, but I had to call Jennie and tell her. Remaining adamant, she again replied, "I will not allow them to operate on my child!" There was hysteria in her voice.

Losing patience, Dr. Ross warned me, saying, "If your wife does not consent to the operation I will be forced to get an emergency court order! Mr. Yablokoff, your son's life is at stake. Can I make that any clearer? He is my responsibility now, he's my patient. If you don't trust me to operate, then get someone else, but do it, dammit!"

I was frantic. Dr. Ehrenberg drove me to the home of my in-laws, and together we finally prevailed upon Jennie to consent to the operation. Losing no time, we took her and Jackie to the Post Graduate Hospital in downtown Manhattan.

The operation dragged on for hours. At last, looking completely spent, Dr. Ross appeared and told us that the operation, thank God, was successful. It was a question of by-passing the most vital nerves.

A few weeks later, his head still swathed in bandages, Jackie was back in school. The kids were most sympathetic and his teacher brought him up to date in his studies. At the end of the term, all vestiges of bandages gone, Jackie was promoted to the next grade together with the rest of his classmates.

* * *

Winter descended upon New York. Attendance at the theater fell off, naturally. But my partners became a little shaky, insisting that we change the play. Twenty-four weeks, they argued, was more than enough in a local house, where people were accustomed to a new show every few weeks.

"What if the new play doesn't go over?" I asked. "Granted, *Papirossen* is not doing the business it did up to now, but we are still covering expenses, our people are being paid their salaries and we are still getting our weekly drawing. The money we saved is still in the bank."

In the long run I had to give in. I produced a new melodrama with music called *The Wedding Night* by Samuel H. Cohen. It did not click, just as I predicted. The phone calls still came in asking for *Papirossen*.

Taking off a hit show that was publicized everywhere for four months was the biggest mistake. And this mistake cost us dearly!

I felt I could still do something with this production elsewhere and strictly on my own. After finishing up at the Hopkinson, I released myself from the McKinley Square partnership.

55

Surprise!

Actors Irving Jacobson and Max Rosenblatt ran the Walnut Street Theater in Philadelphia that season. Barely managing to stay afloat, they awaited the New York attractions for Passover, as a pious Jew awaits the advent of the Messiah.

They booked me into their theater on a percentage deal to star with their company in *Papirossen*. My leading lady, Bella Mysell, was included, and I also brought Chaim'l Parness, the little boy in my show, along with his mother. And, except for my transcribed film, the management supplied everything else I needed for the production: singers and dancers, sets, decor, etcetera.

Israel Mandelkern, whom we called Mandel for short, was the publicity man. While he stirred up the city with his press notices, I did a couple of broadcasts.

The company was exceptionally well suited to the play and *Papirossen* scored the same hit in Philly as it did in the Bronx. We played it through the holiday, and stayed on for many weeks after that, doing Sundays in Baltimore.

At the special midweek matinees, we needed the mounted police to keep order among the crowds that surged around the theater.

I did very well financially, except that, after paying the surgeon and staff of specialists for my son's operation, I was left with pockets bulging with—success! My friends, Dr. and Mrs. Ehrenberg and Counselor Storm, became frequent visitors in Philadelphia.

One Saturday after the matinee, Mandel came rushing into my dressing room flushed with excitement. "Surprise!" he exclaimed. "Do you kow who came to see the show this afternoon? Mr. Edelstein, the owner of the Second Avenue Theater in New York!"

"Edelstein?! Well, well, that is a surprise! What's he doing in Philly? Did he come specially to see my show?"

"What else?" Mandel winked at me. "He asked me to tell you that he's waiting for you over in that big drugstore on the corner. You know, where they have a section of tables for coffee and stuff."

My heart raced as I quickly removed my makeup and changed. I knew that his father, Yosele Edelstein, was old and ailing and that his son, Isidore, a lawyer, was now managing the old man's theater building. Breathlessly, I hurried across the street.

346

"My compliments, Mr. Yablokoff," Isidore Edelstein greeted me and shook my hand as I joined him at a discreet little corner table. "I made a special trip here to catch your show. It's the first time I've seen you on stage."

"You could have seen me in Brooklyn, or in the Bronx, and saved yourself the time and train fare," I joked. "I played *Papirossen* for more than six months at the McKinley Square Theater."

"I know you don't have much time between shows, so I though this was the best place to meet. Well, let me tell you," he said, "during the last few years, we have been renting our Second Avenue Theater to Michael Sachs. We had nothing to do with the production end. Sachs paid us a fixed rental for the house and the rest was his business. Now, as you must know, he died recently, and we are looking for a suitable lessee. There's a lot of talk about you in New York, so I came to see for myself. I must admit, I haven't seen such a crush for tickets in years as I witnessed here today. Yes, sir! The box office! That's what counts! I saw your show this afternoon. Very good. I took special notice of the audience. They ate it up!

"Now, Yablokoff, let us talk openly. Would you be interested in leasing our theater?"

I couldn't believe my ears. Me? At the Second Avenue Theater? Was this a dream?!

"Mr. Edelstein, I thank you for your confidence," I hesitated. "Do you really believe that I am the man to take over your theater? Such a tremendous project demands a lot of capital, which I haven't as yet been able to accumulate."

"I appreciate your frankness," he smiled, peering at me over his bifocals. "Would you care to come into New York for a couple of hours? Maybe we can work something out. Can you see me Monday morning in my office at the theater?"

"By all means," I replied, "I'll be there."

Back in the dressing rooms my colleagues fell all over me. "Well, Yabby, is it in the bag?" "Is mazel tov in order?" "How about engaging me for next season, Mr. Shubert?"

"What did Edelstein say?" asked Bella, eager for the details.

"He saw our performance and liked it. Out of courtesy, I suppose, he asked whether I'd be interested in leasing their theater. Imagine! The Number One House on the Avenue! The temple of Yiddish musicals where all the greats have reigned for decades; a theater that leases for a yearly rental of $75,500, with stars like Molly Picon! Me! With what?" I shrugged. "Nonsense! Anyway, I intend to go into New York early Monday morning. If I don't get to see my son, I'll at least have a long chat with him on the phone. Why not take the train with me, Bella? It will also give you an opportunity to spend some time with your little Anita. We can then meet at Penn Station and be back in Philly for the evening's performance."

Bella

We took the early morning train for New York, and while having a leisurely breakfast in the diner, I said, "You know, I can't help thinking: here I am, dreaming about, thinking about and striving for a chance to make it on Second Avenue, while you, of your own volition, left the so-called Yiddish Broadway. Why?"

"I can tell you why," Bella smiled, "except that I must begin at the beginning. My father, like you, Yabby, also came from Europe as an aspiring young actor. Yiddish theater being so oppressed in Russia, he, like many others, struck out for the land of freedom. Papa was also a poet, a songwriter and playwright."

"I know," I said. "In fact, I took part in one of Hyman Mysell's plays in Lithuania, when I traveled with a wandering troupe. Now I know why the heroine in it was named Bella."

"Yes, my father was a gifted man. In schooling, he stood head and shoulders above his contemporaries, some from his very own town of Odessa. His family had the means to send him to the gymnasia, which was otherwise restricted for Jews.

"In America, he had to begin with menial jobs, like so many others, pressing shirts in a hand laundry. But it wasn't long before he was able to join the Yiddish theater, playing with those who had already made the grade, such as the famed Jacob P. Adler, David Kessler, and others. In later years he wound up his career with Maurice Schwartz at his Yiddish Art Theater. He was outstanding in the roles he played and the critics praised him highly. He was at last involved in the kind of theater he had always dreamed about. Papa also had a book of poems published. I was very proud of my dad and loved him dearly.

"In New York, he met mama, who was from Austria, and they were married. For a Yiddish actor back in the early days, it was a hand-to-mouth existence..."

"Is it any different now?" I chuckled.

"But with mama's uncanny thrift as a homemaker, my parents managed to send my brother Max through law school and provide me—another stage-struck soul like papa—with music and singing lessons.

"I had no thought of joining the Yiddish theater. What for? I asked myself. I am an American, born in New York, why not the American stage?! I auditioned for the Shuberts when I was about eighteen, and was engaged to play minor roles in some musical revivals at the time: *The Chocolate Soldier, Blossom Time,* and *The Rose of Stamboul.* At any rate I was the understudy to the leading lady. But after a while I grew impatient waiting for the prima donnas to take sick, or something. Just my luck, they never did.

"About this time, my father received an urgent letter from his sister in Europe, begging him to help her talented, conservatory-graduated son to come to America, for he saw no future for himself in Russia. And this young man, of course, was my cousin, Alexander Olshanetsky.

My father got all the necessary papers and things in order and sent for his nephew. In the meantime, during all these negotiations, papa's sister and her family migrated to Harbin, China, where countless Jews sought refuge from their restricted life in Russia. Harbin became an oasis for thousands, who regarded it as a springboard to America. So my cousin Shura, as he was called, came to us through Shanghai, by way of the Pacific, instead of crossing the Atlantic as most immigrants had done.

"Shura soon joined the Musicians' Union—officially as a violinist—but he also played the piano like a virtuoso. Until he learned a little English, it was thought that he could play in the orchestra of one of the Yiddish theaters. But even with my father's influence, the Jewish Musicians' Club blocked him. Need I say more? You and Jennie have experienced this yourselves. So the only thing my cousin could do was to play the piano for rehearsals. Naturally, he found this very disheartening, though not for long. His talents as composer and conductor were soon in great demand. And today, of course, he is on the top rung of the ladder, with all kinds of offers from the American theaters.

"Well, one day, while he was still pounding the piano at the National Theater, rehearsing a musical by Peretz Sandler, I came to meet him so we could go home together. I was still his guide and interpreter. Finding me waiting in the office, he told me with great excitement that the prima donna of the show had had a violent disagreement with the management and had left the theater in a huff. So, if ever I had the chance of a lifetime, he said, this was it!

"Before I knew it, I was up on stage, and with Shura at the piano—"Svengali" I called him—I opened my mouth and sang for the producers. With only two weeks to go before the premiere of the operetta, *Mendel in Japan,* I was engaged to play opposite the star, Aaron Lebedeff!

"Shura and I seemed so right for each other, we got married that summer of 1924. After that, with my husband already holding the position of composer-conductor, we worked together at the National Theater season after season. Everyone looked upon us as the ideal couple: 'He writes such beautiful songs for her to sing and smiles up at her from his podium. How charming, how idyllic!'

"Well, it was—for a while. But, after about nine years of marriage, things began to fall apart. We no longer could see eye to eye about a lot of things. I found that under such painful circumstances we could not possibly work together anymore. The managers understood my feelings and—like it or not—they had to let me go. All other theaters on the avenue had their own key people, so when I got a bid from Skulnik, I took the engagement at the Hopkinson, in Brooklyn.

"Now you know why I left our Broadway. My divorce is pending. Luckily, I have my dear cousin Molly and her two little daughters living in the house with me, so I know my child is in good hands. At least I have peace of mind about her when I have to travel."

Bella and I had just meandered back to our seats, when the conductor bellowed, "Penn Station! New York!"

56

Only in America!

A s I entered the ornate and spacious lobby of the Second Avenue Theater,
I was impressed all over again by its grandeur, its capacity of 1,970
seats, the roomy orchestra pit, the loges, the two balconies serviced
by ample elevators. Above all, I was awed by the huge stage, suitable for the
most extravagant production.

In the office just off the lobby, I found Isidore Edelstein, his brother Alex
and the benefit manager, Philip Schneider waiting for me.

"Mr. Yablokoff," said Isidore, "I know you don't have too much time to
spend in New York, so we'll make it short. Are you interested in leasing our
theater?"

"Interested? And how!" I smiled. "My problem is how to swing it moneywise."

"We'll make it very accessible. Instead of a straight rental, which is surely
above your means, we are willing to take a chance and lease the theater to
you on a percentage basis. Let us say, 12½ percent from the top. For our 12½
percent, we will rent you the 'house' only. For the rest, you will be solely
responsible. We are only the landlords."

"Agreed!" I jumped at the proposition, figuring that, on a percentage deal,
I would need less to invest.

I knew well enough that in any deal, the lessee is expected to put down
security to assure the landlord that he will abide by all the conditions in the
lease, but I tried to wriggle out of it.

"Security? Why security?" I played naive. "You can collect your 12½
percent at every performance. Do you need better security than that? If I had
the means, security would be no obstacle. You know my circumstances, Mr.
Edelstein. I told you in Philadelphia that I'm not a capitalist... as yet."

"Look," he said, "as soon as you sign the lease, you will immediately have
access to thousands of dollars from the benefit deposits, which Phil Schneider
has already booked for the coming season. And mind you, this is before it is
known who the star will be in our theater next season. These deposits will
first begin to come in heavily over the summer. So you'll be able to help
yourself..."

"Oh no, not that! I won't touch the benefit money until the performances
have been played off. I'll have a big enough headache scrounging up a loan

to run the theater through the summer while preparing a new production for the September opening. How can I worry now about getting a loan to be tied up in security?"

Isidore and Alex excused themselves and went out into the lobby, while Schneider, without a word took a thick ledger out of a cabinet and showed me a list of organizations that had booked dates for the coming season.

"As soon as we know who our top attraction will be, I can sell benefits and block tickets," he boasted, "to the tune of over $100,000. Look, you can see for yourself. These are the figures for last year's benefits."

"If a Yiddish theater is able to bring in such a fortune from benefit tickets," I asked, "why do we find it so difficult to exist?"

"Well, in addition to the benefits, it is also essential to have a really good play, a strong enough hit to make people run to buy tickets at the box office. With the kind of theater fare that has been cooked up here in the last few seasons," Schneider grimaced, "we didn't stand a chance of drawing people to the box office."

The Edelstein brothers came back. "Would you be kind enough," Isidore asked me, "to come and visit my father? Without his consent we can't do anything, anyway. I think my father should be apprised of what our issue is all about. Please come, it's not far from here and it won't take long."

The door to his apartment on upper Second Avenue was opened by his wife, actress Paulina Edelstein.

"My Yosele, poor dear, is not well," she sighed, "but do come in, Mr. Yablokoff. He is confined to his bed."

And there, in the dimness of his bedroom, lay the legendary pioneer of the Yiddish theater. Beneath the bedclothes, I discerned the shrunken frame of a body no bigger than a child's. Only his head, with the sparse wisps of gray, loomed large as it rested on the pillow. His eyes, alive and penetrating, fastened their gaze on me.

"Papa," said Isidore, raising his voice almost to a shout, "this is the young man, the actor I told you about. His name is Yablokoff. Yablokoff!" he repeated even louder. "My father is paralyzed, and he doesn't hear well. Papa," he resumed, "Mr. Yablokoff wants to lease our theater. He doesn't have any money, no security, either. What do you say, papa?"

Yosele didn't take his eyes from me. Finally, he made the effort to speak.

"Yabokoff," he mispronounced my name, "you want my theater!" I nodded. "In my theater, one must invest money. A lot of money...a lot of security."

"You are right, Mr. Edelstein," I spoke up good and loud. "I wish I had something to invest. I told your son that I have no money. I'm willing to work hard, but..."

"Tell me, Yabokoff, can you get fifteen-hundred dollars, somewhere? A thousand maybe? It's not the money, understand. In business you have to show goodwill. It doesn't look good, otherwise."

"Well, maybe I can scrape together a thousand," I replied in order to show that I was a businessman. "I will need a lot of money to run the theater before we open. The benefit money, as I told your son, I absolutely refuse to touch. That money is not mine," I threw in as a strong point, "until the booked performances are played off!"

"Isidore, give him the theater!" Yosele commanded in a croaking voice. "Yabolkoff, I like you. Come closer. It's hard for me to talk. You can't lease a theater with a yearly rental of $75,000 dollars without security, understand? You get yourself a thousand dollars. Fifteen-hundred is still better! When you'll need the money, Isidore will give it back to you. You hear, Isidore? You should give it back to him! Don't wait too long, young man. I have plenty of bidders for the theater, but I don't want them."

"I'll be back in the office in about an hour," I told Isidore. "If I get the money, we will close the deal this very day."

Taking leave of the Edelsteins, Yosele called after me, "Come to see me Yabolkoff! Come up so we can talk. I like you...you're a self-made man. I was also a self-made man."

With the old pioneer's encouraging words ringing in my ears, I came out on the street completely bewildered. Where on earth, and from whom, could I borrow money on such short notice?! I was fully determined to plunk down fifteen-hundred just to show that...oh, I know! It suddenly dawned on me...the Ehrenbergs! They were the closest friends I had. Finding a booth, I rang them up and related the whole story. To my relief, they were only too happy to let me have the money.

Overjoyed, I hurried to the office and asked Isidore to draw up the lease. As soon as Dr. Ehrenberg arrived with the precious check, we shook hands and closed the deal. I made a quick call to my son and the doctor drove me to Pennsylvania Station. I couldn't believe that all this had really happened.

"Wish me luck, Bella!" I exclaimed when I met her at the train gate. "It's in the bag! I signed a lease for the Second Avenue Theater!"

Excited beyond words, she threw her arms around me and kissed me, as we ran to board the train for Philadelphia. We both knew that we were a team offstage now, as well as on, and that, from here on in, nothing could separate us!

For the weekend, the Ehrenbergs and Counselor Storm came out to Philly. After the show, as we sat in Uhr's Kosher Restaurant, I asked Pat Storm to take charge of the necessary legal arrangements for my enterprise.

"Yabby," said Gussie Ehrenberg, "would you consider taking us in as partners in your theater business?"

"You?! Partners in the theater?" I laughed. "You're my friends! I certainly wish you a better—and safer—kind of business! I'm an actor, so I take chances. Theater business is a bigger gamble than cards or horse betting!"

"Yabby, we appreciate your frankness and we are aware of the risk," said Storm, "but we have great confidence in you and your ability. Dr. and Mrs.

Ehrenberg are looking for an investment and I too would gladly invest as much as I can. To bet on a horse like you," he chuckled, "we're ready to run the risk. As long as I am your attorney, you may as well get used to taking my advice. Let's form a corporation and become partners. Well, what do you say?"

What was there for me to say? We drank to it and wished one another mazel tov!

The April 17, 1936 *New York Press* carried the news: "Herman Yablokoff, new producer-actor and director, leases the foremost Yiddish playhouse in America, the Second Avenue Theater."

"Only in America," I said to myself, "only in America!"

57

Germany, April 1947

Upon reaching the entrance to the Munich autobahn this bright spring day, the ambulance stubbornly ground to a halt. The old military vehicle, having done its hitch in the American Army, was inherited after the war by the JOINT, now functioning in Europe. The large letters on either side of the ambulance read: AMERICAN JOINT DISTRIBUTION COMMITTEE—SPECIAL SERVICE—DO NOT DELAY.

Its four passengers were Hans, the driver, a native of Germany whose parents were Jewish; Arzewski, a pianist from Poland; Mishka, a partisan from Russia; and me, an actor from the United States.

Hands, doggedly bore down on the gas pedal, getting only some spluttering noises. Then, with a huffing and puffing in the transmission, the motor came alive, and off we went.

The autobahn! The same highway over which had sped, so recently, the triumphant mechanized German armies on the blitzkrieg to devastate the entire world. On this magnificent expressway, hundreds upon thousands of martyrs—Jews and non-Jews—were herded together from various countries to breathe their last. By their sweat and blood, the marrow of their bones, they were forced to build this infamous monument to German civilization... the autobahn!

The ambulance, except for its wide windshield and small windows in the side doors, where my chauffeur and I sat, was closed in all around.

I turned to check on the other two in my crew. On a long bench behind me sat Arzewski and Mishka. Stretching his neck over my head, Mishka tried to catch a glimpse of the passing panorama; while Arzewski, his eyes closed, his hands resting on the lid of the upright piano that stood wedged in front of them, looked as if he were playing the instrument in his sleep.

Snuggling into the military greatcoat so solicitously thrown over my shoulders by Mishka, my dresser, I gazed at the picturesque landscape that rolled past me. The autobahn, winding its way through field and forest, curving snake-like around the slopes of the snow-capped Alps, spreads its multibranched intersections throughout the land of the Amalekites—the Germans. Like a keen sword it cut through cities, towns and villages clear to the frontier of its neighboring countries, but transportation to the camps was practically nonexistent.

The Jewish DP camps in Germany were spread out in far-flung, remote regions. In addition to my difficulty in securing the necessary travel orders

from the American Army of Occupation, there was the problem of finding
a suitable vehicle to carry out my mission. Considering we had to cart a group
of three, a piano, a public address system and changes of wardrobe for my concert tour, Sam Gaber, the director of the JOINT in Munich, decided that the
most convenient conveyance for my expedition to the DP camps would be—
an ambulance.

A Mirage

Dusk fell on the autobahn. A pale moon rose and was soon swallowed
by clouds that darkened the sky and the road ahead. It was quiet in the ambulance. Hans put on more speed—a risky thing to do. The ambulance could
easily topple over. The steady droning of the motor lulled me into drowsiness
and my thoughts began to wander. They carried me back across the thousands
of miles home to New York. I thought of my son, Jack, now first cellist with
the Buffalo Symphony Orchestra. I recalled the short visit with him in Buffalo
before leaving for my mission in Europe. I attended one of his concerts at the
newly built Kleinhaus Music Hall, with guest soloist Yasha Heifetz and William
Steinberg, conductor. What joy and pride I felt, having my son, a Juilliard student, now playing with such a noted symphony orchestra!

My thoughts dwelt on my wife, Bella, to whom I was now married, and
her young daughter, Anita, whom I regarded as my very own and who was
devoted to me like a true daughter. Nita, as we call her, was now an English
teacher at Washington Irving High School in Manhattan.

I thought of my sister Mary, her husband, her family...of my colleagues
in the Yiddish theater...

The glaring headlight of oncoming trucks blinded us as they roared by.
Hans flicked on the brights and the ambulance sped on its way to the "valley
of tears," to the 250,000 Jews who were still confined to the concentration camps
of Germany and Austria. No one wanted them, no one needed them...aban-
doned by their liberators and the entire world.

Resting my head against the windowsill, my eyes sleepily followed the
yellow lines that divided the highway into lanes. The ambulance's powerful
headlights threw long beams along the road, piercing the blackness of the night.

Out of the autobahn's endless distances there seemed to emerge mysterious silhouettes. Wraith-like, they floated in and out of a bottomless pit—
appearing and disappearing. Mesmerized, I followed the misty figures as they
took on familiar faces...faces of my dearest ones, whose features are forever
carved in my memory. My mother...father...my brothers, sisters, their husbands, wives...their children...oh, all those poor children! They reached out
to me, "Come my son, my surviving son, my Chaimke! Come, brother, come,
uncle...you have traveled all the way from America to search for our remains?
Our ashes are scattered all over Poland, Germany, Kelbasin, Auschwitz, Treblinka, Buchenwald, Bergen-Belsen, Dachau..."

A screech from the swerving ambulance startled me. It shook me back from this macabre mirage to the tragic reality! Not a trace of any of my dear ones. All of them gone, perished, while I, with the same blood in my veins, nurtured by the same mother, have remained alive. Why? Why was I destined to remain alive?

The motor roared and the wheels, spinning faster and faster, could not overtake the spinning thoughts in my brain. Why have I remained alive? Was it the road I chose to travel after leaving home? The wandering road around the world with Yiddish theater? Where was I when all this horror took place? I was absorbed in furthering my career, seeking fame and fortune, and as ignorant of the massacres as the rest of the Western world.

With the Remnants of the Holocaust

The huge barracks in the German DP camp where I was to give my first concert was packed to the rafters. People stood wedged elbow to elbow, with many of them hanging in at the windows. The wide doors were flung open so that the hundreds who could not squeeze in might snatch at least a look. They could also listen to the goings-on outdoors, over the loudspeakers perched on the roof of my ambulance. The camp police, Jewish DPs themselves, stood helpless, unable to cope with the overwhelming sea of humans. It seemed as if the whole camp of ten to twelve thousand inmates had massed in a protest against the entire world—and against even me.

On a makeshift platform, arrayed in my clown costume, I stood in front of the microphone silent, utterly bewildered. Unaware that my accompanist, Arjewski, had several times repeated the introduction to my opening number, "Let me Live," I remained frozen. Never before, not even when I'd had to do a performance on the very day I learned of my father's death, did I feel so much like a clown! Choking back my emotion I stood face to face with the thousands of despairing DPs in the Hindenburg Kaserne.

Men, unshaven and ragged, women, gaunt and threadbare, children clinging to their mothers in awe, and mothers, with suckling infants at their breasts, were all eyeing me with hostility. They had come to stare at still another "savior!" Their piercing glances seemed to rail: "We are sick and tired of the American committees, delegations and commissions who come to gawk at us as if we were zoo animals! All they do is sigh, cry and cluck their tongues over our misfortune. They promise us deliverance, yet here we are, still rotting in the concentration camps! Today, we have the honor of meeting a brand new guest from America—a clown if you please! Well, clown, have you come to entertain us? That's a laugh! It is we who are the clowns at whom the world laughs! Better tell us, American clown, how long are we to starve and wallow in filth on this bloody German soil?"

I stood there, wishing I could run from this platform, away from their accusing glances blazing with resentment at me—me, a member of the outside world who was keeping them imprisoned. What am I doing here? Why did I come to this "valley of tears"? It had been sheer madness to impose on so many friends in New York, and knock on the doors of the State Department in Washington and the JOINT in Paris, begging them to help me give free concerts in the German DP camps.

They had remonstrated, "Do you suppose the Jews in the camps are in the mood for entertainment? They need food packages, clothing, medication, teachers, homes for the orphans."

How right they were! It was indeed foolish. Here I was, rigged out as a clown, with yet more costume changes in my program down to sporting high hat and tails!

Once again Arzewski attacked the introduction to my opening of the program. Paying it no attention, I took heart and in an anguished voice addressed the crowd:

"My dear fellow Jews, I have not brought you the liberation you have been waiting for. I have not brought you the food packages and the clothing you so desperately need. I have not brought you any British certificates to get you legally to Palestine nor visas to America. In short, much to my great sorrow, I have not brought you the freedom you long for.

"My dear people," I continued, "in all sincerity, tell me, how can I, a Yiddish actor with the stage name Der Payatz bring you the things so vital to you, when a world that kept silent during the massacre of our brothers and sisters, when the representatives of the same world, sitting at the United Nations, spouting hypocritical sermons on brother love, justice and quality for mankind, can still look with indifference at the plight suffered by the remnants of the Holocaust, weltering even now in these miserable camps?

"True enough, the electrical currents in the barbed wires surrounding you have been disconnected and the camps are now known as 'Displaced Persons' camps. But, for you they remain the same gruesome concentration camps as before!"

The applause that broke out was soon quelled by cries of, "Hush! Quiet! Let us hear!"

"You are part of the 250,000 Jewish martyrs," I went on, "broken in health and spirit, cut off from the outside world and sentenced to squat here on this accursed soil, soaked with the blood of our dearest ones—yours and mine. So, I ask you, when the world remains silent, how can I, a native of Grodno myself, who lost his own dearest ones in this horror, bring you salvation?"

The barracks shook with thunderous and appreciative applause. The crowd, like an ocean wave, pressed closer to where I stood, a sort of wonderment in their eyes. My years of professional experience told me that I had struck the right chord. I had openly expressed the despair and anger rankling in their hearts, an anger directed at everyone and at themselves as well.

"My esteemed brothers and sisters," I resumed with more assurance, "I have not come to you as an American philanthropist, or politician. I have come as a Jew to his fellow Jews in despair. As a Jewish actor, I deem it my duty and a privilege to be the first from the United States to appear before you as I have appeared these many years for our people around the world. I fervently pray that we may meet again in the near future when all of you are free. Of one thing you may be certain—the Jewish communities in the free world have not forsaken you, and never will! In my role as Der Payatz, permit me to help you forget for a while your sorrows. I too am a wandering Jew, a displaced person. Even the initials of my stage title, Der Payatz, happen to be D.P."

Nodding to Arzewski, I began my program with "Lost Mich Lebn"—Let me Live. In song and recitation I depicted a meeting at the United Nations, where a Jew is beseeching the representatives of the world to "Let me Live" ...thereby recounting how the Jew had given the world some of the greatest personalities, who had enriched mankind in every phase of life...science, art, music, literature, medicine, as well as the Ten Commandments and, for many people in the world, their Son of God, Jesus Christ! After all that we have contributed to the world, we Jews demand—Let us Live!!!

This intensely dramatic composition was met by a storm of applause. An elderly Jew, standing at the edge of the platform, spoke up. "My son," he said in tears, "you understand us. You feel our misery. Please talk to us. It's been so long since we heard such beautiful Yiddish. Tell us about the free world. About America. Please talk to us!"

"Brothers and sisters," I addressed them again, "I must caution you that, in the outside world, the Jewish people still have many enemies who are waiting for you to lose courage, to give up hope and fall into despair. Do not give anyone this satisfaction. Despair and resignation are the most dangerous pitfalls in your crucial hour. Deliverance will come despite all our enemies!

"And now that we understand each other, let me tell you that I have not come entirely empty-handed. To lift your morale, I have brought you the token gift of a lively little song called "Nisht Gezorgt"—Don't worry...don't despair. I will sing it for you. Now then, my friends, what is the gift the Clown has brought you from America? Let me hear it from the men, women and children!" With sparkling eyes and great gusto, the entire crowd roared, "Nisht Gezorgt! We won't despair!"

All barriers between the audience and me were finally done away with. Breathing easier I launched into the rest of my three-hour program of folk and theater songs, with the crowd joining me in a sing-along. I also did some dramatic excerpts from I.L. Peretz, and Leivik, humorous monologues and anecdotes by Sholem Aleichem and others. At certain compositions women silently wept, while men brushed away a tear with their sleeves. But soon again, the barracks rang with laughter and shouts of "Nisht Gezorgt. We will not Despair!"

* * *

Late at night, after this initial concert for the survivors of the Holocaust, my crew and I packed ourselves off in our ambulance. The camp could not accommodate us for the night; so, tired as we were, hungry and emotionally drained, we sped along the autobahn back to Munich.

Thoughts whirled round in my head. How strange were the paths into which fate had maneuvered me these many years. How appropriate, I contemplated, was my tag title, The Clown, through which I could bring a bit of cheer, by way of laughter and tears, to the thousands of Jewish survivors in Germany, Austria and Italy! Was I destined to come here and share the sad lot of the remnants of Jewry, in order to atone for my spared life?

I could not block out the deplorable picture I'd encountered on this first camp concert. How meaningless, I thought, was man's striving toward ideals, toward building up hope for the future, trying to carve out a life of beauty for our children, when it can all collapse. Did justice mean anything? Did heritage, history, culture and art teach us anything? Didn't Germany's highly cultured and dedicated stage artists sell their theater's very soul to Hitler and convert it into a propaganda machine to slaughter the Jewish race?!

Where was I during the terror when I believed I had attained my goal, and was sitting on top of the world? But was I really?

It seemed only yesterday that I reveled in landing the "big one." That was the season of 1936-37, when I leased the Second Avenue Theater. Yes, ten years had rolled by... and what unforgettable years they were.

58

On Top of the World?

The news that I had taken over the most prominent Yiddish theater in America hit the Cafe Royale like a bombshell. The kibitzers had a field day. "Yablokoff," they joked, "will last there about as long as a snowball in hell!"

Finishing up my engagement in Philadelphia, I returned to New York, whereupon Edelstein and I promptly went up to the Hebrew Actors' Union to report our business deal. Guskin greeted us courteously, but coldly. The nature of our visit was no secret to him. He knew about it before I could even call him from Philadelphia. He was obviously miffed because I had made the deal without having him mediate the transaction.

He informed us that the union was calling a conference of all theater managers, representatives of the United Hebrew Trades and the Yiddish press. The union, he explained, was going to propose a plan to stop the unscrupulous tactics pertaining to the sale of benefits in Yiddish theaters.

It struck Edelstein and me as fishy. Why now, when I had become the director of a theater that sold the greatest number of benefits, did the union suddenly decide to put a stop to the skulduggery that had existed for years?

Guskin also informed me that, according to the union laws, I would have to engage at least sixteen actors with a minimum guaranteed season of thirty-six consecutive weeks.

"What if my play requires a cast of only twelve?" I asked naively. "What will the rest of the actors do?"

"Do? They will collect wages," Guskin smiled. "This working condition in your union agreement is not just for you alone. All the theaters on the avenue must engage the same number of union members."

"Well, meanwhile, I can report that I have already engaged Bella Mysell as my co-star. You have probably heard that Bella and I will be married in the near future. I hope there is no union rule against that. I will bring you a list of performers I intend to engage as soon as I have decided on the opening play."

Back in the theater, Edelstein introduced me to his wife, actress Annie Thomashefsky, a handsome woman with big, black sparkling eyes. I deemed it a privilege to meet the sister of the founder of Yiddish theater in America, Boris Thomashevsky.

* * *

My son, Jackie, was fully recovered from his ear operation, which afforded me great peace of mind. I could now go ahead and work on a play for my Second Avenue Theater. In fact, on one of my visits, my son, who still lived with his mother at the home of his grandparents, surprised me with the news that he was studying the cello.

"Why the cello?" I asked Jennie. "He was studying the piano, wasn't he?"

"Well, it's like this," she laughed, "we organized our own family quartet and quintet. Uncle Max plays first violin, Manny, second violin, grandpa plays viola and Davie and I play the piano. So we needed a cellist, and Jackie was it!"

I was still living alone in the Bronx. Dr. and Mrs. Ehrenberg watched over me with parental care. Bella had taken little Nita and gone to spend the summer in Los Angeles with her brother Max and his family. We often spoke on the telephone and discussed the progress I was making in the theater.

I completed the script for my new production, based on the theme of another of my popular songs, "The Dishwasher." In discussing plays with Edelstein, I learned that, during the years of his father's activity as a producer on the avenue, he always opened the season with a repertory play, holding off the new production until after the High Holidays. An idea struck me. Why should I risk producing a new, untried play at the very beginning of the season? What if it doesn't click? I'd be finished before I had even begun. Why not start the season with one of my tried-and-true successes, which would establish me on the avenue?

I consulted with Edelstein. Since he collected his rent on a percentage basis from the gross income, he of course had the right to object to my opening with a revival.

"What do you think of opening with *Papirossen*?" I tried sounding him out. "My song, 'Papirossen,' is still going strong on the radio, and there are countless requests for the play from my listeners."

To my surprise, Edelstein did not oppose the idea. In fact, he had thought about it himself, he admitted. The only vehement protest against it came from our benefit manager, Phil Schneider.

"You'll ruin the benefit business," he argued. "The organizations will not buy benefits, or block tickets, for a revival. Especially with such competition on the avenue this season. We must have a new show!"

Despite his protests, Edelstein and I decided to open with *Papirossen*. And I went about my business of engaging my company.

Leo Fuchs

One morning, having breakfast at Gus's, a restaurant next to the theater, I saw come in the young Polish guest star, Leo Fuchs. I asked him to sit down and join me.

"What brings you out so early? Haven't you heard that actors are supposed to sleep late? I'm a producer-director now with plenty on my mind to keep me awake nights. But what's your excuse?"

"It's not that easy to sleep in your America. There are many things I have to take care of today. I'm going back to Poland. In Poland, I'm the greatest, but in America, I don't stand a chance."

"Look, my friend, America hardly needs my defense, but I'm sorry to hear that you are leaving with such a bitter feeling. I don't think you have a justified complaint. You made success here, all right. That the impresario, Michael Sachs, who engaged you, died was an act of God, so why blame America?"

"There's more to it than that."

"When do you plan to leave?" I asked, an idea beginning to sprout in my head. "Maybe you should consider taking an engagement with me here, at the Second Avenue Theater."

"Well, I..." stammered Fuchs, looking confused at this sudden proposal. "I've already bought my steamship ticket. The union knows that I'm going back. I'm not a member, you know."

"Leave all those details to me," I said, becoming even more enthused with my idea. "You just decide whether you want to take this engagement. Think about it. Let's meet somewhere this evening. Would you enjoy a really good Russian sweatbath? How about meeting right across the street at the Second Avenue Baths? We can steam ourselves 'po Russky' and talk over my proposition."

That evening, taking advantage of all the bracing conveniences at the Baths, we spent the night there and woke up refreshed. Upon leaving, I had, tucked in my pocket, a signed agreement with Leo Fuchs for the coming season, as another co-star at my Second Avenue Theater.

Ilia Trilling

For *Papirossen,* my opening show, I, of course, had the score. My problem was whom could I engage as composer and conductor for my new, as yet unnamed, production? Bella called my attention to a talented young man who had previously worked with her at the National Theater under Olshanetsky. She recommended him highly, describing him as a jack-of-all-trades: actor, choreographer, composer, conductor and pianist. His name was Ilia Trilling. I had a feeling that he might be just the man for me.

Trilling was a pleasant-looking, sturdily built man in his early forties and uncommonly modest. At the proposition that he become my composer-conductor, he wavered. "The position as conductor I would gladly accept. But, to assume the responsibility as composer... You see, I've been working as a stop-gap for everything: rehearsing the principals and chorus, helping out with the orchestrations and conducting the show when Maestro Olshanetsky had other commitments. I also understudied the actors, so that if one got sick... actually, I came to the United States as a choreographer... not as good as my brother, now a noted choreographer on Broadway. I don't want you to think that I consider myself an expert in all these chores I do, but it's a living. I would love to compose music for the Yiddish theater—it's been my ambition for years..."

"Well then, I'm offering you the opportunity to do just that. My first production is scored and ready, so you will only have to conduct. And you will be able to devote the entire summer toward composing the score for my next show. I will give you the script and you can get to work immediately. I will help you all I can."

"There is yet another problem. I am engaged for the summer as music director at Camp Boiberik. I won't be able to come in to New York very often."

I set his mind at ease, "I will come out to see you. It will also give me a chance to spend a day or two in the country."

That was how I engaged a new and talented musician, whose compositions in the course of a few seasons proved to be the most popular in Yiddish theater—Ilia Trilling.

Yiddish Theater Business

According to the figures presented by Phil Schneider, the benefit sales, covering a season of thirty-six weeks, came to about $400,000—a staggering sum for Yiddish theater in New York. Through the benefits alone, the organizations brought in over a million dollars.

For decades, however, the benefit business had been in a chaotic state. To remedy the situation, the union proposed that the producers organize a mutual pot for the benefits, and that each producer receive a share from this pool whether or not he sold benefits. This would automatically stop the cutthroat competition, and everything would be hunky-dory.

Stable prices were established. And, in order to boost sales at the box office, no theater was allowed to play the current weekend show for the benefits in the middle of the week. Determining the size of the share allotted each theater out of the common pot was no easy task, for each producer claimed that his was the finest theater, the greatest stars and the most expensively elaborate production of the season, which was bound to bring him a fortune in benefit business all on his own. This, therefore, entitled him to the biggest share of the pot. Despite the fact that my theater had a vast capacity, and that Phil Schneider was reputed to be the number one benefit salesman, the other producers demanded an equal share with me.

I visited old man Edelstein again, and he warned me that my competitors would try to "give me the business." Taking his advice, I fought them tooth and nail. Finally, they agreed to divide the percentage of the common pot according to each theater's benefits sales of the previous years. And, since the Second Avenue Theater had always sold the most benefits, I was to receive the biggest share.

Yosele Edelstein, the one-time giant of the Yiddish theater also said, "Don't worry, Yabolkoff, after New Year's, the pot will only be a pot to pee in!"

59

The Thirteen Unions

The Yiddish theaters had to employ a quota of members from thirteen separate theatrical unions: the smallest of which could, if so motivated, call a strike, picket and bye-bye theater! The members of these thirteen unions had to be employed for the entire season, whether or not they were needed. These were the quotas for the theaters on the Second Avenue strip:

1) Hebrew Actors' Union: For the large-capacity houses—sixteen members minimum. Smaller houses—twelve members minimum.
2) Stagehands Union: nine men minimum. (I had played the same show in Brooklyn and the Bronx with five men and even these were far from overworked.)
3) Musicians' Union: ten members minimum. (What if I play a drama with no music at all?)
4) Chorus Union: ten members minimum. (For a musical, I can understand this. But for a dramatic show?)
5) Dressers' Union: three dressers—two men and a woman. (Three people to press and sew on a button?)
6) Ushers' Union: ten ushers minimum. (What if business is so slow that there are very few customers to show to their seats?) No matter—ten ushers!
7) Doormen's Union: three doormen—two stationed at the regular entrance and one for the balcony and gallery. (What will these three doormen do if there are no patrons to admit?) Well, then, they'll kibitz in the lobby... but three doormen!
8) Managers and Cashiers' Union: five members. Two cashiers, a benefit manager, a Yiddish publicity man and, if English publicity is needed, an extra man. And last but not least, a general manager. (Suppose I myself am the general manager? Am I not permitted to manage my own business?) Sorry, a general manager—union!
9) Special Policemen's Union: one policeman. (Thank goodness for that! But what is he needed for?) To keep order, so that the customers behave like civilized people when they line up at the box office. (This gave me a laugh. Thousands of dollars were spent on advertisement, begging people to come to the theater. Must they then be intimidated by a uniformed cop for being too slow to put their money down and pick up their tickets? Why not call out the National Guard?)

The rest of the unions, with their by-laws and working agreements, were:
10) Superintendents' Union (maintenance and cleaning).
11) Billposters' Union (distributing posters and show cards).
12) Printer's Union (posters and all advertising material).
13) Scenic Artists' Union.

Surely, none of us were against unions. The actors and even the bosses, for the most part, were union people themselves. It was the attitude toward the Yiddish theater that was so aggravating.

My biggest struggle was with the Yiddish Chorus, one of the first unions in the United States. At our very first encounter in my office, I made my demands quite clear to their representatives.

"I want young, attractive girls and boys, good singers and dancers for my productions. I will not have your plump mommas cavorting on my stage!"

"What do you mean, you want?! What are we supposed to do with our regular members? Our chorus girls are all right for everyone else, except for you? For you they're of no use anymore?!"

They ran to complain to Guskin and to the United Hebrew Trades. The answer they got was "Yablokoff is a tough customer. Try and get along with him."

The leaders of their union were obliged to go and find some attractive girls and boys uptown, Jewish and non-Jewish, who could sing and dance. Trilling and I selected twelve among them, who became union members. And for the first time in the Yiddish theater, the chorus line was handpicked and well matched. Then I engaged eight men and women from the chorus union with really good voices, to sing only in the background.

When their elderly union leaders were asked by the other producers: "How come you gave in to that Yablokoff?" they replied, "He knows what he wants, 'that' Yablokoff. He deserves credit!"

That was the first credit I received on Second Avenue.

* * *

Ilia Trilling had already begun work on the score of my next scheduled production. He also volunteered to re-orchestrate the score of *Papirossen* according to the instrumentation of the augmented orchestra.

I acquired a second-hand Chrysler and learned to drive. As soon as I received my driver's license, I ventured forth on the open highways to Rhinebeck, New York, to visit Trilling at Camp Boiberik. Arriving there in one piece, miraculously, I asked for the music director, Mr. Trilling.

"You'll find him in his forest shack up there, on that steep hill," I was told. "And better warn him that you're coming. He likes to roam around in his hideaway, stark naked."

"Trilling!" I hollered, as I trudged up the hill. Peeking out to see who had the audacity to disturb his solitude, he spotted me and ducked back in, grabbed a robe and blushing like a bride, explained, "Here, in the quiet of my 'aerie,'" he smiled, "I get my inspiration to compose the music for your new production."

Sitting with him in his little shack and listening as he played several tunes on the weathered piano that had been hoisted up the hill for his work, I whole-heartedly subscribed to his stalking the woods in the nude, à la Tarzan. His catchy melodies were imbued with a freshness that went straight to the heart.

* * *

The idea of opening the season with a revival did, in fact, slow down our benefit business during the summer. Phil Schneider, who regarded himself as a star benefit salesman, took this drop as a personal reflection on his reputation.

"As long as we'll be getting our share of the mutual pot, anyway," said Edelstein, "who cares if we do sell less benefit tickets!"

I tried to reason with Schneider. "Old man Edelstein, himself, told me that, in the beginning of a season, and in the best of times, he lost ten to fifteen thousand dollars. At least I will have the chance of opening with a proven hit; especially now, with a co-star like Leo Fuchs, no less, with dancers, chorus, enlarged orchestra... So, even if I lose money in the beginning, I still have the hope of realizing profit out of the box-office business."

During rehearsal I was delighted with the members of my company. For some, this was their first opportunity to play on Second Avenue. They all put heart and soul into their parts. Leo Fuchs, however, was not too happy with his role. To please him, I padded his part with special material suited to his own unique style.

The premiere of *Papirossen* was a sellout. The audience loved the show and everyone in it. We were thrilled. The advance sales were far better than we expected. Still, I planned to run the show only about three or four weeks; enough to give me time to prepare my new production.

On press night, the house was packed again. The audience, enthusiastic as ever, demanded curtain call after curtain call. We could hardly wait for the reviews in Friday's theater section of the Yiddish press. A black Friday for me! Most of the critics tore the show to shreds. And even those who had praised it when they reviewed it at the McKinley concluded with: "It is too heavy for Second Avenue." A few did find some merit in the production as a whole, as well as in the company. And some even had a kind word for me, the new face on the avenue.

My only consolation was the steady ringing of the telephones, with peo-ple calling for reservations weeks in advance. Feeling crushed, I went to seek solace from my fatherly friend, old man Edelstein.

"Laugh it off. Don't mind the critics. Haven't you heard the old saying: 'Today's newspaper is tomorrow's herring wrapping?' The audience likes your show? Good! So pull yourself together. Mark my words, according to the box office, you'll be playing this show for weeks. And tell my sons, Isidore and

Alex, not to lose their pants and not to listen to Schneider. Let your competitors play for the benefits. You go after the box office. And don't listen to the
actors, either, or they'll step all over you. You're the boss, remember!"

* * *

Despite my black Friday, I instinctively felt that I was on the right track.
For years, most of my competitors had been building their musicals around
plots so feeble they'd never stand up on their own without the tinsel surrounding them. The audience was, of course, diverted by song and dance, laughter
and glitter and—as we say—went home with nothing. I wanted my audience
to go home with something to think about and tell their neighbors. The new
productions and rave notices at the other theaters were doing them no good
at all. They were dependent on a captive audience—an audience stuck with
benefit tickets by their organizations for a show that would, otherwise, not
have lured them to the box office.

Yet people streamed from all corners of the city to see my "played-off"
show because the new and diversified style of theater presentation impressed
them. It seemed that even the Jewish critics had been brainwashed for years,
and could not digest any sudden change. Now, the same organizations, after
seeing my revival, booked dates for my second production, willing to pay the
weekend rates.

Years later, Broadway producers also came around to my way of thinking
that, before anything else, one must have a story to tell. They made fortunes
in converting classics and popular novels into great musical extravaganzas such
as *Kiss Me Kate* (based on *The Taming of the Shrew*), *My Fair Lady* (*Pygmalion*),
The Man of La Mancha and certainly *The Fiddler on the Roof*, which made
theatrical history; a specific Yiddish musical, based on Sholem Aleichem's novel,
Tevye's Daughters. Who would ever dream that this would be performed in
so many different languages, scoring success even in Japanese? Yes, give the
people a story—a good story!

60

The Dishwasher

Considering the cool critical reception my opening show received, I never expected it to run longer than the few weeks originally planned. Still smarting from the blow, I finally settled down to read my new play for the cast. I had built this story around my current hit song, "The Dishwasher." This involves the plight of a man grown. Neglected by his well-to-do-children, he is forced to take the job of dishwasher. My audience, I felt, could easily identify with this kind of situation, judging by my song's tremendous impact on radio listeners.

After the reading, there ensued a heated discussion:

"It's a strong drama, all right! But for a musical?"

"It's too heavy," said another, echoing the critics.

"This, too, won't find favor with the reviewers. To the American press, a drama is a straight drama, a comedy is a comedy and a musical is a musical. They don't go for combinations. To them, even a subplot is superfluous and dated. The patriotic production number you have in this play might be highly appreciated by Jewish people, but the critics lampoon this as flag-waving and corny. To attract youth to the Yiddish theater, it's very important to have a favorable mention in the American press."

When the company heard that I intended to call this production *The Dishwasher,* a revolution erupted.

"A musical should have a romantic title!"

"Now, wait a minute!" I exploded. "Must I trudge the same old beaten path which the Yiddish theater has followed all these decades? Isn't there a limit to the stereotyped titles like *Blind Love, Garden of Love, Sacred Love*? Or the newer editions like *Jaykele Bluffer, Solomontchik from Karapontchik, The Bride from Cracow*? To some of you actors the title *Papirossen* was also ridiculous. Yet, it brought mighty fine business. 'The Dishwasher' is another of my hit songs, and it may very well intrigue my radio listeners to come and see the show by the same name."

"Do you think the organizations will buy benefit tickets for a dishwasher?" Schneider put his two cents in, as well.

The briefing I got from Yosele Edelstein flashed through my mind: "You are the boss!"

With determination, I summed the cast and crew on stage and told them point blank: "The management of this theater is no one's concern but mine. My theater is not a co-op business for everyone to voice opinions and give advice. In this theater no one will miss a penny of his pay envelope—as experienced in other engagements! The moment someone does not receive his full salary on time, he is not obliged to come to work the following day. To those who think my play is too heavy, let me set you straight right now. I did not sweat bullets all summer to prepare some lightweight script of fluff and feathers, so you will have to make do with what I did prepare. Our new musical production will neither be titled the 'Singing,' nor the 'Jolly,' as some suggested, but simply, *The Dishwasher!*"

Exaggerated versions of my speech were quoted in the unions, in the Cafe Royale and in the competitive theaters. It also added to my growing reputation as a "guy you don't tangle with"—a strict boss!

* * *

Rehearsals for *The Dishwasher* were held daily, while we were still running *Papirossen* nine shows a week. But we had to be prepared. Should the box office take a sudden drop, the new show would have to go on the very next weekend.

The work was certainly hard on me, especially since I was still continuing with my broadcasts on WEVD and WBNX. To save time and effort in traveling to the broadcasting stations, I had a radio hookup implemented in the theater, so we could do programs from our own studio—a first in the Yiddish theater.

We were in the tenth week of *Papirossen,* and Edelstein wouldn't hear of taking it off. "You have to be crazy to take off a show that's doing such business. A revival with mixed reviews yet!"

I had planned to have my new show wind up with an elaborate wedding. Yet, despite the efforts I had already put into making this wedding scene more outstanding and different from any ever portrayed on the Yiddish stage, my heart just wasn't in it. A wedding again?! Was there a Yiddish play that did not end in a wedding? Everything else in the show was off the beaten track; completely modern to the extent of portraying a colorful nightclub in Havana, with electric guitars introduced for the first time on a Yiddish stage! So, how could I have blundered into such stereotyped banality as a wedding?!

With the premiere almost upon us, I was still wracking my brain to change the finale for something novel. Finally, I got an idea! My part in the play was that of a blind composer. If I could have the blind composer conduct his own symphony on stage, my, what a sensational ending that would be!

When I told Trilling and my stage manager, Moe Honigman, what I had in mind, they thought I'd gone made. "What?" protested Honigman, "One week before the opening, you expect us to build you a Carnegie Hall?"

"And you expect me to compose a symphony overnight?" cried Trilling. "You think I'm Beethoven or something?"

"Look, Honigman," I tried placating him, "your wedding salon is a splendid piece of scenery, so why can't we use it as a concert hall? We also have enough platforms on which to set up the musicians. And have the crew build a loge at each side of the proscenium. I intend to place the principals in them as part of the audience.

"And you, my dear Trilling," I said, "do you have to be a Beethoven to make a medley of your beautiful motifs in the score and paraphrase them in a symphonic arrangement?"

Bella's problem was that she had an elaborate wedding gown already made and paid for. "I'm sorry, my darling," I said, "the production is costing me plenty, so a few dollars one way or the other won't change my mind. So forget the bridal gown and shop around for the most elegant dress to wear at the concert."

My real obstacle was to get the pit musicians on stage. I finally solved this too. With permission from the Musician's Union, I was allowed to have my entire orchestra perform on stage together with my Cuban combo; all of them in dress uniform. Jointly, they made up an orchestra of twenty-two. With the stage amplified for sound, I was sure they would come across like fifty! In an old shop on the East Side, I acquired extra musical instruments of all sorts. After these were scoured and polished, they shone like new. The musicians rehearsed the chorus men and the extras on how to hold and simulate playing their assigned instruments. After a few rehearsals I had a ready-made symphony, all in the same attire; and it was impossible to tell which were the bona fide musicians and which were the extras.

I carefully integrated this revised finale with the story line, so that it became part of the plot, not merely presented out of the blue for effect.

One of my pseudo musicians, who expertly went through the motions of playing the cello, was a young extra who later emerged as a famous stage and film star, Walter Matthau. In the first act of the *Dishwasher*, he played the incidental part of an immigration officer and doubled at the end of the show as a cellist. In a profile on Walter Matthau that appeared in the *New Yorker* magazine, as in all other interviews on radio, television and personal appearances, he still relates his early experiences with me at my Second Avenue Theater. It makes me proud and happy indeed.

* * *

One of the finest personalities, as well as close friend of the Yiddish theater, was the general manager of *The Jewish Daily Forward*, the prominent writer and poet, Baruch (Charney) Vladeck. For a few years he was also the director of the radio station WEVD.

I had invited him and his wife to see *Papirossen*, and they enjoyed it immensely. Days later, in an editorial in the *Forward*, Vladeck wrote, "Herman Yablokoff, a new face on Second Avenue, has brought much needed freshness to the Yiddish theater. We can expect noteworthy achievements from him in the future."

This was the first encouraging article written about my enterprise since taking over the theater. It filled me with renewed energy to go ahead with my preparations for the premiere of *The Dishwasher*. Soon after this, I went to see Vladeck at his office and thanked him for his kind words.

"Mr. Yablokoff," he said, "your upcoming production will, I presume, be another spectacular. I would like to do something for you. How about arranging for a double page in the art section of the Sunday edition—something that's never done for the Yiddish theater. Have a photographer take the most outstanding scenes of your new production. I will have our artists, Morris Winograd and Louis Sperling, set up a layout of pictures for a double fold in the rotogravure section. I'll see that you get the center fold. The readers will thus get an eyeful of your new show in a two-page spread of pictures, with proper captions and names of the cast. Such a display is sure to bring you good results."

"This certainly sounds very attractive, the question is can I afford it?"

"I can order a double page in Sunday's roto section for one thousand dollars. This would only cover the expenses of preparing the artistic work, the cuts, the setting and printing of the double page. Believe me, I'm not trying to pressure you into it. I'm trying to help you. I like your drive, and you deserve it. I feel that you can realize great returns from this kind of publicity. You can pay it out in installments. On your regular weekly bill for the daily announcements, we will add fifty dollars, so you will have ample time to pay it out. We trust you. I like your record, up to now, as a punctual payer. I wish I could say the same for the other theaters. If we had the money they owed us for ads, we could publish another paper!"

Gratefully, I accepted his advice and ordered a two-page spread. To avoid hard feelings, I went directly to the nearby offices of *The Day* and *The Morning Journal* and told them of my arrangement with the *Forward*. Since these Yiddish dailies did not carry rotogravure sections, I ordered full single pages at $350 for Sundays I would designate later.

As my competitors were preparing new productions for Thanksgiving, we decided not to take any further risks and promptly announced the preview of *The Dishwasher* to be held on Thanksgiving Day. After the matinee and evening performances, we knew we had a smashing success.

The greatest innovation, of course, was the show's finale. When the traveler opened, the audience beheld a dazzling scene illuminated by a sea of colored floodlights, a handsomely outfitted symphonic orchestra on tiered platforms, the principals in sparkling raiment ensconced in the simulated loges on either side of the stage, the showgirls spaced between the columns in the background like statuettes. This magnificent tableau evoked a tumultuous ovation. When the orchestra, under my baton as the blind composer, finished

Trilling's paraphrased arrangement of his score, the applause reverberated in the theater the same as for an authentic symphony in any concert hall.

Reservations for the show began to pour in immediately. Tickets were bought for months in advance. Edelstein admitted that sales of this magnitude had never before been seen on the avenue.

My competitors also opened on Thanksgiving Day with very few cash customers at the window. Mostly, they played off the benefits and block tickets. After that, they began maneuvering to stay open. The actor's salaries were cut to half, paid out in postdated checks.

The weeks I happened to have the bulk of the benefits, I promptly turned my share over to the communal benefit pot in accordance with the agreement. The other theater managers, however, failed to contribute their share. The business of organizing this pool finally cost me $28,000 that season.

Two Sundays before Christmas, the *Forward* carried the pictorial array of the *Dishwasher*. The stunning layout on the colored double centerfold created a sensation. Vladeck was right. He had wanted to do something for me—and he certainly did! Business was fabulous.

On New Year's Day, after the matinee, my chorus girls and dancers, elated at being part of this success, decided to have a Dutch-treat dinner at the Cafe Royale, and swagger a little. They reserved a large table and on the wall behind them, they hung a big sign, painted for the occasion by one of the chorus men, Michael Zwiback. It read: "The Dishwasher Girls—Success of the Decade, January 1, 1937." Inspired they vowed that, no matter where time-and-tide led them, they would meet for an annual reunion every January 1st at the Cafe Royale!

Time rolled on and they became wives, mothers and career women, yet they faithfully observed their reunions for the next twenty years, always inviting Bella and me as their honored guests. Accompanied by their husbands and children, we would meet and celebrate this heartwarming get-together. Recalling with nostalgia the many episodes that made the season of the *Dishwasher* so memorable, we would sing the songs of the show and other songs of my repertoire and enjoy a most delightful family-style reunion!

When the Royale closed its doors, they held their meetings further down the avenue at Moskowitz and Lupowitz's Romanian Restaurant. And when this landmark also faded, it finally rang down the curtain on the annual celebrations of my loyal "Dishwasher Girls."

61

Business is Business

The season on Second Avenue was drawing to a close. Some of the theaters had folded right after the New Year, while our *Dishwasher* was still going strong. We had to add on extra matinees during the Christmas holiday and a midnight performance for New Year's Eve. The plan was to continue up to May. We would then be booked for an eight-week tour of the major cities in the United States and Canada.

The pressure on me—star, producer and director eased up only after I engaged Max Kletter, a tall, handsome actor with a resonant tenor, with the added asset of playing the violin. Remembering his professional courtesy toward me when I was about to be ousted from the Hopkinson Theater, I made him a proposition.

"Would you be interested in taking an engagement at my Second Avenue Theater? Running a business like mine and playing nine shows a week is beyond the strength of any man. I want you to take over my roles for the mid-week performances."

"What?! You mean to tell me that you would be willing to let me play your parts?" Kletter stared, incredulous. "Is there an actor alive, who would permit another to step into his starring roles, in his own theater at that?!"

"As soon as you're ready," I said, "you will take over for me in *Papirossen* and *The Clown*, the shows we're playing weeknights."

Kletter gladly accepted my proposition and was extremely well received by the audiences. We became staunch friends and he worked with me in productions that were to follow.

I was now able to work on a new play to be produced the following season. The atmosphere in the theater was one of elation. Everyone felt a personal pride in sharing our unqualified success.

"Have you any plans for the coming season?" asked Edelstein one afternoon.

"Of course," I replied. "I'm almost finished with the libretto for my new production. Since I've been so lucky with titles up to now, I intend again to name the new show after one of my popular songs, 'Give Me Back My Heart.'"

"Since you intend to remain in the theater, don't you think it is time for us to negotiate a new lease?"

"Why, what do you mean, Isidore? With the kind of success we're having, are you in doubt about my remaining for the coming season? According to our contract, I have fulfilled my obligation to you 100 percent, and promptly. On your percentage, I'm happy to say, you received a lot more than you anticipated. So what have we to negotiate? Draw up a copy of our lease and I will sign it."

"We feel that for the following year we are entitled to better conditions. Instead of the 12½ percent we've been receiving from the gross, my brother Alex and I would like to have 15 percent. And in place of the $1,500 security you placed with us, we would prefer to have a security of $5,000."

"Five thousand dollars! As far as the 15 percent is concerned, I can readily understand. We're making money, so you are entitled to a better deal. I don't think we will have any dispute over that. The thing that really stumps me is your request for $5,000 security! How was it that last year you took the risk with me, a newcomer, trusting me with your theater for almost no security and now, with this fabulous success, you no longer trust me? Now, you are asking $5,000 security? To tell you the truth, Isidore, I'm insulted!"

"Yabby, I'll be candid with you. You are right, but business is business. Rumshinsky and Skulnik are offering me 15 percent of the gross and $5,000 security. You can verify this with Mr. Guskin at the union. We want you, Yabby, but business is business. If you agree to give us these same conditions, the theater is yours, and you can remain with us for as long as you choose."

I was burnt to the core! "I am not quarreling with you over the extra security. I can afford it. It's the principle of the thing! All of a sudden you can't trust me with $1,500, but with $5,000 you can? Is that fair?"

"My, but you're naive! Are you looking for fairness in the theater business? Think it over. Have a talk with your partners, the Ehrenbergs, and let me know your decision. Don't get me wrong, we want you, Yabby," he reiterated, "but business is business."

My partners, Dr. and Mrs. Ehrenberg and Counselor Storm, were as indignant as I over Edelstein's unjust demands. But about one thing, I had to admit later on, Edelstein was right. With all my experience and practice I was still very naive. To think that the big-time moguls of theater business... lawyers by profession... had no scruples, was not only naive, but downright stupid.

How could I suspect that Edelstein was being pressured by every trick of the trade to squeeze me out of the number one house on Yiddish Broadway? I was so riled at the injustice of his demands that, instead of reasoning, I stood firm on my principle of fairness and refused to submit to the pressure tactics that said: business is business!

National Theater

The National Theater on Second Avenue at Houston Street had once been the citadel of Boris Thomashevsky. For the last few seasons it had remained closed. Some had tried running it as a vaudeville and movie house, but without success. Excavations all around the area to build the Second Avenue subway line made access to the theater very cumbersome.

The National was only two blocks from the Second Avenue Theater. Both houses had about the same seating capacity; except that the Second Avenue had elevators to carry its patrons up to the balconies, while the National had no such thing. People were obliged to climb three flights to the topmost gallery. The building also housed meeting rooms available to various Jewish organizations. Atop the building was the well-known Roof Garden that, for a time, featured Minsky's Burlesque. The entire property was owned by the Raynes Realty Corporation.

Nathan Raynes and his wife were devoted fans of the Yiddish theater and were steady patronizers of my productions. Their son, Jules Raynes, often came to buy tickets for them to see my shows in Brooklyn, the Bronx and at the Second Avenue Theater, where they saw the *Dishwasher*.

I called Raynes and arranged to see him at his office.

"To what do we owe this pleasant visit?" he greeted me, warmly.

"I want to rent your National Theater for next season," I came straight to the point.

"So! You want to rent my National Theater! And what will you do with your Second Avenue? Do you mean to say you already need two theaters?" he chuckled.

"Right now I have nothing," I said. "I made such a hit that Mr. Edelstein gave me my walking papers." When I relayed all that transpired between Edelstein and me, I could tell from the grim expression on his face that he disapproved of such business dealings.

"Tell me," he said, "why do you want my theater in particular? You have the Public, as well at the Folk's Theater on the avenue."

"Well, I wouldn't care to do unto others that which was done to me. I know that the Public Theater is under the management of William Rolland, and the Folk's Theater is too small a house for a benefit business. Your National is just tailor-made for me and my production. It's a beautiful house. Sure, it's sort of neglected having been closed for so long. Still, I really can't see why a house like that on the avenue should remain dark."

Raynes called to his son in another office, "Jules, come here a moment. Mr. Yablokoff wants to rent our National. He thinks we have a beautiful theater!" he laughed, amused. "Don't think we have a lack of bidders for the theater. They come and go. You wonder why I'm laughing? All these bidders tell us what a wreck of a theater we have: it's rundown; the subway-digging is making the place a hazard; there are three flights to climb without an elevator. If it's a lemon, we ask them, then what good is it to you? So you see, you are the first one to make us feel that we still have a good piece of property. If you want the theater, you can have it and good luck to you! My son, Jules, will make the necessary arrangements. He handles our business. I'm sure you'll come to terms. As long as we have a 'good theater', we're in business."

That evening after the show at the Second Avenue, I officially announced that for the coming season I would be appearing with my productions at the National Theater.

Winding up our season, we went on the road with the *Dishwasher*. We presented it exactly as it was played in New York. We traveled in two special railroad cars, carrying every stitch of scenery, including the effects for the symphony at the finale. Business was tremendous everywhere. My partners and I realized undreamed of profits.

As for the union's "pot experiment," it did not last more than that one season. Once again there began the old cutthroat tactic over benefit sales. Nonetheless, this experiment, initiated by the Hebrew Actors' Union, cost me a good deal of money and a lot of heartache.

The one gratifying thing for me that season, which made me proud indeed, was the theater award presented to me by the Educational Alliance in New York on February 6, 1937. The first such acknowledgement had been awarded Maurice Schwartz for his production of *Kiddush Hashem* by Sholem Asch.

Give Me Back My Heart

Returning from the road I got busy opening the padlocked National Theater. The Raynes people gave me great co-operation in getting the theater cleaned and back in order. We illuminated the front of the house with electrical signs and huge, colored portraits of the company. I hired Menachem Edelheit as benefit manager, and Abe Cogut as general manager. As cashier I brought Midgit Kantor from Philadelphia with his family. I had promised him an engagement in New York and kept my word.

I did make a few changes in the cast. In place of Annie Thomashefsky, I engaged Yetta Zwerling, an eccentric-type comedienne. Mostly, I engaged the same personnel that had worked with me at Second Avenue Theater. At first I thought they might not care for another season of my strict discipline, but they all admitted that they preferred it to the chaos and laxity experienced in other companies. So, chorus, musicians and crew all came along with me to the National Theater.

I exerted every effort to present my new show on as broad a scale as my previous spectaculars. The production of *Give Me Back My Heart*, also required two children. But, as luck would have it, a new municipal law was enacted forbidding minors to perform on stage. This restriction posed a real snag since the kids in my play were part of the story—not to mention the fact that children are usually such an attraction on stage. How was I going to get around this handicap? I was also uneasy about Leo Fuchs and his actress wife, Muriel, who had gone off to Europe for the summer. I hoped they'd be back in time for rehearsal. I really didn't know what to worry about, first!

"Tell me, Karper," I asked my English publicity agent, "how are the Broadway theaters coping with this child restriction problem?"

"They're using midgets to perform as children."

"Midgets?! I don't believe it!"

"Oh, yes! Some can easily pass for kids on stage. They are exceptionally talented and adaptable. One of them just played the part of a little girl with Helen Hayes. This midget was sensational!"

"In the American theater, of course, they can do it," I sighed. "They can get midgets who speak English. But where do I find midgets who look like kids and speak Yiddish to boot?"

Karper promised to get in touch with the agent representing the midget who played with Helen Hayes. Soon afterward, an elderly, aristocratic-looking woman came into my office leading a child by the hand. If I hadn't already surmised that this must be the midget that Karper mentioned, I would have sworn that she was just a little girl. An angelic face, with a doll-like little figure, she was dressed like a moppet of seven or eight.

"I am Helen Magna," the little girl spoke up in a bell-like voice.

"Hello, Helen," I smiled at her, "tell me, what do you do?"

"What doesn't she do!" interpolated Mrs. Magna. "Helen sings, does any type of dancing, including ballet on toe. She plays the piano and guitar and has appeared in dramatic roles, as well as in comedy."

"Helen handed me a folder of music—her repertoire. With Trilling to oblige at the piano, Helen delivered a song and dance that would have made Shirley Temple sit up and take notice.

"She's a sensation!" I murmured to Trilling. "She'd be perfect for the part. Now, where can we find a talented boy midget for her partner? And what about speaking Yiddish?"

"Learning Yiddish will be no obstacle for Helen," said Mrs. Magna in quick rejoinder. "Helen speaks German, Ukrainian and Spanish. She can master Yiddish as well. Simply write out her part phonetically, and in a matter of days she will know the lines by heart. As for a male partner, Helen has one. They work together as a song-and-dance team. I can bring him down so you can audition him."

Well, I figured, what have I got to lose? I may as well have a look at him, too. I wrote out part of a scene phonetically, and handed it to Helen. She read it well and would do fine, I thought, with a little coaching. When Trilling played the duet which Helen and her partner would have to do in the show, she asked him to write out a lead sheet with the lyrics spelled out phonetically under each note. She and Buddy, her partner, she said, could then study it at the piano at home, and in a few days be ready to audition for us.

Sure enough, Helen and Buddy came prepared. They sang the duet and when they went into their dance, we sat open mouthed. I immediately signed a contract with their agent. We did not broadcast the fact that they were midgets. Certainly not! They were children—and that was that!

Helen, who was about eighteen, was born to Ukrainian parents, both of whom were of normal height, as were the rest of their children. Not well off, her parents placed her in the care of Mrs. Magna and her daughter, a dancing teacher. Helen had also adopted their name, Magna.

Buddy, except for a somewhat larger head and lines in his face, looked like a little boy, not a bachelor of forty. Fortunately, these tell tale signs were not discernible across the footlights. For years, Buddy, with his ringing youthful voice was known on radio and television as the little bellhop who strode through the hotel lobby paging: "Call for Philip Morr...ris...!"

* * *

Having left the Second Avenue Theater, I realized that not only did I cut Edelstein's throat, but my own as well. I was convinced that considering the success I enjoyed that season, the organizations would book their benefits with me no matter where I played. Well, I was mistaken. Most of the committees still dealt with Phil Schneider at the Second Avenue.

My manager, Menachem Edelheit, sold benefits of course, but not in the amount I anticipated. Still, I hoped that with the drawing power of my production I would make up in box office sales during the weekends what I lacked in middle-of-the-week benefits.

Leo Fuchs and Muriel Gruber were still in Poland. Rehearsals were due to begin, yet I had not had a word from them. I sent cables and waited. At long last I received a letter from Muriel.

The American consul in Warsaw, she wrote, was refusing to issue them visas to return to the States. Although she herself was American born, she had forfeited her citizenship by having married a foreign subject. In her case, however, the consul might work something out for her return, providing she could submit certain affidavits. But the consul was refusing categorically to grant a visa to Leo, a Polish citizen.

I was beside myself! Here was I, ready for rehearsal and my star comedian, whose name I had been publicizing all through the summer as co-star to Bella, Kletter and me, was stuck in Poland! Frantic, I ran to the HIAS and pleaded for help. They immediately wired their representative in Warsaw to investigate the case. Then began telegrams there and back, documents there and back. I went to Washington, spoke to a senator, a congressman, and made calls to Warsaw, as if I were calling Brooklyn. It cost me a pretty penny. At last, the American consul in Warsaw agreed to issue Fuchs and his wife the necessary visas. In the meantime I rehearsed the show "around" them. When at last they arrived we had only a week left before the announced opening.

"You saved our lives!" were Fuch's first words when I met them at the boat. "I'll never forget it as long as I live! Conditions in Poland have become intolerable. The anti-Semitism is not to be believed. Jews are mortally afraid to appear on the street. What a joy it is to be back on American soil!"

We opened with *Give Me Back My Heart*, which was an instant hit. Outstanding were Bella Mysell, Max Kletter, Muriel Gruber and Anna Appel. A great asset to the show was the zany comedienne Yetta Zwerling. Her style was so individual, it was impossible to imitate—although many actresses tried. A great portion of the play's success must be ascribed to Leo Fuch's unique artistry. With smooth grace, he employed every self-styled artifice to charm the patrons.

Helen and Buddy sang, danced and delivered punch lines like the true professionals they were. Their Yiddish was certainly no worse than that of most American children I worked with, or the Jewish kids I recruited in the foreign countries in which I played. The audience accepted them as "kids" and one critic wrote: "It's worth the price of admission to see and hear them on stage."

The box office did very well, but as I feared, we lacked the benefits, which were so important to fill out the middle of the week. Expenses were sky-high, publicity ran into a fortune. Once again I paid for a Sunday spread in the *Forward*, plus for single pages in the other newspapers.

We lost quite a few thousand dollars. My partners, who had realized a sizable profit the season before, turned cool when it came to putting some of it back into the business...especially when so-called good friends added fuel to the fire by pointing out that had we remained at the Second Avenue, we would have raked in a mint with *Give Me Back My Heart*." But, because of Yablokoff's stubbornness, they'd lost out on a good opportunity.

Notwithstanding, I started work on a new production planned for the New York.

* * *

We opened on New Year's Eve with a musical drama I called *Sammy's Bar Mitzvah*. It was an elaborate production that was also based on one of the compositions I introduced on radio. The book by Harry Kalmanowitz; music by Ilia Trilling; choreographed by Moe Zaar and directed by me. It soon became the talk of the town. My announcements read: A $50,000 Herman Yablokoff Production—*Sammy's Bar Mitzvah*. It cost me a lot less, but to the audience it certainly looked the money!

The story was written in a realistic style with flashbacks covering a span of thirty years. Some of its characters started young and progressed in age as the story unfolded.

Our show began running late. With cute little Chaim'l Parness as Sammy, the play kept the audience so absorbed they remained glued to their seats no matter what the hour. Still, there was no reason to drag the performance and pay overtime.

The worst thing that can happen to an actor is having his role cut down after the premiere. It's bad enough when this becomes necessary during rehearsal. But, once the show has opened... Actors have a pet phrase: "If you must cut,

cut my wages, but don't cut my part!" Since we kept running late I pleaded with my cast to step up the tempo. "An extra minute or two, stretched by this, or that one, can mean a lag of ten to fifteen precious minutes in the show. So please stop pulling molasses. Step on it!" They realized it was better than having lines cut.

Everyone cooperated except Fuchs. Again, we wound up past midnight. I got warnings from the stage crew and musicians about union overtime.

At one of the performances I caught cries of "Louder! Louder!" while Fuchs was on stage. My blood ran cold. With mikes planted in the footlights across the stage, how could they not hear him?!

"Please Fuchs," I begged after the show, "speak louder. They don't hear you out there!"

"I don't have the strength to speak louder. I work too hard, nine shows a week...this is not for my stamina!"

Most of my aggravation was over his couplet toward the latter part of the show. The first few verses were very good and the audience reaction was terrific. When the following verses were met with a weaker reception, Fuchs went into his eccentric dance, doing double-jointed twists and corkscrew turns. At this hilarious bit, naturally, the crowd wouldn't let him off the stage. And, since he would not repeat this bag of tricks to satisfy them, the only solution was to drop the curtain.

"Leo," I implored, "I don't want to interfere with your success. Your success is my success, since this is my production and my business. You can see for yourself how each of us is racing against the clock. Why can't you go into your dance routine a little sooner and omit the verses that are only so-so? There's no sense in singing encores the audience doesn't want."

"When Lebedeff sings his couplet he does eight encores," Fuchs retorted, "and Itzhak Feld does nine. So I have to do ten! And if I don't do my couplet the way I have been doing it right along, I quit the show as of now!"

At the next performance, Sunday matinee, the theater was packed. Trilling rushed into my dressing room.

"Fuchs is threatening not to go on if he doesn't have his way. What shall I do about his encores?"

"So, let him not go on!" I said, shaking inwardly. I could not believe that a professional actor could find it in his heart to carry out such a threat. Well, he did play off the first act. Then, during intermission, he again threatened that he would not do his number at all in the second act if he couldn't do it his way. He knew that we had to change the scenery while he was out front singing. So how could we possibly manage this without his couplet?!

Little did he know that I had Yetta Zwerling standing by to fill in with another comedy number. At the last moment, however, Fuchs, right on cue, burst on stage and delivered his song and dance the way I had instructed.

Immediately after the matinee I hastened to the Royale, knowing I'd find

Reuben Guskin there. "Sorry to interrupt your dinner," I said, "but I must tell you that as of tonight Fuchs finishes his season at the National Theater!"

"What are you saying?" Guskin gasped. "What happened?"

"I can stand for a lot of idiosyncrasies, but when an audience is seated in the theater and an actor says he is not going on, I refuse to take such unprincipled, unprofessional behavior from anyone, be it even a star like Leo Fuchs!"

"But you have such a tremendous success, how can you afford to throw Fuchs out of the theater in the middle of the season?"

"Whatever the consequences, I am willing to take the risk. Let him go with my blessings. I simply want to know if I have the legal right to dismiss him in the face of what he did today. He is not a union man as yet, and I want to be sure that I'm in order."

"You want to ruin yourself, that's your business. I can only warn you. Such hasty decisions can wreck a business, especially at the beginning of a new production."

"I'll engage whomever I can get. As for Fuchs, I want him out. If he remains in the theater I will no longer have discipline. It will become a free-for-all. Everyone would take advantage, thinking all they have to do is throw a tantrum, grab me by the throat and I will give in. You know, more than anyone, what it cost me to bring Fuchs back to America, not counting the heartache and the effort... and this is the thanks I get!"

During our conversation, Max Wilner came into the cafe. An exceptionally fine young comedian, he had been struggling with a company in Philadelphia and decided to return to New York.

"Max would you care to take an engagement at my National Theater?"

"My God, Yabby, I sure need a job. After Philly, I'm busted!"

"Then listen, here is Mr. Guskin. He will affirm our agreement. You will receive the same salary I'm paying Fuchs and the same billing. You need only do one thing for me. Come to the theater this evening, watch the show, concentrate on Fuch's part, and tomorrow night you will play his role. After the show tonight, the cast and I will rehearse with you all night if necessary. Trilling will teach you the musical numbers and Ostroff will prompt you from the wings. But you must step into the part tomorrow night."

"My God!" said Maxie, bewildered, "If you have that much confidence in me, who am I to say no? I agree."

That same evening after the show, Fuchs got his salary with a note telling him that he was through. Everyone in the theater took this to be a huge joke. Things like this simply didn't happen!

The electricians worked part of the night taking down Fuch's name from the marquee and replacing it with Wilner's. All placards, show cards and signs were redone and repainted, new programs were printed, and when the actors came for rehearsal again next morning, there wasn't a trace that Leo Fuchs had ever played at the National Theater.

Wilner and I got no sleep at all. I helped him cram as much as his head could hold. The cast also gave him as much assistance as possible. Max Wilner did indeed go on and in a few performances fell into stride; he was absolutely brilliant in the part.

The consensus in the Royale was that by dismissing Fuchs I had ruined myself as well as the theater. My partners, too, were nonplussed. Nevertheless, we played *Sammy's Bar Mitzvah* the entire season to the greatest gross receipts. After the season we took the show on the road, covering key cities in the U.S. and Canada.

We traveled with the entire ensemble, plus sceneries, costumes, stagehands, musicians and all necessary trappings. We were received with pomp wherever we appeared. True, we didn't make a penny's profit, but we did manage to stay afloat for forty-some weeks without owing anyone a red cent.

Disregarding the bad feelings which the episode with Leo Fuchs incurred between us, it did not change my regard for his superb talent. It was necessary surgery to save the life of discipline, so sorely lacking in the Yiddish theater! Time brought us together again as very good, congenial colleagues.

That particular season also marked a happy occasion for me. I married off my niece, Sarah, the daughter of my sister, Mary. Since my sister and her husband were not in a position to give Sarah the kind of wedding most girls dream of, I offered, as a token of my gratitude for their help in bringing me to America, to stand the expense of a truly elaborate wedding. Lacking the funds, however, for such an affair, at which I intended to invite the whole theater profession, I fell back on the old, reliable source—a benefit performance! We played *Sammy's Bar Mitzvah*, and the net gross went for the wedding.

Eventually Sarah and her husband, Reuben Sharek, enriched our family tree by three sons: Richard, Bruce and Robert.

62

Buenos Aires

T he European impresario Meyer Winder had seen my productions during his visits to New York. Spectaculars like *Sammy's Bar Mitzvah*, and *Papirossen*, he assured me, could run in Warsaw for months, then tour other cities of mass Jewish population in Poland, Lithuania and Latvia. In fact, Winder was ready to arrange such a European tour for me.

I did have a great yen to be in Poland again and wanted very much to have Bella, to whom I was already married, appear with me in Europe. I also thought of bringing my mother over to Warsaw, so she could spend time with us during our engagement there. I had hoped to bring her to America, but she'd been reluctant to leave my brothers and sisters and their children.

At the same time, I was corresponding with the managers of the Excelsior Theater in Buenos Aires, who wanted Bella and me to guest-star.

The phenomenon of opposite climates in North and South America has always afforded a great advantage to our traveling stars. The difference in latitude makes it possible for Jewish actors to extend their New York or European engagements by going into another immediate theater season in Buenos Aires.

I decided to give up my National Theater and start out with my wife on a world tour. We would begin in Buenos Aires and go on to Montevideo in Uruguay, then Sao Paulo and Rio de Janeiro in Brazil. From there to Johannesburg, London, Paris and for the fall season, to Warsaw.

I wired the managers of the Excelsior Theater in Buenos Aires, and accepted their offer. We would start their "fall" season in April, 1939. In addition to the Excelsior, which was the most prominent Yiddish Theater in Argentina, there were four others: Ombu, Mitre, Soleil and the IFT.

Aside from the Excelsior, where Bella and I were to play, Aaron Lebedeff was to star at the Ombu; Isidore and Hannah Hollander at the Soleil; and David Medoff with his wife, Raya Soloviova, at the Mitre, in a revue program in conjunction with a Yiddish film: *Yankel, the Smith*, starring Moishe Oysher. The IFT, a non-professional group, was directed by the regisseur David Licht.

Negotiations for the North American guest attractions were handled mostly by promptors, Charles Fidelman and Max Friedlander. This extra activity afforded them the opportunity of becoming "personal representatives" in South America. The stars, who really needed no such emissaries to arrange their bookings took them along anyway. They paid their passage, plus a weekly salary in American dollars, because they wanted someone to watch over their percentage from the box office receipts...

I had arranged our engagement directly with the Excelsior on a percentage basis from the gross, I did not take along anyone to represent me, nor to look after my interests from the box office—although I had been warned that, in the absence of a personal manager, I would be "trimmed" but good! I did take along my pianist, David Fleischman, who knew my complex scores note for note. I decided to take my chances as far as the box office was concerned, but to take chances on an unknown conductor—not me. The management had written that their pianist, Simon Tenofsky, was most competent, but if I preferred to bring my own musical director, that was my affair. It is certainly not profitable to take on such additional costs, but that's the way I wanted it.

As my wife and I were not up on Spanish, a young Argentinian, Gregorio Sirota, who also spoke Yiddish, was recommended as my personal representative...an added expense.

Besides our personal effects, I carted steamer trunks packed with costumes for the chorus, plus microphones, a P.A. set, crates full of spotlights, special effects, a dimmer board, a variety of colored gelatins, drapes and drops— equipment not yet available in Buenos Aires. I also took along two prints of the film I used in *Papirossen*, and a portable folding organ for practicing and vocalizing during our extended journey aboard ship.

* * *

We set sail for Buenos Aires on the S.S. Uruguay on February 25, 1939, a frosty day. The next day we shed our winter coats and the day after that we were splashing in the pool. The cruise took nineteen days.

Our shipmates were our "competitors": Aaron Lebedeff, his wife Vera Lubow, his manager Max Friedlander and the Medoffs. It was one of the most delightful sea voyages experienced in my many travels.

Lebedeff, a poor sailor, was sick a good part of the journey despite the smooth sailing. We could not persuade him to leave his cabin and come up on deck. Back home on Second Avenue, Lebedeff was rarely seen without a carnation in his buttonhole. When he finally began showing up on deck, the rest of us exchanged puzzled glances. Where was he getting these fresh carnations to sport on his lapel?! We solved the mystery. Upon boarding ship, Lebedeff had brought with him a boxful of his beloved posies and had the steward store them in the galley refrigerator. Thus, delivered to his cabin every morning, was a fresh boutonniere.

We all became as one happy family, enjoying one another's company. Our closeness continued throughout our entire sojourn in Buenos Aires. The usual tug-of-war among guest artists playing the same town—a situation gleefully exploited by the local theater cliques—did not apply to us.

On the ninth day at sea we reached our first stop—Barbados. Small tenders plying from ship to shore accommodated passengers who wished to visit the island. Bella and I climbed down the rope ladder into a waiting tender and were ferried across the unbelievably blue waters.

Bella turned to me and, in Yiddish, said, "Isn't it just beautiful here? It's like some rare painting!"

"You like it?" a girl seated near us responded. We were astounded! We took her to be a young native of Barbados, riding the tender to and from the ship for the sport of it—a native, and she speaks Yiddish?!

The girl smiled at our surprise. "We live here. We are only ten Jewish families on the island; mostly relatives my father helped emigrate from Poland. The only problem we face here is marriage. There aren't enough Jewish young men in Barbados, so we have to 'import' eligible husbands from Argentina, the States and elsewhere. In fact, I'm waiting for my fiance. He's the ship doctor. We plan to be married soon."

Stepping off the next tender came the young lady's intended, the doctor. The girl invited us to her house in back of her parent's large store, selling the kind of native articles tourists usually go for. On their piano, I found a stack of printed Yiddish songs! Songs by Rumshinsky, Ellstein, Olshanetsky and my very own "Papirossen," "Der Dishwasher," and others. What a strange and wonderful feeling it was to find our songs in such an unlikely corner of the world.

"Whenever my fiance's ship docks in New York," the young bride beamed, "he buys Yiddish sheet music and records at the Metro Music store on Second Avenue. So, every Saturday night all our families get together and enjoy listening to a Yiddish concert. If it weren't for this type of entertainment, life on the island would be a lot lonelier."

* * *

We arrived in Buenos Aires at break of day. The first to hop aboard was our representative-interpreter and what-have-you, Gregorio Sirota. He was a short, slight young man, but obviously a live wire. All the immigration officers seemed to know him. Gregorio took over at once, jabbering away in Spanish with the reporters, photographers and baggage inspectors... not a word of which I understood.

"Don't worry, Senor Yablokoff, I'll take care of everything," he reassured me in Hispanic-flavored Yiddish. "Leave it to Gregorio. Your baggage will not be inspected. I've already seen to that. I have also reserved your rooms for you at the Hotel Passaje Guemes. Everything will be muy bien."

The harbor was crowded with ships flying the swastika and Mussolini's fascist flags; ships that brought in hordes of agitators to spread anti-Semitism among Argentina's populace. Buenos Aires, a cosmopolitan melting-pot, possessed a variety of nationalities, races, colors and creeds, with a sizable number of German and Italian residents. Neither was there a lack of Arabs, who were incensed against Jews by their famed Jew-baiter, the Mufti...

On the Avenida Florida near our hotel, right in the heart of town, we came upon groups brazenly parading large placards bearing anti-Semitic slogans and ugly-featured caricatures of Jews. My blood boiled at these atrocious displays. But to voice a protest was to risk one's life.

A shocking incident stands out in my mind: in celebration of Argentina's Liberation Anniversary, all buildings were draped with the Argentinean national flag. Our Excelsior Theater was no exception. The Argentine flag was displayed, as well as the blue-and-white Jewish flag with its Star of David. Soon enough, a vigilante ordered the Jewish flag removed.

Due to internal, as well as external friction, including differences with the United States, Argentina's economy was not at its peak. Still, the Jewish population enjoyed better living conditions than Jews in Europe. They were well represented in commerce, medicine, jurisprudence, journalism, science, culture, arts and even in politics. Jews owned large factories and other profitable businesses. They owned their own homes, as well as cars that cost a fortune to be imported from North America and Europe.

Buenos Aires had already begun to develop a middle class much as in the States. But in the hinterlands, as in other South and Latin American countries, there still existed the two-class system; the royally rich and the beggardly poor. Later on, when I toured the provincial towns of Argentina and neighboring countries, I was always reminded of the little Yiddish folk songs: "To the rich man, bread is a fresh white roll... to the pauper—oy, the pauper, bread is a hard dry crust." And often, not even that!

During the years of my theatrical globe-trotting, I guest-starred in Buenos Aires six times. The heartiness displayed by its Jewish community toward visiting artists could hardly be found anywhere else. I never felt like a "guest" or a tourist in Buenos Aires, but rather like an old resident.

Pirates in our Midst

Aaron Lebedeff was opening with *Tovarish Liovka*, by Wolf Shumsky; the Hollanders with *Abandoned Women*, by Zolotefsky; the Medoffs with a revue; and the IFT with Sholem Aleichem's *The Bewitched Tailor*.

I had contemplated opening with my production of *Papirossen*. But my hit song had not only been sung to death in Argentina, it had actually been printed without my permission and sold in thousands of copies. So I decided to open with my latest play, *Sammy's Bar Mitzvah*, which had not yet fallen into the hands of the "pirates," who traveled Argentina and Europe with plays and music borrowed from the Yiddish Theater repertoire in the States.

Filching goes on to this day. Artists of guest-star stature have their own exclusive and carefully selected repertoire of plays and music. These are an actor's stock in trade. Playwrights and composers are paid handsome royalties for the rights to perform their works. And it goes without saying that an artist selects the material best suited to his, or her, particular talent and personality.

The smuggling of plays was practiced by several New York promptors. To copy a script was no great difficulty for them. It was even easier to pilfer songs. The catchy tunes of a musical were generally published and sold at a nominal price in the music stores, or in the lobby of the theater.

A copyright did not in any way deter the filchers. They unscrupulously inserted these stolen songs into equally stolen plays, whether or not they fitted in.

Often upon arriving in Argentina or Europe, an American guest-artist would read his new play for the company—a play to which he had the exclusive rights, or which he, himself, had authored—only to be told that the play had already been done.

Shattered at the news, the star would read another of his plays, and still another, only to receive the same devastating reply: "It has already been played off under some other title!" If the play wasn't done in its entirety, the "vultures" picked it clean of its best jokes, comedy scenes, theme songs, et cetera. At this point, the said guest-attraction had no other recourse but to pack up and head back for home.

The biggest shock was to discover that the pirates were fellow actors from the States, one's own pals...union brothers! With certain performers "borrowing" is second nature. When the guilty ones eventually show up in New York, they are taken to task. But, what's the use? The damage is done.

Manana

The theaters in Buenos Aires in need of proper electrical equipment, presented a great handicap in mounting a decent production. No matter how artistic the setting and background, they still had no effect without adequate lighting. I was lucky indeed to have carted my own spots and other electrical paraphernalia. The sound equipment I brought was another innovation in town.

Most of the employees in the Yiddish Theater—stagehands, scenic artists, choreographers and dancers were recruited from the Spanish theaters. They, of course, were non-Jewish. The language barrier posed quite a problem for me. The diversity of language at the Excelsior made communication even more complicated. Our chief technician and his assistants spoke only Spanish; the electrician and his assistants, Brazilians, spoke only Portuguese. And the rest of the crew spoke a variety of Hispanic dialects. How they could understand each other, God only knew. But how, on earth, was I to get across to them?

The promptor, Leon Narepkin, who had only recently begun his career in the Yiddish theater, became my interpreter and right-hand man. Somehow, he did communicate with the crew—or so I hoped. The first Spanish word I caught onto was manana—tomorrow...except in Argentina tomorrow never came.

"Narepkin," I would say, "tell the stagehands I want this, or that placed thus and so." After at least a half hour he took to relay my short directives, in which I thought he must be telling them the story of his life, the answer I invariably heard from the crew was one word—"Manana!"

"Manana!" I fumed. "At this rate we'll never get the show on!" When, at last tomorrow came, the answer was still, manana! I was at the end of my wits. "In heaven's name, Narepkin," I pleaded,"what is the Spanish word for today?"

"Hoy." (The h is silent, reading oy.)

"Oy?! Very appropriate!" I snapped. "That's exactly how I feel. Oy! And what is the word for now... this instant?"

"For now, meaning right away, the word is ahora."

Mumbling my lesson in Spanish, I went to my dressing room, picked up a stick of rouge and in large, red letters wrote across the top of my mirror: No manana... Hoy! Ahora!

This bright idea solved my problem. Whenever I heard the word manana, I promptly steered the guilty party into my dressing room and pointed to my slogan on the mirror. Never again did I hear the forbidden word backstage. If, out of habit, anyone did let the word slip, there'd be a spontaneous burst of laughter. Manana had become taboo.

* * *

The radio in Buenos Aires was most popular and an important publicity medium. Our management thought it wise for us to do a few live broadcasts on the Jewish radio hour. I agreed, on the condition that we be accompanied by the entire orchestra rather than the usual tinkling of a lone piano. They complied, although it did involved much extra expense. It was worth it, nonetheless, for our programs created quite a stir in the community. Bella, doing some coloratura numbers, was hailed as the Jewish Lily Pons. As for me, I sang my "Papirossen," despite the fact that it had been done to death. The novelty of it was my own particular interpretation. And the discovery that I was the composer stirred up a whole new flurry of interest. After our broadcasts, tickets were sold out weeks in advance.

* * *

Our premiere of *Sammy's Bar Mitzvah* was an exciting event. The public must have sensed that something special was cooking at the Excelsior. The little shingle at the box-office window stating "No mas localidades" (S.R.O.) was not taken down during the five months of our engagement. The support of our excellent cast surprised even me. And the two youngsters, Yosele Katz and Kukie Tachman, the daughter of our talented actress, Paulina Tachman, attracted unprecedented numbers of children to the matinees. They hummed and sang along with the actors on stage. It did my heart good to perform for them.

The settings for the twenty-eight scenes in the play, plus the score, the ballet, costumes, lighting, sound equipment and last, but not least, our handsome nineteen-year old maestro, David Fleischman, decked out in his first tuxedo, truly overwhelmed the audience... let alone the señoritas!

Reviews in the Yiddish and Spanish press were filled with praise for the spectacular production, with generous accolades awarded me as an actor, producer and director.

Out of my first earnings in Buenos Aires, I sent off money to my mother, urging her to go to Druskenik for the summer and take the baths for her rheumatism. I also assured her that we would meet very soon in Warsaw.

Descanso

The most welcome day in the week for theater employees in Buenos Aires is Monday. It is the day off—"descanso." After the show on Sunday night up to Tuesday at noon, nobody is permitted to even come near the theater. This regulation is a godsend for the actors in Argentina—a chance to rest the nerves, the vocal chords and relax with family and friends.

The Hebrew Actors' Union in New York tried for many years to establish such a day off, but it never materialized. The Yiddish actors in Buenos Aires owe thanks to their Spanish colleagues theaters for the blessings of descanso. This ordinance came into being because of the dreadful exploitation that formerly reigned in the Spanish vaudeville and revue houses. The vaudevillians were obliged to perform day in, day out, in continuous programs lasting from noon to three o'clock in the morning, if not later. Out of sheer exhaustion, performers sometimes fell flat on their faces on stage. They suffered chronic throat ailments, pulled ligaments and what-not. Finally, the government took a stand against this brutal treatment and ordered a day of rest—descanso!

By the same token, American guest artists awaited Monday with great anticipation. For us to spend part of that precious day just driving through Palermo Park in a hansom cab was no small pleasure. Then, with no show to do, we thoroughly enjoyed the cocktail hour...almost a ritual in that South American city. After that we would invariably attend a late dinner invitation.

* * *

With my second production, *Papirossen*, we beat every previous financial record. It ran for six consecutive weeks—an unprecedented achievement those days in Buenos Aires. For my testimonial performance, I produced *Der Payatz*, and received a surprise gift contributed jointly by the management and the company. They replaced the old S.R.O. sign at the box office with a gold plaque bearing the words: "No mas localidades." This shiny plaque remained at the box office window for the remainder of our engagement. Our competitors at the other theaters had to change their play every week or two, while both our productions ran five and six weeks each for sellouts. All in all the engagement in Buenos Aires was a mighty pleasant and profitable one.

During this time, Adolph Midde, the impresario of the Teatro Mitre, brought over a group of actors from Poland: Chavel Buzgan, Rebecca Schiller, Leybele Friedman, Max Perlman, Gita Galina, Max Bozyk, his wife Reizel Lebrovsky-Bozyk and their little daughter, Ziseleh. They appeared in a musical comedy,

The Village Princess. Buzgan and Schiller eventually returned to Europe. I was to meet them again in 1960, during my concert tour in Poland, where they held prominent positions in the Jewish State Theater.

Max Perlman and his wife Gita Galina, who remained in Buenos Aires, emerged during the war years as first-rate musical comedy stars, appearing in South America, Europe, Israel and the United States.

Bella and I happened to catch *The Village Princess* at the Mitre and were very much impressed. In particular, I found Max Bozyk to be a most talented character comedian, with a style all his own. He had the audience laughing their heads off. At our very first meeting Bozyk asked me, "Panye Yablokoff, how about taking me and my better half to America in one of your trunks? Our Ziseleh can sit on my lap."

"Well, maybe," I replied in earnest. "You never can tell. I will certainly have you in mind."

"I don't want you to have me in mind, I want you to have me in America," he quipped. "I know it is cold lokshn (noodles) but there's no crime in asking. Do you know how many American stars have had me in mind? Your American stars seem to have short memories."

"My dear Bozyk," I said, "don't measure everyone by the same yardstick. Didn't I recently bring over your pal Leo Fuchs from Poland? And there have been others. It's not that easy. At the moment, I can't give you a definite promise. My wife and I are about to set sail for South Africa, Europe, Poland..."

"Poland?!! Are you crazy? Couldn't you pick a better place?"

"My heart is set on playing Poland. My mother expects us there. I promised to be in Warsaw for the High Holidays."

"Well, if I were you," he persisted, "I wouldn't go to Poland. There is big trouble there. Haven't we just gotten ourselves out in the nick of time?!"

* * *

Bella's testimonial evening came due, and I chose to put on *The Queen of Song*, an appropriate play in my repertoire. Our testimonial performances covered the cost of our passage to Buenos Aires. As a bon voyage, the company tendered us a gala banquet and showered us not only with verbal bouquets but some valuable gifts as well.

The prominent artists Joseph Buloff and his wife Luba Kadison followed us into the Excelsior. They had won great prestige during previous engagements and were highly esteemed in Buenos Aires. They began rehearsals for their opening play while we were still finishing up. I promised to leave all my electrical equipment for their use. Thus, I endowed the theater with lighting and sound such as the big Spanish theaters in town hadn't as yet come upon.

Comments on our Buenos Aires engagement are also in the published autobiography of veteran actress Zina Rappel, written by Nehemiah Zukor, *Four Generations of Yiddish Theater*:

Herman Yablokoff came with his charming wife, Bella Mysell, an engaging actress, whose gentleness and refinement warms the heart and wins one's admiration at once. Mr. Yablokoff, with his friendly demeanor and sympathetic understanding, is a most congenial director and colleague, who, at the same time, retains a dignified reserve demanding respect. Watching him at work as he directed his production I was reminded of the time I played at the Coliseo under the direction of Maurice Schwartz. Herman Yablokoff puts forth the same intense effort toward the perfection of his musical extravaganza as does Maurice Schwartz for his literary drama. In the same way that Schwartz strives for an harmonious threesome in his play, namely: lights, settings and interaction, so does Yablokoff seek to implement in his musicals. Taking part in his productions at the Excelsior Theater was a most memorable interlude.

The booking agent, Edwin A. Relkin, whom I had sent ahead as the promoter of my European tour, wrote to me from Europe: "I have made all the necessary arrangements for your appearances in London and Paris. I haven't as yet heard from Warsaw. The political situation in Europe is extremely tense. War is in the air. I feel that you should think over very carefully whether it is advisable for you to venture out on a theatrical tour in the face of such an unsettled atmosphere hanging over Europe."

I wired Meyer Winder in Warsaw and asked him to let me know immediately if our agreement to play Warsaw still stood. In my memorabilia I have Winder's reply dated August 12th, 1939. "There was talk of war...merely talk. All is quiet, thank God. You can safely plan to start out for Warsaw as we arranged. Bring the shows I saw you play in New York. Send photos of Bella Mysell and you and publicity material at once. We will start the Jewish New Year in September with a real bang! Good luck."

September 1st, 1939—Hitler's Nazi Hordes Attack Poland!

How vividly I am reminded of that period in 1939, when it all began. Bella and I were looking forward to our tour of Europe, when a monster in Germany reared its ugly head and launched its bloody crusade. We had to cancel South Africa and Europe, and hie ourselves back home. All communication with Europe was cut off. And while Hitler's henchmen were brutally putting my nearest and dearest to death, I was involved with petty theater politics in New York. What cruel irony!

63

Back to the Second Avenue Theater

The nineteen-day journey on the S.S. Brazil from Buenos Aires back to New York was fraught with apprehension. At night the ship plied her course in total darkness. The ocean, it was rumored, was already rife with enemy submarines and mines.

Life in New York, nevertheless, went on no worse than before. Everything appeared to be normal. In fact, the war in Europe brought prosperity. There was no fuss made over the tidings that trickled through about German atrocities against Jews in the sieged Polish territories. American Jews thought it was just too weird to be true...

Yiddish theater, however, was in the same shaky state as it had been the last few years. The Second Avenue Theater had changed hands during this time, and sadly enough, they lost money. Isidore Edelstein had written me while I was still in Argentina, saying that he was ready to rent to me on my own terms. I was to forget our misunderstandings—"business is business"—he wrote. Jules Raynes was also most anxious for me to take over the National Theater again. In the end I made up with Edelstein. Both of us had paid the piper and I decided to let bygones be bygones. It was a great satisfaction for me to take over the number-one house again and on the same conditions as before: 12½ percent from the gross and $1,500 security.

My new production, *Goldele, the Baker's Daughter*, I completed with the help of my collaborator, Itzhak Friedman. And once again I engaged the composer Ilia Trilling. Taking a copy of lyrics by Chaim Towber, he took off directly for his forest hideaway at Camp Boiberick to work on the score.

* * *

For *Goldele*, I remarked to Bella, "I'd like to engage a top-notch character comedian. The part I have in mind is surefire. In the right hands it would add enormously to the success of the show."

"Do you have anyone in mind?" she asked.

"Of course I have! I had him in mind as I was writing the play, but try and get him!"

"Who, may I ask is it?"

"Sure," I laughed, "Menasha Skulnik!"

"Menasha? That would certainly be a bombshell!"

391

I mentioned the subject to Edelstein and Schneider. They thought I was crazy.

"What are you talking about?! Skulnik accepting an engagement? He's a star and producer on his own!"

"I'm ready to take him in as a partner!"

"And what about the billing?" asked Edelstein, skeptically.

"So I'll give him star billing! At any rate, we'll cross that bridge when we come to it."

"Don't pin your hopes on such a foolish notion," he persisted, pouring cold water on my fantastic idea.

What can I lose? I thought. I can ask the man. There's no law against it. He can only turn the proposition down. I called Skulnik and asked him to join me for a cup of coffee.

As we sat sipping coffee, I came straight to the point. "Don't you think it would be a great idea for us to go into business together at the Second Avenue Theater? I'm ready to take you in as an equal partner."

"A partner?" he repeated, giving me that goggle-eyed Skulnik stare. "I've had my fill of Yiddish theater business. Not me! Not if they paid me would I consider being a boss again. It's high time that I, myself, collected a week's wages!"

"Then maybe you would consider taking an engagement with me," I ventured timidly. "I have a new spectacular. You would, of course, play one of the star roles. What do you say, Menasha?"

"Well, that's a horse of another color," he quipped. "To be engaged without all the headaches of hunting for plays, directing, playing nine shows a week to boot....I tell you, this is something to consider."

"Then listen! The two of us are an ideal combination: you handling the comic roles and me, in the straight dramatic parts. As for salary, I'm sure we'll get along. You know the score in this business, so I'm sure you won't go overboard. There is one point, however, that I find very awkward to discuss with you, and that's billing. You have certainly earned your star status and I can attest to that. I know the sweat it cost you to achieve it. But, according to the way my contract reads with Edelstein, I'm able to offer you top billing, but not "first" billing. Therefore, Menasha, please accept co-star billing that will read Yablokoff - Skulnik - Mysell. If you feel that you can agree to such an arrangement, the deal is made. As for other conditions, just name them and I will sign right now."

After a lengthy pause, he said, "Yabby, let's go and talk to my wife. Me, you've already sold. Now let's hear what Sarah has to say about it, come."

During our talk the waiter had set down several glasses of water—so we wouldn't talk ourselves dry, I suppose. Now, as Skulnik and I rose so hastily from the table, the glasses toppled to the floor, breaking into smithereens.

"Mazel tov!" cried the customers at the nearby tables. These Second Avenue "regulars" had surmised that Skulnik and I were not kibitizing, but were no doubt cooking up business for the impending season. The smashing of the glasses seemed to strike a symbolic note: the traditional breaking of the glass under the heel of the bridegroom...which always brings gusty cries of mazel tov!

Up at the house Menasha explained the details of my proposition to Sarah. In a matter of minutes the deal was wrapped up and we did indeed wish each other a hearty mazel tov! Phoning Edelstein from Skulnik's apartment, I broke the news: "I engaged Menasha Skulnik." Edelstein said I was pulling his leg. So I put Skulnik on the phone.

"Mazel tov! Isidore, I just married Yablokoff! Yes, yes, I'm engaged. The way Yablokoff presented it to me, how could I say no? We'll be together again, but this time with Yablokoff's headache!" he laughed. "Tell Schneider he can start selling benefits for the new star-combination: Yablokoff - Skulnik -Myself!"

Goldele, The Baker's Daughter

As I sat in my office of the theater, engrossed in work, I heard a soft knock at the door. A little girl poked her head in. Looking at me with her big, cherry-black eyes, she asked, "Zindt Zie der Herr Yablokoff?"

"Ja, das bin ich," I responded in German, somewhat amused. "Come in child."

"What can I do for you, my dear?"

"Can I please get a job in your theater?" she stammered, her earnest tone so incongruous with her childish naivete that I was tempted to laugh.

"A job?" I repeated, striving to match her seriousness. "What can you do in the theater?"

"I would like please, to be an actress," she replied with more assurance.

"What is your name, little girl?"

"Marilyn, Marilyn Bieler. My Jewish name is Malkele."

"Malkele! Fine. Tell me, Malkele, have you ever performed on the stage?"

"Ja, many times, in Philadelphia at the Children's Home. I lived there. I was brought over to Philadelphia with a transport of children from Germany."

"Where are your parents, my dear?"

"My mother is downstairs waiting..."

"Well then, I must speak to your mother. Ask her to come up."

This is unbelievable, I thought. Here I am, casting about for just this type of little girl to play the center figure of the play, and out of the blue, she materializes! Malkele soon came back with her mother, a pale, thin, sickly-looking little woman.

From her mother I learned that Malkele was among the first transport of children brought from Europe to Philadelphia by a Jewish philanthropist. She gave her sponsors no rest until they brought her parents over a year later. They had just moved to New York, the woman told me, where her husband found occasional work in a tailor shop. Malkele had taken part in some children's plays at the Home and everyone said she had great talent. As it was known that I featured children in my productions, she'd been advised to bring the child to me.

I was in a spot. While I felt that this kid would be perfectly suited for the part, I hesitated to take a chance on an untrained youngster in such an important role. It is difficult enough to direct a kid who has had professional stage experience. What was I to do about this little girl, who stirred such great pity in me? It was my first contact with an uprooted Jewish family. Who could know the circumstances of the children in my own family with whom I had lost all contact. My heart went out to the Bielers. The child's earnings, I felt would be a great help to them.

"Can you sing, Malkele?"

"Ja, I can sing die Greeneh Kuzineh." Without hesitation she gave out with: "Tzu mir is gekomen eine Kuzineh..." Well, I thought never mind the lyrics—her voice rang true and clear as a bell.

"Very good," I applauded. "Look, I will write out a scene for you in Yiddish, with German letters. You learn the lines by heart. When you know them well, come back here and I will get you an audition. In any case, I will give you a job among the other kids in the show. All right?"

Malkele and her mother left my office, elated.

Next morning, in my office, there came a knock at my door—again Malkele! She knew the entire sequence by heart, and was ready for her audition. She spoke her lines and I sat there amazed. Although she gave most of the words a German pronunciation, she spoke with feeling and conviction—a rarity among children. In the dramatic moments she shed copious tears.

Eureka! I had found *Goldele, the Baker's Daughter*. After a while we dropped the baker's daughter form the title and remained only with Goldele. I kept my discovery a secret. I let the cast and the public keep puzzling for a while as to who would be featured in the title role. Most likely Bella Mysell, everyone thought, never dreaming that Goldele was to be a child.

During the summer I worked with little Malkele until she was letter perfect. After Labor Day, I called rehearsal for the entire cast. That was when I told them that Goldele would be played by a little girl, a DP from Germany. She would rehearse with us only on weekends, since she had to attend school. She absolutely stunned them!

"Well, we can all go home!" quipped Skulnik. "This kid will walk away with the show! Nobody will even know the rest of us are alive!"

The women began pouring motherly affection on Malkele, overwhelming her mother with compliments.

I begged everyone in the company to please refrain from fussing over the youngster. I knew from experience that as soon as child performers begin to feel their importance, they can become unmanageable. There is much to be tolerated, not only from the children themselves, but from their mommas. Stage mothers—with very few exceptions—are a bane, a species unto themselves.

The production opened with a spectacular number featuring the principals, the chorus and dance group. When the curtain rose, the stage came alive with units of boy and girl scouts, and cub scouts in full regalia with flags and banners flying. As they marched in, led by the tiniest cub scout, Sammy Milman as drummer boy, the audience broke into spontaneous and thunderous applause. It was an ovation one might sooner expect at the grand finale of a show!

Since my son Jackie was a boy scout at the time, I was able to purchase authentic uniforms at the official scout outlets. It was a most colorful and exciting opening number. Certainly a first on the Yiddish stage!

The production of *Goldele* scored so tremendously, both with the audience as well as the Jewish and English press, that there was no doubt in my mind that I was in for a mint of money. The cast, the music, the ballet numbers, especially the dream scene with all the fairy tale characters, Snow White and the Seven Dwarfs, Jack and Jill, Cinderella and the Good Fairy, were the talk of the town. The combination of Yablokoff - Skulnik - Mysell was a master stroke.

Malkele, as I expected, was a sensation. When it got around that she was a DP child, she was showered with gifts sent in by our patrons. In the beginning even I could not believe that a child of her tender age could command such an involved role. Then, as good as she was to begin with, she turned just as bad and unruly several weeks later. The very same ladies of the ensemble in whom she had stirred such maternal feelings began to complain that the brat was insufferable. She was impossible to be with in the shared dressing room, as well on stage. It was useless for me to say I told you so. The tens of thousands of people who saw this child portraying the pathetic Goldele would never have believed that this dear, sweet little angel was actually behaving like a demon!

At one of the matinee performances, while Skulnik and I were preparing for the show in our shared dressing room, who should pop up, but Malkele's father. He had a grievance against me, he said.

"The entire audience of two thousand people who have come to the theater today, and to every other performance, come to see my Malkele!"

Aha! Skulnik and I exchanged glances.

"So what?" I asked, nonchalantly.

"So, I want to be a partner to the big profits you are making!"

"I am paying your child almost as much as I am paying the professional union actors. I can't do any better." My words fell on deaf ears.

"If you don't give in to my demand. I won't let her go on. I'd like to see what you would do without my Malkele!"

Skulnik and I felt that this character could very well carry out his threat. I knew I had to handle him with diplomacy.

"Well, all right," I humored him, "I'll think it over." After the matinee, I called Betty Marcus, a sedate little girl who had played with me before. She knew the part of Goldele to perfection from the day the show opened. I had kept this undercover, and engaged Betty as an understudy. What if Malkele took sick, I thought. Why take chances? When Betty came, I ran through the lines and musical numbers with her, and told her to be ready to go on at the next performance if necessary. Betty was thrilled. She'd been waiting for such a break. However, I kept stalling Malkele's father and let his daughter play off the evening show.

The next day, when Malkele showed up for the matinee, the dresser who had herself suffered enough from this little devil, joyfully gave her the message: "You can go home now. Another girl is playing your part."

Before long, Mr. Bieler came running. "What is this? All the people out there have come to see my Malkele and you have another girl playing her part?!"

This time I could not restrain myself and told him to get out. Little Betty went through the performance; the audience applauded; nobody knew the difference. And most important—nobody demanded their money back.

That Monday afternoon, a young man came to my office. He had made a special trip from Philadelphia to see me. If his late father was still alive, he said, he too, would have come.

"It was my father," he explained, "who brought the first transport of homeless children over from Europe. Malkele gave him a great deal of trouble, constantly nagging at him to bring her parents over from Germany...which, of course, was natural and easy to understand. It cost him a fortune to arrange their particular immigration to the United States, for it was no easy process. With their arrival came fresh aggravation. No matter what my father did for them, they were not satisfied. Then, one day, taking Malkele, they up and left for New York.

"Still, it made my father happy to hear that the little girl was appearing in your theater. If this child was enjoying success, then he had indeed accomplished something, after all. It gave him a last bit of contentment before he died. When her mother called to tell me what happened here, I decided to speak with you."

I appreciated this man's coming to see me, and I set down my conditions: "The child's parents are not to come backstage anymore; the dresser and the rest of us will see to her needs; Malkele will have to alternate with Betty; the decision as to which of them is to play, and when, will be designated by me. And if Malkele does not behave according to rules and do as she is told, Betty will take over for the run of the show."

From experience I knew that all of these warnings wouldn't help much. But to send the kid packing altogether, I had no heart. She was an exceptional talent. All I could do was grin and bear it. The only, and most effective, punishment was to have little Betty substitute for her in a performance, now and then.

Men in White

The critics in the Yiddish press, as well as my intellectual friends, often admonished me "Yablokoff, you're a great success this season, making a fortune, we hear... so why not give the intellectuals a treat and also produce a literary drama?"

My reply was: "I have no wish to, nor can I compete with Maurice Schwartz and his Art Theater. He had legitimately earned this priority. I stick to my middle-of-the-road formula and strive to give the public an intelligent performance, a combination of everything. And this, judging by the thoroughly pleased audiences filling my theater nightly, I manage to do. Am I to doubt whether or not I'm on the right track?!"

Still, remembering the Literary Thursdays that were so popular years back in the provinces, and thinking that they might also catch on here, on Second Avenue, I was finally persuaded to produce a special literary drama. This would be given on nights when there were no benefits. It would surely be a worthwhile experiment.

I went about this plan with the greatest of care. No longer a novice in the business. I was only too well acquainted with the assortment of excuses used to explain a flop: "This play is really not of the highest caliber, still if they had had another regisseur, then maybe... But this one is not suited to direct a classic. He only butchered it The cast? These actors are accustomed to their song-and-dance stuff... But where do they come off tackling literary works? No wonder the intellectuals stay away."

Well, I certainly wasn't going to gamble my money on ifs and buts.

About the choice of a play? I bought the rights to Sidney Kingsley's Pulitizer-prize drama, *Men in White*. How could I go wrong?

Regisseur? Bob Harris, who directed the original play on Broadway, also playing a leading role in the English version.

The cast? Barney Kisner, an American-Yiddish actor from Broadway; several well-suited members of my own troupe and others recruited from the American stage—Equity members. Skulnik, Bella and I did not participate.

The Yiddish translation was done by the playwright Meyer Schwartz, a very erudite man. The premiere of *Men in White* was attended by New York's elite—most of them on free passes. The Yiddish and American press praised the performance to the skies. Several critics said it was a finer production and a far better cast than they had seen in English. So, who could ask for anything more?!

The result? The play ran for all of three nights! In protest, the audience created scandals at each of these performances, hurling vociferous complaints at the box office as they walked out in the middle of the show.

The irony of it all was that, even with this cultural endeavor, the intelligentsia found flaws: "This is no play for a Yiddish audience!"

And so, this spiritual pleasure in the name of art—at which I had aimed—cost me over $10,000. Although the press rewarded me with merits for my worthy experiment, the only happy note to come out of this flop was that Barney Kisner, the leading man fell in love—for real—with the leading lady in the play, our own dear Gertie Bulman. They were subsequently married and settled in Los Angeles. Bob Harris, the director, continued as a prominent actor in television and films.

Thus ended my experiment with a Pulitzer-prize play, no less, on Second Avenue.

My Son's Bar Mitzvah

To an actor, the phrase "the show must go on" is often quoted together with malediction, wishing it had never been invented...especially in the Yiddish theater. For we could never afford the luxury of maintaining understudies on the payroll. So, dead or alive...!

My son had been studying Hebrew at the Linden Heights Talmud Torah in Boro Park, where Rabbi Boruch Charney was preparing him for his bar mitzvah. And this happened to come up during the very height of the theater season. So there I was, faced with the actor's lot—a Saturday matinee performance while my only son's bar mitzvah was being held at a synagogue in Brooklyn.

I was heartsick over it. And there was no way I could have planned for any kind of celebration where I could be present. These affairs are usually arranged months in advance. All I was able to manage was to order wine, whiskey and cake for the congregation. Early morning, right after prayers, during which my son did himself proud, I only had time to congratulate him and dash off to the the theater.

I did, nevertheless, ask Jackie to invite all his classmates to the Sunday matinee of *Goldele*. Our daughter, Nita, also came with a bunch of school chums. After taking them all on a tour backstage to ogle the behind-the-scenes "mysteries," and plying them with ice cream and cookies, I felt that this was a greater treat for them than any banquet I could have arranged at the Waldorf Astoria. The kids had a ball! And before they all left, I surprised my son with his bar mitzvah present—a Ferrato cello.

64

What a Project! What a Finale!

Jacob R. Schiff, a man of great wealth and great friendship for the Yiddish theater and its people, bought the Public Theater on Second Avenue. It was later known as the Anderson.

"Mister Schiff has purchased the theater, not for profit," reported Guskin at a general meeting of the actors' union, "but to make certain that the house remains a Yiddish theater. This is a very vital asset for our union." This was met by a rousing ovation both for Schiff and for Guskin.

Throughout the years of the Public Theater's existence, nobody had succeeded in realizing any profits there. In fact, some managers had lost their shirts. The most recognized artists had, at one time or another, played at this theater, producing musicals, dramas...with audiences applauding, critics writing words of praise, yet nobody had been able to stick out a season.

Standing practically across the street from the Second Avenue Theater, the Public certainly offered us no competition.

For the coming season, I was well prepared with a new play called *Live and Laugh* by Harry Kalmanowitz. Ilia Trilling was already at work on the score in his summer hideaway. The combination of our three names—Yablokoff, Skulnik, Mysell—so successful the season before with *Goldele*, kept the organizations flocking to the office of good old Phil Schneider. There were simply not enough midweek nights to accommodate the committees who wanted full house benefits.

Summer was moving along and the Public Theater was still vacant. The popular star comedian, Itzhak Feld, negotiated for it, and so did Yehuda Bleich, but it was just talk—no results.

Reuben Guskin wanted to see me about something, so I met him in the Royale. I could tell right off that he was distraught.

"Let's take a walk," he suggested, "I don't want to talk here in the cafe. You know how things get around..."

We walked up to the little park at Seventeenth Street, and sat down.

"What am I to do?" he started. "Jacob Schiff, as you know, has purchased the Public Theater for the union members. I have already tried every combination possible for someone to take it over. I tell you, I don't sleep nights. Here I can have a troupe of members making a living...and nothing! You, Yabby, are a producer of course, one of our most prominent ones, but you are also

399

a good-standing member of the union. So I can talk to you freely. How will it look for the union, if the Public Theater should remain closed because we have no one willing to play there?! We always cry for help and when someone actually goes to the extent of buying a theater for us, what are we supposed to say, 'Thank you but no thanks?!' Can you imagine what I'm going through?"

"It's a serious problem all right. But how can I help?"

"The union and I, personally, would deem it a tremendous favor if...well, only you could swing it and save the situation. What I mean is, maybe you would consider taking over the Public?"

I gasped, "What are you saying?! I already have a theater. I'm making a nice living there and I'm more than satisfied. I believe that the union, as well as you, are also satisfied with me."

"Very much so, Yablokoff! Why you are the only one among the managers who does not owe the union a penny. In fact, we owe you plenty out of the 'benefit pot.' You have acted like a gentleman. That's why we are turning to you. Every year we seem to lose another playhouse. Pretty soon there won't be a theater left to play in. You are the only one who can help us now. You must take over the Public Theater!"

"You've got to be joking! You, more than anyone should know how difficult it is to pull through a season just in one theater! Are you asking me to take on a double headache?! Besides, what will Edelstein say? There is a clause in our contract that prohibits me from involving myself in any other theater enterprise."

"Edelstein will release you from this clause," Guskin quickly assured me. "Edelstein himself is interested in my idea for both of you to take over the Public as partners. I'll let you in on a secret: there is a question whether the Second Avenue Theater will remain a theater next year. The owners, you see, are deceased. The executors and lawyers handling the estate are giving the Edelsteins a hard time. They are seriously thinking of tearing down the building. So, Edelstein wants to insure himself of another theater on the avenue. I have already spoken to him. You will not have to invest a cent. He will take care of that. Your deal will be exactly on the same principles as now. And both of you will also share the $3,000, derived from the candy-and-soda concession. Consider what it will mean having no competition from a rival theater facing you. Even at its worst, the Public Theater still took in as much as $80,000 a season in benefits. This money too will fall into your general income. You'll make a million...let alone the prestige of running two theaters at the same time! This has never been accomplished in the history of the Yiddish theater!"

I said, shrugging my shoulders, "How can I produce a play in two different theaters at the same time, particularly in my elaborate style? How can I direct two companies, composers, musicians, scenic artists, chorus and dancers, choreographers, not counting all the employees out of the thirteen unions?

And both productions opening within a few days of each other? Don't forget I have to play nine shows a week. Who wants to commit suicide?! For me to take on the responsibility of two such enterprises at the same time, I have to be completely out of my mind!"

"Up to now, Yabby, you've broken down so many barriers and accomplished things I never thought you could! That's why I feel that you can overcome these other challenges as well. I can assure you that the union, as a whole, and I myself, will help you any way we can. We will meet you more than half way on all issues. Mr. Schiff is threatening to give the building away to anyone who will have it. Can we afford that? We will lose another house! It may affect your own future in the business. Who can tell? Let's discuss it with Edelstein. I'll give him a call and ask him to come up to the office."

"Well, what do you think of this development?" Edelstein greeted me with a laugh as he came into Guskin's office. "It's entirely up to you, Yabby. With you in the deal, I'll go partners. Without you, it's off. I won't tie myself up with anyone else."

"I'd like to talk it over with my wife, and Menasha Skulnik," I tried to stall for more time.

Guskin didn't lose a minute calling Bella and Skulnik to please come up. He was determined not to let the matter rest.

Bella, caught off guard and unaware as to how I felt about this zany proposition, said, "I never interfere in my husband's business affairs." Skulnik was dumfounded. And although he liked the idea, he refrained from urging me into it.

"If I should agree to take over the Public Theater," I said, still struggling for an alibi, "I will have to give up acting. It will seem odd, of course: an actor, with two theaters on the avenue, yet not appearing in either of them. First and foremost, I am an actor. I want to play. I was forced into the business end of it for that very reason. No one wanted to give me a chance any other way. If I had considered a career as a businessman, would I have chosen the Yiddish theater business?"

"So for the first season perhaps, you won't play," said Guskin. "Later on, who will stop you from playing in your own theater if you feel like it?"

Again I mentioned the clause in my contract, hoping Edelstein would take the hint and get me off the hook. Instead, his response was, "Yabby, I would prefer having you star at the Second Avenue; but if it is physically impossible for you to play, I won't hold you to it for the first season. How could I? I'll be partners with you at the Public."

After discussing the pros and cons for hours, I couldn't hold out anymore. Finally, Edelstein and I shook hands and wished ourselves happy sailing.

"So tell me, Yabby, who will play Yablokoff's part?" Menasha quipped. "Your part is a knockout. I wouldn't give it up for anything!"

"Don't let it worry you. We'll get a better actor than I to take over. And you'll get the chance you've been hoping for—first billing! As for me, I'll con-

tent myself with my advertised trade mark: A Herman Yablokoff Production—
starring Menasha Skulnik and Bella Mysell. OK, Menasha?"

"OK, Yabby."

And that was how Chaimke from Grodno became the boss of two foremost Yiddish theaters in New York.

My first concern was to search for a suitable play for the Public Theater.
With two separate enterprises to operate simultaneously, I could not very well
take time to sit down and write one myself. I assigned the task to the dramatist
Abraham Bloom and my collaborator Itzhak Friedman. They came up with
a mighty fine script for an elaborate musical-drama, based on the then-popular
film, *Rebecca*. I named the production after one of my hit songs, *My White
Flower*, which I had dedicated to Bella.

For composer-conductor, I engaged the dean of Yiddish composers, Joseph
Rumshinsky. Aside from being a gifted musician, he was a great showman.
In every composition, it was the melody, the theme, that prevailed, never over-
shadowed by the orchestration. I felt that we were geared toward success!

* * *

"When do you intend to start engaging your companies?" asked Guskin
as we sat in the Cafe Royale. "All the actors in the union are waiting for you.
As soon as you make a move, things will get busy."

"Please, let me have a few more weeks, at least, to enjoy being a boss."

"I don't understand," he eyed me, puzzled. "You are boss…of two of the
biggest playhouses we have!"

"Exactly. That's why I have it so good. All the actors give me the big hello
and shower me with compliments on my business acumen. I'm riding high.
But, as soon as I sign up actors for my productions, nobody will give me a
tumble. Those I engage will immediately regard me as the 'slave driver.' And
those I don't will have no use for me at all! So, please let me enjoy my role
of boss a little longer."

I never heard Guskin laugh so heartily. Still, I complied with his request
and began casting my two productions. At the outset I made it clear to each
performer as to which theater he, or she, would be working in, explaining that
these were two completely separate corporations.

Heading the cast at the Second Avenue were Menasha Skulnik, Bella Mysell,
Muni Serebroff.

Heading the cast at the Public were Edmund Zayenda, Miriam Kressyn.
With Skulnik as star comedian at the Second Avenue, I felt a sense of security.
Now who, I wracked my brain, could I possibly engage as star comedian at
the Public? A new face, someone who could lure the people to the box office.
And suddenly, it hit me!—Max Bozyk in Buenos Aires! If I could bring him
to the States, he would certainly fill the bill! Bozyk had already been seen in
Yiddish films with Molly Picon, shown in the states with great success.

Bozyk was elated. When, and how soon, he wanted to know could he, his wife and child leave Argentina for the United States?

When I made this known to Guskin, he warned me that this was sure to start an uproar in the union since several fine character comedians were still unemployed. My intent, I argued, was not to put down any of our talented union members. What I needed was a star comedian qualified to vie with a drawing card like Skulnik. It had to be a new face, an artist with enough stature to share billing with Zayenda and Kressyn.

Nobody believed that I would succeed in getting a visa for the Bozyks. By now, Hitler had laid siege to all of Europe... England was on the brink of destruction... Russia was fighting with her last strength... and America was being extremely wary about granting visas to applicants with Polish documents.

I contacted the congressman for our district, Arthur Klein. He promised to use his good offices in helping me. It was far from an easy mission. But, after much tribulation—and much expense—the American visas were issued.

As we had a long-standing precedent in the actors' union, allowing foreign luminaries the privilege of starring with our companies in the States, I was granted a privilege for Max Bozyk. But, for his actress wife, Reizel? Under no circumstances. She would have to wait. Next, we ran into the problem of transportation. Ships were no longer making frequent journeys from South America, and time was running short. Rehearsals were to begin and I was desperate to have Bozyk in New York. There was only one recourse—Bozyk must fly! And even for this we needed a special permit. Thanks to my friend, Congressman Klein, this too was accomplished. At the crack of dawn, there I was at the airport to welcome him, like a star arriving from Hollywood.

I arranged to have his wife and child follow him by boat. Flying was too expensive. At the time of their arrival, civilians were no longer permitted on the pier. The smell of war hung in the air. With the help of the HIAS I managed to gain permission to board the ship and was the first to welcome Reizel Bozyk and little Susan to the United States.

* * *

Everyone wondered how I managed to produce and direct two such big productions at the same time. Where did I find time to confer with my separate business associates, technical staffs, set-builders and costume designers? "On roller skates" ran the jokes in the Royale.

I did in fact, work like a demon eighteen hours a day, rehearsing both companies in shifts. This of course, left me without a minute to catch my breath. Both theaters had to open within a few days of each other.

65

I'm Riding High

After Yom Kippur, the Second Avenue Theater held its premiere of *Live and Laugh*. It was a sparkling performance, played to a house sold out in advance. The crowd couldn't get enough of Menasha Skulnik and the grotesquely funny Yetta Zwerling. Bella Mysell and the suave Muni Serebroff, who played my part, carried off the romantic and intensely dramatic side of the play, contributing their own professionalism toward the success of the production. We sensed at once that it was going to be as successful as my previous productions and would run a full season.

The Public Theater's premiere—another auspicious event—took place four days later. I invited Congressman Klein and other Washington dignitaries, who helped me bring Bozyk to the States. *My White Flower*, with its strong melodramatic plot and beautiful romance, was another instant hit. Rumshinsky really outdid himself with his melodious score.

Our theater-going public hadn't seen a more handsome romantic lead than Edmund Zayenda, not since the younger days of Michal Michaleso! And Miriam Kressyn, his leading lady, was lovely to behold. She charmed her audience with her multifaceted talents as actress, singer and dancer.

A great source of satisfaction to me was the tremendous hit scored by our guest artist, Max Bozyk. I had picked a winner. To vie with a funny man like Menasha Skulnik, appearing directly across the avenue, one had to gird oneself pretty well! Bozyk was duly acknowledged by the press as a shining new asset on the Yiddish stage.

The consensus of opinion was that I had indeed performed a feat never before accomplished in the profession. Business couldn't be better in either house. "Yablokoff is becoming a millionaire!" they buzzed.

The most heartwarming words I received were from Reuben Guskin. "You have now established yourself as one of our most esteemed and talented directors, one of the most gifted showmen we have. You have made theatrical history and you deserve all the credit in the world!"

From a man not given to flattery, his praise was more gratifying to me. The press also swelled my head, calling me the "Shubert of the Yiddish Theater."

Maurice Schwartz

Sitting in the office of the Public Theater, I was dictating the narration of my radio program to my private secretary, Zelda Bernardi, when the phone rang.

"Hello? Mr. Maurice Schwartz?" Zelda asked, uncertain, "just a moment, please..."

"Hello, Mr. Schwartz," I said as surprised as Zelda. "How are you?"

"Don't ask!" came the answer in his well-known basso profundo. "You have heard, no doubt, that I have had to close my Art Theater. In twenty-five years, this should happen to me! It was impossible for me to go on. They squeezed me to the wall from all sides! I couldn't take it anymore. I'm calling you about a very important matter. I would like to see you... not in your office, if you don't mind."

"Of course," I replied, "just tell me where and I'll be there."

"I'm waiting in Kotlitzky's bake-shop across from you. I would appreciate it if you would come. I'll wait."

"Sure, I'll be right over."

Entering the bake-shop, I hardly recognized him. He was unshaven, his hair disheveled, clothes rumpled and the deep lines around his eyes, clearly indicated sleepless nights. I felt a twinge in my heart at sight of this great artist. How well I understood the pain he felt in having to close his Art Theater now, after the first week of the season! He had opened with *Judgment Day*, by Jochannan Twersky, and had been unable to meet the first week's payroll.

"Do you realize what a catastrophe has befallen me? I will have to traipse all over the world again to earn enough to pay off my debts. And where can one travel in times like these?! Europe is at war. There remains only Buenos Aires. And even Buenos Aires had become difficult to contact. I will have to find a way somehow. But what am I to do about the benefit tickets? Not that we sold very many... as if the organizations need such a thing as art theater! They have already begun to run uptown—to Broadway. English they want! Give them English! But the organizations that did buy their benefit tickets at the Art Theater... how can I leave them high and dry?! Can I rely on the managers of the other theaters, who've already offered to play off my benefits? What will they play for the art theater—their trash? I have read that you have produced two very respectable plays. Last year you produced *Men in White*... so I would much prefer to turn over my benefits of the Art Theater to you and have the performance played off at your Second Avenue Theater, or Public Theater."

"Tell me, is there any advance money left?"

"You should ask such a question?!" Schwartz shook his head. "Don't you know that the benefit money has already been eaten up during the summer? The production cost me a fortune, need I tell you? Well, there are some balances outstanding that will add up to a few thousand dollars, maybe. This money you will collect."

"And what about the federal tax money on the tickets?" I asked, surmising that this was the crux of the calamity.

"Oh, my friend," his voice sank even deeper, "do I ever bother with these things? My managers... they did the managing, and oh, did they manage me. But what's the use of all this talk. It's spilled milk. My biggest headache is the government. How can I have the internal revenue after me with the tax business? I'm appealing to you, play off my benefit tickets. Take this worry off my head. I will return the favor, I give you my word."

"Mr. Schwartz," I said decisively, "tell Milton Weintraub to bring me your list benefits. I will sort them accordingly and accommodate them in both of my theaters. Be at ease, I will do all I can to satisfy them. Brace up now, it isn't the end of the world," I tried to console him. "What's so unusual about hitting a bad streak in the theater business? I'm sure you will overcome this trying interlude and be back again with your Art Theater as prominent as before."

* * *

The war in Europe brought prosperity to the United States. People went about their business immune to the reports from overseas. The Jewish communities in America still continued their social, benevolent and cultural activities unaware of the searing holocaust hovering over the Jews in Europe. Any news that did somehow trickle through, giving accounts of German annihilation of the Jewish people in concentration camps and crematoriums, sounded so preposterous it failed to incite the protests it should have. Utterly incredible! was the reaction. And so, the world remained silent.

Lucky Me

For several days I'd been troubled by a sharp pain in the calf of my right leg. But who paid attention. I knew I'd been doing more than my share of trekking back and forth between my two theaters; to say nothing of the long hours on my feet during rehearsals. Still, the pain did not subside. If anything, it felt worse. I mentioned it to my friend Charlie Cohan, one of my actors and executive secretary of the Yiddish Theatrical Alliance.

"I've had this persistent pain in my leg. I find it difficult to walk. Charlie, you're always helping some ailing member of the Alliance. The doctors on your roster call you 'Doctor Cohan'—so how about helping me too? I'm a member."

"Well, being that you, 'Mr. Shubert,' are not just a plain member," Charlie ribbed, "I don't want to rely on Dr. Cohan's diagnosis. I'll go one better and take you to a professor!"

Letting all other matters rest, we grabbed a cab and Charlie took me to an orthopedic specialist. After a long and involved examination, I assumed he was through with me and started down from the table.

"Where do you think you're going?" the doctor stopped me. "You won't be going anywhere so soon, my friend. I'm going to put your leg in a cast, and you will be confined to bed for four to six weeks. The other leg, I'm afraid is also affected."

"But doctor, what are you saying?" I asked, horrified.

"You have a case of phlebitis. This is a dangerous type of inflammation. Oddly enough, it usually strikes pregnant women. So where do you come off having it?" the doctor grinned.

"Why not?" Charlie piped up, unable to resist a wisecrack. "Didn't he just give birth to two spectacular bambinos? And both of them heavyweights, knock on wood?!"

"Well," Dr. Mandel laughed, "could be those heavyweights are what laid him low. I saw both productions... terrific! So I can well imagine the strain, the physical labor he put in. Now, he's paying for it."

After my leg was encased in a plaster cast, I was lifted into a taxi, given orders not to walk, assisted into my apartment and put to bed. Even in bed, I was advised to have my legs elevated.

Bella and Anita were aghast at sight of me. They thought I'd been in a car accident. I was promptly put to bed and that was that!

Business was going great in both my theaters, although the Second Avenue with Menasha Skulnik was doing better, as we expected. With an extension telephone at my bedside, I ran my two businesses by phone.

According to the reports and box-office statements brought to me by my managers, I figured that, if business continued this way up to New Year's, I was good for $100,000 profit. Summing up the season, I had a chance of netting a quarter of a million dollars... and maybe more. "I'll settle for less," I joked... if only I could put my feet down and walk!

Evenings, when Bella had to leave for the theater, I was left in Anita's tender care. On matinee days, Saturday or Sunday, Jackie would pay me a visit and often brought his cello. He was quite advanced by now and it gave me keen pleasure to hear my son play. Now and then, Guskin as well as several friends from both theaters would come up to see me, to divert me with theater gossip.

One Sunday, after Bella had left for the matinee, I happened to fall asleep and missed the regular Sunday broadcasts, which I sponsored featuring the members of my troupes. About 1:30 in the afternoon, Friedman came up to see me. Glancing at the clock I was rather surprised. He should be at the theater, I thought. But there he stood at the foot of my bed staring at me, saying nothing.

"What's the matter?"

"You don't know?"

"What am I supposed to know? Well, go on, Friedman, tell me!"

"You heard nothing on the radio?"

"No, I slept all morning."

"Then turn on the radio, you'll hear something!"

I switched on the radio and heard: "This morning, at 7:50 a.m., Japanese planes began a treacherous attack on Pearl Harbor, causing severe damage to American naval and air units, with great loss of life. Japan has declared war on the United States."

It was December 7th, 1941.

* * *

Matinee performances at the various theaters that Sunday drew few people. My theaters were no exception. And the evening performances attracted
almost none.

The next day, December 8th, President Roosevelt asked Congress for a
war declaration against Japan and Congress immediately approved it. Men began
hurrying to induction centers to volunteer for military service. In the evening,
streets were steeped in darkness; windows were curtained in black to shut out
the merest hint of light. Theater marquees were ordered to be left unlit. The
lobbies had to be equipped with buckets of sand—a precaution against incen-
diary bombs from possible air raids. All street transportation had to navigate
with the dimmest of lights. A pall descended on the city. Who could even
think of such frivolity as going to the theater, or indulging in any kind of entertainment?

And in this crucial hour, when I should have been at the helm of my two
sinking ships, I was forced to leave them in the hands of others. And to quote
my mother: "With the hands of others, it is good to handle fire only!" There
I lay, confined to bed with phlebitis, forbidden to budge, while I was losing
between fifteen and twenty thousand a week. There was no box-office activity
to speak of in either house. But play, we did. Organizations insisted on can-
celling their dates, especially those with an outstanding balance. Nobody will
come, they contended—and they were right. Yet what could I do? It was an
act of God! Pearl Harbor! War!!!

With the help of crutches I hobbled down to my office. I held conferences
with my managerial staffs, with representatives of the different unions, but no
one lifted a finger to help me in this critical situation. My accountant, Dave
Kulok, advised me to close the Public Theater as soon as possible—for how
long could I go on losing enormous sums every week? Instead, I should concentrate on the Second Avenue Theater; where I could play off the remaining
benefits and block tickets of both houses.

With most of the unions I settled satisfactorily by giving them two weeks
notice. To my cast of the Public Theater I offered an additional two weeks'
salary as a bonus. (The managers of the other theaters had stopped paying wages
to the actors even before the attack on Pearl Harbor). The cast of the Public
Theater refused my offer. Why should the actors of the Second Avenue be
the lucky ones to continue the season, while they should have to close? Why
not the other way around? My argument in the union that the contract I had
with each and every one of them stated that my two theaters were two separate
corporations fell on deaf ears. By right, I should have given them the same
two weeks notice I'd given the other unions, yet here was I offering them an
additional two week's salary and they refused!

"Who knows of corporations? We know only Yablokoff!" they balked. Yablokoff engaged them and it is his responsibility to pay their salaries for a whole season, even if he does close the Public!

Reproaching Guskin, I said, "You, above everyone, know the truth. Did I want two theaters? You begged me to help the union, the profession... is this the thanks I get? Is this how the union is 'meeting me half way?'"

After much haggling I was forced to settle on paying both companies 75 percent of their original wages for the remainder of the season, with a pledge to pay the balance when things improved. Thus, during the worst times for the country, especially for theater, I was compelled to pay wages to two companies of thirty-six members; half of whom would not be performing for the rest of the season. Some, even worked here and there, but still collected their weekly pay from me.

As if I weren't already drowning, the Treasurer's and Manager's Union got after me. Since I was giving the actors such a deal, why not give the unemployed cashiers and managers of the defunct theater at least a bonus of two weeks' pay? If I didn't comply, they threatened to take their members off their jobs at the Second Avenue and picket the theater. So I gave in.

All I could do was try and save my name at least. Skulnik was the only one in full sympathy with me. I never forgot his compassion when I came out of my two theatrical ventures looking no better than Pearl Harbor after the Japanese attack!

* * *

No sooner did I give up my theatrical enterprises, when a sudden reversal took place and America found itself in the midst of a boom never experienced before! People began making money left and right. With the initial shock of war over, folks turned once again to places of diversion. Theaters, dance halls and nightclubs did a land office business with pleasure seekers wanting to laugh and be amused. It was wartime prosperity.

As for "lucky me," I was happy enough to be rid of my phlebitis. Organizing a traveling company, my wife and I went on the road with some of my hit plays and were very successful. To save my reputation, I sent every penny we could spare to my creditors to cover the remaining debts from my two theaters. I may have been down, but far from out. Consoling Bella, I jokingly said, "The capital of eighteen dollars, which I brought to United States in 1924, I still have! At least I did get a taste—if only for a fleeting moment—of standing on the brink of becoming a millionaire!"

* * *

I thought back over all these years as we sped along the autobahn in our ambulance. We finally approached Munich. Hans was exhausted and grumpy.

Maneuvering the timeworn ambulance was a great strain on him. Arzewski and Mishka weren't in a cheerful mood, either.

I really couldn't blame these aides of mine, great fellas! After all, what did they get out of this project? I, at least, was rewarded by applause, while they shared the brunt of the hardships with me for no reason at all. In Munich, without lifting a finger, their status as DPs would get them the very same food rations they were getting me. Arjzewski would prefer staying with his wife and child in Munich, and Mishka couldn't wait to stretch out on his bunk in the DP camp of New Freiman on the outskirts of Munich.

The city was steeped in darkness, not a living soul around. Streetlights were lit only for a few hours in the early evening. The beams of our headlights fell on caved-in chimneys rising out of the rubble, casting grotesque shadows on the heaps of scattered bricks. I had become accustomed to this shocking sight. It no longer affected me the way it did upon my first arrival in Munich from Paris.

66

Passover Seder in Jubilee Hall

I happened to arrive in Munich on the eve of Passover. The train plowed through the wreckage of what was once the terminal and came to stop at a post bearing the makeshift sign: Munich.

I looked around for someone who might have come to meet me, but saw no one. I was sure the JOINT in Paris informed their office in Munich about my coming. What worried me was whether this information had been received since communication with Germany was next to impossible.

The station master, an old man in a ragged uniform, soon came along. How, I asked him, could I get to Sieber Strasse with my heavy baggage? He referred me to a German chauffeur standing by, who drove a jeep for the American Red Cross. This fellow assured me that as soon as he had delivered the passengers he had come to pick up, he would be back to drive me to the JOINT headquarters.

The director of the JOINT in Paris promised that my other large trunks, which I had brought from New York carrying plays, music, costumes and makeup for the surviving Jewish actors in the camps, would be sent on with the special military trucks making the route from Paris to Germany.

I stood there and hoped that the German driver would indeed come back for me, or else I would have to celebrate the first Seder in the bombed-out railroad station. Lighting up a cigarette, I offered one to the station master. Instead of lighting up, the old man wrapped the cigarette in a slip of paper and stowed it away in his pocket like some rare gem. A group of youths, I noticed, hadn't taken their eyes off me. As soon as I tossed away my half-smoked butt, they pounced on it like a pack of wolves. The one who grabbed it took a deep drag on it and look transported.

The Red Cross driver did come back to fetch me.

Since 1181 Munich had held an important place in German history. What I now beheld was a city in ruin. Foremost historic structures, museums, impressive residences were wiped off the face of the earth; a glaring reminder of American air power. Only the towering monument erected near the banks of the Isar in 1871 still stood intact. And high on its steeple, hovered the golden Angel of Peace...what irony!

"How much do I owe you?" I asked the driver in stilted German, as we pulled up at JOINT headquarters.

"Five cigarettes," he ventured. I had a feeling he would just as well have taken three. But I gave him ten. He gaped at me. Bowing, he mumbled, "Danke schön, mein Herr." He never expected such a windfall.

In Paris I had already learned that the unofficial exchange in Germany was the American cigarette. To an outlander, the German mark was of no value at all. Using military currency, scrip, or American greenbacks was verboten to the civilian populace. Consequently, the best and safest exchange was the American cigarette. Not that this too didn't warrant arrest if caught. The brand of a cigarette also determined the price. The moment I set foot in Germany I was convinced that, armed with a pack of cigarettes, one could go places.

In the courtyard of the JOINT building, to my great surprise, I met a survivor from Grodno, Sholom Dreiser! We embraced like long-lost brothers. He was working for the Central Committee and heard that I was expected. "But of all times! On the very eve of Passover, with everyone in the staff gone off to celebrate somewhere out of Germany!"

Even the director, Sam Gaber, to whom I was to report, had taken leave for a few days.

Dreiser also informed me that a number of survivors from Grodno, had set out for France—illegally—upon learning that I, the president of the Grodno Federation of America and Canada, was in Paris. I was beside myself. Of all the foolhardy things to do! Taking such a risk, smuggling across borders to see me in Paris, when I was here, in Munich! A crazy, mixed-up world, to be sure!

Dreiser showed me to the billet where JOINT directors were quartered. The only ones who had remained in Munich for the Passover holiday were Dr. Philip Friedman and his wife, Ada, a doctor herself. These gentle people were among the survivors and were now dedicated to researching and compiling all salvaged documents related to the Holocaust. The Friedmans made me welcome. They invited me into their room, where I was surprised to find a piano of all things. From them I learned that Sam Gaber had not received any communication of my arrival and had, in fact, expressed concern over it.

"Do you have a place to go for the Seder?" asked Ada Friedman.

"No, I don't know anyone in Munich and no one knows me."

"Then you'll join us at the communal Seder prepared by the JOINT in Jubilee Hall. We'll get you a meal coupon at the door. Without the coupon nobody eats!"

The Seder

In the very same Jubilee Hall, where Hitler held his venomous speeches against the Jews, the Seder was held for a thousand Jewish DPs and Jewish military men serving the American Army of Occupation. In shabby full-dress, Germans waited on table, serving them the Passover "feast." The hall was decorated with flags of blue-and-white with the Star of David, and on a special stand stood six tall memorial candles to sanctify the memory of the six million martyrs.

The rabbi's four-year-old son asked the traditional four questions in the Haggadah. This was followed by a little DP boy asking the questions out of a new handwritten Haggadah:

"In what way is this Passover night different from that of the previous year? Why do we remain in the DP camps? What has changed in the world and in the lot of our people after the war? When will there arise a new world of work, freedom, brotherhood and equality? When will we at last be a free nation among free nations? When will dawn the day...?"

At these heartbreaking questions, coming from the mouth of a tiny child, I choked back tears.

The menu of the Seder consisted of matzohs, courtesy of Manischewitz, Carmel wine from Palestine, a sampling of gefilte fish, a forkful of meat and potatoes and a few vegetables.

An actor from Munich Yiddish Kunst Theater stopped by our table. I asked him to let Israel Becker and the rest of the actors know of my arrival. I also learned that a Yiddish daily newspaper was issued in Germany. It was done in Yiddish, if type was available, or else in Latin letters spelled phonetically. No matter. Even in the DP camps, Jews were eager to know what was going on in the world.

A woman at the table remarked: "They ought to put all the Americans into concentration camps, then they would get a taste of what we have endured and what we now endure before we can emigrate to America!"

Well, well, a fine how-do-you-do! I simply couldn't let this go unanswered. "My dear lady, with such an opinion of Americans, perhaps you had better emigrate to China!"

The woman flushed. "It was an ill-chosen remark. After Bergen-Belsen, please don't blame me for feeling the way I do. I have relatives in America. I know they want me, yet here I am, still stuck in Germany. Please forgive me."

Sam Gaber

Early next morning, returning from his short leave, Sam Gaber was startled to find a stranger in his bed, although he soon caught on that the stranger must surely be me.

"Welcome aboard!" he said. "I'm sure glad that you've come to Germany. Sorry I didn't have someone to meet you at the train. Phone connections with Paris are impossible. It was difficult to make out what was being said at the other end of the wire, so I couldn't figure out just when you were due in Munich. But welcome!"

Sam Gaber, an American, was a tall, heavy-set young man. After changing into his military uniform of high-ranking officer, he took me to the JOINT mess hall for breakfast. "By the way," he said with a big smile, "my mother in Philadelphia is a great fan of yours."

The cook, a Jewish DP woman from Poland, fixed us a special matzoh brei. After spending a month in Paris where every bite of food was doled out on ration cards, this holiday breakfast was a gourmet treat for me.

"Getting the military permit for your entrance into Germany," he said, "was a difficult project. Rabbi Philip Bernstein, who attended your concert at the Salle Pleyel in Paris, is the representative of Jewish Affairs on General Lucius Clay's staff. He put forth a great deal of effort in your behalf. They don't want American civilians 'spectators' in occupied Germany. The circumstances of the Jews in the DP camps," he explained, "are pretty tragic. The people are filled with despair. Life is rugged here…even for Americans. And there's no room for prima donnas either, Yabby," he intimated with a grin. "Don't mind my calling you Yabby. I know that's what your friends call you. Please call me Sam. We don't stand on ceremony here. Everything must be accepted with good grace. For expressing any criticism you can be sent packing. Everything is censored by the army of occupation," he briefed me. "You have to watch every word. Just look, listen and keep your mouth shut. My biggest problem now is finding you a pianist to travel to the camps with you as your accompanist."

Gaber told me that I could stay in Rabbi Solomon Shapiro's room since he was away for the holiday. I felt uncomfortable camping in someone else's room, but I had no choice. Didn't Gaber inform that this was no place for prima donnas?

Before turning in that night, Gaber, in a reminiscent mood, recalled that at Passover time, as a youngster back home in Philadelphia, his mother used to take him to Walnut Street Theater to see me. "Imagine fate throwing us together, of all places, here in Germany! My mother won't believe it!"

I debated with myself whether to confide in Gaber about the personal matter pressing on my mind. Somehow, I felt that this was the opportune moment.

"Sam, you're a regular fellow," I began with a compliment, "I fell that I can talk to you about a matter that concerns me deeply. The four weeks I spent in Paris I wore myself out knocking on doors attempting to gain admittance in to Austria. My niece, Dora, a daughter of one of my brothers, is in a DP camp in Linz. Except for me she has no one in the world. Sam, I need your advice and your help. Before I start my concert tour, I want more than anything to find my niece. I want to rescue her from that hell. She has already suffered enough in her young life, and now…" I could barely go on for the emotion that welled up inside me.

Obviously startled by my request, Gaber nevertheless was moved. "Listen, Yabby, your military permit is valid for the American zone in Germany only. Austria is a separate country and is governed by the four major powers. To go there you have to obtain a special permit and travel orders." After a long pause, he said, "I'll try to help you. Tomorrow is the second day of Passover and I'm not working. We'll take a ride to the Austrian border near Salzburg. I can't guarantee you we'll be permitted to cross the borders. First of all, my friend, we'll have to 'organize' an army uniform for you. In civvies you can't go anywhere. For now, let's catch forty winks, and at break of day we'll start out for Austria."

Gaber set his alarm clock so he couldn't oversleep. I, of course, needed no such thing... as if I could even shut an eye! I could not believe that I was on my way to see my niece, the little Dora whom I had last seen in Grodno as a tiny tot. Only through her letters did I learn where she was.

Gaber scrounged up an Eisenhower jacket, a pair of matching pants and an army shirt. Any of Gaber's uniforms would have fit two of me. The only items in his wardrobe that I could wear, were his army tie and overseas cap. Transformed so suddenly into an army man, I hardly recognized myself.

Stowing a few tins of candy, cigarettes and his Leica camera into a knapsack, Gaber and I climbed into his jeep and off we went to the Austrian border.

In the distance, high in the Bavarian Alps, soon emerged Hitler's snow-capped "Eagle's Nest," where he and his mistress, Eva Braun, often came to roost. "Not far from here," Gaber pointed out, "is Berchtesgarden, the resort spot where the historic meeting took place between Hitler and Chamberlain... and his umbrella," Gaber laughed.

On reaching the Austrian border, a few kilometers from Salzburg, we came upon lines of army trucks, cars and jeeps waiting for border inspection. Gaber steered right up to the border patrol's shack. Leaving me to wait in the jeep, he hopped out and hailed the guards like they were old buddies. On an earlier trip to Salzburg, he had taken snapshots of the American MPs at this checkpoint, promising to send them copies. Having brought them along, he passed them around, much to their delight. Again snapping pictures of some other MPs at the post, he promised to bring back copies anew, so that they too could send them to the folks back home. He so distracted them, they never thought to ask for travel orders, and waved us right through to Austria. I breathed a great sigh of relief!

The road from Salzburg to Linz was terrible. All the bridges were out. The detours onto side roads sloped dangerously downhill, or hazardously uphill, before they connected back to the main road.

My Surviving Niece

It was midday when we arrived in Linz. Across the bridge, on the other side of the Danube, lay the Russian zone of occupation. Two red flags flapped in the distance. We somehow found our way to the DP camp in Wegsheid.

Camp Tyler was fenced in by the same barbed wire as it had been under the Nazis—although no longer electrically charged. A military guard stood at the gate, a large sign overhead forbidding admittance to the camp by military personnel and Austrian civilians.

In a shack close by was the office of the American camp commandant, in whose charge were over six thousand Jewish men, women and children. Gaber reported to the commandant, inventing a story about our being on a mission involving the immigration papers for one of the camp's Jewish families. This congenial officer gave us permission to drive into the camp.

I had heard about the conditions in which the remnants of the Holocaust still weltered. But, the unbelievable pictures that met my eyes was beyond anyone's imagination. It had rained the night before and the mud was ankle deep. Outdoors, women stood over tin pots, in which they were cooking something over loosely piled smoldering bricks. Children, in tatters, ran about in the mud. The sudden appearance of a jeep with two men in American uniforms caused an immediate stir. Heads came poking out of the wooden barracks. Some hurried outdoors, agog at the unexpected visitors. Stopping at one of the barracks, we were instantly surrounded by a host of children. Gaber, armed with a supply of chewing gum, passed them out which won us the youngsters' immediate trust.

"Can you please tell me where I can find Dora Yablonik from Grodno?" I asked some of the men and women beginning to crowd around us. "I'm looking for my niece Dora. Don't let our uniforms scare you. We're Jews, from the JOINT. I am Dora's uncle from America. Do you know her? Is she still here?"

"Dor'ke? Dor'ke Yablonik?" repeated one of the women. "Of course, she's here! Where else would she be?! Do they let us out of here? Dora and her husband, Shimon, are expecting a baby any day now."

"Do me a favor," I asked one of the boys, "please go call Dora's husband Shimon. Don't tell them that her uncle is here. I don't want to startle and upset her at this time."

Soon enough, along came a young man in his twenties, with a pleasingly handsome face and a crop of light brown crinkly hair. Shimon hesitated at sight of me, and then, as if by a sixth sense, uttered, "Uncle?!" We threw our arms around each other, too overcome to say a word.

"How is Dora?" I asked, anxiously.

"Very good," he managed to reassure me. "Up to yesterday we lived in the barrack over there. But, it was so congested. I have a roomier place now. We'll have it all to ourselves, and it will be more comfortable for Dora and the baby. Come, uncle. Dora will be wondering why I was called away so suddenly. Come…"

Escorting Gaber and me to their new quarters, Shimon explained, "There was this empty barracks at the edge of camp, formerly a commune of young people who recently took off for Palestine, aliyah beth (illegal immigration). The barrack was falling apart, with everyone pulling out beams, slats and logs for kindling wood. I partitioned off a corner, put in an old door and, despite all the cracks, we're comfortable enough."

On hearing voices, Dora came to the door. She was taken aback by our uniforms for a frightening moment. But she soon recovered and with a cry of "Uncle! Uncle!" fell into my arms.

"Uncle, I had a feeling that you would come, my heart told me so," she murmured. "Aunt Bella wrote us that you had gone on a tour of America and Canada and would not be able to write us as regularly as before. But then I began to wonder why Aunt Bella didn't go along with you on the tour. Besides that, another survivor from Grodno, Leyb Reiser, who is in Camp Bindermichel nearby told me that he'd read in an old newspaper that you were giving concerts in Paris. I somehow knew that you would come to find me. And here are the packages Aunt Bella sent me... all the things I will need for the baby. Bless her, she thought of everything, just like a mother." Tears filled her eyes, but she fought them back.

Dora was indeed due any day. How I wished I could stay with her during this vital hour in her young life!

"I'm sorry but I can't spend my time with you. I must start back. I only arrived in Munich yesterday, and I must try to find a way of getting you out of here. My friend, Sam Gaber is a very important director with the JOINT in Germany. In fact, he took a big chance bringing me here."

"But uncle, you only just got here. We haven't even had a chance to get to know each other..."

"I know, dear, but I'll be back," I reassured her. "I don't know exactly when, but I will try by every means possible to get back into Austria. I promise that I will not leave Germany before I can make it possible for you and Shimon to emigrate to America. You are my children and I will look after you as a father!"

Gaber, in his American-accented Yiddish, also comforted them and explained that we must indeed hurry back. Giving Shimon the address and telephone number of the JOINT in Munich, he told him that, if he needed anything he was to get in touch with the JOINT office here in Linz, which, in turn, would contact him by phone. Gaber said he would call the JOINT director in Linz and ask him to help them any way they could.

With a heavy heart I took leave of my new-found children and pressed a handful of dollar bills into Shimon's palm.

When we walked back to the jeep, eager moppets were climbing all over it. After a fresh distribution of candy and much persuasion, Gaber finally got them to climb down and let us proceed out of camp where all was astir over the news that Dora's uncle had come from America! Followed by the stares of thousands of Jews, hopeless and despairing, we left the grounds and drove out of Austria back to Munich.

* * *

Dusk fell, Gaber stepped on the gas, anxious to get back. In a few days, he said, he would have a surprise for me—the pictures he'd snapped of my first embrace with Dora. He was obviously touched by our emotional meeting.

"If such a scene were to be portrayed on stage," he said, "the critics would lambaste it as sheer exaggeration and overacting." Then he asked me how I first learned that she was alive.

"When Dora was liberated from Auschwitz, she reported to the Red Cross that she was trying to locate her uncle. The last time the family had heard from me was before the war when I wrote to my mother from Buenos Aires. Dora, under the impression that I must still be in Argentina, informed the Red Cross that the uncle she was trying to contact was a Yiddish actor playing in Buenos Aires, and gave them my name. This item in Buenos Aires press was relayed many months later to the Yiddish press in New York.

But in the interim, not receiving any information about me, Dora—together with some other girls from Grodno, lone survivors like herself—set out determined to make their way back to Grodno. However, they were sidetracked to Kovel, under Soviet occupation. During the time she spent there, she met Shimon. After they were married, they decided to smuggle into Poland. A short time later, the pogrom in Kielce sent them, like all other Jews, fleeing once again. On foot, they wandered back toward Germany and Austria, where they were placed in this camp.

"They registered again with the Red Cross. And as soon as I received the news that my niece was alive and was here in Austria, I contacted her.

"From her first letter we learned the tragic truth: my entire family had been annihilated. And Dora described the circumstances that saved her life. Moments before they were all led to their deaths, her father—my brother Motke—told her to run and hide in the woods, as only some youngsters were able to do. Her older sister, with a babe in her arms, could certainly not run anywhere... Should Dora remain alive, her father impressed upon her, she must try to find me—I would take care of her and, as an actor in the public eye, I would not be hard to find.

"Losing no time, I sent all the necessary papers to Linz to bring her and her husband to America, but without results. In the meantime, she wrote that she was expecting. I couldn't live with the thought that my one surviving niece and her husband should languish in a DP camp, and in her condition at that!

"With the help of the Hebrew Actors' Union, the Labor Committee and the HIAS, I applied to the State Department for a visa to Austria. This was denied me. So I left for Paris hoping that from there I could more easily reach Dora. The only way to achieve it was to volunteer to give free concerts in the camps under the auspices of the American JOINT."

"I'm sure that with JOINT's help," said Gaber encouragingly, "you will have no difficulty in getting them to America. Since they come under the Polish quota, it will take quite a while, unless the U.S. government decides to ease up on the immigration laws for the uprooted, homeless Jews in the camps. Meanwhile, they are not accepted anywhere. And Palestine is blocked to them by the British... so there isn't a shred of hope for the Jews who still find themselves in the DP camps. Yabby, if you succeed in bringing a little joy to the despairing remnants of our people, allowing them to forget, if only for a couple of hours, their miserable existence, it will be a sacred mission indeed!"

We made it safely across the Austrian-German border. Seeing an American jeep with two in uniform, the sleepy guards asked no questions. The roadblocks were raised and there we were, back on the German side!

Except for the few stale crusts of bread and a couple of pieces of chocolate, neither of us had had a bit of food in the last twenty-four hours. But at the moment we wanted nothing more than to lay down our weary heads.

At breakfast in the mess hall, Gaber introduced me to the other directors. They gave me a cheery welcome and eagerly asked when I would be starting my concerts. Some of them knew me from the Yiddish theaters in New York. After putting away a substantial meal, we went into Gaber's office to work out the details for my tour of the camps.

We were at work barely an hour when the phone rang. "JOINT office in Linz calling Sam Gaber!" It was Shimon excitedly relaying the good news: "Mazel tov! Dora gave birth to a boy!" ...so when am I coming to Linz, he wanted to know!

My head swam. I thought I was going to faint! Turning to Gaber with an imploring look, I said, "Sam, maybe there is a way I can go back to Linz? I've got to be there! How can I leave my children alone at a time like this?! I beg you, Sam. I'll never forget this favor as long as I live!"

"Yabby, I can't take you to Linz again," Gaber begged off. "In addition to the many pressing issues I have to take care of, I have to prepare your tour schedule. I'll get one of my drivers to take you. Yesterday we made it across the border by sheer luck. Whether you can get away with it again today...well, that's stretching it a bit. Believe me, I understand how you feel and I do sympathize with you. So, go ahead, Yabby, take the chance."

He instructed Alfie, one of the DP chauffeurs, to drive me to Linz. Arming us with a travel order from the JOINT, he explained that anything stamped with a seal was better than nothing. In Germany, he laughed, they didn't bother to read papers. If it was stamped, that was good enough. His order to Alfie was to refer back to Gaber in Munich if he ran into trouble, and he would try to fix whatever it was. Above all, Alfie was to tell the fellas at the checkpoint that their snapshots had turned out great and that he himself would deliver them before long.

Alfie was certainly no dummy. He knew all the ins and outs. Considering all that he had gone through in his young life, the business of slipping across a border was mere child's play to him.

We drove on until we reached Wegsheid. I did not anticipate such smooth sailing. The camp commandant, to whom we reported, remembered me from the day before. I told him about Dora and the baby, and asked if he could please tell me where I could find her. After his inquiry by phone, he told me that at 5 a.m. she had been taken by the camp ambulance to a civilian hospital in Linz. Following his directions we headed straight for the hospital where Shimon, who hadn't left the premises for a moment, looked amazed by my speedy return.

He led me into the ward where Dora lay with some other women. She burst into sobs. "Uncle! Oh, uncle!" she wailed, "where is my mother?! I need her now. Oh, mama...mama!" It was more than I could do to calm her—or myself.

I asked an attendant to please show me the baby. Such a tiny mite! Under these conditions, what chance did he have? I gave the attendant a bar of chocolate and some cigarettes and asked her to look after the mother and child.

"We'll name him Motele, after my father," said Dora, tearfully.

"There will be a problem with the bris," Shimon said. "There is no mohel in the area. We'll have to wait. Will you be able to come back again, uncle?"

"I'll try my best," I promised. "Meanwhile, my chauffeur and I will have to spend the night. Without official travel orders we cannot trake any risks. We start back at daybreak." Taking Shimon with us, we drove back to the camp.

Shimon managed to come up with a herring, a hunk of cheese and a bottle of spirits brewed from pieces of carrots and potato peelings salvaged from the communal kitchen. He opened a box of Manischewitz matzoh, which the DPs had been allotted for Passover and we were all set for a royal feast. Forks were nonexistent, but not necessary. We had our fingers.

Some neighboring DPs offered to put Alfie up in their barracks for the night. And I, not wishing to leave Shimon alone, stayed to sleep on his bed of wooden planks. At least it was wide enough for two.

It was very cold outdoors and even colder indoors. Dora and Shimon slept on a pallet of straw covered by a black, scratchy horse blanket. Shivering with cold, I lay down fully clothed. Though I pulled an old coat over me, my teeth still chattered.

"It's spring already," I said, "and still so cold!"

"I don't feel cold," said Shimon, "I'm used to it now. It's nothing like a winter in Russia!"

"I haven't as yet had an opportunity to talk with you, Shimon. These last few days have been so unexpected, so unreal...I want you to know that you are as close to me as Dora—like a son. Tell me about yourself."

"Well, our home, as you know, was in Kovel. In June 1941, four months before Germany attacked Russia, my father, Shmuel Rosenbaum, died. People kept saying that the war would not last more than a few months. Still, young men in our town were already beginning to flee.

"Leaving my mother at home with other relatives, my older brother Jacob and I set out on foot toward deeper Russia. This was very dangerous because we soon found ourselves close to the front. My brother and I were together for several months. But then, when Jacob was taken to serve in the Russian army, I remained alone in a town near Woroniezh working as a mechanic in a mill. When the front kept moving closer, I fled again and got as far as Turkestan in Central Asia.

"Life in Russia during 1942-43 was dreadful. By the end of 1944, I too was inducted into the Russian army and was immediately sent to the front. I was wounded. But given a short rest I was sent back to the front. I fought at Berlin. And on the very day that victory was finally won, and Germany capitulated, I was wounded again near the German city of Brandenburg, and more seriously this time. My head and arm were badly hurt and I was hospitalized for two months. When I was sent back to Poland, I landed in another hospital where I spent another four months. After that I somehow made it back to Kovel to find my mother and brother.

"My homecoming, after all my horrible experiences, proved to be the most shattering of all. Stumbling among the ruins, I was totally unable to recognize the spot where our house once stood. There was nothing. I just stood there and cried like a baby. After an agonizing search, I found a Jew who gave me shelter for the night and told me that the Germans, with the help of the Ukranian murderers, had led Kovel's remaining Jews out beyond the city and shot them... my mother among them.

"I remained in my hometown. Where else was I to go?! My father was a mechanic and I too followed the trade. That was how I managed to string along until I met Dora, and we were married. But life in Russo-Poland became unbearable for Jews. We dragged ourselves over the Czechoslovakian mountains into Vienna. There we were detained and sent off to the DP camp in Linz. You can imagine the joy we felt when we finally found you, uncle! And now, with the baby, maybe the sun will begin to shine a little for us, too..."

Early dawn I bade Shimon goodbye. To visit the hospital again was impossible. Stopping at the camp gate, I thanked the commandant for his kindness.

I noticed a bearded young man near the gate-house, quietly puffing on a pipe—another DP, I assumed, judging by his clothing and appearance. Sidling up to me, he whispered in English: "Going back to Munich, Mr. Yablokoff? Please tell Nahum Levine of the Sokhnute (Jewish Agency), and also Mr. Dobkin and Dr. Goland, that they are to proceed at once to Paris for an urgent conference. They, in turn, know the others for whom this message applies. It is too difficult to contact Munich by phone. Besides, it's healthier in general not to discuss our affairs. You are known to us—you can be trusted."

We got back into the jeep and Alfie took off at top speed toward the frontier. The jumble of experiences that were crowded into my first three days in Germany kept whirling round in my head. Would anyone in America believe me, I wondered, if I told them that the remnants of our people were still living in such dire conditions two whole years after the global menace had been conquered—the menace that had sought to destroy the Jewish people, and the free world?

67

Returning to Munich

At the border, the approach of our American jeep, with two uniformed occupants, did the trick again. The MPs raised the bars and we were safely across the border.

Sam Gaber was relieved to see us back again in Munich. He was deeply moved when I described the circumstances under which my niece gave birth. I sent Bella a wire, saying: "Greetings from Motele." I knew she would understand that Dora had given birth to a boy and named him Motele. She would also gather that I was safely back from Dora's camp. I shook in my boots lest my escapade leak out. I could be arrested and sent packing from Germany...for after all, how dared I smuggled myself into Austria—twice within forty-eight hours at that—when I had no right to be there in the first place?

* * *

The immediate concern now was to find a pianist to accompany me on my tour of the camps. Gaber located one who happened to be a German. But a German as my accompanist in the Jewish DP camps?! Oh, no, I hesitated, the Jews will surely resent it.

"Many German civilians are employed in our various Jewish agencies," Gaber pointed out, "and nobody protests. So, let's try."

The German pianist arrived. He was a gaunt and ragged man. "I am Professor Kurt Muller," he introduced himself. Dr. Ada Friedman offered us the use of her piano for rehearsal. When the professor sat down and delved into Beethoven's Moonlight Sonata, I was overwhelmed. Gaber and I decided that until we could find a Jewish pianist we would take a chance with this German.

Herr Muller swore that he was never a Nazi—although nobody questioned him. He was solely a music professor, he contended, and music was his whole life. All Germans, I soon learned in the few days since my arrival, chanted the same alibi that they knew nothing of what happened. To me they were all guilty as hell!

I rehearsed with the professor until Gaber called me to lunch. The mess hall was off limits to Germans, DPs and military personnel. So what to do with the professor? I couldn't let him hang around, hungry, with no place to go until my return from a good lunch.

Gaber understood my feelings and led Herr Muller to the mess hall's kitchen by the back door to see that he was fed. The professor was deeply grateful. He hadn't eaten a meal like this in many months, he told us.

We rehearsed through the rest of the afternoon and again during the week. We went through my whole repertoire and my program was shaping up beautifully. During the composition, "Let me Live," my German accompanist shed tears. How ironic. When the Jews pleaded with the brutal murderers "let us live!" they laughed and jeered! Now, a German wept...

At last I was ready to begin my concert tour. Suddenly, no professor. Gone! Vanished! We made inquiries, we looked high and low. All in vain. Finally, we learned that, in trying to board an overcrowded trolley, he fell off and cracked his skull. How awful! The poor man. I was shocked beyond words!

During the time it took to search for another accompanist, I had a chance to acquaint myself with the "Jewish Washington"—Munich! This was where the Central Committee of Liberated Jews in Germany, and all central agencies of the allied countries, were located.

The Central Committee also had departments for culture and education and a historical commission that collected all documentary material on the Holocaust.

From every DP camp in Germany, Jews trekked to Munich for one thing or another; immigration, to search for relatives, or simply to learn what was going on in the world. Transportation presented the biggest problem. From the train depot, they had to trudge the rest of the way into town on foot. And it was quite a hike! The trolleys ran during the day only in limited numbers to conserve electrical power. At night they did not run at all. Fortunately, all these Jewish bureaus were concentrated on Sieber Strasse.

One thing about these scurrying DPs baffled me. What were these briefcases they all carried...an accessory hardly in keeping with the rest of their shabby appearance? They looked like bankrupt businessmen! The mystery became clear to me when the offices closed for lunch hour. Parking themselves wherever convenient—on the steps of buildings or on the sidewalk—the DPs opened their attache cases and out came the allotted calories they'd brought from camp to see them through the hours spent in Munich.

I made the acquaintance of the photographer Kadisch, from Kovno. He was photographing the city's ruined sites and scenes of Jewish DP life in the camps. His work appeared in the *Forward* and *The Day*. General Eisenhower had presented him with a jeep so he could carry on his important work. Kadisch snapped a picture of me in uniform against the background of a ravaged building. Still discernible among the ruins is the sign: Munchen.

A Union for Surviving Actors

Besides entertaining the DPs and rescuing my niece. I had another mission in Germany: to gather and organize Jewish actors among the survivors. Some had already grouped themselves together to give little performances.

I knew of one group in particular, the Munchen Yiddish Kunst Theater (MYKT). The head of this group was Israel Becker, and I went to his camp to seek him out. He was a handsome fellow, with a longish curly mane and large eyes that stared at me in disbelief. My major's uniform put him off somewhat. But in a moment we were in each other's arms like brothers of a clan.

"Forgive me, I should have come to see you," he apologized.

"No matter," I put him at ease, "under the circumstances we can't stand on ceremonies. I wanted to see my surviving colleagues and so I put aside all my activities in America, and here I am. There are trunks on the way, sent by our fellow actors, that are filled with plays, music, makeup and costumes to enable you to carry on with your craft. We know how vital it is to keep up everyone's morale until, God willing, you will be free to migrate wherever you choose. In the meantime, I'm extremely interested in knowing what you are doing."

"I am the director of the representative theater of surviving Jews here in the American zone. We've been giving performances in the big barracks that serve as cultural centers for the DPs. We played *The Bloody Hoax* (Hard to be a Jew) by Sholem Aleichem. Now, we're doing his *Tevye, the Dairyman*. We're restricted to camps in the American zone. We can't tour those in the Russian, British and French zones. Becker also gave me a surprisingly long list of names in the cast.

Through him I met Israel Segal and Abraham Wolovtchik, and we decided to call a conference of all the professional actors scattered throughout the region to lay the groundwork for an actors' guild. This, of course, posed many problems: how would the actors get to Munich in view of the poor transportation? Where would they stay? And what about food? While they were in their respective camps, they each received 1,200 calories per day.

My two assistants assured me that they would "organize" something. Actors who happened to be in camps close to Munich would squeeze together a bit to make room for fellow delegates. As for food—this I promised to organize (a camp expression). No one would go hungry.

Sam Gaber promised JOINT's full cooperation in aiding the convention of surviving actors and actresses, and in facilitating their efforts to perform at the various camps.

I wired the representatives of the Hebrew Actors' Union and the Yiddish Theatrical Alliance in New York and received assurances of immediate help from both organizations.

* * *

The call to the actors' conference was sent out in writing to all the camps. It would be held on Tuesday, May 27, 1947, 10 A.M. at the Cinema House on Melstrasse 45, Munich. The communique also contained the Order of the Day, ending with the following appeal:

The survivors now in German exile, who had built the Jewish social and cultural life in Europe before the war, have already united themselves in various organizations. Only we Yiddish actors are still splintered, not as yet unified. Aside from our social obligations we have our purely professional interests, which we can protect only when we are joined in an actors' guild. We therefore hope that for the sake of our mutual interests you will participate in this vital conference.

* * *

The founding of the Yiddish Actors' Guild was a memorable event. About fifty actors and actresses who had begun their stage careers before the war managed to make their way to Munich... many of them on foot. They gathered, not arrayed in fine feathers to be sure, but making every effort to appear at their best in whatever they had. Like other DPs, the actors carried briefcases and portfolios. Some of these contained a salvaged critique, a yellowed poster, or letters of praise from camp committees, if they had already had a chance to perform for other displaced persons.

This first encounter with other colleagues gave way to heartrending episodes. Tearfully, they hugged and kissed as if risen from the dead. They exchanged tragic tales of others who perished, or tidings of those who had remained alive and were still in Russia and Poland.

I too had an unexpected and touching meeting with the impresario from Romania, Maurice Ziegler. I gave him first-hand news of his daughter Erna, in Chicago, and of his granddaughter Charlotte Cooper in New York. I learned that his daughter Sevilla Pastor had survived and was still in Romania.

The conference was attended by the representatives of the JOINT; Sam Gaber; the chairman of the Central Committee, David Trager; the representative of HIAS, Ort, Unrra and other organizations in Munich. The hall was strung with slogans that read: "Z'chor! (Remember)... In memory of the holy martyrs, artists and people of the Yiddish theater... Never to forget!... Never to forgive!"

At the intonation of the memorial prayer, a wailing broke out in the assembly, soon followed by vigorous singing of the "Hatikvah."

I was scheduled to speak on the four theatrical organizations in New York. Addressing the gathering in the name of the Hebrew Actors' Union, I emphasized: "Although the situation of the Yiddish theater in America is not what it once was because of curtailed immigration, language assimilation and many other facts, the union still seeks ways to sustain the Yiddish theater and protects its more than 300 members who are active on the Yiddish stage. I can assure you, my dear colleagues, that the Hebrew Actors' Union, who always maintained a close relationship with fellow artists throughout the world, will not, in these dire circumstances forsake our brothers and sisters, stage professionals— survivors of the Holocaust!"

With keen interest the gathering listened to my lengthy discourse on our sister organizations in New York: the Yiddish Theatrical Alliance, the socialist-minded Hebrew Actors' Club and the Yiddish Artists and Friends where visiting artists were warmly welcomed, and where they could spend a most delightful evening, with food and entertainment galore!

I summed up my report with the assurance that all these organizations would keep their promise to help fellow artists in this hour of need. This was met by a rousing applause.

We made a break for lunch. I had brought a few bottles of liquor purchased at the P.X. with army scrip. Food was organized by a committee with the help of my American dollars, and acquired aplenty via the black market... may this transgression never catch up with me...

After two days of deliberation, the Actors' Guild in Munich was duly formed. Its by-laws were the same as those before the war at the Yiddish Actors' Guild in Warsaw.

The new guild's emphasis was mainly on forming units to perform in the camps; making contact with other organizations in Argentina and Palestine; and overseeing the distribution of the care packages, plays and music that my fellow actors in the States had addressed to me.

I also presented the newly formed guild with a gift of my Yiddish Corona typewriter. And, full of hope, the convention came to a close with the inspired singing of the "Hatikvah" and "Zug nisht keinmul" (Never say the road you're traveling is the last.)

68

My Tour of the Camps

The pianist Solomon Arzewski was a godsend to me. Before the war, Professor Solomon Arzewski was a well-known concert pianist in Warsaw. He had also gained great popularity with his jazz orchestra, the first to introduce this style of music in Poland. A young man, he looked a lot older than his age. His hands gave him trouble. His fingers had become stiffened in the concentration camps where he had certainly not played the piano. Following liberation he returned to Poland and got married. After the pogrom in Kielce, he fled to Germany with his wife and child, who were now with him in Munich. To help him rehabilitate, the JOINT placed Arzewski in a sanitorium at Eben-See near Salzberg. I had a hard time persuading him to accompany me on my concert tour of the DP camps in Germany. In a matter of days we had rehearsed my program and were off doing the concerts on my itinerary.

To send an ambulance into the camps with more than three people was impossible. The problem was sleeping accommodations. Unless there happened to be JOINT or UNRWA billet in the vicinity of a camp, I would have to make the best of it and bed down with my crew wherever possible—even in the ambulance if need be.

The first leg of my tour was only an experiment, I was told to determine how the DPs would receive me. But after my first concert's success, there was no doubt that my program would lift morale. The JOINT and the Central Committee of Liberated Jews in the American zone got right down to arranging an extended tour for me.

It was late afternoon when we arrived in Camp Beknang. Announcements for the evening concert were already posted. Yet, no sooner did my ambulance pull into the grounds, but the crowd swarmed into the huge barrack to secure seats, prepared to wait no matter how long. Several men, unable to squeeze their way in, gave us a hand in hauling the piano out of the ambulance into the barrack and onto the platform. At least it gave them an excuse to wedge themselves in. I asked to have the wide doors at the side of the barrack thrown open to let in some air. My concern was for the children. I was afraid they'd be crushed. The crowd that remained outside immediately jammed the doorways, hoping to catch a look at what was going on indoors.

For my dressing room, they had strung up a few army blankets at one

427

side of the platform. With no lights to speak of, my driver, Hans, rigged up two large lamps on the platform to throw some light on my face, at least. Arzewski too, had a small lamp on the piano.

Arrayed as Der Payatz, I stepped from behind my "curtain." There was no applause—a reception usually expected. But, after my opening number, "Let me Live," the walls of the barracks shook with a thunderous response.

During the time I took to change and re-do my makeup, Arzewski played the Warsaw Concerto. I noticed that several women left their seats and moved toward the exits. The crowd had applauded with such enthusiasm, so why were they leaving? The women had slipped out to gather wild flowers, presenting them to me after my three-hour concert.

Following this lovely gesture, the crowd began besieging me with questions:

"What's to become of us?"

"How long must we suffer?"

"Do not despair," I tried to encourage them. "Take heart. Your salvation is near. It must surely come and soon!"

Finally, they escorted me and my crew to the UNRWA Villa. The director, Sam Solomon, not only prepared us a fine supper, but arranged it so that Arzewski and Hans could also sleep at the villa. I was most grateful. I would not have felt right sleeping like a lord, while these two spent the night flopping somewhere in camp. When we finally called it a night, it was four o'clock in the morning. I went to bed exceedingly happy. I had scored with the survivors of hell. They accepted me!

In the morning, a delegation of children invited me to the same "concert barrack," where they gave a recital in my honor. They sang, they recited and danced. It was so poignant, I was moved to tears. The youngsters clung around me, kissing and addressing me as "Uncle" Yablokoff—the most heartwarming title I had yet received. Needless to say, I didn't get away with being just a spectator. I had to concertize anew for my special audience of children. I taught them a few folk songs and together we had a ball.

The cultural committee of Beknang presented me with a letter of thanks—handwritten but stamped with a seal, which they had already managed to acquire. This letter of thanks, as all the other hundreds of such letters I received, I would not trade for the diploma of any university. I cherish them as sacred and dear.

We piled into the ambulance with all our paraphernalia and started to leave the grounds, when a host of people began to trail after us. They're escorting us, I thought. We drove out of the campsite and they still trudged after us. I made Hans stop.

"My good people, where are you going?" I asked them.

"We want to follow you to the next camp. We want to hear you again." some called out to me.

"We want to go with you. Take us along! We want to be free! We don't want to stay in camp anymore!" their voices clamored all around me.

"My friends! What are you saying?! Please, go back!" I implored them, my blood running cold. "You're not allowed to leave the camp. You're getting me into trouble. It will appear that I have incited you to rebel. That's all I need! They'll deport me from Germany. I beg of you, go back! Don't forget the slogan: 'Do not Despair!'"

With bowed heads and tear-filled eyes, they wished me Godspeed and reluctantly turned back. Hans drove off and we continued on our way to Stuttgart.

* * *

The countryside was beautiful as it swept by the windows of our ambulance. It was a bright and lovely morning, and as my next concert was scheduled for that evening, we drove along at a moderate pace.

I was unable to shake off the distressing incident with the DPs, who were determined to follow me out of camp, on foot—but where to?

In a little town not far from Stuttgart, with time to kill, Hans decided to stop and fix our P.A. equipment, which had given us a little trouble the night before. This took quite a bit of time. When we finally pulled up at the JOINT billet in Stuttgart, several staff workers upbraided us. "What happened to you? Why so late? The people have been waiting for you at the theater for hours!"

"For hours?! What theater? Where? The concert is scheduled for the evening!"

"Who told you, for the evening! It's now, in the afternoon! It was supposed to start two hours ago! Over 1,500 people are waiting for you at the Schauspielhaus!"

"Oh, my God! Somebody goofed. Step on it, Hans!!" I commanded. "The theater on the double!"

At the theater I hurried backstage, found a spacious dressing room and hastily slapped on my makeup. I heard the impatient clapping that clearly conveyed: "Nu, how long must we wait for this American Payatz?" Marek Gutman, chairman of the camp's central committee, explained the misunderstanding to the audience. In no way was it my fault for arriving late, I was at this very moment preparing to appear, he said.

The theater was magnificent and fully equipped with a lot more than my program required. Fortunately, we didn't have to drag our upright piano from the ambulance, wasting precious time. Already in position on stage, amidst a beautiful setting, stood a Knabe concert grand, which made Arzewski's face light up.

A committee appeared in my dressing room wanting to know more "facts" about me, since they had been delegated to introduce me from the stage. I suggested, instead, they greet me after the concert. "According to my routine," I tried to explain, "I come on cold, and do my own introductions." They were peeved at being denied this honor. (In many camps I found that some committee people prepared such lengthy monologues to introduce me that there was hardly any time left for me to go on. I had to be firm.)

Arzewski was already seated at the piano launching the introduction with gusto, so I gulped water to wet my throat and made my entrance.

I got a very warm reception. The people obviously forgave me for keeping them waiting, and had probably already gotten word via the unbelievable camp grapevine that I was OK.

The theater was packed. I went on with my program giving them all I had, and more. In all modesty I must say they didn't let me off the stage. The place echoed with their applause.

The first to rush up on stage after the concert was my welcoming committee. Their faces beaming, they shook my hand, and made speeches of praise and gratitude for my artistic contribution. Two little girls from the DP kindergarten presented me with a beautiful basket of flowers and thanked me in Hebrew. Of all pictures taken of me in action, I treasure the one snapped with these two tiny girls handing me their flowers.

Here too, as in every camp, people surrounded me with inquiries: "Maybe you know my uncle in America...my aunt...my cousin? Before the war they lived in New Jersey...Chicago...Los Angeles...New York..." And everyone, it seemed, either began or ended, with the same sentence: "I am the only survivor of my entire family." I told them to write names and details to my wife in New York. She would try to locate their relatives if at all possible. After this, during my entire tour of the camps, I prepared dozens of slips of paper bearing my home address, ready to hand out. Bella and Anita carried out this mission with great effort. Evenings and all day Sunday, they ferreted through telephone directories and succeeded in tracking down quite a number of kin in the United States.

The director of the JOINT office in Stuttgart region was Miss Flora Levyne, an American. I had already heard in Munich that Miss Levyne, a small woman, was as tough as any man—a no-nonsense individual. The position she filled left no room for feminine softness. She carried out her duties with sensitivity and understanding, but it wasn't easy to pull the wool over her eyes.

When Flora Levyne came into my dressing room, I felt her appraising eye on me. After our greetings, I offered her the basket of flowers I'd received.

"I can't very well display them in my ambulance," I joked.

"We'll show them off in the mess hall," she said, thanking me and complimenting me on my program. She was also apologetic that someone had forgotten to advise me about the correct time for the concert. It happened that the theater had already been scheduled for an evening performance of Gogol's *Inspector General*. My concert then had to be switched to the afternoon. She was sorry for this merry mix-up. But, she invited me to give another concert, this time in the evening and at the big Theater Metropol.

Others came into the room and Miss Levyne introduced me to the top brass in Stuttgart: chief director of the UNRWA in Germany, Mr. MacNeil; Louis Levitton, another bigwig; and Abe Grossman, chief director of HIAS in Germany.

"I'm sorry that I don't understand Yiddish," said Mr. MacNeil, greeting me warmly. "When the audience laughed so uproariously, I had to nudge Miss Levyne with 'what is he saying?' and 'what is the meaning of nisht gezorgt,'" which the crowd kept repeating after you."

They invited me to join them for dinner at the officers' club. Over a few cognacs they promised to see that I was supplied with whatever I needed in my travels throughout the Stuttgart region. I was elated to meet such esteemed friends, thinking they might be valuable aids in getting my niece out of that hellhole camp in Austria. When I told Levitton of my problem, he said, "Bring them to Stuttgart. I'll do something."

The report of my concerts, which Flora Levyne sent in to the chief, A.J.D.C. directors—Charles Pasman in Munich, Charles Malamuth in Paris and Dr. Joseph Schwartz in New York—stated:

> In this crucial period for the Jews in Germany, the artist, Herman Yablokoff, is a most welcome and significant emissary presented by the JOINT in the DP camps. He practically mesmerizes the people. They are so ecstatic and so inspired by him, they forget their hopelessness and misery. The DPs follow him like Hassidim after their rabbi...

* * *

The Jewish community in Stuttgart was concentrated, not in a camp, but in an area around Rheinsburger Strasse; its focal point was the community center, Beth Bialik.

Mr. Levitton took me on a tour of the city in his jeep, acquainting me with various facilities: the ORT School, Hebrew School, clinic and kindergarten.

My second one-man show in Stuttgart was held a few weeks later. The Metropol, a tremendously large theater was jammed with more people left outside than in.

In the journal *To Freedom*, printed in Stuttgart, I read: "With his two unforgettable presentations, Herman Yablokoff, the goodwill ambassador from the JOINT and the Hebrew Actors' Union in America, brought great cheer to the 'Shearit Hapleita'—Remnants of Jewry. He made them forget, if only for a while, their bleak existence..."

* * *

At Camp Wasser-Alfingen, a throng of DPs from a neighboring camp had already collected at the gates. They had walked several kilometers, afraid I might pass up their camp.

The concert was received with the same enthusiasm as in the other camps. By now it had gotten around that I was a down-to-earth fella—"amcho" (one of them)—not just deigning to amuse them, but regarding it a privilege to perform for them.

I visited their newly formed school and, gathering the children, sang Yiddish and Hebrew songs with them. I was shown around the ORT workshops, a chief project in many of the DP camps. I also participated in the special service for the heroes of the Warsaw Ghetto.

I worked very hard. It was not so much the three-hour program itself as the packing, unpacking and preparing the several changes I made during all of my performance. I was beginning to feel the strain and was afraid I would not be able to carry on.

I decided to put in a call to Gaber in Munich. The connection was frustrating. We could barely understand one another. All I could make out was that two telegrams and six letters from my wife were being forwarded to me by special courier. Under the circumstances it was useless for me to try to get across to him that I had to have someone help me with my changes and packing.

In Camp Schwabisch, I also had to give two concerts. The barrack, with a capacity for 800, was jammed with almost double the people. They sat on the platform, they stood bunched at the sides so that I had to squeeze through them to make my changes. After the concert, during the usual welcoming speeches, I was presented with a large painting in a heavy wooden frame. How on earth, I wondered, was I going to cart this around with me in my erratic travels?! Yet, somehow, I managed. (This still life, a bowl of huge sunflowers painted by Morasch, now hangs in a prominent spot in my home.)

Two young DPs, compatriots of mine from Grodno, asked a favor of me. Since Canada was offering young men a chance to work in the woods of their northern provinces, they were most eager to go there; for, after a certain amount of time felling trees, they would be permitted to settle in Canada. Though the Canadian commission needed brawny specimens for this rugged assignment, and my two compatriots were far from the type, my friend Levitton interceded in their behalf and they were accepted. (A year later I ran into my two lumberjacks in Montreal. Surprised to see them I asked how come they were not at work in the woods. "Let the husky galoots with the muscles chop down trees," they laughed. "We packed ourselves off to the city as soon as we arrived!")

* * *

I continued my journey to Ulm. The director of UNRWA was a tall, angular Englishman who sported a little goatee and seemed rather fond of the bottle. Under the influence of a few snorts, Adams confided to me: "I know the Jewish DPs are being smuggled into Palestine, and that the Brichah (underground) is helping them to flee but me, I look the other way. I know something is brewing in my camp. I expect a Jewish revolt any day now—but you'll find me at the head of the march... and I will probably get the first bullet," he concluded, downing another scotch-and-soda.

In Ulm, I also met the area director, Sol Rabinowitz, a fine gentleman and very able administrator. "In Dornstadt, a German community not far from here," he told me, "there is an orphanage. These are Jewish children rescued from peasant families in Poland. These little orphans never knew that they were Jewish and that their mothers, before being led to their deaths, had left them with the peasants in order to save their lives. The children slaved there, feeding the pigs and doing burdensome chores for bread and shelter.

"After the war these children were either relinquished—at a price—to the Jewish partisans and underground workers, or taken at gunpoint when the peasants refused to give them up.

"At first these rescued orphans presented great problems for their Jewish caretakers at the orphanages. Many were homesick for the farmers whom they had come to regard as their parents. Some, were already imbued with hatred for Jews, having been reared in an anti-Semitic environment."

My first encounter with such orphans was during my stay in Paris. Together with prominent Zionist leader, Yacov Zrubovel, and the European correspondent for the *Jewish Daily Forward*, Israel Shmuleviz, I went to meet the first transport of rescued orphans from Poland.

Upon their arrival, when their attendants formed them in a circle, to sing and dance the hora, some children hung back, sullen and belligerent. A few, when approached, bared their teeth in decision: "Jhidi!" they sneered. Other cried, or cursed and shouted "You, Jews! Christ killers!" It was a most painful experience for me and everyone else.

The cavernous barrack, in which I appeared in Ulm, held as many as 2,000 people. I gave four concerts in this region, the fourth I planned as an afternoon special for children. I was very anxious to include the orphans from Dornstadt. The army headquarters promised to send special lorries to bring these kids into Ulm. Eagerly, I awaited their arrival. But as luck would have it, it rained "cats and dogs" that day and there was no sign of the children. The army had sent out open lorries to pick them up and since it had rained without a stop, the children had had to remain at the orphanage.

I was heartbroken, but had to go on with the show without them. When it was over, I remarked to Director Rabinowitz, "If the orphans of Dornstadt weren't able to come to my performance, is there any reason I can't go to them?"

Although Hans and Arzewski were tired and hungry, I insisted we go and visit these children. So, in spit of the rain, we went. It was quite late when we arrived in Dornstadt. The orphanage was in darkness, the children were already asleep. We knocked and someone soon came to the door. On learning who we were, the place came alive. The housemothers told me about the children's disappointment: how they had looked forward to the concert and dreamed of the exciting ride to Ulm. But, it rained! And down went all their anticipated joys! They even refused supper and with tear-stained faces had gone to bed.

Unprecedented as this was, the director of the orphanage gave permission to awaken the children so I could hold a special "performance" for them. We dragged the piano and my costumes into the dining area and, setting myself up in the adjoining kitchen, I put on my makeup and clown suit.

The older children hastily pulled on pants and shirts, while the smaller ones, rubbing the sleep from their eyes, were brought down in their night-shirts. They were all then treated to milk and cookies, while Arzewski livened the scene with a tune on the piano.

The Clown stepped out of the kitchen. The happy squeals of laughter, and the childish delight at the humorous stories I told, warmed my heart. I sang appropriate songs for them and taught them a charming little ditty, "Tzigele," the story of a little goat. This was written by Israel Rosenberg, and the children loved it. They repeated it with me over and over. The sound of their ringing voices I shall never forget.

At the end, kissing me and bidding me tearful farewells, they made me promise to come again. The smaller tots insisted that I, their uncle, must put them to bed. And I obliged. Singing them to sleep with Gebirtig's lullaby, "Shlufzhe mir, mein Yankele, mein Shyner"—Sleep, my Yankele, my Pretty One—I substituted the name Yankele for the name of the child I was lulling to sleep: Moishele, Chaimke, Rochele, Surale…Their faces shone with content-ment as they reluctantly fell asleep one by one. Tiptoeing out, I could not pull myself together and cried my heart out for the children of my own family and the one million Jewish children who perished from the earth.

I regard this impromptu concert for the orphans of Dornstadt as the most exalting experience in my entire career.

The saga of my "midnight show" for the children spread through the camps like wildfire. I was declared honorary member of every DP camp in which I appeared, and presented with a membership card as a DP, the same as all the Jews in concentration camps. To me, this represents the highest honor.

69

Camp Angels

At the Red Cross in Munich I came upon an article in *Stars and Stripes*, with the dateline Ludwigs Hafen, April, 13, 1947, which related that 270 Jews had left Munich illegally eight days earlier in an effort to reach Palestine. The group, which included pregnant women and children, was packed into four dirty third-class railway cars with broken windows. They had very little money and only rations enough for two days. Their destination was Marseilles, where they planned to hire a vessel to smuggle them to Palestine. Several children took sick from hunger and polluted water. This frantic exodus ended tragically when American and French patrols intercepted the train and sent them back—in the same cold and filthy railroad cars.

I went looking for my landsman, Sholom Dreiser in the courtyard of the JOINT. Not only had he heard about the ill-fated exodus, but he told me that, among the twenty-four Grodners in the group, were my cousins, the two brothers Shillingoff and Joseph Rosjanski.

"We can find out more details about this junket," said Dreiser, "from the Binders. They happen to be housed in the city proper and can tell you all about Grodners here in the American zone. Our townspeople who, for one reason or another, come into Munich from surrounding camps, find the Binders' a good place to rest—and nobody leaves hungry. They share whatever they have."

Catching a jam-packed trolley, we rode into town, straight to the Binders. They knew of my arrival in Munich and were, in fact, surprised that I hadn't visited sooner since it was easier for me to get around. I was promptly offered food, which I declined, knowing their scarce rations.

I knew that there was a Grodno committee in Munich—organized March 12, 1947 in commemoration of the Grodno Ghetto liquidation. It did not take long before several of them showed up at the Binders... as if they knew where they'd find me. They knew all the names of our townspeople, including my cousins who, when learning that I, the president of the Grodno Federation of America and Canada, was in Paris, had struck out—illegally—to locate me there.

Now, that the committee had me face to face, they demanded aid from the Grodno Federation. With so many organizations in America they saw no reason why I, as president, couldn't take every one of them to the United States immediately, and have the Federation take care of them. They complained that our people in the camps were starving and getting mighty little help from America. So what, if anything, did the Federation do?

With understanding and patience I tried to explain the difficulties. With Grodno organizations spread throughout the States, working without any coordinated system between them, no wonder some of our DPs had been receiving food and clothing, while others had not.

"At my own expense," I reported, "I traveled the cities across the United States and Canada, wherever Grodno organizations had long been established. After years of touring these cities with my theater companies, I was no stranger to our contemporaries who had been sending aid to our hometown for many decades. And I was at once urged to make this a united effort. It was decided to call a conference and at this meeting, held in New York, the Grodno Federation of America and Canada was founded."

I assured these Grodno friends in Munich that the Federation and I, as its president, were doing all in our power to help them; I had been entrusted with a sum of money—a substantial part of which I had already allotted in Paris—and was now distributing the rest among them in the camps.

The committee thought it best that I turn this money over to them. They could better distribute it, they contended, for they knew those who needed it most. I could not agree to this. As president, I felt it was my duty to make personal contact with my surviving townspeople wherever possible and, according to circumstances, hand each one a monetary gift from the Federation.

"In every camp, at the end of my performance, I sit down with as many Grodno DPs as there happen to be, and jot down information about them in my book. I take the names of their relatives in America, or some other country, and each one receives a sum of money from me. I also have their signatures. This is a very trying and exhausting task after a three-hour program. Yet, despite the drain on me," I told the committee, "I will have to do it my way."

As we sat discussing these issues, along came my cousins, the two Shillingoffs and "Yoshke" Rosjanski! They surmised they would find me at the Binders. I was overjoyed to see them and relieved that they were back safe.

After listening to their account of the snag that aborted their expedition to Paris, we anxiously asked about the other Grodners.

"Everyone in our group is back in camp," they said, "because during the time we were en route, we were angels..."

"Angels?!" I exclaimed. "What do you mean angels?!"

"When Jews vacate camp, they turn their DP cards over to the camp committee so their provisions can be collected the same as if they're still in camp—a welcome bonus to those who remain, of course. The absentees are referred to as angels; for while they have bodily vacated the premises, their cards proclaim they are still, officially, in camp. Now that the transport has fallen apart, we will simply reclaim our cards, as well as the same old corner where we used to lay our weary heads."

* * *

The chief director of HIAS in Munich, Abe Grossman, and his wife, who was with him in Germany, were most gracious toward me. They were well aware of the one thought that gave me no rest: what to do about Dora, Shimon and the baby. Grossman promised that, should he be in Austria, he would inquire about their emigration status.

I received a letter from Dora—censored. They were holding off the bris (circumcision), as there was still no mohel available. More than anything, they were anxious to know when I would be coming.

Who could tell, I thought. I might not even be permitted to do my concerts in Austria; although Gaber had reassured me that as soon as I had covered the Bamberg region, he would try to "organize" an opportunity for me to get into Linz again to see my children.

The executive director of the JOINT in Munich, Samuel Haber, was an amiable gentleman, who threw himself into the complex job of aiding the Jews in the American zone of Germany. Meeting him at lunch in the mess hall, he gave me the warmest greeting and asked me into his office. He showed me a number of letters from the various camps, even some that had come from Berlin and the British and French zones.

"What sort of magic have you cast over the Jews in Germany?" Haber grinned at me. "All the letters bear the same request: 'Instead of food packages, send us Yablokoff'!"

To think that my efforts were so overwhelmingly appreciated, left me deeply moved.

"Mr. Yablokoff, what can I do for you?" Haber asked. "You needn't hesitate. Tell me, are you comfortable here? Do you get enough to eat? A suitable place to sleep?"

"Everything is OK," I said, touched by his concern. "But, since you ask, well, I would be grateful if you could do me a favor. Most of the time I'm in the camps and I manage to do the best I can about sleeping accommodations. Very often I sleep in the camp clinics. At least it's clean. But when I get back here to Munich, I have to shift from one temporarily-free bed in the JOINT billet to another. Maybe you can arrange for me to have my own room in Munich, no matter where. That's request number one. Secondly, packing and lugging my costumes, and making several changes during my program, is beyond my strength. Would it be possible to send along somebody who could help me?"

"You will have a room arranged for you here, this very day!" came his firm reply. "As for an extra person, well, that presents a bit of a problem. But, at the very first opportunity, we'll get someone to send along with you. If you need anything, and if it is at all possible, we will arrange it. You certainly deserve that consideration!"

Samuel Haber kept his word. A few hours later I was assigned to a room in one of the villas on Sieberstrasse. And in Camp Egensfelden, sure enough, sent to me by special courier from Munich, came Mishka! Mishka was in charge of my wardrobe and helped me with my changes. Judging by his short, boyish, skin-and-bones-frame, he was about eighteen or nineteen years old. When he started talking about his experiences in the ghettos and with the partisans in the woods, it was enough to make my hair stand on end. Mishka could polish off a bottle of moonshine without batting an eye. It only loosened his tongue, and he would wind up singing a Russian army ditty that could turn a Cossack red in the face. In a short time he became my right-hand man. I grew very fond of him, despite all his shortcomings…and Mishka, I'm sure, developed a deep affection for me, too.

Walls of Paper

The director of the JOINT in Bamber, Irving Kwasnik, had his headquarters in Bamberg proper. I had already appeared in the camps of Ansbach, Schwabach, Struht, Weinsbur, Camp Furt and Camp Bayreuth. After one of my late sessions with my Grodno townspeople, I caught a very bad cold. What worried me most was the deep hoarseness that set in. A Jewish doctor in Bayreuth advised me to enter the German hospital for a few days.

I was miserable! How was this to be explained to the people waiting for me in the other camps?! I decided to phone Mr. Kwasnik and ask him to notify the various camps in his region that I was taken ill.

"Hello, Herman!" came Kwasnik's friendly voice over the wire. "I know you from New York…from the Yiddish theater. My parents are your greatest fans. You know the actress Esther Field? Her son Leon and I studied the violin together at Juilliard."

I was relieved to have run into a director who knew me. And I didn't need to explain my dilemma, either. I sounded like a buzz-saw.

"Why suffer in Bayreuth?" he said, "Come directly to me in Bamberg. We'll get you well in no time!"

Such a heartwarming invitation was more than I ever expected. Irving Kwasnik received me like a son welcoming his father. Neither did he allow my crew to knock about somewhere in camp. He made room for all of us at his headquarters in town. We also took our meals with the military staff. The first thing he insisted I do was get into a clean, white-sheeted bed. A Jewish nurse from Johannesburg fussed over me and in a few days had me on my feet as good as new.

Kwasnik had served in the air force during the war and when it was over, he had come back to Germany to help the Jewish survivors. The camps in his region were among the best-run in the American zone. The Germans trembled at his command. He employed a strict military discipline.

I had found a close friend in Irving, one from whom I need not keep any secrets. I told him about my niece and her little family in Austria and asked his advice. He, too, thought it best if they could somehow be brought into Germany, where it would be easier to help them. Austria was altogether a calamity!

* * *

In Bamberg I held my first concert in the Ulaner Kaserne. Up to now I thought I had seen enough misery and suffering in the camps I had already visited, but what I encountered in Bamberg was beyond imagination: people living in cubicles with walls of paper! The huge barnlike Kaserne, formerly used by the German military as livery stables, the walls still studded with iron rings for tethering horses, were now squared off into cubicles separated by paper partitions. Each cubicle, according to size, was allotted as living quarters to a family, or a single person. The paper "wall" could hardly be called opaque; especially in the evening when a lamp or a candle was lit...nevertheless, they were supposed to give a feeling of "privacy"...

My concert was held in a gigantic barrack, where the few benches were not enough to take care of the hordes of people. After the performance, Kwasnik arranged a little party in my honor, inviting the committee members of the camp, including a DP pianist, Tanya Grosman, who often accompanied the local talent in camp. Without much coaxing, she obliged us with several classical compositions including the Warsaw Concerto—Arzewski's solo on my program.

"Her husband was a prominent physician in Lemberg," Kwasnik informed me in a hushed voice. "The Nazis summoned him out of the house and shot him before her very eyes."

My second concert, arranged for the afternoon, was held at the magnificent State Theater. Arriving there I was surprised to find droves of people milling about the courtyard. The theater was closed. I knocked on one of the massive doors, and a German appeared—evidently as the custodian.

"Why haven't you opened the house?" I demanded.

"The Hamburg Symphony is scheduled to play here this evening for the German populace. The stage is set with instruments, chairs and music stands, so how do you expect to give a concert here?!"

I ordered him to open the doors to once, or I would call the American MPs...the sight of whom scared the Germans out of their wits. Without another word, he opened the theater and admitted the Jews.

Carefully, we pushed back some of the instruments and stands and made just enough room for my entrance. And that was how I concertized, backed by a full symphonic orchestra—without the musicians. My audience of Jews was happy enough with my piano accompaniment.

Before leaving Bamberg, my good friend Kwasnik made sure to supply me with extra food for the journey, plus a few blankets, bedsheets and pillow cases for my new lodging in Munich.

Taking a Chance

The room assigned to me was in the quarters that housed the UNRRA personnel. It consisted of a single iron bedstead, an old-fashioned wardrobe and a chair. Grateful for the linen Kwasnik had given me, I spread out the sheet and blanket, covered the pillow, hung my civilian clothes in the closet and felt as if I had checked into a first-class hotel.

Again I pursued Gaber with my urgent desire to slip into Austria to see Dora, Shimon and above all, Motele.

"Maybe I can try making it into Austria on my own?" I ventured.

Gaber didn't oppose the idea. He merely said, "If you run into trouble, contact me here. I'll think of something."

My official permit for Austria and other zones was to be issued later on. Consequently, Gaber could not supply me with travel orders, but since there was no lack of trucks, jeeps and other vehicles on the road to Salzburg, he suggested my best bet was to get out early in the morning and simply thumb a ride—American style.

I followed his suggestion and sure enough I didn't have much of a wait. The first army truck, loaded with sacks of flour, pulled to a stop at the wave of my hand. I invented a story about my jeep breaking down and how important it was for me to be in Salzburg on some military matter.

"Sure thing, sir. Climb aboard." said the driver, jovially.

I hoisted myself up beside him, careful not to get flour on my uniform. As we drove along I got an earful of the driver's life story...but my mind was keyed only on seeing myself on the other side of the checkpoint.

We pulled up at the border and ran into trouble. Our American army truck was not permitted into Austria! "What about the commissioned transport of flour?" the driver argued. But, according to the new regulations, a special American army truck sent out from Austria would have to come to the border and transport the sacks of flour from one truck to another. That would make it legal. This idiotic maneuver was beyond our comprehension. While the driver argued back and forth with the border guard, I sauntered through a small sidegate a few yards from the lowered barricade and was on my way on foot.

When a jeep, driven by an American officer, crossed over into Austria, I hailed him and relayed the story of the flour shipment. "They barred my truck from entering Salzburg," I explained, sounding very authoritative, "so I must arrange for an Austrian truck to pick up the flour."

"Hop in," said the officer and drove me clear into Salzburg. He was kind enough to drop me at the office of the HIAS where I received the warmest hospitality from the director, Mr. Goodwin. I showed him the letter given me by HIAS in New York before my departure for Europe, asking that I be extended whatever help I needed.

Mr. Goodwin was ready to do all he could, except that he had no way of arranging transportation to Linz. Instead, he advised that I take the train. Giving me some Austrian shillings, he took me to the station.

A long line of Austrian civilians were lined up at the ticket window. They made way for me, puzzled, no doubt, that a high-ranking American officer should be traveling on a local Austrian train. As a matter of fact, my heart was in my mouth lest I be spotted by some American MPs. I wasn't even sure that I was allowed to travel on a civilian train. Nevertheless, I arrived safely in Linz, and then had to take several trolleys to get in the vicinity of Camp Wegscheid.

Imagine the surprise of Dora and Shimon at my sudden appearance. Motele had turned into quite a handsome little fellow in the interim. Happily, the circumcision had taken place. A group of Lubavitcher had passed through the camp in transit, and they, of course, had a mohel amongst them.

Dora also told me that the Jewish books I had sent out from New York had finally arrived. The entire camp was elated over them. Most of the people had not laid eyes on a Yiddish book in many a year.

"Everyone in camp is blessing you uncle! And the food packages, the clothing that Aunt Bella sends, have been arriving with more regularity. But the possibility of emigrating—that's still a big question. Shimon is constantly running to the HIAS, to the JOINT, but all the affidavits you sent are still sitting there... In general, very few Jews are able to leave Austria."

A young boy, about fourteen, from a barrack close by came up to me and introduced himself. "My name is Abie Lebowohl. My mother and I hope to go to America. What do you think, sir, is there any chance of a future for me in America? I will have to provide for my mother, you know."

"Yes, Abie," I encouraged him, admiring his spunk. "I believe a boy like you can find a good future in America. A young man like you can achieve many good things." (My prediction came true. Abie is the successful proprietor of the Second Avenue Delicatessen in New York; an upstanding citizen, a devoted family man and a good son to his mother.)

Our Grodno friends Leyb Reizer, his wife and little daughter also had no prospects of emigrating anywhere. I was becoming more and more convinced that my people had to get themselves into Germany... for it was easier to accomplish things from there. The question, of course, was how?

When it was time for me to start back, Dora protested, as she did at my first visit. "But, uncle, you only just got here. Why not stay a while?"

How could I make her understand the anxiety I felt lest I miss the only train to Salzburg, let alone the prospect of smuggling across the border again?

It was evening when I reached Salzburg I found the Red Cross canteen humming with American army personnel. A band played and couples danced. In this cheerful atmosphere I became acquainted with several nurses who worked in a children's sanitorium on the German side of the border. They had come by jeep and got me across the border the same way. A few hours later, there I was, in the JOINT mess hall as smug as the cat that swallowed the canary;

with Gaber winking at me in approval. I took the chance—and I made it! Nothing ventured, nothing gained.

Golden Opportunities

Representatives of the Polish propaganda-machine agitated among the gentile and Jewish DPs. Golden opportunities awaited them there. And they promised them food packages and clothing even before starting back. A number of Jewish DPs, no longer able to endure the hopelessness, the filth and hunger in the camps, allowed themselves to be caught up in the web of these promises, and did indeed return to Poland.

Preparing to continue my tour the following day, I had arranged with Arzewski that we would pick him up at daybreak. Hans stopped the ambulance at Arzewski's house and Mishka got out to knock on the door. There was no answer. He rapped again. Finally, out came a disgruntled German woman, who gave us the news: Arzewski, his wife and child had left during the night and gone back to Poland!

I was stunned. People were waiting for me in the camps and my accompanist was gone! Hans made a screeching U-turn and we sped back to headquarters. Once again we began the mad search for a pianist.

"What are the chances of bringing Tanya Grosman, the pianist from Bamberg?" I asked Gaber. "I'm sure Irving Kwasnik would arrange it for us"

Gaber called Bamberg and, sure enough, Kwasnik was only too happy to help and soon arranged Tanya's transfer to Munich.

* * *

In the meantime, I learned that the Yiddish actors in Munich had reorganized the M.Y.T. players with Alexander Bardini as director. They produced a dramatization of the poem "Shlomo Molkhus" by A. Glantz-Leyeles. The JOINT, the central committee and I helped them acquire the raw materials for the sceneries and decor, including the electrical equipment I had imported from Paris. The performance was received with extraordinary enthusiasm.

A Protest Demonstration

Jews in the American zone in Germany were outraged when they learned of the atrocious British actions in carrying out the hangings of Dov Gruner and his three companions in Palestine. Jews from all ideologies, headed by rabbis and representatives of various organizations, marched on the main streets of Munich in a protest demonstration. The placards they carried bore slogans denouncing the British government, not only for barbarism toward the Jewish people in the holy land, but for seizing ships that transported Jewish immigrants to Palestine and incarcerating them in camps on Cyprus.

A squad of American military police, with automatic machine-guns trained on the demonstrators, surrounded them on all sides. My heart stood still. My

God, Jewish blood will again be spilled. I could not believe my eyes! American soldiers so openly displaying their hostility toward Jews?! American soldiers aiming their guns at the patriarchal beards of rabbis? Must these survivors again stare into gun barrels—of soldiers whose army had only recently rescued these Jews from certain death? But those were the former army transports, who found our people in the most dire conditions. The newer recruits had already found Red Cross centers and places where they could make merry with frauleins, who fed them countertales pertaining to Jews.

The tension was ultimately eased by an American chaplain. Placing himself at the head of the procession, he led them all the way to the British Embassy. The marchers calmed down. If a high-ranking officer of the American army was with them in their protest, then, obviously, not all Americans were against them. It also had a cooling effect on the MPs themselves.

Thus, the dangerous protest march came off without incident; thanks to the quick-thinking chaplain, the director of the JOINT's religious department, Rabbi Dr. Solomon Shapiro.

* * *

The pianist from Bamberg, Tanya Grosman, arrived in Munich. Her appearance was pitiful, but, at the JOINT's storehouse of old clothing, she found a dress suitable to wear at our concerts. I wondered whether she would be able to rough it, dragging as we did, from camp to camp. And where would she sleep? Well, were we in for a surprise! Tanya proved to be a trouper. She took everything in stride with good humor—including Mishka's colorful language. She shared our rations, traveled without complaint, regardless of how long the journey, and slept wherever there was room.

Considering all she had already lived through, she told me, our hardships were a mere snap to her. As long as she was playing the piano again, she felt she was back in civilization!

I gave concerts in Wilseck, Eichstadt, Eschwege and continued on to Kassel. The city was in ruin. It was said that thousands of bodies still lay buried beneath Kassel's rubble. The stench of death hung in the air.

Most of my concerts were held outdoors in the open fields to accommodate the multitudes of DPs. By setting up two or three large tables against a door or window of some building, and covering the tables with a layer of wooden planks, I had a ready-made stage. The piano and amplifier were placed near the platform. The speakers were set up on the roof of the ambulance, so that my voice could carry to every corner of the field. During Tanya's solos, I made my changes inside the building, either through the door and more often through the window. The audience was not at all fazed by my acrobatics. They understood the circumstances and appreciated me all the more.

My first open-air performance in Kassel was attended by more than ten thousand people. During this concert, something happened to my pianist, which gave me an awful shock. In my composition, "Yisroel, der Shomer" (Israel, the Guard), I portray in song and recitation a scene in Palestine where a guard is shot by Arab marauders. Suddenly, Tanya stopped playing. As we were out in the open, I thought a breeze had blown the sheets of music from the piano. I continued singing, hoping she would catch up. But she did not, and I finished without accompaniment. Glancing at her I saw that she was staring into space, as if she didn't know where in the world she was.

"Tanya! Tanya!" I softly called to her. She awoke with a start as if from a trance. I continued with the program and she resumed at the piano.

"What happened to you, Tanya?" I asked after the concert, "why did you stop playing?"

"Did I... again?" she murmured. "I'm sorry. It happens sometimes. Please forgive me. All of a sudden, the horrible scene sweeps before my eyes... I saw the Nazis shooting down my husband..."

* * *

Regensburg. The concert on our itinerary was scheduled for three o'clock in the afternoon, except someone forgot to mark down just where it was to be held. Frantic, we cruised the town up and down knowing that somewhere people were waiting for me—but where? Finally, we came upon a Jew who did know. He was on his way to the concert, himself, and directed us to the State Theater.

The Germans in charge were openly hostile to the Jews who had already assembled for my performance. What's more, I found all the dressing rooms locked. The custodian did me a favor and unlocked a room cluttered with props and old furniture. I managed to clear a corner and began to dress. There was no point in starting a new world war with the Germans.

After the concert my group and I were off on the road again. Most camp committees wanted me to give my concerts in the barracks or in theaters, but I now preferred performing out in the open, where I could play to any given number of people at once, since I could not spend too much time in one place by giving additional concerts, except for children, or hospitals.

Nuremberg. This was where the trials of the Nazi war criminals were being held. My performance was attended by many Jews who had come to Nuremberg from various camps to testify as eyewitnesses against the Nazis.

Heidenheim. Here, I met two esteemed colleagues; the actress, Lola Folman, who had endeared herself to the Jewish DPs in Germany with her charming folk songs, and her husband, the noted writer and poet Itzhak Perlov. Together with their little son, Benami, they managed to leave Germany "aliyah beth" and were destined to live through history's epic chapter of Jewish strife: the Exodus. Happily, we were to meet again in Israel and in America.

I had stopped keeping track of time. In place of days, weeks, months, I was counting DP camps, driving out of one and into another. On my fiftieth performance the JOINT sent my wife a special congratulatory cable. Her reply was: "When is my husband coming home?" How could I contemplate going home when my mission here had only begun? I was in great demand in every zone under occupation by the Four Powers.

The JOINT office in New York contacted the Hebrew Actors' Union with a request to send several artists to aid me in my work. Since nothing came of it, I remained to carry on alone as the "one man U.S.O."

Most difficult for me was having to entertain the tubercular patients in the sanatoriums of Gauting, St. Otilian and others. Patients, who were able to get around, waited for me outside the entrance for hours. The signs they hung on the gate posts read: "Welcome Brother Yablokoff! Nisht Gezorgt!"

The doctors told me that so much excitement was not exactly ideal for the patients. Some were warned to calm down or they would not be permitted to attend my performance. The nurses asked me not to mind the fits of coughing during my program. Those who might be overcome by such a spell would have to be wheeled out. I assured them I understood and had adjusted myself to the situation in other institutions.

Wrapped in hospital robes, my audience for the most part, was settled on the floor, propped against the wall. Bed-ridden patients were brought in nonportable cots, or wheel-chairs, with doctors and nurses standing by, ready to remove a patient at the slightest indication that he, or she, wasn't up to the occasion.

During my entire program there was hardly a cough to be heard. Neither did it become necessary to remove a patient. They were so deeply absorbed that, instead of hacking and coughing, the air ran with bursts of laughter. A phenomenon! the doctors puzzled. Could it be that spiritual treatment, after all, was the right cure for their patients?!

I had been in close contact with many of the gravely ill, never thinking to be cautious. Who could bother under such dire and emotional circumstances? When I did ask the doctors to test my lungs, it was surprising indeed to have the results turn up negative.

* * *

Degendorf. Jews here had beaten up a capo, a Nazi collaborator. I went to the hospital to see him, curious to hear what he had to say for himself. They had beaten him to a pulp. His face and head were swathed in bandages.

"As I sat in the hall listening to your concert," he related, "a man tapped me on the shoulder. 'Were you in the ghetto of Lodz?' he asked me. Yes, I nodded. 'Did you know so-and-so?' he whispered. Yes, I answered. Then, for no reason at all he struck me across the face. I didn't want to start a commotion in the hall, so I left. Outside, they ganged up on me. The fell on me, beat me up and here I am in the hospital. I still don't know what it's all about." He began to cry.

"Why don't you go before the special trial committee in Munich and clear yourself?"

"I have no confidence," he whimpered. "People will be afraid to appear as witnesses in my behalf. My attackers are underworld characters. I'm innocent!"

I left the hospital feeling that this bird was indeed a capo.

Habmille, near Degendorf. I visited Beth Sefer Kovshi Hayam, the school for sailors. The captain of the ship, a German, under whose tutelage the Jewish youths were training as seamen, was highly pleased with his students. They were diligent and quick to learn, he said. I thought if only these boys were allotted a little more than the 1,200 calories per day they were receiving! Young appetites... and doing such rugged work! Some were actually barefoot. But they went through their maneuvers like born mariners.

The captain said he wished they could be outfitted with uniforms. It would be a tremendous lift to their morale. But where could these uniforms be gotten?! My God, I couldn't help thinking, if the Jews in America had an inkling of what was going on here, these boys would be swamped with uniforms! Imagine! Jewish sailors!

These wonderful boys, future Israeli seamen, marched in to see my performance. They were given the best seats up front near the platform. After the concert, a committee of them came up on stage and declared me an honorary member of their marine school, Kovshi Hayam. The certificate is still in my possession. I regard it as a great privilege to have witnessed Jewish youths prepare themselves for the rebirth of Israel. I am sure that many are now high-ranking officers of the Israeli Navy.

Jew Against Jew

Pokking. In a telegram from the JOINT in Munich I was ordered to make a switch in my itinerary and head for the camp in Pokking. An order is an order! So, no questions asked, we made a right-about-face. Pokking was a tremendously large camp filled with Jews of every party and ideology. Many were orthodox with a large number of Lubavitcher, recently from Russia.

Some time before my visit, a celebration had taken place in honor of a Sefer Torah being brought into camp. It was carried under a chupa with all the religious factions reverently taking part in the procession.

Arriving at the gates we found American MPs posted there. They insisted on examining our documents. What kind of newfangled order was this? Why the military police? They were not even permitted in the camps. The lieutenant in charge, a Jewish fellow from Baltimore, explained: a free-for-all had broken out, with Jews knifing one another, and the MPs were called in to bring about order. We drove into camp and found the JOINT director, Bernard Tabb, a compassionate young American Jew utterly desperate over the situation.

"A troupe of players from Munich," he said, "had come to give a performance in camp...which was fine," he added. "The freethinkers among the DPs persuaded them to announce their performance for Friday evening. This, of course raised the roof. The religious Jews protested the desecration of the Sabbath. The freethinkers proclaimed that they did not have to be bound by rules laid down by the fanatics! The actors went about their business and continued to sell tickets for Friday evening.

"Before the performance hundreds of religious Jews gathered in front of the theater-barrack, loudly haranguing those who came to see the show. One angry word led to another until people began pushing and shoving, which finally ended in a brawl. Twenty-some casualties were taken to the infirmary. "It was a tragic and shameful situation. The military police with their jeeps and fire-arms only incensed the long-suffering Jews all the more," deplored Tabb, "and things came close to a blood bath..."

During my entire sojourn in the camps, I never appeared on a Friday night, or a Saturday before sundown. In order not to waste a Friday I would fill in an afternoon program at a children's home, or at some hospital in the region where my Saturday concert happened to be scheduled. I neither wanted—nor would the JOINT allow me—to perform on the eve of a Sabbath.

"Finally," continued Tabb, "I contacted Samuel Haber, our chief in Munich."

Now I understood why I was rushed to Pokking. I was to try to cool the atmosphere. By now the DPs everywhere regarded me as one of their own—"amkho!" The first thing I did was to prevail upon the Jewish MP lieutenant to leave camp. Their presence and their automatic guns, I explained, only outraged the survivors, who had barely escaped with their lives from the German machine guns. Realizing that I was right, he gave the order to pull out of camp.

Bernard Tabb took us to UNRRA headquarters. Shown to our rooms we began to unpack. We were just getting settled, when in strode the UNRRA director, a Jewish fellow from California—who shall remain nameless. Although he wore an American uniform, he sported black Russian boots—a thing I'd never encountered before. With him came his aide, a woman in a British uniform, also wearing Russian boots!

"Who allowed these DPs to occupy rooms at an UNRRA House?!" he demanded. For me, an American, he made an exception. But my crew? These DPs had to remove their stuff at once and vacate the premises.

Tabb was outraged, but couldn't butt in. True enough my little group had no right to lodge at an UNRRA house. They were DPs. But, damn it, this "UNRRA" character with the Russian boots was a Jew himself, and he saw the situation. As long as my people were already there, why not let them stay the few days?! "If my traveling group is not permitted here," I told this UNRRA Jew from California, "then I don't wish to stay here, either. Come on boys, let's go."

We took our belongings and marched. But where to? We were not allowed to lodge with Germans in the vicinity. In the meantime, Tabb took us to his room, where he opened some canned goods and we had a bite to eat. Tabb and I decided that we would not take our meals in the UNRRA mess hall. Many among the UNRRA personnel also failed to show up for meals there to protest the director's gesture toward me and my crew.

When the camp committee heard of the incident they immediately did some juggling and made some room for us to stay among the DPs. I gave Hans and Mishka a whole carton of cigarettes, with which they "organized" enough provisions at the P.X. to see us through.

I went along with director Tabb to pay a visit to the rabbi of Pokking, a gentle but ailing soul. The rabbi was profoundly disturbed by the turbulence in camp. I begged him to appeal to the worshipers during the evening service to make peace. At the hospital too, I went from bed to bed, playing the role of peacemaker.

Our posters announced three concerts: two for adults and one for children. And they stressed, as in every camp, that admission was free. My performances, I'm glad to say, had the desired effect. The air was cleared, nerves were relaxed and there was peace at last. The one who suffered the most flak after the upheaval was the Jewish lieutenant of the MPs, who'd been summoned to camp to quell the riot. Some of the anti-Semites in his outfit kept needling him about Jews killing Jews. Getting back at them, he later told me, he made his name on his office door read: Lieutenant "John Doe"—Jew.

The good rabbi pronounced a blessing upon me for my sacred mission, and prayed that I would return safe and sound to my dear ones. My wife, Bella, firmly believes that the blessings of this holy man did indeed bring me out of the camps alive.

Upon leaving Pokking, throngs of people saw me to the arched gates. A girl, pushing her way to the ambulance, hurriedly tossed a large envelope through the window into my lap and disappeared in the crowd. The envelope contained two sketches: one, the grotesque image of a clown, half of his face crying, the other, laughing. The second, done in crayon, depicted the nude figure of a girl, her long hair flowing, electrocuting herself on the charged barbed wires. Attached was a note: "Dear Clown, Yablokoff, this is the way we look... tell it to the world."

70

Bergen-Belsen

We left for Bergen-Belsen, the infamous German concentration camp where tens of thousands of Jews were massacred during the Holocaust. It was now a displaced persons camp in the British zone.

Sprawled in the midst of a heavily demolished area named Freedom Square, it was one of the largest encampments in Germany, packed with survivors from various countries, most of whom had been liberated right here in Belsen.

This had been the most gruesome of all death camps. Traces of gas chambers and crematorium were still visible. I also saw the unbelievable number of mass graves where lies buried countless thousands of Jewish martyrs. At one of these mass graves of about 30,000 victims, the Central Committee of Liberated Jews in the British zone, had put up an impressive monument with the inscription: "You are now entering the site of the memorial, which has been erected in memory of the many thousands who perished in Belsen concentration camp." Other mass graves were simply marked: "Here lie 10,000 …5,000" and so on, on and on.

My pianist, Tanya, threw herself upon one of these graves and wailed: "My dear sister…my sister…!" It was here that her sister had perished, but having no way of knowing where her body lay, Tanya could only weep anew at every other grave. It made me shudder. It was impossible to shake off the nightmare of this wasteland. Yet, the entire camp with its feverish activity was part and parcel of this vast cemetery.

I gave three concerts in the big Cinema Theater, which held over 1,500 people. The overseer of the house, a German who was a proven friend of the Jewish people, lived on the premises with his wife and family. He happened to be the brother-in-law of the famed film star Marlene Dietrich.

My performances were received with tremendous appreciation and enthusiasm, although the laughter was somewhat restrained. It's not easy to laugh on a cemetery haunted by horrendous memories…

Bergen-Belsen was in the midst of intense activity at the time, preparing Jews of all parties and ideologies for a new life in Palestine, with particular attention on the children. They were the hope of tomorrow. On the limited number of certificates doled out so sparingly by the British government, only a handful of Jews were able to emigrate to Palestine legally.

Before I left, the committee arranged a gathering in my honor and presented me with a letter:

> Most esteemed friend, Herman Yablokoff, the cultural com-
> mittee of the central and local bodies wish to express their deepest
> gratitude in their own as well as in the name of all Bergen-Belsen
> inhabitants, who had the honor and pleasure of attending your
> concerts.
>
> Eight thousand Jews have experienced the joy of sharing laugh-
> ter with you and—with you, the Clown—we also shared tears. You
> brought us into living contact with Jewish communities around the
> world, and recounted our recent past and immediate future before
> us as vividly as in a moving film. You have instilled in us the cour-
> age and the strength to go on. May your future travels be blessed
> with achievement. We feel sure that the Jewish people whom you
> will yet visit will receive you with the same heartiness and esteem
> that you have found here, with us.
>
> Thank You, Brother Yablokoff.

I also deem it a sacred privilege to be mentioned in the subsequent pictorial album, *Holocaust and Rebirth*, published by the World Federation of
Bergen-Belsen Associations, which includes a picture of me at Bergen-Belsen
in 1947.

The JOINT director in Belsen, Sam Dallob, succeeded in wangling the Russian travel orders I needed to pass through the Russian zone. This was the route
that let directly to Berlin. My traveling companions, especially Mishka, were
loathe to venture anywhere in the proximity of the Russians, but didn't protest.

After a pleasant overnight stop in Hanover with a concert at the Stadt
Theater, we reached the boundary that separated the British and Russian zones.
The British guards were friendly chaps, warning us as we rested at the border,
to be cautious in passing through the Russian zone. Many a night, they related,
they had heard shots fired at people attempting to escape into the British side.
The victims were left to rot between the two frontiers, their bodies fouling
up the air.

At the Russian border we were stopped by one of their guards holding
a machine gun. In examining our travel orders and other documents, the Russian kept turning the papers over and over. What's wrong, I wondered, can't
he read? It's written in Russian! Our papers, of course, were so crammed with
rubber stampings, he apparently couldn't make head or tail out of them. Finally,
returning our documents, he saluted and ordered another Russian soldier to
raise the barrier. And there we were—in the Russian occupied zone!

How remarkable! The moment we drove past the barrier, the unmistakable tang of Russian air hit my nostrils. It brought back sharp reminders of my
childhood years under the czarist regime.

The next thing that caught my attention was the sight of shabbily clothed German women, wearing worn Russian boots, cleaning the roadways. They lugged heavy stones, loaded and pushed wheelbarrows and did chores usually performed by men or machinery. The Russians were obviously not pampering the fräuleins the way the Americans were doing in their zone.

Berlin

The JOINT headquarters in Berlin occupied an entire villa, The director, Max Elvarg, was devoted heart and soul to the welfare of the survivors in the Berlin region. Staying at the villa with us was Norman Gilmofsky of the United Jewish Appeal in New York. We had already met in Munich. En route back to the States after his visit to Poland, Gilmofsky had stopped off in Berlin to report to the office of the United Jewish Appeal on the situation he encountered in the Polish DP.

I gave a performance in the camp of Schlachtensee at Mariendorf and another at the Palladium Theater for the community of German Jews in Berlin. During my concert, long lines of Germans had collected for the showing of a Deutsches film scheduled to follow. After my audience left, the crowd of Germans still remained in line, nobody budging. Asked by the doormen why they weren't entering the theater, the Germans replied: "We are waiting for the Jew-stench to evaporate..."

Through the chaplain of the American Berlin Command, Rabbi Meyer Abramowitz, I learned of a children's colony in Vancy, outside Berlin.

"Would you like to come along with me," he asked, "and visit the children?"

"I'd gladly go," I said, "although I can't see how I can entertain them without a piano... and dragging the ambulance up that steep hill, I understand, is out of the question. It must be tough enough making it by jeep."

"I'm sure you can think of something to amuse the kids," the good chaplain smiled.

Well, I certainly couldn't refuse to do my bit for the isolated youngsters on the hill. We climbed up to the tent colony in jeeps and I did, somehow, manage to keep the children entertained minus the piano. Their sheer delight in the songs I taught them and in the humorous stories that provoked their childish laughter, made me doubly grateful to Rabbi Abramowitz for the pleasure of performing for them.

One of my concerts in Berlin was attended by the members of two dramatic groups, Hanodeid (Wanderer) and Baderekh (On the Way), which happened to be playing there. My friends Max Elvarg and Norman Gilmofsky came around after my performance to take me to supper at the Officers' Club. When we entered, the orchestra struck up the opening bars of "Happy Birthday." Whose birthday? I wondered. Surprise! It was mine, and I had completely forgotten. I found my crew already seated at one of the festively decked tables. We were served an appetizing meal of gefilte fish, noodle soup and other delicacies. Elvarg handed me a telegram from my wife and children, wishing me a happy birthday. And as a birthday gift, my friends had arranged an overseas telephone connection so I could talk to Bella in New York.

Before leaving Berlin, I transcribed a broadcast from the military radio station in which I addressed the people of the United States and other countries. I described the tragic plight of the survivors in the camps. I ended the taped message with the composition that had become the highlight of my program, a composition that spoke for itself: "Let us Live!"

It was near daybreak when we finally drove back to Munich. And there, on the door of my room, I found a note from Grossman at the HIAS: "Contact me at once." I could barely wait for his office to open.

"Your niece and her family," Grossman informed me, "were brought into Stuttgart last night with a transport from Austria. They are now in the transit camp of New Freiman. If you have a chance to whisk them out of the camp, now is the time to do it. Once they are registered to be shipped somewhere," he warned me, "it will be too late."

I was bewildered! And as luck would have it, my confidante, Sam Gaber, was away from headquarters. What was I to do? In order to get them out of camp I would need a vehicle. My ambulance would be just the thing, only I would need a special travel order. And for this, I had to give a reason. How could I possibly ask to use the ambulance to smuggle out DPs? Having no other recourse, I had to tell my story to the chief director, Samuel Haber.

He was delighted to see me, and had already received reports on my concerts in Bergen-Belsen and Berlin.

"I must ask a favor of you. Sam Gaber isn't here and only you can help me."

"What is it, Yabby? For you, anything."

Timidly I asked, "Can I have permission to take my ambulance for a day? I need travel orders to visit my niece and nephew in Stuttgart."

"You have relatives in Stuttgart?" he asked, surprised. "Well, no problem. I'll gladly give you a note to the dispatcher at the car pool. He'll make out your travel order for Stuttgart and get your chauffeur to drive you there."

I knew my driver was exhausted after our long journey from Berlin, so I asked Halpern, one of the others. I instructed him to drive to Stuttgart. After explaining my mission there and the chances we were taking, he was extraordinarily moved and more than willing to help me.

Although the entrance gates to New Freiman were guarded by the camp police, they didn't dare stop a JOINT ambulance. I spotted Shimon just inside the gate! Intuitively, he'd sensed that I would show up. Seeing me, he turned without a word and began to walk. Taking the cue, we followed in the ambulance. When he stopped at one of the barracks I understood this was where we'd find Dora and the baby. With an expert maneuver of the wheel, Halpern backed right up to the barrack door. Letting the motor run he went around to throw open the rear doors of the vehicle and in seconds, Dora, Shimon and

Motele in his baby carriage, were all stowed away behind the piano. Closing the doors, Halpern got back behind the wheel and with the same cockiness with which we'd driven into camp, we now steered out and were back on the autobahn.

Along the way we were stopped by MPs. My heart sank. Dora and Shimon, huddling in back of the piano held their breath. And Motele, though wide awake in his carriage, never uttered a peep... as if he understood that this was no time to let himself be heard. I identified myself and the MPs waved us on.

Motele hadn't yet fully recovered from the ordeal of his circumcision, yet he was behaving like a trouper. I asked Shimon to roll the baby-cart toward the back of my seat so the little one could get some fresh air through my open window.

"You see, Motele," I said, glancing at him over my shoulder, "you just came into the world and already you are getting a taste of how great it is to be born a Jew! You have to smuggle across borders... hungry, thirsty, hide behind a piano, tremble at every sound... a wandering Jew before you can even walk!"

Motele's baby-blue eyes smiled up at me as if he grasped my discourse on the fate of a Jew. "So what?" his gaze seemed to imply, "it's fun!"

My driver was hungry and so was I. Dora and Shimon said, never mind, they could do without, but I was worried, knowing that Dora needed the nourishment to breastfeed her baby. Later in the day we came upon a snack bar and decided to stop. I told the fräulein who waited on us that we were transporting a German family in my ambulance; a man, his wife and infant. They hadn't had a morsel of food all day. "Bitte schön, if you could let me have some milk, a sandwich perhaps. The mother has to feed her infant, and she's famished. I'll pay..."

Without a word she pointed to a sign: "It is strictly verboten to take out food."

Putting down several cigarettes on the table, I remarked pointedly, "This is a German family. You are German yourself. My conscience is clear."

We finished eating and as we were about to leave, the fräulein pushed a package into my hands. I thanked her and we returned to the ambulance. Wrapped in an old newspaper was a full carton of malted milk and a dozen doughnuts—typical American fare—which my passengers relished for the first time in their lives.

Toward evening we arrived at a sanatorium in the heart of Stuttgart. Having appeared there in concert, I had prepared a tentative place in case I succeeded in bringing my little family into Germany. My friends put them up in the attendants' barracks and assured me that they would be cared for until I could find them a suitable refuge.

With a heavy heart I took leave of my little trio and started back. Along the autobahn, some time later, we pulled over to catch a snooze, for this too was quite a journey. Before dawn Halpern and I were back in Munich.

71

From Camp to Camp

L andsberg. I visited the jail where Hitler had been imprisoned before he became Ruler of the Third Reich. Here, he wrote *Mein Kampf*, in which he brazenly outlined his aspiration to conquer the world and annihilate the Jewish people. Now, two years after Germany's capitulation, the liberated remainder of Jews were still confined in this large camp.

The DPs at Landsberg were extremely proud of their theater group, Hazomir, directed by M. Khran. When I arrived in camp they were rehearsing *The Golem* by H. Leivick. I was invited to sit in. Realizing that, under the circumstances, they would not be able to do justice to such an ambitious production by themselves, I contacted the JOINT director Samuel Haber in Munich and asked him to please dispatch the noted regisseur, recently arrived from Poland, Alexander Bardini. Thanks to Bardini, *The Golem* proved to be a rewarding success, providing tremendous recreation for the Jews in Landsberg and the camps surrounding the area.

The people had so little to eat, so little to hope and to live for, but, they did enjoy and appreciate their theater groups. And, because actors would rather act than eat, their very drive threw their brothers and sisters a lifeline...the "straw" that kept them from drowning! I shall always regard them as the heroes of the ghettos and accursed camps.

I continued my tour of camps—Mitrakhing, Waldstadt, Leip-Heim, Greifenberg, Föhrenwald. I also appeared in the camps of Windheim, Vlating, Lichtenau, Zels-Heim, Eiring, Ausbruk, Wolheim, Zeitskopen (a T.B. sanatorium), Geredstsreich, Filseck, Masbach, Saltzheim, Lempertheim and on to Feldafing.

Camp Feldafing was known throughout Germany. The Jewish Workers' Committee, the Socialist Federation and the Bund in New York devoted their efforts on behalf of this camp, which was run with exemplary order and bore the look of a small town in Eastern Poland. Their dramatic group, Amkho, scored success with Anski's *The Dybbuk*, another very ambitious undertaking.

To Paris, with Lubavitcher Hasidim

The Jews in the camps suffered the lack of everything but rumors. No one ever knew where, when, or how the rumors originated, but they spread like wildfire. Mostly, they were prompted by wishful thinking. Upon my return to Munich to prepare for my next tour, I heard that Maurice Schwartz, who

454

was concertizing in Paris, was coming to Germany to appear in the camps. The Jewish newspaper in Munich also ran this item. So, needless to say, the people awaited him with eagerness.

When I inquired from Samuel Haber whether he knew anything about this rumor, he shrugged his shoulders. Communication between Germany and Paris was so erratic, it was quite possible, he said, that the JOINT office in Paris had not been able to get through to him about Schwartz's coming to Germany. Nevertheless, the rumor persisted.

"Yabby, I know how tired you must be," Haber said. "You're doing a superman's job. So how about taking a break in your routine and going off to Paris for a few days? At the same time you can inquire about Schwartz. Maybe you can even urge him to come here and impress upon him what a tremendous lift his appearances would give the survivors."

Gratefully I accepted his offer. The weather was beastly hot. Luckily, Bella had sent me a package that contained some lightweight summer uniforms. And when my friend Gaber arranged my travel orders plus train ticket—first-class with sleeper—I changed into one of my summer uniforms and was all set!

Waiting around at Munich's makeshift train station, I was approached by a Hasid in traditional garb. What an incongruous picture he made in these German surroundings.

"Since you are going to Paris, would you please do a favor for the Lubavitcher Rebbe in Pokking?" he asked. "A transport of Hasidim and their families are traveling third-class to Paris on your train. You will earn a big mitzvah by keeping an eye on them. Please see to it that they don't run into difficulties at the border. The Rebbe is blessing you for it."

When I made my way to the third-class section to have a look at my transport of Lubavitcher, I was promptly met by their lively singing of "Shalom Aleichem." Most of them, especially the women, had heard my concert in Pokking and were enormously cheered by my presence on the train. If I, an American high officer was traveling with them, then—God willing—no ill could befall them at the border. They begged me to keep them company until the military inspection was over.

The Lubavitcher, I learned, were refugees from Russia. Their occupation: prayer-shawl weaving. They'd been told they would be able to settle in Paris.

The women had a hard time getting their children bedded down on the wooden benches. Half-naked they pranced about, climbing all over the railroad car with their capers and laughter. Kids are kids! After a while, one of the men softly launched into a lilting melody. Others joined in and it developed into a poignant "nigun," ending in an ecstatic climax that lifted the heart.

I had gathered up everyone's documents and at dawn, when at last the border police showed up, I identified myself as the man in charge of the entire group. I handed over the packet of papers to one of the bleary-eyed inspectors and after a perfunctory riffling, he returned them to me stamped: in order.

With inspection safely over, jubilation reigned in the car. Heaping blessings upon blessings on me and my family, the men donned their prayer shawl-
sand began the morning prayers, praising the Almighty for His Grace.

I finally retired to my first-class section to wash and tidy up. To my surprise, waiting at the station in Paris, were hundreds of Hasidim, come to greet
my transport of Lubavitcher! Joy was rampant, with everyone singing and dancing right there at the terminal. Frenchmen stopped to gawk in amazement.

At the head of these welcomers in Paris was the man dedicated to the
succor of the religious survivors of the Holocaust, the worthy representative
of the Lubavitcher Rescue Committee, Rabbi Benjamin Gorodetzky.

In parting, a delegation of my prayer-shawl weavers presented me with
a gift: a talis woven in Russia.

At the JOINT office in Paris, I was told that Maurice Schwartz had already
left for London, en route to New York. What a letdown!

"Could you possibly connect me with Schwartz in London?" I begged.
This took a little while until I finally heard the familiar baritone rumbling over
the wire, "Yablokoff?"

"Yes! I'm calling you from Paris. I came here from Germany specifically
to implore you not to disappoint the homeless Jews in the camps. They're expecting you. They remember you from the years before the war. All the Munich
papers," I shouted into the phone, "have announced that you are coming!"

"But that's impossible," he replied, "I have to open my season in New York."

"The survivors of the Holocaust are waiting for you! They are just as important as the opening of the Art Theater…and maybe more."

"You're putting me in a terrible spot. A theater man like you, Yablokoff,
should understand that I can't jeopardize my Art Theater. You know what?"
he suggested, "you get all the Jews from the camps together in one place and
I'll fly into Germany and give them a special concert."

"What are you saying!" I gasped at his naiveté. "I have been in Germany
now for more than five months, traveling by ambulance over tens of thousands
of miles and I still haven't reached all our people in the camps. So how can
it be done in one day, in one place, with one concert?"

"I'm truly sorry," Schwartz sighed, "but I can't help it. If someone had only
explained the situation to me earlier—Well anyway, extend my greetings to
all the Jews there. I've heard that you are performing wonders in Germany.
I will write about you in the *Forward* back home. Well goodbye now—and
keep up your good work."

* * *

During my stay in Paris I dropped in to see a Yiddish performance at the
Lencry, with Israel Barenbaum and Esther Zefkina. I have never forgotten that
performance. Barenbaum and his wife Zefkina were singing a duet when, in
the middle of the refrain, Esther suddenly cried out: "My son…my son!" With

his arm around her in a reassuring embrace, Barenbaum bravely sang on to the finish and led the distraught mother off the stage.

"This happens occasionally," he sighed, as we talked after the show. "My wife is haunted by visions of our son, who died in Auschwitz..."

* * *

Returning to Germany, my first mission was to go visit my three refugees. My friends in Stuttgart had settled them with a German family. The man of the house, a postal worker, was a former Nazi. Because of this affiliation, he was now obligated to rent a spare room in his house, if so requisitioned. These Germans went out of their way to make my children comfortable—afraid lest they offend me, the uncle, the major with the American Army of Occupation.

The big problem was food. In addition to the provisions Bella sent me from New York, I brought along articles I was able to purchase at the P.X. I also provided Dora and Shimon with American cigarettes and chocolate bars—enough so they could use them to acquire to some things on their own.

Baby Motele bloomed. The German and his wife fell in love with this exceptionally beautiful boy, pampering and fussing over him.

On one of my visits I arranged to have Hans drive the ambulance directly from Munich to my next destination, Frankfurt. This enabled me to spend another day with my children, and I then proceeded to Frankfurt by train.

Frankfurt-am-Main gave the survivors the feeling of residing in a metropolis. It certainly did not resemble any of the other camps I had seen.

The director, Bella Dalin, and the chairman of the central committee, David Werve (now in Los Angeles), told me that my concerts had already been announced in the camps of that region. Thousands were expected to attend.

It was time to prepare for my first performance and the ambulance carrying my crew and wardrobe hadn't yet arrived. We called Munich and were told that the group had left early in the morning. Where were they? We phoned the MPs patrolling the autobahn, thinking some of them might have encountered my ambulance. No one had seen a trace of them. Waiting outdoors on tenterhooks, I strained my eyes down the road—not a sign! Then, off in the distance, a team of horses pulling a farm wagon plodded into view. Perched on the wagon, calm and unruffled as you please, sat Mishka and Tanya.

"What happened? Where is Hans? Where is the ambulance?"

"The ambulance? Gone! Bye-bye!" replied Mishka flippantly. "It turned over with the wheels on top and us on the bottom. We were lucky to crawl out alive! Hans stayed behind on the autobahn, watching so no one steals the old wreck. But who's got the brains? Me, Mishka! I immediately 'organized' a German wagon with two nags, hauled your costumes and your pianist aboard and here we are. Now, where would you be without me?"

* * *

Next, I appeared in Garmisch, Gabercy, Rosenheim, Prien (a large center for youths, many of whom later settled in Winnipeg, Canada), Bad-Reichenhal, Hof-Salle (a camp of 6,000 Jews), Purtin (a teachers' seminary), Ayning, Wiesbaden, Bad-Naum, Fahrfer and Transtein.

I found the camp in Transtein in an uproar. Everyone was up in arms. The reason? A to-do over four cows! After liberation, when this camp was first set up, there was not much nourishment. And so, the American Army of Occupation rounded up four cows from the surrounding farms. As one man put it, the lean cows described in Pharoah's dream must have looked like elephants compared to these scrawny animals.

A general meeting was called, with one item on the agenda: how to fatten up the poor cows. Aside from the fact that they were pitiful to look at, they gave no milk. So it was unanimously decided that every adult spare a portion of his own meager calories for the cows. Before long the cows filled out so beautifully they were a pride to behold. The milk they now provided for the little ones poured like pure cream. Then all at once—calamity!

The American Army of Occupation decreed that everything requisitioned from the German civilians after the war had to be restored to them immediately! Sure enough, along came the German farmers demanding the return of the four cows. This, of course, started a hue and cry: "What?! Give back our cows?! Where is justice?! Now that we fattened them up they want to take them from us? The cows are so used to us they follow us around. We call them by Jewish names: Malkeh, Shprintze, Sossel, Breineh...We will not give up our Jewish cows to the Germans! No, a thousand times no!"

The women took up a war strategy. Lining up their small fry in carriages, buggies and strollers at the camp gate, they closed ranks and formed a human barricade. Now! they challenged, let anyone dare to lay a hand on any of the cows!

The moment the Germans arrived, accompanied by police, the women set up such a screaming hullabaloo, together with the earsplitting cries of their children, that the Germans and the police remained frozen at the gate. When they realized that there was to be no end to this raucous defense, they backed down and retreated.

Before long, investigations began. The camp committee was taken to task. The Jews, nonetheless, stood their ground. The cows, they said, weren't willing to leave camp where they were enjoying the good life. At sight of the police they had made off somewhere to hide—and go find them.

Unfortunately, the story had no happy ending. The Germans did indeed reclaim the four cows.

New Exodus from Romania

Preparing to leave Salzburg for Munich, I received an order from the Jewish Defense Committee to head at once for Vienna. To do so by ambulance was out of the question. My crew of DPs could not go. And so I sent them back to Munich and proceeded alone to Vienna by train.

My first performance in Vienna was held on the front steps of the Rothschild Hospital, for an audience of pitifully emaciated men, women and children, with barely a stitch of clothing on their backs. They squatted on the ground of the little park facing the hospital and around the side streets. From sheer exhaustion many of them slept through my program, never making a move. I had all I could do to invoke the semblance of a smile from the tragic, bewildered faces of those who did stay awake.

How deeply I felt their anguish! I knew that their woes had only begun. They still needed to smuggle past the Russian zone to reach the Americans, where they would remain stuck in the overcrowded DP camps. Some of them might also make a try for the undercover route, up steep and winding mountains to Italy—and then on their way to Palestine to risk falling into the hands of the British and being shipped off to Cyprus.

Upon fleeing the new wave of anti-Semitism in their homeland, the majority of these Romanian refugees had struck out on foot with nothing but the shirt on their backs. Those who did manage to salvage something fared no better. Waylaid by bandits, they were stripped clean. Barely escaping with their lives, they trudged on to Vienna.

A young man in the crowd came up to me. "Don't you recognize me?" he asked, somewhat surprised. "I am Marcel Kreisler, the violinist who led the orchestra when you guest starred in Romania in 1930 with the Ziegler troupe, remember?" If he hadn't identified himself, I would never have recognized him.

The outside world had not as yet heard of this new Jewish exodus. In order not to strain relations with the Communist government of Romania, the American army censored this shocking news and barred all foreign correspondents from Vienna.

I wrote a letter describing the plight of these refugees and addressed it to the *Jewish Daily Forward*. At the Red Cross, I asked an American officer who was flying to the States to drop my letter into any mailbox in New York. And so, before the news of this latest exodus reached the Associated Press and before the foreign correspondents had had a chance to swoop down on Vienna to cover this latest Jewish tragedy, my letter appeared in the *Daily Forward*—a first in the Yiddish and English language press in New York.

I returned to Munich by military plane. I was being rushed to Munich to film a short of my program, which was to be exhibited in the camps after my departure from Germany. I was also scheduled to give two farewell concerts in Munich before I started out on a tour of the camps in Italy.

Never having flown before, I had quite a few qualms; especially since this plane was an old army freight carrier, a C-47 with long benches along the sides and no passenger comfort whatsoever.

On boarding the plane, the sergeant-in-charge handed me a parachute. For the life of me I couldn't figure out which end was up. I looked to the sergeant for instructions.

"Instructions!" he laughed. "In the event you have to use a parachute, this damn contraption won't do you any good anyway! Just close your eyes and pray!"

* * *

My last two concerts in Germany were held at the Schauspielhaus in Munich. On both occasions the theater was packed to the rafters and attended by top-ranking military personnel.

Addressing me formally on the flower-laden stage, an aide to General Lucius D. Clay, the military governor of the American zone in Germany, presented me with a Certificate of Meritorious Service, "in recognition of magnificent artistic contribution to the spiritual rehabilitation and cultural well-being of the Jewish Displaced Persons in Germany and Austria."

Charles Pasman, director-general of the JOINT in Germany, pinned a gold medal on my lapel. Especially designed and cast for me, it was attached to a little blue-and-white ribbon—the colors of the Jewish flag, that became, only a year later, the official flag of the State of Israel.

The greatest honor of all was bestowed upon me by the Jewish people themselves. They awarded me the title of "Folk Artist of the Shearitt Hapleita (Remnant of the Jewish People)."

I took leave of all these dear friends and my devoted crew: Tanya, my accompanist who, as a DP, could not come to Italy with me; my chauffeurs who had traversed the tens of thousands of miles with me during my tour of Germany and Austria; and above all my devoted friend, Mishka. It was very difficult for me to say goodbye to the cousins I had met in the camps. I could only hope to see them placed in America, or Israel. Even more painful was the parting with my niece Dora, Shimon and Motele who were still in Stuttgart waiting for their visas to emigrate. I was grateful to my friend, Irving Kwasnik, who promised to look after them; a promise he faithfully kept until they were finally able to leave for the United States.

72

My Tour of Italy

Sam Gaber had an important mission to accomplish in Rome. And since he was driving to Italy with a weapon-carrier, I packed my theater wardrobe and tagged along. The rest of my stuff was shipped to Paris.

The shortest route from Munich to Italy was via the French zone. From experience I knew the French border authorities in Germany to be the most unamiable. They only confirmed my opinion. In vain did Gaber beg them to let us pass the French border. They refused. As we had no intention of turning back to Munich, Gaber stopped at a farm in the area and, for a few cigarettes, we were given directions for a detour that bypassed the border checkpoint. We would still be traveling through the French zone, the farmer told us, but along this side route, we would not be bothered.

The detour took us through the Brenner Pass over the Alps. We climbed steadily upward and despite its being summer, we nearly froze to death on those mountainous heights.

It was daybreak when we made the Italian frontier. Unlike the French, the Italian border guards proved to be very friendly. We weren't asked for any official travel orders and were allowed to cross into Italy with nary a snag.

In one of the villages on the way to Milan, we came upon an Italian selling grapes from a little pushcart. Having no Italian lire, we drove a bargain by sign language: a tin of canned meat for a bunch of grapes. Nodding in agreement, the vendor twisted a sheet of newspaper into a cone and filling it with a generous cluster of grapes handed it to us with a smiling "grazie." We would have appreciated some water to rinse our little morning refreshment, nevertheless we drove along enjoying the grapes—unwashed—with neither of us faring any the worse for it. Our weapon-carrier, on the other hand, did begin to ail. We lost half a day trying to perk up the motor. It was almost dusk when we crawled into Milan.

And there, waiting for me at the hotel, was Renee Solomon, the pianist. Mme. Solomon had, in fact, accompanied me soon after my arrival from New York, when I gave my first concert in Paris at the Salle Pleyel. Her husband, Henri Solomon, a noted musician himself, had been taken away during the German invasion of Paris and was subsequently put to death in Auschwitz. Finding shelter with some French peasants in the Pyrenees, Renee and her small daughter, Monique, were able to save their lives.

Mme. Solomon had been sent by the J.D.C. in Paris to accompany me on my concert tour of Italy.

Visibly perturbed, she hurriedly told me that people were already waiting for me in one of the camps on the outskirts of town. Having expected me in the morning, they had gone ahead and arranged for me to give a performance that very evening. How could they possibly know we'd be dragging in so late—and more dead than alive?!

Losing no time, we bade Mme. Solomon climb aboard our truck and an hour later, there I stood on a platform of the huge Camp Adriatica, concertizing for a crowd of about 2,000 Jewish DPs in Italy. Their laughter and shouts of "Nisht Gezorgt"...Don't Despair!...could have been heard way back in Milan!

* * *

There were about 40,000 Jewish DPs in Italy at the time, the majority of survivors from Poland and Hungary. They weltered in what were formerly concentration camps and in all kinds of makeshift kubbutzim, the same as in Germany and Austria. All political parties were engaged in active Zionist undertakings. Once the DPs managed to reach Italy, it meant the last stop in the trek to Palestine—or Cyprus.

I had lost a lot of weight by this time and suffered severe headaches. But, somehow I carried on. My appearances in Italy were held outdoors the better to serve the thousands of people. Many of them now knew me from Germany and Austria. They were on their way to Palestine, aliyah-beth, and were stuck in Italy. Fortunately, the Italian government displayed a benign attitude toward the Jewish refugees. Sympathetic to their aspiration of reaching Palestine, they were well aware of the hordes that filtered in nightly. Yet the Italians closed their eyes to this massive influx into their country, despite the risk of incurring England's displeasure...

Patiently, the people waited for a ship of any kind that would take them to Eretz Yisrael. The recent, heartbreaking drama of the Exodus, with its cargo of Palestine-bound Jews so brutally sent back by the British to the blood-stained soil of Germany, was still painfully fresh in everyone's mind. Yet, this very tragedy fired the Jewish youth with still greater courage and determination to press onward, to the shores of the Holy Land.

* * *

We left for Rome by train. Renee Solomon, Sam Gaber and I, barely managing to push into one of the compartments, wedged ourselves into a corner and rattled along in this fashion all night. And we were lucky at that. Scores of people traveled all the way to Rome huddled atop the railcar roofs.

One of the concerts I gave was held fifteen miles out of Rome, on a field at Castel Gandolfo, the summer home of Pope Pius XII. The enormous crowd, including a host of children from a nearby children's center, simply wouldn't let me off the platform. I begged the kids to come and sit on the grass close to me. After wheedling them into climbing down from their precarious perches on the trees, they obeyed. I was quite relieved.

A rumor got around that His Holiness the Pope, seated at a window of his villa, listened as the amplifiers carried my Yiddish program across the open field. The authenticity of this, however, I wouldn't swear to.

Sam Gaber sent the following letter from Rome to my wife in New York:

> I am writing this letter in a little room beneath the steps of an outdoor balcony, where Yabby, at this moment, is performing for an audience of over 6,000 of our Jewish survivors yearning to reach Eretz Yisrael. It is evening and the only lighting he has is from the dimly lit street lamps.
>
> After covering the length and breadth of Germany and Austria, tonight, here in Italy, marks his one-hundredth performance...his priceless gift to the homeless.
>
> I had the privilege of arranging your husband's tour and it is enough reward for me to see our wretched brothers and sisters able to forget their misery, their knocking about in the corridors, sleeping on straw in every corner of the buildings. Even in a drained-out swimming pool did Yabby hold an Oneg-Shabat with a transport of youths before they ventured forth on their way to Eretz Yisrael.
>
> Yablokoff has been carrying out an extraordinary mission. Only he, and those who work with him, know what he has been accomplishing. As for his reward, it is the reward of having inspired laughter and grateful applause in tens of thousands of Jews who have forgotten how to laugh.
>
> I salute you for sparing us your dear-to-all-of-us husband for these long arduous months. May you both enjoy many, many happy years together. Bless you.
>
>   Sam Gaber

* * *

My last concert in Italy was held from the back of a truck. We were parked in a courtyard jammed with people. Leaning out of the windows of the storied tenements surrounding the court, people vied with each other for a better look at me down below. It was a frightening sight. I shuddered lest someone come hurtling down.

That morning I had risen with a splitting headache. And as if that weren't bad enough, I experienced the most ghastly incident near the compound. A man ran up to me and, falling to his knees, began to lick my boots. I was terrified and utterly sickened! He made the weirdest gurgling sounds in his throat. Fortunately, some men walking with me pulled him away.

"Don't mind him," they said, "he is deranged, you see. He does it whenever he sees a man in uniform. It's a mania with him. He has no tongue... the Germans cut out his tongue..."

Renee Solomon, who had herself seen her share of Jewish anguish during the time her husband was hauled off, never to return, was unable to control her tears throughout the concert as she sat on the truck, playing the piano and weeping...

In the middle of my program, I felt a sudden shock through my brain. Clutching my head between my hands, I fell to the floor, unconscious.

And so, my last performance in Italy remained unfinished.

* * *

My headaches continued as I eagerly waited for my return home to New York—by air this time.

The J.D.C. in Paris arranged two farewell concerts for me at the Sarah Bernhardt Theater. This was for the benefit of the Yiddish actors in Paris. And together they arranged a "folk banquet" in my honor. Hundreds of people, who paid their own way, came to wish me bon voyage.

Hershel Chalef, a boy from Grodno whom I had befriended, was most upset. Hershel, whom I had first come across after my arrival from New York, was about sixteen years old. He was small and looked even younger than his age. Hershel was said to be the youngest member of the fighting partisans in the woods during the war. I was told of his heroism by Grodno survivors. His mother and the rest of the family had all been killed. His father, a partisan, was machine-gunned before his very eyes. Now, a lone survivor, he was knocking about the streets of Paris, a typical street-wise gamin.

Hershel had clung to me, looked upon me as his "father," and I practically adopted him. He had taken my advice about learning a trade. At the ORT School, he was being taught to make ladies' handbags. Since he was convinced that he was coming to America with me, he would be equipped to take care of himself.

"How can you go back to America and leave me high and dry?!" he upbraided me. "You're my adopted father. To please you I learned a trade at the ORT. Take me to America with you. Please don't leave me!"

When I learned from the HIAS representative that a whole transport of orphans was about to be flown to Toronto, we arranged to have Hershel included among them. On the day the orphans were scheduled to depart for Canada, Hershel came running to me.

"I'm sunk!" he panted. "They told me I had to produce an affidavit from the Refugee Committee in Paris that I am an orphan before I can leave with the transport! So I ran to the office to get the affidavit, but the secretary—a jackass of a Frenchmen, a Jew at that—wouldn't give it to me. He doesn't believe I'm an orphan. I'm sunk, I tell you. Save me!"

Sick as I was with my persistent headache, I hurried off with him to the Refugee Committee.

"M'sieu," the secretary informed me, "I must have witnesses that this boy's parents were killed."

"M'sieu," protested Hershel, "where do you expect me to get you such witnesses? All the witnesses are dead! My mother and the rest of my brothers and sisters were burned in Auschwitz. My father, Abraham, was a partisan with me in the woods. I saw him die! I swear I'm an orphan!"

I couldn't bear the boy's torment. Grabbing this thickheaded Frenchmen by the lapels, I yanked him to his feet and said, "M'sieu, if you don't want every bone in your body broken, you better sit down and write out a statement that Hershel Chalef is a fatherless, motherless orphan! I will sign as a witness!"

Hershel snatched up the signed paper, kissed me and ran posthaste to join the group of orphans. He flew that very evening to Canada. (Hershel Chalef now resides in Los Angeles with his wife and children and is a successful hairstylist with his own beauty salon in Hollywood.)

After the nine strenuous months I spent in Germany, Austria, Italy and France, my J.D.C. friends in Paris took me to the airport to see me off at last, on my flight back to New York.

Home, At Last

It took me quite a while to recuperate after coming home. And no wonder! I had lost twenty-five pounds, my pressure was down to zero and my complexion, as my wife commented, was as green as the olive-drab uniform I arrived in.

Dr. Elihu Katz, an esteemed friend of the Yiddish Theatrical Alliance, was very concerned about my condition. After much probing, he concluded that there was nothing radically wrong with me. It was a clear case of exhaustion, lack of sleep and lack of nutrition.

Reuben Guskin, representing the Hebrew Actors' Union, arranged a reception honoring my return. Colleagues and friends, emissaries of the JOINT, representatives of the United Jewish Appeal, HIAS, the Jewish Labor Committee and members of the press all came, anxious to hear a first-hand report from the only one in the theater profession who had spent so many months with the surviving Jews in the camps. I described the tragic lot of the DPs and the hardships of the Yiddish actors among them, who tried so desperately to carry on with their plays to bolster their own and everyone else's courage.

* * *

In September 1948, I was elected president of the Hebrew Actors' Union. Michal Michalesko was vice-president. I considered it a great honor bestowed upon me by my colleagues in the United States.

The J.D.C. invited me on a lecture tour around the country to share my experiences in Europe and make people aware of the vital work being done in the camps by the J.D.C.

The United Jewish Appeal was another national organization which asked me to help with their fund-raising campaign in key cities between New York and California. I devoted all my energy to these missions and fulfilled them most successfully.

My lecture tour also took me to Havana, where I was joined by the Navy commander, Chief Chaplain Joshua L. Goldberg. The Jewish community in Havana flourished. With cultural and social activities, a Yiddish newspaper, many organizations and Yiddish schools, Havana's community was the backbone of Jewish life in sunny, guitar-strumming Cuba. The Jews here also sent generous contributions to aid their surviving brothers and sisters in Europe.

In Havana I addressed a mass meeting attended by the majority of the Jewish population. This demonstration protested Cuba's political stand in the United Nations, in which she displayed little sympathy toward the resolution to declare an independent Jewish State in Palestine. In fact, Cuba voted against it.

The most stirring experience of my life came during my visit in Cuba when David Ben-Gurion made known to the world his Proclamation of the State of Israel on May 15, 1948. There are no words to describe my feeling. I knew only too well what a Jewish Homeland would mean for the morale of the Shea-ritt Hapleita, with whom I had spent so many long months in their gehenna.

When President Harry S. Truman acknowledged the State of Israel, moments after Ben-Gurion's proclamation, there welled up from the depths of my heart the words: "God bless America!"

Jews in Cuba, like others throughout the world, gave voice to the Brocha Shecheyonu—"Blest art Thou Who hast enabled us to reach this moment." They kissed each other, wept and danced with joy and exultation.

Who could have foreseen that, only a few years later, the wheel of destiny would turn? That the hearty and wonderful Jewish community in Cuba would be uprooted by the Castro revolution? And that they, too, would become refugees seeking asylum in the United States? How hollow rings that smug, self-assuring phrase: "It can't happen here!"

73

My Song "Nature Boy"

The executive director of the Canadian Jewish Congress, Saul Hayes, invited me to do a combined lecture-and-concert to aid the fundraising drive in northwest Canada. I was to come to Montreal and proceed from there to Winnipeg, which would be my headquarters for western Canada.

Before my departure, my wife and I sat discussing what needed taking care of in my absence. Her daughter, Anita, a student at New York University, was in her room doing schoolwork, with the radio playing popular tunes of the day. Suddenly, she called to us: "Mom! Dad! Do you hear what they're playing on the radio?"

We stopped to listen and caught part of a beautiful, catchy melody that sounded strangely familiar. For the moment none of us could pinpoint which of my many compositions it resembled. But soon I was convinced that it was indeed one of my songs, only sung in English. At the end of the record, the disc jockey said, "Well, folks, how did you like that one? Super, eh? It's the first time I've heard it myself. A brand new song called 'Nature Boy.' I don't mind hearing it again. In fact, I'll make an exception and spin it once more."

I concentrated on the words and melody and finally pinned it down. No question about it. It was a ballad I had composed and sung in *Papirossen*: "Schweign Mein Hartz"—Be Still, My Heart.

"It's just possible," I remarked to Bella, "that during the time I was away, my publishers gave someone the rights to translate and record my song in English under the title 'Nature Boy.' The announcer will surely mention my name as the composer."

When the record was over, the jockey commented: "'Nature Boy' is sure to be a sensation, a first on the hit parade for many weeks. The song was written by a new composer, Eden Ahbez."

We all looked at one another in bewilderment! Who the devil was this Eden Ahbez? Bella tried to call the broadcasting station and couldn't get through. The lines were jammed with callers, no doubt expressing their enthusiasm and requesting the song be played again.

Since I had to take off on my flight to Canada, it was left up to my wife to contact the publishers, the Kammen Brothers, to find out whether they had indeed given someone the rights to an English version of my song.

Next day in Montreal, Bella called me. "The Kammen Brothers," she said, "have also heard the recording of 'Nature Boy'…as who hasn't?" she added. "It's being played over and over, and it is exactly what the disc jockey predicted…an overnight sensation! The Kammens are convinced, just as we are, that it's your song, 'Be Still, My Heart.'"

"The press," Bella went on, "describes this Eden Ahbez as a yogi with long hair and beard. He wears a flowing white robe and sandals, sleeps in parks and on the beach and lives on fruit and vegetables. The Kammens have turned the case over to Ed Masters, the attorney for the Yiddish Composers League."

From the day I heard my song recorded in English, I suffered the agonies of hell. The first artist who introduced "Nature Boy" on the air was the popular Nat King Cole. He did it the hard way: without orchestral accompaniment. Since the Musicians' Union local 802 in New York happened to be on strike, he used a chorus of mixed voices for background. It did not in any way detract from the success of the record. On the contrary, the harmonious vocal back-up created an ethereal, religious effect. It was soon recorded by others, selling over two million records in the United States. The song was also printed in different languages, selling by the millions of copies all over the world.

For $20,000, Hollywood bought the rights to the song and used it as the background theme for the film *The Boy with the Green Hair.* The news media, including television, played up the bizarre image of the yogi as the personification of Nature Boy himself. The stories were blown up out of all proportion. The alleged composer was booked for a week at the Paramount Theater and people streamed there to see this phenomenon. The publishers bought him a jeep to cruise around New York in his robe and sandals.

While all this ballyhoo was going on, I was "pioneering" in the outposts of northwestern Canada. I traveled from one Jewish community to another, some with only a handful of Jews, describing the lot of our people in the camps. To see these remote Canadian Jews wholeheartedly giving more than their share was indeed satisfying. At the same time, the furor over "Nature Boy," had already reached Canada via radio and television. Even in such far-flung corners as I was able to reach only by dogsled with an Eskimo driver, the strains of "Nature Boy" followed me. The news exploded like a bombshell: "Herman Yablokoff, noted Yiddish actor, files a claim with the New York Supreme Court against Eden Ahbez, his publishers and everyone connected with the song, 'Nature Boy,' charging plagiarism—music and words—of his copyrighted and published ballad, 'Be Still, My Heart.'" (My song had been in print since 1935 and was copyrighted in the Library of Congress.)

The order issued by the Supreme Court stated that all monies derived from "Nature Boy," and yet to be accrued therefrom, were frozen until after the trial.

Attention was now focused on me! I became the most sought-after person by the press. And I was somewhere near Churchill, Alaska.

Heinz Frank, the director of the western division, finally caught up with me. He told me that the lawyers in New York were awaiting my return. Frank agreed it would be advisable for me to take care of this matter. I had to give him my word, however, that I would return at once, as the people in the other Jewish communities of western Canada were expecting me.

* * *

Back in New York during the pretrial examinations, the lawyers from the defense put me through the wringer. But it did them no good. I had ironclad proof that the song was mine, music and lyrics. Ahbez, I claimed, took the text of the verse in which I tell the story of a little boy who wanders the world hungry, forsaken, wanting to love and be loved, and had set it to my chorus of "Be Still, My Heart." The publishers named it "Nature Boy," which had nothing to do with the song at all; except for publicity maybe—to play up the yogi image of the alleged composer.

Eden Ahbez, himself, honored me with a long-distance call from Venice, California, pleading to be as innocent as a babe. The idea of the song came to him, he said, when he heard angels singing in the California hills...

He offered me $10,000 to withdraw my claim. I laughed at him. All I wanted, I told him, was for him to admit that he had plagiarized my song, words and music. And if he heard angels singing it, they had probably bought one of my printed copies from the Kammen Brothers, or from Metro Music on Second Avenue, or any other music store in the United States.

* * *

While the case dragged on, I continued my mission in western Canada. A great source of pleasure for me was meeting once again with the orphans and with the hundreds of other DPs who had finally made it here from the camps. I even helped settle some of the orphans with Jewish families. In the beginning it was very difficult for these youngsters to become adjusted to a conventional way of life; especially for those in the smaller, rural communities. They sorely missed their buddies who had settled in cities like Montreal, Toronto and Winnipeg. In time, however, they became integrated with the families that had adopted them. At my lecture in Winnipeg, about fifty of these kids came to see me. It was a heartwarming reunion for all of us.

* * *

The "Nature Boy" case dragged on. It seemed as if years would go by before we'd come to trial. I was summoned for pretrial examinations: the lawyers for the defense grilled me, my lawyers grilled the yogi. My family and I had nothing but heartache over the entire affair. When I was offered an out-of-court settlement for $25,000, the greatest amount ever settled in a case of this kind, I decided to accept it.

74

Pride in Our Children

Yiddish actors, by and large, never amassed any great capital in the theater. They did, however, manage to raise children who more than compensated. Some followed in our footsteps, becoming successful actors, even on the American stage, and a good many others went off into other fields, but all of them achievers.

My son, Jack, received his musical education at the Julliard School of Music, under the noted cellist and musicologist William Willeke. At seventeen he became a member of the Musician's Union, Local 802, and was subsequently engaged as a cellist with the Buffalo Symphony. He also played with the Radio City orchestra and in Billy Rose's production, "Violins over Broadway." Later, Jack became the cellist with the New York String Quartet and the Palestine String Quartet. Eventually, he joined the Portland Symphony as first cellist.

Before leaving for Oregon, Jack imparted the happy news that he was engaged to marry his school-days sweetheart, Helen Schraub. The family celebrated a traditional Jewish betrothal party at his bride's home.

My daughter-in-law, Helen (Hindy), a wholesome and delectable Yiddish daughter, a student at the Linden Heights Talmud Torah B'nai Israel, was—as she is to this day—a Sabbath observer. When Jack enrolled at Julliard, Helen went on to City College, and their friendship continued and ripened into romance.

Helen's parents Rochel and Israel Schraub had come to America from Poland. Israel Schraub, an insurance agent for many years, was also the president of the Radamishler Benevolent Association and the president of the Sephardic Synagogue in Boro Park, Brooklyn. In addition to Helen, the Schraubs had two sons, Carl and Sol, very prosperous businessmen. Growing up with Jack, in the same neighborhood, they loved him like a brother.

Jack and Helen were married on Saturday, June 18, 1949. And attending the wedding, to my great joy, were my children, only recently arrived from Germany: my niece, Dora, her husband Shimon, and the baby Motele.

Rabbi Sidney Honig and Cantor Kapow-Kagan officiated, with the assistance of Sam Sterner's choral ensemble. With deep emotion and great pride, Jack's mother Jeanette and I escorted our son to the marriage ceremony.

* * *

Anita, Bella's daughter, showed marked talent for the stage as a child. In Kinder-Ring of the Workmen's Circle Camp where she spent her summer vacations, she played all the leading roles under the direction of Leyb Kadison, a veteran of the Vilna Troupe. He considered Anita his mainstay among his group of performing youngsters. Her ambition for the stage, however, faded. After graduating from New York University with an M.A. degree, she was assigned to teach English at Washington Irving High School, from which she herself had graduated.

Soon after Jack's wedding, Anita followed suit and became engaged to Joseph Willens, the son of our theater colleagues Fannie and Michael Wilensky. After returning from military service overseas, Joe attended the Julliard School of Music, and after graduating was engaged as bassist in the National Symphony of Washington, D.C.

Joe's mother, daughter of the veteran musician Max Rubenstein of Montreal, was a pianist for many years in Yiddish theater. In fact, Fannie worked with us on Second Avenue. Joe's father, Michael, born in the Ukraine, started his theatrical career on the American stage with the renowned star, David Warfield and eventually became established as an actor and stage manager in the Yiddish theater.

Anita and Joe knew each other as children from their frequent visits backstage. As grownups they rediscovered one another, fell in love and decided to get married. We arranged a traditional engagement party for them and they were married on December 25, 1949.

Dr. J.H. Lookstein, the esteemed rabbi and leader of Congregation Kehilath Jeshurun, graciously agreed to perform the wedding ceremony in his temple. The Palestine String Quartet and Sam Sterner's Ensemble were conducted by Sholom Secunda. In addition to the immediate family, the wedding was attended by many theater people.

Anita's father, Alexander Olshanetsky, had passed away some time before, and so the bride was escorted down the aisle by her mother Bella and me. I was deeply moved and proud indeed that Anita, whom I consider my own daughter chose as her matron-of-honor, my surviving niece, Dora.

* * *

For a number of years there had been a steady decline in the Yiddish theater. We lost quite a few playhouses. Out of fourteen in New York, only the Second Avenue, the National Theater, and the Parkway in Brooklyn remained. The Public Theater on the avenue had not been functioning.

The slump was disheartening to everybody, especially so to Reuben Guskin. It had a very adverse effect on his health. He saw no way of providing work for his members.

On receiving the $25,000 settlement from "Nature Boy," Bella and I decided to invest the money in the Yiddish theater again for the following season. I rented the Public Theater from the Raynes Realty Corporation for a yearly rental of $30,000, with $10,000 security, and began to prepare for the opening.

Season 1950-51

Irving Jacobson, fed up with the hardships of running vaudeville at the National Theater, had rented the Second Avenue and was operating it as a legitimate house. There, he presented Molly Picon and Jacob Kalich. For the coming season he became partners with the actor, Edmund Zayenda. I realized it wasn't going to be easy to compete with the Second Avenue Theater for benefits after my long absence from the avenue.

At any rate, I adapted a play by Harry Kalmanowitz and called it *The Magic Melody*. To write the score, I engaged the dean of Jewish composers, Joseph Rumshinsky. Unfortunately, we could not agree and called it quits. I set about creating a musical production on a grand scale. Once again I engaged William Rolland as my general manger; Max Kreshover, benefit manager; Jerry Cohen and Rose Goldstein, cashiers; Morris Siegel, press agent; Max Eisen; English publicity.

Besides Bella and me, my company included Aaron Lebedeff, Michal Michalesko, Hanna Grossberg (of the Yiddish Bande), Charlotte Goldstein (of the Art Theater), and other well-chosen performers.

With the invaluable help of my son-in-law, Joseph Willens, the two of us composed the musical score of *The Magic Melody*. Joe did the arrangements and orchestration, and also conducted the show at the premiere performance. After that, he had to return home to resume his work as orchestra contractor for the National Theater in Washington, D.C. My son, Jack, took over the baton from my son-in-law.

My cast was outstanding. It was worth all the money in the world to watch the two veteran stars, Lebedeff and Michalesko, appearing in the same show and lighting up the stage.

Another asset was the character actress Hannah Grosberg. She had already given up acting and had resigned herself to staying put in a remote cottage in a Miami suburb. I brought her back to the stage. Her unique style and temperament added a good deal of spice to each performance. Zelda Kaplan and Feivush Finkel, two refreshingly new faces on the avenue, were another important addition with their youthful verve, their singing and dancing. Still another young actress and fine singer was Freydele Lifschitz. The rest of the cast added their own individual talents in making *The Magic Melody* such a hit.

I felt confident that a spectacular such as this, into which I had poured every possible facet of the arts with a generous hand and which had been so favorably received, would surely bring as much business in the middle of the week as it did on weekends. Well, I miscalculated. The Jewish organizations had begun booking their benefits and theater parties on Broadway...with the excuse that their members did not understand Yiddish.

Those who remained loyal to the Yiddish theater divided their bookings between the Second Avenue and my Public Theater—with the result that neither house received adequate benefits to cover their weekly expenses. I could not stretch the season for more than sixteen weeks. And even this, by the skin of my teeth.

The Magic Melody was, beyond doubt, a grandiose production. Still, as the saying goes: "The operation was successful, but the patient..."

I was blessed, nonetheless, with compensation from quite another source: my daughter-in-law Helen and my son Jack presented me with my first grandson, Randy. Later, came Susan and Robin...so I was a millionaire again!

75

Uncle Sam in Israel

Buying the rights to a new play by Benjamin Ressler, I began preparations for the 1951-52 season. The book appealed to me, because it portrayed a vivid picture of contemporary life in Israel. I saw the possibility of a musical extravaganza on the style of my former productions and called it *Uncle Sam in Israel*.

I interested Sholom Secunda, the noted composer, to do the score. Sholom was no novice in the Yiddish theater. His theater songs had for years enjoyed great popularity. And his liturgical compositions have greatly enriched cantorial and choir repertoire. I could not have wished for a more congenial and adept composer. The lyricist was Chaim Towber, whom I regarded as an expert in the field. So I had this part of my production set.

In order to get the pulse of Israel and to fully absorb the atmosphere and substance of kibbutz-life where the play was to take place, I boarded an El-Al plane and took off on my first visit to Israel.

Throughout my wanderings I'd always experienced varied emotions upon crossing the threshold of a new country: expectancy, curiosity and, at times, even trepidation. But the awe-inspiring heartthrob that possessed me when I first set foot on the soil of our yearned-for and fought-for Jewish homeland was an emotion I'd never experienced anywhere else!

For two thousand years Jews in every corner of the globe have prayed three times a day: "May our eyes witness Thy loving return to Zion. Blessed art Thou, Lord, Who will restore His Divine Presence to Zion."

No wonder then, that Jews so divinely privileged to see this miracle for themselves, kiss the hallowed ground, and through tears of exaltation, murmur the Shekhionu—benediction. And I was no exception.

At the Lod Airport I was met by my lifelong friend, Shimon Finkel, his wife Batami, other artist from the Habima and several Grodno compatriots.

The porters—former DPs who remembered me from the camps—hailed me. They elbowed each other for the privilege of carrying my bags. And, under no circumstances would they accept my offered gratuities.

"Adon Yablokoff, it's our pleasure to welcome you in our homeland," they insisted. "We are honored to carry your baggage. Your 'Nisht Gezorgt' has stood us in good stead. It strengthened us in the darkest hours, until our final deliverance in Israel."

"Shalom, Adon Yablokoff! I saw you in Fohrenwald.."
"I know you from Berlin...!"
"From Landsberg...from Bergen-Belsen.."
"You came to us in Gauting Sanatorium, remember?.."

These were the greetings that came at me from every direction, warming my heart. It was a reception I will never forget.

The Finkels wouldn't hear of my checking into an hotel. They insisted that I stay at their home. Food was being strictly rationed at the time. Upon arrival, tourists were supplied with ration cards for bread and other items. The first meager luncheon I was served consisted of a small, flat, one-eyed fish referred to as a Moshe Rabeinu fishl—Rabbi Moses fish. My initial taste of food in the land of Israel was delicious, but far from adequate.

That same evening I was a guest at the state theater—the Habima—where I saw Hendrik Ibsen's play *Peer Gynt*, with Shimon Finkel in the title role. The performance ran four hours and twenty minutes. After the premiere, the critics advised cutting it down. But the Israelis protested. They bought their tickets and insisted *Peer Gynt* be presented in its entirety, exactly as premiered. And they had their way.

Where, I wondered, can you get an audience to sit through a performance over four hours?! In New York, we have to cut the guts out of a play in order to let the people out as early as possible.

Theaters in Israel, the Habima, Cameri, Ohel, Metateh, and Li-la-Loh, are active all year round. Certain ensembles were divided into two units. One played in Tel Aviv, while the other toured the cities, the outlying settlements and kibbutzim. I was soon convinced that theater in this newborn country was not merely entertainment to distract from life's cares, but an integral part of the culture.

Audiences at the different playhouses I attended were made up mainly of young people, with the Habima taking first preference. This state theater, subsidized by the government and the Norman Fund in the United States, is a magnificent house, built as a temple of art. The stage, suitable for every type of production, is equipped with the most modern prerequisites.

The business end of the theater is run on a cooperative basis and is conducted by a committee with a hired business director. All the artists have equal rights to vote for, or against, a proposed play. According to my experience, I think this is a grave mistake. An actor, who sees no appropriate role for himself, or begrudges another in the company who gets a part which he, or she, has designs on, will hardly vote for such a play no matter how important a particular piece may be for the welfare of the theater.

The center for Israeli theater, of course, is Tel Aviv. Just as actors on the American stage strive for Broadway, and Yiddish actors aspire to be seen on Second Avenue, so is the ambition of every Israeli actor to appear in Tel Aviv.

The great obstacle at the time of my first visit was the shortage of playhouses. Except for the Habima, the other companies had no suitable theaters where they could perform. This was certainly not the time to build theaters. The crucial need was to supply living quarters for the hundreds of thousands of Jews who were still waiting in makeshift refugee camps.

To my surprise, the big movie theaters in Tel Aviv, Jerusalem and Haifa, could easily be compared to those in the States. They ran American films and, to this day, are always packed.

I was particularly interested in the way theater performances were arranged in the kibbutzim. If live theater was such a necessity in the big cities where one could easily find alternative entertainment, it was easy enough to imagine the importance of theater in a kibbutz, or other farflung settlement. The person who works and lives in a kibbutz is a special type of individual. A great number of them are Europeans...idealistic, learned, intelligent, former city dwellers. To them, the theater was always an integral part of life. After the Holocaust, a good portion of these Jews settled in Israel's kibbutzim. But without an occasional theater performance they would truly feel isolated.

These performances are held outdoors in the amphitheaters, where the audience is seated on long benches beneath the starry skies. A troupe carts its own sceneries, furniture, props, costumes, lighting equipment, and orchestra. In order to bring the whole troupe for a performance, several neighboring kibbutzim usually get together, pay the company a fixed sum and whatever the profits go to the kibbutzim. It is almost like a benefit performance in New York, or Buenos Aires, but instead of the audience traveling to see the show, the actors, with all their trappings, come to the people.

This truck-and-bus mode of travel reminded me of my own roamings in Lithuania during the 20's...except that in those days our transportation was accomplished by horse and wagon and, in the winter, by sleigh. Either way, the audience's appreciation of the actors who come to bring them a bit of recreation has not changed one iota. The welcome, the deference and heartiness extended the kibbutzniks more than compensates for the hours of bouncing over the winding highways that lead to the settlements.

The moment a company of actors arrives, they are promptly shown into the communal dining room and treated to a country-fresh meal. The most comfortable rooms are relinquished in their honor. The kibbutzniks willingly double up with a neighbor, or even bed down out in the open. There's a holiday spirit in the air.

I tagged along for one of these performances given by the Habima. It was arranged by Kibbutz Degania. This particular event could have wound up an international conflict.

The kibbutz, close to the Golan Heights, was near the Syrian border. The amphitheater was in Eiv-Gev, a fisherman's village by the sea. Ein-Gev could only be reached through no-man's land—an area constantly patrolled by the Israeli Army, with the Syrian military watching from the Golan Heights.

Toward evening, when the audience began making the trek to the amphi-theater, the Syrians took it to be an invasion of their territory. They cocked their guns, ready to shoot, when the Israeli border guard quickly transmitted the information that these were civilians passing through to attend a Habima performance at the open-air theater in Ein-Gev. At this, the Syrians simmered down. Squatting on the rim of the Golan Heights, their guns at their sides, the soldiers watched the theater performance, fascinated by Aaron Meskin's portrayal of Othello, in Hebrew.

* * *

I brought back to New York many photographs of the various kibbutzim. Using these as models, my scenic artist created a marvelously authentic setting for the Tel Shalom Kibbutz in my production of *Uncle Sam in Israel*.

I called rehearsal and we got right down to work. The cast was greatly enthused over the timely play. Then, in the midst of a rehearsal, Charlie Cohan came running up on stage and in a breathless voice said: "Ladies and gentle-men, I have very sad news, our representative of the Hebrew Actors' Union, Reuben Guskin has passed away."

We were stunned. We all knew, of course, that he was gravely ill, yet his sudden death, just prior to the opening of the theater season, threw a pall over everyone in the profession.

For me, personally, Guskin's passing was a sharp blow. During the time I worked with him as president of the union, there had sprung up a very close relationship between us. It was only then that I became convinced how very difficult it was to "swim against the tide"... to conduct a union of actors and provide them with the opportunity to make a living when treacherous waves were pulling our profession into an undertow.

The committee of the union executive, with the help of the secretary, Rosel Pivar, steered clear of possible chaos before the launching of the new theater season. They did not appoint anyone else to succeed Guskin as salaried bus-iness representative and ever since then, the union has been managed by the prevailing president and the executive board.

* * *

Uncle Sam in Israel was another lavish production. The Yiddish and Amer-ican press praised everything about it; the music, the dances, beautifully chore-ographed by Belle Didja. The scenery was so impressive that a noted critic wrote: "I have just returned from Israel and when the curtain rose at Herman Yablokoff's Public Theater, I recognized every little stone, every little path—so authentic is the setting of the kibbutz depicted in *Uncle Sam in Israel*."

I too came in for a gratifying bit of praise for the staging and directing.

The title role of Uncle Sam was played by the talented character-comedian, Mikhl Rosenberg, an alumnus of the Yiddish Art Theater. When Rosenberg found he could not further his career at the art theater, he turned to freelancing, accepting single engagements in Yiddish-American nightclubs and revues. I brought him back to the Yiddish stage because the role of Uncle Sam was so perfect for him.

Other new faces on Second Avenue were Ben-Zion Witler and Shifra Lerer. These artists had toured the globe together. Witler, tall and handsome, was possessed of a magnetic personality. In America he had been seen in the provinces and in the theaters of Brooklyn. Since I was not playing in this production, I engaged Witler to fill my role, and I could not have made a better choice. (Sadly enough, this gifted man died in the prime of his life.)

A revelation to all her colleagues was the vivacious, young actress Shifra Lerer. Born and bred in Argentina, she, nevertheless, gave a flesh-and-blood portrayal of an American girl born and bred in Kentucky. Shifra sang and danced a la soubrette in one scene, and in the next performed equally as well as a dramatic actress.

Shifra married Michael Michalovic, a talented actor, whom I'd met and also appeared with in Argentina. A fine performer and a really good pal, he and Shifra are a great asset to the Yiddish theater.

In her first straight dramatic role, Bella Mysell gave a memorable performance of a woman desperately searching for her husband, unwilling to accept that he was killed in the Holocaust.

The rest of the cast was also excellent. Yet what good did it do me, when the organization committees claimed that, after New Year's when the Jews all leave for Miami Beach, they can't sell a benefit ticket!

I barely managed to string along for sixteen weeks and came out cleaner than clean...not to mention the $25,000 from "Nature Boy," which I had sunk into the business as well!

Yet here too, there was compensation. Bella and I were blessed once again. This time, our daughter Anita and son-in-law, Joseph Willens, presented us with a grandson, Michael Alexander, named for his grandfathers, Michael Wilensky and Alexander Olshanetsky. Later on Anita and Joe enriched our family tree by a granddaughter, Gina Hope Willens, named for Goldie and Hyman Mysell, Bella's parents.

76

Uncle Sam in Argentina

When the actress Miriam Lerer came to New York on a visit from Buenos Aires, she took in a performance of *Uncle Sam in Israel*. She was so enthused over the production she promptly proposed that I bring it to Argentina and star in it.

I welcomed her proposition. South America was always a good money-making source to help pay off theater debts in New York. Bella could not join me on this trip, because the enterprise could not stand the expense for two. So I flew solo. I was to open at the Mitre Theater, directed by Miriam Lerer and Willy Goldstein. But, on arrival, I learned that my two impresarios had rented out their theater as a movie house and, instead, rented the big Excelsior Theater, where Bella and I had appeared during our first guest engagement in 1939. I was delighted. It was a most advantageous move, since the Excelsior's stage was more adequate for my production's grand scale.

Buenos Aires, the same as New York and even Israel, no longer had private enterprisers to invest in Yiddish theater. The task of operating the theater rested solely on the shoulders of the actors themselves.

Argentina at the time, was ruled by Juan Peron, with the help of his wife Evita. New laws were enacted which affected all theaters. It was forbidden to sell tickets earlier than forty-eight hours before a performance. Phone reservations were no longer permitted, so patrons were obliged to come directly to the box office—first come, first served. At least, it put an end to the cashiers' long-enjoyed free hand to manipulate. No more "propina." I like it.

At the gathering held in the actors' union to welcome my arrival, I expressed my admiration for them for having managed to acquired a summer retreat for the members—an achievement, which we in New York had been unable to accomplish.

They had bought up a farm house with plenty of acreage and turned it into a resort for Jewish actors and their families. As the place could not accommodate all the members at the same time, they took turns, staggering their vacations. Each member was entitled to spend his vacation in this actors' "koch-alein" for free, enjoying a few weeks of country air in camaraderie. This "estate" was looked after by a special committee, which lovingly tended each little tree, each budding flower, every cow and calf.

The members in turn expressed their gratitude to me for my help in this purchase. With permission from the Hebrew Actors' Union and the help of its president, Jean Greenfield, I succeeded in raising a thousand dollars—a fortune at the time—for this summer home in Buenos Aires.

The actors' union in Buenos Aires has always had jurisdiction over Yiddish theater in Uruguay. From Buenos Aires to the Montevideo takes hours by boat but only a scant hour by plane. The Jewish community in Montevideo, and the money exchange there, was truly one of the best for Yiddish theater. But during my engagement, because of political differences, travel between the two countries was restricted. And so for a time the Jewish population in Uruguay was deprived of Yiddish theater. After some of the differences were ironed out, Yiddish actors were again plying by boat, or plane, between the two countries.

* * *

I opened at the Excelsior with *Uncle Sam in Israel*, this time playing the title role. I also had a very able cast. Of my three stage managers, the one who helped me most with my complex production was a young actor, named Bernardo Sauer. Born in Argentina, he naturally spoke a fluent Spanish and was able to communicate with the stage technicians. And his Yiddish was so good I wished some other young performers could do as well.

In 1963, on my last tour of the South and Latin American communities, Bernardo Sauer, an actor in my troupe as well as my jack-of-all-trades stage manager, came back with me to New York. He has since settled here and, I'm glad to say, is doing well both as an actor and skilled technician.

Friendly Competitors

Only a block from the Excelsior where I was fulfilling my engagement, Paul (Pesach) Burstein, Lillian Lux and their twin moppets, Michael and Susan, were starring at the Teatro Soleil.

The Bursteins, appearing as a couple, had been a welcome attraction in Buenos Aires. But now, with the addition of the twins, the attraction was doublefold. These kids sang duets, danced, spouted wisecracks and cavorted, much to the audience's delight.

I felt so akin to the Burstein family as if they were my own, despite the fact that we were competitors working in two rival theaters. Little Mike and Susan called me "Uncle Yabby." The actors loved having a bit of fun with them.

"Michael," they baited him, "who is the president of the United States?"

"What do you mean, who?!" Michael retorted in his broad and authentic Yiddish, "my Uncle Yabby."

"What are you saying?" they teased him further, "the president is Harry Truman!"

"I know!" the boy shot back. "But my uncle is the president of the Hebrew Actors' Union!"

Having indoctrinated the tots with Yiddish theater—for their parents refused to leave them even in the good care of grandparents while they went on tour—the twins developed into talented entertainers. Susan eventually married and left the stage, while Michael remained loyal to the craft. In Israel, Michael blossomed into a great favorite with a very promising and well-deserved future on the Hebrew and American stage.

Radio was still the most popular medium in Buenos Aires. Not everyone could afford a TV set at the time. The disc jockeys emulated their North American counterparts, except that here the strains of the tango held sway on the air, blaring from every station.

Since Jews in Buenos Aires were undergoing the same marked assimilation as we in North America, it was good that one could still enjoy—together with the tango—an occasional Yiddish song on the air.

Before leaving Buenos Aires I was granted honorary membership in the Asociacion Argentina de Actores—the Spanish Actors' Union. And after a farewell party arranged for me by the resident Grodno Federation, I boarded my plane with several thousand hard earned dollars to pay off my debts to the creditors in New York.

77

The Art Theater Resurrected

Louis Siegel, general secretary, and Samuel Bonchek, vice-president of the Farband—a National Zionist Labor Organization—called a conference of cultural and social leaders to revive the Yiddish Art Theater with Maurice Schwartz as artistic director. I participated as the Executive representative of the Hebrew Actors' Union.

The project was represented by the most influential people in the city, with a specially chosen repertory committee. And I was unanimously elected as executive secretary of the project, as well as its general manager. I gave up my own theater enterprises and threw all my efforts into raising funds needed for the Yiddish Art Theater's revival.

The board of sponsors—legally incorporated and registered as a nonprofit, tax-exempt cultural foundation—rented the National Theater and put down $10,000 security. Part of this money was donated by the committee members, and part was realized from several official functions.

The salary I was supposed to receive during the season for my double capacity as executive secretary and general manager (working minus pay all summer as a volunteer) was much less than that of any other theater manager. I did, nevertheless, insist upon one stipulation: I would not interfere with Schwartz's duties as stage director, and he was not to interfere with my business and organizational duties.

The salary which Maurice Schwartz was supposed to receive was the most minimal amount possible. We tried to cut expenses to the bone so the theater could get on its feet. It was the first occasion I had to work with this dynamic individual. Schwartz's energy had no equal. His devoted aide of many years, William Mercur, was practically worn out by him. Not that he spared me, either. Schwartz, Mercur and I worked fourteen to sixteen hours around the clock. And very often, after getting home after half the night, my phone would ring: "Sorry if I woke you...I just want to remind you..." And these reminders usually developed into another hour's conversation.

During the scant year in which I worked with this great artist, I came to admire and respect him more than ever. All the tales I'd heard about his uncompromising dedication to the stage were no exaggerations. He was my kind of man. And so it became my burning ambition to enable him to carry on without any of the monetary worries he'd had to endure during most of his professional life. I hoped this would be shouldered by New York's Jewish community. The press played it up big, quoting appeals made to the public by prominent leaders.

Schwartz came to me with a complaint. "I'm constantly being harassed by hack writers with pretense at dramaturgy! Why don't I recommend their scribblings to the repertoire committee as 'the' most fitting vehicle to open the Art Theater? If only they brought me something worthwhile! The trouble is that each scribbler thinks he's created a masterpiece. Go convince him that it isn't worth the paper it's written on! As for the accepted playwrights—they are a nuisance too. They send me their stooges to drop a little word of advice: 'Mr. Schwartz, so-and-so has a play that would be just the thing for you...'"

"Even when I was the sole boss of my theater, and did as I saw fit, I was pestered. But since this is a community-sponsored theater, it's worse and I'm the one to bear the brunt of it!"

"Send them to the repertoire committee," I said.

"Well, what do you think I've been doing?!" he stared at me. "The committee is already swamped with scripts. They haven't recommended anything. But I heard that an original drama, written by a young unknown, Lazar Treister, has already won an award. Maybe you can contact the author and have him send me a copy."

I made an appointment with Treister to see me at the theater. When he came, it was apparent that he was a very reserved and modest young man. His drama, *The Shepherd King*, was now being published and was due to appear in September. He did not have a clean copy, but he could readily obtain galleys from the printer.

Treister was not anxious to have his drama produced before it was out in print. Who would buy the book? We assured him that, if Maurice Schwartz did indeed produce his play, the book would be sold at the theater during the performance. Could he wish for better publicity?! So it was arranged, Schwartz read *The Shepherd King* and liked it.

I notified the repertory committee and asked that they too read the galleys. They all read the Biblical drama and they believed *The Shepherd King* was the most suitable production to launch the renewed Art Theater.

* * *

Maurice Schwartz began work on the play. And for the musical embellishment I called on Sholem Secunda.

Two weeks later, Secunda, Mercur and I were invited to Schwartz's apartment to hear his adaptation of *The Shepherd King* for the first time. We left around midnight. Secunda, Mercur and I exchanged glances...we understood one another.

"Sholem," I said, "I'll drive you home. There isn't a taxi in sight. Why drag uptown by subway at this late hour?"

I drove Secunda all the way uptown, and during the entire ride both of us remained sunk in pessimistic conjectures about the play. As for the adaptation, neither Secunda nor I ventured an opinion, even between ourselves.

Next morning at the theater, Schwartz, trying to sound me out, asked, "What do you think of the play? I mean my reconstruction? Last night you left and...well, don't you like it?" he suddenly bristled.

"Why do you say that?" I tried to gloss over it. "It was late and I wanted to get home. And to tell you the truth, as director of my own theater, I always play musicals so I'm not much of a maven on serious works. I think we can only rely on the repertoire committee, and what is more important, on you yourself, Mr. Schwartz."

"It's a Biblical drama," he reasoned, "and with the birth of Israel, what could be more appropriate than to produce a modern version of King Saul, of David and the other heroes of Jewish history? And the play has already won a prize. How can we go wrong?"

* * *

We hardly stopped to rest all summer. Schwartz, Mercur and I didn't lose a single opportunity to add new subscribers. We arranged mass meetings and ran special concerts at the summer camps and big resort hotels.

That summer, Schwartz's wife and his children, Marvin and Risa, were away at Unzer Camp. The heat in town was brutal, but Schwartz only allowed himself the pleasure of joining his family in the country on Friday nights. Sunday evening he was back in town.

"Why don't you remain a while in camp?" I urged him. "We'll take care of everything!" But, to no avail. Air conditioning was still way off in the future. The weather continued hotter than ever, until one night, very late, my phone rang: "I can't stand the heat any longer. Sleep is out of the question. The theater...the play...everything is hammering at my brain. I guess I'll have to toss like this till morning and catch the first bus to camp. Please forgive me. Did I wake you?"

Compassion swept over me. "I'll call you back in a moment," I said, and woke up my wife. "Bella, Mr. Schwartz, poor man, is sweltering in his apartment, waiting to catch the early bus for camp. Would you care to go for a ride right now to Unzer Camp and back?"

As we hurriedly dressed, I rang Schwartz and told him to wait for us in front of his house, which was only blocks away. We were coming to drive him up to the country.

"I'll never forget this wonderful gesture!" he cried as he got into the car. Bella let him sit up front with me so we could talk, talk, talk. We brought him up to camp and drove right back. By the time we got home it was almost time for me to go to the office.

With all our sweat-and-blood efforts throughout the summer, we barely eked out $48,000, aside from the $40,000 deposits for the sale of benefits. The largest contributions came from the committee members themselves. The Jewish community, on whom we had placed so much hope, produced very few subscribers. The dues of ten dollars a year entitled the subscriber to cut-rate tickets during the entire season. Who would have believed that with all the publicity; the participation of representatives of the foremost organizations; a special "landsmanshaft" division; special appeals in the Yiddish and English press bombarding the public about their own community-sponsored theater, we only managed to attract 368 subscribers?

* * *

Who is the Jewish Community...?

Under this caption, I published the following article:

For years people have talked about the state of this "fabulous invalid"—the Yiddish theater!—and have always come to the conclusion that the only cure for its sad plight is a community theater. The crisis, which it has been experiencing these last few years, has been blamed on the producers for their choice of repertory. Blame has also been heaped on the directors, the actors—often justified and, more often, unjustified. In each case the theatrical profession accepted without a protest. For, deep in his heart, every professional agrees that the Yiddish theater is a vital branch of our Jewish culture, and every artist is morally responsible to society and to public opinion.

Prosaic as the word "business" may sound when applied to art and artists, one must realize that theater is indeed a business, the same as any other...with investments, expenditures and income. Every businessman understands that when the income does not cover the expenses, even if a theater may be operating on the highest level of art, it is still a losing proposition. In other industries it may be possible to balance the budget. Not so in the business of Yiddish theater. The public, however, does not take such circumstances into consideration.

The Jewish community in New York has awakened at last. Thanks to the representatives of the press, the cultural and national welfare organizations and the individuals who have remained loyal devotees, the renewed Yiddish Art Theater, sponsored and financed by the Jewish community, has become a reality.

With the folding of the Art Theater in New York four years ago, there disappeared the resplendent aura that hovered over our theatrical domain. Out of fourteen Yiddish theaters in New York, only three remained. And if the community was able to allow a situation

where our Art Theater could remain closed after its thirty-year existence, it meant there was no place for a literary Yiddish theater in
America. How sad for us!

Now, with the opening of Maurice Schwartz's production of *The
Shepherd King*, by Lazar Treister, the curtain rises again on the first
chapter of the resurrected Yiddish Art Theater in America. The second chapter must be written by the Jewish community itself with
its financial support of this cultural institution. Who is the Jewish
community? You are!

* * *

A week before opening, my phone: "This is Anna Schwatz. Maurice would
like to see you. It's urgent," she said, sounding disturbed. "Could you please
come to the house? And another thing—this is just between us."

Up at the house, catching one look at Schwartz's face, I knew this serious.

"Come, sit down," he said, "I have something very upsetting to tell you.
I deliberated with myself all day and said to Anna, Yablokoff is one person
I have to tell the truth to. Lately, I haven't been feeling well. Can't sleep a wink
at night. It's my feet. Look at them, swollen like balloons! I saw a big doctor
today, a professor. In his opinion my legs should be operated on immediately."

"An operation?" I gasped.

"Well, you know these professors. Talk to them and talk to the wall—
same thing! He just insisted. What am I going to do? If word gets around that
I've been taken to the hospital, it means the end of the premiere! And after
so much work and money has been invested! It's a catastrophe! The premiere
will have to be postponed. You will have to announce that, due to technical
difficulties or something...Well, anyway, to keep New Yorkers from finding
out, I reserved a room in a Philadelphia hospital under an assumed name. I'll
have the operation performed there. So now you have it. What do you think
of this sudden disaster?"

"I'm so stunned, I don't know what to say! Of course the theater is important," I said, "but your life is more important. If the professor says you must
undergo surgery, there's nothing more to say. But reserving a room in a Philadelphia hospital...I don't agree with that. I also don't think you should rely
on one doctor's opinion. Why not call on our theater-friend, Dr. Michael Steiner,
and have him advise us. If an operation is indeed urgent, then that's that!"

Dr. Steiner took us to one of his specialists. After a thorough examination,
he concluded that Schwartz was in no immediate danger. For the time being,
the operation could wait. What the specialist did recommend was a pair of
elastic hose for support. And these stockings did indeed save Schwartz from
having his legs operated on before the scheduled premiere.

"One thing you'll have to admit, Yabby," he chuckled, "I'll be playing a
very modern King Saul, wearing a pair of elastic stockings!"

The Premiere

The audience attending the opening was mostly made up of representatives and drama critics of the Yiddish and American press and their families. Other invited guests were important city officials and leaders of the Landsmanshaft Division.

As general manger, in my tuxedo, I greeted the guests as they arrived. No sooner was the crowd seated when there began a grumbling: "Why is so-and-so and his missus seated up front, while my wife and I are stuck in the back? Does he rate more prestige than I, in my community-run theater?!"

After the first act I knew the worst. We had prepared flowers for the ladies of the ensemble, but the remarks aimed at our expense were filled with thorns. Several dramatists eyed me with scorn, gloating as they milled in the lobby. I read in their sarcastic glances: "Our dear Mr. Schwartz didn't want to produce my play? Fine! Now you're stuck with a turkey!"

On top of that, the show dragged and ran late, as often happens with premiere performances. No matter how good the second act turned out, I knew it would not save the play. And that's exactly what happened. Many left the theater during the second act. The storm against Maurice Schwartz really began after the show. Complaints were directed at me, as well. "Yablokoff! How could you, a showman for so many years, allow the production of this play?"

I kept silent. I wouldn't even defend myself with the explanation that I had had nothing whatever to do with choosing a play because a special repertory committee had been designated for that purpose. I also knew that the playwright was most unhappy with the reconstruction of his work.

But most deserving of sympathy was Schwartz himself. Instead of receiving his usual after-curtain accolades and bouquets, he just managed a little thank-you speech. When he stepped out from the wings, he found only a few of his friends waiting. All the others had gone home.

The drama critics did not care for *The Shepherd King*. They were within their rights, of course, but it was certainly no help at the box office.

Schwartz immediately began preparations for *The Brothers Ashkenazi*, a play by I.I. Singer. It did prove to be a success, and brought box office, but far from enough to defray the overwhelming costs of the two productions. We struggled through twelve weeks, after which the final curtain was rung down on the Community Art Theater.

Every theater enterpriser will surely agree that he has more failures than successes. Yet, that never stopped anyone. Like the rest of us theater bugs, Schwartz has suffered failure in the past, but, as sole boss of his theater, he carried on for years striking success again and again. The audience was willing to forgive and forget. But this was different. This enterprise was run by the people, and the blame for hammering the last nail into the coffin fell on the heads of the community.

78

Back to Wandering

I received a proposition from impresario Willy Goldstein in Buenos Aires to star with his traveling ensemble in an extensive tour of Latin America. I flew directly to our starting point, Buenos Aires. I had an excellent cast, with the pet of Buenos Aires, Jenny Lovitch, and the handsome actor, Michael Michalovic, playing leading roles.

We opened in Montevideo with my sure fire production, *Papirossen*, and were received with great enthusiasm. We did well both artistically and financially. My Grodno compatriots, long settled in Montevideo, went all out with a reception in my honor. To commemorate the occasion, I was presented with a parchment scroll bearing the signature of all my hometown people now living in Uruguay.

October rolled around and the theater season in Buenos Aires had come to a close. According to its geographical zone, it was summer. Many folks had gone off to the beaches at Mar del Plata, or to the mountains. yet, when the Jewish community in Argentina read that my company was playing in Montevideo, a clamor went up: why not in Buenos Aires?! Oh, no, I balked. This was too risky. Who will come to the theater in the heat of summer? Especially when it has never been done before!

My friends Solomon Stramer and Leon Narepkin, who had been running the Teatro Soleil, also tried to talk me into a two-week engagement. Well, I thought, if they are prepared to guarantee the expenses, OK—but on the condition that I get a percentage from the gross receipts.

We planned to play the two weeks and then go back on the road. But the engagement stretched into two months. Hot as the weather continued, people kept streaming to the theater. It was amazing. So, go be a prophet!

Particularly outstanding was Jenny Lovitch, who possessed all the attributes necessary for her craft: a lissome figure, charmingly defined features, long black hair that swirled about her shoulders with every graceful turn. Some artists are blessed with that certain something known as "it"—in Yiddish referred to as "di rozhinkeh"—the raisin. Jenny's fans lovingly dubbed her "Di Rozhinkeh."

From the Buenos Aires Press

In the main hall of the Wertheim Hotel, the Landsleit Federation of Grodno and Vicinity gave a reception in honor of their com-

488

patriot, Herman Yablokoff. The president of the federation, Shmuel
Winitzki, in his opening address, dwelt on Yablokoff's deep concern and interest in his fellow-Grodners, wherever he may find them.

Among the many others who spoke of this man with great esteem
was the actor Joseph Griminger. With admiration he recounted
Yablokoff's activity in the DP camps of Austria, where he, his wife
and child were confined and where he met Yablokoff for the first
time. The concluding speaker was the guest of honor, himself: "My
friends, if I were not to confess to you how deeply moved I am
at receiving this honor, I would be sorely remiss. Speaking of Grodno,
were it not for the unyielding stubbornness of our fellow-
townspeople—a trait of which I too am guilty—there would be no
one to turn to, no one to unburden one's heart to. Life has a past,
a present and a future. The present and future can be discussed with
anyone, be it close friend or stranger. But in recalling the past one
can only find true rapport and understanding with a fellow compatriot, a landsman.

Our future no longer links us to our devastated home. Our common past, shared together in Grodno, comes to a close with our
generation. Therefore, I say, blessed be the 'stubborn' ones who refuse
to let the future erase the past, refuse to let sink into oblivion the
hometowns in which we were born.

For more than thirty years now, I have traveled around the world
with Yiddish theater. But, aside from my chosen profession, I hold
dear the warm and friendly ties with my landsleit wherever I find
them. No matter how much I may have done for them, they have
paid me doublefold in love and friendship."

"My Son and I"

Before taking my company on the road, I invited several writers, actors
and theater directors to gather at the Soleil, where I read a play I had written,
My Son and I. Everyone told me that it was earmarked for success. Their predictions came true. In 1960, after returning from a European tour, I directed
and starred in My Son and I at the Anderson Theater in New York (formerly
the Public), where it was produced by Irving Jacobson and Julius Adler. The
play—with music by Sholem Secunda and lyrics by Bella Mysell—did indeed
prove to be a triumphant success and ran through a four-month season.

Appearing with me in this show, besides Adler, were Henrietta and her
brother Irving Jacobson. Both were so outstanding in their roles that they were
soon recruited for important parts on the American stage. Henrietta received
accolades as the mother in Come Blow Your Horn. And Irving scored a tremendous hit in the character of Sancho Panza, in the world-famous musical
production of The Man of La Mancha.

In 1962, on my sixth visit to Buenos Aires, I produced *My Son and I* at the Teatro Soleil. It met with the same acclaim as it did in New York. After finishing the season in Argentina, I arranged the tour of a chamber-theater ensemble throughout South America and Mexico. Instead of the customary concert or revue format, I adapted two of my plays, *My Son and I* and *The Magic Melody*. The people in these various Jewish communities received us with open arms. Financially, we did well everywhere. Moving ever closer to the States, a couple of my actors ran into visa difficulty and had to return to Buenos Aires. However, I was able to get my wife and New York actor Itzhak Lipinsky to join us in Florida and step into the two missing roles. From there, we went on to New York and Canada, under the management of Louis and Fay Shochat.

Our tour finally took us to California. In Los Angeles, under the management of Oscar Ostroff and Stan Seiden, we played *My Son and I*, *A Guest from Israel*, and *Papirossen*, staying on for close to five months; first at the Music Box Theater and then at the La Cienega. With *Papirossen*, we beat a record by playing the same show eight performances a week in Hollywood, for a run of twelve weeks.

79

Guest Appearances in Israel

In 1958 I received an invitation from the entrepreneur Joseph Lichtenberg to guest star in Israel. Delighted, I accepted his proposition. Bella would join me later.

How different the Lod Airfield looked to me compared to my first visit in 1952. The country had made unbelievable strides in the short span of years.

Assembling members of the cast, I read my musical play, *Oh, What a World!*, with which we were to open on the second day of Passover. The actors were engaged by Lichtenberg on a monthly salary. Nothing to get rich on, to be sure, but with careful budgeting they got along reasonably well. Most of the actors were recent emigres, and as such, were provided by the government with living quarters at minimal rents. This was a great help.

Shortly after my arrival, the representative of the Writer's association, Moshe Ron, arranged a press conference. I was also interviewed on the Voice of Israel. Both the press and the radio put great emphasis on my mission in the DP camps.

Lichtenberg asked me for the script of my play to send it to Jerusalem for censoring. "A Jewish play in Israel needs to be censored?" I asked in surprise. "Well, if we must, we must." The actor, I. Segal, typed up a copy of the text, using the very same Yiddish typewriter I had left as a gift for the surviving actors' guild before leaving Germany in 1947.

It was the height of the tourist season in Israel. Every time I emerged from my room, I was deluged by greetings from tourists from every corner of the globe, who recognized and fell all over me. I had no time for these sociabilities. I had enough work facing me before I could get my first production on the boards. Besides, they assumed I was such a VIP in Israel that I could at least get each of them a private audience with Ben-Gurion!

Rehearsals were held at the Kursky Library Building in Tel Aviv. Days were pretty hot in this semitropical climate, so we'd start work in the cool of the morning. At the stroke of noon we had to make a break, or there'd be nothing to eat later on. Not because of "tzenna"—rationing was a thing of the past, but because restaurants served only during specified hours. And once the noonday meal was over, it was siesta time in Israel. Everyone went home to relax, or catch a snooze—same as in the South American countries. Then, evenings we resumed rehearsals.

I began to notice that certain actors in my troupe moved about sluggishly, and had trouble remembering lines they had already memorized.

"What gives?" I asked. "Yesterday, everything went as smooth as silk. Today, it falls flat. What's going on?"

"Today, there is a khamseen," I was told. "Don't you feel it? It's a desert wind. It'll get you soon enough. You'll feel a dryness in your nose, a rasping in your throat and a buzzing in your head. Then you'll know the taste of a khamseen! But don't be alarmed, Adon Yablokoff. It's nothing serious. All you do is take an aspirin and suffer a little until the khamseen decides to shift. About the scripts? Don't worry. We'll know our lines inside out."

Whatever free moments I had I spent with Shiman Finkel. Evenings, if there were no rehearsals, I took in the performances at the Habima and other Hebrew theaters.

At the Habima I was deeply impressed with the performance of *Trees Die, Standing* by Alejandro Casona. Hannah Rovina played the leading role of the aristocratic grandmother. I'll never forget the vision of this divinely gifted artist, silently ascending the staircase after a stirring scene. Her face was not visible to the audience, yet in the slow and tense movement of her shoulders, we could sense the utter despair she was suffering. It left the audience spellbound.

I also saw a revised adaptation of *The Merchant of Venice*, directed by Shimon Finkel, in which he himself played Shylock.

Exceedingly popular at the time were the humorists Dzigan and Schumacher. Their hilarious revues and stylized skits were incomparable. Their satirical monologues and barbed witticisms, spared no one, endearing them even to the younger Israelis, who did not much frequent the Yiddish theaters. Simon Dzigan and Israel Schumacher later achieved worldwide acclaim.

* * *

My premiere was held at the big cinema theater in Ramat Gan. We gave a matinee and evening performance, attended by a good number of recent emigres, who remembered me from the camps, and many American tourists as well. My impresario Lichtenberg admitted that, since he had become a theatrical enterpriser in Israel, this was the first time he'd seen such a take at the box office.

The mayor of Ramat Gan, Abraham Krinizi—who is related to me—greeted me formally from the stage. There were also several Grodno friends, including my cousin Simka and her husband Shmuel Kurasz, who finally made it from the camps.

Ohel Shem Theater

Saturday nights we usually played at the Ohel Shem in Tel Aviv. Officially, it is a synagogue; it is also the training institute for cantors. Boys with exceptional voices are given the experience of officiating at the pulpit. While one boy acts as the cantor, the others assist him as choirboys.

A theater performance given at the Ohel Shem could not begin until after the Sabbath evening prayers. Sceneries had to be delivered on stage by Friday afternoon. If the company was scheduled to play on Friday in any of the small settlements outside Tel Aviv, all their paraphernalia was hauled in through the back door under cover of night. The stage was set up in back of a special curtain, conveniently serving as a partition between the Holy Ark and the theatrical trappings.

After Havdala, at end of the Sabbath, the Bima and the Ark were rolled back out of sight. The scenery and furniture were brought downstage and voila! On with the show!

The Ohel Shem, having its own lighting equipment, was a godsend for traveling companies saving them the time and trouble of lugging their own stuff.

Saturday evening, as soon as the worshipers left the synagogue, the theater crowd was ready to pile in for the first show.

During my engagement in Israel, I always looked forward to the performance at the Ohel Shem. I would slip into my dressing room during afternoon prayers so I could listen to the singing of the boy-cantors. Nothing could put me in a better mood. It brought back memories of my own childhood spent as a choirboy in the Great Synagogue in Grodno.

For the second performance on Saturday, the box office would open—if there were any tickets left. There was no break between shows, so before the actors could catch their breath, they were on, doing the whole thing over again.

On my very first visit to Israel, Cafe Kassitt was the hangout for actors in Tel Aviv. Now, the theatrical "stock exchange" had moved to the Cafe Noga. The actors laughingly dubbed it Nega, meaning a plague in Hebrew. It was truly an actors' bedlam.

The topnotch impresarios conducted their business from their offices, arranging their bookings around the country by phone. The lesser managers made their transactions at the Noga, which buzzed like a beehive and sizzled with gossip.

Traveling from town to town was very exhausting. Remembering how I shlepped all over Germany with my ambulance, I now considered a bus first-class transportation. The Israeli bus and taxi drivers are, without doubt, real crackerjacks. Israelis make jokes about it, yet it is indeed a feat to steer one of those lumbering buses, making hairpin turns in ancient streets so narrow that a passenger can actually peer into the kitchen and see what's cooking! All through the war with the Arabs, the buses continued to operate in total blackouts, using no headlights.

The hardest work connected with these one-night stands fell, of course, on the stagehands. After each show they had to strike the set, fold the drapes, remove the furniture, pack up the props, undo the electrical equipment and get everything into the truck. The wardrobe and orchestral instruments were also part of the truckload. The next day all this had to be delivered and set up again in another community.

Some of the seasoned performers in my troupe, Lola Jacobwitz, Sigmund Savitch, Joseph Widetsky and veteran Mordecai Hilsberg told me how this or that star from America would cut up his scripts so that he alone would be doing all the talking and singing. "We," they complained, "would just walk on and off stage like robots. But not in your plays, Adon Yablokoff."

Mordekai Spektor, a handsome young actor with an exceptionally fine voice, quite frankly said to me, "When I heard that you were coming to us as a guest star, I was sure I wouldn't stand a chance of opening my mouth, neither to speak, nor to sing. And here you are, giving me such beautiful numbers to sing and such fine parts to play. I'm amazed!"

"Why amazed?" I asked. "These very parts and songs were done in my productions by actors in New York, as well as in cities around the world. I cast my plays accordingly. Why should you be the exception, my friend? On the contrary, good luck to you. Your success is my success."

Spektor, a native of Bialystok had recently arrived from Poland, where he'd played with the Kaminska Ensemble in Warsaw. His experience in a Russian jail, where he was incarcerated for several years without a trial, made me shudder. (Spektor and his actress wife, Miriam Sandler, now reside in New York. Spektor gave up the stage in favor of his position as cantor.)

* * *

Thanks to the prestige of my friend, Shimon Finkel, I received an official invitation to the Tel Aviv parade in celebration of Israel's eleventh anniversary. We sat in the VIP section reserved for heads of state and top representatives of various countries. The heart of every Jew that day fluttered with pride at the parading Israeli military contingents. That evening I was also invited to a festive gathering attended by some high-ranking Israeli military. During my stay in this reborn country, I enjoyed the warmest hospitality from many old as well as new friends.

The native Grodners, now in Israel, arranged a welcome party for the visiting Landsleit. The get-together was held in the building of the Bet-Zion America, near the impressive structure erected by Grodno compatriots in the center of Tel Aviv. Over its doorway an inscription in Hebrew reads: "In Memory of the annihilated Jewish Community of Grodno." In the entrance hall, a huge bronze plaque proclaims that the building was erected with the help of the Grodno Aid Society of America and Canada. A long list of names includes mine, as first president of the Grodno Federation of the United States and Canada.

* * *

Every Israeli town we played in was new to me, and fascinating, particularly Haifa. This city is magnificent—especially when dusk falls and the lights go on, up and down the mountainside. And beautiful is the word for Bat-Yam, Naharia, Herzlia, Rehovot, Givatayim, not to mention Tiberias and the Kinereth! Dazzling panoramas! Later, when my wife came, we also visited Rishon L'Zion, the fabulous wine cellars, and together with the rest of the tourists tasted the Carmel wine—as much as anyone wanted—for free.

In Ramlah my company and I were booked into a theater directly next to a movie house showing an Arab film. The rattling of tambourines, the lusty bursts of song in Arabic bouncing off the soundtrack could be heard right through the walls. It was a marvel that our audience was able to sit through our performance with all that din going on next door.

One day I received a postcard from Jerusalem. In conclusion it read, "If you, whose pictures I see on the theatrical posters, are the Yablonik I remember from Grodno, then you and I went to Yeshiva together..." The card was signed Rabbi Moshe Bulvin, director of Yeshiva Torath.

I answered at once that I was indeed Chaim Yablonik and arranged to visit him in Jerusalem. The rabbi and I had much to reminisce about, and we have since kept up a regular correspondence. I cherish the friendship that developed between our two families.

On the way to Jerusalem, strewn along either side of the road still lay battered tanks, jeeps and overturned buses... grim reminders of the crucial siege of Jerusalem.

Arriving in this historic city, I was heartily welcomed by the highly respected impresario S. Kahana. Our company was booked into the Edison, a huge, modern cinema theater. My performance brought out the elite of Jerusalem. I noticed that the first row was occupied by a group of blind persons. According to Kahana, they never missed a performance given in Yiddish. Their sighted companions quietly described the decor and visual actions on stage, and judging by their appreciative laughter and applause, their enjoyment was boundless.

My company and I had just arrived in the town of Afula when a busload of people pulled in. They had come all the way from Nazareth to see my show. And wonder of wonders, who should be among them but the long-lost brother of my nephew Shimon... Jacob, and his wife Sarah with their children. They had already been in touch and knew who I was and where to find me. They had arrived from Poland and were planning to emigrate to America. In Tel Aviv, I was later able to help them.

In Beersheba, my cousin Joseph Rosjanski, whom I'd found in the camps was anxiously waiting for my visit. He was now living in Israel with his wife, Julia, and their two little children. Unfortunately, I could not spend too much time with them.

A most unforgettable impression was made upon me by Safed—the holy city of Kabbala Jews. Traveling up those winding roads from Galilee to about 27,000 feet above the sea left me breathless! Safed is also the locale of a famous

and very picturesque artists' colony…a sort of Greenwich Village. Its sanatoriums and lodging houses also make it a popular vacation resort.

Descending those hills at night was a frightening experience. We were winding our way down from Safed, when our eyes were suddenly blinded by a
powerful searchlight…Israeli patrols demanded to know who we were. Iden-
tifying ourselves, we were then allowed to drive on. I can still visualize the
Chagall-like figures of the little Yemenite Jews; small and scrawny, with crinkly
side-curls and wispy goatees. Their slight frames seemed lost in the soldier uniforms they wore. Red kerchiefs around their necks absorbed the sweat that trickled down their faces. Bent under the weight of the heavy army-pack on their
backs, guns slung over their shoulders, they trudged along the road in the dead
of the night, going on maneuvers…holy Yemenite Jews, defending the land
of Israel.

* * *

I was preparing a second production. Our first play, *Oh, What a World!*,
had been seen in every community several times over, so that it had become
necessary to travel to and from the furthest points from Tel Aviv—six weeks
of dragging around in this fashion, getting home in the wee hours. And at nine
the next morning, there was rehearsal!

I decided to do *Papirossen*. This presented a problem. The play calls for
a small boy, and no parents seemed willing to let their child traipse around
the country. The new "olim," who could certainly have used the extra income,
wouldn't hear of it. These people had lost everyone and everything and wouldn't
trust their children out of sight. Besides, the kids had to attend school. Still,
we scoured the area for talented youngsters.

A little girl called Chayele was recommended to me. Her parents were
recent arrivals from Romania. Chayele's mother agreed to let her play, on the
condition that the child's father be hired as a stagehand. In this way he could
look after Chayele, and earn a few pounds to boot.

The little girl, who was about nine, spoke Romanian and was fast learning
Hebrew. Yiddish, she knew not at all. I wrote her part out phonetically in Hebrew
letters. And she read very well indeed, except that I had the same trouble with
Chayele as I had with the kids in Argentina. They would enunciate the letter
b as a v and vice-versa; so that the word bobbe became Vovve and the expression oy vay became oy bay. Chayele, however, was quick to pick up her lines
in Yiddish and before long delivered them like a pro. She was a dear child,
pretty, smart and quite talented. On stage, and dressed for her part, anyone
sitting out front would swear she was a boy.

Since my song, "Papirossen," was already sung in Israel in several different
languages including Hebrew, the title attracted people to the theater the same
as it had in other countries around the world. And so, the success of my second
production topped my first.

Lichtenberg wanted me to extend my engagement for another few months, but I decided to have my wife join me so we could spend a vacation together. And, like other tourists in Israel, we would roam the country, marvel over its historic points of interest, enjoy the company of friends, and then visit other countries on our way home.

When Bella arrived in Tel Aviv, I had only a couple of weeks to wind up my commitments. How surprised she was to step down from the plane and fall right into my arms!

"Well, you don't know what a celebrity your husband has become in Israel!" I swaggered. "No nonsense with customs. Let's go!" I said, and whisked her off, luggage and all, in a taxi.

Next day, my company was scheduled to play in some out-of-the-way town. My wife came along with us on the bus. Only a few hours off the plane from New York, she was inordinately impressed with the Bedouin tents that dotted the landscape. They seemed so incongruous to her, she exclaimed, "Is this for real, or is it an MGM lot shooting an Arab film, maybe?"

"No," I laughed, "this is the real thing, my dear."

Jerusalem

Walking through the Mea Shearim Quarter, observing its inhabitants and its centuries-old atmosphere, Bella softly whispered in awe, "It's as if the breath of yesterday is touching and living side by side with the world of today."

In front of a quaint little prayerhouse we came upon a small group of yeshiva students busily debating some subject—in Yiddish.

"Is it permitted," I ventured in Hebrew, "for a woman to enter and look around the synagogue?" They gave me a look of disdain.

"Listen to that American yokel!" one of them cracked in juicy, Vilna-flavored Yiddish. "Hebrew, he speaks! Can't you speak English? If not, then speak Yiddish."

"And why not Hebrew?" I asked, playing naive.

"Hebrew is the language of the Holy Scriptures, reserved for prayers and for studying the Torah. For blabbering nonsense there are other languages: Yiddish, English, Turkish, or what have you..."

Convinced that these fellows were recent arrivals, I reverted to Yiddish. "Tell me, my young friends, are you new olim? You speak such a splendid Yiddish."

"New olim?!" they burst into laughter. "We are sabras, born in Jerusalem. But our mother tongue is Yiddish."

"Do you go to the Yiddish theater sometimes?" I couldn't resist throwing this in.

"Sometimes?" they laughed, "all the time. Tonight, in fact, we're going to see *Papirossen*. We have our tickets, see? And oh, yes," they added, "the lady can go into the synagogue if she keeps the kerchief on her head."

We Join the Tourists

Several days before leaving Israel, our friends provided us with a chauffeur to take us on a guided tour of the country. We were joined by an Israeli couple who were on vacation. Instead of spending it in one place, they preferred—for the umpteenth time—to observe the newest developments in their homeland. They spoke a British English, and we could not have wished for more congenial company.

Our guide, Paul, was fluent in Hebrew, Yiddish, Arabic, English, French, and what not. Before starting out from Tel Aviv, he asked in English: "Have you read *The Exodus*? If you have, then our tour is wasted, because you probably know all that happened here even better than I do. Not too long ago I took some American ladies on tour. No matter what I showed them, they looked down their noses at me: 'What's the nincompoop jabbering about? In the book it's entirely different!'"

Paul knew every little path from Tel Aviv to Eilat and described everything with accuracy. Then two Israelis traveling with us were also quite knowledgeable on the country's history. They too, had fought for the land. No one could feed them any mythical rubbish, or take them down to the Dea Sea to show them Lot's wife, turned to salt...

We were entranced with each new picturesque landscape. I felt the dynamic impact of this burgeoning land. The air vibrated with building and new kibbutzim emerged on the very rim of the borders that separated Israel from her enemies.

The lifestyle of the Arab, I noted, had undergone mighty little change. Along the road we passed a paunchy Arab astride a donkey. Behind him, on foot, a heavy pack on her head, trudged his better half...In the villages, the men sat around the cafes, kibitzing or playing backgammon, while the women did all the mean and thankless chores.

The stretch of desert between Beersheba and Eilat harbored a good many Bedouin tents. Their herds of black sheep climbed the bare hills nearby. Here too, nothing had changed. Even the Druzes, who had, more or less, adapted to Israel's modern stride, still threshed their wheat as their forefathers had done centuries ago. It would take modernization all around, we felt, to bring everlasting peace to the Middle East.

Back in Tel Aviv, we packed our stuff and made ready to leave. Bidding our many friends a hearty "l'hitraot," we boarded an El Al plane we flew to Istanbul, our first stop as tourists.

80

Yiddish Theater in Paris

After Istanbul, we went to Italy, then Paris. At the Cafe Terminus on the Place de la Republique, we sat chatting the afternoon away with friends, old-time actors, writers and the pianist Renee Solomon, who had been my accompanist in the DP camps in Italy. Several theater lovers had also gathered around to say hello. Most lamented that it had become impossible to organize a theater project in Paris. Others claimed it was a waste of breath to even talk about it—there was no theater in which to play and no one with whom to play, anymore.

Turning to my wife, I said, "I doubt I'd be missing anything in New York. Maybe I ought to try to arrange a few performances here in Paris?" Bella agreed.

The writer, drama critic and editor of *Our Voice*, Abraham Shulman, expressed his opinion, "If a Yiddish theater were to be organized in Paris, the cultural and social organizations would come forward with financial subsidies. They have special funds for theater projects."

"I don't believe in organizational subsidies," I replied, "They'll call meeting after meeting and the project will end in talk. If I could get a theater, I would undertake my performances in Paris on my own!"

"If money is no object," the actor, Poliakoff, spoke up, "you can get the Entrepot."

"Then let's go and find out! I believe in actions, not words."

The air in the cafe began to tingle. Everyone decided to stay put and wait for our return to hear the outcome. An hour later we were back with a three-month contract to play every Saturday and Sunday at the Entrepot!

"Well, this is what you call 'no sooner said than done,'" our friends remarked incredulously.

"And where will you get a troupe of young actors?" asked the inevitable killjoys, "As if there are any Yiddish performers in Paris to speak of!"

"I'll get actors," I assured them. "If I don't, I'll bring a whole troupe from Israel. There will be Yiddish theater in Paris, all right! I have shelled out quite a sum for the Entrepot!"

It wasn't easy but I was able to assemble a first-rate cast, with Renee Solomon as musical director. I paid all of them substantial weekly salaries.

The experiment of reviving Yiddish theater in Paris proved to be a success from every standpoint. Up to the time of my arrival, there had existed a political tug-of-war in the community. The friction only served to make the theater and its actors the innocent sufferers. I was more than gratified to see that the greatest share of my financial success was because the Jewish audience in Paris came to see Yiddish theater, leaving all politics at home.

And thanks to the Zionist Federation of Belgium, I was able to take my company intact, with scenery and stage effects, to perform in Antwerp and Brussels. Belgian Jews were delighted with performances given in Yiddish. They extended us the warmest possible welcome.

A bright and personable young man, Ellis Sela, came to Paris direct from his native Finland. Not only did he speak a pungent, down-home Yiddish, he wound his phylacteries every morning, said his prayers and wouldn't touch non-kosher food if he starved. But, above all, he wanted to be an actor. I took this talented young man under my wing. It was he, in fact, who arranged my forthcoming concert tour of Scandinavia. From there, our tour was to take us to Poland.

Bella and I agreed that, since we'd been gone from home for such a long period, it was best that she fly back to attend to some important things. I planned to be home in several weeks.

81

Scandinavia

My accompanist, Renee Solomon, and I left for Copenhagen to set sail from there to Finland. Ellis Sela had gone on ahead and would be there to meet us. When my wife told friends in New York that I was on my way to a Scandinavian concert tour, their eyebrows went up: "Why, are there any Jews there?" She later scolded herself for not having come along with me.

The ship that was to take my accompanist and me to Finland was solidly iced-in at the pier. An icebreaker crunched its way close to our vessel and crushed the surrounding ice into great chunks, leaving our ship an open water lane. We finally got under way, sailing through a dazzling winter panorama.

Our first concert was to be held in Turku, formerly known as Abo. Ellis, who made all the necessary arrangements for our appearances, was at the port.

"What time is it, Sela? Ten at night, or in the morning?" I asked after we disembarked.

"In the morning!" he laughed, catching on to what I was driving at. "Later on we'll get a little daylight too," he assured me, "but not for long. About three or four in the afternoon it will grow dark again. In the wintertime the nights are long and the days are short. Ah, but in the summer the sun shines almost through the night. So we have very short nights and long days."

"In that case what do the Jewish people do about the blessing of the Sabbath candles?"

"During the winter we light them on Friday about three in the afternoon. And in the summer we have to hold off the Sabbath until sundown, which is usually, after eleven o'clock at night. Our communities in Scandinavia print a special calendar indicating the correct time for our latitude, so that observers won't desecrate the Sabbath, heaven forbid."

It was severely cold, but crisp and dry. Every road in Turku was covered with snow. The quickest and most convenient transportation was, obviously, by ski. People of all ages went gliding by on skis; especially on the outskirts of town.

Sela owned the apartment building he lived in—an inheritance from his father, left to him and his brother. I was surprised to see its ultra modern conveniences. And, above all, something we don't see in America in similar apartment houses—a built-in sauna!

We took advantage of the sauna quite frequently. "During the war years," Sela related, "Finnish soldiers could not very well carry a steambath with them to the front, so they build themselves a hut, blanketed in heaps of snow, so it soon froze solid…a sort of igloo. Then all they had to do was lay a fire, heat the stones and it became a cozy, first-class sauna."

Abo-Turku

Abo, by which the city was originally known, was made up of two Finnish words: "A" meaning river and "Bo" for people. The area's early inhabitants, mostly fur-trappers, had settled on the river banks, making it more convenient to transport their pelts to Russian fur merchants. Thus, they came to be called Abo—River People.

The present community organized itself in 1918. When Finland won its independence after the war with Sweden, Jews received civil rights equal to the Finns. In the Jewish cemetery in Turku headstones date back to 1853 and there are old graves where frayed scriptures and loose leaves of sacred books lie buried.

Many Jewish citizens in these regions are descendants from either the "Nikolai" or the "Kantonist" soldiers. These were two kinds of Jewish-Russian soldiers. The Nikolai soldiers were inducted into the army at the age of twenty-one and served for twenty-five years. The Kantonists were Jewish children, whom the kidnappers sought to convert through every possible means. After the death of Nikolai I, the child-snatching ceased. Once, between afternoon and evening prayers, as Sela and I sat in synagogue, he brought over a man called Stiller, and introduced him as the son of a Kantonist.

"Yes, my father, Abraham Stiller, was a Kantonist. In 1867, when he was only eight years old, he was snatched up in Kritchev, a town in the Mogulevsk Province, and sent away to be reared in the home of a Christian peasant in Kasterna, a village in Russia. He lived with the peasants until he was fifteen and then entered a boys' cadre near St. Petersburg. Kalman Wisotsky, of the famous Wisotsky Tea merchants in Russia, used to visit this home to teach the boys a bit of 'Yiddishkeit.' Ninety percent of these kidnapped youngsters never reached adulthood…"

Stiller related another unique tale. "The Jewish community of Turku," he said, "was famous for its homely women."

"Homely women?" I repeated, intrigued. "How come?"

"The influx of Jews that started from Lithuania, Latvia, Estonia and Poland brought families with daughters, who had apparently been left on the 'vine' a little too long. These daughters became the brides of the lonely Kantonists, or Nikolai soldiers. Even if a family came with as many as five girls, they were soon grabbed up. The best-looking ones were plucked off somewhere along the route—Helsinki, or Viborg. By the time the family reached Turku, they remained with the homelier stock. A Hebrew teacher, a rebbe from Lodz, came here with his daughter. This one happened to be a doll. My father took one look at her and said, 'That's for me!' And the rebbe's daughter became my mother!" Stiller chuckled gleefully.

The bizarre narrative did not convince me. Taking note of the Jewish women and young girls in Turku—descendants of the imported brides, the alleged "uglies," I saw only lovely, radiant faces!

Another son of Abraham Stiller, the Kantonist, I was told, is a famous film and stage director in Sweden. He, in fact, discovered the fabulous Greta Garbo. And the grandson of another Kantonist is the symphony conductor Simon Pergament, a highly acknowledged interpreter of Jan Sibilius's music. His brother is a known music critic in Sweden.

* * *

Turku's entire Jewish community, including its smallest tots, turned out for my concert. Ellis Sela, a native son, went over big, singing Yiddish, Hebrew and Finnish folk songs. Renee Solomon's piano solos were enthusiastically received; especially the Goldfaden Concerto, which she had paraphrased on his beloved melodies.

Before leaving Turku I had a fur collar attached to my overcoat, which I'd had made up in Buenos Aires. And to complete the picture I acquired a fur cap—a "papakha" and off we went by train to Helsinki.

Helsinki

Arriving in the bustling metropolis, we made straight for the Polish Consulate. According to my understanding with Hersh Smoliar, editor of the *Folks Stimme* in Warsaw, as well as secretary of the Culture Federation of Poland, we were to pick up our Polish visa right here in Helsinki.

The Polish vice-consul was most cordial. He had indeed received an order from Warsaw to issue my pianist and me our visas, plus work permits. How soon, he asked, would be prepared to leave, for he was quite ready to stamp our passports.

"In a month," I replied, "just as soon as we have finished our concert tour in Scandinavia."

His face clouded over. "According to the law, you must leave as soon as your visas are stamped on your passports. Your time allowed in Poland starts with the date indicated. A month from now, this will no longer be valid."

My heart sank. If we didn't get our visas now, then my whole project of being in Poland—and maybe Grodno—wasn't worth a damn!

I described my dilemma to the vice-consul, who proved to be very sympathetic. He conferred by phone with the consul-general in Warsaw. To my utter relief, he ordered that our work permits and visas be dated a month ahead. I was overjoyed!

Norway

Up until 1848, Jews were not permitted to reside in Norway. The very first ones—German tradespeople—began to trickle in from Denmark around 1852. Oslo's Jewish community was celebrating its sixty-eighth anniversary at the time of our arrival.

Among the eminent guests invited by the community leaders to my concert were American and Israeli consuls. I noticed that the overfilled hall had quite a number of young people enjoying our program. And when the concert was over, and the chairs were stacked away, the young folks began to dance to a record player. Well, well I thought, maybe this was the attraction after all. The dancing started out with an Israeli hora and progressed to some typically American boogie-woogie.

In our honor, the American consul invited prominent community members to join us at his home for a l'chaim. What a lovely evening! Before we left, our host pushed a package into Sela's hands...two bottles of American scotch. A present for Yabby," he murmured out of my hearing. "It's mighty cold up here in Oslo. These will come in handy for the road."

And come in handy, they did...sooner than expected! On reaching the hotel, I found a telegram containing a mazel tov! My son and daughter-in-law had presented me with another grandchild—a girl named Robin. And according to news broadcasts flashing around the world that same February day, England's Queen Elizabeth had given birth to a son—Prince Andrew!

So thanks to the consul's good scotch, we drank toasts, and I bestowed upon my newly born granddaughter the title—"Princess Robin."

Denmark

The prominent rabbi, Dr. Marcus Melchior, headed Copenhagen's substantial Jewish community. His son, an eminent rabbi in his own right, welcomed us warmly in his home. The elder Dr. Melchior happened to be abroad attending a convention. Young Rabbi Melchior and his charming wife took us to see the historical landmarks of Copenhagen, a city famed for its life-and-death risks taken on behalf of its Jewish citizens during the Nazi brutalities.

I came away awed after our visit to the museum with its picture-exhibition of the bloody reign held by the German infiltrators. Children of all ages are brought here by their schools, so they can see, learn and remember.

Our concert in Copenhagen brought out the elderly, the young adults and the littlest ones. After the concert they escorted us en masse to the ship that took us to our next commitment in Malmo.

Sweden

We arrived in Malmo and found the port a lively place, with ships arriving and departing...the tumult characteristic of any port. Malmo's Jewish community, though small, proved to be a very active one. We were greeted with open arms.

A new little community, Boros, had taken root sixty kilometers from Göteborg. About two hundred young people, survivors of the Holocaust, had come to settle in their own little township. They even ran their own factories and apparently were making a go of things.

Most of the town's settlers had seen me in the DP camps. They invited me and my colleagues to give a concert in their newly built center. I was more than glad that we did. After the concert we got together to reminisce—happily this time—over the bitterly trying circumstances after the devastation.

Stockholm

The most prominent of the four Scandinavian countries is Sweden, of course. Stockholm's Jewish population at the time numbered about 12,000.

Cantor Itzhak Borenstein, the founder and long-time president of the Jewish Youth Organization, told me, "The Scandinavian Jewish Youth Organization, founded in 1919, strives to combat assimilation; encourages and strengthens Jewish culture and unites the Jewish youth of all our Nordic countries into one corporate body. It is Stockholm, naturally, which sets the tone for Jewish religion as well as Jewish cultural and social life in Scandinavia."

According to Swedish law, all the children—in addition to their regular studies—must receive religious instruction in the Episcopalian denomination. Jewish children are exempt from this study only when they bring a written statement from their community center, declaring that they are studying the Jewish religion. Without it they cannot enter the higher schools of learning. Thanks to this ordinance, approximately 90 percent of our children get a Jewish education."

We opened a Hillel School, where children are taught Hebrew by teachers from Israel. The relationship between Jewish and Christian youngsters is a normal and friendly one. Ours is a modern youth. They mature earlier than those of the same age in other countries. And premarital sex is practiced among our Jewish youth."

* * *

In Stockholm I met several girls from Grodno who had been in Auschwitz with my niece Dora. After liberation they made their way to Sweden, another country that offered refuge. They were married now and raising families. I was promptly received as their "uncle."

"The whole time we were together in camp," they related, "Dora had one thought in her mind: she was going to be rescued by her uncle in America. Facing the gas chambers as we did day in, day out, we laughed at her for this wishful thinking. But, apparently, if you are destined to live, your dreams come true. Now that we have lived to see you here with us, then you too are our uncle."

82

Poland 1960

From Stockholm, I traveled to Warsaw. During my three-week sojourn in Poland, pianist Renee Solomon and I gave concerts in the ten largest cities, including Warsaw, Lodz and Cracow. We also gave a concert for the small number of Jews remaining in Bialystok.

We were met with the warmest enthusiasm, whether it was in a hall, a theater, or a club. Each appearance was turned into a special holiday for Yiddish folk-culture...

I was told that it had been a long time since Jews in Warsaw had laughed so heartily as they did at my concert at the Jewish State Theater on Kirlewsky Street. The laughter came from the hearts of the common people, the social leaders, writers, scientists, actors and students alike.

At our farewell appearance in Warsaw, we received enormous baskets of flowers; one of which was from the president of the Cultural Federation of Jews in Poland, with a letter of thanks on behalf of Polish Jews.

The people in our audience were reluctant to part with us and the curtain of the State Theater had to be raised seven times.

Before our departure from Poland, we were honored at a farewell gathering arranged by the president of the federation. Here, I spoke of the impressions made upon me by my visit: "Meeting with the Jews in Poland has been a most profound and meaningful experience. During every performance they sat rapt in attention and this gave me a strength and courage. A most gratifying experience was Bialystok—Bialystok whose Jewish population now stands at a mere hundred souls. Seeing the tears in their eyes, tears of joy at our meeting, was something I shall never forget. Performing in Poland for our people who yearn for a Yiddish word and song has definitely climaxed my last two-year rambling around the world."

The Power of a Theater Pass

"Yablokoff?!" exclaimed Simon Zarzhevsky, surprised to hear my voice over his private phone. "You're still in Warsaw? I was sure you were in Grodno by now! What happened?"

"I was stopped in Kuznica at the Polish border. My Polish visa is valid for one entry and one exit. The officer at the border told me that once I left Poland for Russia I wouldn't be permitted back into Poland. So, at the last moment I decided not to run the risk and boarded the same train back to Warsaw."

"You did the right thing," Zarzhevsky said. "But don't take it to heart. Come to my office, we'll think of something."

"I don't want to impose on you again," I said, guiltily. "I'm afraid it's just a waste of your effort. In order to get a new visa, it takes months, I was told...if it can be accomplished at all."

"Come to my office," he persisted. "I'll try my utmost to get you a re-entry permit to Poland."

As I sat with him in his office, his secretary let him know that the party he'd called was now on the wire. He began a lively chat with one of the government bigwigs. Bantering on the phone, he smiled and winked at me. Zarzhevsky invited him to attend Alexander Bardini's production of *Boris Godunov*.

"No need to thank me," Zarzhevsky said, "be my guest. You'll find the tickets at the box office in your name. Sure, anything for a friend..."

When I heard him touch upon the subject that concerned me, I silently prayed.

"...so I need a little help," he went on. "I need a re-entry permit from Byelorussia back to Warsaw for a close friend of mine, an artist now on a concert tour in Poland." There was a big pause, in which I held my breath. Finally, his face lit up as he said, "Thank you very much. I appreciate it."

"Well, that's that!" Zarzhevsky smiled broadly putting down the receiver. "You of all people, an actor, should know that there's no greater power than a complimentary pair of seats to a smash hit! So, hurry to this address," he prodded me. "You'll get your re-entry permit from Byelorussia to Poland." I wired my Bella in New York that I was on my pilgrimage to the cemetery. I knew she would understand that I'd succeeded in fulfilling the wish I had long nurtured in my heart. Thus, once again I took off for the Polish-Russian border in Kuznica.

Back at the Border

The Polish officer, who had detained me two days before, never expected me to pop up so soon again. When he saw this new re-entry permit on my passport stamped by the secret police, he turned white.

"I was doing my duty," he apologized. Obviously, with my connection in obtaining a permit overnight, after he'd told me this would take months, he took me to be some important political figure. He feared he would get an order from high echelons to vacate his post and go, the hell knows where.

I assured him that I understood his position. On the contrary, I was very grateful, because in the end, everything had turned out for the best. I could now go to Russia with an easy mind. When it came to the inspection of my valise, he gave the order: "Don't touch."

So there I went, through the narrow exit, past customs to the waiting Soviet train, with its huge letters on the sides locomotive reading U.S.S.R., and flying the hammer and sickle.

The train soon moved toward the no-man's land leading to Byelorussia and Grodno.

Every section in the car had two wooden benches facing each other, a small table between them. The wooden lids that covered the benches, stood open, as the conductor made sure that there were no "free-hitchers" hiding there, or beneath the benches—so reminiscent of the czarist days, when Jews redistricted from traveling beyond the Pale, used to stow away under the benches—hardly ever fooling the conductor.

Sharing my compartment were two students from East Germany. They were studying in Moscow and were returning there from their vacation. Both spoke English. After closing the bench-covers the conductor ordered our baggage placed on them and opened for inspection.

Two uniformed inspectors, reinforced by two military men with automatic rifles, appeared. One inspector took our passports, giving mine with its Soviet visa, an extra glance.

"What is the purpose of your trip to Grodno?" the inspector asked me.

"I'm going to visit the cemetery," I replied in English, after the students were kind enough to translate for me. "My father and the rest of my family are buried there."

Two more uniformed inspectors showed up—a man and a woman, who promptly inspected my small valise. Right on top of my things was a paperback book, which I had been carting with me all the way from Norway to pass the time during my long journeys.

"What kind of book is this?" the woman inspector snapped at me in Russian. I understood, but I waited for the English translation.

"Just an old detective story to pass time on the train."

"Who is the author?"

"Ellery Queen, a popular writer of detective stories."

"Is it a book on American espionage?"

"What do you mean?" I said, becoming confused and looking to the students to interpret for me.

"Answer!" commanded the other inspector, as he leafed through the paperback. "Are you carrying a book on espionage?!"

"On my travels...I always carry something to read..." I stammered, nervously remembering that, wrapped in one of my shirts, I was carrying a book in Yiddish, a gift for Scheikowksy in Grodno. If they were making such a to-do over an innocuous whodunit, what would happen if they came across the Yiddish book?

"Don't you know it is strictly forbidden to bring in that capitalistic propaganda?" they raged at me through my interpreters.

"I don't need the book," I pleaded. "Please take it!"

"What else do you have in your luggage?"

"A sweater, some underwear...a few shirts..." and now it comes, I cringed. My knees buckled. They will began searching—and I will be done for!

"Where were you born?"

"In Grodno."

"And you don't speak Russian?!" This really unnerved me.

"So many years, away in the United States...I don't remember the language..." I floundered, knowing that they didn't believe me, and that I'd better watch myself and stick to English.

To my surprise, the woman inspector gave my things a superficial riffle, while the other impatiently tossed the Ellery Queen book back in my valise and slammed it shut.

I realized that, unwittingly, I'd make the mistake of pretending that I did not understand Russian. Now, I was obliged to continue the pretense. I would have to stick to English, or Yiddish, as the case might be. The experience with the Byelorussian officials filled me with a terror that grew from minute to minute. I was so upset I could hardly calm down. Slowly, the train came to halt. Squinting through a little spot in the window, I could barely make out a sign on the snow-laden roof of a shack. In large Russian letters, it said: Lasosno. Here ended no-man's land and from this point the train entered White Russia.

Armed Polish and White Russian soldiers stood guard to make sure none of the few passengers aboard could sneak out of the locked cars...

83

Grodno, At Last

The train rattled on. We were coming closer to the iron trestle that spanned the River Niemen, and my pulses quickened. Everything lay blanketed in snow. A few more minutes and the trained screeched up to the station in Grodno.

As the doors opened, my ears were suddenly assailed by strident martial music blaring from loudspeakers. I had arrived, of all times, on Women's Day—celebrated on March 10th—and the women were being saluted via the radio.

The station's platform was lined with soldiers, their breath curling in the frosty air, their feet stomping to keep warm.

I was the only passenger shown off the train. I was directed to a small room in the station, where I was left to wait. I was very perturbed that I had not been given back my passport after it was taken from me on the train. I noticed a small buffet in the waiting room selling various drinks. My throat was parched from nervousness, only I had no Russian rubles, nor did I want to venture speaking Russian. Whoever was in charge had sent for someone who could speak English to communicate with me.

Finally, a woman came along and introduced herself as an interpreter. Her English was fairly good. From her tone, I gathered she wished I'd sooner gone to the devil before showing up on her holiday of all days, causing her to be burdened with me—an American tourist out of the blue!

A few moments later, a man in military garb appeared. From the flutter of attention at his arrival, I understood him to be a high-ranking officer.

"It surprises me that you were issued a visa to come to Grodno," he said, which my interpreter translated for me. "We are not yet prepared to accommodate tourists. I don't really know what to do about you. Do you have anyone here?"

"I have no one," I said, "But perhaps I can find a Jew, who may have known my family. I was born here. I left Grodno a good many years ago."

"How will you manage to communicate?"

"In Yiddish. To my regret I have forgotten Russian after so many years away in America..."

He murmured something to my interpreter. She balked. It was Woman's Day after all, she pointed out, and her husband and family were waiting dinner.

Well then, he said he would contact Moscow and have them give the necessary instructions about what to do with me. I was the first such visitor in Grodno. The currency exchange was also not clear to him. In the meantime, he instructed her to settle me at the Hotel Byelorusse. She was then to take me somewhere to eat and after she had escorted me back to the hotel she would be free to join her family.

Dusk had fallen by the time we reached the hotel. Driving along, I was struck at the innovation of traffic lights. My, my! I thought, traffic lights in Grodno!

I was shown into a large room with four beds. Looking askance at my interpreter, she assured me that I would have the room to myself and could choose any bed I preferred.

I asked her to excuse me so I could wash up and change my shirt. The moment she stepped out of the room, I fished the Yiddish book out of my valise and quickly hid it underneath a wooden wardrobe that stood against the wall. In any case, I figured, it would not be found on me.

My escort took me to a restaurant, The Nieman. Just inside the entrance my coat and papakha were taken to be checked. I still felt the frost in my bones and would have preferred to have kept my overcoat. Besides, I was already thinking of ways to shake off my escort and get out on the street by myself, so I could look up Sarah Dworetzky, Michel Trilling and Scheikowsky. But there I was, without my hat and coat—and a companion who watched me like a hawk.

The main dining room was beginning to buzz. Preparations were already under way for the evening's celebration of Women's Day. Long tables, decked with silver and flower decorations stood ready.

I was famished. I hadn't eaten a thing since the day before. Food had been the furthest thing from my mind. My nerves were taut. I had to be on guard so I wouldn't accidentally drop a word in Russian. In this atmosphere the words came to the tip of my tongue almost beyond my control.

The restaurant manager offered to serve me privately, in a small anteroom, but I preferred to eat in the main dining room. I knew my companion was impatient to be off as quickly as possible. I asked her to order a 100-gram measure of vodka. (In Russia, hard liquor is ordered by measure). The menu listed a great variety of dishes. I asked for some pumpernickel bread and a portion of salt herring as an appetizer. After downing the vodka, I bit into the black bread with relish. The waiter brought me a whole herring—enough for more than one person—but I ate it.

Guests began arriving and the place took on a festive atmosphere. Young couples breezed. The young women wore thin, summery dresses, though it was winter. No doubt these were the only party-type "platyes" they owned. The guests made toasts praising the Soviet Union. Surprisingly enough, all of them spoke Russian rather than the somewhat differently accented Byelorussian.

After devouring the herring and vegetable soup, I would have been satisfied to forgo the rest. Not that the food wasn't tasty, only who could eat such portions? I begged my escort to please join me and eat something, but she refused. The only favor she wanted was for me to hurry up and finish my meal so she could go on home to her family.

"I can find my way to the hotel," I assured her. "It isn't that far. Why should you sit around for no reason at all? As soon as I finish eating I'll go back and go to sleep."

She finally let herself be persuaded. She thanked me for being so considerate, I, in turn, wished her a happy holiday and she left. I remained alone at my table, and now, I thought, how on earth could I sneak out of here? I had no desire to spend the rest of the evening in my shabby hotel room. Maybe I could still succeed in finding someone—anyone of the several Jews for whom I had brought regards from Warsaw.

The tumult in the restaurant grew louder still; drinking, singing, laughing, dancing to the strains of an orchestra. In sign language I indicated to a waitress that I'd had enough to eat. I wanted my check so I could sign it, as my "guardian" instructed me to do. I also added a good sum to the total as a tip—which was taboo as I later learned. Then, I threaded my way among the dancing couples to the foyer. At the checkroom I made the woman understand that I was tired and mentioned the word, "Byelorusse." She understood, and smiling, handed me my hat and coat.

Once outside the restaurant I started toward the hotel. I looked back to see if I was being followed. There wasn't a soul on the street. I made a sharp turn into a side street and began to walk briskly in the opposite direction...a ready alibi on my lips: "I lost my way. I'm looking for the Hotel Byelorusse..."

A full moon shed some light on the dark city streets. The biting frost pinched my face. My nose felt numb. Remembering the antidote for frostbite from childhood, I picked up a handful of snow and rubbed it over my face and nose. Drying my face with my handkerchief, I walked on.

A man came toward me and mumbled a greeting in Russian. For a moment it gave me a turn. But in order not to draw suspicion, I answered him in kind. Taking heart, I asked him, in Russian of course, how I could get to Sotzialistichskaia #54. He gave me directions and I thanked him. With his chin dug deep into the collar of his fur coat and his cap pulled down to his eyes against the frost, I knew he wouldn't bother giving me a second look. He went his way and I continued to the address I needed.

I stopped in front of the houses on the street. Every strained nerve in my body told me that this must be it but I couldn't find the number. I entered a dark little hallway. Groping along the wall my hand touched a banister, which indicated a stairway. Yet I remained in a quandary: which way should I go? It was so dark I couldn't even find my way back to the street. Even if I found a door, how sure could I be it wasn't the door of some disgruntled Russian? He would surely hand me over to the police. Who was I, knocking on his door at night?!

As I stood in the dark, a gramophone began to play. I inched my way up the stairs in the direction of the music. I heard a woman speaking...and my relief was unbounded! She was speaking Yiddish. I fumbled for the doorknob. Then, taking courage, I rapped softly. The music stopped. I waited. The stillness continued. I knocked again, a little louder this time.

"Kto tam?" a woman's voice asked in Russian. (Who is there?)

"Don't be afraid," I murmured in Yiddish. "I'm a Jew from Grodno...just arrived from Warsaw. Please tell me where I can find the apartment of Sarah Dworetzky. It's so dark I can't find the number."

Again, all was silent. I waited, and after a few moments, I heard the fumbling of a chain and the door opened. A woman stood there observing me warily for moment before she let me in. It was a dimly lit one-room flat. An elderly woman sat on a cot. Both she and a man, who stood near her, took me in with curious glances.

"I am Sarah Dworetzky," said the elderly woman. "Are you looking for me?" I handed her the letter of reference given me by Hersh Smoliar in Warsaw. Sarah Dworetzky adjusted a pair of old-fashioned spectacles and perused the letter.

"Thank you for bringing me this letter," she said, looking up at me. "Such a dear friend, Hersh...and a dear co-worker for a better world. We went through a lot together. Take off your coat, my dear Yablonik," she said courteously. "Will you have something to eat? Today is a holiday. So in honor of us women, you too may as well indulge yourself. We haven't prepared any specialties. Who could have anticipated such a guest! All the way from America...a Yiddish artist at that! You're welcome to share the little we have."

The table was set with a platter of sliced bread and three bowls filled with a thin barley soup.

"Madame Dworetzky," I said in apology, "please forgive my intrusion of your supper hour. I can't stay too long. More than anything I wish to meet other Grodno Jews, especially Michel Trilling and Lazar Scheikowsky. If you think I can harm you in any way by my visit, I will leave immediately. I won't take it amiss..."

"My dear friend, don't disconcert yourself," this venerable revolutionary smiled, "and please call me Sarah. Nothing can harm me anymore. You see before you an aged, sickly woman. So what have I to fear? You are my guest, a very welcome guest. Your apprehensions are completely unfounded. We have nothing to fear now in our country. We are a free people and free citizens."

"This is Asna Levine,'" she introduced the woman who opened the door for me. "She lives here with me. I couldn't do without her. Asna, please run over to Trilling and Scheikowsky—they don't live far from here. Also, perhaps, the Pomerantzes. Tell them that I have an esteemed guest. He can't stay too long. Let them come and pay me a visit.

"And this," said Sarah, introducing the man, "is a friend of ours, Hershel Plaskov."

"I was formerly a cantor," said Plaskov, extending me a warm handshake, "as well as the editor of a Yiddish paper in Groniedzsher, near Bialystok."

"Madame Dworetzky, I mean Sarah, please tell me, how many Jews are there now in Grodno?"

After a long pause—not in calculation, but in deep emotion—she said: "About sixteen. Some Jews hail from other parts, many of whom don't let it be known that they are Jews. A few native Grodners are in Vilna, Minsk and Moscow. Some of them occasionally come to visit us in Grodno.

"Yes, we've come to a fine end," she sighed. "And you, my friend, still remember our Grodno? How old were you when you left to go out in the world? Seventeen or eighteen? Of course. What do you know of the horror that came down on our heads?! The former Grodno—the Jewish Grodno, is gone and never again to be. I survived the Holocaust, but my loved ones, my dear ones…I remember every detail of the devastation. It is all burned into my brain. I shall remember it to the last day of my life."

She told me the plight of the Grodno Jews. "On September 1, 1939, Grodno was bombed by Nazi planes. There were countless casualties. The Polish populace evacuated the city. Local hooligans took advantage of the anarchy to make pogroms and murder Jews. After the Soviet army marched into Grodno, the pogromists were meted out their well-deserved punishment. In accordance with the Hitler-Stalin pact, Grodno remained under Soviet rule for almost two years, but in 1941 Nazi Germany attacked the Soviet Union, and the Nazis occupied Grodno. They began murdering Jews. At the German field gendarmerie on Ivanovski, they beat Jews to death. People were covered with excrement. And when winter came, Jews were forced to clear the snow with teaspoons and toothbrushes. For disobedience? Death! Jews were also drowned in water-filled bathtubs."

"Grodno was feeling the impact of the Nuremberg Laws. A detail from the Gestapo arrived in Grodno. They immediately arrested people from among the Jewish intelligentsia, and shot them. Grodno was annexed as part of White Russia under Governor Becker, who later annihilated Minsk Jewry."

She paused, then continued, "Within the next few hours, all Jews had to evacuate Grodno's main streets. Grodno was removed from White Russian territory and was incorporated together with the entire Bialystok region into the Third Reich. On November 2, 1941, It was a bleak day, with wet snow. A day so completely shattering, it was subsequently memorialized in a song, created in the ghetto."

"Into the two areas now designated as 'the ghettos'—where once 10,000 peopled lived in congested quarters—there were now squeezed 23,000 together. The ghettos were fenced in by barbed wire, guarded by German gendarmes holding machine guns. A year after the Jews were driven into the ghettos, the Gestapo took over control.

"In Kelbasin, on the outskirts of Grodno, there was a camp once used for prisoners. Approximately 28,000 Jews were rounded up. Kelbasin became the transit camp. From there, the Jews from around Grodno were transported to Treblinka, Auschwitz and Majdanek. The Jews were driven from Kelbasin to their death. In order to ensnare them, the Nazis told them that they were being sent on work assignments. They supplied these transports with second class railway cars and provided the Jews with bread and other food for the journey.

"Out of more than 23,000 Jews in the Grodno ghettos, only 10,000 were left by 1942, and of the 28,000 in Kelbasin, only 4,000. The next year, about 10,000 Jews were led out of the Grodno ghetto, where they had been wallowing in the streets. The snow was red with the blood of those who had been shot, or wounded. The corpses were ravaged by black crows. To bury the dead was forbidden. We only got permission a week later to bury the slain in the old ghetto cemetery. After "Operation Ten Thousand," only 3,000 Jews remained in Grodno (legally) and over 2,000 in hiding somewhere...

"Not all Jews from Grodno went like sheep to the slaughter. A number of them succeeded in escaping from the transports. They leaped from the moving trains, risking the hail of machine-gun bullets. The survivors fought like heroes and fell, defending Jewish honor and dignity.

"Some of Grodno's youth became part of the general resistance movement, a Jewish underground to combat the Nazis. Comrades, mostly of the Zionist Movement, planned a unified uprising of both ghettos against the enemy and many a courageous hero lost his life on the way to Treblinka during their revolt.

"In March of 1943, the last one thousand Jews were driven like sheep to the slaughter of the German 'Schutzpolizei' astride his horse. Followed by huge trucks jammed with the elderly, the sick and the smallest of the children, German brutes, wielding the whips, switches and rifle butts, drove the bedraggled, barefoot skeletons on, forcing them under threat of death to sing and dance along to the tune of the Jewish wedding march: 'Khosn-Kalle Mazel tov,' and the jolly song, 'Yidl mit'n Fidl.'

"Grodno's non-Jewish populace—neighbors for so many decades—congregated on balconies, rooftops and trees to watch the 'parade.' Even the peasants, drove in from their villages to view this spectacle. Sitting on their farm wagons, they joined the others in laughing and applauding the death march of Grodno's last Jews.

"The Nazi heroes photographed the jubilant spectators, as the Jews were being driven to the freight depot. There they were crammed ninety to a boxcar on their way to death, singing, 'Khosn-Kalle Mazel tov' and 'Yidl mit'n Fidl.' And on the very next day—March 13, 1943—a large sign at the Grodno railroad station proclaimed: 'Grodno—Juden Rein'!"

* * *

A few of my compatriots did come to see me at Sarah Dworetzky's home: Lazar Scheikowsky, and Shlomo Zhukowsky, my chum from Cheyder

Mesukon, a schoolteacher now. (One of his pupils, I was told in strictest secrecy, had recently slapped his face and called him, "zhid proklyati" (accursed Jew). Sonya Pomerantz and her husband Yasha also came along and told me about the few others in Grodno.

Leaving Mme. Dworetzky's house, I was accompanied back to Byelorusse by Scheikowsky. In my hotel room I quickly handed him Smoliar's book which I'd smuggled in from Warsaw. He promptly hid it in his overcoat and hurried out.

"Yidl Mit'n Fidl..."

The scene of the deathmarch dragging through the streets of Grodno kept moving before me. My ears rang from the blood-chilling singing of "Yidl mit'n Fidl" and the wedding march, "Khoshn-Kalle, Mazel tov..." My brain refused to grasp it! Why did I come here?! How could I bring myself to look upon Grodno, the slaughter city, stained with the blood of my dearest ones and of the entire martyred community.

I tried to sleep. It was useless. I could not dispel the macabre spectacle that tore at my heart.

By which death-route did they drag my brother Velvel, the revolutionary? He who sacrificed his life to save the world for the proletariat! The unforgettable episode I witnessed as a child flashed before me: Velvel in chains, made to trudge with the others in the etape to the Grodno depot; sentenced to ten years hard labor in the Schlusselberg Fortress. Ten years! Then Siberia! And my dear brother, for what? To be driven after years of exile, along the same route with your dear wife Heitche and dear little children to the gas chamber forced to sing "Yidl mit'n Fidl?!"

I tossed and turned, but sleep was out of the question. When at long last, things were astir in the hotel, I dressed, and before my guide could call for me, I decided to get out on the street—alone!

Saborna Street. In the little park near the Magistrate, I came upon a massive statue of Josef Stalin set on a broad base of black granite. A statue of Stalin? How come? In Russia proper, there were no longer any vestiges of Stalin to be found. Yet here, in Grodno—White Russia—there were three statues of Stalin, and only one of Lenin. Could it be, I pondered, that Grodno was still under the influence of Stalinism?

All the houses at the corner of Saborna and Schmukler Streets were gone. The Russian Church across the way look dilapidated. And the Polish Church looked no better.

The boulevard was deserted. Where, oh where, were the familiar faces of the Jewish workers who waited around in the wee hours hoping to earn something? I silently mourned their passing. No droshkies, no Jewish drivers to be seen anywhere.

There was no sign of the market-stalls, above which I'd played with the firemen's band. Everything was flattened, so that standing on the boulevard,

I could actually see as far as Fehrstadt on the other side of the Niemen. The old and new marketplaces...erased as if they'd never been.

"Slavka," I murmured, "dear sister...Itchke...and the dear children. No trace of anyone. Gone in the death-march, forced to sing 'Yidl mit'n Fidl'..."

Skidler Street, Politzeiski and the gruesome prison. The prison was still standing, a silent witness to the torture of Jews dating back to the czarist and Polish regimes.

I looked for the house with the garret where my sister Rochele, the half-twin, lived with her family. "Rochele! Dear little sister...children!...Hershel, you, also dreamed of a new world, of brotherhood, of justice and peace. Were you also in the death-march?"

On Slobodka, everything remained the same as before; there were no signs of the bloody ghetto. My eyes searched among the houses, imagining that, at any moment my brother Shayke would emerge with his wife, Yenta, and their children. The Gentile residents eyed me with suspicion.

Passing the State Theater, where I trod the boards for the first time as the young aspirant, I saw a poster announcing a Russian troupe playing *The Three Sisters*, by Chekhov. And in front of the theater stood another life-sized statue of Stalin on a massive foundation of black granite.

The "Brikhalka" was buried in snow, its brook below, frozen. Oh, what memories this tree-shaded dell awakened in me! People began to appear on the streets hurrying to work. I doubted that there were any Jews among them. A bus came along and stopped for passengers. A police car cruised by the main streets, its loudspeaker warning: "Pedestrians, do not walk in the middle of the street! There are sidewalks! Wait for traffic signals!"

The Niemen was frozen solid. People strode across its surface to Fehrstadt as they had always done, and I followed suit. A row of newly built houses with the uniformity of military barracks ran all the way to the iron railroad bridge. Fehrstadt was unrecognizable, except for a few houses that still remained. In vain did I search for the one in which my brother Motke lived with his wife, Sheine-Libbe, and their children...

I took the footbridge back to town. There was no sign left of my Uncle Shillingoff's complex of buildings—simply wiped from the face of the earth—such a landmark in Grodno! The entire area I had been told was marked for the construction of a culture center for thousands of people. And how many Jews? Sixteen?...

On Zamkova Street, I passed the house where my mother and brother Velvel lived during my short visit in 1930. I didn't have the heart to enter the yard. What was it my niece, Dora, the only survivor, told me in the Austrian DP camp, when she spoke of my mother? "Grandma was a saintly woman. Her eyes did not witness the bloody end." Although where and when my mother breathed her last, Dora did not know.

With a pounding heart I turned into the vast Synagogue Courtyard. It was here that I'd spent my childhood; studied at the yeshiva; sang with Cantor Kaminetzky. And here was the Great Synagogue! This holy house of worship, the pride of Grodno's Jewry, was now a warehouse.

All the synagogues and prayer houses in the city, including those in the court of the Great Synagogue and big Hayyei Adam, where my father, rest his soul, served as reader of the Torah and where I was Bar Mitzvah, were now living quarters for Christians.

I had left the visit to my father's grave for last. Trudging the distance out to the New Cemetery, as it was known, I suddenly stopped. Half of the broad gate opening onto the burial ground was gone. The hut, for ritual purification at the entrance, had been left with one wall standing.

I walked through the half-gate, and couldn't move any further. My feet felt paralyzed. Where am I?! Where is the cemetery?!! I stared in disbelief! From what I recalled as the center lane, two far-reaching fields spread out—barren and snow-covered. No sign of tombstones, no sign of graves. Off at a distance, placidly rambling over the snow-patched fields, were several cows and pigs...

Oh God!...Oh God!!...

How long I stood there in shock, I don't remember. But, as if in a trance, I stooped and gathered up a handful of little stones, which I slipped into my pocket.

Where did the gravestones disappear to? The tombstones, the mausoleums, the monument depicting an angel with crumpled wings on the grave of the young poet, Leyb Neidus? Where is my father's gravestone? Where?...

All at once, a horrible thought struck me! The statues of Stalin! Lenin! I realized that the black granite bases from our Jewish cemetery were used to support those statues. And the other monuments? Were they used for building material? For road paving?

With mounting hysteria, I cried out, "Yis ga del, v'yis ka dash, shmey rabo"—Exalted and Honored by the Name Almighty God. Merciful God! How could you allow this to happen? Merciful God? No, no—Vengeful God! I will not recite the Kaddish anymore! I too, want to sing, as my dearest ones were made to sing in the deathmarch—"Yidl mit'n Fidl"..."Yidl mit'n Fidl"..."Yidl mit'n Fidl"...

Little Stones

Back at the hotel I found my guide rather peeved at me for having wandered off by myself. "Take me back to the railroad station," I begged her, "I want to leave this very day."

The chauffeur who drove us to the station, grumbled, "Born in Grodno, yet he doesn't speak Russian? Hogwash! The bastard understands every word we say! He's an American spy, an American warmonger!"

I sat stoned, in complete resignation. Nearing the depot, I could visualize the huge sign, proclaiming: "GRODNO JUDEN REIN!"

In one of the rooms at the station, inspectors examined my valise.

"Have you taken anything with you from Grodno?"

"Yes."

"What?"

"Little stones."

"Stones?!"

"Yes, from the cemetery."

"What do you need them for?"

"In memory of the desecrated and devastated cemetery, once the site of my father's grave."

"It's against the law to carry stones out of our country!" interposed another inspector. "Hand them over!"

"I will not give up these little stones! You can do whatever you like with me. These little stones are my treasures. They are all that remains of my mother and father, my brothers, my sisters, their children, my family, my youth, my home, the entire martyred Jewish community of Grodno! Please, I beg you, spare me these little stones."

"It's against the law!" insisted the inspector. "Hand them over!"

"Aw, let him keep them and go to the devil," mumbled one of the inspectors, as he handed me my passport. "Tell him," he said to the interpreter, "if he wants the stones so badly, he can have them!"

I climbed the steps of the wooden railway car that was to take me back to the Polish frontier. About to sit down and get myself settled, along came a woman inspector, followed by two soldiers carrying automatic guns.

"Give me the stones!" she commanded. "Don't make such a to-do over it. It's forbidden, and that settles that! Give them to me!"

They took the little stones from me, and left.

I remained alone in the car. Utterly drained. I sank to my seat, and with my head buried in my hands, bewailed my precious little mementos, as the train carried me across no-man's land and back into the world...

Postscript

Herman Yablokoff died on April 3, 1981

Bella Mysell Yablokoff died on January 17, 1991.

INDEX

Edelstein, Yosele, 345, 351, 359, 362, 365-367
Educational Alliance, award to Yablokoff, 375
Efron, Ketti, 182
Ehrenberg, Gussie, 343, 345, 351, 360
Ehrenberg, Max, 343, 360
Eisen, Max, 472
Eisman, Goldie, 200
Eleazor of Verbelov, 11-12
Ellin, David, 228
Ellis Island, 168-178
Ellstein, Abe, 252
Elvarg, Max, 451
Elving, Bernard, 333
Englander, Chanineh, 199-201, 203-204, 209, 212
Entin, Al, 315
Epstein, Esther, 320
Epstein, William, 308, 318
Eternal Jew, The (Herman Heiermann), 119, 209

FADA (Farein fun Yiddische Dramatische Artisten in Vilna). *See* Vilna Troupe
Family Ovadis, The (Peretz Markish), 182
Farband (National Zionist Labor Organization), 482
Feder, Moshe, 249
Feld, Harry, 233, 238, 243
Feld, Itzhak, 339, 379, 399
Femova, Aniuta, 64
Fidelman, Charles, 382
Field, Esther, 258, 438
Field, Leon, 438
Fields, W.C., 311
Fineman, Dinah, 61
Fineman, Sigmund, 61
Finkel, Batami, 474-475
Finkel, Feivush, 472
Finkel, Morris, 257
Finkel, Shimon, 8, 136, 142, 286
   childhood in Grodno, 107, 109, 112-114, 119
   in the Habima, 267, 285
   in Israel, 474-475, 492, 494
Finland, Jewish population, 502
First Byelorussian Infantry Regiment, 118
Fishzon, Misha, 204, 258, 264-265, 267, 277, 283-285
Flaum, Julia, 181
Fleischer, Nathan, 334
Fleischman, Chaya, 206, 246
Fleischman, David, 206, 324, 334, 383, 387
Fleischman, Fay, 206, 218, 246, 257, 261, 264
Fleischman, Jeanette (wife), 257, 261, 266, 285, 295, 470
   accompanying Yablokoff at audition for the Hebrew Actors' Union, 299-303
   birth of son Jacob, 240-242
   courtship with Yablokoff, 207-208, 217-220

engagement to Yablokoff, 220-222, 224-225
illness of son Jacob, 306, 232
in Los Angeles, 233-244
at the Lyric Theatre, 264, 287
orchestra conductor in Los Angeles, 238
as a pianist, 206, 229-230
pregnancy, 232-234
radio performances, 238-239
separation from Yablokoff, 343
tensions in marriage to Yablokoff, 248-249, 252, 259, 323
wedding to Yablokoff, 229-230, 248-249, 252, 259, 323
Fleischman, Manny, 206, 225, 324, 334, 338
Fleischman, Max, 206-207, 225
Fleischman, Shaya, 202, 206-207
Fleishman, Sol, 206
Fogelnest, Pauline, 238
Fogelnest, Sam, 238
Folman, Lola, 444
Four Generations of Yiddish Theatre (Nehemiah Zukor), 389-390
Frank, Betty, 292
Frank, Heinz, 468-469
Freiman, Adolph, 238
Freiman, Annie, 238
Friedlander, Max, 337, 382-383
Friedman, Ada, 412, 422
Friedman, Isidore, 340
Friedman, Itzhak, 391, 402
Friedman, Leybele, 388
Friedman, Philip, 412
Fuchs, Leo, 339, 360-361, 365, 375-377, 379, 389
Furman, Norman, 319, 331-332, 337
   and Der Payatz, 314, 324
   radio representative of Yablokoff, 310-312, 314-315

Gaber, Sam, 422, 432, 452, 461-463
   assisting Yablokoff with rescuing niece, 417, 440
   as director of JOINT, 354, 412-415, 419, 425
Gable, Harry, 209
Gable, Max, 209-212, 251, 292, 304-305
Galina, Gita, 388-389
Garber, Smulke, 105
Garbo, Greta, 503
Garden of Love, The (Siegel and Olshanetsky), 296
Gehrman, Lucy, 297-298
Gehrman, Misha, 297-298
Gensher Cemetary (Warsaw, Poland), 181
German Theatre Company, 106-107
Gertler, Anna, 198, 287
Gertler, Sam, 195-196, 198, 204-205, 212, 222-223, 301